30 ILLEGAL YEARS TO THE STRIP:

The Untold Stories of the Gangsters Who Built the Early Las Vegas Strip

BILL FRIEDMAN

30 ILLEGAL YEARS TO THE STRIP:

The Untold Stories Of The Gangsters Who Built The Early Las Vegas Strip

Published in 2015 by
Old School Histories
www.OldSchoolHistories.com

www.BillFriedmanAuthor.com

ISBN: 978-1508529453

THIS BOOK IS DEDICATED TO MY WIFE, GLADYCE,

WHO GAVE ME UNENDING ENCOURAGEMENT AND SUPPORT.

OUR MARRIAGE INCLUDES THE LAST 39 YEARS

OF THIS 49-YEAR PROJECT.

SHE REINFORCED ME DAILY

WITH THE INSPIRATIONAL CHALLENGE,

"WHY DON'T YOU FINISH THE DAMN THING!"

TABLE OF CONTENTS

CHAPTER 10 - LUCIANO IN PRISON

CHAPTER 11 - THE ACTION CROSSED THE HUDSON RIVER

CHAPTER 12 - THE ACTION MOVED INTO CAJUN COUNTRY

CHAPTER 13 - JOE E. LEWIS & COSTELLO'S COPACABANA

CHAPTER 14 - THE ACTION SETTLED UNDER THE PALMS

THE PURPOSE OF & THE SOURCES FOR THIS BOOK

WHY THIS HISTORY?

This is the untold story of America's most powerful gangsters. It describes for the first time how organized crime came into existence. It details the organizational structures of the key gangs, and the interrelationships between these independent territorial gangs. This is the inside story of the four gangs who dominated the underworld across the country for five decades like no other criminals before or since.

Early in Prohibition during the Roaring '20s, three of these gangs became the country's largest in order to import astonishing amounts of the world's finest liquors. Their freighter ships stopped at sea idling just outside U.S. territorial waters. At night their speedboat fleets loaded the contraband and then raced through the darkness to shore trying to evade lurking pirate craft and Coast Guard cutters. At shore these speedboats transferred their cargoes to a long line of trucks. This convoy then drove to storage depots with its guards ever vigilant for hijacking gangs who could be hiding in ambush in the shadows all along the route.

With the Repeal of Prohibition, these three gangs began operating illegal casinos across the nation that were wide-open to the public just like today. Most were elegant facilities that catered to the wealthy with high-wagering-limit table games. These casinos often offered the area's finest restaurant or top nightclub entertainment to create a great mood before their guests proceeded on to the gambling room. These high-rolling players were accompanied by their wives who were adorned in magnificent evening gowns, lush fur coats, and exquisite jewelry.

Seven leaders of these three premier gangs developed close associations with each other and became known in the underworld as the Young Turks. These seven included the five partners of the largest importing gang - Charlie "Lucky" Luciano, Giuseppe "Joe Adonis" Doto, Meyer Lansky, Ben Siegel, and Vincent "Jimmy Blue Eyes" Alo. The second biggest Prohibition gang was led by Frank Costello. Even though these two gangs were based in Manhattan and they competed for its wealthy market, Costello was tight friends with each of the other gang's five leaders. The third largest gang was based in the Midwest and partner Moe Dalitz took the lead in dealing with the nation's other gang leaders. All the names of the five partners in the largest gang are well known to any one interested in early organized crime, but this is the first time it has been revealed that they were partners.

Likewise no one until now has known which bootlegging gangs were the biggest. I personally interviewed members of these three gangs, and all agreed who was one, two, and three because they knew the amount of firepower each employed to move and protect their liquor inventories. However none of these participants had any idea how many bottles they brought into the country, because they handled every transaction individually in cash and never wrote anything down.

These seven leaders of the three leading gangs partnered in legal and illegal businesses, and they formed underworld political alliances that were every bit as complicated, calculating, and treacherous as the politics of the overworld. These seven leaders, or the Young Turks, shared values that were unique to the underworld. They applied standard business principles to their Prohibition and illegal casino operations, while rejecting gangland's core values of violence and monopoly. They were convinced everyone could make more money and live longer by competing in business and cooperating politically than they could by fighting, killing, and dying for exclusive territories.

One would have expected that these peculiar underworld values would have kept the seven Young Turks on the sidelines of underworld influence, but major territorial gang wars inadvertently thrust these improbable men to the pinnacle of organized crime leadership. As foreign as their values were to the nation's traditional violent gangsters, these seven men achieved far greater respect and stronger support from the rest of gangland than any gang bosses in history.

The country's fourth biggest Prohibition gang was headed by Al Capone in Chicago. This was the country's most murderous gang and the one focused on expansion. Their values could not have been more contrary to the Young Turks, especially in their proclivity for violence and monopoly. Despite these extreme differences, the Chicago gang's first eight successive leaders (Capone was the third) and their close associates admired the Young Turks of the three largest gangs and remained loyal to them for many decades. Thus these four gangs partnered together in business ventures, allied in underworld politics over which they were the dominant force, and later developed in concert the gambling resorts of the early Las Vegas Strip. The leaders of these four gangs and their associates built 80% of the fabulous Strip resorts from the *Flamingo* in 1946 to *Caesars Palace* in 1966. This was the Strip's Golden Era when it was the world's gambling and entertainment mecca, the greatest adult playground ever created.

Unbelievably the Young Turks of the three largest gangs were able to restrain Chicago from committing even more murders than their awful total, and the political intrigue surrounding these disagreements over the use of violence is presented in this book. In addition the Young Turks demanded Chicago behave like normal human beings when dealing with anyone in Las Vegas. The Young Turks kept Chicago in check from the time the Windy City gangsters established a beachhead on the Strip in the late 1940s. They enforced this until the early 1970s when the Young Turks and their associates had sold their Strip gambling resort interests. Since the people associated with the other three gangs were gone from the business, all hell broke loose in Las Vegas as Chicago brought in its penchant for gangland violence. These types of murder had been prohibited from occurring in the city before. Only a few of these bad incidents were depicted Hollywood-style in the movie *Casino* (1995).

Las Vegas residents and the media have long used the term "the mob that built the Strip." This phrase merely referred to the licensed owner/operators of these marvelous gambling resorts. No one in Las Vegas ever had the slightest suspicion that there might actually be an interrelated criminal mob hidden behind the scenes calling all the shots in the vast gambling-tourism industry along the Strip. Then 20 years into this research project, the Young Turks or their associates who directed everything had finally built up enough trust in me to let me into their inner sanctum, so I could write the whole amazing story of what actually occurred and how it all worked. Now the world is about to be exposed to this gripping and exciting exclusive look inside as these gangsters followed their varied paths to the Strip.

This is the thrilling story of these gangsters' three decades of astonishing adventures negotiating their way through the intricacies of gangland to finally arrive at the Strip. It describes their business challenges; competitive conflicts; underworld political intrigues, clashes, and gang wars; law enforcement prosecutions and persecutions; and threats by powerful and unscrupulous politicians with Machiavellian personal agendas.

To this day old Las Vegans who were residents before 1980 talk about the town's mob with fond memory. They invariably say, "The town was a lot better when the mob ran it," meaning before corporations took over the industry. This is because the casino leaders up until then adopted the core values of the unusual gangsters known as the Young Turks who you are about to meet.

FICTION MASQUERADING AS TRUE CRIME

Vincent "Jimmy Blue Eyes" Alo was the best friend of Charlie Luciano, and also the best friend and lifelong partner of Meyer Lansky during Prohibition and in running illegal casinos (although when Ben Siegel was alive he was the closest to Lansky). At the beginning of my first interview with Jimmy, he asked why I had been researching for so many years the history of the Nevada gambling industry and the gangsters who populated it. I described my passion for discovering the truth about what actually happened. After listening he advised, "I'm fascinated by history. I'm only talkin' to you because I respect your searching for the truth. But the lies have been told about Meyer (Lansky) and Ben (Siegel) and Charlie (Luciano) for so long and so many times, you can't change anything. The lies are now the world's reality. No one's gonna believe you." [i]

Jimmy Blue Eyes' statement triggers two questions. How did so many lies about these gangsters come into existence and then become perpetuated, and why does history have an almost total void about the actual early development of organized crime? The answer to the void is because no one investigated it. Big city police departments did their job of identifying the local gang members, but they acquired little knowledge about these gangs' organizational structures or their underworld alliances and political interactions with the gangs in other cities that were outside their jurisdiction. Federal law-enforcement agencies like the FBI, IRS, and FBN (Federal Bureau of Narcotics) investigated a rather small number of cases that focused on gang leaders, so they learned nothing about these gangs' organizations or relationship interconnections. [ii]

The only meaningful information about the inner workings of gangs in that era was obtained by local newspaper investigative reporters. They usually developed close personal relationships with their area's gang leaders who traded information about competing gangs' activities in the hope of receiving better press for themselves. The investigative reporters of this era were very effective and uncovered much of the information contained in this research. However they usually developed little information about the local gangs' relationships with other gangs throughout the country. It was the merging of the information from all these local sources and my interviews with key participants during this research that allowed me to finally put together for the first time this era's nationwide gangland interrelationship structure.

A number of biographical books have been written about these early organized-crime leaders, but all are seriously flawed for the following reasons. Not one of these writers ever interviewed their criminal subjects or their few close associates who had any knowledge about their illegal behavior. Unfortunately our knowledge is so limited because these Prohibition gang leaders were the most tight-lipped criminals in history. Total silence protected them from criminal prosecution by state's witness testimony, and also from accidentally divulging a clue about their mass liquor transportation methods and plans and storage facilities. The only time they ever talked about their activities was with their most trusted gang associate (or very few associates) who were also involved, but even with them these gangsters never talked about their legal or illegal businesses in which the other was not involved. Thus, while all the former hoods I interviewed later in their lives were surprisingly open about their pasts, not one was able to tell me anything about any of his associate's activities except for those in which he was also a participant.

The few gangsters of this era who commented to the press were publicity-hounds like Chicago's Al Capone and Los Angeles' Mickey Cohen, but they offered reporters only self-serving one liners that were too often untrue denials. Because of this ingrained absolute code of silence among the gangsters of this era, not one of them ever sued an author no matter how untrue and libelous his lies. Thus, unscrupulous writers knew they could manufacture any fiction about these gangsters and publish it as "factual" biography without fear that its authenticity would ever be challenged, and oh my gosh did these writers ever take advantage of this opportunity.

Two writers claimed their books were autobiographies, but even they failed to obtain any interviews with their subjects about their criminal activities. Thus, the writers of the fraudulent autobiographies about Charlie Luciano and Meyer Lansky were totally discredited by the press upon publication. Despite these damning revelations, which are buttressed by additional strong evidence in this book, especially in the addendums, later writers about organized crime in this era continued to quote many of these two books' proven bogus assertions.[iii]

A biography can be a great historical work even without obtaining an interview of the subject, if it is well researched from relevant documents. However, writers about early organized crime rarely studied their subjects' lives. Their standard approach was to look at a small collection of major headlines from newspaper morgue files, and around these events write pure fiction about their behavior, motives, interpersonal relationships, and personality traits. These writers presented each gangster's childhood, early teenage years, family life, and introduction into the underworld, even though practically no record exists about any of this except for their birth certificate or arrival in this country, years of school attendance, and police record. These early organized-crime books also list dramatically different police records for the major gangsters meaning at the most only one book can be factual.

This is why few of the books about early organized-crime have footnotes identifying their source of information, because they are imaginary tales. The books that are footnoted depend primarily on earlier published undocumented organized-crime biographies. Many of the other listings in these books' footnotes typically cannot be confirmed or they turn out to be false, not exactly the stuff real histories are supported by. Sadly, this genre of books about early organized-crime has been based on repeating the falsehoods by previous writers and then introducing new fanciful embellishments to expand upon and sensationalize these fairytales.

Two blatant examples demonstrate that these writers did not seem to even read the articles attached to the few headline events they incorporated because their books reversed their subjects' roles. Arnold Rothstein and Joe Adonis were illegal casino operators based in and around New

York City and both were big-stake players in high-limit private games. Rothstein and Adonis made separate headlines when each became associated with financial crimes. The book writers who discussed either of these hoods not only attributed the financial crimes in the headlines to them, but went further by claiming Rothstein and Adonis spent their careers specializing in these types of crime. However, if these writers had bothered to read the articles below the headlines, they would have learned that in every one of these cases Rothstein and Adonis were either the victim or an innocent bystander. In fact law enforcement publicly credited both gangsters with helping to bring down the actual culprits. This is how the incredibly ridiculous fantasies about each of these Prohibition and illegal casino gangsters was created, and then book after book repeated and embellished these fictitious accounts. The grossly false information about each of these gangsters in the early organized-crime fictions is exposed in this book not only in the text but also with additional revelations in the addendums. Unfortunately, today's writers about this era continue to rely on these old books, rather than researching the raw material as I did, so they continue to perpetuate all these fabrications.

Because all the books written about early organized crime are almost pure fiction, practically nothing you have ever read about the organized-crime leaders of this era appears in this book. Likewise almost none of the information presented in this book have you ever read before or seen in a Hollywood production. But these are the events that actually did happen. These gangsters' lives have finally been exhaustively researched and documented with the source of every statement footnoted so it can be easily confirmed by any researcher, historian, reader, or critic. You are about to learn the whole unvarnished truth about these gangsters' careers and values, and the reality is very different from the fabricated myths that have been written about them. You are about to embark on a truly unique and amazing real-life adventure packed with riveting and exciting action and filled with intrigue in a place far away from anywhere you have ever visited before.

Jimmy Blue Eyes' two grandsons lived in Las Vegas, and for years I put out feelers to them that I was interested in interviewing their grandfather. Finally during one visit he agreed to talk with me. At the end of my first meeting with Jimmy, I pointed out that he had never once during his long career given out a single comment to the press, so I asked him why he had finally agreed at age 91 to talk to me. He answered, "Because everybody I know is dead. You're the only person left whose lived in my world, who knows what it was like, who relates to my values, who knew the people I did. You're the only one who can understand me. Besides, you've got some great stories and facts about the people I knew that I never heard before." At the end of my interview he said he needed to get some rest before going out dancing that evening. He was still sharply alert, amusingly quick-witted, and an excellent ballroom dancer who regularly went out to a club to charm the silver-haired girlies and to spend the evening foxtroting and waltzing with them.[iv]

THE EXTENSIVE NEWSPAPER RECORDS

Besides being complete, this presentation is wholly different from previous histories because for the first time the newspaper article accounts of these gangsters' activities are included. These were written by reporters from interviews of the eyewitnesses at the events, police and detective descriptions of their findings and handling of investigations, and the trial testimonies that included the victims, the criminal cohorts who turned state's witness, and the people who harbored some of these gangsters during their fugitive manhunts. The many individual facts collected about each of these incidents create a dramatic step-by-step flow that produces an incredibly exciting and fast-moving adventure story. It is like a movie that is made up of many individual pictures flashed one after the other to produce the motion, but in this case it allows the reader to follow the moving action through his or her imagination.

Newspaper reports are primary source material for biographies about politicians, business leaders, and criminals, and also for law enforcement in criminal investigations. The U.S. Attorney in Chicago who successfully directed the IRS investigative team that prosecuted Al Capone and his lieutenants for income-tax evasion, George E. Q. Johnson, testified to a Senate Judiciary Subcommittee on April 2, 1932 about the importance of newspaper articles in building these cases. He explained, "I made up a card index. Newspaper men have amazingly accurate information. It was rather astonishing. It was not evidence, but it was very accurate information as to who the gangs were and the leaders [and their activities], so I had a newspaper man make a card index of all the gangs, taking it from newspaper stories." This was the IRS' principal source material to identify and locate the criminal associations and financial holdings of Capone and his lieutenants.

In that era many newspapers specialized in publishing organized-crime exposés, and their articles were a useful law-enforcement source tool. For example, from the 1920s through the 1980s, about half the pages in the FBI files concerning members of organized crime were reproductions of newspaper articles. (I did not study the FBI files after the 1980s because they were no longer relevant to the Nevada casino industry since the FBI directors who succeeded J. Edgar Hoover eradicated this type of crime by driving all organized-crime hidden interests out of this business.)

Nevada's early gaming controllers depended heavily on press reports to determine whether casino license applicants should be approved or denied. In the 1940s through the 1960s, Nevada knowingly licensed illegal casino owners and executives from other states for two reasons. First, Nevada had no home grown operators, so the only experienced and knowledgeable casino managers available were illegal operators. Second, a high percentage of casino dealers and executives in that era were accomplished slight-of-hand cheats. Thus, casino officials had to be very knowledgeable about card and dice theft techniques or their operations would have been severely ripped off. This was illustrated by those legitimate businessmen who were licensed as owners in this era but who did not employ a qualified casino manager. Soon after opening, these casinos experienced a high-rate of bankruptcies due to employee theft.

Thus the goal of the early gaming controllers was not to keep experienced illegal casino operators out of Nevada, but as they told me, "our job was to determine the good hoods from the bad gangsters." This meant Nevada wanted licensees to have been involved only with the crimes of gambling and Prohibition, while keeping out all those who had committed crimes involving dishonesty, theft, threats, or violence. Hence this book presents the early backgrounds of the good hoods before they began building the Las Vegas Strip. It is the story of these men's careers, lifestyles, and survival while running huge illicit liquor and gambling operations in the midst of America's toughest and most dangerous gangs.

To distinguish the good hoods from the bad gangsters, gaming controllers interviewed crime reporters in the cities the applicants came from. The first Nevada Gaming Control Board Chairman, Bob Cahill, told me, "Newspapermen were a very important arm of my law enforcement program. There were the out-of-state newsmen. Every town has a reporter who specializes in hoods and syndicated crime. I got more information from newsmen than from official law enforcement agencies. They have access to information the police do not have through personal acquaintance with the criminal element." [v]

Nevada's early gaming controllers also depended on four dedicated in-state investigative reporters who had a passion for chasing down dirt about hoods. They were determined to ferret out the facts, all the facts. And they never interjected personal opinions that have become the style of so many of today's newscasters. They worked for the state's four largest newspapers, two in Las Vegas and two in Reno. They had personal relationships with the local casino operators, who revealed the backgrounds of the various applicants they deemed to be undesirable for Nevada, and defended the ones they knew to be "legit" no matter how bad their reputations in their home press. All four Nevada investigative reporters also had close contacts with some out-of-state reporters in major cities who followed this criminal element in their locales, so these local newspapermen not only wrote the news but they occasionally dramatically influenced the licensing process by covertly supplying their inside information to the gaming authorities. I was fortunate to have had in-depth interviews with all four even though two had left the state by the time I began my research. They were Ed Olsen, Bob Bennyhoff, Bryn Armstrong, and Frank McCulloch. I discussed with each one much of the information they had learned from their sources especially the many scandals they exposed in shocking headlines.

A major part of my research program was to study the microfilms of six archived daily newspapers. Three covered the gambling industry, politics, and economic trends in Nevada, and the other three newspapers were key home cities for many of that era's major license applicants. I read the relevant articles in a total of 123,200 newspapers from the following years:

- The *New York Times* - 1910 through 1959 (50 years)
- The *Chicago Daily Tribune* - 1910 through 1959 (50 years)
- The *Los Angeles Times* - 1920 through 1949 (30 years)
- The *Reno Gazette-Journal* (I used the *Nevada State Journal* until its merger with the *Reno Evening Gazette* on October 7, 1983) - 1931 through 2006 (76 years)
- The *Las Vegas Review-Journal* - 1931 (the year Nevada legalized casinos) through 2006 (76 years)
- The *Las Vegas Sun* - its first edition was on July 1, 1950 to the final edition on September 30, 2005 (55 ¼ years)

The *New York Times* is an exceptional newspaper that had a liberal editorial page but employed both top liberal and conservative reporters to obtain balanced news coverage. Its articles gave in-depth analysis of most issues and included much historical information. The *Times* is a researcher's dream because its articles often lead to other sources and related issues and individuals.

The *Chicago Daily Tribune* was staunchly conservative, but the publisher valued law and order and honest politicians more than his political agenda. Thus, this paper led the fight to topple Al Capone and exposed Republicans as readily as Democrats when it found them to be corrupt. It even endorsed Democrats against the worst-offending Republican candidates and elected officials.

The *Los Angeles Times* during this era was a huge research disappointment. It carried sparse coverage of Prohibition and illegal gambling in Southern California, even though casinos operated openly in Los Angeles and Palm Springs. The *Los Angeles Times'* articles did not list all the facts from police reports, and often did not list the address or even the city where illegal casinos were busted or were having legal problems. Its reporters did almost no research, so unlike the other five newspapers, which frequently exposed the activities of major criminals in their communities, the *Los Angeles Times* produced almost no crime exposés during the 1920s through the 1940s. At least part of the reason can be found in the paper's political agenda. It endorsed and supported the most corrupt politicians and DA's during this period. It even editorialized in news stories on behalf of the crooked officials who protected the serious criminal element in the Los Angeles metropolitan area. The *Los Angeles Times* contained some useful information, but unfortunately buried much more.

The three Nevada newspapers effectively covered the casino industry and its leaders in Las Vegas, Reno, and Lake Tahoe. They also reported on the strength of the economies, market trends, and state politics, including actions and decisions by the state legislature and city councils, courts, and state and local gaming control authorities. Each newspaper had an aggressive investigative reporter who specialized in the gambling industry and politics. (There were four excellent ones until the merger of the *Nevada State Journal* with the *Reno Evening Gazette,* when it was reduced to three.)

It is important to note that reporters sometimes write inaccurate information because some of their sources lie, and reporters are occasionally required by press deadlines to submit articles before fully completing their investigations, which can result in incomplete or distorted information. Thus my research of many other types of documents and my in-depth oral histories with Nevada's gambling-industry pioneers for their first-hand eyewitness' accounts was invaluable in confirming, correcting, and expanding upon these newspaper reports.

I also read the *Kansas City Star* and the *Kansas City Times* for the years 1923 through 1950. Both newspapers had excellent investigative reporters who exposed the city's unusual and unbelievable political and gangland history and its influence on developments in the Nevada gambling industry. These findings were presented in the first book in this series - "All *Against* The Law: The Criminal Activities of the Depression Era Bank Robbers, Mafia, FBI, Politicians, & Cops" (2013).

ORAL HISTORIES WITH NEVADA'S GAMBLING PIONEERS

This book is based on the only extensive in-depth, comprehensive interviews ever conducted of the pioneers who distinguished themselves by making important contributions to the Nevada casino industry. These 582 people were resort owners, hotel and casino management and marketing executives, organized crime gang leaders and their close associates, attorneys, accountants, bankers, gaming control and law enforcement officials, political leaders, and newspaper investigative reporters.

The vast majority of the men who developed Nevada's legal casino industry had previously been involved with illegal casinos, many with Prohibition as well. They always refused requests from reporters and authors for interviews about their lives. Part of the reason for their silence was a remnant of their strict secrecy to avoid exposing criminal activities, but most of this reticence was a reaction to the frequent misquotes by reporters and the lies by authors whose books were fiction thinly disguised as organized-crime history.

Once these good hoods settled in Nevada, their penchant for privacy was counterbalanced because they were now legitimate, licensed, law-abiding businessmen. These men harbored a deep resentment toward the terrible stigma still tainting their names, and they wanted their families to have an accurate record and image of their lives.

My oral histories began with a few bold pioneers who hoped the truth would finally be told. Satisfied with the depth of my research and my determination to dig up the truth, they convinced other pioneers to speak to me. Over time I earned acceptability from virtually every pioneer. All but a handful eventually participated in my oral histories.

They accepted me to be their official historian because I was a dedicated, well-prepared academic researcher and a fellow Nevadan, unlike writers from out of state who stayed briefly and moved on. I had attended the University of Nevada, Reno, and was a casino dealer for three years before beginning my research. They knew I had become part of the casino industry and loved it.

I was surprised to find that these gambling-industry pioneers actually wanted an accurate record - warts and all - rather than a puff piece. The most negative information I got about some of them came not from documents, associates, or enemies, but directly from them. When I would point out that what they had just related to me was quite unflattering, they invariably admonished me with a remark like, "That's me. You can use it, but just tell the truth, the whole truth. Tell it the way it really was!"

Each of these oral history interviews lasted at least two hours. I interviewed key figures from six to 50 hours over several years. Before I sat down with the most relevant individuals, I tried to interview each one's best friends, worst enemies, attorney, and accountant. I prepared a detailed list of relevant questions based on the previous interview statements and all the documentation I had assembled. I explored every important event and issue they were part of, and the policies and their experiences at every casino with which they were associated.

This historical research includes only first-hand, contemporary experiences that are based on eyewitness' observations of each event or issue covered. When an interviewee repeated what he had heard from someone else, the information was almost always highly distorted compared to eyewitness accounts of the same event. So I consigned any second-hand, hearsay information to a special file that I used to prepare questions for future interviewees. Then I sought people who had been at these events or who were involved with these issues so I could obtain their eyewitness reports.

THE SCOPE & UNIQUE FEATURES OF THIS RESEARCH PROJECT

This 48-year research program involved searching through 123,000 old newspapers, numerous books and magazine articles, 200,000 pages of FBI Headquarters and agent internal reports, Congressional hearings, legislative and court records, federal and state government agency historical records archived on the internet, and University of Nevada Reno oral histories of Nevada gambling industry pioneers and political leaders. I combined and organized all this data into source material by topic, and then I conducted in-depth, comprehensive interviews with 582 people who distinguished themselves by making important contributions to the Nevada casino industry. I integrated these detailed interviews with the enormous volume of collected documented records, and then I crosschecked all facts and sources to verify their authenticity and create the first academic analysis of the development of organized crime in the U.S. and the Nevada casino industry.

This great variety of sources produced the facts for the text and the 30 addendums. When each fact is presented, its source is identified either in the text with it, or in the extensive endnotes, such as "in testimony before the U.S. Senate Kefauver Committee." This is to assist historians, researchers, readers, and critics interested in further study or to confirm the accuracy of their use. For every quote, the name of the person who said it and the source where it was found are identified either in the text, addendum, or the endnotes. Quotes that are from gambling-industry pioneers who participated in my oral histories are listed as "my interview."

The facts presented in most consecutive sentences are from different sources, so a complete documentation in the endnotes would require a book much longer than this one. The simple but effective solution when dealing with newspaper reports was to not identify the specific sources when it was obtained from the following six daily newspapers - the *New York Times,* the *Chicago Daily Tribune,* the *Los Angeles Times,* the *Las Vegas Review Journal,* the *Las Vegas Sun,* and Reno's *Nevada State Journal.* For every event dated in the endnotes, these six newspapers usually have an article about it in the next day's edition, but sometimes in the same day's edition.

This historical presentation has special features intended to make it easier to read. While a history is a chronology of events, multiple incidents that occur simultaneously can make it difficult for the reader to clearly focus on the specifics of each one. Thus, each chapter section follows a single gang or individual and takes one event or issue after another in its entirety to its conclusion.

Only key participants' names are presented in the text to make the storyline clearer and easier for the reader. The names of people who appear briefly in a single incident are listed only in the endnotes to be available for historians, researchers, and interested readers without cluttering, complicating, or slowing reading of the text. Each of these people's roles is clearly identified in the text according to their relationship to the event or the key subject. For example "an eyewitness" or "his girlfriend."

Dates in the text are replaced with the length of time in days, weeks, or months between pairs of related events to make the time frame clear. The date of every major event is presented in the source notes, and the key dates for interrelated events are listed in chronological order to create clear historical timelines for other academic researchers.

When the FBI releases document pages under the Freedom of Information Act, the names of everyone except the file subject are usually redacted (blacked out). Thus, quotes of FBI documents in the text and in the endnotes may contain five small x's as xxxxx to indicate a redacted name was part of the quote in an FBI document.

And now here are the amazing drama-filled adventures of the most incredible gangsters in history along their routes to the Las Vegas Strip, and also the many interesting characters they encountered. These are their mind-boggling untold stories!

AUTHOR'S BIOGRAPHY

THE LEGAL RAMIFICATIONS OF HANGING OUT WITH HOODLUMS

This author's biography describes the unparalleled, historical research program that took me inside organized crime and led to this book. It also resulted in my careers in Las Vegas Strip casino management and worldwide casino consulting. The unusual circumstances surrounding them were filled with seemingly impenetrable roadblocks that were opened up by unexpected opportunities.

My fascination with Nevada gambling began at age 7, when my parents started taking me on summer vacations to Lake Tahoe and the Las Vegas Strip. I was required to stand at a distance behind the players at the twenty-one tables to study the proficiency of the dealers and the gambling action. The first time I watched, I knew I wanted to be a twenty-one dealer when I grew up.

At age 21, I spent my summer break from San Francisco State University working in downtown Las Vegas as a dollar-an-hour shill at the *Fremont Hotel,* which had a large clientele of high-rolling players. The shills gambled with house-supplied money at the tables to make them seem busy during slow daytime and evening business periods.

The next summer, I began my career as a twenty-one dealer at the new *Sahara-Tahoe Hotel* at Lake Tahoe. I worked Friday through Monday at the casino and completed my college degree by attending classes in San Francisco every Tuesday and Thursday. I then attended graduate school at the University of Nevada, Reno (UNR), while continuing to deal at South Shore four days a week.

After work, I often had a nightcap at the bar with one of the table-game executives who worked behind me. I listened intently as they described their incredible career experiences. Most of these men had previously worked in the wide-open illegal casinos found throughout the country during the 1930s and 1940s. Then around 1950, local political reform movements and law-enforcement closed down almost every illegal casino in the country. The unemployed executives and dealers moved to Las Vegas because positions were readily available for experienced employees in the rapidly proliferating gambling resorts along the Las Vegas Strip and also in Reno and Lake Tahoe.

These men had lived very different lives than I had been exposed to in the genteel, middle-class, nonviolent milieu I was brought up in. Most had grown up in poor neighborhoods and had grammar-school educations at best. But they had very savvy street smarts and keen perception about people. Although they had worked in illegal operations that bribed the police to avoid arrest and closure, the police offered them no protection for their large cash bankrolls. These illegal casino operators had to defend themselves from robbers and also from gangs trying to take over their territory. They were fiercely independent individualists, the last of the frontiersmen, standing alone against a tough predatory underworld.

I was so intrigued by these men's stories that I wanted to learn more about their backgrounds, life in the illegal-casino world, and how gaming control had developed in Nevada. It was a new and unique form of law enforcement that existed only in Nevada. I spent my limited free time in UNR's library searching old newspapers for articles about the development of the industry. I realized the mass of available material on the subject demanded a full-time effort, but I had no way to finance a serious chronicling of this information to satisfy my curiosity or to write a book about it.

Then the Vietnam War got underway, and I soon received my draft notice. I declared conscientious-objector status and the FBI conducted the required investigation of my life to determine if I warranted this classification. Then the Selective Service System approved my application. It typically ordered conscientious objectors to spend their two years of alternative service at a hospital near their home cleaning bed pans for about $300 a month. But the FBI investigation and Selective Service interviews about my background had brought my research interests to light. It turned out that I was the only academician who had developed close personal relationships with members of organized crime. This was especially impressive at that time, because it was years before the FBI would insert an undercover agent into an organized-crime gang.

As a result, I was introduced to Joseph D. Lohman, Dean at the School of Criminology at the University of California, Berkeley. He was a highly-respected criminologist, who proposed to take advantage of my trio of assets – personal contacts in the underworld, a passion for casino gambling operations, and a university degree in social psychology. He proposed to transform my research dream into a structured sociological historical study about the development of organized crime, its impact on Nevada's casino industry, and the creation of Nevada gaming control. To encourage the former illegal gambling operators to cooperate and to demonstrate my research was not a law-enforcement sting, every question I would ask was about events at least 10 years old, so participants would know their answers were well beyond the statute of limitations for criminal prosecution.

Since Dean Lohman's proposal would potentially expand law enforcement's and academia's limited knowledge about the structure and operation of organized crime, the Selective Service System quickly approved this study. It ordered me to report for two years of alternative service with the School of Criminology at Berkeley. Dean Lohman directed me to read relevant archived newspapers and other documents in UNLV's library, interview gaming-control authorities, and hang out with hoodlums for interviews. Between mid-1967 and mid-1969, I enjoyed the glorious wonders of Las Vegas on my $300-a-month salary. I completed my two years of service and received an honorable discharge from the Selective Service for majoring in hoodlums. Yet I had barely tapped the surface of the available information. So during the next 47 years, I devoted every spare moment to finishing my research and writing this first book in a planned historical series about the Nevada gambling industry. My personal life-long research is in memory to Dean Lohman who was a very special mentor. (The Selective Service and School of Criminology draft-order and discharge documents are presented at www.BillFriedmanAuthor.com)

After discharge, I spent the next 10 years making a living as the leading after-lunch and after-dinner speaker for Las Vegas convention groups. About once a week, I taught groups of 50 to 5,000 people how to play the table games, or I told them intriguing historical inside stories about the Nevada casino industry. I also taught the pioneer course Casino Operations and Management for the College of Hotel Administration at the University of Nevada, Las Vegas under Dean Jerome J. Vallen. I wrote the book *Casino Management* (1974 and updated it with Atlantic City in 1982). It became the seminal work in the field, and the *New York Times* reported it was the most expensive required reading at Cornell University's School of Hotel Administration. All these endeavors provided a livable income and left me with five days a week full-time to continue my research.

I did not attempt to conceal my feelings like a reporter or a psychiatrist. On the contrary, I was a young man captivated by the subject and intently searching for the truth, and I was very open about my opinions and beliefs. My candor was important because law-enforcement policies, judicial decisions, and Constitutional interpretation in the period I was studying were very different from the times I lived in. Many times, Nevada's top gaming and law enforcers, as well as the hoodlums who owned and operated the casinos, told me, "If you don't get back into our world, you will never understand why we made the decisions we did and why anything happened." They were right!

Learning about their world caused a major life and career adjustment. An encounter I had with Benny Binion, one of Nevada's premier pioneer casino operators and marketers, best describes how I made my occupational decisions. Benny was an early supporter of my research, and he advised me on my career like a father figure. Because I was developing so much knowledge about the operation of the industry and I was getting to know top executives in the limited number of casinos, in 1970 I was offered executive positions by two casinos that would have paid me far more money than I had ever dreamed of earning. I turned both down because I would have had no time to continue my research. My goals and values had changed from my youth, when one of the attractions to Las Vegas was the affluent lifestyle. One day at lunch, I told Benny about these two opportunities and my decisions to pass on them. This older Irish gentleman stared at me intently for some time, shook his head, and said, "You are the only Jew I have ever met who absolutely does not give a damn about money." Then, as now, my consuming passion for knowledge about this fascinating industry and these remarkable men directed my career decisions.

Then, seven years after discharge by the Selective Service System, an opportunity came along that was too enticing to pass up. Summa Corporation, owned by tycoon Howard Hughes, appointed me to be the only person to ever simultaneously manage two casinos on the Las Vegas Strip - the *Castaways* and the *Silver Slipper*. Both positions required I apply for my first state and county licenses as a key employee. This was a crisis situation because the Nevada gaming control authorities denied every one who had any association with organized crime figures, unless these were minimal and accidental. In the few cases they approved, they prohibited any further contact as a condition of licensing. If my applications were denied, it would have ended my career in the casino business, and if I were restricted from further contact, it would have ended my historical research. This was a scary prospect because I had spent my whole career researching hoods to understand what makes them tick and why they do what they do.

Fortunately, I had interviewed the key state gaming control officials extensively throughout my research and kept them posted on who I was seeing but not what I was learning. I also discussed my research with Las Vegas Metropolitan Police Department detectives, including its Organized Crime Bureau. The licensing authorities and their investigators knew me well and wholeheartedly supported and contributed to my academic research into the underworld's involvement in Nevada. They wanted me to complete my history in my spare time, so they encouraged me to continue my research. Thus, I became the only Nevada gaming licensee who was allowed to associate with hoodlums as long as they were associated in some way with the casino industry or Las Vegas.

I quickly transformed the *Castaways* and the *Silver Slipper* from long-time money-losers into top Nevada profit makers. When the figures came out for my third month of operation, Summa's leaders called me to a corporate meeting to tell me that the month's profits were greater than any of them had imagined possible. Except for months in which the players had big wins, the profits went up significantly every month for the next twelve years. In the process, I achieved the highest average win per slot machine in Nevada. Under my leadership, the cash flow from these two old, smaller casinos financed the entire corporate structure of the world's largest privately-owned company.

At the first corporate meeting, Frank Morse, who was Summa's second in command and the man to whom I reported, pulled me aside because he said they wanted to inform me who my friends were. He said, "We told you up front that you were an experiment for us. We knew you had never supervised anyone or managed anything, when we made you president. Your five references were reputable professional people who were good character references, but we knew none of them knew anything about the gaming business. We still did our due diligence and talked to them. We also went to the two biggest gangsters in town for their opinions, because we know they know the most about this business. We think you should be aware that Summa has had tens of thousands of applicants over the years, but Benny Binion gave us the finest reference that we have ever received for anyone, and Moe Dalitz was just one step behind. Both were confident you were ready. You can thank them for making this job available."

I was already grateful to both Benny and Moe for having made all their key executives available to assist my historical research for the previous decade. The vast knowledge and experiences they had shared with me had prepared me well for the many challenges I faced in turning both casinos around. My professional and business careers were truly made possible by my penchant for associating with hoodlums. It should be noted that Moe Dalitz is a key figure in this book because of his large Prohibition operation, illegal casinos, and great influence in organized crime nationwide, before he built two major Las Vegas Strip gambling resorts.

I operated the highly-successful *Castaways* and *Silver Slipper* casinos for 13 years before they were sold because of Hughes' death. (Nevada law requires that all assets be sold when the deceased has multiple heirs.) The two casino-sale contracts gave me complete unfettered control over the operations for one more year to produce additional profits for Summa. Despite assuring generous severance packages to the employees who stayed until the closings, both casinos came close to producing record profits because the regular tourist and local players who visited each one did not search for a new home until we threw a huge goodbye party and closed the doors at their favorite hangout. The *Castaways'* property was developed into the first megaresort, the *Mirage.* The *Silver Slipper* was purchased by the adjacent *Frontier Hotel* to become another megaresort, but the state appropriated much of the *Silver Slipper's* property for a freeway.

Since then, I have worked as a consultant to casinos across the country, including being licensed as a key casino executive in five states. At the same time, I consulted to casinos in countries around the world, including almost all that catered chiefly to high-rollers. Between consulting assignments, I continued to focus on my historical research, except when I wrote another business book, *Designing Casinos to Dominate the Competition.* It was published by my alma mater, UNR's Institute for the Study of Gambling and Commercial Gaming, in 2001.

Two decades after being licensed in the heart of the Las Vegas Strip at the *Castaways* and *Silver Slipper,* I was involved with another unique licensing situation. This resulted when I signed a five-month contract to manage and turn around the once profitable 1,000-room *Oasis Hotel and Casino* resort, with its world-class Arnold Palmer golf course. It was located in Mesquite, Nevada, 85 miles northeast of Las Vegas near the Utah border. The landlord was Si Redd, who had created giant slot manufacturer IGT. As landlord of the *Oasis,* he had taken over the operation from the lessees who had defaulted, and he called on me to save the operation because he was well acquainted with my great turnarounds of the *Castaways* and *Silver Slipper.* I replaced the general manager who had held the only license at the *Oasis* after the lessees had departed. The Gaming Control Board waived the legal requirement for me to apply for a license upon taking the position because the investigation could not have been completed during my five-month tenure, and the Board did not want to waste everyone's time for what would be mere window dressing. As the Board told the *Oasis'* attorney, "We already know everything about Friedman, and we are comfortable with him." This decision was practical and justified, but it resulted in an irony. Nevada has allowed just this one casino to ever operate without anyone holding a state gaming license, not an owner nor a manager, and it just happened to be controlled by the man who was known for his relationships with hoodlums.

I have lived my life in a unique twilight realm that allowed me to seamlessly move back and forth between two separate opposing worlds that loathed each other. I was successful in dealing with both the law enforcers and the criminals because, until this book, I never repeated anything I was told. Everyone in the underworld knew I never reported about my research interview findings or personal discussions. Everyone in the overworld knew I never participated in a felony and also never revealed anything about their investigations and suspicions. The gaming controllers also knew my casino operations scrupulously followed all regulations, and I worked closely with agents to address their occasional concerns.

Since closing the *Castaways* and *Silver Slipper* 25 years ago, my consulting and writing pursuits have given me more than half of each year to devote full time to my historical research. It has been a wonderful odyssey exploring the casino pioneers' unique and intriguing lives, struggles, and achievements along with the economic, political, and legal context in which they occurred. Now it is time to tell their astonishing stories. I hope you enjoy sharing their adventuresome lives as much as I have.

CHAPTER 1

THE PROHIBITION OPERATIONS OF LUCIANO & COSTELLO

BEN SIEGEL'S GLORIOUS DREAM

Ben Siegel opened his fabulous *Flamingo* casino on the evening after Christmas 1946, when the fledgling Las Vegas Strip consisted of just two other hotel/casino resorts and four tiny restaurant/ bars. Beyond these few buildings was nothing but pristine desert, extending outward over the huge valley to the surrounding mountains.

The *Flamingo's* opening was the first exciting event to hit Las Vegas since the town celebrated the Allies' victory ending World War II 16 months earlier. Local residents and guests staying at the town's few hotels jammed the new casino from wall to wall. That first night the *Flamingo's* hotel rooms were still unfinished and unoccupied, but the casino was jammed without any in-house tourists.

But what appeared to be a great success was a disaster in the making. Wealthy tourists rimmed the crap tables, shooting one long winning streak after another. By 11 p.m. practically every player was a big winner. Then one gambler's wife, concerned that her husband's luck might change, thought of a clever way to get him out of the *Flamingo* while he was still ahead - she demanded to see the midnight show at one of the other two hotel/casinos on the Strip. The wife of every other big winner quickly followed suit.

As the shows ended at the *El Rancho Vegas* and the *Last Frontier*, all the *Flamingo's* earlier winners rushed to the crap tables just outside the showroom doors to try to parlay their previous luck into bigger winnings. Unfortunately, as sizzling as the dice were earlier that night at the *Flamingo*, they were frigid at the competitors' tables. Just about every player went to bed a loser for the night, denying the *Flamingo's* owners an opportunity to win back their losses.

The *Flamingo's* staggering opening night losses, compounded by an already overwhelming debt to its construction contractor, turned Siegel's dream into a monumental nightmare. But while his glorious venture appeared to have been a serious miscalculation, this bleak time turned out to be just a temporary glitch in Siegel's farsighted plan to develop the tiny town of Las Vegas, Nevada into the gambling capital of the world.

Siegel was the most visionary entrepreneur to ever gamble on the Nevada casino industry. In addition to building his fabulous *Flamingo,* he envisioned a panorama of luxury hotel/casinos stretching along the Los Angeles highway expanding away from the city limits of Las Vegas. He proselytized the potential riches of his magnificent dream to his life-long underworld associates, all legendary gangsters from the days of Prohibition and illegal elegant casinos. When he was murdered, just six months after the *Flamingo's* opening, his old friends and partners in crime, one after the other, stepped in to participate in the construction of his blueprint. Over the next two decades - from the 1946 opening of the *Flamingo* to the 1966 opening of *Caesars Palace* - they would build 80% of the Las Vegas Strip's resorts.

Turning Siegel's vision into reality made the 1950s the Las Vegas Strips' greatest growth period as it became a wondrous, neon-lit, beckoning sight. Single-story gambling resorts sat far back from the two-lane highway. The front and sides of each casino building were lined with a broad swath of beautiful foliage and behind were meandering walkways of single-story and two-story bungalows. The early resorts were about a half mile apart from each other with few buildings between them. Along with the clear air, this isolation turned each gardened resort into a tempting oasis surrounded by undeveloped natural desert covered by shimmering native vegetation - sagebrush, creosote, and yuccas - as far as the eye could see all the way to the distant mountains.

During this glamorous era, Las Vegas' showrooms and restaurants were filled with men in well-tailored suits and women in elegant evening gowns and furs. For pleasure-seeking adults, the Strip was America's naughty playground, the only place in the country with legal 24-hour gambling and drinking, readily-available beautiful call girls, and the greatest entertainers in the thrilling era of the dinner nightclub and showroom. This uninhibited paradise was visited almost exclusively by serious gamblers and rounders, men and women escaping the responsibilities and humdrum realities of everyday life.

Here for the first time are the real stories of the amazing criminal careers and social worlds of Ben Siegel, his partners, and close associates up to the time each made the decision to invest in the fledgling Las Vegas Strip. It covers three decades beginning with Prohibition in 1920. Of all the liquor-peddling gangs, three were by far the biggest and most successful. The premier gang had five partners – Siegel, Meyer Lansky, Charlie Luciano, Joe Adonis, and Vincent Alo. A leader from each of the other two major suppliers – Frank Costello and Moe Dalitz – became their close underworld and overworld allies. During this era, the territorial gang wars inadvertently thrust these seven improbable men to the pinnacle of organized crime leadership, making Luciano America's most powerful gangster. After Prohibition ended in the 1930s and 1940s, these seven became the biggest operators of illegal wide-open high-end gambling casinos across the country. Then in the late 1940s and early 1950s, they pioneered the rapid development of the Las Vegas Strip gambling resorts, which they would oversee for the next two decades. The astounding truth about their careers and lives began with the implementation of Prohibition.

PROHIBITION - IDEALISM WITH UNINTENDED CONSEQUENCES

National Prohibition began in 1920, but two centuries earlier the forces that created and opposed this massive social experiment were introduced to colonial America. One group of immigrant settlers wanted to prohibit alcohol, but another group desired to drink, while a third was willing to illegally supply this demand. The opposing values of these groups was illustrated at the inception of the colony of Georgia way back in 1733. Its founder banned "demon" rum and brandy in the colony, but the enclave was far from dry. Some of the original settlers built illegal stills in the woods distant from the colony to avoid detection of the telltale aroma, and they worked under the cover of darkness by using moonlight, leading to the name *moonshiners.* Other settlers smuggled boatloads of these beverages from nearby colonies and were labeled *rumrunners,* while the retail distributors, who often hid their illicit contraband in their clothing or broad boots, were termed *bootleggers.* The net result was total failure of Georgia's early alcohol prohibition and lifting of the ban after nine years.[1]

The utter failure of this social experiment did not deter colonial moral crusaders from developing local prohibition movements, whose goal was the complete eradication of alcohol from the country. These groups' political influence grew over time, and in the last half of the 1800s, they succeeded in having laws passed prohibiting the manufacture and sale of alcoholic spirits in more than half the States, while getting many counties in wet states to go dry. When the U.S. entered World War I, the temperance movement capitalized on the public's aroused patriotic spirit. The reformers claimed alcohol interfered with this national commitment by diverting grains needed for the war effort and by reducing production due to many workers suffering from hangovers. The 18th Amendment to the U.S. Constitution outlawing "the manufacture, sale, or transportation of intoxicating liquors" was ratified following approval by the 36th state, and to give it teeth, Congress passed the National Prohibition Enforcement Act, called the Volstead Act, which took effect a year later on January 16, 1920. The Volstead Act established penalties for production and sale of alcohol, but none for consuming it. (See Addendum A)

A large percentage of Americans still wanted liquor, including many politicians and law enforcement officers, and they were willing to violate the law to get it. Up against this resistance to the law, the number of federal Prohibition law enforcers, known as *Prohis,* was inadequate from the beginning, and although their numbers increased during Prohibition, so did consumption. The Prohis were not able to make a dent in national alcohol sales, and the feds convicted few major Prohibition gang leaders. Local authorities made the vast majority of arrests against the big violators, but they invariably received nothing more than a trivial fine of about $100, making the penalty akin to a city business tax or licensing fee.

While the temperance movement succeeded in criminalizing alcohol distribution and drastically decreasing legal alcohol supplies, Prohibition produced several unintended effects. Amazingly, alcohol consumption per capita rose substantially. Violating Prohibition became a national obsession in the flapper party atmosphere of the Roaring '20s stock market boom, and illegal speakeasies sprang up across America.[2]

Violating Prohibition was incredibly lucrative, so it was not surprising that enterprising criminals jumped in to fill the gap between the limited supply and the large demand. Ambitious street gangs expanded their territories and acquired business proficiency in manufacturing, importing, storing, and wholesaling large quantities of booze. These gangs' status during Prohibition was elevated from vile villains to national heroes. These gangs grew into powerful and lucrative organized crime syndicates, some of which continue to plague many cities today almost a century later.

Government officials were aware of the country's great thirst and the broad public opposition to Prohibition. It was easy for many to deceive themselves that allowing violation was merely carrying out the will of the people. Major criminal gangs strengthened their connections with politicians, police, prosecutors, and judges by offering unprecedented large bribes that expanded the breadth and depth of government corruption throughout the nation.

While banning alcohol was supposed to empty the prisons, the jail population quadrupled during Prohibition. Two-thirds of new federal prisoners were convicted of alcohol or drug offenses. Federal expenditures on prisons increased more than 10 times during Prohibition, yet prisons were severely overcrowded. Even with more men sent to prison, crime increased nationally. Most striking was the steady rise in the number of murders. Prohibition violation was highly competitive and dangerous. Gang disputes erupted over territories, and gunmen rode shotgun on the truck convoys to protect the liquid contraband from violent hijackers. Fierce shootouts at storage depots and ruthless killings of competitors were also ongoing problems. After Prohibition was repealed, America's murder rate fell for 11 consecutive years.[3]

PROHIBITION'S MANY NEW SOURCES OF ALCOHOL

The Volstead Act had serious loopholes such as allowing the sale of alcohol for priests to use during sacramental religious services and for *medicinal* purposes. The Act required liquor companies to store millions of bottles of liquor in bonded warehouses, supervised by federal agents. This alcohol was sold to drug companies for distribution to drugstores. The drugstores could dispense medicinal pint bottles of hooch for all manner of curious illnesses, but only if a patient possessed a doctor's special prescription.

The rest of this "bonded" alcohol was sold to companies that manufactured a myriad of government-approved products from antifreeze, paint, and varnish to toiletries such as colognes and anti-dandruff hair tonic. Alcoholics that were desperate enough drank denatured alcohol products or illegally manufactured alcohol, which was more likely to be adulterated with toxins. Many became seriously ill, and the death rate from poisoned liquor quadrupled during the first five years of Prohibition, prompting humorist and social commentator Will Rogers to remark, "Governments used to murder by the bullet only. Now it's by the quart."

These bonded federal supplies met much of the nation's demand for liquor during the first year of Prohibition. For example just one hour after the law took effect the first Prohibition violation was reported. Six armed masked men stole $100,000 worth of whiskey stamped "for medicinal use" from two freight cars in a Chicago railroad switching yard to sell illegally. The liquor business was quickly entered by enterprising professional street gangs who bribed corrupt federal officials to withdraw huge quantities of bonded alcohol using false manufacturing permits. Other gangs obtained these medicinal stocks by bribing the major drug companies that had shown no concern for the health of the public it was supposed to serve. Six years before Prohibition went into effect Congress had passed the Harrison Act that criminalized the use of narcotics without a physician's prescription to prevent these drug companies from routinely spiking their *patent medicines* with heavy doses of morphine to addict unsuspecting consumers. Whatever their ailment, these elixirs made them feel a whole lot better.

One year after Prohibition went into effect Republican Warren Harding was inaugurated President, and he appointed Roy Haynes as Federal Director of Prohibition. He in turn appointed many dishonest or ineffective state prohibition directors. Frank Wilson, who would build the government's case against Al Capone, wrote in his memoir, "State directors appointed ward politicians, crooks, or protégés of the bosses as federal prohibition agents. None of them had civil service status. The prohibition directors enjoyed great power and heavy responsibility. It was their special function to issue permits for the withdrawal from distilleries of whiskey for medicinal purposes and alcohol for manufacturing purposes." [4] (See Addendum B)

As the bonded alcohol supply was depleted, many families augmented their income with small alcohol operations. The Volstead Act allowed home winemakers to ferment 200 gallons a year for their own use, an average of more than two quarts a day. They could not be prosecuted unless their home or vehicle contained more than 200 gallons, or unless law enforcers observed them accepting payment. While U.S. commercial wine production plunged from 51 million gallons to just 3 million during the first five years of Prohibition, a quarter of California's wineries survived by shipping grapes and concentrated grape juice across the country to the big cities' home markets. Grape-growing acreage in California actually doubled during this period, and grape prices increased dramatically. Paradoxically the loophole in the Volstead Act that made prosecution of home winemakers extremely difficult increased American wine consumption substantially. Home winemaking flourished as these family enterprises began supplying restaurants and individuals. [5]

Tens of thousands of small, decentralized home manufacturers churned out an enormous volume of corn liquor. Criminal gangs not only profited by buying and distributing the output of these home producers, but by supplying them raw materials as well. The raw materials market was so lucrative that territorial disputes soon arose between the large suppliers. One such conflict, the Sugar War, erupted over supplying corn sugar, the principal ingredient in corn liquor.

One of Prohibition's unintended effects was a shift in consumption from beer to spirits. A much larger quantity of beer had to be produced, stored, and transported to equal the volume of alcohol contained in a bottle of wine or liquor, making it a much riskier venture. This caused the price to get a buzz from beer to rise higher than for wine or spirits, so many consumers switched to the harder stuff. While most gangs stayed away from beer because of the greater risk, its high price made it very profitable, so it became the specialty of a few major crime gangs like Chicago's Al Capone and New York City's Waxey Gordon.

As the bonded liquor supply was exhausted, the organized-crime gangs moved forward by calling upon an American heritage created by two wars during colonial times. It began with the British defeat of the French to take possession of North America east of the Mississippi River. This victorious seven-year war drove the British government into heavy debt, so it imposed new taxes on the colonies. The tea tax became the rallying cry for the revolution, but the tax on liquor manufacturers was much larger as was the opposition to it, so many immigrants made moonshine from their traditional recipes and sold it to neighbors. After the eight-year Revolutionary War, the new U.S. government was deep in debt from the money borrowed to fight it. It had to institute taxes to pay off this obligation, but it repeated the English Crown's mistake of placing the heaviest tax burden on liquor manufacturers, so the moonshine industry continued to flourish. This tax placed an unfair burden on the many western-frontier farmers who moonshined to increase their income, and their opposition led to three years of sporadic violence against government revenuers.

Finally the Whiskey Rebellion erupted with 5,000 armed rebels gathering in protest in the small frontier settlement of Pittsburgh. This mob challenged the authority of their democratically-elected federal representatives to tax, just as they had confronted the British Crown. This forced President Washington to muster an overwhelming force to march against these insurgents. This 13,000-man militia was larger than Washington's army most of the time during the Revolutionary War. The

President's goal was to scare the farmers back to their homes without violence, and his massive approaching army and artillery units accomplished the crushing of the tax rebellion.

Now the still operators had to either pay the tax or shut down. Many of the primarily Scot and Irish western Pennsylvania farmers instead rejected federal authority. They moved to the back wood areas in the unsettled mountain regions of the Southeastern and mid-Atlantic states, especially Kentucky, where they continued to ply their illicit trade. Six years after the Whiskey Rebellion, Thomas Jefferson defeated incumbent president John Adams by campaigning to eliminate the alcohol tax, which he did. Moonshining became a family business in these parts of the country, and some of their descendants during Prohibition directed the operation of the organized-crime gangs' large distillation plants that replaced the output of the closed giant legal distilleries, or taught the hoods their craft. (See Addendum C)

Prohibition moonshiners made an important impact on modern technology. They carried their loads from the hills to market in standard cars with revved-up engines to outrun the Prohis along the route. They tested their swiftness in races at Daytona, Florida, where one world record after another fell as speeds approached 300 miles per hour at the end of Prohibition. These races led to the birth of NASCAR (National Association for Stock Car Auto Racing) in Daytona Beach, and many of this sport's early legendary drivers were moonshiners. (See Addendum D) The moonshiner's craft is a fascinating process akin to baking bread at home, but it produces a very different product. (See Addendum E)

SMUGGLING FOREIGN LIQUORS

Soon after Prohibition began there was no shortage of small gangs distilling some type of hard liquor and fermenting wine and beer, but these illegal concoctions were raw and rough. Understandably affluent drinkers wanted the type of quality barrel-aged liquor they were used to, and they were willing to pay premium prices to get it. Small rings of smugglers emerged to fill the supply. The nearest legal source was the Caribbean Islands, making rum the easiest to obtain. Therefore it became the first type of illegally imported liquor. Budding rumrunners bought up every available vessel that looked seaworthy, as well as many that looked like they should have been condemned as possible deathtraps. The cargoes were transported mostly from Cuba to isolated shores along the U.S. Gulf Coast.

Since many drinkers preferred whiskey, the bigger smuggling operations began buying large quantities of expensive Canadian and European whiskeys and scotches for wholesale to nightclubs, upper-end speakeasies, fine restaurants, leading hotels, and underground retailers across America. They replaced the small boats that were adequate to transit the Caribbean Sea or Gulf of Mexico from Cuba with larger cargo ships and freighters. They purchased their merchandise legally in the Bahamas, then transported it to offshore locations along the Northeastern seaboard. These ships stopped just outside the three-mile territorial limit so as not to officially enter the United States and thus avoid seizure and arrest by the Coast Guard or Navy.

In darkness of night, each freighter stopped at a specific spot, and independent speedboat operators pulled up. All vessels kept their engines running, on the ready to make a fast escape from Coast Guard patrols and pirate ships that lurked in the darkness at a distance. The din of revving engines drowned out conversation, so the freighter captains stood on deck under floodlights, holding up signs listing their prices. Speedboat crews handed over bundles of cash, loaded their cargo, and then sped to remote shore enclaves and isolated docks to transfer the shipment to waiting trucks.

Piracy was an ever-present threat, so freighters were armed with cannons and speedboat crews carried guns. Raging battles were fought on the water, but the surviving combatants - rumrunners and pirates alike - never admitted participation or knowledge about these violent, sometimes deadly conflicts to the authorities. They rarely even told their associates, so acts of Prohibition piracy rarely appeared in newspapers.

The areas where the freighters lined up along the east and west coasts just outside the three-mile limit became known as *Rum Row.* Newspaper pictures of the stationary-boat displays hammered home the failure of the Noble Experiment. To push this embarrassing failure far from public view, federal lawmakers stretched the limit of America's legal territory to 12 miles offshore. This unilateral action violated treaties, but the U.S. Supreme Court allowed the seizing of smuggling vessels up to this expanded limit during Prohibition. The new 12-mile limit made rumrunning more dangerous. It was four times further to shore, and the longer distance meant the boats had to be faster and sturdier to protect the crews and cargo from both pirate ships and Coast Guard patrols.[6]

During Prohibition's early years, the Coast Guard was only a minor obstacle. It had few patrol boats, and its old vessels could not keep up with the smugglers' swift ones. In addition to lack of resources, the Coast Guard lacked motivation, reflecting the public's hostility to Prohibition and apathy among local authorities. But the agency's role changed in 1924, when it was fortified with more and better boats and given a mandate to stop the smuggling. The Navy loaned a couple dozen destroyers that were faster, had larger cannons, and carried crews armed with machine guns and rifles. In addition, construction began on specially designed cutters, which were armed to deal with the rumrunners' violent crews.

The fully-equipped Coast Guard spread its ships along several hundred miles of coastline, forming a territorial screen. At night their searchlights were trained on the large, motionless freighters, so small boats dared not approach. This tactic effectively closed down the Rum Rows, but the smugglers adapted an effective counter strategy. Liquor freighters began traveling alone with each arriving at a specific spot at a designated time in the dark of night with lights out. Speedboats arrived at the same moment, hovered alongside while they rapidly loaded their cargos, and then quickly sped to shore. The Coast Guard's expanded role took a toll on the less sophisticated operators, but there were enough successful rumrunners to keep the Jazz Age speakeasies in full swing.

THE LUCIANO & COSTELLO IMPORTING OPERATIONS

Charlie Luciano and Frank Costello headed Prohibition's two giant illegal importing gangs. Even though they competed for the Manhattan market, where the majority of America's wealthy people were concentrated, they became life-long close friends and gangland political allies.

Costello's operation is well documented. His smuggling ring was started by Bill Dwyer, who owned racetracks in Montreal and Cincinnati. The allure of Prohibition's tremendous potential profits tempted Dwyer and other legitimate businessmen to cross over into crime. The implementation of the Volstead Act led Dwyer to build a massive illegal importing business with Frank Costello as his manager and eventually partner. Dwyer and Costello employed five full-time agents to purchase fine liquor in foreign capitals and a sales staff in Manhattan to wholesale their inventory to distributors, middlemen, and speakeasies. The Manhattan high-end drinking market's greatest demand was for the world's best whiskeys and scotches with lesser demand for fine champagnes, sauternes, and cognac.[7]

Dwyer and Costello contracted with legitimate shipping firms to transport their inventory across the Atlantic to Bimini in the Bahamas. The goods were reloaded onto their own fleet of two-dozen freighters which ran the final lap to the edge of U. S. territory. They anchored along the nation's largest and most famous Rum Row off New Jersey, and offloaded their cargo onto the ring's string of speedboats for transport into New York Harbor.

The tremendous volume of alcoholic beverages Dwyer and Costello transported into the country was an embarrassment to U.S. authorities, so they successfully pressured the British Government to close down the Bahamas' pipeline. Since the Canadian authorities helped the U.S. enforce Prohibition in the early years, Dwyer and Costello relocated their freighter-transfer operations to a French possession securely out of their reach. Their new safe haven was the island of Saint Pierre off the Miquelon Islands near Newfoundland. There the pair built a long pier, a deep-water dock, and a large warehouse, and they paid the municipality of Saint Pierre $2 for every case they transshipped. They moved more than two million cases annually through this way station, providing the tiny town of only a few hundred residents with revenues exceeding $4 million a year for a decade. (This equals $50 million a year in buying power today.)[8]

Luciano's gang amassed an even bigger bankroll to lease a larger fleet of freighters that traversed the Atlantic directly from Europe to New Jersey's territorial boundary. The source of their funding was never revealed, but their annual volume clearly eclipsed the more than 24 million bottles of fine European liquor that Costello's ring moved through Saint Pierre.

To safely pass through U.S. territorial oceanic waters, Dwyer and Costello corrupted Coast Guard personnel from the highest to the bottom ranks. They especially targeted captains, radio operators, and observers. A radio operator could delay reporting to his captain rumrunning sightings that came in from other cutters, and defer broadcasting his ship's smuggling sightings to the rest of the Rum Row Coast Guard fleet. Observers and captains who saw smugglers speeding off in the distance could simply look in another direction.

Officials at Coast Guard headquarters were bought off so they would dispatch the bribed cutter crews to the positions where the ring's freighters were headed. They dispatched the crews that were not receiving graft to areas far from the smuggler's path. Coast Guard officers updated the smuggling ring about the assigned area and hours of every patrol crew. This assisted the gang's speedboat crews who were running late from the freighters to alter course if necessary for safe entry into the harbor. The gang's crews were told by their employers, "You need not be afraid of the Coast Guard in the harbor. If they shoot at you, they will only shoot in the air, but outside, it is the survival of the fittest."

Smuggler-friendly Coast Guard crews telephoned the ring's headquarters to find out the nightly rumrunning ship schedules. This enabled these crews to redirect any freighters that were off course to the location of their speedboats. It also allowed these crews to pull up and remain near the heavily-loaded freighters to protect them from pirates. Some Coast Guard crews even ran alongside the speedboats to protect their dashes for shore. On occasion Coast Guard crews helped load the ring's speedboats to get them quickly on their way in bad weather or before the Navy came along. Coast Guard cutters also warned the rumrunners when Navy destroyers were nearby. When a speedboat ran into a destroyer and a corrupted Coast Guard patrol crew, the cutter would dutifully fire its small, one-pound gun in the direction of the speedboats and undertake hot pursuit at less than full speed.

Dwyer and Costello used codes to communicate between corrupted Coast Guard cutters and rumrunning vessels. The cutters flashed a light three times for "all O.K. to transfer." A steady light on a freighter indicated it was already protected by a Coast Guard cutter. Guardsmen could recognize the ring's smuggling boats by the dory each one carried on its stern. They also shared information about patrol and rumrunning routes and the payoff locations and times via telegram and cablegram. Ship names were spelled in reverse, and common words were used to encode the four compass direction points and the landing locations.

As a fail safe, a pilot at Curtiss Field in Mineola, Long Island was employed to fly his plane along Rum Row and direct ring smuggling vessels to the correct position for unloading. The pilot also found ships that lost their bearings trying to get to Rum Row or the desired speedboat-contact point. Pilot Edward Caperton was the only "air bootlegger" ever indicted. His illegal activities were revealed at the ring's July 1926 trial and captured the public's imagination. Airplanes were still considered a novelty for hobbyists and for shows. The first commercial passenger plane flight had occurred just two months earlier, and Charles Lindbergh's dramatic nonstop solo flight across the Atlantic was still a year in the future.

The ring's identification and accounting system was simple but effective. A speedboat leader gave the freighter captain a dollar bill, and he compared the bill's serial number against a list to validate that the speedboat crew was part of the ring. The list also enumerated the amount of liquor to be offloaded onto each hovering craft and this inventory was confirmed upon arrival at the pier.

Some of the ring's boats had armor plate covering the pilothouse, engine room, and gasoline tanks, so they could navigate under heavy fire in running sea battles. The armor was needed for protection from pirates and any Coast Guard boats whose guns the ring had not silenced with bribery. The ring's speedboats were built and repaired at the Marine Garage on the East River in the Bronx, where the boat crews were also recruited. When authorities seized the ring's speedboats, the charges against the crew usually disappeared. In at least a couple cases, the confiscated boats inexplicably reappeared in the hands of the smugglers.

The leaders of truck crews made sure the piers were clear of law enforcement prior to signaling trucks to pull up and boats to land. In addition to unloading the speedboats and heading the truck convoys, the truck leaders handed out protection money to the policemen encountered along their routes. At the Long Island piers, corrupted uniformed NYPD patrolmen were occasionally present while liquor was being transferred from boats to trucks.

The Coast Guardsmen, who were poorly paid and often dissatisfied with their jobs, demanded large bribes. The ring paid each cutter crewman as much as three-years salary for every speedboat allowed to land safely. Cases of whisky, champagne, and ale frequently accompanied the cash, which often turned the remainder of a patrol into a drunken celebration. The ring regularly hosted Guardsmen in royal fashion at the finest restaurants, theaters, and illegal brothels. Dwyer owned the Sea Grill Restaurant.

Costello and Luciano were Prohibition competitors, but they were tightly associated professionally and personally throughout their careers. They had common business interests and goals, shared their vast New York City political and law enforcement influence, and aligned in their dangerous criminal underworld against violent, menacing enemy gangs. However their Prohibition operations were very dissimilar. They had different liquor suppliers, smuggling routes, and corrupted law-enforcement protection. Costello landed his contraband at numerous Long Island piers - including the Bellevue Hospital pier - and certain shore areas. Luciano used New Jersey's isolated beaches.

Vincent "Jimmy Blue Eyes" Alo, who joined Luciano's partnership later in Prohibition and was his best friend, said, "Charlie was partners with Meyer (Lansky), Ben (Siegel), and Joey A. (Adonis) importing whiskey. They had ships out beyond the 12-mile limit with speedboats delivering it. The fix was in. The cops guarded their trucks." [9]

Luciano had by far the most extensive police protection for his convoys. His trucks were often guarded the entire trip from New Jersey's beaches to his Manhattan warehouses by marked NYPD patrol cars driven by uniformed policemen. Not only did police escorts give his convoys more firepower, but they were intimidating to hijackers. Every one in the underworld knew that anyone who killed a New York City cop would surely be assassinated by the NYPD. The police got away with retaliation killings by making them look like legitimate officer-self-defense shootings, or by writing these crimes up to cast suspicion on the victim's criminal associates or adversaries. Luciano's gang did not want any police officers killed because of their activities. When one of their convoys lacked police escorts and was attacked, the lead car fired a flare high into the blackened night to warn friendly local police that this was a criminal-versus-criminal battle so they should ignore the gunfire and stay away.

All this protection was necessary because hijackers on land were an even greater threat than pirates at sea. Smuggling boats were only vulnerable in open water when a speedier pirate boat pulled near, or when they passed close to a legitimate-appearing vessel that attacked by surprise. However, hijackers could ambush a truck convoy from any number of hiding places along most roads. Thus, smugglers protected their truck fleets like army convoys with a car in front and in back armed with shotguns and machine guns. Underworld folklore includes tales of furious gun battles fought on the roadways, but the smugglers and hijackers who might have participated never confirmed or denied such incidents ever occurred. Even after a load of liquor was stored in warehouses that could cover acres of land, it had to be protected from the threat of burglary, law-enforcement, and hijacking until it was delivered to its final destination.

Luciano and his close associates survived in this dangerous world because they had guts and were tough in a fight, but every one of them always opted to run away from conflict and battle when pursued or confronted by police, Coast Guard, hijackers, or pirates. They resorted to combat only when the threat was imminent and inescapable.

THE COSTELLO & DWYER RUMRUNNING TRIALS

Big Bill Dwyer was eventually arrested and charged with heading the nation's largest liquor-smuggling operation. Federal prosecutors quickly followed with 60 more arrests in what they announced was "the greatest round-up in the history of Prohibition." Most of those charged lived in Manhattan, but many also lived on Long Island, where the ring imported the liquor.

The government erroneously believed Dwyer and Costello were ringleaders of different organizations, so they were tried separately. Dwyer was prosecuted first because the case against him was stronger. On opening day of the trial, Dwyer pleaded with the judge to postpone it because he had changed attorneys the night before, and because he wanted to attend the season opening at his Coney Island Racetrack in Cincinnati which was two weeks away. The judge denied his motion and proceeded to jury selection. However, most potential jurors had to be "excused for cause." They said significant things like, "My feelings against Prohibition are so strong, I'm afraid they'll influence me. I consider it a different class of crime from others I might've been asked to sit on."

Of the 17 defendants scheduled for the first trial, six were either ill or fugitives, one pled guilty at the outset, and two had charges dismissed for insufficient evidence. Of the eight remaining defendants the jury acquitted six. Dwyer and the man who delivered his bribes were each convicted on one of three counts for conspiracy to violate the federal Prohibition law. Both were sentenced to two years in the Atlanta Federal Penitentiary. Dwyer remained free on bail pending a decision on his appeal, but an automobile accident broke his jaw in two places. Soon afterwards he lost his appeal and the judge ordered him to be treated by the prison doctor instead of his own. The fractures never entirely knitted so he had surgery while in prison, and then spent more than two months in the prison hospital for stomach ulcers. His health problems got him paroled after serving 13 months of his two-year sentence.

When Dwyer went to prison, he gave his share of the rumrunning partnership to Costello. Once a wealthy man, Dwyer claimed that he was "not only broke" but owed more than $150,000 because of two expensive attorneys. The government pursued an income tax case throughout the 1930s for his unreported early-1920s Prohibition profits, and it finally won a $3.7 million judgment. However the Assistant U. S. Attorney said the government did not know whether Dwyer possessed anything to pay his debt.

After his release from prison, Dwyer promoted various sporting endeavors by using investment money from friends who trusted him. He purchased racetracks in various parts of the country, and built Tropical Park in Miami. He put on prizefights, and he bought three professional sports teams - the Montalvo Stud and New York Americans hockey teams and the Dayton, Ohio Triangles when the National Football League had just 12 teams. He moved his NFL Triangles to Ebbets Field in Brooklyn and renamed them the Dodgers, the same name as the major league baseball team that owned the stadium. Big Bill Dwyer disbanded his NFL team a year before he died of natural causes at age 63.

At the second big Prohibition trial, the jury acquitted eight minor defendants and deadlocked on Costello and the remaining six. Several jurors said they never considered conviction, saying they resented the poor caliber of the government's witnesses and its "undercover" investigation practices, which included kidnapping the defendants, denying them their Constitutional rights to call or consult with their attorneys, and blatant torture. Later, other prosecutors decided to retry Costello, but their case evaporated as witnesses had moved without leaving forwarding addresses, and records and evidence had unexplainably disappeared during the course of endless delays. The lack of convictions from the Costello-ring trial was a severe blow to the government's methods of prosecuting liquor conspiracy cases.[10] (See Addendum F)

THE BIG THREE IN LIQUOR & GAMBLING

Prohibition spawned abundant bootlegging rings across the country, but only three grew to be "super" importers, transporting far greater volumes of liquid than any of the rest. These partnerships were headed by Charlie Luciano, Frank Costello, and Moe Dalitz.

The Luciano and Costello gangs competed for the Manhattan market and became the nation's two top importers. They shipped Europe's finest liquors across the Atlantic Ocean and Canadian whiskey south along the eastern seaboard. The Dalitz gang became third. Speeding in the dark of night across Lake Erie from Canada to Detroit, Michigan and later to Cleveland, Ohio, they imported the same quality foreign liquors as their Manhattan counterparts. Then they distributed their goods by truck and boxcar throughout the Midwest.[11]

During Prohibition, Luciano and Costello also reached the pinnacle of organized-crime leadership and became New York City's two most powerful political kingmakers. After Repeal, the three gangs used their business and political savvy to open elegant but illegal casinos across the country. These were fronted by high-end nightclubs and fine restaurants with a gambling room attached in the back. This was during the 1930s and 1940s before they went on to pioneer the Las Vegas Strip.

The Luciano, Costello, and Dalitz gangs became the most successful in the fields of illegal alcohol and gambling because they conducted these crimes using modern business methods. While other gangsters used violence, or the threat of it, to attain monopoly in a defined territory, the three elite rumrunning gangs became far bigger than their competitors by providing their clients better service. They raised significant financing to acquire fleets of large freighters, ultra-fast speedboats, and trucks, and they also obtained massive secret storehouses. They purchased the finest foreign liquors in unprecedented quantities, developed wholesaling skills to sell to the many upper-end liquor outlets in Manhattan and the Midwest, and built large distribution systems to ensure quick delivery.

These three smuggling giants also became America's first criminals to establish alliances with other underworld gangs. Prohibition made cooperation between gangs in different territories practical, but none branched out like the big three. The Luciano, Costello, and Dalitz gangs formed a coalition, collaborating closely with each other throughout Prohibition and for decades afterward.

They assembled extensive networks of corrupted law enforcement at all levels of government in every jurisdiction they transited including the ocean within territorial limits and the Great Lakes waters, isolated shores, piers, country roads, small towns, and the congested inner cities.

During the Roaring '20s Manhattan was home to more than half of America's wealthiest citizens. It featured the country's finest hotels, restaurants, nightclubs, and entertainers. Broadway was aglow with several times more brightly-lit show marquees than it has today. Manhattan's affluent residents and tourists and its exciting evening attractions made the island the ultimate Prohibition marketplace. The Luciano gang and the Costello-Dwyer tandem both aimed to dominate this dream market, but a major obstacle stood in their path. Tough street gangs had already staked out key parts of Manhattan as their exclusive criminal territories, and they violently protected them from intrusion by outside lawbreakers.

CHAPTER 2

THE HISTORY OF THE AMERICAN MAFIA

AMERICA'S POWERFUL STREET GANGS & THE DEVELOPMENT OF THE MAFIA

With the advent of Prohibition, Charlie Luciano and Frank Costello dreamed of having open access to the lucrative Manhattan fine liquor market. But standing in their way was New York City's large street gangs, who had long before earned the reputation of being the most violent criminals in the nation. To understand the entrenched Mafia gangland culture blocking Luciano and Costello, their struggle to conduct their illegal business begins with a brief history of these crime syndicates' development and values.

In the early years of America, youthful street gangs sprang up in the poor neighborhoods of the larger towns. Over time these young punks developed into well-organized packs of career criminals who preyed upon defenseless immigrant residents and businessmen. These thugs profited from many crimes including purse snatching, grabbing produce from street carts, shoplifting, burglary, strong-arm robbery, shakedowns of fellow countrymen, extorting "protection" money from merchants, loan sharking, and operating gambling establishments and brothels.

By the early 1800s New York's street gangs found they could become professional criminals by bribing crooked police in their local precinct and doing the bidding of shady politicians in their district. Repeated political scandals and official investigations for more than a century documented that many cops in the notoriously corrupt New York City Police Department (NYPD) readily accepted bribes to ignore these gangs' criminal activities. It was revealed that Police Department officials paid politicians several times the amount of their annual salaries in exchange for their positions and for promotions. These police officials not only took graft from criminals, but they also insulated their elected political sponsors by acting as go-betweens with the street gangs in arranging questionable deals and collecting bribes. With each exposure of political or police payoffs the public reacted with outrage, but this subsided as the next shocking revelation commanded the headlines and public indignation, so this corrupt system continued unabated.

For professional gangs, survival depended more on dishonest elected officials than the police. In a system that began decades before Prohibition, corrupt Republican and Democratic political party machines openly paid bail money for gang members and supplied them defense attorneys free of charge. The politicians told crooked judges – many of whom they had appointed - which toughs to let go. Sentences for major street-gang members were unbelievably short except in a few cases. Judges sent most home with no more than a verbal reprimand for their "youthful indiscretions," using the artful legal dodge that they were minors.

In return for this court protection, the gangs supplied their political sponsors with services in their wards. Many of these professional street gangs showed up en mass at polling stations in their districts and threatened those voters who objected to being observed filling out their ballots. Other gangs operated political clubs that assisted the neighborhood residents who had financial or job-related problems. This enabled these gangs to deliver a large block of their grateful fellow countrymen's votes on election day. In return, the winning officials rewarded the gangs with law-enforcement immunity in their district during their term in office. In addition many politicians owned or controlled casinos and brothels, and the gangs protected these operations while destroying competing facilities.

Fortunately some NYPD officers were honest, dedicated professionals. They arrested street gang members often enough to tag most of them with extensive police records. These arrests and the newspaper reports about them are the basis for most of today's knowledge about these early criminal organizations' activities.[12]

New York City's five most formidable street gangs were in Sicilian neighborhoods. They fashioned their enterprises after the deep-rooted Mafia criminal culture developed on the Italian island of Sicily, just off the mainland's southwestern tip. The Mafia was created because the people of Sicily were oppressed for centuries by a succession of foreign military conquerors. In response Sicilians formed a small secret society of guerrilla warriors to protect civilians from pillage and rape by the occupying forces and to avenge the crimes of the occupiers. Unfortunately this gallant band of freedom fighters, known as Mafia, soon turned their physical prowess against the very people they originally intended to protect, as they degenerated into one of the most vicious criminal organizations in history. They brutally oppressed, preyed upon, and impoverished Sicily's hardworking inhabitants. The Mafia was worse than any conqueror. Destroying business competition and siphoning off prospective investment capital through extortion, these brutal thugs destroyed this island's economic potential. The grim consequences are obvious to this day.

Sicilian culture was unknown in America until 1887, when an agricultural depression in Italy spurred the first mass Italian/Sicilian migration to the U. S. Seeking work, immigrants settled in large cities - New York, Chicago, Cleveland, Buffalo, Detroit, and Milwaukee - and, like previous ethnic groups, the Italians and Sicilians banded together to share the cultural values and language they had brought with them.

Unfortunately the earliest-arriving Sicilians included criminals who imported their tradition of Mafia. In each large Sicilian neighborhood, the meanest bully established himself as a Mafioso-style leader, dominating residents and businesses alike. Later arrivals who embraced their criminal heritage joined these Mafioso gangs. These U.S. Mafia street gangs were wholly independent from the gangs in Sicily, who had originated the name. But they adopted their three main features - the threat of violence as the primary tool to rule over neighbors, vendetta against anyone who opposed them, and monopoly for the businesses they supported.

When Prohibition began, the Sicilian mobsters were the best organized to exploit it and quickest to do so. Not only were they the tightest-knit criminal gangs in the country with their blood-oath initiations, but the Sicilian culture gave the Mafiosi two advantages over other ethnic gangs – a ready supply source and a distribution network. Sicilian immigrants brought their tradition of *alky cooking,* which was a method of producing moonshine from corn sugar using primitive household stills. Since immigrant Sicilians had an inherent mistrust of outsiders, especially government and law enforcement officials, due to centuries of foreign and domestic domination, they dealt only with their own countrymen. Thus they sold their moonshine output strictly to Mafiosi.

Mafia street gangs quickly created large neighborhood networks of alky-cookers. Each gang supplied families in its community with alcohol-distilling equipment that fit in a bathtub, then sold them raw ingredients. A family could supplement its income by producing a relatively small amount of hard liquor daily, which was transported in five-gallon pails. Alky cooking became the cottage industry of Sicilian neighborhoods, and the smell of sour mash hovered over residential streets for blocks.

The total production was substantial, giving Mafia gangs the largest liquor-distilling capacity during early Prohibition. In Chicago Alky was so profitable that it led to a murderous war between two gangs from different regions of Sicily that also involved their gangland allies residing in New York City. Political alliances between Mafia gangs from Chicago and New York brewed conflict in both cities throughout Prohibition.

New York City had five Mafia street gangs, with three in different sections of Brooklyn, one of the closest poor areas to the immigration processing center on Ellis Island. All three street gangs later expanded into parts of Manhattan because of its wealthy residents and thus its greater profit potential. Two of these professional gangs enjoyed great success, and before Prohibition they had grown into the country's biggest criminal organizations. They demanded tribute from any illicit business seeking approval to operate in their territory without interference.

Since the Luciano and Costello rumrunning partnerships had no interest in manufacturing booze, they were not in competition with the Mafia's operations. Instead, Luciano and Costello wanted to import the finest foreign liquors into America's wealthiest market, the island of Manhattan. Thus, both Luciano and Costello cut deals to give a share of their profits to the most powerful Mafia gang leader in Manhattan in return for being able to distribute imported liquor without interference. This gang is generally referred to by law enforcement and the media as the *Genovese* crime family.

JOE MASSERIA'S MANHATTAN/BROOKLYN MAFIA GANG

The Genovese crime gang was started by Ignazio "Lupo the Wolf" Saietta. He grew up in the province of Palermo, Sicily where he was first arrested in 1899 at age 22 for the murder of a fellow Corleone townsman. While awaiting trial he fled to the U.S. where he settled in Brooklyn. He soon married the sister of the notorious "lottery king" of Harlem named Ciro "The Artichoke King" Terranova. Then at the beginning of the 1900s Lupo built the country's biggest professional street gang. Lupo's Mafia gang plundered, terrorized, and murdered the Italian merchants on Manhattan's East Side. Yet few details about their activities were ever officially recorded because the citizenry were afraid to talk.

Lupo was notorious for traditional *Black Hand* anonymous extortion notes that the Sicilian Mafia and Italian Camorra had used for generations. These notes were written in black ink and included a crude drawing of a hand and sometimes a skull and crossbones. They threatened the affluent victim with bombing, kidnapping, torture, or death unless he left a specific amount of cash at a certain location. In an effort to try to stop Lupo's gang activities, a NYPD Lieutenant went to Sicily to encourage the Palermo authorities to activate the old murder charge against him and initiate extradition proceedings. Sadly the dedicated unarmed detective was shot to death by Lupo's old Sicilian associates. A year later in 1910, the Secret Service raided Lupo's large counterfeiting factory in Brooklyn and he was convicted in federal court, receiving a 30-year prison sentence.

From his prison cell that was his home for years, Lupo continued to lead his gang by delegating responsibility for day-to-day operations to his assistant, Giuseppe "Joe" Masseria. He was born in Sicily about 1887 and immigrated at age 16 with his family to settle in Brooklyn about 1903. A large, aggressive youth, he soon joined Lupo's gang and made himself feared by his countrymen. At age 20 he was arrested the first two times for burglary and extortion, but he received suspended sentences. Six years later he attempted to rob a pawnshop and was sentenced to four and a half years in Sing Sing. When Masseria went to prison, Lupo was still incarcerated so he had his brother-in-law, "The Artichoke King" Terranova, handle the gang's daily affairs.

When Masseria was released from prison, he resumed as Lupo's conduit to the gang. One task assigned him was to cut a deal with U.S. Attorney General Harry Daugherty to obtain Lupo a Presidential pardon. Daugherty was America's top prosecutor, but his tenure was embroiled in scandal. He would later be tried but acquitted for his role in the Teapot Dome Scandal, a corruption case in which oilmen close to Republican President Warren Harding stole from the huge government oilfields in Wyoming.

Shortly after Harding took office in 1921, AG Daugherty submitted the pardon application for Lupo and the President approved it. This was just a year into the Noble Experiment, but Prohibition's huge profits had already financed corruption all the way to the White House. Lupo was released with 20 years left to serve on his counterfeiting sentence, even though he was the prime suspect in ordering the execution of a defenseless NYPD official and numerous neighbors. His pardon was unique because it contained the condition that he had to cease criminal activity forever. Since the President retained authority to return Lupo to prison to serve the remainder of his sentence, this condition converted the pardon into a parole, and made the President of the United States Lupo's personal parole officer.

While AG Daugherty claimed that Lupo had reformed and forsaken criminal activity, he never bothered to explain the source of this prescient knowledge. This condition of Lupo's pardon gave President Harding political justification for releasing Lupo, but it also benefited Masseria because it allowed him to assume uncontested leadership of the nation's largest criminal organization. Only the two men who cut the pardon deal ever knew whether the AG demanded this condition to protect the President politically, or the ambitious criminal Masseria proposed it to remove Lupo from leadership of his gang. In any event Masseria became absolute boss of the country's biggest gang.

Because of the conditional pardon, Lupo steered clear from associating with his former gang's leadership, but with Masseria's blessings Lupo went back into crime in his old territory. Fifteen years after he was pardoned, a group of independent Italian bakers in Brooklyn wrote to Democratic New York Governor Lehman pleading for an end to Lupo's extortion racketeering activities. The state AG launched an investigation, but the bakers who testified were bombed, beaten, and driven out of business by Lupo's gang. A police investigation discovered that Lupo was also running the Italian lottery and had a stranglehold on wine-grape sales in the Italian/Sicilian neighborhoods. This was a major enterprise because so many residents fermented large quantities of their own wine. The DA was unable to bring charges because no resident would testify, but in his study of the case he became aware of former President Harding's 15-year-old conditional pardon. The state petitioned

Democratic President Franklin D. Roosevelt to revoke Lupo's parole, and FDR signed a warrant returning the 60-year-old to prison to serve the outstanding 20 years of his counterfeiting sentence.[13]

THE AMERICAN UNIONE SICILIANA POLITICAL POWER BASE

When the poor Sicilian immigrants landed in New York City the only jobs available to them were the lowest paying, and they had no idea how to seek help from the limited government services. Their lack of resources was coupled with their centuries-old inherent distrust of government and outsiders, so Sicilian immigrants in the Big Apple turned to established Sicilian intermediaries known as *padrones* because they spoke English and understood the system. These unofficial community leaders were replaced in 1895 by a new benevolent mutual-aid fraternity called the *Unione Siciliana*. Charging reasonable dues, the Unione found Sicilian immigrants places to live, connected job seekers with employers seeking cheap labor, offered its members life insurance and loans, and navigated them through the intricacies of citizenship applications, the imposing government bureaucracy, and the complexities of American society. Unione meetings gave Sicilians from every profession and strata of society an opportunity to network. Branches opened in every sizeable Sicilian neighborhood in the country, and as these communities grew the regional Unione became a potent organization in local politics.[14]

Immigrant Sicilian Mafia members also joined the Unione Siciliana because they were bewildered by American customs just like their fellow countrymen. As the Unione became more politically influential in these communities, Mafia gangs worked to control the leadership of local branches. Early on Lupo the Wolf and his large gang took control of the Unione's New York City leadership, acquiring political influence with their fellow citizens and clout with their district's elected political leaders. The Unione's legitimate officers claimed to know nothing about this gangster infiltration. But just like the gangsters, these law-abiding Sicilian businessmen - as well as politicians, judges, prosecutors, local and state government officials, and also businessmen who were neither Sicilian nor members - benefited from networking with all types of Sicilian society. Few people in the larger, non-Sicilian society were aware this organization existed, and those who did knew little about its activities.

When Lupo was pardoned in 1921, Masseria not only inherited control of Lupo's gang but also his influence with the local branch of the Unione in New York City. Now called "Joe The Boss," Masseria's ascension to power was apparent in his demeanor. He pompously swaggered through his terrain like a celebrity. Despite this posturing, he was able to shroud his criminal activities in secrecy and maintain a low profile with the outside world. The police said he was in "every kind of racket in existence," but he publicly distanced himself from these activities, so he could stay under the radar of the press and the citizenry.

New York Prosecutor Thomas Dewey's public relations official was Hickman Powell, who spent his career playing up the law-enforcement effectiveness of his employer and friend. However, Powell had to admit that Dewey knew nothing about Joe Masseria even though he was leader of the nation's biggest criminal gang and operated right under the Prosecutor's nose. Powell later wrote that Dewey "didn't know much" about Masseria. "Hardly anyone had heard of Joe Masseria…After that summer of 1922 Joe Masseria had dropped into obscurity." Even though Sicilian gangs by then were the nation's largest and most successful criminal gangs, the public knew only the names of that era's infamous New York City non-Mafia underworld leaders such as Arnold Rothstein, Dutch Schultz, Legs Diamond, Owney Madden, and Bill Dwyer, who were either Irish or Jewish.[15]

In the summer of 1922, a year after Masseria assumed power, a long-simmering territorial dispute between his gang and Umberto Valenti's gang erupted. The conflict had started eight years earlier over gambling and brothel jurisdictions when Lupo was leader. Valenti was the upstart criminal in the neighborhood, and while he was arrested on a variety of charges he always got off. Lupo wanted exclusive control of his territory, so he sent four of his principal leaders to meet with Valenti and warn him under penalty of death to stay out of their bailiwick. Shortly after the meeting, Valenti responded to the death threat by murdering two of Lupo's representatives. Lupo's gang retaliated by firing shots at Valenti, but he was not hurt. Detectives eventually linked Valenti to more shootings than any other man in the city, and because of his demonstrated great propensity for violence, Lupo finally negotiated a peace accord with him.

This détente lasted for eight years until they butted heads over leadership of the Unione Siciliana. National Unione leader Valenti wanted total control of the organization including the local branch in New York City that was under Masseria. This political battle led to Masseria's only notoriety outside the Sicilian community, when Valenti launched a major assault against the Masseria organization. He started it early one afternoon when he had his henchmen shoot down and kill Lupo the Wolf's nephew, Vincent Morelli. That evening at 6 p.m., Masseria and an unidentified associate were walking along a busy sidewalk. In the path ahead of them were three well-dressed "Italian-looking men" loitering in front of a cheese dealer on Grand Street, a block east of Police headquarters. When Masseria and his associate got to within two shop doors of the trio, each loiterer pulled out two automatic pistols and started shooting. Masseria and his companion immediately returned revolver fire. The five gangsters fired a barrage of 60 bullets at each other on that crowded sidewalk. Innocent pedestrians tried to flee, but when the smoke cleared, an 18-year-old girl, a 23-year-old woman, and four men were lying on the ground, most seriously wounded but none fatally.

The chaotic shootout shocked New York City. From the beginning of Prohibition, Chicago gangs were notorious for shooting wildly from a distance in crowded locations, but New York gangsters typically did not shoot until they got within a few feet of their targets. And they shot accurately so bystanders were almost never hurt. When all those shots rang out on Grand Street, two detectives were standing within 75 feet of the two targets, and they pursued the pair who made their getaway along Mulberry Street. The detectives captured Masseria, but his unknown associate escaped. They also recovered the .38-caliber pistol Masseria threw away during the chase, and four of the 10 cartridges had been discharged. They would have arrested him for carrying a concealed weapon, but a crooked judge had preempted that charge by improperly issuing ex-convict Masseria a pistol-permit three months earlier. The permit card had "unlimited" written on it, authorizing Masseria to carry a pistol in any part of the state. Masseria refused to make a statement to the police beyond telling them that he was an automobile dealer. Since the startled pedestrians caught up in the gunfire could not identify the shooters, no arrests were ever made.

A month later Valenti's associate Silva Tagliagamba was killed at Grand and Mulberry Streets. Police dubbed this corner "Bootleggers' Curb" because imported booze stocks were wholesaled and bartered there. Police assumed Masseria was retaliating, so they promptly charged him with the homicide but he was released on a $15,000 cash bond. Two months after Tagliagamba's killing, at one o'clock in the afternoon a blue Hudson pulled up to a restaurant directly across the street from Masseria's home and two of its four occupants got out. The two men entered the restaurant, sat down at a table near the door, ordered coffee and cake, and kept watch on the three-story brownstone across the street. A hour later Masseria descended the stoop of his home and turned north along Second Avenue, and the two men speedily walked out of the restaurant and crossed the street. At the curb they faced Masseria, and one of them produced a 45-caliber automatic. The victim saw the weapon and ran toward the Mathilda Millinery Company shop, then changed direction turning back toward his home past the Henley Brothers' women's wear shop. One of its proprietors witnessed what happened next: "The man with the revolver came close to the other fellow and aimed. Just as he fired, the man jumped to one side. The bullet smashed into the window of my store. Then the man fired again, and this time the man being shot at ducked his head forward. Again the man fired, and again his target ducked his head down. The third shot made a second hole in my window." [16]

As a crowd ran out from the tenements, the two assailants sprinted across the street. One attacker jumped into the backseat of the car with the two waiting accomplices, as the other hopped onto the running board holding revolvers in both hands. As they tried to escape by driving west on Fifth Street, the residents ran out into the street in the vehicle's path. The attacker standing on the running board fired shot after shot downward to frighten off the pursuit in front of them.

A little further down Fifth Street, striking cloak makers of the International Ladies' Garment Workers' Union had just left a strategy session at their hall. About 50 of them were milling on the sidewalk near Third Avenue, when they heard yelling and saw the residents chasing a car coming toward them. The union members ran into the street to block the fleeing vehicle, but when the car's occupants saw their escape route cut off, three opened fire. They poured 25 shots at the crowd, hitting six people. As these men dropped to the ground, the rest of the strikers ran back into the hall, trampling two men in their rush for cover. The street emptied, and the car turned the corner on Third Avenue and sped away. The next day one of the six wounded cloak makers died. Police found the stolen getaway vehicle but no arrests were ever made.

Two of the three bullets fired at point blank range at Masseria passed through the crown of his straw hat, meaning he had needed every bit of his astonishing agility to duck those shots. A detective went to question Masseria at his home because he had run there for shelter. The detective found the victim sitting on the edge of his bed still wearing his bullet-pierced hat. Masseria's ability to bob, weave, and duck to avoid bullets became legend, earning Joe The Boss a new nickname, "The Duck." New York crime leader Joe Bonanno would later fight a long, violent war of attrition with Masseria, and then he wrote, "He gained a reputation as a man who could dodge bullets." [17]

Immediately after this second close shave with death, Masseria called for a peace conference. Masseria and Valenti, each accompanied by two bodyguards, negotiated a treaty over lunch at an Italian restaurant. It appeared to witnesses like Masseria capitulated giving Valenti a seeming victory. Valenti looked pleased when the two gang leaders shook hands. Masseria, Valenti, and their four bodyguards seemed friendly as they walked together along the busy sidewalk. As the group paused at a stoplight on a crowded corner at Twelfth Street and Second Avenue, without warning Masseria and his two associates drew pistols and opened fire. The suddenness of the attack caught the other three by surprise, and they immediately started running in different directions. The three assassins pursued Valenti, two of them nervously firing wildly. Valenti attempted to get into a stopped taxicab, but one assailant planted himself in front of the vehicle in the street and took careful aim. Valenti leaped on the running board, drawing his revolver to fire back, but the shooter emptied his revolver first. A single bullet hit Valenti near his heart. He fell dead on the running board. One witness said, "It was the coolest thing I ever saw. People were shrieking and running in all directions, and this fellow calmly fired shot after shot. He did not move until he had emptied his weapon." [18]

The three gunmen loosed a salvo of more than 20 shots. A street cleaner was pushing his broom along the gutter when one wild bullet hit his neck causing the seriously wounded man to fall to the street. Another stray bullet narrowly missed a four-year-old girl, but struck her eight-year-old sister, who was playing in front of her grandfather's store. The bullet hit her in the chest and lodged in her left arm. She cried out, "I'm hurt, mamma," as she fell toward the ground and her mother and father ran out of the store to catch her. The girl and the street cleaner were rushed to the hospital in critical condition, but both ultimately survived. The parents and their two daughters were in New York to visit family. [19]

When Valenti fell, the three assailants ran through the crowds and disappeared into different buildings. Despite the presence of hundreds of bystanders, no one was able to furnish descriptions of the murderers beyond, "They were stocky and well dressed." Masseria, already out on bail for the Tagliagamba murder and known for his animosity with Valenti, was arrested for Valenti's murder and held without bail. At the time of this shooting, false alibi witnesses claimed Masseria was home, and said he was proudly sporting a well-fitting new hat with no holes in it. Both the Valenti and Tagliagamba murder charges against Masseria were ultimately dropped for lack of evidence.

During the three months of this warfare, a few bootleggers from both gangs were killed. Gang leaders Masseria and Valenti were either fighting over Prohibition territory, control of the Unione Siciliana, or both. Whatever the reason, Valenti's murder made Masseria, who already headed the nation's largest criminal gang, the unrivaled New York leader of the Unione Siciliana. This was the first of repeated killings of Unione leaders across the nation by rival Sicilian gangs that continued throughout Prohibition. The Unione was an extremely valuable political plum, and to savor this fruit, one Sicilian man after another risked his life to be its national leader. [20]

LUCIANO & ASSOCIATES BECOME RANKING MAFIOSI

Luciano, Costello, and their colleagues grew up and lived amidst the toughest of New York's professional street gangs, so they understood these gangsters' culture. Both Luciano and Costello decided their best option was to forge an accommodation with the city's most powerful Mafioso, Joe the Boss Masseria. Both rumrunners turned over a share of their profits to him for the right to wholesale imported liquor to the whole lucrative Manhattan marketplace unmolested by anyone.

When Luciano and Costello allied themselves with Masseria, they received his protection. He led the country's biggest band of thugs, and they guaranteed fierce and deadly retribution against anyone who interfered with these two importing groups in New York City. This kept the city's four other Mafia gangs and all other criminal organizations from molesting them. Masseria also offered Luciano and Costello the services of the city's corrupt politicians, judges, and police who were on the Mafioso's payroll. This was an important door opener that would help Luciano and Costello become powerful overworld political kingmakers.

Masseria's underworld alliances with Luciano and Costello fit a classic business-merger model when a large established firm absorbs a small specialty company. The big gang retained its identity as the umbrella organization with Masseria entrenched as The Boss, and both smaller partnerships were allowed to continue operating as independent divisions under the leadership of Luciano and Costello. Luciano's total independence from, and great influence over, Masseria impressed rival New York City Mafia leader Joe Bonanno. He later wrote, "Luciano, who up to then had operated independently with his associate Meyer Lansky, and was absorbed by Masseria into his Family. At first, Luciano had mainly contributed his business acumen to Masseria."

Luciano became the chief of staff of America's largest criminal empire. The Boss' organizational structure insulated him from exposure to any state's witness testimony because no member of the organization had first-hand knowledge about the man giving the orders. Masseria separated himself from his gang members' crimes by having each one report to a division leader who in turn reported to his lieutenant Luciano. This illustrated the great faith Masseria had in Luciano because he was the only person who was in a position to put The Boss in prison for life, or who could manipulate all the members he directed to follow his personal agenda or even a coup.

Fortunately for Masseria, Luciano was a honorable man whose only ambition was to enjoy each day to the utmost. This arrangement bestowed power and status on Luciano with the rest of gangland, but he exercised his power judiciously. His ability to arrive at mutually-beneficial arrangements with those he dealt with was legendary in the underworld. He and his four Prohibition partners were even cooperative with competitors. Costello, the nation's second biggest importer, and Vito Genovese, who had a small distributorship, were both direct competitors with Luciano for the Manhattan market, but they were also his two closest and strongest underworld political allies. The life-long bond between these men never wavered. Masseria absorbed both Costello and Genovese into his organization as independent division leaders who reported directly to Luciano. Masseria demanded that all members pay him a percentage of their revenues, but Luciano made sure his two close friends were always allowed independent control of their operations.

Masseria and Luciano were a study in contrasts. Masseria was a caricature of the traditional Sicilian Mafia culture and its isolation within Sicilian communities. The sophisticated and worldly Luciano was comfortable working with people from every ethnic background and every economic stratum. For him, ethnicity was irrelevant. The Boss took advantage of their differences to benefit his gang. Masseria personally dealt with the other Sicilian Mafia leaders, while he had Luciano deal with all the other Prohibition gangs. Masseria also had Luciano along with Costello handle his gang's lobbying in New York City politics long dominated by the Irish.

The only people who ever knew when and why Luciano, his two Italian partners Joe Adonis and Jimmy Blue Eyes, and Costello, joined Masseria's Mafia gang were its leaders and the inductees. Both sides certainly benefited from these arrangements. Masseria established formal control over all crime in his territory and ensured himself a continuing share of the profits from Prohibition's two giant fine-liquor importers. By making Luciano and Costello loyal blood-oath members he felt safe bringing them into his inner sanctum as chief advisers.

Every Prohibition-era Mafia member always denied that any such secret crime organization as the Mafia existed. However, New York City mobster Henry Hill described the benefits of Mafia membership in his autobiography after he became a federally-protected state's witness. "The guys who worked for Paulie [who was the gang's division leader Paul Vario] had to make their own dollar [and give him a share]. All they got from Paulie was protection from other guys looking to rip them off. ... what Paulie and the organization offer is protection for the kinds of guys who can't go to the cops. They're like the police department for the wiseguys." "The other reason you have to be allied with somebody like Paulie is to keep the cops off our back." He bribed the police, judges, and politicians. "Corrupt cops on [Paulie underling] Jimmy Burke's payroll tipped him off about informants and potential witnesses." "Usually the lawyer has the kinds of contacts that can keep you free on bail as long as you want. They can keep you from running across some hard-nosed judge who sends you inside or rushes the case along. Then you've got the private detectives who work for the lawyers. ... They had good contacts with cops, and arrangements can be worked out so that testimony or evidence is changed just a little bit, only enough to make a tiny hole through which your lawyer can help you escape." "Everybody reaches the jury. ... Where a guy works means his job, and that always means the unions, and that's the easiest place to make the reach."[21]

LUCIANO'S ECUMENICALISM IN AN INSULAR SICILIAN CULTURE

No one associated with Charlie Luciano ever talked about his own background or criminal activities to anyone. For example, Luciano, Meyer Lansky, Ben Siegel, and Joe Adonis became partners early in Prohibition, and later Vincent "Jimmy Blue Eyes" Alo became the fifth partner. Even though Jimmy Blue Eyes became the best friend of both Luciano and Lansky, Jimmy admitted in my interview, "I have no idea how Charlie and Meyer met." Not one of the original four partners ever told Jimmy about anything that happened prior to his joining them. Personal and criminal backgrounds were always taboo subjects. The point is that while a lot of ridiculous fiction purporting to be biographical or even autobiographical has been written about these gangsters, what follows is all the documented information that exists about them.

The original four partners of Prohibition's largest foreign-liquor importing and wholesaling operation grew up in New York City. Three were raised in Brooklyn where they became friends. Two of these three then moved to Manhattan's Lower East Side where they met the fourth partner, Luciano. He had immigrated with his family who settled there when he was 7. Joe Adonis was 6 when his mother brought him and his three siblings to join their father in Brooklyn, and Adonis remained there until after the repeal of Prohibition. Lansky's father came alone to Brooklyn, and after two years he had saved enough money to pay for the trip so his wife and their two sons could join him when Lansky was 9. Three years later Lansky moved with his family to Manhattan's Lower East Side. Siegel was the only one of the four who was born in America. He grew up in Brooklyn and moved away from home at 14 to join his pal Lansky on the Lower East Side. All information about how these four partners first encountered each other was kept in their private remembrances and died with them.

When Prohibition began, Luciano was 22, Lansky and Adonis were both 17, and Siegel was just 13. This made Luciano the oldest of the original four partners, but age had nothing to with his becoming leader of America's largest rumrunning operation. After all Genovese was also 22 and Costello was older at 28. Yet these two Prohibition competitors for the Manhattan market readily became Luciano's close underworld subordinates. They respected him as their leader and gave him lifelong loyalty.

When the four partners joined forces to create Prohibition's largest liquor-importing enterprise, Luciano was the only one who had business experience, even though it had all been illegal. For eight years beginning at age 14, he had run crap games and booked horseraces. These operations allowed him to develop broad contacts with New York City's diverse ethnic gangs, but the core reason he ascended to power was his personality. He spoke slowly and thoughtfully. He had a quiet, calm, firm disposition, and he never got emotional in times of danger. His aura of self-assurance gave others confidence in him. His personality, and his ability to effectively negotiate to satisfy the other person as well as himself, would go on to make him the most respected and influential underworld leader in U.S. history.

Luciano's Prohibition partnership was made up of several ethnic backgrounds. Luciano was Sicilian, Adonis and Alo were Italian, and Lansky and Siegel were Jewish. Luciano's close underworld allies from the early days of Prohibition, Costello and Genovese, were both Italian. This mix contrasted with the nation's street gangs, virtually all of which were composed of a single nationality or racial group that lived in the same poor neighborhood.

Sicilians were inherently mistrustful of outsiders due to centuries of foreign domination, so they were the most isolated ethnic group. They only wanted to deal with their own countrymen, and the Mafiosi even insulated themselves from the non-Sicilian residents in their neighborhoods. They did not accept non-Sicilians into Mafia membership, not even Italians from the mainland.

Luciano alone among his close associates possessed an ethnic pedigree acceptable to the Mafia leaders. He was Sicilian and born in the old country. Once he earned Masseria's trust, he was able to induct his two successful competitors as independent division leaders. Before then they had to pay tribute to The Boss to operate in Manhattan unmolested, but they did not receive the advantages of membership. While Costello, Adonis, and Genovese would go on to become top Mafiosi, it was Luciano who led the way and influenced the Sicilian Mafia chiefs to accept leadership by these three mainland Italians.

Lansky and Siegel received all the benefits of association with a Mafia gang because their five comrades became initiated members. These two Jewish partners were close friends with all five of their Sicilian and Italian associates and were also highly-respected, life-long advisors to each one of them. However they could not participate with their buddies in secret Mafia dealings. They may have been trusted with inside information and their advice may have been highly regarded, but they were excluded from dealing directly with Masseria and the other Mafia leaders. The other four New York City Mafia gangs and their Sicilian leaders in that era avoided any contact with them. Los Angeles bookmaker Mickey Cohen was an associate of Siegel, and he later wrote, "Being Jews, Benny and me and even Meyer couldn't be a real part and parcel of that [the Mafia]." [22]

For decades, America's Mafia gangs had been ruled by stiff-collared Sicilian despots whose handlebar mustaches earned them the nickname "Mustache Petes." Insular and bellicose, they shunned alliances with non-Sicilian gangs and admitted no mainland Italians. Masseria typified the Mustache Petes. Except for inducting the four Italian super-profit makers - Adonis, Costello, Genovese, and Jimmy Blue Eyes - he observed strict Mafia orthodoxy.

Luciano and his Americanized-Italian associates became known as the *Young Turks.* They wanted to ally themselves with other gangs without consideration to ethnicity. This attitude set off major long-term friction with the other four New York City Mafia gangs. As the Young Turks gained power, tension between them and the Mustache Petes festered and ultimately exploded into warfare.

Long after Prohibition ended, New York City's other four Mafia gangs maintained their isolationism. During the 1930s and 1940s, when illegal casinos proliferated across the U.S., these Mafia gangs opened small sneak operations in their own territories, but they failed to participate in the national spread of wide-open illegal casinos. They also did not participate in the 1940s through 1960s boom on the Las Vegas Strip. In contrast Luciano and his colleagues reached out from their early teenage years to develop relationships with people of diverse ethnic backgrounds and varied professional skills. This ecumenical attitude allowed them to not only participate in the growth of the nation's illegal casinos and the Strip's legal resorts, but to take the lead in the development of both.

ETHNICITY IN U.S. CULTURE, PROHIBITION, & CASINO DEVELOPMENT

America's street gangs and Prohibition rings were typically made up of a single ethnic group. This was because the vast majority of immigrants arrived penniless and knew no one in this strange new land. They moved into the cheapest housing in ethnic districts made up of their fellow countrymen so they could share their cultural and linguistic heritage with their neighbors, and help each other make a life in their new fatherland. These families' teenagers and young adults were often marginalized by the larger society, and some joined street gangs to affiliate with their own kind. Over time many of these families' breadwinners obtained higher-paying jobs so they were able to move into more affluent neighborhoods and assimilate into the larger culture. Then these people demanded that the police control the teenage criminal activity of the newly-arrived poor immigrant groups who had moved into their former housing.

From the 1840s through the 1920s, foreign-born residents living in New York City fluctuated as a percentage of the city's population between one-third to one-half. Thus, the city's ethnic balance and culture changed dramatically every few years as large numbers of immigrants from different countries arrived. Since street gangs were usually made up of the youth of the poorest and most recently-arrived families, gang ethnicity also changed over time. Between 1840 to 1890, the largest immigrant group was German, most of whom moved to small Midwest communities, where their youth spent long hours working on farms and were not exposed to inner-city gang life. The second largest immigrant group during this half-century was the Irish and many settled in New York City. By 1850 they were by far the largest ethnic group in town and their youth belonged to the toughest street gangs. However four decades later, the Irish made up more than half of the city's police department and dominated much of its political structure. (See Addendum G)

Between the 1890s through the 1920s, the two largest immigrant groups were Jews and Italians. Some of the youth of these newly-arrived slum poor established street gangs prior to the introduction of Prohibition. When the Noble Experiment began, most of the men who would go on to become Prohibition's major gang leaders and their close associates were around 20 years old, because they had been born between the late 1890s to the early 1900s. Thus, most New York City alcohol rings were Italian or Jewish, along with some Irish and a smattering of other nationalities.

While almost all street and Prohibition gangs were made up of a single ethnic group, four were racially diverse. These unique gangs socialized and conducted business with every nationality and race. Three became Prohibition's biggest liquor suppliers - they were, in order of sales, Luciano and his associates and the Costello-Dwyer team, both in Manhattan, and the Moe Dalitz partnership in Cleveland. Each of these three groups were joined by friends who formed their business partnerships to take advantage of Prohibition's profit potential, whereas most other liquor violators were part of preexisting street gangs. The fourth multi-ethnic gang was Al Capone's in Chicago. He and his successor leaders aligned in business partnerships and underworld politics with the top three suppliers throughout Prohibition, and all four gangs remained closely associated for the next half-century.

All four of these gangs' leaders came from at least two ethnic groups. For example Luciano's partnership was composed of Sicilian, Italian, and Jewish. Dwyer was a native New York Irish, and Costello was an Italian immigrant who started as an employee, then became a partner, and finally sole owner. Dwyer had influence with the Irish New York City political hierarchy, and Costello was associated with the Italian and the Sicilian neighborhood leaders and their political connections.

Dalitz's gang had five partners, four Jewish and one Irish. In their many other legal and illegal business deals over a half century, they included many additional partners from a wide variety of ethnic backgrounds. Their early predominantly Jewish makeup and their nightly rumrunning excursions across Lake Erie to bring in the world's finest liquors from Canada caused the underworld to nickname them *The Jewish Navy*.

Capone was an illegal brothel operator and beer brewer, and he headed the only other major multi-ethnic gang. He was a vicious thug, but a racially tolerant one. He was prepared to befriend or beat up anyone irrespective of their nationality. This gang operated brothels for almost two decades prior to the inception of Prohibition, and its top hierarchy always included several nationalities making it the most diverse of any of the gangs. Capone and his boss Johnny Torrio were both Italian and had Irish wives. Even though New York's Costello was Italian, law enforcement and the press never suspected him of being a Mafioso because he was well known to associate primarily with Irish and Jews, and his wife was Jewish.

These four Prohibition gangs would later pioneer the Las Vegas Strip and they would be the only underworld gangs to make major inroads there. Thus, the resort-casino owners during the early two decades of the Strip's development were predominantly Jewish and Italian, with a few Irish and other nationalities. Instead of owning and operating separate hotels, these different nationalities partnered in the same establishments, just as they had during Prohibition and in their many illegal casino operations.

A key element in these four gangs' history is interracial brotherhood. My systematic study of the hidden Nevada casino interests held by Sicilian and Italian underworld criminals during the four decades the Mafia was involved revealed that every Mafioso was fronted on the license and in the operation by a Jewish owner. This began with Siegel's early investment in the mid 1940s to the mid 1980s when law enforcement ousted the last mobsters from the industry.

Ecumenicalism ran through the Las Vegas gambling fraternity including the downtown casino partnerships that had a different mix of cultures than the Strip. The three men who had the greatest impact on creating the special ambiance of the downtown casino center were Irish - Benny Binion opened the *Horseshoe Club,* Guy McAfee opened the *Golden Nugget,* and Jackie Gaughan owned a number of downtown casinos along with his flagship *El Cortez Hotel.* (During my young adult years I occasionally spent an evening enjoying one of these three exceptional casino operations by first savoring one of their great signature menu items and then gambling.) Interestingly, the second biggest partner in all three of these casinos was Jewish, but it was the Irish operating/marketing partner in each one who created these popular casinos' unique atmospheres that made the downtown casino center such a special place to play for devoted gamblers. Prior to coming to Las Vegas, each of these three Irish casino leaders was involved in a small illegal gambling operation. This is in marked contrast to most of the early Strip casino resort owners who previously had operated large elegant illegal casinos.

America's large Sicilian Mafia gangs were about to become involved in a nationwide conflict. Luciano and the Young Turks would end up right in the middle of this violent war.

CHAPTER 3

THE YOUNG TURKS EMBROILED IN CONFLICT

PROHIBITION TESTED THE TOUGHEST

The big profits and quick returns of Prohibition attracted both professional criminals and men who had never committed a felony. All began manufacturing and/or distributing booze, and some also stole others' inventories. Luciano, Costello, and their associates were unassuming businessmen who threatened no one, but they had to have tremendous guts to compete and survive in this violent industry. Bribing the legal authorities to ignore their operations gave them no protection from the persistent threat of pirates at sea, hijackers on the roadways, and robbers at warehouses. During my interviews Luciano's best friend and partner, Jimmy Blue Eyes, spontaneously pointed out his vivid memory of this constant threat several times. "You had to be tough during Prohibition. There were a lot of tough people. I had to do things to survive. You had to be lucky to make it, and I was lucky."

Jimmy's toughness and luck were evident even at age 88. While showering, he felt a large, hard bump on his shoulder. Concerned about this new growth, he went to the doctor. Unsure what it was, the doctor cut his skin open to find a corroded bullet. Years earlier Jimmy had been shot in the shoulder, but he left the bullet in. He did not become aware of it again until it finally worked itself out the muscle to beneath his skin. He never explained how he happened to get shot. It may have happened more than a half century earlier, while defending cargo from an attempted hijacking.

Frank Costello's attorney, George Wolf, wrote of his client's toughness. He "was one of the 'legitimate' bootleggers. By that I mean he imported the liquor which the 'illegitimate' bootleggers attempted to hijack." He concluded with, "a remark an old friend of Costello's made to me recently: 'If you're writing a book about how nice a guy Frank was, don't put too much in there about the Twenties.'" This statement almost certainly applies to all major rumrunners. When facing gun barrels, they survived by either shooting first or shooting more accurately.[23]

Organized crime spans many different types of specialties and a range of personalities. For example illegal gamblers, who manage casinos or book horseraces or sports, want to get other people's money, but they do not want to hurt them physically. Violence is not part of the gambler's trade. Las Vegas residents learned the distinction decades ago, when the nation's illegal gamblers moved into town to build the casino industry. Unlike organized gangs in other cities that preyed on the local residents and businesses, the Las Vegas casino operators treated the townspeople decently and courteously and became highly respected and well-liked members of the community.

When the legitimate public corporations began their takeover of the casino industry in the 1970s, long-term residents who had either worked in the business or were its customers started a popular refrain, "The town was better when the Mob ran it." Older residents still say it today. It may sound crazy to the rest of the country, especially cities exposed to the exploitation and violence of organized gangs, but Las Vegans are sincere. What Luciano, Lansky, Siegel, Adonis, and Costello did during their long careers, is done now by modern gaming corporations and Native-American tribes across the country - offer gambling games and sell booze.

The only association these illegal casino operators had with what we call organized crime was to pay a share of their profits to organized gangs for the right to ply their trade in their territories. They paid the gangs and the police in whose territories they operated to be left alone, but they received no protection of their large cash bankrolls from anyone. Since their operations were illegal, they were on their own. They could not dial 911 when they were robbed. They had to defend themselves against such attacks without outside assistance.

When I became a dealer in the mid 1960s, most of the table pit executives I met had already spent years working in illegal casinos across the country and on Caribbean islands. I regularly went out with them after work to have a drink and listen to their experiences. A substantial percentage had been knifed or shot in robberies during their careers, and some had killed to protect their bankrolls and their lives.

Luciano, Lansky, Siegel, Adonis, and Costello became some of the most infamous mobsters in American folklore, but they were first and foremost businessmen. They worked in an underground world that was populated by the most dangerous and treacherous goons of their time, but dealt with them without either compromising their personal values or flaunting their fearsome power. Their demeanor was unassuming and courteous, never self-important or swaggering. Even Siegel, despite his high-energy, intense personality, was always considerate, accommodating, and polite. No one would have ever surmised from their social bearing that these were men of awesome power and status in the underworld.

Luciano's attorney Moses Polakoff said years later, "Lucky was a nice guy. The old timers were well behaved. They were not like the present mob. If Lucky was walking down the street and he bumped into you, he would apologize to you." He loved the haunts in his Manhattan province, and he frequently walked the busy sidewalks. Whenever he accidentally bumped into another pedestrian, he was indeed quick to apologize, but when someone bumped into him, he was also known to apologize just as quickly. Quiet and unassuming, he never threw his weight around. He went to great lengths to defuse potential trouble and would back away from confrontation whenever he could.[24]

VENGEANCE IS NOT MINE

When Luciano was the well-established number-two man in the powerful Masseria gang, one evening at the dinner hour he was walking the streets of the city he loved, when a car pulled up beside him. Three passengers leaped out, shoved gun barrels into his back, pushed him into the car, and tore off. They quickly covered his mouth with adhesive tape. When they reached their destination, Staten Island's Huguenot Beach, they yanked him out of the car. All four men pummeled him with fists and gun butts until he fell to the beach, where they kicked him into unconsciousness. He remained comatose for seven hours. At 2 a.m. he woke up, sprawled near the surf that was rolling in and out.

Seriously injured, he pulled the tape off his mouth, got up, and stumbled toward the lights in the distance looking for a pay phone to call someone to pick him up. He made it almost a mile before a patrolman saw the struggling man near the police booth at Prince's Bay Avenue. Luciano pleaded with the cop, "I'll give you fifty bucks [then a week's salary] if you get me a taxi, and let me go my way." Instead, the officer took the badly battered man to Richmond Memorial Hospital and called a detective.

Luciano told the patrolman the facts presented here, but he denied recognizing the men who had taken him for that ride and insisted he had no enemies. He did say, "Don't you cops lose any sleep over it. I'll attend to this thing myself, later." Detectives speculated to the press that Broadway racketeers had thrown him on the beach and left him for dead. A gun butt or heel stomp to his face caused a disfiguring scar from the corner of his right eye to his chin and caused his right eyelid to droop, which added a slightly sinister quality to his expression.[25]

Jimmy Blue Eyes explained to me in an interview what Luciano had told his partners had happened that night. It was exactly what he had said to the patrolman, but he added that he recognized his assailants as four plain-clothes NYPD detectives. Jimmy related to me, "The cops were mostly Irish, and they hated the Italians. The "Broadway Squad" were detectives in plain clothes and an unmarked car. These were tough, rogue cops who may have had some private agenda, or just been angry that night, trying to demonstrate their prowess, as is the case with most brutal police. They used to beat the shit out of Italians, even in their neighborhoods. They picked Charlie up where there was an elevated train, where Radio City Music Hall is today at 50th and 6th Avenue. They crossed to Staten Island, beat the shit out of him in the car, and then threw him out into the gutter. They left him there, probably thinking he was dead. He was close." When I raised the possibility that the cops were demanding information about another hood, Jimmy responded, "Charlie would never have told them [the cops] anything, even to save his life." (See Addendum H**)**

Police of that era typically fell into three categories. Some were honest, dedicated professionals. Some readily accepted bribes from street gangs and Prohibition gangs. Some were racists, meaning besides being corrupt they were filled with hatred toward minority and immigrant ethnic groups and disrespected their constitutionally-guaranteed civil rights. During Prohibition, a contingent of Irish NYPD police brutally discriminated against Italians, Sicilians, Jews, and Africans, and it did not matter to them whether their targets were criminals or law-abiding citizens. Such intolerance against minorities and the poor has existed to some degree in virtually every large U.S. city police department at some time.

The infamous Broadway Squad was composed of 14 detectives. When a new Police Commissioner took over, he disbanded this Squad and two other NYPD units by transferring the members into two existing units because they all bungled the murder investigation of gambler Arnold Rothstein (see Chapter 5). Even though the unit transfers occurred a year before Charlie was beaten, Jimmy correctly identified the guilty detectives, who continued patrolling the same area of Broadway together in an unmarked car.

Jimmy told me you had to be lucky to survive in Prohibition, and his pal Charlie certainly was lucky to be alive. The *New York Times* story about the beating gave Luciano's nickname as "Lucky." It was the first time anyone who knew him heard the term used, but it stuck. Perhaps the reporter heard someone say, "He's lucky." From then on, his friends and associates called him *Charlie Lucky,* and the entire underworld picked up the moniker.

Three years later, it was Siegel who was lucky when he survived an attack described in an FBI internal report. "On November 9, 1932, Siegel while attending a meeting of the organization in the Hard Tack Social Club at 547 Grand Avenue, New York City, suffered rather severe head injuries as the result of a bomb explosion. He and some other members of the mob were taken to a hospital for treatment. An Italian named Fabrizzo had lowered a bomb down the chimney, but failed to take into consideration that the chimney had a right-angle offset which caused the bomb to become stuck before reaching the proper elevation. [11 days later] Fabrizzo was shot and killed on November 20, 1932 for this attempt on the lives of the mob. Siegel still has the scars on his head caused by the flying bricks. One of these scars, about 1.5 inches long on the upper side (left) of his head, is visible through his thinning hair." [26]

This report is enlightening for what it does not say. It does not identify the other crime figures who were present or any possible relationship or conflict they may have had with Fabrizzo. Most significantly it does not suggest that Siegel was considered either the target of the bomb or a suspect in killing the bomber. Jimmy Blue Eyes was unaware of Ben and the perpetrator being on the outs.

Luciano did not retaliate against the detectives who nearly murdered him, and the FBI did not believe Siegel avenged the bombing that was intended to kill every one in that room. Neither man sought vengeance for the vicious assaults, even though Mafia culture demanded it. The original Sicilian Mafia warriors centuries before defended their countrymen, and they retaliated when they were harmed or victimized by occupying foreign forces. Avenging maltreatment and injustice was an important part of their honor code. Unfortunately, when the criminal element took control of the Mafia, they brutally intimidated their neighbors and threatened to silence anyone who objected to their exploitation.

When the Sicilian Mafiosi immigrated to the U.S., their heritage of vendetta became a key tactic in dominating their fellow countrymen. But while Luciano and his comrades were closely associated with Mafia gangs and their culture throughout their Prohibition and illegal-casino careers, these Americanized Young Turks emphatically rejected vengeance as counterproductive, because it only fuels a never-ending cycle of violence. Their Las Vegas associates explained to me in various ways the logical conclusion of the philosophy of an eye for an eye - everyone ends up blind.

The Young Turks were stoic in the face of injustice, even when police and prosecutors framed three of them for crimes they did not commit. None of the seven ever sought vengeance, even though all endured violent attacks, including being shot at point blank range; being beaten close to death; and having a cousin, a son, a partner, and/or several close associates murdered. (The details of each incident is presented in chronological context in this and future volumes.) They knew the perpetrator in all these attacks, but never sought retribution. The seven even refused to supply information to the police or testify against the perpetrators in court. This was a key trait of the Young Turks, and it made them by far the hoodlums most respected by both the underworld and overworld. Throughout their lives, all endured violent tragedies, grave injustices, and terrible affronts yet reacted passively. They drew a strong line between self-defense and murder - to them, vengeance was calculated and premeditated murder.

Even though hundreds of Masseria gang members had taken a blood oath to murder upon the command of Luciano, he and his colleagues never used this power to avenge an attack or affront. Luciano, who could have issued a one-sentence edict to any of his underlings to spray machinegun fire at the four detectives who beat him, simply put the vicious beating behind him. His lack of vindictiveness was typical of the gamblers who pioneered the Las Vegas Strip, most of whom were associated with him or the other Young Turks.

During my years of research, I developed close relationships with a number of major casino operators who had acquired infamous mobster images as Prohibition violators and illegal casino operators and also the gangsters in the background of the Strip operations. They told me shocking tales of dastardly deeds committed by competitors, thieves, and even trusted friends and relatives. Still each man renounced vengeance, pointing to the futility of tit- for-tat as an effective way to resolve or relieve antagonism. They passed on to me the unique perspective they had learned during years in the violent underworld while they possessed awesome power to retaliate. They emphasized to me that real power is not possessing the ability to hurt or to control others. It is having the ability to hurt or to control others, and to be able to restrain yourself from doing it. Real power is being able to control oneself. They counseled me whenever I vented frustration and anger that unless I planned to retaliate, then hatred is a devastating negative force, consuming the hater rather than effecting the hated. They lectured me to put aside the desire to get even, and instead concentrate on positive pursuits - my research, developing new ideas, and writing.

I was deeply impressed with the tremendous capacity of these men to accept adversity, put it behind them, and move on. Interestingly, except for Ben Siegel, virtually all the major former illegal casino operators who became involved with Nevada gambling, lived to a peaceful old age and died of natural causes.

THE YOUNG TURKS CAUGHT UP IN THE SICILIAN-AMERICAN WAR

When Fascist leader Benito Mussolini became dictator of Italy in 1924, he appointed a special prosecutor, with sweeping powers to imprison any suspected Mafia member in an attempt to rid Sicily of the Mafiosi's iron grip over the politics of the island. This caused some Mafiosi to migrate to the U. S., and the rest hid in the hills until the waning days of World War II. As American troops fought through Sicily and then Italy, the Mafiosi trailed behind the advancing U.S. troops, filling the political power void left in the war's wake. Thus, the Mafia became much stronger politically in Sicily and throughout Italy than it had been before the war.

One Mafioso who immigrated to the U. S. was Salvatore Maranzano. He entered the country illegally in 1927 at age 47 and started an import-export business as a front. This was to cover up joining both a major bootleg distilling ring, and the Brooklyn/Manhattan crime gang whose members were all from the region bordering the Gulf of Castellammarese on Sicily's northwest coast. Maranzano's son later said that his father was in the fishing business, and his fishing fleet was based at Sea Isle, New Jersey.

A fellow Castellammarese, Joe "Bananas" Bonanno, who had fled Mussolini's regime three years earlier, went to work as muscle for Maranzano's moonshine still operations in Pennsylvania and upstate New York. Bonanno's job was to protect the stills from fire, sabotage, and extortion in the form of protection demands by other hoods. When the stills were hit, Bonanno's job was to carry out Maranzano's edict - retaliate with force. Bonanno later wrote in his autobiography that a "common occurrence was the hijacking of delivery trucks by rival bootlegging gangs. For the transport of alcohol we used vehicles disguised as milk trucks or fruit trucks or, as in this case, furniture-moving trucks. ... All the Irish cops took payments. ... The tolerant relationship between the police and the bootleggers existed not so much because of bribery as because of a similar attitude toward Prohibition. The Irish cops of the day, as well as the public at large, adopted a laissez-faire attitude." (See Addendum I)

Immigrants have always stuck together, but the Castellammarese immigrants were more clannish than even the other tightly-knit Sicilian gangs. Bonanno recalled, "We had our own distinct neighborhoods, not only in Brooklyn and Manhattan, but also in Detroit, Buffalo and Endicott, New York. Not only did we all know each other, but we were often related to one another."

When Bonanno entered the U. S. in 1924, Stefano Magaddino of Buffalo and Gaspar Milazzo of Detroit were the two most powerful Castellammarese Mafia leaders. Both had close ties with Brooklyn's large Castellammarese community, where Bonanno's boss Maranzano was based. The nation's Castellammarese gangs would eventually band together and fight a war with America's other Sicilian Mafia gangs for ultimate underworld power.

Opposing the Castellammarese gangs was Luciano's boss, Joe Masseria. Like many of his gang members, he was born in Sciacca on the west coast of Sicily. Their dispute was not over clan quarrels from the old country. It was driven by competing ambitions to obtain supreme control over the underworld. As the conflict heated up, most American-Sicilian gangs were forced to pick sides. The war's causes and the resulting impact on the hoods who would later develop the Las Vegas Strip follow, but the individual acts of violence in the tit-for-tat fighting were too numerous to mention each one here.

From the late 1800s, when Sicilians began arriving in the U. S. in large numbers, their professional street gangs fought over territory. These disputes were always between adjacent gangs who coveted the "no man's land" separating their territories. This type of localized rivalry continued during Prohibition, but the need to obtain raw ingredients and to market bottled inventory created networks of associates nationwide for the first time. During this period Sicilians competed and fought far more often with other ethnic gangs within their territories than with nearby Sicilian gangs.

Sicilian gangs in different geographical areas during Prohibition formed mutually-beneficial business alliances so when two gangs that each had nationwide alliances got into a dispute it made widespread conflict inevitable. Chicago had many bloody gang wars but these did not affect the nation's other Sicilian gangs because the Aiello brothers were always aligned with Al Capone. But when Joe Aiello and Capone started competing for the Unione Siciliana Chicago branch presidency, their allies were drawn into the conflict. All the Castellammarese clans had close ties with Joe Aiello and supported him. Capone's multi-ethnic gang had always supported the nation's biggest Mafia gang leader, Joe The Boss Masseria. Thus, he reciprocated and threw his support behind Capone and most Sicilian gangs followed Masseria's lead.

This war began in Chicago when the Aiello brothers tried to kill Capone, but instead succeeded in murdering his appointed Unione Siciliana Chicago branch president, Tony Lombardo. This battle raged until Joe Aiello finally captured the presidency and Capone killed him (detailed in Chapter 6), setting off the Sicilian-American War that quickly involved the New York gangs and the other Castellammarese Mafia gangs around the country.

Of the nation's two powerful Castellammarese leaders, Gaspar Milazzo of Detroit was geographically closest to Chicago. Masseria had him killed in a fish market causing the gangs in other cities, who had taken sides in the Chicago conflict, to scurry to the mattresses. Masseria maneuvered to have his supporter in Milazzo's gang, Chester "Big Chet " La Mare, take over leadership. But less than a year later, Castellammarese gangsters killed La Mare in his home, as the two factions continued to eliminate opposition leaders and install their backers in the vacated positions.[27]

Milazzo's killing in Detroit made Buffalo's Stefano Magaddino the most senior leader of the Castellammarese clans. However, the clans' prime enemy in the conflict switched from Capone to New York City-based Masseria. Thus, it fell upon Maranzano's Manhattan/Brooklyn gang to lead the fight, with Buffalo and Detroit supplying money, arms, ammunition, and some manpower. The powerful Masseria gang had a huge manpower advantage over the combined Castellammarese clans, whose much smaller gangs were spread throughout different cities. Masseria also enjoyed the support of Capone and several non-Castellammarese Mafia gangs.

Once Aiello ignited the conflict with Capone, both sides assumed the other had unrestrained ambition and malevolent intentions. Thus, Masseria and Magaddino rejected each other's proposed truce meetings, fearing they were really murder traps. How many members were killed on both sides is not known, but the fighting escalated to include the strategic murders of key leaders. The two warring chieftains made no effort to try to find a peaceful resolution.

Organized crime, especially the Mafia, is a world of secrecy, intrigue, and treachery, and there is no better illustration of these traits than the actions of the two principal adversaries in the Sicilian-American War. Three of the New York City Mafia gangs' leaders were not directly involved in this fight, so the two warring adversaries ordered two of the three neutral Mafia leaders killed and replaced with their backers. Masseria first had one leader killed, and Maranzano in turn had that leader's replacement killed by his trusted lieutenant. Maranzano then had the two leaders of a second gang killed, and Vincent Mangano ultimately took over.[28]

Gang wars were tough on the fighters and their families. Bonanno wrote, "You had to leave your family, you had to abandon your business and you had to put your life in danger." During the American-Sicilian War, the fighters were separated from their wives and children for an entire year. The gangland term for *war* is *going to the mattresses,* a description of how they lived. The fighters camped out in unfurnished apartments, offices, or warehouses with only mattresses on the floor for sleeping. It could be days, weeks, or months between face-to-face battles, time filled with boredom, waiting, and tension. To make matters worse, female companionship was a no-no for the gang members, who are typically womanizers. They could not visit their wives or mistresses because enemies might have them staked out, and they could not frequent hookers since they might know someone associated with the adversary and sell them out.

The Sicilian-American War occurred decades before television and the Internet, so the fighters had no entertainment in their austere bivouacs. Their sole pleasure was food, so a primary imperative was to have a good cook in the group. Food gave the Sicilians and Italians a great advantage over other nationalities because so many of their men were outstanding cooks. Their barren rooms were always filled with the aroma of slowly simmering fresh marinara sauce, garlic, and other delicacies made from old-country recipes.

Combatants were most vulnerable when they left their shelter. Every time someone left, he had to be careful the enemy had not found their safe house and set up an ambush outside. He had to remain alert every minute he was out, watching to make sure no one showed recognition that might tip off the enemy. He had to take long, circuitous routes back to the safe house. Some made it a policy to follow the same long route over and over for a hour to two hours, or drive the wrong way on one-way streets, forcing enemy followers to give up the chase or tip their hand by going the wrong way too. Sharp, fast U-turns in the middle of blocks served the same purpose. Such maneuvers made for a thrilling ride. Going very slowly or very fast also revealed a tail unless they called it off.

Supplying the safe house with enough food, clean clothing, and other living necessities also posed great danger. Married women during that era tended to be full-time housewives who did all the domestic chores. It was unusual to see a man carrying large bags of groceries out of a market. It was a tip-off he could be living with other men at the mattresses. Every one associated with the enemy looked for such behavior. Bonanno wrote, "Within our Family, only a minority were combatants. The majority were noncombatants such as bakers, butchers, undertakers, masons, doctors, lawyers, and priests. They all pitched in, helping us out with their special skills."

LOOKING FOR AN EXODUS TO A QUAGMIRE

This gangland war strategically resembled a chess game with the goal to knock out the other's king and win total dominance over the Sicilian underworld. The Masseria-Maranzano dual was not going to end until one gang killed the other's leader. Five months after the beginning of all out war, Masseria and seven lieutenants held a strategy session in the Alhambra Apartments in the Bronx. Upon its conclusion, Masseria walked through the courtyard towards his armored car with his bodyguards leading the way. In the quiet still of the night an explosive burst of machinegun fire poured from a ground floor apartment window towards the group. Two guards fell dead, but Masseria escape unscathed. The legend of "The Duck's " miraculous survivals grew.

Ambition and greed have always been the two primary causes of violence among Mafiosi. For Masseria, unbridled megalomania to dominate all major American crime was added to this narcissistic stew. He took the nickname Joe The Boss seriously, and he was willing to wage war even when there was no chance for victory in sight. Luciano and the other Young Turks had loyally obeyed and followed The Boss for more than a decade, but Masseria refused to even consider the possibility of peace meetings. He was totally committed to fighting this duel until he either won or lost, no matter how long it might take nor how many men might die.

Luciano held clandestine discussions to evaluate the bleak situation with his six closest associates, his four Prohibition partners - Adonis, Lansky, Siegel, and Alo - and their two close business competitors - Costello and Genovese. They had now been at the mattresses for a year in a conflict that had begun more than two years earlier. To them it was a war without purpose since they never coveted anyone else's territory, power, or wealth. Worse, it was a war that might never be won. They longed to return to their families, to their businesses, and to fully enjoying each day.

None of this was possible, maybe not even their very survival, as long as Masseria remained in command. Despairing over the futility of their situation, they realized their only option was to make an independent peace with Maranzano. But as Costello's attorney George Wolf wrote, "They were in a bind; they weren't Castellammarese so they couldn't be accepted by that gang. At the same time they were against Masseria's pointless war."

Switching sides was not an option because the war would continue to go on. They wanted out of the war and the only way out was for the war to end. But Maranzano only dealt with Sicilians, preferably Castellammarese. Worse, he was vocally outspoken against, and refused to deal with, Luciano and his Young Turks. He disliked everything about them. There was only one Sicilian in the gang, Luciano, and the rest were mainland Italians and Jews. All seven rejected the Mafia lifestyle and its superficial, meaningless *code of honor*.

Luciano's gang was trapped on the horns of a life-and-death dilemma, torn between two malevolent forces. It cannot be overemphasized that, unlike these two megalomaniac dictatorial leaders, Luciano always relinquished power over others whenever he was offered it throughout his career. The only power that was ever relevant to him was to be strong enough to make others back off and leave him alone, as in this case.

Then Maranzano created an opening. He sent word to Luciano that the quickest way to end the war was for Masseria's men to kill their boss. In return Maranzano swore that he would seek no vengeance on Masseria's supporters and soldiers. Luciano accompanied by Genovese met with Maranzano and his lieutenant Bonanno at a Brooklyn home. Luciano agreed to Maranzano's proposed resolution to the gangland war. Luciano would kill Masseria and replace him as head of the nation's biggest gang. Luciano would continue to operate independently of Maranzano with the condition that Luciano would pay the man who would become the new Boss of Bosses an on-going tribute from profits. In return, everyone's safety was guaranteed. There would be no retribution. Bonanno later wrote that Maranzano made it clear the olive branch would only be extended after Masseria was dead. Until then, Luciano and his buddies remained Maranzano's warring enemies.

Both Masseria and Maranzano were arrogant, overbearing Mustache Petes who clung to the isolationist, dictatorial traditions of the Sicilian Mafia. While Luciano and his gang held a special place with Masseria, they did not really know how Maranzano would treat them. But when Maranzano offered hope for peace, he became the lesser of the two evils confronting them.

Luciano and his comrades were Masseria's closest and most loyal members, but once they decided to risk trusting Maranzano, they became a potent and lethal force set to destroy their misguided leader. They prepared their trap. Masseria liked to lunch at his favorite Italian restaurant, the Nuovo Villa Tammaro, on Coney Island. They waited for Masseria to follow his usual routine of parking his massive steel-armored sedan with its inch-thick plate-glass windows in a nearby garage and walking with three companions the short distance to this little mom-and-pop restaurant on a quiet narrow street near the bay. The four lunched for a hour until all the patrons had emptied out. One of the three bodyguards went to the men's room. As he returned to the dining table, he suddenly jumped behind Masseria and shot him three times in the back. The other two men quickly pulled their guns and opened fire. The man sitting across the table shot Masseria just above the eye, and the man to his side shot him once in the neck. Even The Duck could not dodge bullets coming from three directions at once.[29]

The three killers quickly staged the setting to look as if they had been at a social meeting. They overturned a few chairs and tossed a deck of cards and approximately $35 in bills and coins on the floor. Masseria lay on his back, and they adjusted his left hand to clutch a brand new ace of diamonds to complete the card-game scenario rather than to send some symbolic message. The three shooters then quickly exited, leaving behind their hats and coats. They got in an escape automobile strategically parked at the curb in front and drove off. Four hours later the police found the car abandoned about two miles away. It had been stolen five months earlier and fitted with new, unregistered plates that were untraceable. Three pistols were found on the back seat; a single cartridge had been fired from each one. The weapons were not consistent with the murder scene - five bullets, not three, were fired into Masseria. Two revolvers found in the alley beside the restaurant opened the possibility that two additional assailants, posing as diners, may have joined the one returning from the men's room, and the three each shot Masseria once in the back. If this is what happened, the excessive firepower could indicate that the assailants were truly apprehensive about Masseria's legendary ability to bob, weave, and duck.

The police investigation failed to discover a meaningful clue except that the hats and coats left behind had been purchased in Brooklyn. Witnesses put up the usual blank wall of terrified silence. The restaurant owner said he had gone out for a walk at the time, and his mother-in-law said she was in the kitchen, leaving the restaurant empty. The police were never able to identify the three men who accompanied Masseria to lunch, nor did they discover a motive, although they were disinclined to believe he was shot over a card-game quarrel. NYPD Detectives expressed fear that this murder might set off the worst gang warfare in history, so they clearly had no idea the purpose for the killing was just the opposite, to end a long and bloody gangland conflict. Nor did they realize there was a pattern and relationship between Masseria's death and the city's gangland murders of the preceding year of this war

Detectives announced Masseria was 45 and was "the biggest of 'em all - bigger than Al Capone." The NYPD Commissioner explained to the press that Joe The Boss was known to have several rackets including an interest in horseracing, a dice game, and leadership of the New York branch of the Unione Siciliana. All these activities made it difficult for them to establish just which one had led to his death. Masseria's family told police that he had been partners in a racing stable of 20 horses with Little Augie Pisano (successor of Frankie Yale in Chapter 6) and had been interested in a bookmaking enterprise.

Authors about organized crime have gone to great lengths to guess who the shooters were, even through no evidence or identification of any kind was ever uncovered. They tend to just repeat each other's wrong conclusions - that Luciano accompanied Masseria to lunch and told police he was in the restroom washing his hands when he heard the gunshots. In reality the police never learned who the three dining companions were. Luciano always denied he was there, an assertion that the detectives did not disbelieve. No other information surfaced, but since Luciano must have known he could become the prime suspect, he likely was surrounded by strong alibi witnesses far away at the moment Masseria was killed.

Organized-crime authors who have written about the Masseria murder clearly failed to consider the most obvious facts surrounding this event. It occurred at the height of a major gang war. Masseria would not have ventured out from hiding without a strong security force, especially to his favorite restaurant, which he knew the enemy would likely stake out. He and the companions he most trusted would not have sat frozen as strangers or outsiders approached the table, pulled guns, and then fired five bullets. The companions would have instantly returned fire, and the cluster of bodyguards parked outside would have charged and fired at the assailants as they tried to leave. Not one previous author who has covered this gangland killing grasped the obvious conclusion - absent a major gunfight, Masseria's luncheon associates had to be the shooters and all his security had to have been in on it. Luciano was the man they reported to and the man they most respected.

FROM THE FRYING PAN INTO THE FIRE

Salvatore Maranzano defeated the enemy, but he did not bother to establish peace with the opposition's survivors. His lieutenant Bonanno complained in his book that Maranzano had replaced Masseria but continued his worst dictatorial traits to dominate the Mafia underworld and subjugate the other gangs. Bonanno described his boss' lousy people skills. "Maranzano had qualities that made him a great conqueror but a mediocre statesman." He was aristocratic, imperious, and prone to temper tirades. He crushed opposing views, and he believed it irrelevant to accommodate other people even if they were powerful.

Maranzano even changed leadership of some of the five New York City gangs to install either war allies or supporters. Maranzano did keep his word with Luciano and Genovese to replace the vanquished Masseria as the leader and lieutenant of the nation's largest criminal gang. But Maranzano's old-world Sicilian Mafioso temperament and style clashed with Luciano's gang of Americanized Sicilian, Italian, and Jewish Young Turks. Maranzano dictated with a condescending attitude to the leaders of a gang that was probably three times larger than his.

Six weeks after Masseria's murder, Maranzano established his dominance by convening the first meeting ever held of all the leaders of the American Mafia gangs, and he chaired the convention. About 300 Mafiosi gathered in upstate New York's Hotel Congress. All were Sicilian except Genovese, who was Italian. Maranzano approved Luciano's request to bring his Jewish advisor Lansky, but the new Boss of Bosses required he sit outside the meeting-room's closed doors.

At this so-called peace conference, Luciano and Genovese quickly realized that Maranzano was making himself dictator of the Mafia. They knew none of the other gang leaders would be safe, most especially themselves because they had long made their opposition to such leadership well known. They had successfully ended the war, but in the process they had replaced one violent, tyrannical leader with another. They had murdered to be able to have a life filled with peace, family, and enjoyment, but it turned out to be one clouded with discontent and wariness over Maranzano's actions and intentions.

The Young Turk's fear peaked one day when Luciano received a command request from Maranzano to come to his office the next afternoon. By then Luciano undoubtedly sensed the meeting was a rouse, setting him up for murder. More importantly someone who had to have been very close to Maranzano to have been privy to the information about the planned murder betrayed the Boss of Bosses by forewarning Luciano to beware. And Luciano later admitted that he had known Maranzano was expecting an IRS examination of his business accounting records.

Maranzano's Eagle Building Corporation maintained a suite of offices on the ninth floor of the Grand Central Building on Park Avenue. The next afternoon at about 3:45 p.m., 15 minutes before the scheduled meeting with Luciano and Genovese, seven men and Maranzano's secretary were sitting in his office anteroom when four men impersonating IRS agents entered in a businesslike manner. Suddenly all four pulled out pistols and every one threw up their hands as one gunman ordered the eight to line up against the wall. Then the other three burst into Maranzano's private office, and as the startled Boss of Bosses leapt from his chair to defend himself, the first man stabbed him repeatedly with a stiletto to avoid gunfire that might be heard in nearby offices. As Maranzano fell backward, screaming epithets and trying to reach for a gun in his desk drawer, another intruder shot him three times. Maranzano slumped into his chair dead.

The four men ran out of the suite, through the hallway, and down the nine-story fire escape. Occupants from other offices dashed into the hallway at the sound of the shots and saw the men fleeing, but nobody interfered. The seven men who had been in Maranzano's waiting room lost no time in disappearing too. The secretary later told police they were clients waiting to see Maranzano, but police were unable to identify any of them. The four killers had dropped the murder weapons as they fled and vanished. The stiletto was on the office floor; a .38 caliber pistol from which three cartridges had been discharged was on the sixth floor of the fire escape; and a fully-loaded pistol was on the second floor of the stairwell.

During the struggle in Maranzano's office, the hats of two assailants were knocked to the floor. Both were expensive and featured labels from Chicago hat stores. These hats could have been plants to misdirect police because Luciano's gang had many initiated members who were unknown to the city's other four Mafia gangs, but Al Capone idolized Luciano and would have readily supplied shooters who were unknown to anyone in New York, especially to the police and press. This is likely what happened because a small piece of yellow paper fastened to the lining in one hat contained Maranzano's Brooklyn home address. Local shooters often drive by the hit location a few times to familiarize themselves with it, while out of towners would more likely want the exact address in a foreign setting.

Maranzano was 51 when he died. He left an estate of $54,000 ($760,000 in today's dollars). Among his personal papers, detectives found a book listing the names of 51 prominent people including a judge, a politician, and a female employee of the U.S. Naturalization Bureau, but every one of them denied knowing him. At the time of his murder, authorities were attempting to stop a nationwide alien-smuggling ring and it became evident that Maranzano was deeply involved. Detectives found documents about evading immigration laws, and his secretary said his office had exchanged correspondence with the Department of Immigration in Washington, D.C. It was learned that at least one person went to Maranzano for a visa extension believing him to be an attorney. The police concluded that he was engaged in providing forged or counterfeit credentials such as false U.S. baptismal certificates. Maranzano had corresponded with a number of officials in the U. S.

immigration service, but the investigation was hindered by the smuggled aliens who feared they would be killed if they talked. Soon more than two-dozen people would be prosecuted exposing corruption by Federal employees. Maranzano's naturalization records were missing from the Federal Naturalization Bureau files in the Manhattan, Brooklyn, and Washington. D.C. offices. It was assumed that the official who signed them destroyed them to cover up his or her tracks.[30]

According to underworld folklore, as the four killers fled down the fire escape, they passed well-known cold-blooded murderer Vincent "Mad Dog" Coll walking up. The shooters not only did not kill the intended assassin of Luciano and Genovese, but they extended Coll the courtesy of telling him to beat it because the cops were coming. When Luciano later met with the top Mafiosi, he explained that he had acted in self-defense in killing Maranzano because he knew Maranzano had hired Coll to kill him. Bonanno later admitted that Maranzano had planned to have Coll kill Luciano and Genovese that afternoon in his office. Bonanno concluded, "The truth is that in August 1931, Maranzano and Luciano simultaneously were plotting to kill each other."

Luciano's motive was clearly preemptive self-defense, but no one ever found a rational explanation why Maranzano instigated the murder of two gang leaders who had no ambition for his position and already shared their great Prohibition profits with him. Two possibilities offered by Bonanno and authors about early organized crime are merely vague conjectures - Maranzano wanted even more power and his values about violence differed too much from Luciano. Most importantly, these writers failed to explain how Maranzano could possibly benefit. If he had succeeded in killing Luciano and Genovese, he would have reignited the two-year gang war. It had ended in a treaty because the two large factions were stalemated, but Maranzano's opposition was in a much stronger position than their former boss Masseria had been during the war. While Maranzano was disliked by the other Mafia gang leaders, Luciano and Costello were the underworld's two most revered men. If Maranzano had succeeded in killing Luciano and Genovese, their lieutenant Costello and their Italian and Jewish comrades would have added to their gang's three-times advantage in shooters by reaching out to large gang allies. Mafia gangs that had sat out the war, even some who had previously aligned with Maranzano, would have joined Costello out of fear for their own safety from what had become a power-thirsty madman, personal loyalty to Costello, and vendetta for Luciano. Gangland reverence for Costello was so great that later in his life the entire underworld would unite to avenge him, even though he did not want retribution, and practically none of these supporters who wanted to act in his name had ever met him.

Maranzano's decision to attack these two powerful leaders bordered on suicidal, so what compelled him to do it? Maranzano's motive for wanting the two leaders dead can be discovered through analysis of what his lieutenant Bonanno later wrote and did not write in his autobiography. Bonanno found Maranzano contemptible as a leader and as a man. Bonanno also complained bitterly about the mutual animosity and competitive intrigues between his boss Maranzano and his cousin Stefano Magaddino in Buffalo. Magaddino was the senior Castellammarese leader, and he was the most powerful until Maranzano became the self-elected dictatorial Boss of Bosses, or capo di tutti capi. Bonanno was shocked, disgusted, and sickened by both of these seemingly insatiable, ambitious leaders, and said that Maranzano might have "become intoxicated with power." He wrote, "What grisly games these older men played! Didn't they ever stop maneuvering? " Magaddino was especially offended when Maranzano spent the two months after Masseria's murder jockeying to succeed the slain gangster as leader of the New York branch of the Unione Siciliana. When Maranzano was elected the new head at a Coney Island meeting, Magaddino felt upstaged.

It is interesting and surprising that Bonanno denied knowing Maranzano planned to kill Luciano and Genovese or what his motive was. He also claimed he did not learn Maranzano hired Coll to do it until he heard this from other gang leaders after the fact. His assertions are not credible. Actually, they were not remotely possible given the realities of his gang's organizational structure and loyalties. Maranzano had great trust in his lieutenant Bonanno and no one else. Bonanno ran Maranzano's largest business interest of the moonshine stills and alcohol distribution, he alone talked to Maranzano and passed his orders on to the other gang members to insulate his boss from possible informer testimony, and he assisted in the "grisly" intrigues against his own cousin. Yet Bonanno claimed he was kept out of the plans to murder the leaders of the nation's biggest gang and to prepare the defense against the inevitable massive, actually overwhelming, warfare that was about to occur. Given what we know, another scenario makes immense sense.

Consider the facts - Bonanno held his boss in utter contempt and coveted his position as leader, and his cousin Magaddino was angry with the mounting power and status of Maranzano. Both Bonanno and Magaddino were admittedly involved in secret discussions about political intrigue against Maranzano and both obviously wanted him dead. But they could not afford to act themselves. If Bonanno killed his boss, and Magaddino as the highest-ranking Castellammarese leader then approved Bonanno's ascension to the throne, both men would have been disrespected by the whole Sicilian clan for the disloyalty of a lieutenant to his leader. They needed an outsider to kill Maranzano.

Consider how easy it would have been for the highly-trusted Bonanno to convince Maranzano that he had learned Luciano was planning to assassinate him to become the Boss of Bosses. This false intel would have compelled Maranzano to try to kill Luciano first, and as soon as the Boss of Bosses had employed Coll, Luciano was notified that Maranzano had contracted to kill him. Maranzano would have trusted only Bonanno to contract with Coll, and Bonanno was the only gang member to benefit from warning Luciano because it made him the gang's new leader. The almost certain conclusion from all these facts, along with the one supposition that the two cousins falsely convinced Maranzano that Luciano was a threat, means that Luciano and Genovese were merely hapless pawns in the sinister connivings of Bonanno and Magaddino to force members of another gang to unwittingly kill Maranzano for them. It is relevant to note about Bonanno's character that he was not respected by the other gang leaders because he was not a man any one trusted.

Most writers about early organized crime reported that following the afternoon murder of Maranzano, America's gangland suffered its bloodiest night. They claim that Luciano sent death squads out to kill Sicilian Mafia leaders across the country, and that Lansky did the same to Jewish and other ethnic gang leaders. They supposedly wiped out 50 or more gangland leaders who did not support them so they could become the kings of organized crime. Yet no author ever named even one infamous hood that was supposedly killed, even though such killings could have filled many chapters in their books.

Bonanno would have been Luciano's first target of retribution after the year-long war, but Bonanno wrote that he was unaware of any gangland slayings occurring after Maranzano's murder. "What I know for a fact is that after Maranzano's death no member of my Family suffered reprisals. The peace between Luciano and me held," Bonanno said. On the contrary, he reported that Luciano gave his recent enemy valuable positions in the Amalgamated Clothing Union in the lucrative garment district. Bonanno said Luciano asked nothing in return because he did it as an expression of friendship. But Luciano's gift was more likely an "atta boy" and reward for Bonanno having warned him about Maranzano's planned hit against him.

Jimmy Blue Eyes recalled in my interview, "Each Sicilian group had its own Mustache Petes, the old criminals who brought their ways from Sicily. We eliminated [two of] them. This brought peace to New York for a long time. There were no conflicts. Everyone had their own piece and got a fair shake. The Italian-Americans took over the leadership and hooked up with the Jews."

Luciano claimed the mass murder-vendetta story was "pure fiction," and former Chicago Crime Commission Director Virgil Peterson backed him up when he wrote that his organization listed just two minor gangland killings in Chicago that month. An analysis of newspaper articles for the two weeks before and after Maranzano's murder by Dr. Alan Block, in which he canvassed eight major cities for those four weeks, found only three minor gang-linked killings were reported: two in Newark and one in Pittsburgh. According to newspaper records, not a single major hood was killed anywhere in America during the one-month period surrounding Maranzano's demise. Not only were there no other killings of other gang leaders around the time of Maranzano's killing, but Luciano and his Prohibition partners had always cooperated with their competitors like Costello, Genovese, and many others, all of whom sung their praises. Now they were ascending to the pinnacle of gangland power, and for the rest of their careers they strongly advocated for open competition and cooperation between gangs. Their values and actions were exactly opposite to the bull pucky dished up about massive slayings by these organized-crime writers.[31]

Luciano and his pals now hoped to return to having fun every day like they had enjoyed before the Masseria-Maranzano gang war. What a different time it had been for them just three months before that war commenced as Luciano and Masseria partied together in Miami Beach. They visited a gambling room that occupied the entire floor of a hotel. The police raided and arrested the two hoodlums and the 14 other players. All were fined for gambling and vagrancy.[32]

CHAPTER 4

LUCIANO'S ERA OF PEACE – LEADERSHIP & LIFESTYLES

CHARLIE LUCKY & THE YOUNG TURKS LEAD THE UNDERWORLD

The seven Young Turks killed gangdom's two most ambitious and aggressive Mafia leaders five months apart in mid 1931. The Young Turks acted in self-defense to ensure their survival against two tyrannical Mustache Petes, but in doing so they also inherited enormous underworld power. Masseria's death handed Luciano leadership of the nation's largest Mafia gang. Following Maranzano's assassination, Luciano convened the most powerful Mafia leaders to justify why he was forced to take out the Boss of Bosses. After his explanation, the assembled Mafia chiefs unanimously proclaimed him the new Boss of Bosses.

Luciano never had an interest in acquiring power beyond being able to protect himself and his organization. As Jimmy Blue Eyes told me, "Charlie Lucky didn't want to be a big boss. The other hoods wanted him to be, but he wouldn't take it." Actually he did accept the title, but he immediately gutted the power of the Boss of Bosses. Using his new authority as Boss, Luciano reorganized the Mafia hierarchy into the unstructured form the Young Turks had been advocating for years. He eliminated the one-man dictatorial powers Masseria and Maranzano had instated by unilaterally abolishing the Boss of Bosses' absolute authority over other gangs. This action effectively made the Mafia gangs independent organizations so they could negotiate and compromise with each other as equals.

Luciano had always resented paying tribute to Mafia leaders, and he refused to continue this extortion even though he would have benefited greatly in his new position. As Boss of Bosses, he ended making tribute demands upon the other Mafia leaders, just as he had ended collecting payments from his own Mafia gang's members when he became their head five months earlier. Luciano opposed extortion in any form, but more importantly, he wanted no connection with, or benefit from, the many exploitive crimes he abhorred that other members committed.

Jimmy Blue Eyes emphasized, "Under Charlie, everybody was on their own." Joe Bonanno, who had been second in command against Luciano in the long gang war, wrote that "[Luciano] mainly wanted to be left alone to run his enterprises. He was not trying to impose himself on us as had Masseria [or Maranzano]. Lucky demanded nothing from us."

Luciano had long wanted to be left alone by other gangs, and by granting other Mafia leaders autonomy and unilaterally dethroning the Boss of Bosses, he made his dream of an independent and undisturbed lifestyle possible. While Maranzano created friction by forcing his will on other Mafia leaders without consideration of their position, Luciano avoided tension with everyone else.

Bonanno wrote of the man he had warred against, "On the personal level, I always got along with Charlie." Luciano's likeability was one of his great strengths. He commanded far more respect from America's underworld than any other hood, and the gang members of every ethnic group took notice when he spoke, making him much more influential than just the Mafia Supremo.

As part of his democratic reforms, Luciano created the National Crime Commission that has been made up of between five to eight powerful Mafia chiefs elected by all 24 American Mafia leaders. The Commission had no authority to interfere in any gang's internal affairs. It could only mediate conflicts between gangs to prevent the kind of broad-based gang warfare they had just gone through. It was a forum for discussing mutual concerns and influencing but not dictating major policy issues. Chairman Luciano established the agenda and led the discussions, but like every other member, he had only one vote. He replaced the old dictatorial structure with a committee of gang leaders who had to reach consensus, while at the same time restricting the gang leaders' authority except as it pertained to their own gang's affairs. The Commission was to meet every five years or as circumstances dictated.

At the conclusion of that first Commission meeting, the Mustache Pete leaders were stunned to realize that their society was no longer led strictly by Sicilians with old-country values. Overnight outsiders had been promoted to leadership. Luciano was Sicilian, but his six close partners included four mainland Italians who were high-ranking leaders in his gang and two Jewish associates who were his advisors. (Officially his first and second lieutenants were Vito Genovese and Frank Costello, and his chief advisors were Meyer Lansky and Jimmy Blue Eyes.) Even more disturbing to the Mustache Petes, all seven of the Young Turks had Americanized values and attitudes and held Mafia tradition in contempt.

Luciano's recommendation that Mafia gangs cooperate more closely with the other ethnic criminal gangs was too alien to be accepted by the Sicilian Mafiosi leaders. Thus, their gangs would remain separated from and fail to participate in the approaching two decades of illegal casino proliferation across the country, and the subsequent two decades of development of the Las Vegas Strip.

Luciano may have become Chairman, but even he did not dare to suggest allowing a non-initiated member into the inner sanctum populated by old-country Mustache Petes. Lansky as a Jew was still relegated to sitting alone outside the closed doors of the Commission's meetings. Luciano capitulated on this issue because he could step outside the room and confer with Lansky about contentious issues, and because he had prevailed in establishing the important changes he wanted in the Mafia's hierarchal structure and authority.

MAFIA VIOLENCE, CLEVELAND & MOONSHINE, & THE CRIME CONFERENCE

Right after Luciano voluntarily relinquished most of his power as Boss of Bosses, he shifted into his new role as Chairman of the newly created National Crime Commission. He called the assembled leaders to order for their first official meeting. From that moment on, all Mafia policy changes were made by vote of the Commission membership. Luciano placed just one agenda item on the table that day. He proposed eliminating much Mafia violence. His Prohibition partners and their underworld allies had been passionately advocating this policy to every gang in the alcohol business from the earliest days of the Noble Experiment. The Young Turks used standard business principles and never exploited or victimized anyone with their illegal alcohol and gambling activities that they offered to willing customers. Thus, they had no more need for violence than do today's U.S. gaming corporations and Native-American tribes, who supply gambling and alcohol to the American public.

The Young Turks' chief concern from the time they began smuggling liquor was gang violence. They totally opposed it and argued that violence was senseless because it produced nothing positive, always begot more violence, and increased rather than decreased one's number of enemies. Luciano knew the only meaningful way to reduce violence was to befriend the other criminals, thereby diminishing potential foes. This also provided protection for the Young Turks because their large circle of criminal friends warned them whenever they heard an adversary expressing hostility.

Luciano and his partners always practiced the cooperation and non-violence that they preached. Their greatest allies and closest friends throughout Prohibition were their two main competitors for the Manhattan fine-liquor market, Costello and Genovese. While most gangs fought at times over territory, these three business rivals assisted each other, banding together to maneuver through the treacherous politics of the underworld.

The leaders of these three smuggling rings joined the same Mafia gang because it controlled Manhattan, the territory they all supplied. As the gang's lieutenant, Luciano always protected the autonomy of Costello's and Genovese's divisions from The Boss Masseria. When Luciano became the gang's leader, he promoted his two competitors to be his lieutenants, despite the three continuing to vie with each other in business for America's most coveted illegal liquor market.

Although they now headed the country's largest gang and had absolute control over this lucrative territory, they never had conflict with, or attempted to block, competition by other Prohibition gangs. As Jimmy Blue Eyes proudly explained, "We defended ourselves, but never bothered anyone else." They dominated in business over the other importers by offering quicker, more reliable deliveries. They would later become known throughout the underworld for welcoming competitors into every one of the illegal and legal casino jurisdictions they would open up - the antithesis of the gangland concepts of territory and monopoly.

Luciano was unemotional, patient, and logical, especially in contentious situations. He was particularly low-key in presenting peaceful resolution to gang conflicts which was antithetical to career criminals. The Young Turks were cautious and soft-spoken but steadfast as they campaigned against violence for almost a decade. Then in early 1929, Al Capone's gang slaughtered seven competing gangsters in a Chicago garage (detailed in Chapter 6). In what has become known as the St. Valentine's Day Massacre, the Young Turks were shocked and determined to stop such violence. To better understand the Prohibition chiefs' troubled reaction to this brutal incident, Moe Dalitz's standing among gangdom's leaders, particularly those in Chicago, needs to be understood.

Moe Dalitz was a key participant in the underworld response to Capone's slaughter on St. Valentine's Day because of his Prohibition associations with major gang chiefs. Dalitz's Cleveland gang worked closely with John Torrio, Capone, their successors in Chicago, and with Luciano and his buddies in New York City for a half century beginning with Prohibition. The Dalitz gang was the nation's third largest liquor importer, trailing only the two biggest in the huge affluent Manhattan market, Luciano and Costello.

The Dalitz gang smuggled liquor from Canada across Lake Erie, rather than across the Atlantic. More liquor came through his Lake Erie border crossing than any other area except the New Jersey shore. They were known as the *Little Jewish Navy* because four of the partners were Jewish and the fifth Irish. The gang was tight-lipped until partner Morris Kleinman testified about their activities after pleading guilty for failing to file income tax returns. No charges could be brought against his rumrunning admissions because the Prohibition law was being repealed. Regarding the stature of Dalitz's gang, an FBI internal memo stated about his partner, "One of the reports in the file of the United States Attorney at Cleveland, Ohio, refers to Kleinman as the largest illicit liquor dealer in the United States." [33]

The Little Jewish Navy legally purchased the finest Canadian and European liquor and had it legitimately delivered to the Canadian side of Lake Erie. Then his gang ferried it by ultra-fast boats to Ohio. The *Sambo-G* was the largest of the gang's boats captured by the Coast Guard. It was clad with one-quarter-inch armor plate thick enough that .30 caliber bullets bounced off it. The armor plate covered the pilothouse, engine room, and gasoline tanks, so the rumrunners could navigate even while under heavy fire in a running sea battle. This protected them from their gravest threat, pirates. It was powered by twin diesel engines to travel more than 40 mph fully loaded. She could transport 2,000 cases (24,000 bottles) a night. The Coast Guard seized the boat, but while it was in custody the gang stole its large booze cargo, resulting in four coastguardsmen being fired.

Transporting the booze took all night. The gang members filled the boats and crossed the lake to docks within Detroit, Michigan or nearby little towns and later in Cleveland, Ohio, where the cargos were transferred to trucks. Some convoys delivered their inventories to various warehouses in different cities for local distribution to retail outlets during the day. Other convoys loaded into boxcars on waiting trains that pulled out before daybreak. Once or twice a year, the ice on Lake Erie would freeze solid, and they would drive entire convoys of trucks across the lake unmolested by the Coast Guard whose boats were also immobilized.

Unlike the top Manhattan rumrunners, who were strictly importers, the Dalitz gang operated huge distillery plants, mass-producing less expensive, un-aged, domestic whiskey and beer. Kleinman admitted the gang had operated three large distilleries that each contained a number of vats with capacities of 18,000 to 44,000 gallons to store their daily output from the huge boilers until bottling. Cleveland police seized some of these vats late in Prohibition. Dalitz's moonshine operations were the nation's biggest because they required substantial capital investment, significant quantities of raw materials, a major distribution system, and far-reaching law enforcement protection. He had the personality and business acumen to arrange such large financing, operate these enormous enterprises, and ingratiate himself with law enforcement.

The existence of illegal stills had to be concealed from honest law enforcement. Two telltale signs of a plant were the strong aroma and a steady stream of delivery trucks. To mask the odor, stills were usually situated in industrial areas near stinky smokestacks. Some were built in isolated oil fields. The building façades had to be disguised to cover up the illegal business inside, so entrances sometimes led to legitimate businesses that had hidden doors and secret passageways leading to the production area. Despite such precautions, it was relatively easy for law enforcement to identify illicit plants because the moonshiners sold their liquor and beer production through illegal speakeasies and liquor stores whose locations were well known in every neighborhood. The uncorrupted Prohibition "dry agents" just had to stake out the speakeasies or stores and tail the delivery trucks back to the stills.

To elude detection, moonshiners often parked their unloaded trucks in storage yards far from their stills. When they pulled out to load up at the warehouse, they took circuitous routes with cars trailing to make sure no law enforcement vehicles were following them to the distillery plant. Dalitz went further by innovating another wrinkle. He placed his truck-loading terminals at a different site from the stills, and he moved the booze through underground pipes or tunnels connecting the two sites. The pipes ran from the plant vats to the terminal where the liquid was bottled, boxed, and shipped. The bottling plant was usually next door or across the street from the still. Then Dalitz went even further. He connected a major distillery with a gasoline station miles away by building an underground pipe line through an abandoned city sewer. At the station, gasoline trucks frequently pulled in to fill up with whiskey. Dalitz counted on the fact that no one would pay attention to the station for a long period of time and realize that trucks were pulling in and connecting into the ground connections far too often to be servicing the station's needs.

Moonshine and beer were usually sold in the geographical area surrounding its manufacture, but Prohibition motivated organized crime gangs in different parts of the country to cooperate for the first time. Some areas had limited production or great demand, and production in others was occasionally interrupted by law enforcement. So supplies were moved as needed across the country by truck, train, or boat. Orders were sold in boxcar loads, but occasionally an entire trainload of hard liquor crossed the country. Some plants specialized in supplying far-off markets, so they were located near railroad sidings for easy access to transportation. They typically produced 190-proof straight grain whiskey, which the purchasers diluted and then added color to make it look aged.

Because moonshiners had to purchase large quantities of raw materials, sugar and molasses used to ferment grain became major black market products. The demand was so great that these commodities sold for several times more per pound in bulk than the retail price on grocer's shelves. The profits for every one involved in the production and distribution chain were tremendous.

Dalitz and his partners were not only the third biggest importers, but they were by far the biggest domestic whiskey distillers. They had the largest, most sophisticated stills, and although law enforcement discovered a few of them late in Prohibition, no one was arrested in raids because the buildings were always empty except for the vats. (However the raids did succeed in providing historical records of the enormous size of these illegal stills.) The Dalitz gang also had an extensive distribution system. They supplied domestic moonshine and foreign liquor to much of the Midwest including Capone and the other gangs in the country's second biggest city.

The Little Jewish Navy had one major Prohibition competitor in Cleveland, the Sicilian/Italian Mayfield Road Gang. Key figures in the Mayfield Road Gang were Frank Milano and the Polizzi brothers. These three were partners in many Little Jewish Navy business deals during and long after Prohibition. Big Al Polizzi grew up in a neighborhood where an unrelated family also had the surname Polizzi. This family adopted a young Jewish orphan named Leo Berkowitz and changed his name to Chuck Polizzi. Since both families lived near each other, Big Al and Chuck grew up together and created the public fiction as children that they were brothers. This let them put the street gangs on notice that if they messed with one of them, they messed with both. Few people knew about their true relationship. Dalitz used this example during my first interview with him to warn me when conducting my historical research to remain alert for criminals presenting false imagery and status of themselves because they typically do. He cautioned, "Everything in the underworld is not as it seems." [34]

The Jewish Navy always cooperated with their competitors in the illegal liquor and casino businesses and their many legal enterprises. Like Luciano in New York, Dalitz kept his competition close as friends and allies. Dalitz partnered with many more organized-crime leaders across the country than anyone else. He worked closely with Luciano's Young Turks during and after Prohibition, joined Ben Siegel in opening up illegal gambling in Southern California, and became one of the most important developers of the Las Vegas Strip. In fact Dalitz was the closest thing to a Godfather that Nevada would ever have. In the 1950s and 1960s, he was the only person in Las Vegas who could assemble all the pioneer Strip casino operators to work on common issues. The respect the underworld had for Dalitz would make his endorsement and support important adjuncts to Luciano's peace initiatives and response to the St. Valentine's Day Massacre. This slaughter of seven gangsters in a garage occurred two-and-a-half years before Luciano would be proclaimed the Boss of Bosses, when he was still lieutenant to The Boss Masseria.

The outrage of the Young Turks over that slaughter spurred them to do something corruption-riddled government at all levels had failed to do. They planned an underworld showdown with Capone over his predilection for senseless violence. Luciano's Mafia gang leader, Joe The Boss Masseria, authorized Luciano to lead this bold, extraordinary action. This underworld summit was unprecedented because it was the only inter-gang conclave ever headed by a gang's lieutenant. Subordinates just did not stand up to leaders of other gangs. It was the only gathering of all the nation's major Prohibition leaders and also the only national multi-ethnic criminal meeting. This unparalleled coming together was possible only because Luciano commanded such universal admiration. In ensuing years, the powerful Mafia chieftains met on occasion but never with other ethnic groups.

Luciano sent verbal invitations to America's top Prohibition gang leaders to attend a national crime convention in Atlantic City, New Jersey to discuss pressing mutual problems. Every one invited showed up except for his boss Masseria, who did not even make an appearance. The insular Masseria dealt only with Sicilians, and he was not about to greet leaders of the other ethnic gangs as equals.

The three-day conference was the biggest gangland gathering in U.S. history. The 1959 hit movie *Some Like It Hot* adapted the well-publicized meeting as a backdrop for comedy, but the real event was grim and serious. Luciano hosted the gathering and chaired the meeting. Sitting on both sides of him were gangland's two other giant liquor importers and strong voices for peaceful resolution of conflict through negotiation and compromise, Frank Costello and Moe Dalitz. (It is an interesting footnote to history that the three men sitting beside each other and Capone sitting across the table from them led the four Prohibition gangs that would go on two decades later to build the Las Vegas Strip.)

In a quiet, steady but firm manner, Luciano carefully explained to the homicidal Capone that the bootleggers survived because they were heroes to the drinking public. But his frequent, vicious murders and shootings in the vicinity of innocent civilians were turning the public (even those who drank), politicians, and law enforcers against them. Unless this stopped, it would cause the toppling of their domains and imprisonment for them all. Facing this unified trio and the icy stare of every major Prohibition leader, Capone agreed to end the violence.

Luciano knew that once Capone returned to Chicago and was again surrounded by his large gang's security umbrella, he might return to his old ways. Thus, Luciano told Capone to back up his words to the assembled gang leaders with a tangible guarantee of his intentions. Capone replied with an offer to lower his press visibility in a manner they accepted. Capone upheld his promise. The moment the conference concluded, his bodyguard drove him 60 miles to Philadelphia. There Capone approached two detectives, pulled out a pistol, handed it to them, pled guilty to carrying a concealed weapon, and remained silent as the judge imposed the maximum sentence of one year. (Capone's contrived judicial process and prison time are detailed in Chapter 6).[35]

Realistically Capone had no option. He may have headed the country's third largest gang - an army of brutal killers - but he could not fight the entire underworld. Every gang leader at the meeting had execution squads they could send after him, but Capone actually faced a far greater danger than these other gangs. A number of his high-ranking underlings likely wanted to replace him, and a gang war might lead one of them to carry out a coup, just as Luciano would do a couple years later. Anyone responsible for protecting him could have easily cut a deal during a meeting or over a meal with Luciano to eliminate Capone in return for Joe The Boss Masseria's approval for the perpetrator to take over the Chicago gang. But it is doubtful these serious potential gangland threats were the major motivation for Capone's decision to yield. He had enormous respect for and loyalty to Luciano. Capone had consistently aligned himself with Luciano and supported all his underworld political positions during the first decade of Prohibition up to this incident. After his release from jail, Capone remained close to Luciano and was a chief backer of his anti-violence policy. Of course by then, Capone had already killed or absorbed most of his territorial opposition.

The Atlantic City meeting enhanced Luciano's gangland stature with all ethnic groups, but it would be the country's last multi-racial crime gathering. After repeal of Prohibition, there were far too many gangs for the available crime revenue. The Sicilian gangs were the largest and had established territories and the other ethnic groups were not big enough to challenge them. Some of these smaller gangs' leaders moved to virgin criminal territories to open illegal casinos, several were killed off by other ethnic non-Mafia gangs, a number went to prison, and the rest retired from organized crime, returning to burglary and other standard street-gang felonies.

Two-and-a-half years after this Atlantic City meeting, the Sicilian leaders met to unanimously proclaim Luciano Boss of Bosses. His final agenda item the afternoon of that first Crime Commission meeting was the culmination of more than a decade-long campaign against the use of violence, except for self-defense. His position was logical, but he faced a leadership of old-country Mustache Petes, whose power and position were derived primarily from violence or at least the threat of it. Their number-one cultural imperative was vendetta. Luciano's nonviolence policy flew in the face of their core identity, but he commanded enough respect to push his policy to a victorious vote. Luciano and his successor as Boss of Bosses, Costello, went on to keep their nonviolence policy in force for a quarter of a century. During this time, there was almost no violence between Sicilian Mafia gangs, especially the five in New York City with overlapping territories. This nonviolence policy allowed the Young Turks to finally enjoy their personal and professional lives without worrying about the threat of attack, at least most of the time.

THE YOUNG TURKS MAKE FRIENDS

Living in a dangerous underworld, Luciano and his colleagues went to great lengths to avoid discord with anyone. This was even acknowledged by Hickman Powell, who was the career-long publicist for Manhattan DA Tom Dewey and was his close friend. Powell wrote a book glorifying his DA boss to promote Dewey's ambitions for the governorship of New York and then the White House. Thus, Powell badly tarnished gangster Luciano's image, but Powell could only maintain his credibility with New York readers by admitting, "As a leader and a ruler, Charlie Lucky discouraged bloodshed. He was a peacemaker and that was one reason why he was so popular." Regarding Costello, author Peter Mass conducted in-depth interviews with him late in his life and concluded, "[Costello] was a man who would go way out of his way to avoid violence. He believed that, with serious effort, there are few things that can't be worked out peacefully." [36]

When conflict developed, Luciano and his associates used reason to resolve their differences. They got to the top of the underworld, survived there, expanded into new territories, and died in retirement of old age because they were exceptional negotiators and compromisers. Every one who dealt with the Young Turks said their hallmark was fairness - they respected other people, recognized their needs and rights, and put themselves in the other person's shoes. They negotiated relentlessly as long as hope for a mutually-agreeable resolution existed. They compromised whenever the terms were reasonable, or at the least, tolerable and preferable to mob warfare.

Whenever serious conflict developed between two gangsters, or when a thug planned to kill an innocent victim, the Young Turks tried to mediate a peaceful resolution. Even though author Hickman Powell was Luciano's biggest detractor, he described how Charlie saved the life of mobster Ciro "Artichoke King" Terranova by talking him into retirement. Terranova remained appreciative of Luciano for extricating him from certain death by his subordinate "Trigger Mike" Copolla. As the new leader, Copolla forever valued Luciano for getting him the position he coveted without having to resort to murder for which there was no statute of limitations.

Luciano's closest friend, Jimmy Blue Eyes, was renown for six decades as the "peacemaker" on the East Coast by the underworld and those in the overworld who encountered him. He was exceptionally successful arbitrating potentially violent disputes between mobsters and protecting those targeted by hoods. He acknowledged to me, "I was the mediator. I was respected because of the strength of my word and my sage advice. Since I was an honorable man, not interested in taking anything from anyone else, I had no vested interests when I helped guide a man in his decision making."

I interviewed Jimmy when he was 91 years old and found him to be a very alert and highly analytical thinker. He lived up to his reputation for being exceedingly perceptive and having a penetrating gaze. He looked directly into my eyes with a long, piercing stare, evaluating everything I said. In contrast to the underworld's cold-blooded killers, whose eyes chillingly screamed at me whether I lived or died was of no matter to them, Jimmy's stare was very different, although deeply infiltrating. He locked his eyes onto mine so intensely that he seemed to be peering inside my head to ascertain what kind of person I was and how accurate my words were. I have no doubt this unnerved those people who lied to him.

Jimmy's insight into people was of great value to his associates because he could effectively evaluate both friend and foe. When I mentioned people whose lives I had been told by others that he had saved, he said, "I like to help people, and I helped a lot of them during my life. I stopped many from getting hurt by others. You meet a lot of ingrates in this world. I helped them, and later they forgot they knew me." He concluded, "I believe I led a good life. I'm proud of what I've done. The [federal] government framed me. The press lied and vilified me. But I'm the one who sleeps good at night. I know I always tried to do the right thing."

While the Young Turks rejected the values of the brutal, exploitive American Mafia, none of these U.S.-raised youths may have known about its origins as protectors and avengers of their countrymen. Yet they reestablished the ideals and goals of Sicily's original guerrilla warriors to protect the weak and helpless, especially women. They especially opposed beatings over money. Like the many pioneer Las Vegas casino owners and executives who had previously worked in illegal operations, they wanted to make a comfortable income without hurting anyone. These values were in direct opposition to criminals who profit from hurting or threatening people, a position popularized in Mafia movies with the phrase, "It's not personal. It's business." This translates to, "I'm killing you to steal your money, or to take over your business and steal the profits." Such greed was exemplified by modern-era New York Mafioso Sammy "The Bull " Gravano, John Gotti's lieutenant, who admitted in court to killing sixteen men, most of them friends and associates, to steal their profitable businesses.[37]

During the hundreds of hours I interviewed and socialized with the early Las Vegas casino executives, we occasionally talked about historical or current acts of violence. Every single one of them ranted and raved at the outrageousness of hurting someone for financial greed or to avenge theft. Their values are exemplified by an incident involving Jimmy Blue Eyes and Meyer Lansky, who became partners a year after Prohibition ended in the *Plantation,* an illegal Florida casino.

Jimmy told me, "The second season we operated [in 1936], we hired eight or nine good dealers from Steubenville, Ohio. They included Dino Cellini and Dino Crocetti. They were all bust-out people [cheaters], and they carried the joint out. The season ended in April [because the northeast, especially New York thawed out], and February was traditionally our top month. That second year, we didn't make money during the height of the season. In February we only broke even, and we couldn't figure out why. We never suspected at the time that we were being cheated. We did catch some people stealing at other times and tossed them out."

Over time Dino Cellini was promoted and became their casino manager running the whole operation. Jimmy told me that years later, "I told Dino that the month he came we didn't make any money. He started laughing over it and admitted they robbed us pretty good. We continued to employ Dino because he knew the business." I asked Jimmy how he could trust Dino after that. "That's the way it was," he answered simply.

The other dealer in on the theft was Dino Crocetti who had been 19 at the time. Jimmy's close friendship with Crocetti continued long after the dealer had transformed himself into multi-talented super-star entertainer Dean Martin. After Jimmy learned about the scam from Cellini, the next time he drank at a bar with Martin, he asked about it. Martin readily admitted it and they both had a good laugh.

As Jimmy finished the tale, he laughed wholeheartedly for a long time. When I asked him how he could laugh about being ripped off. "I laughed when I was first told about it, and that man continued to be my friend," Jimmy said. Then he explained, "My attitude about stealing is, so what, they probably needed the money. I'm not going to kill someone over money. If a person is busted or needs money, he's going to steal. You have to know human nature."

I spent many hours listening to these casino men's attitudes, but I was never able to decide whether they reflected tolerance or practical realism about human weakness. Both Jimmy and Lansky remained close lifelong friends with both Dinos, and the two casino owners employed Dino Cellini to run their operations throughout their careers. Said Jimmy, "You must get into the other person's head. If they steal from you, they must have a reason. They must need it more than you do, or they wouldn't take it."

BACK TO A NORMAL LIFE

Having finally achieved peace, the Young Turks returned to making a good living and to having fun. Luciano and his original three partners were close friends with Costello, their major Manhattan competitor, but these five men were a contrast in styles. Luciano, Lansky, and Costello dressed conservatively, impeccably, and expensively, whereas Siegel and Adonis dressed flashily but stylishly. Lansky and Adonis lived in small, modest homes, while Luciano, Siegel, and Costello lived in expensive apartment suites in the swank Waldorf-Astoria Hotel.

Luciano conducted his illegal Prohibition business and his political activities in the morning. Joe Bonanno wrote, "He was a bachelor who conducted his business out of a suite in the Waldorf-Astoria under the name Charles Ross." He spent the afternoon at the racetrack, afterward had a classy call girl visit his suite, and then took a refreshing nap before going out for a late dinner. His evenings were spent in the finest restaurants and nightclubs hobnobbing with friends and concluding unresolved business.

When out-of-town hoods visited, Charlie invited them to finish the evening at Polly Adler's brothel, which featured New York's most beautiful and expensive prostitutes. Adler later wrote, "I never found him (Luciano) to be other than gentlemanly. He was always quiet, clean-talking, and considerate of the girls and maids." The city's call girls liked the quiet Luciano because he was pleasant, accommodating, and generous. Jimmy Blue Eyes quipped to me, "The boys used to say, 'He could make a $50 whore out of a $2 whore.'" [38]

No one around Luciano ever mentioned a romantic interest as his sexual activity was exclusively with prostitutes. The Boss of Bosses was bashful with women. He understood friendship, business transactions, and tense underworld discord, but he seemed to find emotional intimacy difficult. Jimmy Blue Eyes remembered, "Charlie was timid with girls, so he turned to prostitutes for companionship, and he was very generous with them." Interestingly gangster, Ben Siegel, before he became a bon vivant in Hollywood in his 30s (Chapter 16), was more shy with women than Luciano.

Underworld figures intentionally maintain a serious or tough persona when in public, especially when a camera is around. That is why they always look grim, even sinister, in police mug shots. In reality many top underworld figures have had a great sense of humor, especially Luciano and his associates. Siegel was a serious businessman, but also a kibitzer. Every one close to him socially, and those who partied or gambled with him, said he "was a fun-loving guy." Four of his close associates told me in separate interviews, "Ben was an intense character, but he also had great humor." "Benny was very serious, but he loved to tell jokes and be good to his friends." "Ben loved to joke around. He enjoyed practical jokes." "Ben laughed a lot, and he never threw his weight around." [39]

As for Jimmy Blue Eyes, I learned firsthand how funny he could be during my interviews with him. Humor, especially telling jokes, takes a quickness and attentiveness that many senior citizens no longer possess. Maybe that is why some can appear to always be serious. But Jimmy still remained sharp thinking and energetic at age 91. I was usually too focused on the interview issues to remember many of his jokes, but I do remember one quick-witted response. When I mentioned that Jimmy was involved with *organized crime*, Jimmy retorted indignantly, "I was never part of it. The only organized crime I know about is in Washington, D.C., and I swear to you that I have nothing to do with any of that."

Joe "Joey A" Adonis, was Jimmy Blue Eyes' partner who loved to party and gamble. When I asked Jimmy what Joey A's business was, he replied, "gambling and broads." I explained, "I was not referring to his personal predilections but to what business he was in." Jimmy grinned and repeated, "gambling and broads."

Adonis did love to gamble. He openly acknowledged that he would bet on anything, especially craps, prizefights, and the horses. Adonis was passionate about horses, and rode his own every morning. Adonis and Luciano also liked to take time off every afternoon to bet on other people's horses at the tracks, while Jimmy enjoyed a round of golf at his country club. In contrast, Costello and Lansky preferred to tend to business the entire day. And Costello also managed to fit in a good deal of New York City politicking.

Lansky and Siegel began dating two close friends, Anne Citron and Esther Krakower, in 1927 and the two couples married three months apart in the spring of 1929 when Lansky was 27 and Siegel was 23. They stood as best man for each other. The Lanskys had two sons followed by a daughter, and the Siegels had two daughters. Jimmy Blue Eyes Alo adopted his wife's two sons, but he did not change Florence Miller's son's last names so they would not be stigmatized by his hoodlum image. The Alos often socialized with the Lanskys and Siegels. The three women liked to shop together during the day and employed the same interior decorator. The three couples frequently spent evenings together at one another's homes or in nightclubs, always seated at the best table. Some nights the three men got together with other bootleggers they were close to like Adonis, Doc Stacher, and Longy Zwillman. They played low-stakes gin rummy but mainly kibitzed. When these boys got together, humor flowed.

THE REPEAL OF PROHIBITION

A little more than two years after Luciano's gang killed Maranzano, the careers of the Young Turks and all the other Prohibition violators changed drastically because of the presidential election on November 8, 1932. The overriding issue in Franklin Delano Roosevelt's defeat of President

Herbert Hoover was the crushing economic collapse of the Great Depression that rendered 25 percent of America's workforce hopelessly unemployed. Roosevelt's landslide victory gave him a mandate from the people to correct that national economic catastrophe, and he used his election momentum to quickly push through Congress his campaign pledge to end Prohibition.

A month after Roosevelt took office on February 20, 1933, Congress submitted to the states a proposed amendment to repeal Prohibition. Even though Utah had a state dry law, it became the 36th state to vote the country wet by approving the repeal amendment to the Constitution. After 14 years of Prohibition, President Roosevelt proclaimed that the 21st Amendment had been ratified to repeal the 18th Amendment. The 20 states that did not have their own Prohibition laws began serving alcoholic beverages, and many other states soon abolished their dry statutes as voters who wanted the right to drink swung the political pendulum in the opposite direction to overwhelm the long-term efforts of the temperance movement.[40]

When the Young Turks had entered Prohibition, they were between the ages of 14 and 28. When the government with a single edict wiped out their sole source of income, they were forced to embark on new careers because they were still young men. Siegel was 27, Jimmy Blue Eyes 29, Lansky and Adonis 31, Luciano 36, and Costello 42.

Since alcohol was the only business they had known, they initially switched their focus to distributing fine liquor to legal wholesalers. New York's Young Turks reached out to the close business contacts they had developed across the country, especially Cleveland's Little Jewish Navy, to form a strong working alliance. These men shared important values. They dealt honorably, refrained from unnecessary violence, avoided publicity, and effectively used the bribe to fend off law enforcement and control their political environment.

From the moment of Roosevelt's victory, Luciano and Dalitz knew alcohol would soon be legal, but they also knew it would take time for legitimate manufacturers to develop large-scale domestic production. Ten days before Prohibition ended, the Jewish Navy and the Young Turks formed a new company in Ohio to be the first to fill this void. They built the largest liquor distilleries and beer fermenting plants to that time, enterprises in which Dalitz's gang already had a great deal of operating experience. America's first and third biggest illegal importers joined forces to produce un-aged moonshine or colored whiskey on a massive scale. They scrupulously did everything legally and properly except for one thing. They placed counterfeit federal and state alcohol tax stamps on their bottles and ignored paying these new post-Prohibition liquor taxes. This made their alcohol product as illegal as it had been during Prohibition if they were caught.

Since a key attribute of organized crime is greed, one might assume they pocketed this stolen savings. But these were adept businessmen who instead passed these savings on to the consumer by cutting their price by the amount of the new taxes. They produced an excellent un-aged product, but they created a competitive marketing edge by selling it much cheaper than the legitimate liquor manufacturers. The consumers benefited and these distillers still maintained the same profit per bottle as their competitors, courtesy of their illegitimate government subsidy. Thus, they became the country's biggest manufacturers selling to wholesalers across the nation. Since they were interested in total profitability through volume sales rather than profit per unit, they introduced a nationwide low-price, quality marketing method almost three decades before Sam Walton opened his first Walmart in 1962. Their scheme also expanded the potential market because, at the height of the

Great Depression, the large mass of unemployed could only afford cheap alcohol to dull their despair.

The new company's officers were made up of members from both gangs, but the investors in addition to the two gang's partners, or fronts for them, were also from their previous Prohibition competitors, as both gangs always reached out to cooperate with other gangs. Dalitz's Jewish Navy brought in the Sicilian/Italian Mayfield Road Gang including the Polizzi brothers of Cleveland, Peter Licavoli of Kansas City, and Capone associate Charles Baron of Chicago, who would go on with them to build the Las Vegas Strip. Luciano brought in Costello and other New York and New Jersey gang leaders. The partnership was made up of gangsters who resided in five different states and was a balanced mix of Jews and Italians/Sicilians with one Irishman.[41]

Their company's name, Molaska, referred to molasses, which was used as a substitute for sugar in the fermenting process and was the only ingredient they had to import. Two months before incorporation Lansky met with Fulgencio Batista, who had assumed the dictatorship of Cuba in September 1933. They cut a deal to assure the company an ample supply of raw molasses. The company shipped molasses by the hundreds of thousands of gallons, built large manufacturing plants to dehydrate the raw liquid, then shipped the finished product by train to phony candy and ice-cream makers fronting the largest illicit alcohol stills that were ever discovered by the Alcohol & Tobacco Tax Unit of the Internal Revenue Service. The Molaska partnership supplied much of the country's domestic alcohol, wholesaling it to their traditional clients and selling it to many newly created legal liquor distributors. Seven months after repeal, the Federal Alcohol Control Administration Director announced that about half of the liquor consumed in the U.S. was manufactured illegally to avoid paying federal taxes. The American revolution had been fought primarily over alcohol taxation and this opposition to booze taxes continued a century and a half later.[42]

More than a year after Prohibition ended, the largest illicit alcohol plant ever found was raided in Zanesville, Ohio. Another plant was raided a few days later in Elizabeth, New Jersey. Each one was producing tens of thousands of gallons of whiskey and beer daily. Several other Molaska plants were raided, but the politically-influential partners were usually long gone because they were warned by revenue agents. Before every raid, the plants were emptied of all evidence except the huge stills and steam boilers that were not illegal to own. A month after the two big raids, the Molaska Corporation declared bankruptcy. The partners subsequently declared business losses on their income-tax returns. But before the Molaska Corporation formally went out of business eight months later, a similarly named Molaska Company, Inc. was incorporated. It appears to have remained in the molasses moonshine business in other cities around the country for some time, but no charges were ever brought against these huge illicit operations.[43]

The top rumrunners were perturbed for the rest of their lives that they were branded as hoodlums. Their sullied reputations were in marked contrast to those of the three men who sold them the legitimate Prohibition liquor at the Canadian border and in Europe - Lewis Rosenstiel, Samuel Bronfman, and Joseph P. Kennedy. After Prohibition, two of these three went on to operate some of North America's largest legal distilleries, and were revered as respectable businessmen, joining the social and political elite. Rosenstiel founded Schenley Distilleries that became America's leading distiller, and he was linked to hoodlums Costello and Lansky by government committees and authors. Yet he managed to maintain a surprisingly close relationship with FBI

Director J. Edgar Hoover, donating millions to Hoover's charities. Bronfman built Canada's worldwide whiskey conglomerate Joseph E. Seagrams & Sons that made his heirs all billionaires and allowed them to become philanthropists. He was the main liquor supplier of Prohibition's largest rumrunning gang headed by Luciano. Kennedy was the main supplier to the next two biggest gangs headed by Costello and Dalitz. Not only was Kennedy another major contributor to Hoover's charities, but he saw three of his sons become U. S. senators and one reach the White House. All three men who built their empires on profits earned from Prohibition deals with Luciano, Costello, and Dalitz became revered, socially prominent businessmen, while their Prohibition partners were vilified by the FBI's Hoover and the media as public enemies for the rest of their lives, even as retired old men.[44]

With the advent of reform, Luciano and his associates pursued new secondary careers. Luciano became a partner in casinos operated by colleagues. As the most influential person in the Big Apple with his extensive political, business, and union contacts, he could have received substantial fees for bringing various people together. However, he only helped people he liked as a gesture of friendship. Despite his incredible power and influence, Luciano is known to have enjoyed only one personal perk from his awesome gangland and political power. The many Broadway shows of that era gave him four front-row, center seats to every performance gratis. After all with one phone call, he could create a union strike by a delivery service, or he could create a nuisance from the city digging up sewers or repaving the street in front of the theater.

One can only imagine the high prices the little mob ticket agency commanded for the best seats in the house for the most popular, sold-out shows. According to the FBI internal report on Siegel, "He visited the Hollywood Theater Ticket Agency a notorious hang-out for racketeers, almost every day. ... While Siegel is in New York City he frequents the Hollywood Theater Ticket office located on 46th or 47th Street just off Broadway... 225 W. 46th Street. ... The agency is engaged in the sale of theater tickets, amusement tickets, and tickets for sporting events."

In another example, Costello's Washington, D.C. criminal-defense attorney Edward Bennett Williams visited his client in prison after Costello had become Luciano's appointed successor as Boss of Bosses. Williams mentioned to Costello he wished he could see the sold-out *My Fair Lady* while he was in New York. When the attorney returned to his hotel later that afternoon just a few hours before curtain time, the concierge stepped into his path and handed him an envelope containing four front-row-center seat tickets for the show that night.[45]

By the time Prohibition ended, Costello already had major bookmaking and slot machine operations run by partners; Adonis had a restaurant and several legitimate businesses; and Jimmy Blue Eyes had a Harlem policy-number operation, also run by partners. Within a few years all three, along with Lansky and Siegel, would develop major casino operations in different cities around the country. The experience and expertise gained from these casino operations would lead them to later develop the legal gambling resorts along the Las Vegas Strip.

A WORD THAT OPENED DOORS

The mob who built Las Vegas - Siegel, Lansky, Jimmy Blue Eyes, Costello, and Dalitz - stood out in the underworld, the business community, and political life because they were excellent negotiators and compromisers. People from all walks of life dealt readily with them and their close associates Luciano and Adonis because they possessed another essential trait: they were trustworthy. They always lived by their word. Everyone knew that they honored their commitments, even when a verbal obligation turned out to be a costly mistake for them. For these men, it was honor before anything, including profit.

Attorney George Wolf wrote about his client Costello. "He was just. To this day his former underworld associates speak of him with respect, as one of a kind, a man who gave everyone a fair shake. ... He was able to adapt to any situation he was in, to see the possibilities, and to exploit them." [46]

Jimmy Blue Eyes described his associates' values to me in very basic terms: "I always lived by the same idealistic principles I had as a school boy throughout my whole life. Every one in our group was principled, and this is why we had the respect of other hoods from coast to coast."

Every one I interviewed in the underworld, the business community, and the financial world who knew or dealt with any of these men had the utmost respect for and trust in them. Lansky could put together large deals between partners who had no experience with each other, or who lacked confidence in each other, because everyone trusted him and knew he lived by his word. Further, he saw to it that others honored his word when he gave it on their behalf. Jimmy said simply, "Meyer was trusted because he had a good reputation."

Downtown Las Vegas *Horseshoe Club* partner and casino manager Ted Binion said about the Las Vegas casino pioneers, "The very first thing you learn from the older guys (in the casino business) is that you have to have honor. A lot of people wonder why the people who have graduated from illegal gambling operations are the best-loved operators in town. Well, that's the reason. Compassion and honor are what literally kept them alive in the states where gambling was illegal." [47]

The Young Turks and Dalitz had a multitude of different business partnerships across the country during their careers, yet none ever had an ethical conflict with a single partner. In my interviews, every colleague considered himself fortunate to have been associated in business with one or more of them. Siegel's Las Vegas attorney and friend Lou Wiener recalled, "No one in town used to have a contract to do business. All the business deals I made, I did on a handshake, and every one kept their word. Everyone lived by it." Then he lamented about all the hoods retiring from the business. He told me "Since 1980, I write the most protective contract I'm capable of, and I wonder as I'm signing it how they're going to screw me. And they always do." No wonder Las Vegans who lived in the city before 1980 say "The town was better when the mob ran it." [48]

The Young Turks would become deeply involved with New York City politics. At that time the chief underworld influence in the city's politics was Arnold Rothstein. He was the greatest gambler of all time, and the operating style of his illegal casinos in the heart of the Broadway show district became the standard for the early Las Vegas Strip gambling resorts. Rothstein's life and career follow.

CHAPTER 5

NEW YORK CITY POLITICS & THE MOB

THE CORRUPT POLITICAL MACHINES

During Prohibition in the Roaring '20s, Charlie Luciano and his associates had great influence on politics. With their candidates in office, they had immunity from government interference. But during the Great Depression of the 1930s, public sentiment shifted. As the rival parties' politicians and prosecutors came into office, they waged overwhelming political and prosecutorial campaigns against the gang leaders that had risen to power during Prohibition. The Young Turks were able to fend off underworld threats and challenges, but they were much less successful against determined politicians.

The political system Luciano and the Young Turks manipulated was instituted more than a century before they came upon the scene. Powerful metropolitan political machines began coalescing soon after America was established. These political machine bosses derived their power from large, loyal voter-constituency blocks made up to a great extent by the expanding immigrant populations in poor neighborhoods. These local politicians offered the immigrants in their districts a host of social services and provided their only access to the city's government bureaucracy. They found the new arrivals places to live, provided them food baskets, kept their children out of jail, listened to their problems, and treated them with respect. They made life more bearable for the most disenfranchised, lowest-income working families. In return these political machines' professional bosses amassed power.

One of the earliest political machines was the Society of Tammany in New York City, founded when George Washington was America's first president. It was a business organization that quietly dispensed its political largesse to its constituencies' neighborhoods. Early on its influence was less obvious than many other early big-city machines. Then in the 1830s Tammany began representing the expanding immigrant workingman neighborhoods, and as immigrants continued to pour in, it became the city's dominant power structure. Renamed Tammany Hall, the machine controlled the Democratic Party, which ruled New York City for many years. Tammany became headquarters for the city's big-time political bosses, who also used their power to assist businessmen by lowering tax assessments and protecting them from government regulation in return for raking in graft to enrich themselves and their friends and to finance the party organization.

New York City's politicians in every party began forging alliances with the professional street gangs in their districts in the 1820s. The gangs supplied campaign funds, election workers, and muscle at the polls, threatening voters who objected to being observed filling out their ballots. They also stole ballots, and they recruited needy people to vote repeatedly in exchange for a cash payment for every ballot they dropped in a ballot box. The gangs operated the casinos and brothels owned or controlled by politicians, while destroying the competition. Their election day efforts assured government of, by, and for Tammany, at least most of the time. In return, the politicians protected the casinos, brothels, and many predatory criminal activities of the professional street gangs in their wards by offering a clubhouse to meet and hide from police, protection from law enforcement and prosecutors, compassionate and lenient judges, defense attorneys gratis, and bail money. Not surprisingly, Tammany Hall politicians were connected repeatedly to major graft scandals beginning as far back as the early 1800s.[49]

A hundred years later, the powerhouse behind-the-scenes director of Tammany Hall in the generation ahead of Luciano and Costello was big-time gambler Arnold Rothstein. He developed the casino operating model used by the Prohibition mobsters for their second careers of illegal gambling before going on to build the Las Vegas Strip resorts.

A HIGH-STAKES GAMBLER EXTRAORDINAIRE

Arnold Rothstein pioneered wide-open, high-limit, illegal casinos two decades before Luciano and the Young Turks adopted his up-scale operating style and spread it across the country. Rothstein was the nation's biggest poker, craps, and horse bettor, and his no-limit wagering in the first quarter of the 1900s made him a legend during his lifetime.

Born in New York City in 1882, Rothstein quit Boy's High at 16, worked a short time in his father's dress-goods business, and then spent his afternoons at the racetracks studying how to beat the odds on the ponies. He became so successful at it that he had to stop placing large bets with the track cashiers because his wagers drove down the size of the potential payoff ratios. So he began placing a good portion of his total wagers with the illegal bookies who serviced those track bettors who did not want to have a record made of their gambling wins. Then Rothstein turned around and also booked wealthy track patrons' biggest wagers on the horses on which he had not bet. When the other bettors wanted to bet on a horse he had already bet on, he refused with the explanation that he was "overloaded with action and had to keep his book in balance." Thus, when one of Rothstein's picks triumphed, he won the wagers he had made on it and also every win bet he had booked on the other horses in that race.

Rothstein used his track winnings to bankroll a no-limit casino operation in the heart of the Broadway theater district. It was around 1910, and the city was dotted with tiny illegal casinos that the police occasionally raided, usually when newly installed police officials or politicians wanted to replace existing illegal casino operators with their own cronies. Then the nature of New York's illegal casino business changed because of a long-running feud between a police official and Herman Rosenthal, who operated two small high-limit illegal casinos. Rosenthal bribed key politicians but he refused to give anything to Lieutenant Charles Becker who headed the NYPD Strong Arm Squad. For three years Lt. Becker chafed at not receiving bribery payments that he thought were his due, and then he decided to challenge the political leaders protecting Rosenthal by directing his Squad to raid both of Rosenthal's establishments, one being in his apartment residence. The raids led to opposing accusations between two groups of politicians, one supporting the police action but the bribed office holders defending Rosenthal.

Then Lieutenant Becker took the unprecedented action of declaring Rosenthal's apartment residence as a gambling resort and assigning a policeman to permanently stand around the clock guarding inside the apartment residence to prevent any more gambling activity. Rosenthal complained to political authorities and fought in court about the guard's intrusive presence in his residence, especially the many filthy cigar butts the cops left around. Rosenthal got no satisfaction from three months of complaints so he decided to take matters into his own hands. His apartment's front and back doors had dead bolts that were keyed on both sides of the door and he had not given a key to the police. One evening he walked out the front door and latched the dead bolt behind him to lock in the cop who watched through the iron-barred front window as Rosenthal walked away. After eight hours of partying, he returned to find the guard's relief standing outside the apartment along with a reinforcement squad that was preparing to batter down the front door. Rosenthal pulled out his key and let them in.

A few nights later Rosenthal spent the late evening in the dining room of the Hotel Metropole on 43rd Street near Times Square. When the evening out wrapped up, he walked out onto the sidewalk where six loiterers were standing around individually staring into the distance. Without warning, all six suddenly turned while reaching into their pockets to draw pistols and shoot him. Two bullets hit his head, one piercing his forehead, and the other shattering his nose. Both slugs were fatal. The six assailants ran to a large white car waiting at the curb and sped into the darkness. The DA won quick convictions of four men as the shooters, and they were executed in Sing Sing's electric chair. Rosenthal's nemeses Lieutenant Becker did not participate in the shooting, but he was convicted for ordering the assassination. A year after the shooting, he was electrocuted in the same hot seat.[50]

The Rosenthal case resulted in a major scandal leading to an investigation of graft paid to the NYPD for ignoring small casino operations. The police tried to cover up their involvement by conducting numerous raids, but public scrutiny and the arrests of operators and players dealt a deathblow to permanent gambling parlors. Stationary casinos were too visible and vulnerable to raids by police or politicians out to enhance their crime-fighting image. Rothstein and other gambling operators were forced to close their stationary casinos.

Rothstein began rotating his high-stakes games from one hotel suite to another in an innovation that would become known as the floating crap game. Since no player could afford to gamble big every night, he operated only on designated nights. He would wait until a prescheduled time to let the regular players know the new location. Recalling those nights when he ran his floating crap games, criminal lawyer William Fallon, who was on retainer to Rothstein for years, told the press: "Rothstein is a man who dwells in doorways. A mouse standing in a doorway, waiting for his cheese." [51]

After Rosenthal's murder, few stationary illegal casino operations continued to operate in New York City, even during the 1930s and 1940s when much of the rest of the country had wide-open casinos. But the Big Apple was the nation's capital for high-rolling floating crap games. New York City Mafia gangs still operate some high-limit floating games today in strong competition with the large Atlantic City and Connecticut tribal casinos for the most valuable Manhattan players. Wealthy men like these games because they are more convenient, more personal, and the IRS learns about neither their cash wins or losses.

I learned how a typical floating crap game operates from Hallie Tutino who was an illegal sports bookmaker in Miami and Las Vegas, where I knew him well. As a teenager in 1943 he worked in a New York City game operated by Frank Costello's brother. Hallie explained to me, "When I was

16, I served sandwiches in a floating crap game for Tony Costello. The players were mostly Jewish and had big money. They gave me $5 tips for sandwiches. That was huge money, upwards of a week's salary. There'd be a *meet spot* at a drug store or a bar. If there was any heat, they'd change it. They'd tell the regular players [at the meet spot] to go to a different spot each week for pick up, or sometimes by calling them. A limousine would pick up eight players with their cash in hand. Another limo followed. It was filled with guards carrying Tommy guns (Thompson submachine guns). If the players were ever robbed, the operators would have lost all their business. They would drive miles out of the way to make sure no one was following them. They were more concerned about robbers than the law. Then they'd pull into the site of the game. It was usually a dark spot that looked deserted. They selected unbelievable places like a mining site that was closed at night. The players would walk up a long flight of stairs in the dark to the shed on the top of the heap. When they opened the door, everything was lit up and in action. The games were played in cash and they were big action for their time. In many games the operators didn't bankroll the game. They sold the bank to different players and then took a percentage of his winnings. [With this approach, the sponsors stood to win much less, but they eliminated any risk of losing.] If no one wanted the bank the operators would take it. Above the players ringing the room sat the guards with their Tommy guns to prevent a robbery. They then drove every one back to the pick-up site, and they escorted the winners home to make sure they arrived safely. Many of these games were run honestly. The players were always protected from robbery, no matter how much cash they were carrying."

When not serving players, Hallie would watch the action and he realized some of the dealers were pocketing money. Being around Mafiosi his whole life he knew not to be a snitch, but Tony Costello had given him a great opportunity to make money. Thus one day when he was alone with his boss, he warned him. But Tony admonished the teenager, "Don't worry if they steal a little. They all do. Never kill over money." Tony believed this message so important that he occasionally reminded the lad that he should never use violence to solve problems. Tony clearly shared the values of his brother Frank Costello and the other Young Turks. Hallie most remembered Tony for that repetitive lesson. Hallie always lived by this code and he chilled me out more than once when I was in a heated clash with someone out on the mean streets.[52]

Rothstein was an old-fashioned compulsive gambler. In addition to his floating crap game in New York City, he was a partner during the 1910s and 1920s in the *Brook* casino in upstate New York, outside the town limits of Saratoga Springs. It catered to wealthy Manhattanites during summer evenings. He parlayed his racetrack winnings and casino profits at private no-limit poker games. He was America's biggest player, participating in games during the 1920s where individuals won or lost a quarter to a third of a million dollars at a sitting (equivalent to $3 to $4 million in spending power today). He was reputed to have wagered as much as $.5 million on boxing championships, and he always played the maximum limit at other operators' casinos.[53]

Suave and composed, Rothstein remained unruffled even when he won or lost great sums. Money seemed to mean little, at least when he was gambling. It was the thrill of chance taking that was life itself for him. In an era when Freud's writings, psychiatry, and the concept of the powerful influence of parents on character development were becoming popular notions, he told a newspaper reporter, "I always gambled. I can't remember when I didn't. Maybe I gambled just to show my father he couldn't tell me what to do, but I don't think so. I think I gambled because I loved the excitement."[54]

Rothstein was well mannered, seldom raised his well-modulated voice, and rarely exhibited anger, depending on his linguistic ability to drive home his point. He dressed expensively but quietly and he did not like jewelry. He never smoked and hardly ever drank. His hours were irregular but he always managed to get enough sleep. He was tight with his money except when the opportunity to make a bet arose. He had friends, but far more detractors.

A creature of the darkness in a chauffeur-driven limousine, Rothstein frequented the top restaurants, nightclubs, and speakeasies. He was recognized wherever he went, and he knew every one who inhabited the night, both in the underworld and the overworld, giving him a shadowy aura. On the many nights he did not gamble, he typically hung out at Lindy's delicatessen and restaurant on Broadway, dining or sitting at his private booth sipping coffee refills until the wee hours. He held court with the gamblers, criminals, politicians, businessmen, and show people who dropped by to see "A. R." He seemed to have connections everywhere, and he was rumored to be able to arrange anything, provided he benefited. The self-impressed gambler liked to tell his coterie stories about his life and exploits.

Rothstein's lifestyle inspired major novelists. He was fictionalized as gambler Meyer Wolfsheim in Scott Fitzgerald's *The Great Gatsby*. His friend Damon Runyon romanticized him in a series of short stories that were the basis of the Broadway musical *Guys and Dolls*. In them Runyon transformed Rothstein's persona into Nathan Detroit, operator of the "oldest established, permanent floating crap game in New York."

A. R. held court nightly amid *The Great White Way* of glowing lights that outlined Broadway's enticing multitude of theater marquees. The 1920s are famous for the *Ziegfeld Follies* with its beautiful showgirls, novelty acts, and comedians when twice as many people thrilled to the shows that profiled that street than any decade since. Business fell in the 1930s due to competition from the new talking movies and the Great Depression. Ziegfeld's last production was in 1931. By the time the economy recovered during the Second World War, the Broadway casts had unionized. Performers were finally earning decent wages, but their higher pay drove up show prices, greatly reducing the number of people who could afford tickets.

Rothstein was never arrested or charged with a crime. He is most famous for having fixed the 1919 World Series when the Cincinnati Reds beat the heavily-favored Chicago White Sox. Evidence based on confessions, grand jury testimony, and depositions of those involved indicate that three of the players were unhappy with their pathetic pay and brought the idea to Rothstein and other gambling figures to pay the players $10,000 each to throw the Series.[55]

While Rothstein neither dreamt up the swindle or financed it, the evidence (including his own written statement to the grand jury) indicates that he was approached about the scheme during its planning stages by every player and gambler/bookmaker who was involved. Although he discussed it with each of them, he tried to discourage them because they were too likely to get caught. When he refused to get involved, the players backed out. They wanted him to be the mastermind because he had the big bankroll and a good reputation for keeping his word. Thus, the bookies falsely swore to the players that Rothstein was directing the fix from behind the scenes. As the three players had feared, the bookies never paid the promised payments. This scam almost destroyed the game of baseball, and it ruined the reputations of some great players who may not have been involved, but a jury never heard the evidence because most of the documents had somehow disappeared before trial.

Rothstein always swore that he never bet on that World Series, but he wagered privately and secretly with illegal sports bookies, so it was impossible to either verify or refute his claim. More interesting than whether he wagered is whether the consummate gambler could pass up what appeared to be a sure thing.

At the height of the World Series scandal, Rothstein complained that he was tired of being considered a "social outcast." And he said, "My friends know that I have never been connected with a crooked deal in my life, but I am heartily sick and tired of having my name dragged in on the slightest provocation whenever a scandal comes up." Then he announced that he was going to dispose of his gambling games to become a real estate operator. He closed his floating crap game and sold his interest in the Saratoga Springs *Brook*, but he continued to play poker and the ponies. He also bucked the odds by patronizing the crap games that continued floating up and down Broadway.[56]

An early archetype of the men who would later lead Prohibition's major gangs, he never told anyone about his business interests or political wheeling and dealing. At the time of his death, his bank safety-deposit boxes and the 60,000 pages of personal documents in his home contained nothing indicating illegality nor any ties to politicians, with one exception. Rothstein possessed a note for a $20,000 loan from one of his companies to Bronx City Magistrate Albert Vitale that had been paid in full on its due date. The Appellate Court removed Vitale from office for this indiscretion of dealing with Rothstein.

A man of mystery, Rothstein led a venturesome life, enjoyed the privileges of wealth, and was well connected with both criminals and the powerful. Idle speculation about his lifestyle eventually became accepted as fact. He was assumed to be the financier of the underworld and an influential political fixer. It was popularly believed that he financed criminals' activities for a piece of the action and also offered them some kind of political/legal protection. His name was linked by rumor to all manner of mysterious double-dealing.

After his death, writers about early organized crime exaggerated the common gossip and escalated his image to the level of a mythical super villain. Not one of these writers ever listed a specific arrest or identified a credible source about his supposed activities. Yet they depicted him as New York City's most powerful political manipulator, and made him responsible for most major crime, including financial crime. One such alleged crime was financing *bucket shop* brokerages, which specialized in selling securities during Prohibition's booming stock market and then declaring bankruptcy before delivering the purchased shares to the investors. Another was fencing securities stolen at gunpoint from messenger boys who delivered them to brokerage houses and banks. The authors likely derived their conclusions that he was the bad guy because he testified in a brokerage bankruptcy and his name was interjected by a defendant in one stolen securities case. But no one in either case ever accused Rothstein of wrong doing. In fact, the judges, the DA, the NYPD, and the attorneys for the brokerage's creditors all agreed that Rothstein acted legally and honorably in both cases. (See Addendum J)

Despite these larger-than-life portrayals of Rothstein as the city's dominant crime figure, he was always a lone-wolf operator. He had no organization nor staff to back him up or protect him in a city divvied into large gang territories.

ROTHSTEIN'S TIES TO THE YOUNG TURKS

Rothstein achieved success, influence, and notoriety a generation ahead of the Young Turks, but they were well aware of each other because they were all denizens of Broadway's nightlife. Luciano and his associates shared two major interests with Rothstein. All had a passion for big-money gambling, especially Costello, who had an interstate illegal bookmaking operation and was a frequent bettor at the tracks where Rothstein personally booked his elite clientele. In addition, Luciano, Costello, and Adonis, like Rothstein, became deeply involved in Tammany Hall's back-room political jockeying for leadership of the Democratic Party and the endorsing of candidates.

While Rothstein maintained a large, diverse circle of acquaintances, including many politicos, first and foremost he was a gambler. The bond between Rothstein and Costello was based on surviving in the gambling culture. Gamblers who play high-stakes poker are flush one day and tapped out the next. They survive by being able to borrow large sums of money from fellow gamblers and wealthy businessmen. Trading funds back and forth is how these gamblers get through the inevitable downturns. (See Addendum K)

People loan gamblers money for two reasons - they are rated as the best players, and they honor their word to pay their debts as soon as they win. For dedicated gamblers, scrupulously paying off debts is far more than a matter of integrity - it is survival itself. Having readily available cash when they go broke is their lifeline. Otherwise, when they go busted they would have no way of acquiring a large bankroll to play again. It would take months to turn a small bankroll into a large stash by playing and winning at progressively higher-limit games, so they survive the inevitable long losing streaks by loaning to each other when they are riding high.

When Rothstein played in big poker games, he often paid with IOUs and then settled later when he had the cash. From his booth at Lindy's, he frequently loaned money to, and borrowed from, other devoted players who hung out around Broadway. When he died, his files contained a handwritten list of many people who owed him various sums of money. However, his estate could not collect on these outstanding loans because the initials associated with each dollar amount could not be identified as specific debtors. The initials were likely his personal nickname for each person so his records could never be used to embarrass them.

In the brokerage case in which he testified, Rothstein had borrowed cash from the company to pay gambling losses. He used securities as collateral, and he paid in a timely manner when he started winning again. He had no involvement with the company's bankruptcy. He was just getting funding in a properly recorded manner to support his financially volatile and insecure lifestyle.

Costello got caught up in Rothstein's estate because of the way the two big bettors handled their cash infusions. Five months after Rothstein died, his estate entered judgments against Costello, ordering him to pay two promissory notes totaling $35,000 that he had previously signed over to Rothstein. This case sat dormant for 13 years, and then the estate served Costello court papers about his long-pending liability. Costello filed an affidavit asking the court to vacate the 1929 judgments, contending that he was never served in the original actions resulting in the decisions and that the statute of limitations had run out.

Costello forthrightly admitted signing the notes and that he and Rothstein frequently lent large sums to each other. But he also claimed that he did not hand cash loans to Rothstein when he too was short. Instead he gave signed IOUs to Rothstein, who converted them into cash by discounting them to loan sharks, and Rothstein later paid back the face values. Costello's IOUs were used like a co-signed note to guarantee Rothstein's payment, meaning Costello's word was held in much higher esteem in gambling and financial circles. Thus, Costello contended he never received or owed any money from these transactions. The IOUs looked like loans, but he would have had to cover them only if Rothstein had failed to repay which never happened. Costello's IOUs were simply tools, much like a promissory note is used as security to borrow and repay other people. Rothstein should have destroyed the two IOUs when he paid them off, but they remained in his files. When he died, they appeared to record debts owed by Costello. Despite Costello's protestations, the arbitrator ruled in favor of Rothstein's estate, and Costello made the final payment of the $35,000 obligation less than three months later.[57]

THE MAN & THE MYTH

Arnold Rothstein and his wife Caroline appeared to be happily married for 18 years, and then they amicably separated. She was rumored to have left because he would not quit nights out gambling. Six months after their separation, he executed a new will that gave her half his estate.

Then a girlfriend surfaced. Inez Norton was a blond former Ziegfeld Follies showgirl who lived at the Fairfield Hotel which Rothstein owned. His attorney handled her divorce from her husband. As soon as it was finalized, Rothstein told his attorney to draw up a new will giving Norton one-sixth of his estate and reducing his estranged wife's trust from one-half to one-third. Two weeks later he was shot and his estranged wife Caroline sat long hours by his bedside in the hospital.

The shooting of Rothstein was discovered when two Park Central Hotel employees found him lying bleeding in a back-of-the-house hallway. Rothstein told them to tell his attorney to bring his will and gave them his phone number. At the hospital Rothstein was rushed into emergency surgery. The .38 caliber-bullet had ripped through his abdomen, rupturing his bladder and perforating his intestines. The doctors stopped the bleeding, but the wounds had caused fatal sepsis (blood poisoning from pathogenic organisms), and two days after entering the hospital Rothstein died at age 46.

Shortly before Rothstein died, his attorney presented the new will to his client for his signature. Two nurses on duty who witnessed him sign later testified that the attorney guided the dying gambler's hand to produce the wavering cross mark, and that Rothstein drifted in and out of lucidity and was not rational at the time he signed. Yet when asked "Whose will?", he weakly mumbled, "My will."

Rothstein's estranged wife promptly contested the new will, challenging the attorney's questionable actions at the signing and his profiting from a new clause that made him the third executor. By agreement of all parties, the judge denied probate of the deathbed will, and Rothstein's attorney relinquished his role as executor in return for a guarantee of $102,500 in legal fees. Rothstein was always popularly rumored to be worth upwards of $25 million, which would have made him one of America's wealthier men, but by then it was clear the estate had limited resources. Rothstein's real-estate investments were small and heavily mortgaged. He owed three years back property taxes on most of his holdings, and the estate lacking cash, fell behind in mortgage payments. The administrators auctioned his holdings to cover the outstanding obligations and obtained judgments on a number of cash loans, but they were impossible to collect because the debtors were gamblers, who were either without assets, bankrupt, or incarcerated. His IRS debt for back taxes made his estate insolvent. Nobody ever received a penny from Rothstein's estate. His wife's large separation agreement was wiped out, but she had remarried. Three years after he died, girlfriend Inez Norton was awarded $20,000 from a life insurance policy.[58]

Rothstein may have been flush earlier in his life, but his choice of investments in later years indicates that he probably never rose above the level of a street scuffler who gambled high stakes. His compulsion kept him teetering on bankruptcy. Had he lived, he would have had to book a winner in his next few plays or the gambling fraternity would have stopped loaning him money. It appears that he spent his life living on the brink of ruin, but whenever his back was against the wall, he was able to win and keep his well-polished façade intact.

Rothstein used his gambling daring and expensive lifestyle to create the image of an affluent bon vivant. His highly leveraged buildings created the impression that he was wealthy, an image he parlayed into acceptability as a socialite and advisor to politicians. In reality he was a man of illusion.

THE LEGAL & POLITICAL MACHINATIONS OF THE ROTHSTEIN KILLING

The killing of Arnold Rothstein was a headline story in New York City. Who did it? Why? The NYPD, the DA, the press, and all his friends and associates speculated, but they were stumped. The case developed into a major political scandal when revelations about the inept police investigation came to light. The police immediately zeroed in on one suspect, George McManus, a partner of Rothstein in one of the city's largest floating crap games. Their suspicions were based on three facts. Someone using McManus name had called Lindy's not long before he was shot and left a message asking Rothstein to meet him at the Park Central Hotel. McManus had rented a room at that hotel the day before the shooting, and he had used a fictitious name. Both McManus and Rothstein had recently participated in what was about to become the most publicized and dissected poker game ever played.

What at first glance appeared to be incriminating facts soon turned out to be mere coincidences. The person who made the telephone call steering Rothstein to the shooting scene identified himself as McManus, but the two Lindy's employees who took the message denied recognizing his voice. This was significant because Lindy's employees knew McManus almost as well as they knew Rothstein. Furthermore McManus' attorney argued, "The courts have held that a telephone conversation is inadmissible where the witness is unable to recognize the voice speaking on the telephone."[59]

McManus' use of the fictitious name "George Richards" to obtain the hotel room the day before the shooting seemed suspicious, especially since he paid in cash for a three-day stay in a two-room suite. But an alias was not much cover for a man who openly floated his crap game along Broadway and was well known among the area's habitués. More importantly, the prosecution's own witnesses would testify that McManus always registered under different aliases when he played in high-stakes poker games to prevent the government from learning how much he won or lost.

Even though the initial suppositions of the NYPD and DA Joab Banton soon fell apart, the investigation continued to focus exclusively on McManus, the only suspect they ever considered. Just minutes after Rothstein was shot, the NYPD rushed to judgment. No matter what the evidence, or the lack thereof, the NYPD and the DA repeatedly told the press they possessed overwhelming evidence in "an airtight case," even though they took no action to arrest anyone. It seemed to many New Yorkers that the NYPD and the city administration were less interested in finding Rothstein's murderer than in losing the records he was rumored to have kept about politicians. In a letter to the editor of the *New York Times* published a week after the shooting, political humorist Will Rogers wrote, "We got one of the most stubborn murder cases here in New York. It seems the fellow that shot Arnold Rothstein is just bullheaded and won't come in and give up. There was some little talk of even going so far as to arrest him, but that's been squashed." [60]

Even though DA Banton maintained, "We have an airtight case in this Rothstein case," he also hinted at some weakness. Banton also said, "I think that the shooting actually took place in McManus' room in the hotel," and at the same time indicated that the evidence had not definitely established where in the hotel the shooting took place. Still Banton proclaimed from early on that the case he presented to the grand jury was so complete that he was ready to go to trial immediately.

Actually DA Banton's whole case was based on just one fact - room service had delivered four drinking glasses to McManus' suite a little while before the shooting. Thus, a month after Rothstein died, Banton brought a first-degree murder indictment against four men - George McManus, Hyman "Gillie" Biller, "John Doe," and "Richard Roe." Biller was targeted as an accomplice because he was the man who paid McManus' gambling debts, and because he was a close friend of Rothstein who also frequented Lindy's. The evidence linking Biller was his visit to McManus' hotel room the afternoon before the shooting, and his misfortunate timing just after the shooting, when he walked into the room looking for McManus after the cops had arrived to begin their investigation. The two John Does were thrown in just because there were four glasses. [61]

After all of DA Banton's posturing about the strength of his case, he announced a week after the indictment that he would not try McManus until the NYPD had arrested Biller and the mysterious John Doe and Richard Roe. He made no effort to explain why he needed to wait when he alleged to have had such a strong case against McManus, but he still blamed the NYPD for the postponement.

It was soon revealed that the detectives had been utterly derelict in their investigation. Their lack of professionalism began from the moment they entered McManus' room where they thought Rothstein was shot. They failed to dust the fingerprints on the two whiskey flasks and four glasses. Even if they had, they would have been unable to place victim Rothstein in the room, because they never recorded his fingerprints, though they had plenty of opportunity while Rothstein was in the hospital and then in the morgue. The detectives failed to find any indication that the crime was committed in McManus' room because there was no evidence of a struggle or a shooting. Finally, detectives failed to place the victim or either of the two defendants, McManus and Biller, in the room or even on that floor of the hotel anywhere near the time of the shooting.

While the DA and the police kept saying publicly that they had strong evidence, the case stalled. Five weeks after Rothstein died, New York Mayor Jimmy Walker, fed up with the NYPD's failure to uncover the motive for the shooting or to arrest the perpetrators, forced Police Commissioner Joseph Warren to resign. During the first week his newly-appointed replacement Grover Whalen was in office, he expressed dissatisfaction with the police activity in the Rothstein murder and reorganized the detective force, merging five special squads into two. The 5th Avenue, Pickpocket, and Broadway Squads were combined into a new unit. (Ten months later four of the members who were transferred from the Broadway Squad almost beat Luciano to death.) In addition, five inspectors, a deputy inspector, two captains, and a lieutenant were transferred "for the good of the service." This was six weeks after Rothstein's death. The *New York Times* reported that "It appeared that the mystery of how Rothstein met his death is still as far from solution as it was when Mayor Walker called upon Joseph A. Warren, former commissioner to resign." [62]

Two weeks later new Commissioner Whalen went public with formal charges against a detective who had been awarded the Medal of Honor for valor and forced the retirements of a detective, a chief inspector, two inspectors, and a deputy chief inspector. They were disciplined for failing to fingerprint McManus' room, to report interviews with potential suspects, and for other aspects of the investigation. The two primary detectives who failed the worst in the Rothstein investigation were demoted to uniformed patrolman pounding a beat, including the West Side Detective who failed to fingerprint Rothstein. He was also fined a month's pay and sent to Queens. Five years passed before he was restored to detective rating. Commissioner Whalen promised the whole story of the NYPD investigation would be aired when there was no longer danger of embarrassing DA Banton in his prosecution of the murder indictments.

Almost a year after Rothstein's killing, the case still languished. Then DA Banton's campaign for reelection brought it back to the public's attention, when his opponents charged that politics did not cause the murder, but covered it up. He responded that "politics had nothing whatever to do with" the inactivity. The most vocal candidate for DA, Judge Thomas Crain, promised a renewed vigorous investigation, but it was U.S. Representative Fiorello LaGuardia, the Republican mayoral candidate, who broke the issue wide open. LaGuardia claimed that Rothstein had loaned money to City Magistrate Vitale and possibly others associated with Tammany Hall. The revelation about a link between the victim and the DA's political party was scandalous, forcing Democrat Banton to announce that he would try McManus at once. Banton's move was confusing because he had been insisting for the better part of a year that to convict McManus, the NYPD had to first arrest Biller who was the other named suspect. However Biller was still evading capture by New York's finest.

Shortly after the shooting, the NYPD and DA Banton had claimed that they had the fingerprints off the four glasses found in McManus' hotel room, so they knew the identity of the four men who shot Rothstein. DA Banton stuck with this story in his opening statement to the jury, declaring he would present fingerprint evidence that really did not exist. As Banton presented his smoke-and-mirrors case in court, the story unraveled. Contrary to the claims of an airtight case by Banton and the NYPD from the day Rothstein was shot, law-enforcement had no evidence about how or where the crime was committed, no clue as to the motive, and nothing to link McManus to it.

With no evidence to present at trial, DA Banton proposed a hypothetical motive. The linchpin of his argument was the outcome of a no-limit poker game played on a Sunday two months before the shooting. Banton called only seven of the nine players to testify because the two other players were the defendant and the victim, McManus and Rothstein. The seven witnesses testified that big-time poker players from around the country had engaged in high-stakes games in various New York City hotel rooms and residences during the two months prior to the shooting, and they kept changing the location to reduce the threat of robbery.

The game in question started at 10 p.m. in the apartment of commission bookie Jimmy Meehan and broke up the next night about 8 p.m. The nine gamblers played bridge for about a hour, then switched to stud poker. Bets ranged up to $5,000. At one time Rothstein owed Nathan "Nigger Nate" Raymond $40,000. (This is the name everyone used for this white man.) Then the pair wagered double or nothing at one hand of *high spade,* in which each player cuts one card from the deck and the highest spade wins. Rothstein cut himself a deuce to double his losses to $80,000.

Even though Rothstein kept the score for the game, he was the heavy loser at $303,000, followed by McManus at $51,000. Nigger Nate was the main winner at $219,000. Unfortunately, Rothstein had been losing regularly in poker games during the evenings and picking the wrong horses at the tracks in the afternoons. Not only did he have no cash with him, he asked if he could have the $19,000 in cash Nate had lying on the table in exchange for IOUs for both the 19 grand and his losses.

Nigger Nate never collected a cent before Rothstein was slain. He testified, "I won in paper, and I lost in cash." "In all, I won $219,000 in paper from Rothstein. In addition, I let him have $19,000 in cash. ... When the game was over, I asked Rothstein for the money I had won, or for IOUs. I guess I made a faux pas. The others laughed at me and said, 'Oh, he's all right for it.' I was a stranger from the West, and I didn't know. I never collected a quarter [25¢] of the money." [63]

Nigger Nate was referred to in court as a "wealthy sportsman" from the West Coast. In reality he had been barred from all baseball parks in the Pacific Coast League in 1919 and 1920 for alleged complicity in a baseball bribe scandal, and he was blacklisted from racetracks. Three years after Rothstein's shooting, he was finally sentenced to five to 10 years in Sing Sing for having forged two stolen stock certificates two months before Rothstein's murder. He apparently used money from the stolen stock certificates to finance his New York City poker forays, including the 22-hour stud-poker game with Rothstein. At his forgery trial Nate admitted winning the money, but declared he had not collected any of it before the shooting took place. Even if Rothstein had paid, Nate would have had to deny it to avoid the income tax consequences. However, in this situation Nate's testimony is undoubtedly true, because if Rothstein had paid he would have told his friends in the gambling fraternity in order to maintain his reputation as a man who paid his debts. But the other eight players always denied the debt was paid before Rothstein's death.

In their initial investigation, the NYPD quickly conjectured that Rothstein feared that he had been cheated and refused to pay. This led McManus to lure Rothstein to his hotel room, where McManus had three associates threaten Rothstein to collect the debt. McManus was to receive a percentage of the collections for supplying the muscle, but in the resulting melee, Rothstein was fatally shot.

DA Banton in his opening statement at the trial argued that McManus as the second biggest loser also believed the game was rigged, but the DA never explained why the rigged game would turn McManus against Rothstein who was the far bigger loser. This speculation was Banton's entire case, but he had no meaningful evidence to back any of it up. Every player testified that Rothstein never brought up the possibility of cheating at the time of the game or during the intervening two months before he was shot. They all also argued that the game was on the level, and they gave credible reasons that the way the game was conducted made cheating unlikely.

All seven players testified that they had no idea who shot Rothstein, and they did not know any possible motive. Some players pointed out that Rothstein had so many enemies it would be difficult to pick the real motive. Every player, including Nigger Nate, denied he had threatened Rothstein for payment, and none ever heard of anyone else doing so. A dead Rothstein, they emphasized, would mean they would never be paid. This is exactly what happened.

During the second *World Series of Poker* tournament at Las Vegas' *Horseshoe Club* casino in 1971, owner Benny Binion said to me, "I'm going to introduce you to a piece of history." He called over three old men playing in his tournament. They were the only members of that infamous poker game still living - Nigger Nate, Joe Bernstein, and Alvin "Titanic" Thompson. It was 43 years after Rothstein's murder, and all three told me they still had no idea who might have done it.

At the trial, the poker-game participants testified that McManus never got upset over losing. He "always paid his losses with a smile, as much as $100,000 in other games." They all agreed, "He never complains." In addition, other witnesses said McManus and Rothstein, the two big losers in that game, continued to dine together regularly at Lindy's from the day after the game until his death, often chatting late into the night. They always seemed to be on good terms.

DA Banton's opening arguments contained numerous incongruities to the testimony his prosecution witnesses followed him with. A highlight at the trial was the testimony by a Park Central Hotel room attendant Banton had kept locked up for months as a material witness. The DA claimed that the woman had received threats and asked for protection, but she emphatically denied having been threatened. In prison, she demanded freedom from protective custody and, despite her meager salary, hired an attorney to obtain her release. She was openly hostile to the DA, and spectators at the trial reported that she seemed to relish the opportunity to ruin his case. According to her testimony, McManus could not have been in his hotel room or even on his floor at the time of Rothstein's shooting.

Before the defense began presenting its case, the judge concluded that the prosecution had not produced a single piece of substantive evidence or testimony, had failed to show motive, was unable to place the defendant, or even the victim, in the hotel room at the time of the shooting, and failed to connect the defendant to the pistol found on the street outside the hotel. The judge directed the jury to acquit McManus. Even though the jurors never heard the defense's case, when they were polled, all chorused, "We would have found him not guilty on the evidence anyway."

The *New York Times* reported, "When the foreman formally rendered the verdict that cleared him a year and three days after he had been indicted, McManus tried to smile, but tears filled his eyes. He blew a kiss to his wife, waved to his brothers, and said, 'Tell mama right away.' His only comment to the press as he left the courtroom was, 'Right now I am going to see my mother.'" [64]

When the judge directed the verdict of acquittal on grounds of insufficient evidence, the court clerk returned McManus' overcoat which had been taken into evidence. The first three detectives to arrive in McManus' hotel room to investigate the shooting found the black overcoat neatly folded over the back of a chair. It had McManus' name in the lining.

In DA Banton's reelection effort, he was defeated by Judge Thomas Crain, who claimed he would effectively prosecute the Rothstein case. Upon winning, Crain announced that he would study the Rothstein case during his first two weeks in office, and said, "I do not think there will be anything unknown about the Rothstein case." The DA-elect kept his word. DA Crain announced that during his first 13 days in office, he had revived the Rothstein investigation. He released a lengthy, thoughtful, legally sound analysis of every aspect of the case, which concluded that the authorities did not know who shot Rothstein, why he was shot, or where. He declared that the first-degree murder indictment returned by the Rothstein grand jury 13 months earlier against McManus, Biller, and two others was founded on illegal and incompetent hearsay evidence. "I find that the John Doe and Richard Roe of the indictments are myths – at least in the sense that the grand jury minutes made out no prima facie case against unnamed persons. I conclude that the indictment against Biller should be dismissed." [65]

In an unprecedented move, DA Crain planned to call McManus before the grand jury. "I think that he will believe it to be to his interest to make full disclosure. He cannot, no matter how guilty, be punishable under the law. Being immune from prosecution, he can claim no privilege. Continued silence in the face of official request that he speak will rightly be considered a confession. It is inconceivable that if innocent, he will be willing to live under a cloud. It would seem more likely that, for the sake of his wife and family, if for no other reason, he will speak." [66]

Three months later McManus appeared voluntarily at Crain's office, and the DA questioned him privately for more than two hours, but not under oath. Crain reported, "[McManus] said he had no idea at all as to who shot Rothstein." But McManus had no alibi. He claimed he had gone to see a movie by himself. Crain concluded that McManus had been frank and truthful, so he did not need to honor the grand jury subpoena that led to their meeting. In doing so, the DA lost a unique opportunity to question under oath a defendant who was found innocent and did not testify at trial. [67]

After his long ordeal, McManus returned to living his life. Almost a year later his wife Amanda, who sat behind him throughout the trail, was crossing the street when a speeding 19-year-old driver ran her down, killing her almost instantly. Police arrested him for homicide at the scene. McManus later remarried but shortly after the couple's daughter was born, he was diagnosed with a failing heart. His health gradually declined and he died two years later at 47. His fellow gamblers stayed away from his funeral out of respect for his family, but 300 friends and relatives showed up to send off the likeable gambler, whom the gambling fraternity described as happy even when he was a loser.

WHO SHOT A. R.?

Arnold Rothstein's shooting had an enormous impact on many other people's lives. It wiped out a sense of financial security for those who were dearest to him, panicked political allies who feared exposure of their relationship to him, wrecked the existing NYPD administration, vexed the next one, and became a persistent issue in a municipal campaign the year following his death. While his murder had serious consequences, no one ever addressed who did it. Because of the botched investigation, little evidence was uncovered. The NYPD, the DA, the press, and true-crime writers were never able to piece these limited details together in a comprehensible way.

In a murder case, detectives typically focus first on the spouse because he or she is so often the killer. But in an odd contradiction, no Mafioso's wife has ever been considered a possible suspect in her husband's gangland-style slaying. This is peculiar when one considers the lifestyle a Mafia wife chooses for herself and her children. She selects a mate who lives in a world encircled by violence and who has sworn an oath to murder on his leader's orders. Even more chilling, she expects he will raise their sons to have his values. It is not difficult to believe that a woman with such a great affinity to having a violent family is more likely to kill her husband than a typical wife, especially when considering one additional fact. A Mafia wife knows the police will never suspect her if she waits for a period of conflict between her husband and another hood, and she uses an untraceable small-caliber pistol that she leaves at the murder scene. Such weapons can be easily obtained in any low-income street-gang infested neighborhood. Thus, it is likely that some of the unsolved killings of major organized-crime figures during the last century were committed by the wife who dutifully honored her marriage vow to stay with her husband "until death do us part."

In Rothstein's case, the police made the usual supposition that the culprit had to be an underworld character. But to this conjecture they added two bizarre elements. First, they considered just one man, and then they tried to make the evidence fit this knee-jerk assumption even though none of the evidence presented at his trial could be connected to him.

Fifty years after the crime was committed, I took a fresh look at this cold case by compiling every relevant known fact about the shooting from the grand jury and trial testimonies and the press interviews. I searched for one or more explanations that would unify the assembled evidence. I looked at what the evidence said without any preconceived notions that might block consideration of any possibilities. I discovered the following scenario that connects every individual factual dot into a coherent pattern.

The NYPD traced Rothstein's activities that fateful Sunday evening. His personal chauffeur and confident for nineteen years drove him to Lindy's and then waited outside in the parked Rolls Royce. Later Rothstein came out and told his driver to "get some dough" from either his home or office, and then he went back inside and sat alone sipping coffee in his private booth. Ten minutes later at 10:45 p.m., a restaurant cashier received a telephone message and went over to Rothstein to inform him, "McManus wants to meet you at the Park Central." He put on his overcoat and hat and left for the hotel a mile away.

It is important to note that Rothstein had felt threatened a few times during his career, and he had hired a bodyguard for long periods. However, during the entire year before the shooting, he lived his life unguarded. Gambling buddies and Lindy's employees who dealt with him regularly said he had recently appeared as untroubled and buoyant as ever, even though he consistently lost great sums gambling during the two months prior to the shooting. While he could have waited just a few minutes for his chauffeured Rolls to return and drive him, he instead walked the streets of Manhattan a mile. He walked alone late in the evening, so he clearly did not think any one might be out to waylay him.

Twenty-two minutes after leaving Lindy's at 11:07 p.m., Rothstein was next seen by a Park Central Hotel electrician. The employee was operating the service elevator located in the hallway near the employees' entrance at 7th Avenue and 55th Street. The elevator had been sitting stationary on the ground floor for five minutes, and the electrician testified in court to what happened next. "I was standing inside the door of the [elevator] car, and people were passing in and out, when I hears a man about three feet beyond the door say that he had been shot. He was bent over like this, and was moving toward the timekeeper's office." [68]

This raised the big question - where was Rothstein coming from to try to determine the location of the shooting? Under cross-examination, the electrician explained that he had stood in that ground-floor location about five minutes prior to seeing Rothstein. Since he had a commanding view of the stairway doors above, he testified he could not have avoided seeing Rothstein if he had come through those doors from the hotel above. However, the timekeeper admitted that if Rothstein had come in the 56th Street entrance, he could have entered the hotel without the electrician, or anyone else in the service hall, seeing him.

Rothstein continued walking unsteadily past the elevator and down the hallway towards the timekeeper's desk at the 55th Street entrance, where both the timekeeper and the night watchman testified they were standing and talking. Suddenly, both saw Rothstein on the floor partly propped up by a wall. The timekeeper telephoned for an ambulance as the watchman ran out the exit to fetch a policeman at the corner. Neither employee had any notion of how Rothstein got to that spot in the hallway.

No matter how intently the police and DA Banton focused on McManus' hotel room as the shooting scene or postured publicly about their airtight case, they finally had to admit that they really did not know where the shooting occurred. NYPD detectives had no evidence whether he had been shot inside or outside the hotel building. Rothstein was conscious in the hallway and later at the hospital, but he flatly refused to reveal the location of the shooting or the identity of the shooter. He told detectives only his age and address and refused to answer all other questions.

Rothstein was almost certainly shot close to where he was found in the ground-floor employee hallway because he was incapable of walking very far. In addition a detective testified, "I found no bloodstains anywhere in the hotel." There was no blood trail in the hallway leading to where he supported himself against the wall, but plenty of blood was discovered underneath and next to him. When he arrived at the hospital, he needed two blood transfusions. Bloodstains on Rothstein's clothing could have indicated how far he walked after he was shot, but the detectives amazingly discarded all apparel and shoes without examining them. The medical examiner testified that Rothstein was probably in anguish from his guts being torn up. Thus, he was almost certainly shot somewhere near where he was found, either along the hotel employee hallway or right outside the nearby 56th Street entrance. [69]

No one reported hearing a gunshot. The detectives questioned hotel guests on McManus' floor, employees near where Rothstein was found, and the crowds on 7th Avenue, where the gun was later found. But the pedestrians who had been walking on the sidewalk were long gone before the police questioned anyone, and Rothstein probably entered the hotel on 56th Street, where the police questioned no one. Thus, he could have been shot on the sidewalk, but if so, the pedestrians witnessing it kept right on walking without telling anyone. Rothstein and McManus most likely stepped into an unoccupied room along the hotel's employee hallway and closed the door to transact business in private near where he was found, at a time when no employee was near enough to hear the shot.

The first patrolman dispatched to the scene was approaching the Park Central Hotel when he was hailed by a waiting taxi driver. He told the cop that as he was driving north past the front of the hotel on the 7th Avenue side at 55th Street, a revolver flew in front of his car and landed on the pavement between the trolley tracks in the middle of the street. He thought it could have been tossed from a sedan ahead of him in traffic or hurled from a pedestrian on the sidewalk.

The .38-caliber two-inch barrel Colt Detective Special revolver the cab driver found indeed turned out to be the gun that fired the bullet removed from Rothstein. The pistol's history was untraceable, and McManus was never linked to it. The handle had been chipped as if to hide fingerprints. The police later found the cartridge cylinder in the gutter. It had fallen out when a pin holding it in place was knocked out, along with five loaded shells and one exploded cartridge. The gun apparently broke apart from the impact of either the shooter banging the handle against the hotel wall or hitting the pavement.

After DA Crain assumed office and analyzed the case file, he remained uncertain whether the shooting had been intentional. He surmised, "I think that this latter fact, namely, that but one shot was fired, although the pistol was fully loaded, indicates either that the one shooting had no intent to kill or that the pistol was wrested from him by a bystander." [70]

If the shooter's intention was to kill Rothstein, he would not have assumed that a bullet to the groin would ultimately be fatal, and he would have shot him again. If the shooter wanted to threaten Rothstein to pay a gambling debt, he might have hit him with his fists or some object to inflict pain. However, he would not have sent him to the hospital with a bullet wound that would lead to a police investigation and an attempted murder charge if Rothstein decided to testify against him. Thus, the shooting was almost certainly unintentional.

The case for unintentional becomes stronger when realizing Rothstein was not shot either over nonpayment of a debt, as the police and DA Banton had speculated, or in a robbery. Nonpayment and robbery can be ruled out because he had $6,500 in his pants pocket, and his chauffeur was to deliver more money to him at Lindy's within minutes. Had it been intentional, the victim would have used all this available cash to bargain with the perpetrator not to shoot him. Rothstein obviously planned to make a payment to someone that night.

The gossip about Rothstein's shooting traveled up and down Broadway's haunts with lightning speed. His chauffeur returned to Lindy's five minutes after Rothstein was discovered at the hotel and every one there already knew about it. The detectives interrogated the chauffer later, and the DA questioned him under oath. Unbelievably all of them failed to ask how much cash he had brought for Rothstein, which would have indicated something about the victim's plans that night. This was just one of many pieces of evidence the NYPD and the DA let slip through the cracks.

According to the medical examiner's autopsy report and trial testimony, the bullet entered the front of the abdomen three inches to the right side of the middle, moved downward, and lodged near the base of the spine. The medical examiner wrote, "The course of the bullet was a slanting one downward. It looks as if Rothstein was shot by someone standing to his right. It seems very probable that he was seated at the time and perhaps talking to someone in front of him. It is purely speculation, but the man who fired may have been quite out of sight of Rothstein," meaning behind the victim's right shoulder.[71]

The medical examiner assumed that a gangster intended to either shoot or at least threaten Rothstein, so he concluded that Rothstein had to be seated for the perpetrator to be able to stand above and behind him and shoot downward and forward at an angle toward his abdomen. However, it is inconceivable that an assailant would have stood in such a position. He would have been off balance, close to the victim, the gun close to the victim's hands, and in a position making it impossible to effectively aim higher than the victim's abdomen. Gangland gunmen tend to stand more than an arm's reach away, while keeping direct aim at a victim's vitals to maintain dominance and control.

Actually the autopsy evidence gave no indication whether Rothstein was sitting or standing when he was shot. The bullet did not touch his right thigh muscle as it ripped through his abdomen downward and inward toward his spine, so there was no way to determine the relative position of Rothstein's right leg to his torso.

The medical examiner concluded Rothstein was seated because the bullet's trajectory was physically impossible if he was standing. The perpetrator would have had to be standing behind Rothstein, reached his arm over his right shoulder, held his arm in front of Rothstein, held the gun high enough to be six inches to two feet in front of his body, aim the gun back toward the front of the victim's body, and shot both downward at his groin area and leftward at his spine. The perp could have accomplished this awkward right-arm-and-right-hand contortion only by levitating one to two feet above the floor, depending on his height.

If both men were standing, if the assailant was behind Rothstein, and if the bullet had passed completely through Rothstein's body, it would have also struck the perp in the abdomen. It is highly unlikely anyone would be foolhardy enough to point a gun toward his own midsection whether or not the victim stood between him and the weapon.

My investigation is the first to combine all these evidentiary facts which I believe tie together into a unified whole. The facts allow us to deduce every relevant detail that must have occurred at the ill-fated meeting between Rothstein and McManus.

Rothstein wagered large amounts, and it was well known that he often carried as much as $100,000 in cash. He knew he was an attractive robbery target, and he undoubtedly survived by vigilantly protecting himself. One way was to place a gun in his pocket on top of his bankroll, so if he were robbed and ordered to hand over his money, he could reach in, pull out his pistol, and fire before his assailant recognized that he had something other than cash in his hand.

That night Rothstein arrived at Lindy's carrying two guns. Jimmy Meehan, at whose home the infamous no-limit poker game was held, testified that he was sitting with Rothstein when he received the message at Lindy's to meet McManus. The two men went into the men's restroom, where Rothstein gave Meehan the long-barreled revolver and kept the short-barreled one. As

Rothstein departed for the Park Central Hotel he remarked, "I will be back in half an hour." He obviously planned to have a very short meeting with McManus.

During the winter Rothstein carried a gun in his pants pocket to protect himself indoors, and one in his overcoat pocket to protect himself out on the mean streets. This way he was always ready to draw down on the city's toughs, no matter where they tried to rob him. For this quick meeting, Rothstein only needed one gun in his right overcoat pocket because he never planned to remove his overcoat. Presumably he kept the short-barreled gun, even though it was not as accurate a weapon, because his pocket contained too much cash for the long barrel to fit.

Rothstein and McManus were close friends who frequently dined or talked late into the night at Lindy's. That evening Rothstein's announced schedule gave him just enough time to deliver something at the Park Central Hotel and return to Lindy's, and the only thing these dedicated gamblers ever exchanged was cash. Rothstein was planning either to pay off a loan or debt to McManus or loan him money.

When Rothstein, who was right-handed, reached into his overcoat pocket for the cash, he first had to remove the revolver. If it was a double-action weapon, he probably snagged it in the pocket lining and, as he kept trying to pull it upward with his finger on the trigger, caused the gun to discharge accidentally. If it was a single-action gun, he had to cock it to fire. He could have given McManus the money and, as he slid his gun back into his pocket, the hammer caught on the lining. When the hammer snapped free of the lining, it could have slammed the firing pin into the bullet. In either case, Rothstein would have had to have his finger pressing on the trigger, a dangerous way to hold a gun. But people who lack proper training often hold a gun this way when trying to maneuver it in the tight confines of a pocket.

The autopsy report said the gun was six inches to two feet above the lower right side of Rothstein's abdomen when he was shot, exactly where his hand would have been if he were trying to pull the gun out of his overcoat pocket. He would have angled the gun barrel to the left, as he tried to pull it out of his right pocket, causing the bullet to enter three inches right of the center of his body and to angle left lodging near his spine. My surprising conclusion - Rothstein shot himself with his own gun.

Meehan described the revolver that Rothstein was carrying as a .38-caliber Colt Detective Special, with a two-inch barrel, identical to the gun the cabby found in the street and which ballistic tests identified as the weapon used in the shooting. This had to have been the gun Rothstein had been carrying because if the assailant had been carrying an identical model gun, the police or the employees would have found a second weapon somewhere inside or outside the hotel. The idea of the perp carrying a gun also makes it impossible to explain why he shot Rothstein with the victim's gun and still left the money. In addition, an assailant leaving the scene with a gun covered with Rothstein's fingerprints would have been carrying incriminating evidence that he would have wanted to dump fast. And while the gun was found, police and hotel employees never found Rothstein's overcoat. Rothstein could not possibly have ditched his gun nor hidden his overcoat because there was no blood trail and he could not walk. Thus, he had to have been shot near where he was found slumped against the wall. This means his friend McManus tossed the gun in the street outside the hotel and dumped the overcoat elsewhere because it would have had a telltale bullet hole in the lining of the right pocket. Remember, the $6,500 was in Rothstein's overcoat pocket when he left Lindy's, and it was in his pants pocket when he was found shot in the hallway with no overcoat. It was not an enemy or someone Rothstein owed money to who staged this convenient scene.

Rothstein wanted the overcoat ditched because it proved that he shot himself. A robber or assailant would have had no reason to take it, especially since possessing it could have been a ticket for a trip to the electric chair at Sing Sing. An assailant almost certainly would have gotten Rothstein's money before shooting him or quickly pulled it out of his overcoat pocket immediately after. If for some inexplicable reason he did take the coat, he would have dumped it quickly near the hotel. The killer would not have had any reason to hide, bury, or burn it so that it would never be found. The only reason to permanently make the coat disappear was that Rothstein shot himself and wanted to cover up his blunder.

McManus certainly had the opportunity to dump the gun and the overcoat. Remember, newly elected DA Craig had a two-hour interview with McManus before exonerating him. The DA's lengthy statement contained a stunning admission - "[McManus] claimed he learned of Rothstein's shooting while he was buying a glass of malted milk in the drug store of the Park Central Hotel at the southwest corner of 56th Street and 7th Avenue. This was about a quarter past 11 Sunday evening [8 minutes after Rothstein was found shot]. In the store at the time was a group of people talking about it. He took no part in the conversation. He said he went out of the store, got into a taxicab, and went to the home of his uncle." Thus, McManus' belated alibi to the DA established that he was at the scene at the time of the shooting, and he admitted having a malted milk a half block away from where the cabbie saw the shooter's gun flying near 55th Street and 7th Avenue.[72]

After the shooting, Rothstein steadfastly refused to identify an assailant or divulge any information about the incident. Clearly he was embarrassed by his dumb mistake. He must have begged his friend to get rid of the two pieces of evidence so he could maintain the illusion that he was the victim of an attempted murder. At the hospital as Rothstein lapsed into unconsciousness, three detectives waited at his bedside even though his physicians insisted he be left alone. When he momentarily regained consciousness, his doctors advised him that he was dying and did not have long to live. He acknowledged that he understood. As detectives began to question him, he faintly shook his head. The only thing he would say was, "Got nothing to say. Nothing. Nothing. Won't talk about it."[73]

Does Rothstein's strong refusal sound more like someone trying to protect his attempted murderer, or to save his own ego from embarrassment? He refused to name the person who had shot him, to identify witnesses who might have observed the shooting, or even say where it happened. He snubbed requests for information from family, friends, his attorney, hotel employees, patrolmen, detectives, ambulance staff, and the hospital's medical and surgical personnel.

Rothstein had no reason to shield an assailant. He was always an independent loner who never belonged to a gang and never took an oath of secrecy. He was not known to be a loyal man, and he would have wanted to get even with an enemy, not protect him. It is hard to believe that he would have kept his mouth shut during the two days that he knew he was dying, unless he shot himself. He prided himself on his superior intellect and savvy, and he could never have admitted to the world that he had made such a sucker blunder.

McManus, who had to have seen Rothstein accidentally shoot himself, remained quiet during the months he spent in jail and throughout his trial. McManus would not have kept silent out of loyalty to his dead friend's reputation, but rather fear. He could not have convinced anyone that Rothstein accidentally shot himself. He also knew that if he admitted trying to protect his friend's image by getting rid of the overcoat, the only evidence that would have proven him innocent, the DA would have belittled such a feeble explanation and destroyed his credibility. After all, it would mean admitting that he was the only person at the scene and admitting that he destroyed the only critical evidence. He knew that telling the truth would almost certainly lead to a conviction and a possible death sentence.

At the shocking moment when McManus saw Rothstein shoot himself, he instinctually decided to toss the gun and ditch the overcoat for his wounded, frantic friend. McManus had no concern for legal ramifications because he could not conceive of anyone dying from a bullet to the groin. All McManus needed to be safe from prosecution was for Rothstein to deny McManus shot him. However, Rothstein lapsed into a coma and died quickly. It was only afterwards that McManus was named a suspect, so Rothstein had neither reason nor opportunity to clear him. This forced McManus to dummy up, face the consequences of his trapped situation, and hope for acquittal.

The Rothstein death case had many victims. The most tragic was the innocent George McManus, who suffered prolonged persecution by the police and DA. The ultimate irony is that over an accidental self-inflicted shooting, a police commissioner and more than a dozen top NYPD officials either lost their jobs or were demoted for years, nine key NYPD officials were transferred from their cushy Broadway environs to squads in less desirable parts of the city, and the DA lost his reelection campaign.

LUCIANO & COSTELLO AS POLITICAL KINGMAKERS

A century before Prohibition, New York City politicians of every party became closely tied to the criminal element, so in the early 1910s Rothstein and his cash contributions were welcomed by the leaders of Tammany Hall despite his being a high-stakes gambler, operator of an illegal Broadway casino and a floating-crap game, and being friends with underworld figures. Gambler Rothstein became an influence with key leaders of Tammany Hall.

The interaction between politicians and criminals was clearly revealed years later by a lieutenant in Las Vegas' Mafia professional street gang of the 1970s and 1980s that is depicted in *Casino,* the 1995 movie and book. Las Vegas Police Department Detectives wanted to know how the hoods approached politicians to corrupt them, and gang member Frank Cullotta explained, "We didn't do anything. They approached us looking for what was in it for them." He elaborated that many people run for office primarily to get the opportunity to rip off the very people who vote for them. Some elected officials need to be bailed out of a problem by organized crime, and they sell their souls and are owned forever by the criminals. Others come with the pitch, "I need money, and I can do you guys a lot of good." Criminals need favors from politicians, and at their private meetings, the office holders have an easy opportunity to proposition them for help. In none of these situations are politicians seduced. Rather, these politicians are innately corrupt, greedy people looking to take advantage of a potentially lucrative situation.[74]

Early in Prohibition, New York City's politicians inevitably approached Luciano and Costello as they were becoming the country's two most successful rumrunners. Because the Young Turks came from working-class, highly Democratic, Italian-Sicilian-Jewish neighborhoods, they aligned with Tammany Hall and established tight bonds with the leaders. They had financial resources, respect from the people in their neighborhoods, and were personally likeable. Moreover, they were great negotiators, and they had no personal agenda or vested interests in conflict or competition with the political leaders. As the Young Turks developed large Democratic voter constituencies in their neighborhoods, they became political kingmakers. Costello became the political powerhouse of Manhattan, the country's largest city and its financial center, Adonis rose to be the dominant power in the working-class borough of Brooklyn, and Luciano was the respected quiet man who commanded attention from everyone when he spoke.

Government investigations revealed the great influence Rothstein, Luciano, Costello, and Adonis had in Tammany Hall and New York City politics. The four were associated with different Tammany leaders, so they closely allied in their political endeavors, controlling a majority of Tammany's 12 voting members. It was after Luciano and his colleagues developed their own power bases that they aligned with Rothstein. He was never their mentor in any fashion despite the typical false claims made by writers about early organized crime. (See Addendum L) No other tie was ever established between Rothstein and the Young Turks except for their personal passions for gambling.

Before Rothstein's death, the citizenry did not know who wielded the most powerful political influence in New York City. Most people assumed Rothstein had to be the top political fixer because he received so much press coverage about his intriguing gambling activities, but he was a lone wolf. In contrast Luciano and Costello belonged to the country's largest criminal organization based in Manhattan. They had their own power base, large amounts of available cash, and political, business, and union contacts. They worked closely with Rothstein when they needed his political support. His death created a power vacuum for the Tammany Hall leaders aligned with him, so Luciano and Costello quickly brought them into the fold. Between them, the two closely-knit associates controlled a majority of Tammany's leaders.

Luciano was recognized as a major power in New York City, and when he spoke, everyone listened. But it was Costello who was the primary contact man with politicians, government officials, businessmen, and union leaders. He could deal with the overworld without creating questions because few people in New York City realized that he was a Mafioso, let alone such a powerful one, until after his death. Costello did reveal something about his powerful political influence and his long criminal and legitimate-business background in testimony he gave at a New York City magistrate's 1943 disbarment hearing. He admitted knowing a couple dozen of the biggest Prohibition gang leaders including Al Capone.[75]

During the 1951 Kefauver Committee hearings in the U.S. Senate, Senator Tobey asked former New York Mayor Bill O'Dwyer what he considered to be the basis of Costello's appeal to politicians. O'Dwyer replied, "It doesn't matter whether it is a banker, a businessman, or a gangster, his pocketbook is always attractive." Costello never registered to vote, but he influenced which potential candidates' campaigns that Tammany Hall would endorse and finance.[76]

Luciano's and Costello's political power crested during the 1932 Presidential primary elections. The country had been mired in the Great Depression during most of President Herbert Hoover's first term. Hoover had shown little public sympathy for the quarter of the work force mired in hopeless unemployment. His Treasury Secretary, Andrew Mellon, announced that recessions could be morally uplifting with statements like, "High costs of living and high living will come down. People will work harder, live a more moral life." Rather than stimulus packages and enhanced unemployment benefits, he proposed "Liquidate labor, liquidate stocks, liquidate the farmers, liquidate real estate." It was clear the voters intended to liquidate Republican leadership by electing the presidential candidate the Democrats nominated at their June convention in Chicago.[77]

The two leading contenders were former New York Governor Al Smith and current Governor Franklin D. Roosevelt. FDR entered the convention with a large delegate lead, but not the two-thirds he needed to secure the nomination. Every political watcher knew the key force maneuvering in the background of this campaign was New York City's corrupt gangster-influenced Tammany Hall political machine. Tammany's leaders were antagonistic to FDR because he considered them unsavory and had always distanced himself from them. As Governor, he had not only refused to compromise with these leaders to accomplish things for the city, but he had taken action to restrain Tammany's local affairs when disgraceful scandals hit the newspapers.

At the beginning of the convention in this tense atmosphere, Costello and Jimmy Hines, the leader of Tammany Hall, met privately with Governor Roosevelt at the same time that Luciano and Al Marinelli, the number two at Tammany, met behind closed doors with former Governor Smith. Ironically both candidates were decidedly Wet, meaning they wanted to end Prohibition, a platform that would put the two hoods out of business. Luciano and Costello failed to win any concessions from either candidate, so Luciano told Tammany's delegates to vote their consciences. Thus, the New York delegation declined to endorse a candidate at the 1932 Democratic presidential nominating convention. Even though Roosevelt's efforts to control Tammany's worst excesses had been limited, these created enough animosity inside this large political organization for the New York delegation to vote more than two-to-one in favor of runner-up Smith. In addition, Tammany's leaders who supported Smith, openly and aggressively lobbied other state delegations to defeat FDR's bid.

When a candidate cannot carry his home-state delegation, nominating conventions usually reject him, but most of the other delegations had such great distrust of Tammany Hall politics that its opposition may have benefited FDR. The political wheeling and dealing by both candidates with the various state delegations went on for four ballots, when California and Texas switched to Roosevelt, giving him the nomination. He went on to become the 32nd President of the United States.

Not surprisingly, the 1932 Democratic presidential-candidate intrigue with the underworld was exposed by a Republican. Between the time Manhattan Deputy Assistant DA Tom Dewey won the 1937 election for DA and when he entered office, he released a sworn statement as an unofficial *report* about Democratic County Clerk Al Marinelli. In addition to revealing the meetings with the two leading Democratic presidential candidates, he charged that Luciano and Marinelli traveled together by train to Chicago for the 1932 Democratic convention, attended Arlington racetrack, "and jointly entertained in Martinelli's room at the Drake Hotel." Dewey also noted that Costello and Jimmy Hines had suites in the same hotel.[78]

The politically-ambitious Dewey issued his *report* before taking over the DA's office, because he was already laying the groundwork for a campaign against incumbent Democrat Governor

Herbert Lehman less than a year away. Dewey lost that 1938 New York gubernatorial election, but he continued to vociferously campaign against Tammany Hall's ties with organized crime.

Luciano and Costello had originally become entrenched with Tammany political leaders in order to protect their smuggling business, and to represent their Italian/Sicilian/Jewish constituency. But the Democratic politicians dominated the city and continued to become embroiled in one scandal after another. When the public finally cried for reform, New York City's political climate was in for a radical change that would greatly impact the lives and careers of the Young Turks.

CHAPTER 6

CAPONE'S CHICAGO & THE UNIONE SICILIANA

THE CHICAGO EMPIRE OF JIM COLOSIMO & JOHNNY TORRIO

The Chicago gang that became so infamous under the leadership of Al Capone established strong ties early in Prohibition with the premier liquor importing groups of Charles Luciano and Frank Costello in New York and Moe Dalitz in Cleveland. These interpersonal gangland bonds continued for a half century, all the way through the development of the Las Vegas Strip's Golden Era.

Although the leaders of these four gangs were located in three different states, they partnered in various business enterprises over the years. As Prohibition ended, Chicago invested in the newly formed Luciano-Dalitz interstate legal alcohol production partnership, and when Ben Siegel began expanding illegal gambling into the Southwest, both Chicago and Dalitz had their associates join with him in the move. Siegel then partnered with Chicago in the nationwide wire transmission of horserace information named Trans-American Publishing & News Service. While Siegel was developing his Las Vegas gambling interests, Meyer Lansky and Jimmy Blue Eyes partnered in Florida with a long-time Chicago casino operator.

Siegel impressed his Chicago partners with his vision of a shining ribbon of fine gambling resorts in the Las Vegas desert, and Chicago's leadership became a principal partner with Dalitz in building the world's largest resort hotel and biggest casino, the *Stardust*. Two decades later, Chicago became the most important financier of Strip gambling resorts because of its influence with the Teamsters Union Pension Fund, and the gang became one of the state's biggest owners of casinos, all through hidden interests.

Prior to these four gangs venturing into Las Vegas, the leaders were close allies in underworld politics including the influential Unione Siciliana (see Chapter 2). During Prohibition the Italian Capone often had one of his gang's Sicilian members or allies head the Unione Siciliana Chicago branch, while a division leader in Luciano's New York Sicilian Mafia gang headed the Unione's national leadership.

The gang that is typically associated with Capone's name and ultimately dominated in Chicago was begun by "Big Jim" Colosimo. His family emigrated from Calabria, Italy to Chicago when he was 10. They settled in the low-income Levee area just south of the Loop that was home to the raucous and brawling brothel district. These illegal red-light establishments were officially tolerated by political leaders to keep vice concentrated in one area of the nation's second largest city.

The Levee was in the 1st Ward, and it became the political stronghold of two Democratic Aldermen. They were elected to the Chicago City Council in the 1890s and served for a half century. Mike "Hinky Dink" Kenna was the schemer, and John "Bathhouse" Coughlin (nicknamed because he had once been a rubber in a Turkish bath) was the spokesman. They protected the huge established brothel industry for a price. Police did not interfere with brothels that bought their liquor from Bathhouse John's company, their insurance from a certain firm, and their food from four specific grocery stores.

The Levee saloon that Hinky Dink Kenna owned for the three decades prior to Prohibition featured the city's longest bar and biggest beer schooners. At election times, Dink served free food to hoboes and drifters and slept them in his flop house on the floors above his bar. He also paid his complimentary guests to register and vote Democratic multiple times. Dink organized a rather unique voter base from the 1st Ward's large floating class of transients, derelicts, and criminals by giving each one a numbered membership card in his First Ward Democratic Club. This card assured the bearer of a helping hand "in time of sickness or distress" and a pass from arrest by the police in the district he controlled. His election day voting contingency was the underbelly of society - his flop-house misfits, criminals of every variety, and the saloon and brothel owners who demanded their employees vote under the watchful eyes of Dink's representatives.

Colosimo grew up in this milieu and went to work as a menial laborer. He carried a shovel and pushed a little cart down the city's streets to clean up after the horses. Then he became a bouncer for the madam of an upscale brothel. He married his boss and expanded her chain. Both madam and husband had political influence. She was a close friend of Hinky Dink, and Big Jim was a vote-swinger for the two 1st Ward Aldermen. Colosimo organized a political-social club, and he was appointed 1st Ward Democratic precinct captain and vote deliverer. This made him the man to see whenever anyone in the district wanted favors from an Alderman or a police captain. He collected and bagged the brothel pimps' bribes to the politicians and police after taking a cut for his collection services. Any brothel that refused to pay was shut down by police after officers used a fire axe to refashion the furnishings and piano.

After Colosimo became the criminal and political overlord of the Levee, Mayor Carter Harrison Jr. repeatedly closed the brothels during his five-year term. The Mayor's actions came as a surprise to the illegal Levee operators because when Harrison Jr.'s father had been mayor a quarter century earlier, he had created the Levee's red-light district to concentrate all vice. When the publicity over each closure subsided, the vice squad surreptitiously let them reopen.

Colosimo survived these brothel business downturns because his Colosimo's Café was one of Chicago's finest nightclubs. It offered fine food, rare wines, an orchestra and dance floor in its center, and high-limit gambling on the second floor that went on until dawn. Colosimo's was in the heart of the red-light district, and it became a famous hangout and rendezvous for people of every class with politicians, industrialists, union leaders, and celebrities sitting at tables next to gangsters. This gave Colosimo's a roguish image, but few got out of line because misbehavers were quickly booted so as to never offend the genteelness of the upper crust.

Colosimo's growing wealth made him a target of criminal bullies in the Little Italy neighborhood. These thugs extorted by using traditional Sicilian Mafia and Italian Camorra Black Hand notes. These slips of paper anonymously threatened serious harm to the affluent victim unless he left a specific amount of cash at a specific location. Since the Black Handers were murdering nearly 40 Little Italy residents annually, Colosimo sought protection by importing his 31-year-old nephew Johnny Torrio from New York. He had been born in Naples, Italy in 1882, and his family immigrated to Brooklyn when he was a teenager. By the turn of the century, Torrio belonged to the Five Points street gang, and it was a step up for him to move to Chicago and become a bouncer in his uncle's brothels. Torrio relocated a decade before the inauguration of Prohibition.

Shortly after Torrio's arrival, a trio of Black Handers approached him and demanded Colosimo bring a ransom payment to underneath an Archer Avenue viaduct. Torrio agreed and sent a car with four men. As it stopped at the appointed location, the three extortionists walked out of the shadows for the payoff. Sawed-off shotgun fire riddled them. Torrio was suspected of additional killings of Black Handers until the threats against Colosimo finally ceased. Torrio was physically short, but his ruthless gunplay soon raised his uncle's standing among the Levee pimps.

Colosimo preferred to devote himself to his Café, so he turned the operation and protection of his upscale brothels over to Torrio, who also developed his own chain of a half dozen low-end Levee brothels. While Colosimo was rough and vulgar, hosting his diners with a loud and unrefined humor, Torrio was businesslike and quiet with a soft low voice, beguiling smile, and mild gentlemanly manners. This whoremaster went home to supper in his flat at 6 p.m., and he stayed in for the night. He shunned alcohol, tobacco, and foul language, but the crafty and ambitious pimp wholeheartedly embraced murder in order to rule with an iron fist. He explained to those he dealt with, "Crime is a business, but if you do a wrong to me in our business, we'll settle it without going to court. You know the consequences." Police knew that the suspects in a number of Little Italy murders, including one attack against policemen, had ties to the brothels of either Colosimo or Torrio.[79]

Mayor Harrison's orders to close the Levee's red-light district went unheeded by the four police detectives of the Vice Squad who were bought off by Colosimo and Torrio. Thus, the frustrated Mayor created the Morals Inspection Bureau to get the job done. This division investigated independently of the Police Department, and it was headed by two dedicated law enforcers. Major M. C. L. Funkhauser was given the new position of Second Deputy Police Commissioner, and his assistant was Inspector W. C. Dannenberg. Backed up by the fifteen detectives in the new Morals Bureau, these determined officers' success in closing one brothel after another was a threat to the pocketbooks of the whoremasters and to the reputation of the existing Vice Squad.

In contrast to the Vice-Squad's raids that were pre-arranged with the pimps to pick up just two or three prostitutes, the Morals Bureau raids of the same places captured 10 to 20 women including the madam. Torrio tried to solve the problem by having an ex-cop represent him in offering monthly bribes to these aggressive new vice enforcers. When Torrio's man delivered the first payoff, the Morals Bureau arrested him for bribery as two newspapermen stood nearby observing the transaction. This infuriated the megalomaniac Torrio, who reacted like practically no other 1900s U.S. gang leader. He began planning the murders of Inspector Dannenberg and his dedicated incorruptible Morals detectives.

Torrio brought in his cousin Rocco Vanille to lead the assassination plot. He was the business manager at Colosimo's Café and owner of a brothel. One night Inspector Dannenberg and four of his plainclothes Morals detectives raided The Turf brothel and arrested the inhabitants. Then two detectives strolled down the sidewalk to observe the activity of the hangers on. Unbeknownst to them, Vanille was setting his plan into motion by inciting a group of Levee brothel thugs and local habitués into a frenzy, and then he exhorted them to chase down and attack the two Morals detectives. All of a sudden the two detectives became aware the jeering crowd of 600 behind them was getting louder. The two detectives turned their heads and saw the mob charging them so they began running. Realizing they could not get away, they spun around with their hands on their guns ready to draw to hold the mob at bay.

The detectives had stopped in front of Freiberg's Dance Hall, and watching from its steps were Colosimo, Chicago PD Vice-Squad leader Captain Michael Ryan, and another corrupt cop, who were there to be witnesses in defense of the dirty cop killers. Another man standing beside Colosimo quickly ran over to Vanille yelling, "Not here!" The two detectives slowly advanced step by step toward the mob backing them up. Beside the front of the mob, Torrio's car had slowly inched along with them. His car had likewise backed up as the two detectives pushed the mob a block away from the Dance Hall. There Torrio's car parked at the curb which was apparently the signal to kill, because one man threw a brick that just missed the head of one of the Morals detectives and hit a nearby woman knocking her unconscious. Vanille pulled a pistol and fired at the two detectives.

In the meantime, the sound of the loud howling crowd had drawn two regular police detectives to the scene, and they charged in with guns drawn. Unfortunately, a tragedy was about to ensue. Both pairs of plainclothes detectives thought the other pair of men with drawn guns were Levee thugs shooting at them, so the detectives commenced firing at each other. All four detectives were hit. Regular Police Sergeant Stanley Birns was killed instantly from a bullet to the torso. He left a wife and three young children. His partner, Detective John Sloop, took a serious injury to a hip. The two Morals detectives had lesser wounds.

While Vanille was killing Sergeant Birns, he somehow shot himself in the foot. He hopped over to Torrio's car that was waiting to whisk away the cop killers. Torrio drove swiftly to Colosimo's Café for a short stop, and then took Vanille to the hospital for emergency treatment. Shortly after the doctor extracted the bullet from Vanille's foot, Torrio tried to pocket it, but the police guard grabbed his hand. It matched the bullet that killed Sergeant Birns. This case illustrates the ferocious ruthlessness of Torrio six years before the infamous Al Capone joined his gang.

The most reprehensible actions that evening were by Chicago PD Vice-Squad leader Captain Ryan. He stood beside Colosimo and watched the menacing crowd chase and attack the two detectives without doing his sworn duty of stepping in to protect them. He then lied to the press by claiming Inspector Dannenberg's detectives were "green," and asserted one of them had killed Birns, which was disproved by ballistics analysis. Departmental charges were quickly brought against Captain Ryan for being either grossly corrupt or grossly incompetent, and Police Chief James Gleason transferred him and the other detectives of the Vice Squad to other divisions. This led to vigorous protests by the officers in the new districts because they did not want tainted cops in their respectable neighborhoods.

The typical pattern in police departments is for honest police officers to transfer to legitimate divisions or precincts where scandals never erupt, while dishonest cops congregate where graft freely flows from criminals or politicians. While gangsters offered bribes to the cops on their beat, their primary goal was to corrupt either the captain of the local precinct or a politician who controlled that captain's career because he had the authority to assemble a staff of bad cops beneficial to the donating gangster. A week after the transfer, Captain Ryan resigned. State's

Attorney Maclay Hoyne put together the facts of what happened that night from witnesses, but none could absolutely identify Vanille or Torrio to make a criminal case. Two weeks later World War I was declared in Europe, and this sensational murder of a detective case disappeared from the papers and the minds of Chicagoans.

Mayor Harrison replaced vice-squad leader Captain Ryan with a dedicated detective who repeatedly shut down the Levee brothels, and Prosecutor Hoyne successfully prosecuted the offenders. Their determined efforts suppressed organized vice more than at any other time in the city's history, forcing Torrio to seek alternative locations. This led him to adopt a new trend that evolved during World War I when America started becoming a country on wheels. The wealthy were the first to buy cars and travel, leading to the development of roadside restaurants along highways. As the less affluent began buying cars, Torrio innovated a new marketing concept for vice. He created highway joints offering booze, girls, and gambling. He placed operations in a number of tiny rural hamlets outside Chicago's city limits where he bought and owned the local politicians and police forces. The main floor of his places featured a bar and drinking lounge. Some also had a nightclub or dance hall, while others offered slots or casino tables in the backroom. Upstairs all had up to 50 bedrooms for girls. His payroll included the employees at the gas stations and diners within miles of each establishment. These employees would press a button to warn madams that patrol cars were heading their way, so they could empty the building before the raiders arrived.

Torrio's first vice village was Burnham, 18 miles southeast of the Loop near the Indiana state line. It was easily accessible for an evening's entertainment from southern Chicago, Gary, Hammond, Calumet, and other cities. Just a mile square, Torrio controlled the town's tiny police force and notorious "Boy Mayor" Johnny Patton who managed Torrio's dance halls, nightclubs, gambling dens, and brothels. Torrio's Burnham Inn had 90 women plying their trade upstairs.

Colosimo followed by buying Ike Bloom's Arrowhead Inn and converting it into a vice den. Other criminals opened brothels and gambling halls, and Torrio established a slot-machine route in the local brothels and bars. Torrio may have owned the politicians, but they could only be reelected if Torrio very publicly closed down all vice before elections and whenever activist citizens and reformers protested loudly. These disruptions made Torrio regularly move his operations to different areas of Chicago and between rural suburbs.

When Chicago Mayor "Big Bill" Thompson succeeded Harrison in office, he immediately permitted all criminal activity for which he received bribes. He allowed Torrio to place thousands of slot machines manufactured by Chicago's Mills Novelty Company around the city, making him the gambling king. For three years Thompson threw obstacles in the way of Major Funkhauser, head of the Morals Inspection Bureau, and then falsely blamed him for the wide-open vice conditions the Mayor himself had created. The dedicated Funkhauser got into trouble for overzealously tapping the home phone of Police Chief Herman Schuettler, who was Thompson's appointed corrupt lackey. Mayor Thompson had the Civil Service Commission use this wiretapping as the basis to fire Funkhauser and his inspectors and to disband the Morals Bureau. A lower court ruled Funkhauser was fired arbitrarily, and more than three years later the Illinois Supreme Court refused to review this decision. By then Mayor Thompson had the town operating wide open like never before.[80]

Republican Thompson was well known to be the crookedest Mayor in the Windy City's history when he ran for reelection. However he capitalized on his image of wide-open criminal permissiveness and corrupted police leadership by running on a wet platform that appealed to the many drinkers of the city as Prohibition was set to go into effect in a matter of months. Since Thompson's Democratic opponent Robert Sweitzer also headed a corrupt political machine, the honest and vigorous prosecutor Maclay Hoyne also ran for Mayor as an Independent. Assassins, probably under the direction of Torrio, hid in a vacant house across the street from the Hoyne family home. They laid in wait for the Prosecutor to enter or leave. Hoyne's son returned home and the assassins, mistaking him for his father, fired a shot at him but missed. Despite this shocking attack on his family, the incredibly brave and determined Hoyne refused bodyguards and pressed aggressively ahead to finally close down the wicked Levee brothel district. Unfortunately, Hoyne and Sweitzer divided the anti-Thompson vote, returning the corrupt Mayor to office.

The next year, Sweitzer exacted vengeance against Hoyne for having run against him for mayor. During Hoyne's reelection bid for Cook County State's Attorney, Democratic Sweitzer supported the Prosecutor's Republican opponent. This led to the election of Thompson's ally Robert Crowe, and then the Mayor and new Prosecutor teamed up to sell their offices to Torrio and the other dangerous Prohibition gangsters. If Hoyne had been elected either as mayor or again as prosecutor, his track record indicated he could have kept gangster Torrio from terrorizing the voters, union members, and business owners during Prohibition. Chicago voters had an authentic law-and-order leader in its midst, but instead twice put his totally dishonest gang-beholden opponents into office. Those two elections would cause Chicago to become the most lawless and violent city in America.

Torrio's key aid was Jake Guzik. Born in Chicago, he stood 5-feet and was roly-poly with a flabby face and baggy eyes. He started his career as a waiter in a brothel and moved up to direct all the brothels of both Torrio and Colosimo. Jake Guzik's brother Harry also spent his whole career working in brothels, beginning as a bartender and becoming the managing pimp with his wife Alma at various Torrio brothels that were in Alma's name. One day an 18-year-old farm girl who had just moved into the city unfortunately approached Harry for a job doing housework at his home. He enticed her by offering an alleged maid position at Torrio's Roamer Inn, an illegal roadhouse brothel in Posen. When she arrived, Harry stole her clothes and frequently beat her until he forced her to endure constant rapes by lines of men. The victim's father searched for his missing daughter, and after a few days tracked her down and rescued her. She had the chits, or receipts, for which the brothel was to pay the prostitute $1 for each trick, but in her case the accumulated chits represented 131 rapes. Harry offered to pay the irate father the rape money owed her as a bribe, but he prosecuted instead. A jury found Harry and Alma guilty of white slavery and they were given a one-year sentence. After the Appellate Court ruled the decision was just, Governor Len Small took the unprecedented premature action of pardoning them before the Illinois Supreme Court heard their appeals. The Governor hid the couple's signed pardons from everyone until Attorney General Edward Brundage demanded the Guziks' file be turned over to him to fight their appeals. The Pardons and Paroles Division refused to release any information to the AG except to notify him that the Governor had commuted their sentences three months earlier. The Governor took this action even though the Judge had refused to sign a letter recommending the pardons, and Illinois AG Brundage called their crime "the most repulsive offense imaginable."

During Governor Small's reelection campaign, it was revealed that he had released more criminals from the state's prisons during the previous year than the number of new convicts who were incarcerated by the judicial system. This is particularly astounding because Prohibition arrests were escalating. Worse than these shocking numbers was the prisoners he released. He let the most heinous and dangerous criminals go instead of using his power to pardon in order to correct injustice as it was intended. The newspapers escalated their exposes and attacks, but Illinois reelected him, allowing him to continue his large wholesale business of selling pardons to the most vicious.

Republican Small served as governor for eight years starting a year after Prohibition began. The Republican trio of the state's most dishonest governor, Chicago's most corrupt mayor in Thompson, and Prosecutor Crowe teamed up to sell out the people to the most violent gangs. Many political figures spoke out against State's Attorney Crowe's failure to prosecute and his improper actions during his reign. They complained he never sought convictions in "really important cases," and he purposely permitted errors to be introduced in trial records for the Supreme Court to reverse on behalf of the gangsters. Judge Edgar Jonas protested that Crowe's Prosecutors regularly agreed not to object to defense motions for unnecessary continuance delays. Jonas had quit as Crowe's Assistant because "conditions were such that I couldn't stand four square with my conscience."

It cannot be overstated that organized crime cannot exist without strong protection by crooked political leaders, police officials, prosecutors, and judges. There is no better example of this awful truth than the nightmare created by the wholly corrupt Thompson-Crowe-Small political machine. Chicago became the world's most violent city because these officials turned the machinery of government over to the criminals so they could assault and exploit an unprotected and defenseless citizenry.[81]

America's laws are strong enough to wipe out organized crime unless these gangsters are protected by the politicians and law enforcement. This would later be proven by Mayor Thompson's successor Anton Cermak. Even though he inherited Thompson's highly-corrupted police department, Cermak would quickly and effectively shut down wide open gambling and brothels in the city (see Chapter 15). Whenever major crime exists, the elected officials, no matter how inspiring the law-and-order hyperbole with which they camouflage their total lack of integrity, should be summarily voted out of office by the electorate, one after the other until honest dedicated representatives finally get the job of defeating criminals completed. In contrast to the fraudulent law-and-order promises of dishonest politicians and law enforcers, Cermak never hinted during his campaign that he was planning to drive the gangsters out of town until after he took office. Then he soon forced them to move out to the surrounding communities.

In the totally corrupt political and police atmosphere of the Thompson-Crowe-Small administrations, Harry and Alma Guzik returned to exploiting women. In the three months from the time their pardons were granted until the public learned about them, the Guziks built the Blue Goose Inn roadhouse just beyond the Chicago city limits in the Village of Burr Oak Inn. It housed 60 women. During the next year, Harry was arrested there twice for pimping. After a court injunction permanently padlocked the building, Torrio ordered his goons to burn it down in the pre-dawn hours to collect the fire insurance.

Even though the Guziks bribed the police, Harry was arrested four other times for similar charges. Fifteen years before his conviction, Harry was fined $100 for purchasing a 16-year-old girl who had been repeatedly and brutally raped until she was demoralized into submission, and then he held her prisoner to do his bidding. Five years later, he was charged with employing underage girls. Two years after that, Harry was charged with operating a clearing house that recruited girls from out-of-state and distributed them to the Levee dives, but police failed to get sufficient evidence to convict him. Two weeks after Harry and his wife were convicted in the case in which Governor Small pardoned them, Harry was arrested at a different brothel, the Roamer Inn in Chicago Heights, for holding another girl captive in identical circumstances. The last three charges were apparently dropped by either the Prosecutor or the Judge. Such were the hideous slavery pimping operations of Torrio, Guzik, and later Capone.[82]

The two Guzik brothers were not the only depraved sexual sickos in the family. Jake's son Charles pled guilty in Phoenix, Arizona to unnatural sex acts with teenage boys. He was 41. The outraged judge said, "His activities were widespread, extending all over the country. He induced children to pose in various positions, then took movies of them, and used the pictures as a trap and a club over them." The judge then sentenced him to the maximum 60 to 100 years. His father's money and political savvy turned this punishment into a homosexual pervert's dream. In prison, Jake's son carried large sums of money in violation of the rules to buy sex from the other male prisoners, and he employed a private bodyguard who accompanied him whenever he left his cell and mingled with other prisoners. Heaven forbid he should be raped by another man.

His cell was actually a private, air-conditioned apartment that was furnished with a television set, refrigerator, and stove. His groceries were delivered in, and he cooked whatever he wanted whenever he wanted it. At the time of his arrest, police seized thousands of pictures he had taken of naked teenage boys, many having sex together, so based on this skill set, the Warden assigned him to be prison photographer. His apartment was furnished with a photo lab, and in a novel approach to incarceration, a lock was placed on the inside of his apartment door to make prison officials knock and wait until he and his fellow inmates put their clothes on before opening it. When the press exposed this situation, Arizona's Governor fired the Warden. The warped men of the Guzik family seem to have been drawn from the most exploitively and violently perverse of human gene pools.[83]

TORRIO BROUGHT IN AL CAPONE & THE CICERO MOVE

Months before Prohibition began, Torrio brought New York bar bouncer Al Capone into his Chicago gang. Like Torrio's family, Capone's family had also emigrated from Naples to Brooklyn, where he was born on January 17, 1899. He attended the same grammar school as Charlie Luciano, but did not get past the sixth grade. He drifted through a series of menial jobs before joining the New York City Five Points street gang Torrio had belonged to. Around 1917 Capone went to work as a bouncer and bartender at the Harvard Inn, a low-end bar and dance hall near Coney Island. It was owned by Frank Yale, who was born Francesco Ioele in Calabria in 1893 and came to the United States as a child. Yale, like Luciano, was a member of the gang headed by The Boss Masseria, with Yale operating primarily in Brooklyn. Yale, Capone, and Torrio were feared for being as murderous as any Prohibition thugs. Even though all three embraced the monopolistic and violent orientation of the Sicilian Mustache Petes, each personally revered and supported Luciano, despite his very different businessman anti-violence values.

One night Capone was playing pool and a sore loser pulled a knife on him. Capone threw a right to the man's chin, knocking him unconscious. Capone went home, but a short time later a misinformed poolroom friend arrived to tell Capone that his opponent was dead. Capone incorrectly believed he had killed his opponent and went to his boss Yale for advice. He got Capone away from the local police by arranging a Chicago job with former Five Points' member Torrio. Capone started out as a chauffeur-bodyguard, was transferred to bartender-bouncer in Burnham, and soon managed the brothel. About this time, he was fined $100 after pleading guilty to operating a slot route in his name on behalf of Torrio in the tiny village.[84]

The Chicago gang's leader Colosimo was content with his life. He had divorced his wife at age 42 and devoted all his energy to his 19-year-old bride, singer Dale Winter. His brothels and Café income were greater than his living expenses. With the advent of Prohibition, he continued to serve the finest wines and liquors at his Café and to retail booze at his brothels. He had no interest in wholesaling liquor because he had no ties with federal Prohi agents and judges to prevent arrest and prosecution.

In contrast, Torrio and Capone were consumed with insatiable greed and lust for power and went after the potential profits of Prohibition. Torrio and Capone were soon brewing beer for their brothels and distributing it to speakeasies. When the ambitious Torrio had gone to work for his uncle's brothels a decade earlier, he had told associates what he concluded from his study of his new pimping trade. "A monopoly of all Cook County is the only way to handle the brothel business, so it'll really pay. I'm going to start operating wherever I get a chance all over the city and in the suburbs, too, even if Jim won't come along." This goal for total control and domination over the whole County would become a morbid obsession with both Torrio and Capone.[85]

Colosimo often worked till dawn, and he returned late each afternoon after the luncheon crowd had emptied out to start preparations for the evening clientele. One afternoon he arrived to talk briefly with his secretary and bookkeeper in the office, and then he walked out to the empty front lobby. An assailant in hiding came up behind him and fired two shots. One bullet hit his head behind the ear and he fell face down dead. At the sound of gunfire, the restaurant staff came running, but the shooter had vanished. There were no clues and nothing was stolen. Big Jim's body still had his diamond cuff links, diamond studded garters, watch, and money. The killer fled immediately having no time to search for a box containing 250 $1,000 bills that Colosimo once showed his partner Mike "The Greek" Potsin. This alleged money was never found.

This crime was clearly a premeditated assassination by someone who had inside information about Colosimo's daily routine. Colosimo and his Café partner Potsin regularly argued about all the time Big Jim was spending with his new bride instead of focusing on business. Most of his estate went to his former wife, and his new bride Dale Winter relinquished all claims. She continued her singing career successfully on Broadway and then had a successful marriage. The police never considered any of them a person of interest, but they observed the actions of Colosimo's nephew Torrio. He alone continued to search for the alleged missing box of cash for months after his uncle's death. More importantly, he had taken over leadership of his uncle's criminal gang.

The only witness to the Colosimo killing was a porter who saw a man run out after the gunfire. His description fit Frankie Yale, the former boss of Torrio and Capone. The porter may have confirmed his photo as being the man, but when he was later taken to New York to face Yale, he became frightened and refused to identify the suspect as the man who ran. While highly suspicious, it is unknown whether the porter had already been intimidated by Yale's Chicago pals. Yale was a likely possibility for two reasons. All of Torrio's associates had been previously arrested and any witnesses could have easily identified them from their mugshots, while the New York-based Yale had never been photographed by the police or newspapers in Chicago. In addition, Torrio and Capone later supplied killers for Yale and his associates in high-profile New York murders for the same reason of making identification difficult.

Gangdom always believed Torrio had Yale kill his uncle. Organized crime is a world of secrecy, intrigue, and treachery, and many trusted lieutenants have killed their gang leaders because they wanted it all. Torrio no longer needed Colosimo because Torrio managed and protected both his own and Colosimo's brothels. He had also developed contacts with all the relevant dishonest politicians and police officials.

Colosimo, Torrio, Capone, and the other Prohibition gangs did not create Chicago's political and police corruption. They simply bought their way into it. Mayor Thompson had conspired with the new breed of gangsters to make booze and prostitution plentiful everywhere in the sprawling city. Prohibition forced Hinky Dink to close his two saloons because as an elected official he could not openly flaunt the law, but as Aldermen, he and Bathhouse John turned their Levee red-light district into the wettest place on earth by allowing a proliferation of hundreds of speakeasies, nightclubs, brothels, and casinos as long as they bought all their booze from Torrio, who employed Hinky Dink's precinct workers to sell and distribute it.[86]

After the elimination of Colosimo, the ambitious Torrio made Capone his lieutenant and began expanding his uncle's Chicago gang into what would become the nation's third largest criminal organization behind only the two biggest in New York City. When Torrio had Colosimo killed, Prohibition was just four months old, but the Prohibition territories had already been claimed by other gangs. The city had three major geographical sections separated by the winding Chicago River to the east. The North Side contained affluent residences, the South Side featured ethnic areas, and the West Side was a mostly industrial area bordering the rural Midwest. The three areas intersected in the city's central business district where the elevated and underground railroads arced, so it became known as the Loop. Torrio's strength was with the Italian immigrants concentrated in Little Italy and Chicago Heights, a separate municipality south of town. Over the next two years he focused on turning the law-abiding suburban communities to the south and west of town into hotbeds of vice by corrupting the municipalities' officials. To these quiet neighborhoods' existing speakeasies, he added back-room gambling and women upstairs.

Three years after Colosimo's murder, Capone visited his old haunts in New York City where he made an insulting remark to a female customer in a bar. Her brother, Frank Galluccio, pulled out a pocketknife and slashed Capone's face, leaving three long scars on the left side. This led to the underworld nickname of "Scarface." He hated this nickname because it represented his humiliating defeat in a fight. Before the slashing, Capone had become concerned about his appearance. Having balded by his early 20s, he always wore a hat. Capone believed in vengeance, making it surprising that the two men later reconciled and the slasher became Capone's bodyguard.[87]

After eight years in office, Chicago's scandal-ridden Mayor Thompson faced certain defeat and did not run for reelection. His successor was a honest man. Mayor William Dever directed his handpicked Police Chief Morgan Collins to close vice operations, disrupting Torrio's Levee revenue stream. Torrio was already dictator of vice in the tiny village of Burnham, and he decided to expand into Cicero, a suburb southwest of Chicago and the fourth largest city in Illinois. The residents were predominantly industrial workers, meaning Cicero was always a wet village, and Torrio wanted to offer girls as well. He introduced himself to the community in a most bizarre way. He acted like he did not know it was impossible to operate illegal wide-open vice without police protection. Instead of making contact with the city's police, politicians, or underworld leaders, he made his bold move unannounced.

He drove two carloads of painted women to a storefront, where they ran upstairs to set up their cubicles as he walked a block away to observe the reaction. Within hours, the Cicero Police backed up their patrol wagons, arrested the girls, and threw all the furniture out the windows. Torrio remained undeterred. The next day he repeated this scene at another storefront and watched the police wreck the place. A few days later Torrio went downtown to quietly observe the big 500-machine slot concession of Eddie Vogel. It was suddenly raided by the Cook County Sheriff. As Deputies carted the slots out to trucks, Torrio introduced himself to Vogel and explained, "You have the Police Chief. I have the Sheriff. If I can't have prostitutes, nobody's going to have slots." They quickly reached mutual agreement, and the Sheriff returned Vogel's slots, which were quickly reopened.

In return, Vogel tried to rally his political allies behind Torrio's brothels, but the town leaders were adamantly opposed to prostitution. Instead, they gave Torrio the right to open speakeasies and casinos, which he operated during the afternoon as horserace-bookmaking parlors. These were managed by Capone. Torrio moved his tainted women into small nearby county hamlets like Stickney where his Harlem Inn had a saloon in front, a back room full of scantily-clothed waiting women, and 50 rooms upstairs. It featured a selection of 35 women on weeknights and 80 on weekends. At times as many as 500 workingmen waited in the bar area for women to come back downstairs. Known as a $3 joint, the girls got only one-third.[88]

To create a safe haven from Chicago's reformist Mayor Dever and to expand his criminal enterprises, Torrio moved his headquarters into Cicero's Hawthorne Inn, where he and his lieutenants and bodyguards worked and lived. Capone placed bullet-proof steel shutters on the windows of his hotel garrison. Torrio formed an alliance with the long-time Village Board President Joseph Klenha and his cronies to use their political and Police Department support along with his thugs' violence to expand and control all vice in Cicero. Over night Torrio turned Cicero into America's most wide-open, notorious, and toughest vice center, with scores of speakeasies, brothels, and casinos operating around the clock. Torrio opened three casinos within a few blocks, but he usually had only one or two open. When the citizens' outcry became too loud, the police would raid and close the casino to cover up involvement by the police and politicians. Within a hour the operation was going full blast in one of his nearby closed casinos. Torrio placed slots in every cigar store and candy shop and built brothels upstairs of his Cicero speakeasies and casinos. He licensed other gangs to operate gambling and saloons in Cicero, but they had to buy his beer.

Early in Prohibition, Torrio had leased two closed breweries to supply his brothels, and then he began distributing to other speakeasies. To avoid Chicago Mayor Dever's invigorated Police Department, he built complete breweries in or near his brothels in the tiny outlying hamlets. Torrio established a monopoly for beer distribution to Cicero's 143 speakeasies by killing competing brewers, beating their salesman, and bombing, slugging, or having Prohibition agents shut down speakeasy operators who did not buy from him. At the same time, he killed the leaders of the smaller competing gangs on the South Side of Chicago until he had a monopoly on wholesale beer in half the city. Torrio and Capone became infamous for producing dreadful tasting beer and diluted whiskey. The pair charged the highest wholesale prices in the country for their swill because saloons did not dare buy from anyone else.

Six months after Torrio's arrival in the village, competing Cicero beer runners decided to combat Torrio's domination by having the Democrats run a separate slate of candidates in the election against Klenha's machine. He responded by having Chicago Election Commissioner Czarnecki, who had jurisdiction over the Cicero election district, scratch many Democratic voters from the registry lists and replace large numbers of election watchers and judges. Then the night before the election, Torrio initiated a violent campaign by having his plug-uglies invade the office of a Democratic candidate, beat him up, and shoot up the place. As the polls opened the next morning, an armed invasion of more than a dozen cars of rival beer-running gunmen flaunted either Republican or Democratic banners and sped up and down the streets terrorizing the whole town. Thugs raided polling places and attacked election workers and voters. Intimidation, sluggings, shootings, kidnappings, and illegal voting were the order of the day, all to establish control over vice in the city. A Cicero policeman in front of a polling place was beaten so badly he had to be hospitalized, as did some election workers. This type of savage domestic terrorism had never occurred in any Cook County election, and an alarmed County judge called Chicago Mayor Dever to quell this riot. Dever sent 100 policemen to the judge, who swore them in as County Sheriff's Deputies. Two officers guarded each of Cicero's 35 precincts, and the rest cruised the streets to drive the marauding gunmen to cover. The judge later questioned election officials at all levels and concluded, "Chicago's best gunmen were there to kill or terrorize whatever voters and workers were opposed to whichever candidates were the friends of the gunmen." [89]

At the height of this terrorism, three thugs were standing on the sidewalk near a polling place to intimidate voters. The three were Al Capone's brother Frank, his cousin Charles Frischetti, and an unidentified gangster. Two Chicago Police plainclothes detective squads, who had been sent in by the Judge to protect voters, pulled up across the street from these three men. The detectives jumped out of their cars with guns drawn. The three gangsters drew their guns and ran in different directions. The unidentified gangster escaped. Frischetti ran into a vacant lot, but quickly saw the futility of the situation and surrendered. Frank Capone ran down the street, and one of the two pursuing detectives shot a bullet through his heart dropping him dead on the spot. Witnesses, including his gangster cousin, were unsure whether Frank had fired or not, but his revolver cylinder contained three empty shells. Both Frank Capone and Frischetti carried concealed weapon permits issued by a Cicero justice of the peace. The Cicero Coroner's Jury declared the shooting of Frank justified and commended the Chicago detectives.

Klenha's incumbent political machine won every office, and the first Democratic candidates to ever run in the village claimed the election had been stolen. That election was only the beginning of serious violence in Cicero. It gave Torrio complete control over the vice den operators, and he maintained it with intimidation, sluggings, and murders. Once Torrio owned Cicero's political leaders and moved his gangster army into town, Capone and his henchmen berated, bullied, and even slugged officials at public meetings. The village's officials and Police Department were subverted to the best interests of Torrio's criminal endeavors, and both the Cook County Sheriff and State's Attorney Crowe turned a blind eye to the municipality of Torrio. The intimidation got so bad that the *Chicago Tribune* reported two years after the election takeover, "It has come to the point now in Cicero where one is reliably informed that there is hardly one of the town officials but would gladly resign if he dared. But the gang won't let them quit; the mob will make them run again – and elect them, too." This was written two months after Capone was charged with practicing domestic terrorism at the polls in the village of Stickney on primary day, but this case seems to have gone nowhere.[90]

Jake Guzik ran Torrio's brothels and he also kept the financial records for his brothel and gambling empire with a 25-man auditing office in the Four Deuces. This name was taken from its address at 2222 South Wabash Avenue. It was an unobtrusive four-story building that looked like a rooming house. The ground floor had a speakeasy, café, and cigar stand, while the second and third floors featured a casino and horserace book. The fourth floor housed Guzik's large accounting department.

Five weeks after the Cicero election terrorist riot, Guzik finished work for the evening and walked out of the building. On the sidewalk he encountered Joe Howard, a tough burglar who hung out in the area. Howard shoved a gun into Guzik's ribs, pushed him up against the wall, and robbed him of $1,500. Guzik went back in and told Capone, who was outraged anyone dared rob him. He ordered three thugs to go around town to find Howard and invite him for drinks at Heinie's Saloon. They found Howard and took him for social drinks at the cigar counter. When Howard was intoxicated, they telephoned Capone. He and an associate walked in and went up to Howard while he was telling Capone's three thugs about his liquor hijacking successes. One gang member called out a friendly "Hello Al!" as Capone's accomplice suddenly grabbed Howard from behind, and Capone pulled a revolver out of his coat, pressed it against Howard's cheek, and shot six times into his face and shoulder. As the robber collapsed dead, the murderers ran out the front door and the witnesses quickly disappeared through the side door. Howard was 28, had a long police record, and lived above his mother's fruit store. The witnesses later told police what happened, but were too afraid to testify against Capone.[91]

The most influential man in Chicago during the early years of Prohibition was Mike Merlo. His family immigrated from Sicily when he was 9 years old and settled in one of the low-income areas where many of the future Prohibition gangsters were growing up. Merlo rejected the street-gang life, and instead developed fine humanitarian values and people-handling skills. A personable family man, he began his career as a laborer and then created 10 major companies. He became the chief spokesman for the needs and concerns of his fellow Italians by developing close ties with the city's top politicians and the gang leaders of every nationality because their political clout impacted the lives of his constituency. His unique leadership status was enhanced a year into Prohibition when he was elected President of the Chicago branch of the Unione Siciliana after labor-union leader and political powerbroker Anthony D' Andrea was murdered. Even through Merlo was legitimate, he won the position over the Sicilian gangsters who coveted it, because he was wiser and more popular.

Merlo believed in the peaceful resolution of conflicts and was strongly opposed to murder or any other violence. Even though his values were counter to Chicago's Prohibition gangsters, he was so revered by the gang leaders of all nationalities that they turned to him to arbitrate their gangland disputes because he was evenhanded and a man of great persuasion. Merlo sat opponents together, decreed there would be no warfare, and pushed them to negotiate territorial peace treaties. As a result, relatively few gangland murders occurred in Chicago during his reign, and those that occurred were between the smaller gangs that fought over the leftovers. What Merlo accomplished in Chicago early in Prohibition, Luciano and his colleagues would successfully do in New York a few years later, after they achieved gangdom's respect for their peace advocacy.

Chicago might have had a very different history if Merlo had lived, but complications from a gland operation on his neck slowly dissipated him. He died five years into Prohibition at age 44, leaving behind his wife and six children. At his home 10,000 mourners passed by his casket. Then a procession of 1,000 cars, 20 filled with floral displays, blocked traffic in the Loop for a hour on their way to the cemetery. The Monsignor's eulogy explained why the funeral crowd had been so large. "His gentle kindness made him loved by all his people." [92]

Every major Prohibition gang leader honored Merlo's peace initiatives except for the megalomaniac Torrio. He was committed to the old-fashioned Sicilian Mafia values of monopoly, domination, murder and vengeance rather than Merlo's ideals of negotiation, compromise, and peace. Torrio accepted Merlo's peace truces with the other large gangs because he was not yet strong enough to go into combat, but he refused peace with the small gangs on the South Side and in the outlying towns who he considered poachers in his territory. He systematically wiped most out during Merlo's reign.

Torrio's biggest opponent was the North Side gang led by the Irish Dion O'Banion who lived in a predominantly Irish district. He and his key aids had been minor burglars and robbers prior to Prohibition. Like Torrio on the South Side, O'Banion manufactured beer and distributed liquor. However, he rarely consumed them, was never late for dinner, and spent the evenings at home. He was liked by some in the community because he was generous with the needy and loyal to friends. But he was also cruel to enemies and greedy. Unsatisfied with his enormous Prohibition profits, he continued with armed robberies and safe cracking and occasionally hijacked booze from competitors. Two years into Prohibition, the police caught him blowing a safe in the Postal Telegraph Building, but juries twice acquitted him. Two years after that, a Detective Bureau squad caught the incorrigible thief transporting 8,000 cases of bonded whisky just stolen from the legal Sibley Warehouse. O'Banion also violently attacked picket lines and bombed businesses, depending on which side in a labor conflict paid him. Finally, he intimidated the 42nd Ward voters who opposed his political benefactors during elections.

On the evening of Merlo's passing, someone called O'Banion's flowershop for a $10,000 funeral wreath to be picked up the next day ($125,000 today). At the appointed pickup time, O'Banion was working in the back room of his shop when three men entered. He came to the front greeting them, "Hello boys. You from Mike Merlo's?" The big man in the middle answered "Yes" as he extended his hand and grasped O'Banion's in a viselike grip. The two outside men fired five shots rapidly into his chest, larynx, and right cheek. He collapsed and one shooter bent over and shot him in the left cheek. The three white chrysanthemums O'Banion had been cutting lay blood red beside his body. The four employees working in the back only saw the three shooters backs as they ran out and leapt into a car. As the driver sped away, three cars pulled from the two curbs to block the width of the street to stop traffic, and a few blocks further three more cars again blocked the whole street. The six drivers stood beside their idling cars until the escaping killers were out of sight, and then they leisurely got back in, tooted their horns, and drove off.[93]

O'Banion had always been extreme wary of strangers and had always refused to shake hands with anyone he was not well acquainted. He always stood with feet apart, hands on hips, and thumbs to the rear ready to draw guns from the three holster pockets in his tailor-made suits. The three pockets were inside the coat under the left armpit, in the outside left coat pocket, and in the front right trouser pocket. To make O'Banion feel comfortable with the men who picked up the floral display, the caller requested it for Merlo's viewing, and a man called shortly before the attack for confirmation the wreath would be ready at the appointed time, while expressing his great concern he honor Merlo in a timely manner. The killers correctly assumed that O'Banion's deep respect for Merlo would make him believe no one would disrespect him by violating the truce before Merlo's body was interred. This allowed one of the killers to apply the powerful hand grasp that denied O'Banion the opportunity to reach for any of his guns. As the 32-year-old O'Banion laid in state at the funeral chapel, his ambidextrous gun hands clutched a rosary. A priest denied him last rites and a church funeral by explaining, "A person who refuses the ministrations of the church in life need not expect to have the ministrations of the church in death." [94]

Police Chief Collins announced, "Chicago's arch criminal is dead." He testified to the Inquest Jury that O'Banion had committed seven murders, had been a robber and hijacker, and had an evil temper. All this made many possible murder-motives equally plausible. Two early suppositions by the press were that Torrio found out that O'Banion had set up the police raid on the Sieben Brewery, in which both O'Banion and Torrio were arrested, and also double-crossed Torrio in an alleged sale of the brewery to him. However, both hypotheses were untrue. [95]

The facts are that the two gang leaders were partners in the large Sieben Brewery where they produced the beer that Torrio distributed in south Chicago and O'Banion disseminated in the northeast. Six months before O'Banion's murder, 30 policemen burst into Sieben and arrested 29 underlings along with Torrio and O'Banion, who were working in unison side by side. The police closed the Brewery, but the two partners soon reopened the facility as the Milk Maid Brewery. Thus, it is nonsense that O'Banion ever sold his share of Sieben to Torrio and then created the raid to hurt his former partner because the Sieben partnership continued on as Milk Maid.

As a result of the raid, Torrio later did go to jail, but if O'Banion had been alive he would have gained nothing because the murderous Capone would have stepped forward to represent Torrio's interest. Besides, Torrio went to jail because of a plan by reform Mayor Dever and his honest Police Chief Collins. These two officials were after all the gangsters including O'Banion and were never criminal allies of any of them.

In realty, Torrio and O'Banion had never threatened each other and were on excellent terms despite the inevitable disagreements that occur between two aggressive competitors. Torrio and his gang's leaders all bought very expensive floral displays from O'Banion for high-profile gangland funerals, and key O'Banion gang members hung out at Torrio's Four Deuces speakeasy and casino deep in his territory. O'Banionites came in unarmed and drank heavily with their backs turned to Torrio's shooters. Clearly, neither feared or distrusted the other.

It became popularly believed in gangland that Angelo Genna was the assassin who grasped and immobilized O'Banion's gun hand that fateful morning. This treacherous act stood out because it was the first time a gun hand was clasped in supposed good fellowship to immobilize a victim. Eight months later Genna's involvement in O'Banion's murder seemed to be confirmed, when two men walked up to Angelo's brother Tony and grabbed his gun hand before shooting him to death. Because of Angelo's involvement, some writers about early organized crime believed the conflict was over Torrio's allies, the Sicilian Genna brothers. Their territory was a small Italian enclave surrounded by O'Banion's vast Irish territory. But Merlo had successfully negotiated a peace treaty to stop encroachments into each other's territories that the three parties were honoring until the moment of Torrio's sneak attack against O'Banion.[96]

Crime writers also typically make Frankie Yale the primary O'Banion shooting suspect because he has always been the prime suspect in the killing of Torrio's uncle Joe Colosimo in Chicago, and he had employed Capone in his late teens as a bouncer and bartender in his Harvard Inn. But Yale, as the Unione Siciliana national leader in New York City, arrived in Chicago two days after the O'Banion shooting to attend the funeral of Unione Chicago branch President Merlo. No evidence was ever uncovered that Yale arrived prior to the murder.

O'Banion's gangland murder actually resulted from an argument over morals. While his killing set off a long-term conflict between the two gangs that became known as the "beer war," it started as a disagreement over the morality of prostitution. Torrio's primary business was pimping, so he had proposed placing brothels in O'Banion's North Side territory and giving him a cut of the profits. O'Banion always bragged that what separated him from Torrio was his vocal denunciation of any man taking money from a woman. Thus, O'Banion was deeply offended by the proposal. Torrio tried to address this objection with his next offer to operate North Side brothels by not having O'Banion profit from them. Instead he offered to trade O'Banion the right to sell beer in some of his territories, but O'Banion would not allow any one to exploit women in his terrain. His strong idealistic conviction cost him his life. The resulting gang war may have started over brothel territory and it was popularly believed to have been fought over beer terrain, but it was actually a long-term ongoing battle for leadership of the Unione Siciliana Chicago branch.

Immediately after O'Banion's murder, the Cook County Sheriff and the various city Police Chiefs darkened all vice in the County for a few days. When these dens reopened, it was anything but business as usual. Peacekeeper Merlo was gone, Torrio had violated the peace treaty without warning, and O'Banion's successor "Hymie" Weiss swore vengeance for his fallen leader. Weiss was a Polish Catholic who was baptized Earl Wajciechowski before his family shortened their last name. With both sides at war footing, the peaceful streets of Chicago were about to be turned into one big shooting gallery. During the last year of Merlo's life, Chicago had 11 bootlegger killings, and this number included the deaths of O'Banion and others in the ensuing gang war. The next year 43 were killed and the death toll increased in the following years as the conflict intensified.

Following O'Banion's funeral, the leaders of both gangs left town for a month and a half. The North Siders could not retaliate until Torrio lieutenant Capone returned. North Siders soon fired at him but the bullets missed their mark. Police heard rumors about the shooting and called Capone's home to find out if he had been shot or killed. His cryptic answer was, "Greatly exaggerated." Three weeks later Capone's chauffeur was driving through an intersection when his car was riddled with 30 machinegun bullets. All missed the three occupants except one that went through the chauffeur's clothing to sear his buttock flesh while he was driving. Capone was not in the car. During the next year and a half, the North Siders made 10 more recorded attempts to kill Capone, but all failed.[97]

Reform Mayor Dever cleverly had directed the Sieben Brewery raid so leader Torrio would face a much bigger criminal problem than the other defendants. First, the Mayor had his honest Police Chief Collins select officers from outlying precincts because he knew the local district police were protecting the brewery. Sure enough, when the raid occurred, the district's Police Sergeant and three cops were standing guard and were arrested. While the local violation was a minor fine, the Mayor, in a highly unusual move, had the Police Chief turn Torrio over to the U.S. Attorney for prosecution, because this was his second federal Prohibition offense and required jail time. A year earlier Torrio had pled guilty to operating a beer brewery in West Hammond and paid a $5,000 federal fine. The Federal Judge in the Sieben raid said Torrio and the deceased O'Banion were the chief conspirators of the 31 men arrested and sentenced Torrio to nine months, giving him 30 days of freedom to arrange his affairs.

One week later a car with three men drove on the far side of the street past Torrio's apartment building and turned at the corner to their right and parked. The occupants remained sitting inside for a half hour until Torrio's chauffeur-driven car pulled up and parked in front of his apartment. Torrio got out and was collecting the parcels the couple had purchased, as his wife Anna walked toward the steps. At that moment two men jumped out of the surveillance car. One ran to the front of Torrio's car and opened fire with a .45-caliber pistol wounding the chauffeur in the knee. The other attacker with a shotgun sent a charge of buckshot, through the rear missing Torrio. He dropped the parcels and ran toward his front door. Both assailants fired again. A pistol bullet hit Torrio in the arm, and he spun around to face them while trying to pull out a pistol. Shotgun slugs broke his jaw and struck him in the chest. Torrio slumped to the sidewalk, and the goon with the pistol reloaded to finish the job. But something frightened the two attackers, and they fled to their car and sped away.

Anna dragged her prone husband to the building's vestibule and attempted to stop the flow of blood. A motorcycle cop heard the shots, saw Torrio's condition, and hailed a passing cab to take him to the hospital. Hearing the news, Capone rushed to the hospital in tears. The next day surgeons removed the five slugs and worked on Torrio's shattered jaw that prevented him from speaking. There were a number of witnesses, but only a 17-year-old neighbor boy would or could identify O'Banion lieutenant George "Bugs" Moran in a lineup as the first of the two men to jump from the car and fire a revolver into Torrio. The judge freed Moran while the police sought more evidence and the case died there. All the gangs had bought off the police, prosecutors, and judges.

For two weeks Torrio recovered in the hospital with his fever spiking dangerously high. When he went before a federal judge he was weak and begged him to let him go directly to jail instead of enjoying the 30-day stay and to be placed in any county jail but Cook's. He was clearly a terrified gangster and the judge had him taken directly to the Waukegan Lake County Jail. His cell soon had a special large bed, a thick carpet, and a dresser. He quickly installed a bullet-proof mesh screen outside each window with opaque shades inside to hide his location in the cell. He paid the salaries of two deputy sheriffs for the duration to protect him from assassins inside the jail.

Upon his release, he turned his gang over to Capone, retired, and took a vacation to Italy with a long sojourn in Paris before settling back in New York, never to return to Chicago except when subpoenaed by a grand jury. Torrio was accompanied on his European vacation by bodyguard James Genna, who also feared assassination by O'Banionites. While Torrio had served his jail time, three of Genna's brothers had been killed, two in retaliation by O'Banionites and one in a battle with police.

Torrio needed protection from others because he admitted he had never fired a gun. He easily ordered others to kill anyone in his way, but he deserted an empire, in which he could have afforded as many bodyguards as he wanted, because of cowardice. Torrio spoke quietly and did not appear threatening, but he was the most expansionist and murderous of all the Prohibition gangsters. His insatiable greed and hunger for power, combined with his lack of concern about how many people might get hurt, led him to set off the bloodiest era of gangland war the country had ever seen. He apparently never considered that he could be one of its earliest casualties. After he fled, his gang's successor leaders would systematically murder the heads of the competing Chicago gangs over the next decade to make his former gang the only one left standing.

A decade after abandoning Chicago, Torrio was a principal in a large White Plains, New York moonshine ring. He was arrested for affixing counterfeit internal revenue stamps on illicit booze, but he was never convicted. Three years later he pled guilty to income tax evasion and spent 30 months in prison. After parole he lived a quiet life and died of a heart attack in a barbershop chair at age 75.[98]

CAPONE AFTER TORRIO

Torrio had introduced rampant killing to Chicago's gangland, and as he departed the city for good, he turned his vicious gangsters over to Capone to continue his ambitious and sinister master plan of total dominance over the city's underworld and overworld. Capone was an overweight gluttonous slob who was one of his own best customers. He drank, gambled, and whored in his own joints, contracting gonorrhea probably in one of his brothels. Except when angry, his soft spoken and mild, pleasant manner was not particularly scary, but whatever mood he was in had better be the mood of every one around him. He never belonged to a Mafia organization, but he behaved as if he were Chicago's boss of bosses. If anyone frustrated him, he ordered them killed. And not just other gangsters, but people whom almost every other notorious Prohibition gangster would never consider harming - politicians, police officers, prosecutors, government employees, IRS investigators, legitimate businessmen, newspapermen, and even innocent everyday citizens who had the bad luck to sit on trial juries, vote on election day, or get in the way of a hit.

Not long after the shooting of Torrio, Capone applied for a $50,000 life insurance policy ($12 million today). He listed his occupation as "dealer in antiques," which is not rated by insurance companies as particularly hazardous. It was easy for the actuary to deny the gangster, but pity the plight of the sales agent who had to inform Capone in person that his company did not consider it very likely he would be around the following year to make the second annual payment.

Capone loved the limelight and talking to reporters. He especially liked the reporters who accused him most strongly in print of being a murderer. Every time he was called a killer, it increased his fearsome image and his income. He always gave the press phony, sophomoric defenses for his crimes, but one of his sayings became famous - "It's bootleg when it's on the trucks, but when your host hands it to you on a silver tray, it's hospitality."

Capone found it fun to talk to reporters about crimes in which law enforcement could not prove he was involved, but he could not tolerate factual exposes about his illegal activities. One of the few courageous voices to protest against Capone was Robert St. John, the young idealistic publisher of the *Cicero Tribune*, a small weekly newspaper that reported on Capone's criminal operations with the intent of driving him out of town. St. John refused to be silenced by harassment and intimidation of his paper's advertisers by law enforcement and other city agencies.

St. John wrote an expose of Cicero allowing the reopening of wide-open gambling and booze and of Capone opening the new Stickney Inn less than a mile away, where 117 girls plied their trade. That night four of Capone's thugs and his brother Ralph spent the night drinking and celebrating their newfound success at the Inn. The drunken brutes were speeding back to the Hawthorne Hotel where they all lived when they spotted St. John walking toward his office. Angry over the article publicizing their new illegal Stickney brothel, they leapt out and beat the newspaperman senseless. St. John recalled in interviews, "They gave me a real working over. The butt ends of revolvers and blackjacks, but the interesting weapon that they used was a cake of soap stuffed into a knitted woolen sock. This was one of Capone's favorite murder instruments, because they hit the base of the skull in the back of the neck. They could kill a person." "Then they left me for dead at the side of the road." Though badly hurt, St. John survived. Al Capone paid St. John's hospital bill before he was released and offered to pay him for his damages, but St. John did not want Capone's blood money beyond selling him his paper so he could leave town. He went on to have a fine career in TV reporting and book writing.[99]

Soon after Capone's takeover of the gang, detectives raided his liquor-sales office, arresting Frank Nitti and six of his accountants and seizing the extensive accounting ledgers of Capone and Guzik that they were after. These contained the names of who they bought from, sold to, and bribed. Unfortunately, the detectives did not turn these records over to the U.S. Attorney before a local Municipal Judge impounded them the next day and secretly handed them back to Capone. The U.S. Attorney told the Judge how important inspection of these records was for their pending bootlegging case, but he had no power over the local judge except to complain about his outrage. This was a tragic blow to federal law enforcement who probably could have imprisoned Scarface within a year.[100]

Shortly after the Cicero election riots, an earnest young minister, Henry Hoover, organized a small group of concerned citizens to drive Capone out of the western suburbs. These were family men who spent what available time they could spare gathering evidence about the wide-open operation of brothels and casinos in Cicero and Stickney, but these village's administrations refused to act on their complaints. After a year of such frustration, this group was assisted by the American Legion to secure a search warrant and obtain a constable to escort them in a raid of Capone's Cicero casino and horserace book on a busy Saturday afternoon during the Kentucky Derby. This raiding party first drove out the bettors and then spent two hours carting out the gambling paraphernalia into a truck for demolition. While they were emptying the place, Capone was woken up and the agitated gangster rushed down to the casino unshaven and with his trousers only partially covering his pajama bottoms. One of the minister's raiders blocked Capone at the entrance door, and the gangster admitted, "I'm the owner of this place. Why don't you fellows lay off me?" Capone tried to negotiate with the minister by offering bribes and even the closure of his Stickney brothel for peace, but the pastor stood firm that all vice must go. Then Capone toughened and warned, "You've made your last raid." That is when Capone's associates hit several raiders in the face with brass knuckles, breaking one man's nose.

In the days after the raid, Capone thugs approached several raiders at their homes and terrorized them with verbal threats. This did not deter Hoover's investigator, who kept visiting Capone's casinos and brothels to record eye-witness evidence. This led Capone's thugs to confront the investigator in front of his home garage and savagely beat him up. A neighbor had become alarmed by the strangers hanging around waiting for the investigator to come out and he had called police. As they showed up, the scared goons took off. No one doubted that the goons were planning to kill the investigator. Scarface's goons set other raiders' homes in Stickney aflame. They twice bombed the Chicago home of another crusading minister eight months apart, but neither blast injured him or his family members.

Minister Hoover's daring actions seemed to have had little effect. The Capone casino and horserace book that was closed by the crusading raiders was back in full swing within hours, and then Capone's gangsters terrorized this brave group of citizens into crushing submission. But what appeared to be a total defeat at the time would actually produce amazing results years later. No one realized then that this small valiant band of crusaders had gathered up the essential proof needed to end the criminal career of Capone. They acquired the only evidence the government would ever find that proved the well-shielded Capone owned vice dens, and overcoming great fear, they would someday face the glaring faces of Capone and his gangsters in court to present the testimony and evidence that would finally bring him down.[101]

Capone viciously crushed crusading newspaper publishers and citizen activists to safeguard his remaining territorial strongholds in Cicero and the surrounding rural towns after reform Mayor Dever closed the gangsters' illegal brothels, casinos, and horse books within Chicago's borders. Capone tried to make up for this lost vice revenue from the Windy City market by expanding his share of the beer market in South Chicago. He attacked the small distribution gang of Ed "Spike" O'Donnell and his four brothers whose territory was an enclave located further south in Chicago than any other competitor. This assault was provoked by Spike encroaching outside his established area by terrorizing speakeasy operators into switching beer distributors and by hijacking Capone trucks. This resulted in a two-year beer war until Spike's brother Walter was killed and Spike sued for peace with Capone, who accepted. The war may have ended in a draw, but it was very costly to Capone because the ongoing murders prompted Mayor Dever to order the police to halt booze running in Chicago and to revoke more than 2,000 licenses of so-called soft drink parlors that fronted speakeasies. With this action Mayor Dever and his Police Chief effectively closed all gangland vice in the Windy City despite the corruption of many in the police department and the total sellout by Prosecutor Crowe. Several government and press investigations found that during Mayor Dever's tenure, the only vice operations were outside the city limits, where Cook County State's Attorney Crowe and a succession of corrupt sheriff's allowed unrestricted speakeasies, brothels, and gambling.

Organized crime has never been more powerful in America than during Prohibition, and crime writers and Hollywood have shown the huge Chicago gangs of Capone, O'Banion, and others to be totally dominant. They present these gangs as having total control over the entire society. Yet when one determined reform Mayor with one honest Police Chief went after all these syndicated gangs, they quickly drove them completely out of town. There is no better example of how strong America's state and municipal laws are to completely wipe out organized crime if the elected officials and law enforcement are honest, dedicated, and work in concert.[102]

Torrio had started another long ongoing war after he was ousted from Chicago and moved into Cicero. His ultimate goal of monopoly was frustrated by an assortment of underworld leaders who had already divvied up every type of crime in the village. Torrio's first target was Klondike O'Donnell, whose gang controlled Cicero's beer distribution, but this was put on hold because he was an O'Banion loyalist, Torrio's major North-Side opponent. O'Banion avoided war with Capone by having Mike Merlo negotiate a beer-brewery partnership between Torrio and O'Banion and a treaty for exclusive rights for each gang to specific territories in Cicero and Chicago. A year later Torrio had O'Banion killed and then abdicated his power to Capone, who continued the systematic extermination of North Siders and their allied gangs. One night Capone's goons were roaming Cicero's streets and spotted the car of one of Klondike's gang members. As the three occupants got out of their car to enter a bar, the Capone car pulled up alongside and machinegun sprayed all three to death on the sidewalk. Two were Klondike gang members, but the third was 27-year-old star Assistant Prosecutor William McSwiggin. The resulting newspaper exposes revealed the shameful malfeasance of State's Attorney Crowe's homicide prosecutors.

Upon his death, Prosecutor McSwiggin's illustrious professional image was exposed to be a carefully crafted sham. He was renowned as "the hanging Prosecutor" for racking up death sentences in nine murder trials in less than a year, but no one had noticed that none of these trials was against a gangster. In cases against gang members, McSwiggin's pathetic prosecutions successfully freed them through acquittal or reversal by the appeals court. His most shocking defeat came in the death-penalty case against one of the two gangsters who were killed alongside him. It turned out that the Prosecutor and the hoodlum had been friends from childhood, and McSwiggin saw to it that his friend walked despite a strong case. State's Attorney Crowe was so beholding to Capone that he had no sense of loyalty on behalf of his slain "star" prosecutor, as Crowe surreptitiously prevented murder indictments from being issued by the grand juries he officially called.

Despite the disturbing revelations about McSwiggin's friendships with gangsters and his horribly pathetic prosecutorial performances against them, the public remained outraged that a prosecutor had been slain. This forced the Sheriff to deputize Chicago policemen to shutter and wreck all of Capone's casinos and brothels in Cicero and the other suburbs. Four months later Cicero finally allowed vice to quietly reopen, but it was only a few weeks before another incident made the village slam Capone shut again.

Shortly after a Capone member shot at but missed North Sider lieutenant Vincent "Schemer" Drucci in an intersection, O'Banion's gang, now led by Hymie Weiss, retaliated with a public display of force. An eight-car convoy crawled in front of Capone's Hawthorne Hotel headquarters and residence as three machine gunners in the lead car sprayed the first floor with hundreds of bullets. At the sound of gun fire, every one in the front bar fell to the floor so just two people were wounded. Ironically, one of the wounded was the thug who had shot at Drucci. Minutes before this attack, Capone had departed the hotel. Crime writers have made much speculation about how this attack had some grand strategy, but it was a goofy splashy move that offered virtually no chance of hitting the gang leaders, who were either in their back offices or upstairs apartments.

Three weeks later Capone responded. His machinegunners had rented upstairs apartments on both sides of the street with windows overlooking the street near the gang's flowershop headquarters formerly owned by O'Banion. When successor leader Weiss got out of his car and was just about to walk into the flowershop, Capone's machinegunners fired from the upstairs windows on both sides of the street to kill him only feet from where the former leader had been murdered two years earlier. Only one of Weiss' relatives appeared at the Coroner's Inquest to fill in the basics about his life. His brother Fred told the Jury, "I saw him only once in 20 years." It was at a family reunion celebrating Fred's return from WWI service in France. "That was when he shot me three years ago."[103]

The day before the 1927 mayoralty election, the police were ordered to pick up known trouble makers, especially North Siders because they had already begun a violent campaign against reform Mayor Dever's officials and workers. Drucci had succeeded Weiss as gang leader, and five policeman stopped his car at an intersection and arrested him for carrying a concealed .45-calibre automatic pistol. They took the gangster and his two associates in a large Detective Bureau Car to the Criminal Court Building. Along the way, policeman Dan Healy suddenly shot Drucci three times. At the Coroner's Inquest, Drucci's two associates maintained he was sitting with his hands in his lap and had not provoked the policeman. The five policemen claimed that Drucci reached for Policeman Healy's gun, but it is impossible to reconcile this assertion with their seating locations in the back of the vehicle, based on all the witnesses' testimonies. It was never explained how Healy could have been in danger or why he needed to shoot the unarmed suspect three times to back him away.

As soon as Drucci was shot, the five cops ensured his death by driving first to an emergency room to have the three profusely bleeding bullet holes dressed and then driving him to another hospital to have the bullets removed. At the second hospital, Drucci was pronounced DOA. No one asked the obvious question - how much did Capone pay for this police assassination of his gangland opponent? On election day, the police braced for trouble with an unprecedented 5,100 men standing watch at the city's 2,394 precinct polling places and patrolling the city, but the city's gangsters understood that this was murder by cop and were afraid they were all under police attack. This resulted in Chicago's only non-violent election during Prohibition. Not a single thug or gun toter made an appearance near any polling place that day.[104]

Reform Mayor Dever's reelection opponent was former Mayor Thompson, whose reputation was so bad he had decided against running for reelection against Dever four years earlier. Thompson was the rotten essence of greed and dishonesty. He would die with $1.5 million in unaccounted for cash in his safe deposit boxes ($18 million today), and he once lost a lawsuit for having pocketed $73,000 that he had raised on behalf of the Red Cross for victims of the 1927 Mississippi flood. As the state's top investigator concluded, "A huge amount of money was needed to defeat Dever, who was honestly trying to stop crime and prevent gang rule." To defeat Dever's reelection campaign, Capone gave a $250,000 cash contribution to Thompson ($3 million today), and the gangster bombed the homes of city officials. Thompson campaigned on a promise for booze and saloons - "When I'm elected, we will not only reopen places these people have closed, but we'll open 10,000 new ones." The public voted for the right to drink and the lawless terrorism that came with it. In addition to wide-open saloons, Thompson allowed brothels, gambling, and 6,000 slot machines to flourish. He proudly proclaimed to the international press that Chicago was the wildest, wickedest town in the world.

After winning, Thompson appointed Capone lieutenant Daniel Serritella to be City Sealer and let him run the Mayor's administration including walking arm in arm with him to meetings, causing most of Thompson's key appointees to resign. Except to preside over City Council meetings, Mayor Thompson never went to City Hall. He instead conducted his business of corruption in his bathrobe in his Sherman Hotel suite, known as City Hall Number 2. The *Chicago Tribune's* attorney filed a taxpayer's suit against Mayor Thompson and won a judgment requiring him to return $2.25 million he and three henchmen misappropriated from the city treasury for themselves. A year into Mayor Thompson's term, Chicago's public voiced its unhappiness about the renewed and unrestricted gang violence with resounding reelection defeats of his two Republican cohorts in lawlessness, County Prosecutor Crowe and Governor Len Small.[105]

In return for Capone's huge election-contribution bribe, Mayor Thompson gave the gangster police immunity for the exclusive right to sell booze and to operate casinos, slots, and brothels south of Madison Street where his territory bumped into the North Siders. During the second year of Thompson's administration, Capone started encroaching on territories north of Madison Street in a conflict that would culminate with the St. Valentine's Day Massacre.

LEADERSHIP OF THE UNIONE SICILIANA & THE MASSACRE

Capone's battle of attrition with the North Siders flared up periodically over several years in what were called the beer wars, but much of this violence and treachery resulted from ambition to possess the presidency of the Unione Siciliana Chicago branch. This prized position was coveted by the leaders of the two most important Windy City Sicilian gangs – the Genna brothers and the Aiello brothers. Each gang controlled crime and politics in one of the city's two Sicilian-Italian neighborhoods. Even though these two small enclaves were encased by the mostly Irish North-Side gang territory, both Sicilian gangs aligned themselves with the Italian Capone on the South Side. These two gangs operated the two major alky-cooking businesses in the city.

When Mike Merlo was the Unione Siciliana Chicago branch's president, he kept peace between the large South-Side and North-Side gangs. After his death, his open position as president was filled with the election of Angelo Genna. He was the leader of the six Genna brothers' gang that controlled the Little Italy colony. Capone supported Angelo's election because he was the assassin who had grasped O'Banion's hand while his two accomplices shot him to death in the flowershop.

Six months after the O'Banion slaying, his North Side gang successor leader Weiss noticed Genna shooters John and Albert Anselmi trailing him. To protect himself and to avenge O'Banion, the next morning Weiss had four goons pump 12 slugs into Angelo Genna. During the following six weeks, police got into a shootout with Angelo's brother Mike, killing him, and then Weiss' North Siders murdered brother Tony using the handshake routine Angelo had done to O'Banion. These three killings caused the three remaining Genna brothers to leave Chicago for good after they turned their gang over to independent Little Italy gang leader and close ally Samuel "Samoots" Amatuna. He also succeeded Angelo as Unione President. Six months later, Amatuna was sitting in his barber's chair when he was shot to death.[106]

Capone's specific motive for having Amatuna killed never surfaced, but Capone's next move destabilized his long-term alliance with the other small Italian-Sicilian colony. Capone had been friends and allies with the enclave's two political powers – Tony Lombardo and Joe Aiello – and he lent the two substantial start-up money to partner in a large importing business and wholesale produce market, Antonio Lombardo & Co. Aiello managed these businesses, and he headed his brothers' large alky-cooking operation. Capone selected his close advisor Lombardo to succeed Amatuna as Unione branch president, devastating Aiello's dream of having the position. The distraught Aiello relinquished his valuable wholesaling investment, went into competition with his former partner, and switched his loyalty to the large surrounding North Side gang now headed by George "Bugs" Moran. Capone soon expressed his displeasure over renewal of gang warfare by sending a car loaded with four goons past the front of the Aiello & Co. Bakery to machinegun riddle the windows, mirrors, and furnishings with 200 bullets. New York City gangster Jimmy Blue Eyes told me, "The Chicago group was 'crazy.' Chicago would put a show on. They would have six or seven cars drive by a hotel and spray the place. It accomplished nothing but a lot of press. New York would never do that. The Chicago guys believed New York was the strength."

Aiello plotted to dynamite Capone's headquarters and then to poison him and Lombardo by lacing prussic acid in the grated Parmesan on their pasta at their favorite restaurant, but these plans were leaked to Capone. A total of 13 men were charged in these plots, but the cases against the gang were later dismissed. While none of Capone's enemies was ever able to put a bullet into him, Big Al did shoot himself during this period. After finishing a round of golf one morning, he was getting into his car and somehow managed to discharge the .45-caliber pistol in his right hip pocket. The bullet plowed through the fleshy part of his right upper thigh, narrowly missing his abdomen as it passed through his groin and imbedded in his left thigh. Capone was hospitalized, and the four rooms surrounding his room were occupied by 15 bodyguards.

At the height of the bombings and shootings in the North-South gang war, Capone decided to visit Los Angeles with his family and two bodyguards, but LAPD detectives pressured the Biltmore Hotel to kick him out. Capone told the press he wanted to visit cities in other states, but all loudly declared the gangster to be unwelcome. He then bought a palatial estate in Palm Island near Miami and spent most of his time there to escape his legal and gangdom problems in Chicago. Capone's large Miami estate always had a car with gunmen parked at both entrances, and a large contingent of bulky hard-faced bodyguards roamed the house and grounds that had no trees or shrubbery where enemies could lurk. The City of Miami, the State of Florida, and the neighbors tried to oust the gangster as an undesirable resident. The gangster complained that police shadowed him around the clock and trained a searchlight on the front of his house all night, ostensibly to protect his neighbors from an attack by Capone's Chicago enemies. Various types of Miami police harassment and court legal skirmishes went on for the rest of his career.

As Chicago's North-South war continued, number six of the nine Aiello brothers was murdered, so the surviving three brothers padlocked their cheese and bakery business, and fled the city to hide in Buffalo, New York under the protection of Mafia leader Stefano Magaddino, ending their rebellion to Capone.[107]

Frankie Yale was a New York City Masseria division leader and the longtime Unione Siciliana national President. One day on a residential street in Brooklyn, a passing car fired a machinegun fuselage into his new Lincoln, killing him instantly. This was the first use of a machinegun in a New York murder, making the three weapons found in the car abandoned by Yale's shooters the most popular exhibit in the NYPD Police Academy Museum of archived evidence. The revolver in the car was traced to a purchase by Capone at a Miami pawn shop. Capone would never have challenged the two largest Mafia gangs in their home territory, and Joe the Boss Masseria would have gone after the culprit who took out his important division leader and surrogate national leader of the Unione Siciliana, but he ignored Yale's killing. Capone clearly did this as a favor for Masseria, but the conflict between the Boss of Bosses and his subordinate was never uncovered. The NYPD also had no explanation for three serious attempts on Yale's life during the four years prior to his killing.

Eight years later, NYPD detectives were sure they had figured out the case, but the evidence supporting this claim was never released to the public for evaluation. When the Brooklyn DA requested that President Roosevelt return Lupo the Wolf to prison to serve out his long sentence, the DA included minutes from a NYPD departmental trial of a detective. It concluded that Lupo the Wolf had Capone kill Yale to take over his rackets in the Bath Beach-Coney Island district of Brooklyn, especially over the area's bakeries. Lupo had been Masseria's boss and appointed him his successor, but Yale had been Masseria's Unione Siciliana national leader, so even if this supposition is true, we would need far more facts to understand the motive and politics involved in the Yale murder.[108]

If there is truth to this scenario, it means the treachery between these closely-knit associates is staggering. Just Capone's involvement in killing Yale demonstrates that there is no limit to gangland betrayal. After all Yale had gotten his employee Capone the position with Torrio that ultimately made him Chicago's biggest gangster, and then as a favor to Capone, Yale had killed Torrio's uncle Colosimo. Capone repaid these two huge favors by killing his benefactor as a goodwill gesture to Yale's boss Masseria.

While the Aiello brothers hid in Buffalo under Magaddino's protection, Joe Aiello continued to aspire to lead the Unione Siciliana Chicago branch, a goal his new North Side ally Bugs Moran also wanted for his Sicilian comrade. Aiello moved forward by having Capone's surrogate, Unione President Lombardo, murdered. Then four months later, Moran had Capone's successor representative, Pasqualino Lolordo, killed by his best gunners, the brothers Peter and Frank Gusenberg and Moran's brother-in-law James Clark. The repeated killings of Capone's surrogate presidents intensified the friction towards a showdown. Joe Lolordo demanded vengeance for the deaths of both his brother, Pasqualino, and for his predecessor, Lombardo, who Joe Lolordo had failed to protect as his bodyguard four months earlier. "Machinegun" Jack McGurn was Capone's primary enforcer and bodyguard, and he supported Joe Lolordo's rage because McGurn had somehow miraculously survived three up-close machinegun sprayings by Moran's lethal trio. He was seriously shot in one of them, and several bullets passed through his hat in another (details in Chapter 13).[109]

McGurn earned the nickname "Machinegun" because he became its leading user in resolving Capone's many gangland disputes. The first machinegun went into production months before Prohibition began. It was called the Tommy Gun because it was the World War I brainchild of General John T. Thompson, who was U.S. Army Acting Chief of Ordinance. He wanted to develop an automatic rifle for trench fighting, but the conflict ended before he finished his weapon. After the war Thompson began manufacturing it, intending it for the military and law enforcement, but its potential to spray nearby innocent civilians made it too powerful a weapon for law enforcement to use in trying to control crowds or in gun battles against pistols. However, this weapon turned out to be a gangster's dream – light and concealable, with awesome firepower. In addition to Chicago's gangsters, it became the preferred weapon of the successive Midwestern Public Enemy Number 1 bank robbers of the early 1930s. These bank robbers' and the Chicago gangs' use of machineguns forced many law-enforcement departments to carry them to match these criminals' firepower. The FBI began purchasing them following the Kansas City Massacre. This is a little known incident today, but it was the most shocking crime of its time, as four lawmen were slaughtered and two more wounded, with half of these six being FBI agents. Public outrage led Congress to transform the FBI from an accounting agency of government funds into a secret national police force. All the gangster and law enforcement machinegun purchases combined were relatively small, so the Thompson Company's initial inventory was not exhausted for two decades until World War II, when the world's armies started buying the weapons in substantial quantities. After that, war sales again lagged, but then markets developed from right-wing domestic American extremists and foreign drug-smuggling criminal gangs.[110]

Returning to McGurn's criminal career, he was born on Chicago's Near South Side and became a tough prize fighter. He whipped every amateur fighter, but his manager Emil Thiry later said, "He bowled over the bums of the ring by the dozen. But every time he got up against a real good boy with a heart, he was knocked over and laid there kicking." Thiry finally told him to quit because "When you get a set-up, you fight like a champion, but when the going is tough, you're yellow." With the advent of Prohibition, McGurn joined a neighborhood beer-running gang and moved up to lead Capone's large contingent of bodyguards and to become his boss' side-by-side companion in public.

With McGurn's forces protecting him, Big Al resided and made his headquarters at the Metropole Hotel, where he was registered as "Mr. Ross." He lived in a five-room suite, and the four surrounding suites were reserved for 24-hour bodyguards, frequent guests, and offices. Three or four guards always lived in Capone's suite and one stood outside his front door surveying all passersby. Then Capone took over the third floor of the Lexington Hotel, where his henchmen guarded the lobby, the elevator, and stairway around the clock. No one got to the third floor until their identity was verified, and once there ,they had to go through four rooms of Machinegun McGurn's guards for friskings for guns and approval. Capone had the eight suites on the floor. He lived in the finest one, which housed his bedroom, office, and lounge. The other suites were occupied by his bodyguards. When Mayor Dever drove Capone out of Chicago, Big Al moved his residence and headquarters to Cicero.

McGurn was also Capone's favorite executioner. Chicago police rated McGurn the city's worst killer. Thus, police selected him as the first criminal to be tested for insanity and low-grade mental ability to see if he could be incarcerated in a mental asylum. The police used the insanity tests to try to humiliate the gangsters out of town, but McGurn merely complained to the press that the building blocks, puzzles, and drawings "made me as nutty as a fruitcake." Six years later police again chose McGurn for the first test of the new "criminal reputation" vagrancy law that was intended to stop Prohibition's "mad dog" gunmen. They charged him with being a habitual criminal, and it took a jury just 19 minutes to find him guilty. This was McGurn's first conviction in a state court, but the Judge immediately sentenced him to the maximum six months. Months later the Illinois Supreme Court declared the law invalid because "there must be proof that he is in fact an habitual criminal." The Supreme Court accepted the defense attorneys' contentions that the state must prove wrongdoing, not merely reputation, and the burden of proof should not be placed on the defendant.[111]

McGurn paid a visit to Capone in Miami where he had been living for some time. McGurn was seeking approval to finally have it out with Moran's North Siders and to obtain the cash to pay the hit team during the planning and preparation. McGurn wanted vengeance against the three Moran shooters who had come close to killing him three times. He also presented Joe Lolordo's demand for vengeance against these three shooters over the murder of his brother Pasqualino. Capone had his own long list of grievances against Moran that extended well beyond the slayings of his two Unione Siciliana leaders. Ever since Torrio had shattered the peace with the killing of O'Banion, both the North and South Siders regularly encroached into each other's territories, attacking each other's members, hijacking each other's beer and liquor convoys, and muscling in on each other's speakeasy clients and casino operations. Capone was the more sophisticated at this. He bribed telephone company employees to tap competitors' lines to learn when their trucks would roll and also learned the identities of their speakeasy customers so he could strong-arm them, as learned by the IRS during an investigation.

Capone and Moran were also competing with dog tracks and in the dry-cleaning business. Two Moran goons had killed a Capone union leader who headed the Laundry and Dye House Drivers and Chauffeurs' Union. Moran was also challenging political control of the Bloody 20th Ward in Capone's South Side, which would have meant Capone would have no political or police support to protect this district from penetration by Moran booze sellers. Capone had finally established a monopoly on crime in the South Side, so he approved the attack to protect his current territory from continuing incursion and to make possible major expansion into the North Side.

Capone had close ties with the notorious and murderous Egan's Rats gang in St. Louis, Missouri. They were his chief source of out-of-town killers when he did not want either the gangland targets or possible witnesses to recognize approaching men as Caponites. From the Rats gang, Capone had absorbed Claude Maddox as a division leader to establish a beachhead and headquarters at the Circus Café, which was wedged between Capone's two biggest North-Side enemies, the Aiello brothers in Little Sicily and Moran's North Siders. To give Maddox strength, Capone assigned two enforcers, Machinegun McGurn and his driver Tony Accardo (who would head the Chicago gang during the early development of the Las Vegas Strip). McGurn and Accardo were once arrested in a taxicab for carrying concealed weapons. McGurn frequently ventured into Moran's territory to shake down bookmakers for protection payoffs and beat saloonkeepers to force them to buy Capone's beer. Moran finally struck back against McGurn's incursions into the North Side. McGurn was the combination manager, bouncer, and bookkeeper of the casino in the back of Barsotti's Restaurant until Moran had it bombed while it was closed. Moran also had the intruder to his territory sprayed with machinegun bullets three times.[112]

Capone approved McGurn's attack and continued to remain far from the action in Miami for a long stay. McGurn returned to Chicago to call a council of war at Maddox's Circus Café. Maddox brought in two of Egan's Rats to rent the front apartment across the street from a Moran beer-truck garage that was a favorite meeting place of the gang leaders. For a week, the pair watched for Moran and his key aides to rendezvous. They observed each man who entered the garage and compared his facial features to a picture of Moran. Then one day, seven of Moran's associates entered the garage individually. From the distance, the watcher at the window apparently mistook the seventh man, Moran's lieutenant Al Weinshank, for the boss because the two gangsters had similar physiques and favored tan fedora hats. The watcher telephoned the Café that the gang leader had arrived, and the patiently-waiting seven-man assassination squad swung into action.

The killers had obtained two black Cadillacs that were the same model used by the Detective Bureau for its unmarked squad cars. They equipped both cars with a clanging bell on the running board to look like the real thing. The two fake detective cars left the garage near the Café and took different routes toward the garage so as not to attract undue attention by looking like a raiding team. One of the bogus detective cars carried two men who quietly positioned themselves in the alley behind Moran's garage where the truck entrance was located to kill anyone who tried to run out of the building that way. The five other men drove the second car towards the front office entrance of the truck depot. The three who sat in the backseat wore civilian suits like detectives, while the two in the front seat wore fake patrolman uniforms with brass badges.

When this replica detective car turned onto the street with Moran's garage, it sideswiped a truck but kept right on going causing witnesses in that block to look at the occupants' faces and write down their license plate number. The assassins parked directly in front of the garage's office entrance. The three killers in suits remained sitting in the backseat waiting, as the two men dressed as patrolmen in the front seat got out and walked toward the truck depot door. As they did, the intended target Moran was walking and rounded the corner at the end of the block. Seeing the two patrolmen go in, he assumed he was looking at a standard Prohibition harassment police raid, so he turned around and walked back to his home a few blocks away.

The two bogus uniformed patrolmen ordered the seven men drinking coffee to line up facing the brick wall with their hands above their heads like this was a routine arrest and weapons' frisk. As Moran's men calmly complied, the three killers in the back seat of the car walked in, pulled out from beneath their overcoats two machineguns and a shotgun, and let go a withering fuselage of hundreds of bullets. One machinegunner sprayed the seven men from left to right while the other machinegunner went from right to left. One aimed at their heads, and the other at heart level. They reversed directions with one aiming at their butts and the other at their knees. The third killer fired a shotgun into the heads of two fallen victims who must have seemed to still be alive. Confident all seven victims were dead, the five assassins walked away from the flowing river of blood towards their parked car. The three shooters in suits put their hands up in the air like they were under arrest, as the two uniformed patrolmen took their machineguns and directed the three into the back seat of the car to make it appear this was an arrest. Then the five drove off. This was gangland's bloodiest slaughter, and it was quickly dubbed the St. Valentine's Day Massacre.

Both fake police cars were soon found. The ownership of both was traced to people associated with Capone. The first was torched and burned to destroy ownership identification, and the second had only the hood and radiator wrecked by a feeble bomb, so the red notebook belonging to a Massacre victim containing gang business records would not be damaged. The book had likely been laying on the coffee table at the Massacre scene, and Capone's goons placed it in the car to cast suspicion that Moran had killed his own disloyal men to counter the public-relations beating Scarface was taking in the press and public opinion. After the Massacre, both Moran and Capone told the press that only the other killed liked that.

The purpose of Moran's meeting was never discovered. Folklore has it that a man called the garage claiming he had hijacked a load of Capone's liquor and wanted to sell it to them, but this is inconsistent with the facts. All but the mechanic were in expensive suits, hats, and overcoats, one wearing a carnation, inappropriate dress for unloading. In addition, they had little cash to conclude the large transaction, and the garage had no room for another truck and storage of liquor cases.

Besides, it is doubtful Moran would have joined his Prohibition crew for the purchase of a single truck load of hooch. In addition, McGurn would not have needed the observation room across the street if he had been able to set up what time the gang leaders would congregate, nor would he have needed the fake police cars to gain entry. The alleged hijack truck driver would have simply pulled into the garage, walked to the back of the truck, and opened the door to display the expected cargo to the waiting un-loaders, allowing the three shooters standing inside to quickly mow them down.

McGurn immediately became the chief suspect because three of the victims had previously and repeatedly attempted to kill him, but he had strategically remained holed up in a hotel suite with his girlfriend having all meals and newspapers delivered. He did not leave once during the two weeks prior to and the two weeks after the Massacre when he was arrested for the murders along with John Scalisi.

Five days after the pair was released on bail, the bodies of Scalisi and two of his close associates were found in an isolated spot in Indiana. The three men were an inseparable trio. Scalisi and Anselmi had been the Gennas' top killers until the surviving brothers left town, and then they joined McGurn's crew guarding Capone and killing for him. Scalisi and Anselmi were almost certainly participants in the Massacre, and they had earlier been freed by corrupt Prosecutor McSwiggin and his successor in what should have been easy death-penalty cases against them for killing two police detectives. The third victim, Joseph Giunta, was Capone's choice to succeed murdered Pasqualino Lolordo as Unione Siciliana President. The victims had enemies galore, but the police never found any motive or clues. It is noteworthy that Capone, who put on a big show of retaliation every time high-ranking gang members were killed, remained silent about the assassinations of these three close associates. The killers must have been angry at these three victims because they took the time to severely beat them with gun butts or baseball bats before finishing them with bullets, and McGurn had a penchant for viciously beating enemies who he perceived to be disloyal. As leaders of the Unione Siciliana and bodyguards to Capone, the trio was always armed and had regular access to Big Al. No one, who has studied this case, ever considered that the native-born Sicilians might have been planning a mutinous coup to take over the gang with the support of Capone's last major opponent, the Aiello brothers, also Sicilian.

While it is all but certain that McGurn was in his hotel room at the time of the Massacre, State's Attorney Crowe's homicide Prosecutor had the judge drop the charges against the St. Valentine's mastermind with the fallacious argument, "We haven't enough on McGurn alone to proceed to trial at this time. If John Scalisi were alive and on trial we could present evidence against both of these men." This is untrue because the only evidence against either man was eyewitnesses, and the death of one defendant did not have any affect on their testimony against the other. Scalisi's murder gave the Prosecutor a reason to free McGurn that sounded legitimate, even though it was irrelevant to the strength of his case. The gangster quickly returned to his violent labor-racketeering endeavors.

McGurn's girlfriend Louise Rolfe so staunchly accounted for his movements on the day of the Massacre and alibied his whereabouts each time he was accused of later crimes that the press nicknamed her "The Blonde Alibi." She whimsically entertained reporters during interviews. For example, when he was arrested for the Massacre, she pointed out the tiny gold bracelet on one ankle "with my name on it, so the police can't lose me." When the State's Attorney dropped charges against McGurn, exasperated federal prosecutors charged the couple with violating the Mann Act for immorally having unmarried sex across state lines during their car trip to visit Capone in Miami after the slaughter. The two-day trial included 60 government witnesses from seven states who confirmed they had indeed cohabitated. The defendants had wed before their trial, but this did not sway the judge, who found them guilty of making love before the ceremony and sentenced him to two years in prison and her to four months in jail. This conviction was reversed by the U.S. Supreme Court because these esteemed justices concluded any immorality was incidental to the trip rather than the purpose for traveling because they had previously cohabitated in Chicago. This ruling redefined the federal crime of having unmarried sex on the other side of a state line to doing if for the first time in a state other than your residence. As silly as this ruling seems in this era of the hookup, it was one of the first major decisions to override the thousands of laws across the country that let governments at all levels imprison heterosexual adults for consensual sex in the privacy of their bedrooms.[113]

Only one other person was charged with the Massacre murders, but this would happen later. Fred "Killer" Burke had been a member of Egan's Rats in St. Louis. At the time of the Massacre, Burke was a fugitive running from bank robbery and murder charges in a half dozen states. After the Massacre, he remained on the run. While he was passing through St. Joseph, Michigan, he had a minor fender bender. A patrolman heard the crash and approached him to issue a traffic ticket when Burke shot him dead and fled. After the horrific slaughter, the fugitive eluded police for two years until an amateur sleuth saw his picture in a detective-story magazine and notified Milan, Missouri police that Burke was living under an assumed name on the nearby farm of his wife's parents. In the middle of the night while every one in the farmhouse was asleep, eight policemen armed with machineguns burst in and took him without resistance. In examining Burke's seized machineguns, it was found that one had fired some of the bullets taken from the Massacre victims, so Chicago detectives showed his photo to the witnesses who saw the fake police cruiser sideswipe a truck as it continued on to Moran's garage. They identified him as one of the two fake uniformed patrolmen because of a missing front tooth. It is believed that Burke led the assault because of his status with the Rats gang and his closeness to Maddox, along with driving the lead vehicle that day.

Of all the jurisdictions that wanted to prosecute Burke, Chicago had the preeminent claim because this was the most shocking slaughter in America's history. The Chicago Prosecutor offered to drop the death penalty if Burke would testify against the planners of the Massacre, but the prisoner rejected the deal. Instead of going ahead and trying Burke on a capital-murder charge as he had publicly announced he was going to do, the Chicago Prosecutor inexplicably and without explanation deferred his right to take Burke to trial to the DA in St. Joseph, Michigan, where Burke was wanted for killing a policeman during a routine traffic stop, a non-death-penalty case.

The only way to make sense out of the Chicago Prosecutor's inconsistent posturing and weird decision is with the following scenario. First, it was well known that successive Chicago Prosecutors had sold out their office to Capone because they never once during their tenures successfully prosecuted any of his major gang members. In addition, this was a jurisdictional or extradition issue, so the Chicago Prosecutor's conflict was with the St. Joseph DA, not the defendant. Still, the Chicago Prosecutor held a private meeting with Burke. Nothing is known about what occurred in that meeting, but hours later the Chicago Prosecutor officially relinquished his right to try Burke and then the prisoner immediately pled guilty to killing the St. Joseph patrolman. If their rapid actions make it seem like they cut a deal, the only explanation is that the Chicago Prosecutor warned Burke that if he ever fingered their mutual employer Capone, his office would institute a death-penalty prosecution against him, but if Burke would plead guilty in Michigan and keep his mouth shut, he would still have the possibility of winning parole some day.

This scenario became more credible when it later became public that Capone's bodyguard Philip D'Andrea, under an alias, accompanied Burke's attorney into his client's cell shortly before the Chicago Prosecutor met with Burke. This meeting ties Capone to Burke's decision making, and it seems pretty evident that it was D'Andrea who offered Burke the deal to have the Prosecutor dismiss the charges for silence, and soon afterwards the Prosecutor met with Burke only to confirm he would indeed honor Capone's deal for possible freedom versus the death penalty. Then the Chicago Prosecutor quickly relinquished his claim and Burke pled guilty in Michigan. Burke was sentenced to life at hard labor. Nine years later, before he had become eligible for parole, he had a fatal heart attack at age 54 in Marquette Prison. During those nine years, he never talked to anyone about any of his crimes.

In the New York City Frankie Yale murder, the NYPD always suspected Capone had ordered it as a favor to some powerful Big Apple gangster. Years later NYPD detectives became convinced that Capone had chosen Burke to take Yale out, just as he had him lead Chicago's St. Valentine's Day Massacre, but the NYPD never revealed to the public the evidence on which their conclusion was based. In another parallel between the two cases, it was in the Massacre case that the infant science of ballistics came of age. But seven months earlier in the Yale murder case, one of the two NYPD detectives who compared the bullets taken from the victim at first misidentified them as having come from one of Burke's machineguns.

Although Chicago detectives had a long list of possible suspects in the atrocious slaughter, they developed strong evidence against only two. In addition to Burke, separate evidence identified Byron Bolton, who had been Burke's chauffeur/bodyguard when he had been with the St. Louis Egan's Rats. In the abandoned apartment the pair had rented to observed the entrance to Moran's garage for a week, detectives found a letter addressed to Byron Bolton bearing a postmark from Virden, Illinois. A Chicago detective went to the return address in the central part of the state and found Bolton's parents living on a farm. The father turned over a picture of his son and Massacre witnesses identified him as one of the men who had rented the death-watch room. This was supported in FBI files by two redacted sources who said Bolton was the lookout who had given the gunmen the premature go-ahead to roll in their fake police car. Detectives also learned that Bolton had purchased a machinegun, and after the slaughter, he had run back to his St. Louis base.

This is apparently where Bolton became associated with the Alvin Karpis and the Barker brothers gang. This gang committed two of the most infamous kidnappings in history of two St. Paul, Minnesota businessmen, William Hamm Jr. and Edward Bremer (detailed in "All Against The Law" by Bill Friedman). Bolton only participated in the second kidnapping, but he was the prosecution's chief witness to send 15 of his underworld pals involved in the two crimes to prison. Bolton's testimony had serious credibility problems, but these men were almost certainly guilty because of corroborating witness testimony. In return for testifying, the Federal Judge reduced Bolton's life sentence to four three-year concurrent sentences, meaning with the time already served of 20 months while he waited to testify and then getting time off for good behavior, he had to serve only a few more months.

As soon as the FBI's arrest of Bolton made the newspapers, the Chicago Police Detective Bureau expressed interest in interviewing him because they revealed they had long suspected him in the six-year-old St. Valentine's Day Massacre in which seven Prohibition gangsters were murdered. Detectives claimed they never issued an arrest warrant because they were afraid of driving him further underground, but he was not wanted by any jurisdiction and thus not a fugitive who needed to hide, so their position made no sense. In addition, the FBI has used the same rationale for keeping secret certain fugitives' indictments because they had no idea where they might be located, but this strategy worked effectively for the FBI because agents continued to quietly follow leads nationwide until they did locate them. In contrast, the Chicago detectives' silence gave them no way to search outside of Chicago, so this subterfuge was a dishonest way of trying to justify simply keeping the case under wraps and letting it die.

When the FBI arrested Bolton six years after the Massacre, the Chicago detectives and Prosecutor should have demanded the prisoner be turned over to them to face a capital-punishment case for the worst butchery of all time, especially since the FBI kidnap charges against Bolton involved neither physical harm to a victim nor the death penalty for the perpetrators. But Chicago law enforcement again remained silent. Three years after the FBI arrested Bolton, he was given federal parole for having been a state's witness, but the Chicago detectives and County Prosecutor failed to prosecute him because they did not want to risk upsetting their gangland masters. Capone's gang had evolved into new leadership, but the key men who directed the Massacre were still in power. Capone's gang had bought and paid for this complete and appalling breakdown of the Chicago justice system.

An odd sense of justice in this case might be found in the fact that the Chicago detectives questioned 22 men suspected in connection with the slaughter and all but two of these died violent deaths. Unfortunately, it is precisely these two that create the terrible sense of injustice because they were the only ones known for sure to be guilty, and they could have been convicted and executed at any time. Instead, Burke died in prison with parole possible if he had lived long enough, and Bolton lived the rest of his life a free man.

Capone clearly initiated the slaughter, but he was never questioned because he was well-alibied in Miami when it occurred. Prosecutors could have only gotten to Scarface and his top aides by going through the two suspects they could have convicted with an executable offense, Burke and Bolton. While Capone may have skated by this hellacious crime, he faced other problems. The wave of civic indignation over the Massacre caused him unintended consequences. Police shuttered his illegal businesses for months, the IRS launched a determined investigation, and the rest of the nation's Prohibition leaders exacted their own retribution. They were disgusted because Capone had aroused national anger that turned public opinion against all bootleggers.[114]

CAPONE'S PHILADELPHIA STAY & BACK IN CHICAGO

Following the St. Valentine's Day Massacre, Luciano called the Atlantic City national crime conference. He wanted to put an end to Capone's violent ways to stem all the negative publicity about his atrocious behavior that was turning the public, politicians, and law enforcement against all bootleggers. A week before the conference, the Young Turk's objections to Capone's violence were compounded by the brutal beating murders of the three Unione Siciliana Chicago branch leaders,

President Giuseppe Giunta and his lieutenants, John Scalisi and Albert Anselmi. When Capone faced the nation's assembled gang leaders, Scarface agreed to lower his press visibility (detailed in Chapter 4).

At the conclusion of the Atlantic City conference, Capone and his bodyguard drove to Philadelphia to board a train to Chicago. Arriving two hours before departure, they went to a movie. As the two gangsters walked out of the theater, they encountered two police detectives who flashed their shields. Capone voluntarily blurted out, "Here's my gun," as he carefully held the barrel and handed the handle of a blunt-nosed .38 caliber pistol to a detective. His bodyguard did the same. This began the swiftest and most bizarre prosecution in history. During the next 15 hours, the two gangsters were arraigned, pled guilty, and were sentenced. All the while, the usually mouthy crime boss stood silent. His bodyguard had to take the fall so he could share Big Al's cell and protect him from the other inmates.

This was Capone's first conviction, but the nation's press and many law enforcers immediately cried "foul" because it was so obvious Capone had framed himself. Then investigative reporters uncovered the following information about the case. Big Al knew the two Philadelphia detectives because three months earlier he had hosted them for dinner at his Miami home and given them tickets to the Sharkey-Stribling fight. The case also had bizarre legal twists. First, the two gangsters voluntarily announced they were carrying concealed weapons even though the police had no grounds to frisk them. Then the pair quickly waived their legal defenses, and their attorneys requested no legal delays and gave no defense. The gangsters even pled guilty without asking for a deal to reduce the maximum sentence. This was especially astonishing since no major criminal had ever been jailed in Philadelphia for the misdemeanor of carrying a concealed weapon.

All this led the country's press to incorrectly assume that Capone set up his arrest and agreed to the long sentence to seek safety from enemies. But this resulted in rumors implying cowardice that damaged Big Al's standing in the underworld. To counteract this bad press, his attorneys and his lieutenants quickly denied these rumors, decried this miscarriage of justice, and immediately began appeals of their guilty pleas. Three appeals were quickly pursued even though it was clear to the legal profession that they were futile because they had entered guilty pleas. The purpose for these appeals was so Capone could announce to the press at his release from prison a strenuous denial that the arrests were planned, "I tried every kind of writ made to get out of prison."[115]

Capone made no other comments to reporters during the entire episode. However, just after he was arrested, he talked for two hours to police officials in the presence of a stenographer. It was after midnight, and he explained that he had just come from the President Hotel in Atlantic City where he had successfully concluded three days of negotiations with Bugs Moran to prevent another bloodbath in Chicago. Capone never discussed any details about the conference or its attendees, so no one realized the assemblage had actually required Capone to take a cooling-off period in jail.

After being imprisoned, Capone proudly showed a reporter his "comfortable" cell. He had chintz curtains on the window, paintings adorning the walls, a beautiful rug covering the floor, a lamp sitting on a polished desk, his personal bed, an easy chair, a chest of drawers, and a finely-finished cabinet radio. The prison allowed inmates no phone calls and just two censored letters a month, but Big Al made long-distance telephone calls and sent telegrams at will. Guards vied to run errands for him and supply him goodies from the canteen. The resulting article embarrassed the warden, who denied everything in it, but he was clearly in Scarface's pocket. When the day for Capone's release arrived two months early for good behavior, a mob of reporters and photographers stood outside Eastern Penitentiary from dawn until sundown. Then this warden came out and laughed at the crowd as he announced that the previous day he had secretly transferred the gangster 30 miles to Graterford Prison, from where he had surreptitiously departed hours earlier.

In response to Capone's release, a hostile Chicago Chief Detective John Stege threatened he would be arrested on sight even if he was not wanted for a specific crime, and Florida's Dade County Sheriff boldly ordered the gangster to stay out of the towns in his jurisdiction because he planned to arrest him. A reporter knocked at the Chicago home door of Capone's mother to inquire what festivities were planned for Big Al's return. His 12-year-old nephew Ralph Capone Jr. told him to go away and he refused to open the door until the reporter dangled a bag of candy to entice him to talk. Upon opening the door, the youngster looked at the bag and blurted, "Say, I won't tell you anything. Another paper sent some people out here to play marbles with me. I won 90¢ from them and didn't tell them a thing." Whereupon he grabbed the bag of candy out of the reporter's hand and slammed the door shut.

This smart-talking wiseguy child had a very difficult life. Ralph Capone Jr. earned a college degree, but he seemed to be stricken with bouts of depression over the impact his family's name had on school, jobs, and girlfriends' lives. The notoriety of his father and his uncle Scarface led him to get permission from the family as a youngster to change his name to Ralph Gabriel. He became a bartender in Chicago at the Trade Winds restaurant, where he was reputed to be a retiring personality, but personable and a hard worker. He was a heavy drinker, and his only conviction was for attempting to burglarize a grocery store, likely for booze late at night. He was placed on probation, but a year later he was arrested for being drunk and was sent to prison on the burglary sentence, for which he served eight months. A year later his infamous father testified about his criminal background before the U.S. Senate Kefauver investigating committee, and Ralph Jr. soon committed suicide with alcohol and cold pills at the age of 33. Nearby his body was a scrawled sheet of paper that was apparently an attempt to write a letter to his girlfriend. At the inquest, a Coroner's physician said he found Ralph Jr.'s internal organs "flooded with alcohol." His father Ralph Capone Sr., Big Al's lieutenant, attended the funeral with other family members after flying from Mercer, Wisconsin where he operated a nightclub. Ralph Jr.'s divorced wife went to court to change the last name from Capone to Gabriel for herself and their 17-year-old son "to give her son a chance in life," according to her attorney.[116]

After Capone was released from the Pennsylvania prison, he remained as loyal and close to Luciano as ever, even becoming a primary supporter of his anti-violence policy. Of course by then Capone had already killed or absorbed many of his territorial opponents. Capone and his successors also continued their strong business ties for the next four decades with Cleveland's Dalitz even through he backed Luciano's move at the Atlantic City meeting. Capone's successors would later partner with Dalitz in building the *Stardust* gambling resort on the Las Vegas Strip, and for years it would be the world's largest hotel and casino.

While Capone had languished in the Philadelphia prison for 10 months, society had changed dramatically as the Roaring '20s dissolved into the Great Depression. Public perception of Capone had changed from being the roguish supplier of a public desire to being the exploiter of the poor and unemployed who wanted escapism through alcohol more than ever, but could no longer afford his inflated prices. The public continued to be appalled by the Massacre, and the IRS had an intense investigation of the gangster underway. In an attempt to win back public opinion prior to possible jury selection, Capone tried to demonstrate solidarity with the working man by proudly announcing the setting up of a free-soup kitchen in the 1st Ward to feed Alderman Kenna's indigent voters. After a few weeks of operating the kitchen, Capone quietly turned its financial burden over to the United Charities with the condition he continue to be named as the sponsor to the public.

Even though Capone now had the city's only major gang, his income was hurt by both Depression unemployment and the racketeer investigation by Criminal Court Chief Justice John McGoorty that kept his key men hidden from sight to avoid subpoenas. Capone's response to this diminished revenue was to further crush the competition. He sent his union racketeers to approach McGoorty and the State's Attorney's Office with a proposal to withdraw from labor crimes in return for being allowed to peddle beer in Chicago unmolested by the law. The Judge and the State's Attorney condemned these overtures to a grand jury and the press, blocking the gangster's plan.

Two weeks later Capone's goons threatened "to blow the heads off" California's grape growers if they shipped to Chicago their new grape-juice concentrate that fermented into wine. But he soon backed down when the U.S. Justice Department approved the new product and offered the grape growers protection. Interestingly, Prohi enforcers did not molest California's wine-grape growers for selling to fermenters. In addition, these grape growers received a sizeable annual federal subsidy for a product destined for illegal use. Capone's thugs soon threatened death to every Chicago fine-liquor distributor who bought from anyone else. His import inventory was piling up in warehouses because it was not only overpriced but also watered down with lots of moonshine. Finally, Capone took advantage of his wholesale beer monopoly by short-pouring each 32-gallon barrel by two or more gallons, thereby raising the cost per glass.[117]

Alfred Lingle was Chicago's premier investigative reporter because of his close contacts with every top law enforcement officer, the leading politicians and officials, and the gang leaders. He wrote exclusive interviews with most of them. One afternoon the *Chicago Tribune* reporter took off from work for some recreation at the racetrack. As he walked into the Illinois Central tunnel at Randolph Street to catch a train, a lone assailant closed in behind him and shot him in the back of the head, killing the 38-year old. Coverage of the Lingle killing rivaled that of the St. Valentine's Day Massacre, and Capone quickly became everyone's favorite suspect because he was the city's dominating gangster and had such a penchant for killing. State's Attorney John Swanson conducted an extensive investigation financed and assisted by Lingle's embarrassed employer, the *Chicago Tribune,* because it wanted the truth unraveled about its ace reporter. He was clearly living beyond his salary, but no hint of its source or any improper activity was ever uncovered. Lingle's tight friendship with Police Commissioner Bill Russell from boyhood forced Lingle to repeatedly deny rumors that gangster acquaintances frequently sought his influence to obtain police protection for their activities. One week after the murder, the insinuations in the press caused Commissioner Russell to resign his position for a demotion to Captain.

On the day of Lingle's killing, a new ownership group planned to reopen Bugs Moran's elegant Sheridan Wave casino, and underlings told police Lingle had demanded a large payment or he would have the police line the curb with a string of squad cars. Leo Brothers was convicted of Lingle's murder by eyewitness identifications, and Brothers just happened to be working as a bouncer in the Green Mill speakeasy whose owners were associates of the new Sheridan Wave partners. Brothers never revealed who had paid him to kill Lingle. It is possible he remained silent because the person who paid him to kill also tampered with his jury. One juror appeared to have been bribed because he refused to vote guilty unless the other 11 exhausted jurors agreed to a 14-year prison sentence instead of life. This was Chicago's only conviction for a gangland slaying during the 14 years of Prohibition.

Capone may not have had anything to do with the Lingle killing, but about that time Scarface did rub out several business associates whom he suspected of disloyalty. Mike de Pike Heitler was a disgruntled brothel employee who sent a letter about Capone's activities to State's Attorney Swanson. Before a case could be developed Swanson's office warned Capone, and Heitler was found burned in his car.[118]

While the Massacre had greatly weakened Capone's arch rival Moran, the ensuing Atlantic City peace conference gave another adversary the opportunity to get back into action. A week after Capone entered the Philadelphia prison, Joe Aiello returned with his wife and children to settle down in the Windy City after 10 months of hiding in Buffalo. He was finally able to achieve his cherished goal and be elected president of the Unione Siciliana Chicago branch. He also ran the Italian wholesale grocery import house he took control of after killing his former partner and Unione President, Lombardo. Joe Aiello ruled with an iron hand, forcing all North Side Italian retailers to purchase their commodities solely from him, especially sugar that was used in large quantities by alky cookers.

Aiello quickly built up his armed forces from among alien Sicilian laborers by offering them big salaries to compensate for the danger of working for him. Aiello was now the strongest opposition to Capone, and he was joined by West Side brothel lord Jack Zuta and the remnants of Moran's gang. Moran's gang had been dissipated by the Massacre because the seven victims were two lieutenants, the three fiercest shooters, the beer-truck mechanic, and an optometrist with a fixation about hanging out with gangsters. The only top Moran members who missed the extermination were his alcohol and gambling leaders. Records show Aiello and Moran became partners in the Fairview Dog Track in Franklin Park, bookmaking, punch boards, and slots. In their Loop headquarters were a half dozen enlarged prints of newspaper pictures showing the outstretched bodies of the seven slaughtered victims. These reminded them of the ever present threat and helped reinforce their hatred of Capone and his murderous crew.

The Aiello-Zuta-Moran gang peacefully co-existed with Capone's gang during Scarface's 10 months in the Philadelphia prison, and this continued for two-and-a-half months after his release. Then a clash of unknown origin escalated into violence. Detectives brought Zuta to the Detective Bureau for questioning, and as he left, he walked into a withering machinegun assassination attempt from which he somehow escaped. He went directly into hiding at a Wisconsin resort, where a month later he was shot to death.

The war escalated, and two months afterwards a worried Joe Aiello went into hiding in the apartment of his Italio-American Importing Company partner and manager. Aiello did not venture out for two weeks, but McGurn either somehow learned he was there or assumed he was. The enforcer planted five machinegun nests behind windows in the adjacent buildings surrounding his partner's apartment building to cover all four exits. Two of these nests were across the street from the front entrance and offset, so they had about a 45-degree angle from both sides of the walkway to be able to follow him no matter where he tried to run. One evening Aiello decided to venture out, so following dinner he asked his partner's daughter to call for a Yellow Cab. As he walked out to the cab, the two machinegun nests in the building across the street riddled him in a deadly crossfire totaling 57 bullets. During the eerie silence that followed, his partner and the taxi driver placed the still conscious man in the cab and raced him to the hospital, where he was pronounced DOA. The inquest conducted the day after the shooting concluded that Aiello was killed by his one-time friend Capone based on their well-known mutual hostility and the modus operandi. Machinegun nests surrounding every escape route from a building was vintage McGurn. With Aiello's gang finished, Moran's gang was no longer strong enough to go it alone against Capone's forces. His gang dissolved and Moran left town for good. He went back to his pre-Prohibition career of burglaries and armed robberies and spent the last decade of his life in prison.

In killing Joe Aiello, Capone eliminated his last major Chicago rival and the President of the Unione Siciliana Chicago branch. This infuriated Aiello's ally, Buffalo's Stefano Magaddino, who was the most senior leader of the Castellammarese clans. In response, Magaddino set off the Sicilian-American War for ultimate power within the American Mafia. It quickly involved the New York City gangs and the other Castellammarese gangs around the country. This thrust the nation's Mafia gangs into a long and violent conflict (details in Chapter 3), while Capone enjoyed this major victory in his ambitious goal of dominating all of Chicago gangland.

Writers about early organized crime invariably claim that Capone was now all-powerful in Chicago, but this was never true. He inherited the south half of the town from Torrio, and then Capone systematically wiped out or absorbed all the gangs in the northeast third of the city, giving him gangland control over two-thirds of the Windy City. This put Capone's boundaries adjacent to the tough little gang of "Terrible" Roger Touhy, who controlled the western two-thirds of the North Side (one-third of the entire city) and part of the western suburbs. Despite Scarface's ambition for total domination and his advantage of many times more shooters, he never challenged this gang, always avoiding territorial conflict and mortal combat with them (see Chapter 15 for after Capone).[119]

The Chicago Crime Commission compiled the names of the city's 28 worst "Public Enemies," attached a short criminal background of each, and sent this list to local law enforcement agencies and the newspapers. The goal was to glare the light of publicity on them and encourage Police Commissioner Russell to harass them in every way possible in an effort to drive them from town. Most Chicago Criminal Court judges were of no help. They failed to enforce the anti-liquor laws because they were either on gangsters' payrolls or opposed Prohibition.

Then five months after the Public Enemies list was issued, politically-ambitious Municipal Judge John Lyle issued each gangster on it a vagrancy warrant. This was the type of harassment the Crime Commission was hoping for. Until each case was ultimately dismissed, these gangsters were arrested and some of their illicit funds were tied up as the Judge set the highest cash bonds possible at $10,000 to $100,000 [$130,000 to $1.3 million today]. With reporters present, Lyle signed the first warrant for the top name on the list, and headlines branded Capone *Public Enemy Number 1.* This action generated unprecedented nation-wide publicity against criminals and aroused citizen support for a war on crime. President Herbert Hoover acknowledged the Chicago list, pointing out to reporters that the IRS had just convicted Ralph Capone and was hot on the trail of his younger brother Al. This led J. Edgar Hoover to plagiarize the Chicago Crime Commission's concept by declaring a succession of Public Enemies Number 1 and then creating an FBI register of the nation's *Ten Most Wanted Fugitives List.*

The Chicago gang leaders on the list faced arrest, high bail payments, and attorneys' fees, so all went into hiding or on vacation. The day the warrants were issued, which was just a month after Capone had been released from the Philadelphia prison, he and some of his lieutenants fled to his Miami home for a long retreat. The Judge then coordinated with the Detective Bureau to develop a list of the names of the lieutenants of the Public Enemies to get them off the streets too. But an IRS raid of a Capone-gang hangout found the gangster was controlling this police process. The Detective Bureau gave the Judge a list containing 23 names, but the IRS confiscated from Capone's hideout the Bureau's originally prepared list. It had 31 names, with the eight names of Capone's gang members crossed off. None of these names appeared in the Bureau's amended list to the Judge.

Lyle's vagrancy warrant and high-bail campaign kept the major gangsters under cover, but their criminal activities continued at a record pace as other judges reduced their bails and let them off. When Capone finally surrendered to face the vagrancy warrant, he asked for a change of venue on the ground the Judge was prejudiced against him, and Lyle proudly admitted in court to being "prejudiced in the extreme" before granting the motion. Another Judge then approved Capone's request to have Lyle's designation of him as "Scarface Al" removed from the vagrancy warrant before dismissing it.

A few weeks after beginning his well-publicized gangster vagrancy-warrant campaign, Judge Lyle announced his candidacy for the Republican primary opposing Mayor Thompson. He ran aggressively as a foe of gangsterism and crime. His entire campaign was directed against Capone's control of Thompson, but the Mayor's voting base was the city's drinkers, and his campaign conveyed the message that a vote for him was a vote for wide-open booze and vice. Thompson won the primary by surreptitiously conniving another of his Republican enemies to run in the primary and siphon away enough anti-Thompson votes from Lyle to give the incumbent the winning edge. Then in the general election, Mayor Thompson was defeated by Democrat Anton Cermak.

Upon Thompson's defeat for reelection, his horrendous administration was summarized in an editorial by the *Chicago Tribune*. "For Chicago, Thompson has meant filth, corruption, obscenity, idiocy and bankruptcy. He has given the city an international reputation for moronic buffoonery, barbaric crime, triumphant hoodlumism, unchecked graft and a dejected citizenship. … He made Chicago a byword for the collapse of American civilization. In his attempt to continue this he excelled himself as a liar and defamer of character. He's out." In the three-quarters of a century since Thompson's defeat, every Republican Chicago mayoralty candidate has been defeated.[120]

THE IRS IMPACT ON CAPONE

Shortly after the St. Valentine's Day Massacre, *Chicago Tribune* Publisher Colonel Robert McCormick met with newly inaugurated President Herbert Hoover. McCormick complained that the Prohi Agents were arresting the little fellows and ignoring Capone. The President had never heard of the gangster, so McCormick filled him in. He also suggested that non-payment of income taxes was likely his Achilles' heel.

The income tax law went into effect in 1913, but it was unclear whether it applied to illegal income. Then the U.S. Circuit Court of Appeals held in 1926 that income from illicit sources was not taxable based on the Fifth Amendment that people could not be required to report on their criminal activities, but a year later the Supreme Court reversed that decision, giving the federal government a powerful weapon to go after the underworld. The following day President Hoover wrote Treasury Secretary Andrew Mellon, "Please see to it that Al Capone goes to jail." Mellon directed IRS Intelligence Section Chief Elmer Irey to get the job done, and Mellon regularly reminded Irey that President Hoover began and ended every meeting by emphasizing he wanted Capone imprisoned. Irey surrounded himself with honest, dedicated, passionate men to conduct the long, tedious, number-crunching investigation.[121]

The responsibility for directing the IRS investigation fell on the Justice Department's U.S. Attorney in Chicago, George E. Q. Johnson. He did not have access to Capone because since the Massacre, the gangster had remained in Miami to avoid questioning by Chicago police detectives. So U.S. Attorney Johnson used a subterfuge to force Big Al back to town - a subpoena for the gangster to appear before a Chicago Federal Grand Jury concerning bootlegging operations. In response, Capone's Miami physician obtained an eight-day delay by sending Federal Judge James Wilkerson an affidavit that Capone's life would be endangered by traveling with bronchial pneumonia. When Capone returned for the Jury appearance, he did not play emperor like he usually did in his old haunts, but he remained in hiding because of the citizenry's continuing shock over the slaughter.

The U.S. Attorney suspected Capone's doctor had lied and requested the FBI to investigate, as the FBI was an agency in the Justice Department. Agents found that during the eight days Big Al was allegedly bedridden, he was actually visiting his liquor-smuggling bases by flying to Bimini and sailing to Nassau, Bahamas. When he was in Miami he attended the Hialeah horseraces and watched the Sharkey-Stribling fight. The FBI discovered numerous witnesses who said he looked and acted like a healthy man. Agents never discovered the reason Capone wanted that short delay, but the Judge cited Capone with contempt of court for lying and held a week-long trial in Chicago.

During the trial, a police detail drove Capone between the hotel and the courtroom instead of protecting the witnesses who testified against the vicious gangster. The first morning of Capone's contempt trial, several police detectives stopped the gangster and served him with Judge Lyle's outstanding vagrancy warrant. Then Judge Wilkerson found Capone guilty of contempt and gave him six months in jail but allowed him bail during his appeal. This was the first time a court had legitimately convicted Capone (unlike his phony concealed weapons guilty plea in Philadelphia), causing the stunned thug to mumble to the press, "We'll get another court to overrule this court," but none would. Even though the U.S. Attorney initiated and completely directed the Capone contempt charge, J. Edgar Hoover falsely handwrote on two official FBI reports that it was he who had motivated the government case.[122]

Chicago U.S. Attorney Johnson had IRS Special Agent Frank Wilson sent from Washington to lead the income tax investigation and backed him up with local Agent-In-Charge Art Madden. They had 25 agents travel everywhere Capone had been to question more than 1,000 people who knew him in a search for information about his activities and for potential witnesses. They also hunted for all available accounting and ownership records. The agents faced what seemed like an impenetrable wall because Capone owned nothing in his name, never signed anything, and paid cash for everything. Most of his business transactions and profits were handled by Jake Guzik, Frank Nitti, and Ralph Capone, so Johnson first convicted those three subordinates separately for tax evasion during a five-month period and then locked up six more key Capone associates for tax fraud.

Two years of dedicated work analyzing numbers produced little good news for the agents to forward to President Hoover. They still could not tie Capone into his illegal operations or income. Then one evening, Agent Wilson worked late and ran out of cabinet space. To store his current documents, he emptied the old records from a filing cabinet in a storeroom and found a heavy package tied in brown paper that roused his curiosity. It contained three accounting ledgers that listed the results for casino games. They turned out to be the income records for *The Ship* casino in Cicero, picked up in the raid by the Berwyn Minister more than five years earlier. They had been ignored by previous investigators because they could not decipher the code.[123]

Agents quickly discovered that the Minister's raid had produced the key evidence they had been diligently searching for. In addition to confiscating the casino accounting records, the raiders' testimony could tie Capone to them. When Big Al showed up that day of the raid in his pajamas, it was the only time outsiders saw him exercise authority in any of his illegal enterprises - he admitted to the Minister and two of the raiders that he owned the casino. Although badly frightened by Capone's ensuing terrorism against them years earlier, these stalwart citizen raiders would stand firm during their Federal Grand Jury testimony.

The final piece to this puzzle was supplied by Capone's racetrack operator Eddie O'Hare. The agents had built a tax evasion case against O'Hare like they had the other lieutenants of Capone's gang, but his single overriding goal in life was to get his 12-year-old son Butch into the U. S. Naval Academy. This was a dream that could easily be dashed by a father's affiliation with a gangster, so O'Hare approached Agent Wilson and offered to expose the Capone gang if he were kept anonymous. Wilson later wrote, "I considered the leads and advice [from O'Hare] the most important single factor resulting in the conviction of Al Capone."

O'Hare identified casino bookkeeper Lou Shumway as the man who had written the ledgers and knew how to decipher the coded numbers and also casino cashier Fred Ries who could identify who received the profits. *The Ship's* profits had been turned over to Jake Guzik, which led to his IRS conviction and a five-year sentence, but Capone had also signed and cashed some of the checks made out to Guzik to buy things. Agents had to hunt down the bookkeeper and cashier in different parts of the country, and then secretly hide them under 24-hour guard in different states and even in South America for a time.

The travel and living expenses for the witnesses and guards were paid by the "Committee of Courage" that the press dubbed "The Secret Six." They were six wealthy Chicago vigilante citizens who established a large fund to combat the gang's violent intimidation of the justice system and bring down Capone and his lieutenants. They financed independent private criminal investigations that circumvented the corrupted Police Department, contributed to the IRS investigations, and gave witnesses protection in secret hideaways. Their spokesman was Robert Isham Randolph, who was President of the Chicago Association of Commerce, but he never identified these six influential citizens for their anonymous contributions.

The Ship records, along with the testimony of Capone's two employees and the Minister's three vigilante raiders, were the core evidence, but the agents built an enormous case involving many witnesses concerning the gangsters' large cash purchases and his associates delivering him huge cash profits. Wilson's success as the lead investigating agent was later rewarded with appointment as U.S. Secret Service Chief to protect President Franklin Roosevelt.[124]

Upon being indicted for tax evasion, Capone immediately tried to make the criminal case go away by offering to pay $4 million ($56 million today) restitution for back taxes owed. Prosecutor Johnson quickly rejected Capone's offer, and countered with an offer to recommend to the judge a two-and-a-half-year sentence in return for Capone's guilty plea. Prior to Johnson's going after the Capone gang leaders, sentences for income-tax fraud were short. Johnson's offer of two-and-a-half years was more than the longest sentence on record for a guilty plea, and if convicted everyone thought Capone would get no more than a three-year sentence. Besides Johnson had concerns about the legal sufficiency of key elements of his case. Capone accepted the deal because he was facing more than 30 years if convicted on all counts, and he knew the federal government was fed up with his butchery. Four days before he was to plead guilty and be sentenced, Scarface threw a farewell party in a hotel with 50 gangsters. It was held in Benton Harbor, Michigan so none of the attendees would be subjected to arrest under Judge Lyle's vagrancy warrants.

Capone began a press blitz to make it look like he was celebrating having beaten the legal system. This imagery was intended to solidify his leadership of the gang and political clout while he would be in federal prison, just as he had maintained his standing during his 10-month stint in Philadelphia. The terms of the plea bargain were to remain secret until Judge Wilkerson made his decision whether to accept it, but in his PR frenzy Capone had the length of the proposed sentence anonymously leaked to a newspaper that headlined it. The article said this was how the Judge was going to rule, as if the Judge was in the gangster's pocket, which created a great deal of negative comment in the nation's press. At the same time, Capone flaunted his pleasure with the deal in newspaper photographs by sporting big grins in racetrack front boxes and while shaking hands with famous baseball players at games.

All of this outraged Judge Wilkerson, who at the court hearing prohibited the prosecution from exposing its case to the defendant, and instead stunned every one present by his statements directed to Capone. Wilkerson said he would give due consideration to the recommendation but made it clear the court was not bound by agreements between the two parties or the U.S. Attorney's judgment. The Judge emphasized, "It is utterly impossible to bargain with a Federal Court." The Judge then admonished Capone for his "unbelievable arrogance" and "brazen actions." Faced with the enraged and intimidating Judge, Capone withdrew his guilty plea. The press photos of Capone's expression at the beginning and conclusion of the hearing told it all. His ear-to-ear grin was replaced with sullenness as he slunk from the courtroom, escorted as usual by a squad of police.[125]

As the IRS investigation heated up, Capone tried to kill, intimidate, or bribe the key IRS agents to make the case go away. Informant O'Hare twice called Agent Wilson to warn him that hit men were on their way to kill his agents. These efforts were effectively blocked because the targeted agents quickly moved to other hotels and changed their commuting patterns. In a third attempt, agents overheard on tapped telephone lines of the gang's leaders that four out-of-town killers had been imported. An agent visited Torrio, who had returned to town for the first time since abdicating power to answer a subpoena from the Federal Grand Jury concerning Capone's income. The agent warned Torrio that agents would raid the gang's headquarters and kill Capone if it were not called off. Two hours later Torrio called the agent and told him, "They are gone." When these murder threats failed, Capone offered a $1.5 million bribe to prosecution-team leader Irey, but he rejected it. These unheralded IRS agents who dedicatedly stood up to planned gangster hits and rejected huge bribes proved themselves to be true untouchables.

Two weeks before Capone's trial was to begin, informant O'Hare made another call to IRS Agent Wilson for a meeting by warning, "The big fellow is going to outsmart you." O'Hare revealed that the gang had the list of prospective jurors. "They're fixing them one by one" with cash bribes, promised political or church jobs, and front-row prize-fight tickets. Wilson accompanied U.S. Attorney Johnson to presiding Federal Judge Wilkerson's chambers, and Wilkerson found Capone's list indeed matched his own. The Judge's response was simple. "Bring your case into court as planned gentlemen. Leave the rest to me."

The morning the trial started, the Judge took the bench, called his bailiff over, and told him, "Judge Edwards has another trial commencing today. Go to his courtroom and bring me his entire panel of jurors. Take my entire panel to Judge Edwards." The Judge then ordered the jury sequestered at a hotel to prohibit communication with anyone and instructed all references to the trial be deleted from the newspapers they received. A nervous, sweating Capone rose to plead not guilty and almost buckled at the knees.[126]

The trial went as the Prosecutor had planned. Every state's witness stood his ground, confident and determined against the blistering glare of Capone and his goons. Agent Wilson was especially concerned with the intimidating looks of Capone's bodyguard Philip D'Andrea, who looked like he was an attorney sitting behind Capone throughout the trial. Wilson kept his focus on him, and when he stretched during a recess, the agent noticed what seemed like the bulge of a gun on the gangster's right hip. When D'Andrea walked out, Wilson and two other Agents prevented the possibility of gunfire in the crowded hallway by grabbing his arms, pulling him to the door of the Judge's nearby chambers, and shoving him in. They confiscated the .38-caliber revolver stuck in his belt. The Judge interrupted the trial to cite the thug for contempt and held him without bail until a hearing the next day.

At the hearing D'Andrea threw himself at the mercy of the court. The incensed Judge stared at him while announcing, "This band [the Capone gang] exercises a coercive influence over those with whom it comes in contact, which is nothing less than insurrection against the laws of the United States. The activities of this gang were a menace to the court and its officers, and to the due administration of justice." The Judge then sentenced him to six months in the County Jail to begin immediately. When D'Andrea was arrested, he was carrying a star and an expired Municipal Court Deputy Bailiff credential. He also had cards from three high-ranking police officials attesting that he was to be extended the courtesies of the department. The bust raised D'Andrea's stature with the gang. He would later obtain some profitable city contracts including hauling garbage, and for seven years he would become President of the Italo-American National Union, the successor to Unione Siciliana. He was a rare president in that era who survived his tenure.[127]

When the jury completed its deliberations and announced its verdict "Guilty!" the courtroom erupted. The reporters, gangsters, and lawyers ran out of court, but Capone slumped forward as if he had been slugged on the back of the head. A week later Judge Wilkerson sentenced him to 11 years in prison, more than double the longest previous sentence for someone convicted of tax evasion. He was taken directly from the courtroom to jail. When his cell door locked behind him, he had a temper tantrum over the length of his sentence, sulked on his hard cot, and refused the evening supper of corned beef and cabbage. He scowled as the jail radio floated into his cell the strains of *The World Is Waiting for the Sunrise.* The life of the 32-year-old gangster in any meaningful sense was over.

Capone's nightmarish criminal domination of a city had been made possible by a government edict that prohibited the popular American habit of alcohol consumption, and the government ultimately punished him not for his gangsterism but for his failure to share part of his criminal profits. The horror of Prohibition was summed up by Michigan's *Bay City Daily Times.* The paper had always stood for law and order and was an ardent supporter of Prohibition, but during Capone's prosecution, it editorialized that it must end because there was no law and no order, and because the country's prisons and legal system were overwhelmed by dry-law offenders. The official proclamation announcing repeal of Prohibition was issued two years later.

A few days before Capone was sentenced, he tried to manipulate his punishment by having his political lackey Dan Serritella approach an associate of Judge Wilkerson and guarantee that the Judge's rumored nomination for the U.S. Supreme Court would not be opposed by the American Federation of Labor, if Capone were given the two-and-a-half year plea deal. The Judge ignored the offer of political support, and three months after Capone was sentenced, President Hoover, who had ordered his administration to bring down Capone, proudly nominated Judge Wilkerson to the U.S. Seventh Circuit Court of Appeals. The Senate Subcommittee gave two favorable reports on his nomination, but the labor unions controlled by Capone had the political clout to block action by the full U.S. Senate. At the end of the year, Judge Wilkerson wrote the President asking him not to resubmit his nomination to the next session of the Senate because "there seems to be no reason to expect a different result at the coming session." This was both Capone's revenge and a warning from his cell to all federal judges to tread lightly on Chicago gangdom in the future.

Six months later, the U.S. Supreme Court rejected Capone's appeal, but gave him hope by ruling in a Boston case that tax evasion somehow did not constitute fraud, thus the statute of limitations in civil cases of three years, rather than the six in the tax law, applied. This standard wiped out most of Capone's convictions. He hired highly-respected attorneys to handle his new appeal, but Federal Judge Marvin Underwood was a step ahead of them. He ruled the Capone case was different by citing the following wording in the statute, "The time during which the person committing the offense is absent from the district wherein the same was committed shall not be taken as any part of the time limited by law." Since Capone was in a Philadelphia jail or in his Miami refuge for periods totaling several years, the limitation period the trial Judge applied was correct. Upon dismissal of his appeal, Capone was transferred from his luxurious abode in the Cook County jail to the Atlanta Federal Penitentiary for hard-core criminals.[128]

After Capone entered the Atlanta Penitentiary, the Warden requested that the FBI investigate his activities. He was suspected of directing the Chicago gang from his prison cell and managing a contraband ring that he created among the other prisoners. This investigation produced nothing meaningful beyond the likelihood that certain convicts, with some guards keeping witnesses away, extorted large sums of money by "strong-arming" Capone on a number of occasions. If true, Capone's gang associates would have delivered the cash to the guards outside the prison.

A year and a half after Capone was convicted, the War Department released Alcatraz Island to U. S. Attorney General A. G. Cummings, who wanted it to house the country's most vicious and dangerous criminals. When Capone found out he was going to be moved where he could no longer talk to the outside world and no longer control his empire, he went crazy. Capone's inability to control the prison system further increased his vulnerability with prisoners in Atlanta who hated his pompous arrogance. The beatings increased, including a scissor stabbing that sent him to the infirmary. Almost a year after being notified of the move, Capone was among 43 prisoners transferred from the Atlanta Penitentiary to the new Alcatraz Island Federal Prison in San Francisco Bay. They were herded into two specially-constructed steel-barred train coach cars to travel across the continent. Then the two train cars were rolled onto a large barge and towed to the prison dock.

Alcatraz was a stressful experience for the gangster whom the other inmates called the Emperor. They mocked him, and small-time criminals attempted to prove themselves by whipping the now obese infamous bully Big Al. He remained aloof from this hostility most of the time, spending his days working in the laundry and his nights in lonely thought. Two years into Capone's confinement at Alcatraz, a Texas bank robber stabbed him slightly in the back for refusing to lend him money, and he spent five days recovering in the prison hospital. After that, two other convicts tried to kill him; one put lye in his coffee and the other attempted to strangle him in his cell. He feared for his life, lost weight, and regularly requested to be moved to another prison. He attended church services, but the visiting ministers were not permitted to talk to the inmates except for giving sermons to the group. No one had any idea whether Capone had gotten religion or if it was simply the only diversion on the desolate ocean rock. Capone's mother came to see her son, but she was banned from further visits because she spoke only Italian and the guards could not censor the mother-son conversations.

Another aspect of Capone's past was about to catch up with him. A year before the St. Valentine's Day Massacre, Capone's young Greek mistress, a prostitute from one of his brothels, was diagnosed with syphilis and was treated. But when a doctor urged Capone to take a blood test, he withdrew in dread. The doctor graphically described the awful consequences of avoiding treatment, but the brutal gangster could not face a needle prick. A decade later Capone started showing signs of mental impairment from syphilis by starting to mechanically make up his bed hour after hour, refusing to leave his cell for meals, and cutting up dolls. Then the model prisoner burst into song in violation of prison rules and attacked fellow prisoners. This violent phase quickly disappeared, but he deteriorated quickly. He meekly obeyed all orders, was often in a daze, and was unable to remember his name at times. For awhile the disorder was intermittent between long periods of being lucid, but it finally became chronic.

Two years after Capone's mental deterioration became obvious, he was released from prison. He was broke and lived on the generosity of his brothers. He retained his homes from the outstanding IRS claims only because the 25-room Miami estate was in the name of his wife Mae and the Chicago home was in his mother's name. He spent the last seven years of his life moving slowly and unsteadily with dull eyes and sagged jaws and was mute except for occasional muttering. He was fearful of people and imaginary ghouls. He craved constant companionship, but his syphilitic-ravaged mind feared all but a few people, and even them he did not always recognize. The vicious thug and whorehouse pimp died at age 48 with his mother present.

Torrio did not attend Capone's funeral because they had had a falling out. About the time Big Al's behavior had become obviously erratic from syphilis in Alcatraz, he assisted the IRS with a lengthy deposition about the activities of his former boss. The IRS said convict Capone's "assistance was immeasurable" in a 50-page deposition with information only he knew about Torrio, but he could not testify at the trial because he had been judged insane. Torrio was no more loyal. One of the men charged with Torrio for tax evasion had been a key informant in Capone's tax conviction. He had been a collection agent for the gang and had testified which leaders he gave the cash to. Yet Torrio subsequently hired him as his secretary.

Capone died still owing the IRS huge unpaid taxes. The IRS filed two large liens against the Miami home for the income tax claims he never settled. Just before it was to be sold out from under his widow, Al's brother Ralph Capone paid them both times.

Two decades after Big Al died, his only son was arrested in Miami for stuffing two bottles of headache pills and a package of flashlight batteries into his pants' pocket at a supermarket. This was the only arrest of his life. The divorced father of four had a good job as a tire salesman so police asked why he did it. He replied, "Everybody has a little larceny in them." Eight months later, he legally changed his name by dropping Capone and keeping his first two names of Albert Francis. He explained to the judge the reason for the change with, "When a $3.50 shoplifting charge puts you on the nation's front pages, it's time to change your name." Regarding the glare of publicity he had endured for minor incidents he told the judge, "I should have done this years ago."[129]

Eddie O'Hare was Capone's lieutenant who secretly assisted in his boss' IRS prosecution. His son Butch went on to graduate from Annapolis, and five years later was awarded the nation's highest honor, the Congressional Medal of Honor, by President Roosevelt. Butch had shot down six Japanese bombers off the Gilbert Islands. The following year, Lieutenant Commander O'Hare's plane was shot out of the air, killing him. Four years after the War ended, Chicago's Old Orchard Field (Chicago-bound baggage tags are still marked *ORD* for Orchard) was expanded and renamed O'Hare Airport. Unfortunately, the hero's father did not live to see his son's honors. Eight days before Capone was released from prison, O'Hare's father drove to the Chicago airport to operate a Florida dog track during the winter for the gang. Two men drove alongside his car and fired two shotgun charges through the driver's window, hitting him in the head and neck to kill him instantly. His car careened for a block before crashing into a light pole.

It is clear O'Hare was murdered by the gang because they would have avenged their key lieutenant's killing if an outsider had done it. The gang's motive was never discovered. O'Hare had helped the IRS build the case against Capone, but vengeance can be ruled out. Capone had had no contact with gang members during the six years he was on the Rock, and he was now insane. Besides, the succeeding gang leaders had no loyalty to their former leader, never offering financial aid to his family who were supported by Big Al's brothers. Most important, O'Hare's assistance in prosecuting Capone was kept secret while O'Hare was alive. Furthermore, no attempt was ever made on the lives of the bookkeeper and the cashier whose damaging testimony imprisoned Capone. The gang may have caught O'Hare stealing, decided to rob his assets in their greed, or feared he was still an informant. This was a possibility because O'Hare died with a note in his pocket that had been handwritten by his secretary that indicated he had a close association with the Chicago FBI. The memo said the FBI wanted to know what he knew about a fugitive bank robber and counterfeiter. Current gang leader Frank Nitti had personally known O'Hare's secretary for many years from the time he had begun auditing the gang's books. She may have been the one who warned Nitti, since he married her three years after he had approved the murder of her boss.[130]

ELIOT NESS & THE FBI VERSUS CAPONE

When President Hoover ordered the Treasury Department to launch an IRS investigation into Capone, he also had Treasury direct the Alcohol Tax Unit to confiscate and destroy Capone's beer production equipment and trucks and arrest the workers. Agent Eliot Ness was assigned to head the alcohol Tax Unit squad in Chicago. The IRS and Ness investigations could not have been handled more differently or with more divergent results. The IRS agents operated in total secrecy, and they even infiltrated an undercover agent posing as a hood into Capone's gang. In contrast, Ness was a publicity hound. He kept the press informed of his activities and notified cameramen about his pending raids so they could photograph him walking into a brewery or distillery. Despite the photographic imagery, his raids were mundane busts in which the non-violent workers never drew a gun. Ness captured many trucks but few breweries. In fact, it took him almost three years before he found the location of the first brewery to seize, even though this was easy to do. By that time, the IRS had already completed its difficult, complex investigation and charged Capone with tax evasion. Ness' raids were nothing more than a minor nuisance to Capone and his successors and resulted in no convictions at all. Ness' best efforts never caused any Chicagoan to want for an alcoholic beverage. The sad reality is Ness never made a case against a major hood during his entire career.

Three years before Ness started his investigation, the IRS Special Intelligence Unit responded to the murder of Chicago Prosecutor McSwiggin by capturing more Capone trucks, breweries, and workers in five months than Ness did in three years. Ness' sole responsibility was to get Capone's operations, while the IRS Unit had achieved far more impressive results even though they were busy attacking Chicago's other booze gangs as well. Before going after Capone's operations, the IRS Unit agents learned Capone's modus operandi by keeping one of his major breweries under surveillance from a distance. The loaded truck convoys were not given the go-ahead to pull out until up to nine Capone goon scout cars and two police cars and motorcycles drove the surrounding area making sure no dry agents were hiding in wait. Just two weeks after McSwiggin's killing, the IRS busted a Capone brewery at his Arrowhead Inn in Burnham where vats were brewing more than 50,000 gallons of beer. It was a major bust because it was owned by Capone and Burnham's Mayor, and the IRS also charged Cicero's President and Police Chief. Unfortunately, the IRS had to drop this case because two key Cicero state's witnesses were murdered.[131]

After Capone was convicted of income-tax evasion, Ness applied to become a FBI agent, but J. Edgar Hoover denied him because he did not respect his performance as a lawman. Ness went on to hold several law enforcement positions before Cleveland's newly-elected reform Mayor Harold Burton appointed him to be the city's Director of Public Safety, with a directive to close wide-open vice operations. Cleveland had several well-known brothels and casinos, but Ness failed to shut down a single one. Following Prohibition, Moe Dalitz and the Little Jewish Navy operated wide-open high-rolling casinos, but Ness never disrupted one of them. It was like he was the only person in town who was oblivious to their existence.

At the same time Ness was ignoring his Public Safety responsibilities, he created a personal sideline business. Shortly after the outbreak of World War II in Europe, he organized the Industrial Safety Committee, within the nonprofit Cleveland Safety Council, to prevent wartime sabotage and espionage. He informed the leaders of Cleveland's 1,200 industrial plants that the federal government lacked the funds to properly protect their plants in wartime. Ness charged the industrialists a fee to employ a telephone operator to take calls from the member companies about suspicious employees and individuals. The operator then forwarded this information to the Cleveland Police Department. Incredibly, Ness conned concerned companies into buying his service even though the police answered such security calls directly from businesses and citizens at no cost. Ness charged a fee and made a profit for a free service that actually slowed down the reporting process to the police

In addition, Ness' agency violated the Presidential Proclamation requesting that all police organizations refer matters relating to espionage and sabotage directly to the FBI without charge. Director Hoover was deeply concerned that forwarding potentially critical calls through three agencies rather than directly to the FBI could greatly reduce available response time to prevent a pending catastrophe. Hoover relayed his worries to the U.S. Attorney General and to the Secretary of President Roosevelt, but Ness continued to collect fees while falsely claiming that the FBI and the Navy approved his agency. FBI internal reports noted that Ness controlled the organization's funds and drew a salary: "All monies are to be expended only with the approval of Mr. Eliot Ness who is acting as adviser to the Industrial Safety Committee."[132]

Cleveland's newspapers did not find anything about Ness' Public Safety work to be newsworthy, but they covered his nightly drinking and womanizing, even before he divorced the first of his three wives. His behavior was always scandalous, but then it became criminal. After a night of drinking, he skidded his car on an icy road and crashed into another car, injuring the 20-year-old driver. Ness fled the scene, but not before the victim wrote down his license plate number. Ness had enough political power to evade prosecution for drunk driving and hit-and-run, but he resigned in public disgrace.

Ness next used his government contacts to get appointed to the U.S. Office of Defense Health and Welfare Services. His role was to protect military personnel from venereal disease by eliminating prostitution near domestic military installations. He created a department named the National Police Advisory Committee that allowed him to travel the country speaking at law enforcement meetings. He claimed to have new methods of detecting prostitution, but law enforcement officers advised the FBI, "Ness' outfit was nothing but a lot of wind and had accomplished absolutely nothing." Every time Ness appeared at these meetings, his underling handed out a prepared resolution praising Ness' contribution which the organization was expected to approve. However, he was held in such low esteem that at some meetings not a single official would sponsor it. Hoover handwrote on one FBI report, "This is Elliot [sic] Ness outfit. I am opposed to any cooperation."[133]

When the government eliminated Ness' position, he kept moving to new jobs and new bars. He was on a downward spiral when he visited New York and happened to meet sportswriter Oscar Fraley, who talked Ness into writing his autobiography. Months before their book *The Untouchables* was scheduled for publication, Ness had a fatal heart attack. He was 54 years old and in debt. Despite the book's premise, he did not make a single contribution to the IRS case against

Capone. His autobiography was filled with gross inaccuracies, distortions, and exaggerations, and it credited him with much greater achievements than any report to his boss documented. Worse, a number of people who knew him suspected that even his official reports to his boss were highly inflated.[134]

Even though his book was a work of fiction, ABC television ran a hit series loosely based on it for five seasons beginning in 1959. Robert Stack played a confident, determined Eliot Ness in the series, but the real Ness was an unprofessional publicity hound and a serious alcoholic who failed at every job. Ness' widow received royalties on the book, but they were unfortunately so small that she qualified for food stamps and had to use them.

Ness' wholly inadequate prosecution of Capone was rivaled by J. Edgar Hoover. He became Director of the FBI in 1924, and during his half-century tenure he inexplicably did not allow his agents to investigate America's organized-crime gangs that developed early in Prohibition and expanded and proliferated throughout his directorship. Hoover could have easily brought down Capone's empire by proving he was importing large numbers of prostitutes across state lines. It is significant that while President Herbert Hoover rode the IRS to carry on a full-court press against Capone for three years, the President never bothered to mention the serious gangster or his administration's dedicated campaign to J. Edgar Hoover and his FBI or try to involve that agency in any way. The size of Capone's 2,397-page file might sound impressive, but the FBI failed to take official notice of the notorious gangster until more than eight years into Prohibition. Almost two years went by before a second report was prepared. These were the only documents in his file just 15 months prior to his conviction for tax evasion, when the FBI was directed by the Chicago U.S. Attorney to investigate Big Al's alleged illness in Miami. Over half of Capone's file pages are clippings of newspaper articles, and most of the report pages resulted from three FBI investigations that were initiated by other government agencies. For example, it took a telephone call from the President's Secretary for Hoover to instigate an investigation into the Capone gang's extortion of California grape growers and the Federal Farm Board. The gang was delaying these companies' interstate train shipments, causing the grapes to rot. The FBI generated much paperwork, but the reports developed no substantive evidence of criminal conduct.[135]

CHICAGO JOINED THE MOB TO BUILD LAS VEGAS

The Chicago gang was one of the four large Prohibition gangs that would go on to become the principal creators of the Las Vegas Strip during its Golden Era from the mid 1940s through the 1960s. The other three were the giant fine liquor importers headed by Charlie Luciano, Frank Costello, and Moe Dalitz. The leaders of these three importing gangs were recognized by both the underworld and the overworld as men of exceptional ideals – they always kept their word. They abhorred and rejected violence, vengeance, and monopoly. In addition to advocating peaceful coexistence and cooperation, the Young Turks welcomed competition and only participated in the victimless crimes of rumrunning and gambling. All were outstanding negotiators and compromisers who extended their hands in friendship to every one with whom they had differences.

In contrast, Chicago's plug uglies were brutally violent, ruthless, exploitive bullies who fought to build and enforce monopolies to nourish their insatiable greed. They were America's most expansionist and murderous gang. Their macho world was all about a mean reputation and had nothing to do with character, a word they likely did not know the meaning of nor how to spell it. Remember, at the Atlantic City national crime conference, Capone sat directly across from Luciano, Costello, and Dalitz, who were Big Al's biggest antagonists because of the extreme disparities between their values and behavior. Despite these differences, Capone aligned himself politically with all three leaders throughout Prohibition, and his successors also allied themselves for the next four decades. Capone's chief foreign liquor supplier was Dalitz, and Capone's successor leaders later partnered with Dalitz in building the *Stardust* gambling resort on the Las Vegas Strip.

Capone did have one rare underworld trait that he shared with Luciano, Costello, and Dalitz. The leadership of every other major gang in the country was made of one nationality, and they preferred to deal with their fellow countrymen. The four gangs who built the Strip had multicultural leaders as well as memberships, and they did business with every nationality and race. Capone and his predecessor Torrio were mainland Italians, but they absorbed their many Chicago area competitors, regardless of nationality, once each of those competitors concluded that submitting to the command of Capone and Torrio and paying them a tribute portion was preferable to being killed. Thus, Chicago was not a conventional Sicilian Mafia gang. Interestingly, the Italian Capone and Torrio both married Irish women while the Italian Costello had a Jewish wife.

During the 1950s and 1960s Luciano's associates headed by Costello built the vast majority of the Strip resort hotels and were the dominant force in the community. Dalitz headed the two most successful gambling palaces, the *Desert Inn* and the *Stardust.* And he was the town's most influential personality, the only man who could persuade every casino owner to come together for a common interest. Both groups protected the city's residents from underworld interference.

When in Las Vegas, the Chicago gangsters honored the Young Turks values for two reasons - they held the other two groups in high esteem, and they could not afford any negative publicity. The relatively clean Chicago gang members, who held state gambling licenses as casino owners or key executives, faced revocation if their underworld associations were exposed or their behavior became inappropriate. Thus, the Chicago representatives in Las Vegas during the Golden Era led low-profile, respectable lives, and the townspeople never realized these officials were ranking members of the Windy City's notorious Capone gang.

In the 1970s, Chicago's role in Las Vegas changed. The Prohibition leaders who had built the Las Vegas Strip were in their 70s, and they sold their resorts to super wealthy entrepreneurs, large public corporations, or licensable Chicago-gang front men who were financed by the Teamsters Union Pension Fund. These casino front men distanced themselves from the community, but they did not bother the locals. The one exception was Chicago gangster Tony Spilotro, who moved to Las Vegas and brought with him the exploitive horrors of organized crime present in many large American cities. Spilotro was not involved with the casino industry, and his gang was a totally different breed from the gamblers who created the Strip. These developers lived by exceptional ideals and were concerned with the welfare of the community, making them accepted and admired by the townspeople. In contrast, Spilotro's thugs organized street crime for the first time by using violent takeovers, burglarized local homeowners and businesses, and blew up popular non-union restaurants. (The dramatized role of Spilotro in the 1995 movie *Casino* was played by Joe Pesci.)

During the 1920s these New York, Cleveland, and Chicago gangs specialized in alcohol distribution. In the 1930s and 1940s the Luciano, Costello, and Dalitz gangs operated wide-open, elegant, high-limit casinos across the country. Capone and his successors were also in gambling, but their main endeavor during Prohibition was prostitution and afterwards it was big-time labor racketeering. These four gangs' business endeavors, mainstream political activities, and lifestyles from after the repeal of Prohibition to their arrival in Las Vegas follow. We begin with the two Young Turks who never made it to Las Vegas, but who so influenced the five who went on to build the marvelous early gambling resorts of the Las Vegas Strip.

CHAPTER 7

LUCIANO & TOM DEWEY

SPECIAL PROSECUTOR TOM DEWEY

The Great Depression's economic collapse began during Republican President Herbert Hoover's administration. Thus, in the next couple of national and state elections, voters across the country replaced many Republican office holders with Democrats. However, New York City reversed this pattern because the Tammany Hall Democrats had long been dominant in the city, and its politicians had been embroiled in one scandal after another. Like the voters in the rest of the country, the Big Apple wanted change, but it wanted reform by bringing Republicans into power. Thus, a year after America overthrew President Herbert Hoover's reelection bid with Democrat Franklin Roosevelt, New York City elected its first Republican Mayor in two decades, Fiorello LaGuardia.

Even though New York City now had a Republican mayor, the Manhattan District Attorney's (DA's) office remained under the control of the corrupt Democrats in Tammany Hall. However, Democratic Manhattan DA William Dodge was challenged by a determined grand jury. These jurors were hearing evidence about policy-number-lottery operations, and they asked the DA to allow them to investigate the many other prevalent rackets in the city. The DA ignored their request and continued to limit their activities. The frustrated jury revolted and demanded Democratic Governor Herbert Lehman replace DA Dodge with a special prosecutor to lead their panel. The Governor simply sat on their request, so the indignant grand jury protested by going directly to the judge to demand he dismiss them. The judge obliged and let them go on their ways.

The negative publicity resulting from the grand jury's accusations against DA Dodge forced Governor Lehman to authorize a sweeping racketeering inquiry by a new grand jury to be headed by a special prosecutor. The Democratic governor wanted to demonstrate impartiality by submitting the names of four distinguished Republican attorneys to the DA for consideration. But the four attorneys on the list refused the offer and instead recommended a young up-and-coming Republican firebrand named Thomas Dewey. At first the Governor resisted by stating for the record that Dewey's name was not "sufficiently well known to inspire public confidence." His real motive was to slow a Republican juggernaut that had politicized the criminal inquiry. But the mounting Republican publicity campaign forced the Governor to order DA Dodge to appoint Dewey.

Dewey selected his first target to resolve personal unfinished business - as an Assistant U.S. Attorney. Dewey had failed to convict the infamous Arthur "Dutch Schultz" Flegenheimer. The gangster was Bronx-born and of German Jewish ancestry despite his nickname of "Dutchman." He was the beer baron of New York city and operated a lottery in Harlem. Although his gang was much smaller than Al Capone's, he was New York City's version of the bloody Chicago murderer. He used the Tommy gun and achieved the most notoriety for violence of any criminal in the Big Apple. Late in the Roaring '20s, Schultz had a long-term gang war with John "Legs Diamond" Nolan. To finally end the conflict, Diamond moved his base of operations to Albany, New York, but one night two unknown assailants entered his rooming house and shot him to death. Earlier that year Schultz had also waged war against his own underling, Vincent "Mad Dog" Coll, for having gone into competition in the beer business. In one battle Coll started shooting at Schultz's gang members, but they fell to the ground, so Coll hit all five children playing in the background. He killed one, a five-year-old boy. Schultz's associates retaliated. They trapped Coll in a drugstore telephone booth and machinegunned him to death.

When Schultz heard that Dewey was focusing on his criminal activities, he informed Boss of Bosses Luciano about his plans to murder the Special Prosecutor. Luciano and the Young Turks tried to talk sense to him. Not only did they object to the killing of a law enforcer in principle, but they feared the reaction to killing Dewey would be far more devastating than any harassment he could wage. They were concerned the killing would turn public opinion against all rumrunners and generate tremendous governmental pressure to close their illegal operations and prosecute them.

But the impulsive Schultz proceeded with his homicidal plans. When Luciano and the Young Turks realized a hit was imminent, they felt compelled to prevent it from happening. One evening Schultz and three close underlings were going over their policy lottery records while seated at a round table in the backroom of the Palace Chop House and Tavern in Newark, New Jersey. Two intruders burst in and shot them. The three associates were killed instantly, but Schultz remained alive in the hospital comatose for another 24 hours before dying.

Charles "The Bug" Workman and Emanuel "Mendy" Weiss were later convicted of the murders of Schultz and his associates and received long prison sentences, but they never talked about who had given them the orders or why. Dewey's political ally, Brooklyn Assistant DA Burton Turkus, wrote of the Schultz killing, "The mob actually ordained that it would rub out a mobster – to save a prosecutor!" Dewey's memoir validated the underworld rumors that Schultz planned to "assassinate me." He wrote, "The director of the FBI, J. Edgar Hoover, wrote me a letter warning me about it." "*The Valachi Papers* gave the credit [for saving my life] to Luciano," and Dewey said he believed the Valachi documents were "authentic." Thus, Dewey clearly knew Luciano had saved his life.[136]

DEWEY TURNS HIS SIGHTS ON LUCIANO

Regarding the killing of the Dutchman, Luciano's best friend Jimmy Blue Eyes told me, "Shultz was in the beer business. When he was killed, it was the worst thing that ever happened to Charlie because he then became Public Enemy Number One. Dewey was running for president with his anti-racketeer campaign." Frank Costello's attorney George Wolf wrote about Schultz's murder that "Lucky Luciano, the man who saved [Dewey], would soon have second thoughts, Dewey was going after the Boss of all Bosses."[137]

Dewey had an unbridled ambition for power. He was then a candidate for Manhattan DA, but the following year he planned to run for New York governor while dreaming of the presidency. He targeted Luciano and manufactured a case by ordering a shocking number of illegal persecutorial actions. Then he used this made-up case as the cornerstone of a racket-busting, political-propaganda campaign.

Dewey was a publicity hound. He gave certain newspaper reporters access to inside stories in return for being allowed to edit their "news" stories and make them more flattering to himself. When Dewey lost the 1938 New York gubernatorial election, he kept his publicity campaign going. His PR man was his good friend Hickman Powell, a *New York Herald-Tribune* crime reporter. He wrote a book that cast Dewey's fanatical persecution of Luciano as heroic, and glorified his racket-busting image in preparation for the next gubernatorial campaign. Powell's book may have been extremely biased in favor of his boss, but amazingly he still acknowledged most of the sordid details that follow about the gross miscarriage of justice Dewey masterminded. Powell's reward was to become Dewey's speechwriter and a researcher and consultant to various governmental office staffs.[138]

Dewey publicly admitted that he made the decision to "break" Luciano on the night he learned that Dutch Schultz had been shot and was dying. Over the next two months Dewey quietly developed a prostitution case that he tried to link to Luciano. Dewey ordered 160 detectives and policemen to be assembled, but they were not told until the last minute that their assignment was to simultaneously raid 40 tiny, independent, illegal brothels that were operated out of women's homes and apartments in Manhattan and Brooklyn. When the widespread arrests began, Hickman notified the selected reporters so they could photograph the women being brought in and publicize the case.[139]

The NYPD arrested one hundred prostitutes and madams along with four *bookers*. These were independent agents who charged a fee to rotate girls between brothels every week so each madam could constantly offer her clientele fresh faces and bodies. Every Sunday the madams called in and gave the number of women they would need for the upcoming week, and every Monday the bookers gave the girls their new work addresses. The madams took half of each prostitute's gross earnings (a practice continued to this day by Nevada's legal brothels), and then madams paid 20 percent of their share (or 10 percent of each prostitute's total take) to the booker. Each girl also paid $10 a week to the booker (equal to 10 tricks at their share of $1 of the $2 rate) as a "referral" or "agent" fee that included insurance in case of arrest. In return the bookers employed bondsmen and lawyers and paid for quick bail bonds, legal fees, and bribes to judges.

Dewey built his case against the bookers rather than the madams or prostitutes. In his public statements Dewey left out the complicity of certain judges, but he did point out to the jury at trial that the bookers assured the girls they would be protected against going to jail. Four of the 13 defendants were bookers, and Dewey explained that they alone ran the booking service. The rest of the defendants had various support or leadership roles in the group, such as *general manager* and a *chief assistant*. He then contradicted himself by conceding that Luciano and the other eight defendants never collected or received any fees paid by the prostitutes and madams. He also failed to explain why they would be involved in an illicit enterprise from which they received no payment.

Compounding the confusion, Dewey explained to the jury that the defendants were charged with violating the *compulsory prostitution* law, but the case involved only *voluntary prostitution*. The compulsory prostitution law had nothing to do with the use of force, but rather it was applied against the people to whom prostitutes willingly paid money such as pimps and madams. Since Dewey admitted to the jury that Luciano had not been involved with the booking operation nor received any money from prostitution, it was unclear what crime he had committed under the compulsory prostitution law or any other law.

Dewey disclosed that every prostitute in the case was in the profession of her own volition and that every one associated with this case including the prostitutes, madams, and bookers had acted voluntarily. In fact, Dewey admitted no defendant actually compelled any woman to prostitute herself. Thus, none of the defendants was charged with using force or even the threat of force.

With this basic knowledge about these unusual charges, the twisted legal process of the pretrial and trial can be understood. Once Dewey had issued the indictments against the 13 defendants, the legal process took a detour through the State of Arkansas courtesy of Owney Madden. He had been a New York City beer baron and partner in Harlem's famed *Cotton Club* nightclub during the Roaring '20s. It was the Big Apple's late night hot spot, featuring the finest entertainers of African heritage, performing exclusively to wealthy New Yorkers and tourists of European ancestry. Near the end of Prohibition, the Irish Madden left the Sicilian-dominated New York City crime scene and moved to Hot Springs, Arkansas, which had been the south's most wide-open illegal gambling center since the mid 1800s. He quickly became a political power in the small town and county seat. Jimmy Blue Eyes, who had worked for Madden's beer operation before becoming a partner in Luciano's importing partnership, said of his old boss, "Owney was alright, but he was overgrown. He was another one who believed his own press reports." In other words, he took his self-importance too seriously.[140]

The Sheriff and key government officials in Hot Springs were not only very casual about enforcing the gambling and brothel laws, but they also made the town an accommodating hangout for top hoods fleeing prosecution. Luciano and his pals often vacationed in Hot Springs when the snow piled up in New York City or the heat was on. When Luciano found out he was Dewey's target, he traded his long-term suite at the Waldorf-Astoria for an indefinite winter vacation at the Hotel Arlington in Hot Springs. There he became well known as a free spender and a bettor at the racetrack. He had mistakenly thought that under his old friend Madden's leadership Hot Springs was a legal safe haven.

On April Fools Day Luciano was in route from his hotel to the racetrack when he was arrested. At Dewey's request a Manhattan court had issued the warrant. Luciano was well aware that Dewey was a determined and cunning prosecutor, so he promptly marshaled the strongest legal defense available in Hot Springs to fight extradition to New York. His actions set off a rapid series of contentious proceedings that pitted Arkansas Governor Junius Futrell and Attorney General Carl Bailey against the combined forces of Luciano's attorneys along with the judiciary, prosecutors, and sheriff's department of the little town of Hot Springs and surrounding Garland County.

Luciano's attorneys first instigated a habeas corpus proceeding which a judge quickly quashed. Dewey realized that a legal tussle was erupting so he immediately had several assistants board a train for Little Rock, Arkansas. At the same time, Luciano's defense attorneys took the unusual step of resurrecting an old New York charge to have a fugitive warrant issued against their own client, and they submitted it to the Hot Springs municipal court. This made Luciano a prisoner of the local legal system. In response, Dewey's assistants appealed to a Little Rock court for custody. The judge dispatched state rangers to Hot Springs to demand Luciano's surrender, but a Garland County Chief Deputy Sheriff blocked the doorway to the jail where Luciano was lodged. He refused to budge until he received court clarification of the prisoner's status. An enraged Governor Futrell announced that he would provide all the rangers necessary to secure turnover of Luciano, and they would march into the city armed and ready to employ force against the local lawmen and officials.

The next morning at dawn, the Arkansas Attorney General weighed in against the court actions of the corrupted Hot Springs city and county governments. A Little Rock judge quickly ruled that the Garland County authorities in Hot Springs were holding Luciano unlawfully and issued a fugitive warrant. The Attorney General had it delivered to the Hot Springs chancellor, who dismissed the local warrant protecting Luciano. The Little Rock judge also issued contempt citations against Luciano's counsel (who just happened to be the Hot Springs City Attorney) and the Chief Deputy Sheriff for interfering with the state rangers.

Early that same morning, 20 machinegun toting state rangers climbed into five cars for the 55-mile trip to the Hot Springs jail. They carried the Little Rock judge's order to surrender the prisoner. When they encountered the Chief Deputy and the City Attorney guarding the doorway, the 20 rangers brandished their machineguns and threatened to use them if Luciano was not surrendered. But it was logic that won the day. The rangers were able to convince Luciano's local protectors that the Little Rock court overrode any judicial decision in Hot Springs.

As prisoner Luciano departed with the state rangers, he smiled while asking the reporters watching the armed drama unfold, "Is it necessary to call out the National Guard to take me to Little Rock?" Hot Springs jail guards told reporters about Luciano's stay with them. He had bought packs of cigarettes for every inmate and generously tipped every one he encountered including the jail's porter and the barber who shaved him in his cell.[141]

The next day the legal maneuvering continued in Little Rock. Dewey invoked a relatively-new 1934 federal statute that made flight from one state to another a federal offense. Anyone accused in one state of murder, rape, arson, robbery, or extortion with threats of violence could be charged as a fleeing federal prisoner and returned to the state issuing the charge. This legal machination was prepared as a backup should the standard extradition proceedings fail, or should Luciano attempt to wage a drawn-out legal battle in the Arkansas state courts.

Since the Manhattan indictment against Luciano was a minor voluntary-prostitution charge, Dewey spiced up his indictment with another charge that allegedly involved a threat of violence in order to elevate it to federal status to strengthen his extradition request. Dewey swore out a complaint before a Manhattan chief magistrate that charged Luciano with extorting money by threatening one Al Weiner who was then serving time in Sing Sing penitentiary. Of this additional charge, Attorney General Bailey said, "Arkansas cannot be made an asylum for criminals. Officers of Hot Springs seem to have issued an invitation to criminals to come to that city, where they are told not to worry, that they will be given protection, and that they will not be compelled to return to answer for crimes committed elsewhere." In response Luciano presented a number of Hot Springs citizens to testify that he was a long-time visitor who regularly socialized at the hotel, golf course, and restaurants. His defense attorneys used this testimony to make the point that he not only was not in hiding but frequently appeared around town in the open.[142]

Concerning the new Manhattan extortion-threat charge, Luciano insisted that he had been in Cuba on that date, but three NYPD detectives testified in Little Rock that they had seen him at the Jamaica racetrack the day of the alleged extortion. Luciano begged for time to get affidavits or testimony from reputable Cuban hotel and nightclub operators that he was at a hotel and enjoying the tourist attractions of Havana, but Governor Futrell cut him off. He ruled, "This requisition is granted. There is no ground for continuance in this case. Guilt or innocence cannot be inquired into here. I have sought only to determine whether he was in New York the day of the charged offense. These witnesses brought from New York settled that."[143]

Sadly, Dewey had ordered the cops to lie under oath that day, and Luciano was not given the opportunity to properly defend himself. Dewey's extortion charge later proved to be false which meant that Prosecutor Dewey, three NYPD detectives, and the accuser all perjured themselves. Dewey's entire presentation before the Arkansas Governor was a fraudulent illegal charade to get Luciano at any cost. As soon as Luciano arrived in Manhattan, Dewey dropped his concocted extortion-by-threat charge. At trial it became clear just how false and made-up Dewey's extortion charge really was. Dewey presented in court Luciano's complete NYPD criminal record, but the Prosecutor had already expunged the nonexistent extortion charge that would have been the only serious arrest on his record.

Then in Luciano's trial Dewey had the audacity to call the perjuring extortion victim as a state's witness against the co-defendants. Dewey did not question Weiner about the false extortion charge, even though Dewey had attested to it in courts in two states. However, Dewey's questioning backfired when Weiner contradicted the Special Prosecutor's basic premise about Luciano's involvement. Finally deciding to tell the truth, Weiner testified he had never even met Luciano.

Luciano was charged with *felony* compulsory prostitution, even though New York prosecutors and judges treated the charge as a *misdemeanor* unless coercion was involved. While this case involved illegal prostitution, Dewey clarified to the trial jurors that even though the word "compulsory" appeared in the name of the law the defendants were charged with, they had used no force. The bookers, madams, and prostitutes were involved in voluntary, mutually-beneficial business transactions. But earlier at Luciano's bail hearing Dewey handled his explanation of the case very differently. He portrayed this minor infraction as the most heinous crime possible. He demanded a state-record $350,000 bail ($5.5 million today) by accusing Luciano of having committed most of the major crime categories on the books without offering any convictions or any evidence. Without presenting any proof whatsoever Dewey asserted that Luciano's "interests were far-flung and that his annual income was colossal," greater than any bail a court could set. Luciano's attorney contended the high bail amount was tantamount to holding Luciano without bail, which turned out to be true. He languished in jail until his trial because he had been living on his Prohibition savings since the Noble Experiment had been repealed.[144]

Dewey's broad criminal accusations against Luciano turned out to be totally false despite putting out maximum investigative effort to find him guilty of something, anything. The Prosecutor goaded the NYPD to assign more officers to investigate Luciano than any defendant in history, and Dewey ordered his own large staff of legal assistants to investigate and interview every possible witness, often using extralegal pressure. They ferreted out every potential underworld source trying to learn about Luciano's criminal background, but found no evidence of any type of illegal involvement other than Prohibition and gambling violations, which he readily admitted to at trial.

Dewey's investigative staff not only was unable to link Luciano to any other illegal activities, but they were not able to tie him to the prostitution-booking case for which he was charged. Dewey's Investigator Dan Danforth later wrote that he worked several months undercover posing as a Boston brothel owner who wanted to open an operation in Manhattan. He drank nightly in a bar where two of the four prostitution bookers hung out, and he got close to them. However, Danforth,

Dewey's other investigators, and the NYPD never saw Luciano with these two men or any of the other 10 defendants. With no evidence and no reason to believe that Luciano was involved with the bookers, Dewey still claimed Luciano had vague ties to every major crime committed in the city. Even if Luciano had been guilty of Dewey's charges, the courts of that time like most courts today treated voluntary prostitution as a misdemeanor, warranting only a minor fine or in rare cases brief jail time.[145]

Dewey stressed to the trail jury that the case involved no force, that Luciano never received money from anyone involved with prostitution (including from the other defendants), and that Luciano was not involved with the booking operations. Yet astonishingly Dewey characterized the case as the crime of the century and demanded life sentences. In his opening statement to the jury, Dewey said that "Lucania [his name's real spelling] will not be shown to have placed women in houses or taken money from them. Instead, he set up his apartment at the Waldorf-Astoria and was the czar of the organized crime of this city. His word was sufficient to terminate competition." Dewey previously admitted to the assembled jury pool, "We will show you in the case [Luciano's] function was not as the operator of anything, but merely as the man whose word, whose suggestion, whose statement, 'Do this,' was sufficient; and all the others in the case are charged as being his servants."[146]

Despite the rhetoric about Luciano's power, Dewey presented no evidence at all of Luciano's underworld influence. Rather, his position was that Luciano should be convicted of every major crime that occurred in New York simply because Dewey had branded him *Public Enemy Number 1* in an extensive factually-unsupported media campaign.

Had Luciano been tried alone, Dewey would have had no case. Instead he built a case against other defendants, and then claimed that Luciano was somehow mysteriously related. However this was not allowed by state law. New York prosecutors were not permitted to combine a number of related incidents into a single indictment instead of scattering them among separate true bills, as had long been permitted under federal law. Thus, while Luciano was fighting extradition in Arkansas, Dewey pressured New York's Governor and legislature to pass an appropriate statute. While the U.S. Supreme Court has affirmed that a person may not be charged with a crime that occurred before the law criminalizing the specific conduct was passed, a judge may apply procedural laws passed after a crime was committed or a suspect was indicted. This was the first arraignment under the new law permitting the joinder of a series of related events in one indictment.

Luciano had had nothing to do with the prostitution bookers, and he was visibly shaken when the judge announced the staggering bail amount. He pled not guilty. To the reporters attending the police line-up earlier, he frankly professed complete ignorance of the charge against him. He denied knowing anything about the business of prostitution, compulsory or voluntary. Awaiting arraignment in the courtroom, he added, "I'm in a fog."[147]

In Dewey's fanatical obsession to break Luciano, he ran roughshod over every one involved with the case. The standard bail for prostitution was $300, but Dewey badgered the judge into assessing a $10,000 bond on each of the more than 100 prostitutes and madams picked up in his raids. None of these women could afford this extraordinary bond, so Dewey kept them locked up like prisoners as *material witnesses* for three and a half months prior to Luciano's trial, and then for another four weeks during the trial. (Today material witnesses are allowed to give depositions and then remain free.) Holding the women as material witnesses was legally dubious because they were not co-conspirators. Judges assessed only small fines for prostitution, and the rare jail sentence never came close to the four months each one of them was forced to serve.

At the end of the trial Dewey announced, "The handling of more than 130 prisoners, including 120 material witnesses, in the various jails in this city has been a major problem calling for almost daily conferences with [Deputy] Commissioner [of Correction] Marcus, and for extraordinary cooperation on his part." Dewey was proud of imprisoning all the women, many of them single mothers whose children Dewey left abandoned and no means of support, without one woman having been charged or convicted of any crime, for much longer periods than any judge would have ever sentenced them if they had been tried and convicted.[148]

The DA's staff grilled the captive prospective witnesses relentlessly for long hours in isolated rooms in the House of Detention. They were denied their Constitutional right to have an attorney present. When Dewey wanted to really put the screws to one of them, he personally got involved with the grilling. The prosecutors' tactics alternated between threatening long jail sentences and offering bribes in exchange for their cooperation. Most of the madams and prostitutes were drug addicts, so they would be denied drugs cold turkey, and then they would be illegally supplied with illicit substances if they repeated what the DA's staff told them to say. Those who cooperated were permitted to live in apartments under police guard, and in the evenings were taken to movies and even bars for some heavy-duty drinking. The prostitutes were paid $3 a day, the equivalent of a half share of three $2 tricks. Despite all of the DA's manipulation and coercion, and the extended isolation, only 68 of the 120 potential witnesses testified in the trial, but unbelievably just six were broke down enough under these terrifying interrogations and internment to testify they knew anything about Luciano.

Treatment of the women was rumored around town to have been so bad that Dewey found he had to defend his actions in his trial summation. "There has been a great deal of implication in this case, sometimes frankly stated, usually by innuendo, that I have been running a subornation-of-perjury factory over in the Woolworth Building [where the women were imprisoned]." He later wrote that his office was aware during the whole affair that some people believed, "our investigation might be infringing upon civil liberties." His only defense was to quote an alleged verbal statement made by a young deputy assistant, Harris Steinberg, who was not involved in the interrogations and thus had no knowledge of what happened. He quoted Steinberg as saying that Dewey was under immense pressure because the citizenry was in uproar over this case, which was totally untrue. Steinberg did add a forthright and scary conclusion by saying that it would have been easy for Dewey to have "ridden roughshod over civil liberties," and that if he had, "he would have gotten away with it." This was the strongest defense of the case and his actions that Dewey could muster, and it was offered by an inexperienced side-line-sitter offering an uninformed opinion because he had no knowledge about the issues.[149]

Luciano testified at trial that he fought extradition from Hot Springs to New York because he had heard that Dewey intended to put him on trial 48 hours after his return, and he needed to give his lawyers time to prepare his defense. The information Luciano received was pretty accurate because the trial began less than six weeks after he arrived in Manhattan.[150]

It is doubtful that anyone in the courtroom was prepared for the Runyonesque characters who followed one after another into the witness box. Good-Time Charlie was supposed to be the first witness, but before he was to take the stand he told Dewey that everything he had told him and the grand jury was a lie. Dewey replaced him with two prostitutes who provided a description of how the business operated. One said she had worked for madams named "Jenny the Factory," "Cokey Flo," "Nigger Ruth," "Little Jenny," and "Gussie."

Brothel madam Florence "Cokey Flo" Brown admitted her nickname derived from a serious narcotic addition. When Dewey called her to testify, she was too emotionally distraught to get up on the witness stand. To settle her nerves, Justice Philip McCook permitted her to swig brandy in the courtroom before being sworn in on both days she testified. This is one of the most bizarre procedures to achieve a just and fair result in the annals of American jurisprudence.

Cokey Flo's testimony under cross-examination by the defense was stunning and should have led to Dewey's disbarment. She testified she had not known anything about Luciano, until the Prosecutor had cut off her drugs and denied her medical and psychiatric support. This terrible treatment was described by Dewey's own biographer Powell as "torture." She explained that on the fifth day of this hell she signed a statement in return for drugs, but she did not agree to become a witness until the last minute, when the Prosecutor threatened to again cut off her drug supply. Under cross-examination Cokey Flo testified that a few days after her arrest for drug possession, she contacted Dewey and offered information in return for drugs and a suspended sentence. While held as a material witness, she sent her boyfriend Jimmy Fredericks numerous love letters. However, she still denied that she had come forward in the hope of saving herself or her boyfriend from prison.

In total contradiction to her cross-examination testimony, the well-fortified Cokey Flo's direct testimony was that at several dinners Luciano had discussed his criminal conspiracy in detail with her and Fredericks. She claimed that America's most powerful criminal socialized and spilled out his guts to two serious addicts, one a prostitute and another a minor street punk. Her boyfriend Fredericks was facing serious but unrelated charges, so Dewey tried to get him to turn state's witness. But Fredericks had maintained all along that he would tell the truth in court, thus rebutting Cokey Flo's assertion that he had met Luciano. Not only did Fredericks testify for the defense to discredit his girlfriend's direct testimony just as she had done, but Fredericks' attorney Samuel Siegel corroborated his client by testifying that Cokey Flo, during a visit to his law office, had declared that she had never met Luciano. After the trial, even Cokey Flo signed an affidavit supporting Luciano's appeal by admitting her testimony was deceitful. She swore that she agreed to testify only because she was desperate for drugs, and because the prosecutors had broken her down over several nights of high-pressure questioning.

Prostitute Nancy Presser admitted she was a serious opium addict, and she testified that she visited Luciano in his suite many times. She spiced up her story with a denigrating remark that he only wanted to talk to her because he could not perform sexually. Under cross-examination Presser was unable to explain why all of the many employees who worked around-the-clock in the Waldorf-Astoria lobby had never seen her. She replied that Luciano never told anyone when she visited. This was refuted by a hotel assistant manager who testified that all late-night visitors to the Towers apartments had to be announced by the guest to the staff in the lobby to gain access. Her vague recollections of the hotel were not similar to any area in it. In addition, she could not describe where the elevators in the lobby to the rooms were located, nor anything about Luciano's suite, the bedroom where she spent so many hours talking. She could not even remember the location of the hotel or even what part of the city it was in.

Presser got so nervous during cross-examination that she ran to the ladies' room to vomit. Reentering the courtroom, she refused to return to the witness stand. When she refused to complete the cross-examination, the judge should have stricken her entire testimony from the record. Moreover, when a witness like Presser presents such critical evidence that it is impossible to "unring the bell in the jurors' ears," the judge is obligated to declare a mistrial. Instead, the judge let her testimony stand unchallenged, depriving Luciano of his constitutionally guaranteed right to confront his accuser through cross-examination.

After Presser improperly fled the courtroom in the middle of cross-examination, her boyfriend Ralph Liguori rebutted her testimony. He also testified that the Special Prosecutor had offered to drop the charges he was facing if he perjured himself with statements created by the prosecution. Liguori's mother and sister corroborated his testimony by confirming that he told them about Dewey's threats at the time they were made.

Prostitute Thelma Jordan admitted during Dewey's questioning that she was using a fictitious name and refused to discuss her background because she feared retribution for testifying. During cross-examination she revealed the actual reason for not using her real name was because it would expose her occupation to her unidentified "distinguished Kansas family." Dewey admitted in his autobiography that hotel-room attendant Marjorie Brown was also allowed to use a false name. The American legal system requires the identity of every prosecution witness to be revealed to the defense so their background may be investigated. Even in modern street-gang-member trials, the furthest the courts have gone for a fearful witness is to empty the courtroom of spectators and the media, seal the record, and admonish the defense attorney and the defendant not to identify the witness to anyone, although the defendant can do whatever he wants with this information surreptitiously. Thus, Jordan and Brown, whoever they were, are possibly the only witnesses to ever testify in an American courtroom anonymously.

Joe Bendix was a thief and a Sing Sing lifer who volunteered to testify in return for sentence mitigation. He claimed Luciano had given him secret inside information about his crimes. The defense brought out that Special Prosecutor Dewey himself had publicly accused Bendix of lying in a previous case. The defense also produced a letter Bendix wrote to his wife begging her to verify his story exactly as he put it in the letter, proving that his testimony was concocted and he needed her to perjure herself exactly as he was doing.

Madam Mildred Harris admitted being an opium smoker and morphine addict. She said her former boyfriend Gus Franco had introduced her to two men who mentioned in her presence the name "Charlie" with no last name. Under cross-examination Harris committed perjury by denying that Dewey had given her a letter of immunity to testify. Worse, her former boyfriend Franco took the stand and rebutted her testimony by denying the "Charlie" event ever occurred. Even Dewey's publicist Powell wrote that Harris' testimony was questionable because of a glaring inconsistency. She first testified she had never met Luciano, and then she told the jury he recognized her at a bar.

Ignoring that all six witnesses against Luciano were rebutted by someone close to them, what was Dewey's case? Only six of the 68 prosecution witnesses mentioned Luciano, and three of these could only contribute that someone had mentioned in passing the name "Charlie" with no last name. They admitted they never met him and could not recognize him in the courtroom. All six admitted either being hopeless drug addicts or receiving immunity from serious criminal offenses. A year after the trial, Dewey even admitted in a series of *Saturday Evening Post* articles of having unduly pressured all six to testify.

Several hotel employees did testify that they saw various defendants enter or leave Luciano's suite. However, this testimony did not connect him to illicit prostitution activities, suggesting an acquaintanceship at most. And even this limited prosecution testimony was called into question. For example, the assistant manager of the Hotel Barbizon-Plaza testified that he told the prosecutor he had never seen any of the defendants while Luciano was a guest there. Under cross-examination the hotelman said Dewey's assistant told him during the interview, "You must have seen that one and that one." He said the prosecutor "persisted in telling me so. He warned me about jail if I didn't tell the truth. There were three or four in the room. They were very insistent about my identifying the pictures. When I said I couldn't do it honestly, they threatened me. They hinted that Mr. Dewey was very powerful and could do as he liked." His testimony implied that the other hotel employees who testified may have perjured themselves because they feared Dewey's illegal extortionist threats. Some bookmakers and bettors who appeared for the defense also testified that they never saw any of the co-defendants in Luciano's Waldorf-Astoria Towers suite even though they visited him every day.[151]

The audacity of Dewey's prosecution of Luciano extended to anyone who got in his way. Dewey not only used extralegal tactics to intimidate potential state's witnesses into lying, but he punished anyone who told the truth when it was harmful to his case. An example was NYPD Patrolman George Heidt, who was called as a defense witness. Heidt testified that he was stationed in apartments guarding the prostitutes and madams being held as material witnesses. On several occasions he had taken Mildred Balitzer to nightclubs and had permitted her to become intoxicated. Heidt's honesty and forthrightness earned him the fury of both Dewey and Police Commissioner Valentine. They brought rumors about the large size of Heidt's bank savings accounts compared to his salary to the attention of Mayor LaGuardia, who called for a Departmental Investigation. The Commissioner held the hearing one week after the patrolman testified at Luciano's trial and suspended him two weeks later. With the trial still ongoing, the resulting newspaper headlines were intended to intimidate the remaining witnesses and the jurors.

Nine weeks later Heidt was dismissed from the department for failing to satisfactorily explain his finances. He was also fined 10-days' pay for having given an unauthorized interview to a newspaper about the police work involved in his investigation, which they claimed "tended to defeat the end of justice." Until the department persecuted him for his unflattering testimony about prosecutorial and police misconduct at Luciano's trial, his 20-year NYPD career had been spotless.

Heidt remained unemployed for a year and a half while a lawsuit against the NYPD worked its way through the system. Finally, the state Appellate Court unanimously reinstated Heidt with back pay, remission of the 10-days-pay fine, and condemnation of the actions of the NYPD. The court ruled that the policeman's talk with a newspaperman "did not tend to defeat 'the ends of justice.'" The court concluded that his wife had received money from her mother during the period in question, and it asserted that there was no evidence that the bank deposits or withdrawals were not legitimate. Six weeks later Commissioner Valentine, who had fired Heidt, complied with the court order reinstating him with full back pay.[152]

LUCIANO'S TESTIMONY ABOUT HIS BACKGROUND

Luciano took the witness stand in his own defense. He swore he did not know any of the witnesses who testified against him, and that prior to the trial he had met only one of the defendants who was charged as a co-conspirator. When he categorically denied ever receiving a dollar from prostitution, Dewey got more specific by asking, "Did you ever take a dollar proceeds from any whore or prostitute, directly or indirectly, in your life?" Luciano's response was forthright, "I always gave. I never took."[153]

Practically everything that is known about Luciano's background came from the testimony at this trial because the low-profile hood had been almost invisible to the authorities. The first time his name appeared in the press was late in Prohibition. At the time of his trial, his FBI file contained just one document, an internal memo that had been written almost two years after Prohibition was repealed. This memo revealed the total knowledge possessed by the nation's premier police agency. It consisted of his police record and the comments, "Is a general gangster and racketeer - is a boss of a Lower East Side gang. Operates chiefly in beer and liquor. ... Is apparently wealthy. ... The Bureau's files reflect no further information in connection with this individual."

A decade later Luciano's FBI file still contained just three documents. This is truly surprising considering that he had headed top illegal alcohol and gambling enterprises for three decades and had been the Mafia's Boss of Bosses for 15 years. His FBI file later grew to 548 pages because of political intrigue that grew out of the prostitution-booking case.[154]

Virtually no record exists about Charlie's childhood, early teenage years, or introduction into the underworld, as is true of all major Prohibition crime figures. Only a few top hoods from Luciano's era ever talked publicly about their own activities, and it was not until they were old men. These few hoods all admitted they had no idea what businesses Charlie was in and knew nothing about his background.

What is known about Luciano is that he was born in Lerecara Friddi, Sicily on November 11, 1897, and he was baptized Salvatore Lucania. He was seven years old when his family immigrated and settled in a slum tenement on Manhattan's Lower East Side in 1905. He later Americanized his name to Charlie Luciano.

Luciano stood 5-feet-8 and weighed 158 pounds. His failure to attend school at age 14 landed him in the Brooklyn Truant School. Afterwards he quit school to go to work as a shipping clerk in a hat factory for $5 a week, the only legitimate job he ever held. He soon quit and hung around crap games. He had one major conviction at age 18 for selling one packet of opium to an undercover agent for which he spent six months in the reformatory. Not long after his release he went to work for Joe Gould's floating crap games. After three or four years he began running his own games and frequenting racetracks, where he became an expert handicapper and eventually booked horses from other bettors at the tracks. In his testimony he referred to himself as a Bootlegger, a term adopted during Prohibition to mean any type of alcohol supplier but correctly described the practice of concealing liquor in the upper part of the boot or the lower part of the leg. His only legitimate occupation as an adult was as the owner of "a piece of a restaurant" at Broadway and 52nd Street in the late Roaring '20s before the stock market crash.

Luciano's testimony was supported by a succession of defense witnesses. Several bookmakers testified that Luciano was a bookmaker at racetracks and some of his clients were socially prominent. Convicted crap-game operator Fred Bachmann said Luciano had been his partner in several dice games in Westchester County, New York. That ended because he explained, "When a town got hot, I closed."[155]

One bookmaker said he patronized a wide-open dice game run by Luciano in Saratoga Springs in upper New York. "It was a low-class house" where bets as small as a dime were taken. A music publisher testified while he was visiting Saratoga, "One night, I saw my friend Sam Rosoff, the subway builder, lose his money and make a loan from Lucania. I asked Lucania whether I could do the same, and he loaned me $500." Luciano handed both players interest-free loans so they could get back into the action at his tables.[156]

Luciano admitted that he spent his career in three illegal activities – crap games, booking horses, and bootlegging. Witnesses backed him up. This defense testimony was in stark contrast to Dewey's vilification of Luciano in his press barrage during the six months leading up to the trial and in his opening and closing statements to the jury. Dewey frequently proclaimed that Luciano was Public Enemy Number 1, the man behind all major crime in New York City and the most dangerous man walking. But Dewey's rhetoric was never supported by the exhaustive, long-term investigations by his large staff and the NYPD contingent, who found no evidence that Luciano ever committed any illegal act other than the gambling and Prohibition violations he readily admitted. In fact, Dewey's publicist Hickman Powell wrote that for six months the NYPD and the Special Prosecutor's staff studied police reports and questioned hoods about Luciano's background, but they never found a single bit of information to shake or impeach Luciano's trial testimony. (See Addendum M)

Dewey's staff presented evidence at trial that Luciano had 25 arrests during his life. Almost all were so inconsequential that his name did not appear in the *New York Times* until a decade after Prohibition began when he was 31. Dewey's documents corroborated Luciano's testimony that his record contained just two convictions – an arrest for gambling at a crap game while on a Miami vacation at age 33 that resulted in a $1,000 fine, and the conviction at age 18 for selling one packet of opium.[157]

The opium conviction stands out as a serious crime compared to his gambling and Prohibition violations. Yet in the early 1900s a meaningful percentage of the U.S. adult population was unknowingly addicted to drugs. America's major drug manufacturers sent traveling salesman to rural areas with large quantities of potions and elixirs they promoted as general cures "for whatever ails you." Tests later proved that these secret *patent-medicine* formulas contained up to 50% morphine. No matter the ailment, a couple swigs made one feel a whole lot better. Most rural addicts were middle-aged white women. Another cause of unintended addiction was the use of morphine as a general painkiller. It was frequently given in hospitals, especially during and after operations, and the military dispensed it for battlefield injuries. By the time many patients were released from a hospital or military service, they were addicted.

Two federal laws changed all this. The 1906 Pure Food and Drug Act created the Food and Drug Administration (FDA) which approves all drugs. The new agency tested patent medicines, and it refused to approve them unless they had a prescription label stating "Warning – May be habit forming." This pharmacological law effectively prevented unwary addiction, and it reduced America's addiction rate more than any criminal statute passed since. In 1914, a year before Luciano was arrested for selling opium, passage of the Harrison Act criminalized the non-medical use of drugs for the first time. The law applied to opium, morphine, and cocaine, but it did not mention amphetamines, barbiturates, marijuana, hashish, or hallucinogenic drugs.

The target market of illegal drug pushers at that time was not impressionable, innocent teenagers, but rather the desperate adults who had been addicted by the drug companies, the medical profession, and the military, and then were denied a legal source by the federal government. Congress failed to offer these unfortunate victims a withdrawal program to wean their craving for the addictive drugs it criminalized.

Luciano was arrested a second time for drugs eight years later in 1923. A federal informant claimed Luciano sold him a packet of morphine. Yet by that time Charlie was the country's largest Prohibition wholesaler and a wealthy man, so this accusation is highly suspect at best. Since the prosecution at that trial failed to produce any federal agent or any other witness to corroborate the incident had occurred, the judge concluded that the informant, who was a serious addict, was not credible and quashed the charge. Years later during his 1936 prostitution-conspiracy trial, Luciano told the jury that he had been framed and accurately presented the facts in that case.

Dewey countered Luciano's testimony by subpoenaing the federal agent who had brought the drug charge 13 years earlier. The agent testified that he believed Luciano did it, and that he let Luciano go only because he informed on the location of a large drug cache. However, on cross-examination the agent was unable to explain why no record existed of the alleged big-time drug seizure, or why he failed to arrest the people from whom he allegedly confiscated this large cache. The agent's claim that Luciano had been his informant 20 years earlier angered every one who knew Luciano. America's underworld supported Charlie's rise to the peak of organized crime because they trusted and respected him, particularly because he would never reveal information about anyone for any reason. Remember, he chose almost certain death from a vicious police beating rather than disclose the hideout of a hood he had nothing to do with and did not even like.

Luciano testified in his 1936 trial that he sold a packet of opium to three separate people, including his 1915 drug arrest, and he never sold dope again. He spent the rest of his career warning the members of his group and the rest of the underworld about the dire consequences of handling illegal drugs. His one exception regarding drugs was alcohol during Prohibition because of its widespread public acceptance. Luciano's Prohibition partner Jimmy Blue Eyes told me emphatically, "After Charlie Lucky served his time for violating the new Harrison Act, he stayed out of drugs the rest of his life. He was very opposed to involvement in the drug business."

Luciano and the Young Turks never talked publicly about dope, but Luciano's reformatory incarceration clearly had a profound impact on him. When Luciano became Boss of Bosses, he issued just two edicts - no murder and no drugs - policies that were continued by his successor Frank Costello. Under their combined quarter-century reign, both men made it known that no Mafioso was to deal in or take drugs. Associates of the Mafia were well aware of both men's strong opposition to dope. Under their leadership, Mafiosi were rarely arrested for dealing in or using drugs because they shunned touching it. Several in-depth federal investigations later in the lives of Luciano and the Young Turks failed to find any link between any of them and drug pushers. Jimmy Blue Eyes told me, "Our group was utterly opposed to drugs. We were only in liquor and gambling. We made more money after Repeal, when we all (the members of his group) went into gambling."

THE VERDICT

During the trial's closing arguments, the defense hammered away at Dewey's prosecutorial misconduct. Defense Attorney Caesar Barra told the jury, "You are not to launch or boom a political campaign. One witness said Mr. Dewey expects to be Governor. You're not nominating him for public office." Attorney Barra cited the false testimony given by booker David Marcus, who had been a co-defendant until he took a plea deal to turn state's witness and then lied on the stand about his conviction record. When the defense presented detectives from Pittsburgh to expose Marcus' perjury, Dewey quickly stipulated to the judge that after Marcus had testified he had admitted his lie to Dewey. He stipulated to the perjury to make the detectives' testimony irrelevant, because their proof that Marcus had perjured himself would have further undermined Dewey's case.

However, Barra continued, "Not until Dewey saw on the witness stand a chain of policemen from Pennsylvania did he make it known that Marcus had committed perjury. I always understood that the best traditions of the bar and the canon of ethics of the profession required that when a lawyer called a witness and later learned the witness had willfully and deliberately committed perjury, it was his duty to report it to court and jury immediately. I have known a lawyer to be disbarred because he retained and concealed that information. If a lawyer for the defense had done it, he would have been cited for contempt and brought before the bar association." He lamented that "Perjury is not a crime, when it is committed for the State of New York and for the holy cause of justice."[158]

Following four weeks of what was likely the most curious and perjured testimony ever presented in a U.S. court, the judge gave the case to the jury at 9:30 p.m. on Saturday night. The jurors first order of business was to enjoy a leisurely social dinner before the judge sent them to deliberate just before midnight. They quickly considered the almost 600 separate charges against 11 defendants, including 90 against Luciano, and returned every verdict before 5:00 a.m. This means the average decision time for each verdict was 30 seconds. Prosecutor Dewey's specially selected jurors slapped Luciano with 62 separate felony guilty verdicts for voluntary prostitution that was a victimless crime. The *New York Times* reported, "Lucania maintained his customary composure," unlike the other defendants who displayed reactions from anger to tears.[159]

Prosecutors often overstate a case during opening arguments and fail to back it up during trial. But during closing arguments, a prosecutor is not permitted to treat as fact anything that was not admitted as evidence or testimony. However, in this case the judge allowed Dewey to refer to Luciano as "Public Enemy Number 1" and as possibly "the greatest gangster in America" despite Dewey's own extensive investigation and the facts he presented proving his hyperbole to be untrue.

After the decision the jurors told the press that at the end of the defense's 13-hours of summation they were doubtful about the verdict, but their minds were composed by Dewey's seven-hour final address. This means the jury convicted because of Dewey's entirely untrue presentation about Luciano being involved in a host of other unspecified major crimes and the big-time-hoodlum image he painted. The judge should never have allowed such statements because no evidence was presented during trial or at any other time to back them up.

The fact that the jury had any doubts at all about Luciano's guilt indicates just how weak Dewey's case was. He had selected "a blue-ribbon panel of jurors" by using an aberration in the jury-selection process arising from a unique and bizarre New York law that allowed a prosecutor to stack the panel with his political supporters and cronies. This law revived an archaic tradition of the English justice system which that country had abandoned 1,000 years earlier as inherently biased and unfair. Kings and church leaders once ensured a verdict by handpicking blue-ribbon jurors who were predisposed to their position. It was in this era that England also tried and abolished trial by the ordeal of torture because it also was found not to be probative of guilt.[160]

When it comes to grand juries rather than trial juries, blue-ribbon panels in which judges or prosecutors select their friends or prominent citizens have been common in the U. S., because those who are accused are afforded at their criminal trials the protection of a randomly selected *petit* (or *petty*) jury of their peers. New York state went much further than this tradition by passing a law in 1896 that allowed prosecutors to also handpick criminal trial "blue-ribbon" petit jury pools for specially selected cases - meaning those that were politically sensitive, the ones in which the prosecutor had to convict someone for political imagery no matter how weak the case.[161]

New York's law required that these special-panel jurors be selected from lists of people of high income, wealth, social position, and educational levels, or in the professions or arts. The purpose was to obtain jurors of more than average alertness, intelligence, and common sense. The argument for selecting only "middle-aged business and professional men" was "to insure a jury of a high order of intelligence," which was alleged somehow to be linked with the qualities of more impartiality and fairness. No evidence was ever presented during debates about the merits of this law to show how any of these traits bore any relationship with each other.

A year and a half after Luciano's conviction, the State of New York's Judicial Council in a report to the Legislature advocated abolition of these special juries. The Council pointed out that the DAs who invoked this law would not allow consideration of jurors who had previously served in a case ending in acquittal or deadlock. Thus, "special juries are particularly chosen to be convicting juries" and therefore produce unfair and unjust trails. The report included a study of every homicide case in 1933 except for those involving insurance or automobiles. Of the 47 defendants tried for homicide before special juries, 83% were convicted and 17% acquitted. In contrast of 156 homicide defendants tried by ordinary impartial juries, 43% were convicted and 57% acquitted. This significant difference in outcome is even more dramatic when considering that blue-ribbon juries were used to obtain convictions in the most important cases, meaning those that were politically charged for the DAs and for which evidence was weak.[162]

The Judicial Council later held that the use of a special jury system "becomes distinctly un-American and not consonant with a trial by one's peers." It found the selection process was undemocratic because these juries were not cross-sections of the community. The law lacked any objective qualifications, so the selections were at the whim of the DAs. The report also contended that general or regular juries proved they could handle any type of case.[163]

Two weeks later the New York Senate acted quickly upon the Council's findings by passing a bill to abolish the blue-ribbon jury law. The issues seemed clear-cut, so the bill provoked no discussion or dissent. However, Manhattan DA Dewy had used blue-ribbon juries to win convictions in every single one of his racketeer and politician prosecutions. Thus, this bill posed a serious threat to the future success of his racket-busting record, without which his ambitious political goals were unobtainable. Thus, he immediately went public with his opposition to this bill, and he rallied influential and vocal political allies who caused Judiciary Committee Chairman Charles Robinson to call for hearings in the Republican-controlled Assembly.

DA Dewey sent a written statement to the Assembly Committee in order to rouse fear of crime in the public and befuddle the issues of justice and fairness. He claimed that repeal of the special jury law would be a "wanton injury to the already beleaguered administration of criminal justice." Despite overwhelming statistical evidence to the contrary, he claimed that it was only the handpicked juries who were without bias. In reality Dewey packed his juries with people seeking his political favor - the most biased of all potential jurors. Yet he wrote to the Committee, "It is hoped that all jurors will ultimately possess the qualifications and the freedom from prejudice that the law today requires of those on the special jury list." Committee Chairman Robinson carried the Republican fear mongering much further, declaring the bill "a life and death matter" because "if a desperate criminal is released by a sympathetic jury, it might mean the life of some citizen or policeman."[164]

More critics of blue-ribbon juries soon stepped forward to assail many other problems with this system. For example, the DAs selected only certain people from the upper classes refusing to allow any women at all and any men with the following heritages - Italian, Jewish, African, or Puerto Rican. The established majority social order and power structure used the democratic process to preserve a justice system that dominated and controlled, while at the same time excluded, the more recently arrived immigrants and the entrenched poor. Not surprisingly, these blue-ribbon juries were particularly harsh on defendants from minority groups.

One interesting sidelight was the inequity in the use of blue-ribbon juries between New York's counties. The law applied to only those counties that had a population of one million or more, which meant that of the 57 counties, it could only be used in five, with four being boroughs in New York City - New York (Manhattan), Kings (Brooklyn), Queens, Bronx, and Westchester (White Plains) Counties. This led a citizen in a letter to the editor of the *New York Times* to ask the obvious question, "One may well ask why blue-ribbon juries are limited to the five counties. Is the average intelligence in the remaining fifty-two counties of New York State of a superior brand?" The letter writer accentuated the following facts. No county's assembled list of qualified jurors for special service contained more than 2,800 people. The 1940 census showed Manhattan had a population of 1,890,000, and Brooklyn's was 2,698,000. Thus, a pathetically small percentage of these two populations were deemed fit for jury duty in politically charged cases and all were of the same class, race, and gender.[165]

Although blue-ribbon juries were legal for 70 years and made it so much easier for prosecutors to convict, the vast majority of the DAs in these five boroughs refused to use them except for the two Republican cohorts - Dewey in Manhattan and Burton Turkus in Brooklyn. Dewey used the system with great success in his racketeer and politician trials, as did Turkus in his Murder, Inc. trials. In all these trials the evidence was weak and the cases were based on claims that the defendants were part of large, dangerous, secret organizations for which no substantiation was offered during these trials. Dewey and Turkus exploited the blue-ribbon jury system to dramatically pump up their conviction rates, especially first-degree murder cases to add more executions to their records.

Despite all the information presented in the hearings about the injustices of handpicked juries by prosecutors, the Republican-controlled Assembly Judiciary Committee killed a bill that would have abolished them. DA Dewey and other Republican leaders used the scare tactics of the threat of crime and the alleged ignorance of common jurors to successfully mobilize the business community, the wealthy, and the powerful to oppose the bill.

A decade later the U.S. Supreme Court ruled in two different cases that there was nothing wrong with the classism, racism, or sexism of blue-ribbon juries. These Supreme Justices shredded the Constitution by finding in contradiction to overwhelming evidence that the demographic differences between the make up of blue-ribbon juries and the overall population to be "unintentional" coincidences, and it rejected all arguments about the Constitutional right to a trial by a jury of one's peers. This Court's same majority membership in this era found in other cases that oppressive racial discrimination and exclusion that was enforced by domestic terrorist groups like the KKK was acceptable treatment for Americans of African descent.

Every year from 1938 to 1965, the New York State Democratic Party had a campaign platform plank supporting repeal of the law allowing DAs to pack kangaroo juries, and they backed this up by submitting a bill to the New York Legislature. The bills were supported by bar associations and civil liberties groups, among others. Dewey strongly opposed eliminating elitist juries from the time he was DA and even when he was Mayor and Governor of New York until 1954. During the decade after Dewey left office, the Republicans continued their long-term support of his anti-civil-liberties and anti-criminal-justice cause. The Democrat's bills failed to pass the Legislature until the year after President Lyndon Johnson pushed the national Civil Rights Act through Congress.[166]

Dewey, in defense of blue-ribbon juries, admitted that he had used them "extensively." He later wrote, "I argued [before the Legislature] that the blue-ribbon jury was simply the selection from the rolls of regular jurors of people who had sat through one or more criminal cases. ...The purpose was not to get bankers or businessmen on the panel. There were as many laborers and clerks on blue ribbon panels as on any other panels." Court records prove his statement to be a blatant lie.[167]

Dewey's core defense was just plain weird. He argued that schizophrenics were frequently on juries, which "could defeat justice," and that jurors who were claustrophobic became mentally ill during deliberations preventing "justice." His flimsy position was that schizophrenia, claustrophobia, and "hysterical" anxiety attacks were common among jurors, and to prevent this, it was essential to bar 99.99% of citizens from sitting on juries. Actually, effective solutions to such infrequent problems were already in place - attorneys can weed out certain prospective jurors; judges can remove erratic jurors; and jurors have alternates who can replace them if they cannot continue.

Dewey concluded, "I argued that one of the best methods was simply to put on the grand jury panel people who had previously served through a long criminal trial." He falsely implied that blue-ribbon juries were selected randomly from previous panels. He totally avoided the two biggest complaints, especially with his panels, that prosecutors selected people who had never acquitted defendants and who were politically beholden to the DA.[168]

Dewey also wrote other extremist anti-American legal positions. Despite being chairman of the city Bar Association's Committee on Criminal Courts Law and Procedure, every one of his proposals was voted down for consideration. He fought passionately to grant prosecutors the authority to tell the jury that a defendant's failure to testify in his own defense implied guilt. This proposal would have wiped out one of the most basic Constitutional rights, the Fifth Amendment to refuse to testify against yourself.

At the defendants' sentencing in the prostitution-bookers' case, the judge allowed Luciano to say in a clear, low voice, "Your Honor, I have nothing to say outside the fact that I want to say again I am innocent." Then the judge commented on the charges and evidence that involved no violence, force, or intimidation of any kind. Yet he told Luciano that he was one of the most vicious criminals who had ever come before his court despite not a shred of evidence to this effect in the trial. The judge sentenced him to prison for 30 to 50 years, tantamount to a life sentence for the 38-year-old Luciano. In contrast, the judge directed that all the state's witnesses who committed perjury in the framing and mischaracterizing of Luciano be set free.[169]

Costello's nephew Leonard Katz wrote that Luciano's attorneys complained to their friends that "The trial was a travesty of justice. Dewey was guilty of subordination of witnesses, inflaming public opinion against Luciano, and rigging the trial in such a way that the defendant didn't stand a chance."[170]

Jimmy Blue Eyes told me, "Dewey framed Charlie. All of the women testified falsely against him. He didn't know one of 'em. He wasn't involved with prostitution, except as a customer. He hated pimps. Then Dewey went after the 'mob', charging illegal gamblers with being atrocious monsters." Ironically, Dewey undermined his basic contention about Luciano when he made observations that were similar to Jimmy Blue Eyes' about the scorn New York City's crime leaders had for pimps. Dewey wrote that the top mob leaders would visit a prostitute, "But the same men would never eat with a pimp." Thus, Dewey himself admitted Luciano would never have associated with the pimps in this case. Dewey found the behavior of the gambling men he prosecuted and persecuted inconsistently curious only because he never understood that for them consensual involvement with women was wonderful, but taking money from a woman was the lowest thing a man could do.[171]

Dewey further weakened his main premise by writing that he believed a popular book about the Mafia, *The Valachi Papers,* was an "authentic" firsthand account of organized crime. Ironically, in doing so, Dewey was tacitly admitting Luciano was not associated with the prostitution bookers he prosecuted. Dewey even quoted as factual in his own book, Joe Valachi's statement, "'I was stunned. Charlie Lucky wasn't no pimp. He was a Boss [of Bosses]!'"[172]

Dewey also undermined the position he had presented during the trial and in his public attacks when he wrote that organized crime leaders did not associate with or talk to underlings, and he admitted that the subordinates were the ones who did all the work. Dewey's whole case had been based on testimony that Luciano - who never discussed business with anyone except Jimmy Blue

Eyes, Lansky, Costello, and Adonis - repeatedly spilled his guts to minor street punks, prostitutes, and strangers.

Polly Adler, who ran New York City's finest and most expensive brothel from the beginning of the Roaring 20's until the end of World War II, wrote in her autobiography that she was "astonished" that Dewey tried to tie Luciano to the prostitution business. She found it "inconceivable" that such a link existed. "For one thing, I used to supply the girls when Charlie Lucky entertained in his plushy hotel suites, and it hardly seems logical that if he had the alleged tie-ups he would patronize a madam outside the combine [the prostitution bookers]." She wrote that underworld leaders openly talked about Luciano in front of her at her house of joy, "But not once was it ever even implied that he derived any part of his income from prostitution." Adler added, "Certainly I believe that in the many years I was associated with prostitution if there had been even a hint of a rumor of a tie-up between Charlie and the [prostitution booking] combination, I would have heard of it."

Polly Adler pointed out that Dewey's whole case was "the word of frightened, ignorant prostitutes, many of them alcoholics and drug addicts." She knew Dewey's witness Mildred Harris, and remarked about her testimony, "I could not accept a word of this story." Adler also knew the city's top mobsters, and she emphasized that a pimp, a man who shares a prostitutes earnings, "is considered an untouchable by big racket men."

Polly Adler wrote that one evening during Luciano's trial, a limousine drove her to an office conference room. In attendance were the city's top racket leaders. She had never seen them all together - or all fully clothed for that matter. An attorney with the group explained that every man there was doing everything he could "to prove that the testimony being given by certain women was false." They were attempting to find facts that would "discredit that testimony." She and the men there knew who headed what rackets and all believed the charge was false. Guilt would have meant that Luciano talked freely about his illegal businesses to strangers and street punks, but remained secretive with the other top mobsters. Unfortunately, none of the prosecution witnesses had worked for Adler, so she could not help.[173]

In preparing Luciano's appeal, his attorneys wanted to talk with all the prosecution witnesses, but the Special Prosecutor could not stand to have his handling of them scrutinized. Every witness had moved and left no forwarding address. Dewey's PR defender Hickman Powell wrote that those who testified against Luciano were given a four-month, first-class vacation to Europe after the trial and then moved to other areas of the country, all financed by Dewey's political supporters.[174]

Jimmy Blue Eyes said, "Meyer [Lansky] was determined to get his friend Charlie out of prison. He spent a great deal of effort tracking down several of the women. All had disappeared with government assistance, after they perjured themselves against Charlie. Meyer got affidavits from them, and possibly other documentation, proving that Lucky was framed."

Nine months after Luciano's conviction, his attorneys were finally able to assemble the information to file a motion for a new trial. Dewey's three key witnesses - Nancy Presser, Mildred Harris, and Cokie Flo Brown – completely repudiated their trial testimony as untrue fabrications. Luciano's attorneys did not have them sign the affidavits recanting their testimony until after they had been released from a private sanitarium for drug addicts paid for by Luciano's associates. The affidavits were obtained by impeccable third parties, two former Department of Justice agents who had become private detectives. Lansky employed them to eliminate any consideration that the girls had been pressured. When the women testified again, the attorneys wanted them sober and not influenced by the customary threats and bribes from DA Dewey or anyone else associated with his injustice system.

A month later at Justice McCook's hearing for a retrial, Dewey attacked Luciano's attorneys for funding the women's treatment for drug addiction in order to obtain affidavits - a marked contrast to Dewey's tactic of alternatively denying and illegally supplying the women drugs in return for their perjured testimony. The Judge had to maintain the legitimacy of his tainted handling of the case, so it was predictable that he refused to recuse himself and denied the request for a new trial. In the midst of these proceedings, the Department of Immigration in Washington ordered Luciano be deported to Italy at the conclusion of his prison term if he lived that long.[175]

Five justices of the Appellate Division of the New York State Supreme Court unanimously upheld the decision. The Court of Appeals also upheld Luciano's conviction 5 to 1. Appeals courts usually ignore the later recanting of testimony because they want finality of decisions. In addition, witnesses sometimes recant their testimony for bizarre reasons, such as women who are assaulted by strangers and later try to get their rapists released because they have fallen in love with them since their convictions. The U.S. Supreme Court refused to hear Luciano's final appeal for justice. Rebuked by the entire U.S. justice system, Luciano appeared destined to spend the rest of his life in jail. Charlie's lucky streak had run out. But then again maybe not, as truth can be so much stranger than fiction.

DEWEY'S FOIBLES & PROSECUTION OF POLITICAL OPPONENTS

Well before the Luciano persecution back early in Dewey's career, he began using his anti-racketeering platform as he set his sights on the presidency of the United States. While an Assistant U.S. Attorney, he had sent Irving "Waxey Gordon" Wexler to federal prison for income tax evasion and he had a tax case pending against Arthur "Dutch Schultz" Flegenheimer at the time Luciano had him murdered to stop him from carrying out his plan to kill Dewey. But Dewey's political career was put into high gear with his conviction of Luciano. A year-and-a-half afterwards, Dewey handily won election as DA in New York County for Manhattan.[176]

Even though Dewey built his political reputation by prosecuting gamblers, he liked to indulge in this illegal activity himself. He frequented the Harding Republican Club, which was the GOP's counterpart to the Democrat's Tammany Hall. There Dewey wheeled and dealed politically and joined his cronies at the illegal crap table in the lobby. Besides, Dewey had no problem with hoodlums just as long as they were his political supporters. Dewey may have improperly rigged the trials of those hoods who were not his friends, but he zealously protected the criminal behavior of mobsters who were personal friends by never prosecuting them. It was not only the height of hypocrisy, it was the ultimate abuse of his office.

After the Luciano trial, Dewey went after Luciano's first lieutenant Vito Genovese. Dewey announced that he had two underworld witnesses who claimed that Genovese had ordered the murder of small-time hoodlum Ferdinand "The Shadow" Boccia three years earlier. Genovese quickly sailed to Italy, where he remained for almost a decade. That put Luciano's second lieutenant Frank Costello in charge of the gang and acting Boss of Bosses for the imprisoned Luciano. Dewey's PR man Hickman Powell later wrote that Dewey left Costello alone because he had no clue until two decades later that Costello was even in the Mafia let alone so powerful a leader.[177]

The year after Dewey was elected Manhattan DA, the Republicans nominated him as their candidate for governor, but he lost to incumbent Governor Lehman, the man who had made Dewey's career by appointing him Special Prosecutor three years earlier. It was a close election, so Dewey returned to the DA's office to bolster his corruption-crushing image for the gubernatorial election four years hence. He focused on Tammany Hall's top two political powerhouses, Al Marinelli and Jimmy Hines. They were the politicos who had joined Luciano and Costello in private confabs with the two leading candidates at the 1932 Democratic presidential convention. During Dewey's losing campaign, he accused Marinelli of meeting in private conferences at his political club with gangsters such as Luciano. After the election Dewey offered enough specific details to cause Marinelli to quickly resign as County Clerk, although he continued to be a Tammany leader.

Dewey then went after Hines. The DA pressured attorney Dixie Davis to testify truthfully that Hines had been paid off to give legal protection to the Harlem lottery operation of Davis' former client, beer baron Dutch Schultz, who had been murdered three years earlier. Dewey also presented evidence that Hines had selected William Dodge to run for DA and used gangster contributions to elect him. Hines was convicted and sentenced to four to eight years in Sing Sing, while attorney Davis got a year in prison for his involvement in the Dutchman's illicit activities.

Sadly, there is little to differentiate between Dewey's actions to become president of the United States and Capone's actions to become dictator of Chicago. Both completely corrupted the legal system and destroyed anyone who got in their way. As for Luciano, the man Dewey castigated as Public Enemy Number 1 and who the judge also called vicious in the extreme, he behaved like a perfect gentlemen in accepting his utterly unjust fate of life in prison. Even though he headed the country's largest criminal organization in which every member had taken a blood oath to murder under the boss' orders, not one person who was involved in the lies to frame him was killed, hurt, or even threatened. Luciano did not exact vengeance against the corrupt DA, his dishonest staff, the shifty judge, the hand-selected biased jury, the lying witnesses, or any of the other conspirators who had systematically destroyed his life. Not one of the Young Turks ever reacted vengefully during their lifetimes, despite having incredible firepower to do so, and all seven certainly had good reason at times because of the horrific offenses and injuries each endured during his life.

Manhattan DA Dewey's transgressions against the legal system were horrific records of prosecutorial malfeasance. He perpetuated his type of abuse by teaching a protégé how to use these improper prosecuting tactics and one-sided Kangaroo-court blue-ribbon juries. The Manhattan DA's student was Brooklyn Assistant DA Burton Turkus who learned his lessons well, and this made possible his equally-preposterous Murder, Inc. trials. DA Dewey had destroyed Luciano's life, and now Assistant DA Turkus was about to make another one of the Young Turks the key defendant in his Murder, Inc. trials. Turkus' actions would wreck havoc on the life of Ben Siegel.[178]

CHAPTER 8

MURDER, INC. & LEPKE BUCHALTER

A DA INVENTS MURDER, INC.

Four years after Manhattan DA Tom Dewey convicted Charlie Luciano in the trumped up voluntary prostitution case, Brooklyn began separate prosecutions for three homicides that were about to become infamous as the "Murder, Inc." cases. Manhattan and Brooklyn were independent legal jurisdictions, but the Manhattan DA frequently spoke to the press about these Brooklyn cases as if he were involved. Dewey saw these cases as an opportunity to enhance his racket-busting image for political gain, so he surreptitiously manipulated these prosecutions from behind the scenes by coaching and guiding the Murder, Inc. prosecutor, Brooklyn Assistant DA Burton Turkus. Student Turkus would learn well Dewey's techniques to thwart justice, and use them to create the biggest and most outrageous myth about a huge nonexistent criminal empire in history. These prosecutions would further tarnish the reputation of Luciano, falsely connect the names of the other Young Turks to these killings, and lead to death-penalty criminal charges against Ben Siegel.

The saga of Murder, Inc. began six years earlier when Alec "Red" Alpert was shot in the back in a residential courtyard in Brooklyn's Brownsville district. The 19-year-old victim was a violent burglar who, it was believed, was assassinated because of rumors he talked to the law about activities of the local street gang he belonged to. A few days after his killing, three gang members were charged, but a judge dismissed the case for lack of evidence. The case lay dormant for six years, until newly-elected Brooklyn DA Bill O'Dwyer took office. A month later he obtained a new first-degree murder indictment against three gang members.

Politically ambitious DA O'Dwyer immediately made this case a cause célèbre. He announced to the press that these arrests were the beginning of his keeping a campaign promise to rid Brooklyn of "vicious criminals and cheap punks." O'Dwyer publicly displayed intense interest in the case. After the three Alpert homicide defendants were arrested, the DA questioned them, stood nearby at their booking, watched over their fingerprinting, and conducted the arraignment. DA O'Dwyer proudly proclaimed, "This is a clean-cut charge. I have an air-tight case against these punks, and I want them to know it right now." He said he was personally ramrodding the case, but he declined to disclose the nature or source of his evidence. O'Dwyer would take credit publicly for the three Murder, Inc. trials throughout the rest of his career, but he actually stepped aside and turned the cases over to his newly appointed Assistant DA Burton Turkus.[179]

Despite DA O'Dwyer's public braggadocio about the strength of his case, Assistant DA Turkus knew the case was too thin to take to trial because he had just one accomplice willing to testify as a state's witness. Prosecutor Turkus later wrote in his book *Murder, Inc.* that when he interrogated defendant Abe "Kid Twist" Reles, the suspect just laughed at him because he knew there was no second witness for corroboration as required by law. In his youth Reles had been a tough neighborhood bully, and then became notorious as one of the most vicious members of his gang.

During the six years between his two indictments for Alpert's murder, Reles racked up 42 arrests including his sixth charge for homicide, but he was never convicted of a major crime.

Even though Reles was confident he could not be tried for the Alpert murder, he soon sent word to Prosecutor Turkus that he would testify against major Brooklyn gangsters and provide corroborating witnesses. In return he demanded immunity from prosecution for 11 murders he would admit participating in. He wanted amnesty because he knew the statute of limitations would never run out on these cases, and other gang members might turn state's witness against him if charged with major crimes. Even with this explanation, Reles' offer to testify was puzzling. He gained nothing because the prosecutor lacked evidence to try him for any of these murders. Yet he voluntarily put his life in long-term jeopardy by fingering brutal gang members and leaders.

Even Prosecutor Turkus described Reles' offer as bizarre and irrational, emphasizing that he could never figure out Reles' motive. Turkus later wrote, "What made Kid Twist sing? As far as I know, no one ever got the answer." Turkus speculated that the most likely reasons were that Reles enjoyed the limelight or was simply crazy. Prosecutor Turkus should have heard an alarm sound in his head about an informer's veracity with the peculiar motivations of either wanting the limelight or craziness. But instead of being leery of everything Reles said, Turkus bought the gangster's entire yarn because the Assistant DA was as politically ambitious as Dewey. Assistant DA Turkus was seeking to win a judgeship in the next election.[180]

A decade later DA O'Dwyer testified in a U.S. Senate hearing that Reles had good reason to cooperate - he had been indicted for car theft and O'Dwyer promised him a fair-sentencing deal in return for naming higher-ups. Whatever Reles' actual motive was, from the moment Democratic Brooklyn DA O'Dwyer gave Republican activist Assistant DA Turkus free rein in handling the Alpert murder case, Turkus quietly turned for guidance from Manhattan DA Dewey, the Republican's most powerful state leader. Dewey had recently come close to winning the New York gubernatorial election and had successfully prosecuted Luciano in the sensational brothel-booking trial. In the Luciano case Dewey displayed his no-holds-barred prosecutorial style when having weak evidence. He stacked the blue-ribbon jury with political allies; offered plea deals to criminals for prepared and perjured testimony; dazzled the jury with a detailed description of a nonexistent, large, dangerous, secret criminal organization without offering any substantiation; and exaggerated the case's significance to the jury and the press. Dewey's actions were designed to foster his image as a powerful, racket-busting super-prosecutor in order to win the governorship, furthering his long-term plan to become President of the United States. To bolster his chance of winning the governorship the second time around, Dewey helped Turkus develop a prosecutorial strategy in three separate murder cases and kept his own name associated with them in the press.[181]

Dewey taught Turkus his four extra-legal prosecution techniques, so that the first murder case could be upgraded from a violent local-street-gang dispute into the crime of the century. Thus, Prosecutor Turkus gave Reles a walk for 11 murders in exchange for concocting the existence of a massive murder-for-hire organization fancifully named *"Murder, Inc."* The purpose of Reles' ludicrous saga was threefold - to dazzle the jury so they would ignore the lack of evidence, to qualify the case as first-degree murder which carried an automatic death sentence, and to allow Assistant DA Turkus to exaggerate the case's importance to the press to enhance his political image.

It was difficult for a prosecutor in that era to get a first-degree murder conviction that carried the death penalty against a defendant who had committed a single homicide. For example, during Turkus' career as a defense attorney, he had represented 30 murderers and saved every one from capital punishment. Turkus was determined to get a first-degree murder conviction because execution sentences enhanced a prosecutor's crime-buster stature. Since this case involved only one murder, Turkus had to do two things to win. He had to make it part of a larger organized-crime conspiracy to justify the first-degree murder charge, and he had to have a blue-ribbon jury who would believe it. Turkus and Dewey were the only two prosecutors in the state of New York who relied on such juries in every one of their organized-crime cases because their evidence was always so weak.

THE STORY OF MURDER, INC.

Separate street gangs operated in different districts of Brooklyn. All crime along the extensive docks was controlled by the nation's second largest gang that was headquartered in Manhattan and headed by Brooklyn's most powerful gangster, Albert Anastasia (see Chapter 9). Reles' street gang was based in Brooklyn's Brownsville district, whose residents were primarily Jewish, Italian, and Sicilian. All the Sicilian street thugs associated themselves with Anastasia's large dominant Mafia gang. By default the Italian and Jewish neighborhood punks joined Reles' small but violent gang, which had three Jewish leaders. Reles' gang leaders worked closely with Anastasia to avoid ever challenging his overwhelming firepower. Reles' gang became major New York City labor racketeers, plundering several unions' treasuries and using their strike power to extort the employers who had contracts with these unions.

Four years before the second indictments were handed down in the Red Alpert murder case, DA Dewey had improperly used his opening and closing statements to lecture the jury about Luciano's alleged criminal offenses, even though they were never introduced into evidence or substantiated by witnesses or evidence. Turkus copied Dewey's strategy of confusing the jury with big-time gangdom falsehoods by using an established courtroom procedure. He got the judge to declare informant Reles an expert-witness about organized crime, allowing him to testify about critical conspiracy information for the record.

Reles' testimony to the Murder, Inc. trial juries was a long dissertation on the history of organized crime in the U.S. The problem was that Reles had no possible access to such information. He was a shooter at the bottom of a small gang's chain of command. His only familiarity with the underworld, even within his own gang, was limited to crimes he committed himself. No one in the underworld ever had knowledge about the inner workings of other gangs. Yet Reles testified about the structure of the country's major gangs, all of it fabricated by Assistant DA Turkus to fit the facts of his first Murder, Inc. case to upgrade it into an organized-crime conspiracy.

To qualify Reles as an expert witness, Prosecutor Turkus had to turn the hierarchy of organized crime upside down. Since Reles was a shooter, Turkus claimed that the strong-arm men were the most influential and knowledgeable figures in gangland, totally ignoring the reality that gang leaders do not commit crimes; the members at the bottom of the totem pole do. In addition, low-ranking gangsters are rarely informed of the motive for violent acts so they will be less effective as witnesses if they later turn state's evidence.

To explain how Reles could have such detailed knowledge, Prosecutor Turkus drew an organizational chart of large crime gangs that was identical to the standard structure for American business. Both the Prosecutor and the informer claimed that crime gangs had a dictatorial leader who directed and authorized all employee activity. The jurors experienced this type of structure in their work world, so they readily accepted the concept. But it was a complete misrepresentation.

Members of large crime gangs are not employees in any sense of the word. They receive no money from the gang. Members never get paid even when the leader orders them to carry out services in the interest of the gang such as murder. Instead, every member pays a percentage of all his criminal income to the leader as a fee for membership. The criminal benefits because a gang gives him an army of support strength on the mean streets, a network of potential criminal relationships, and some protection from the police, prosecutors, and judiciary. In actuality a member is an independent operator in a loosely-knit trade association who pays a steep fee to belong. He selects, plans, and carries out every crime he commits, and he chooses his crime partners who may not even be members of his own gang.

Members must abide by a small number of gang rules, and they get limited guidance from the leader. He assigns each member, or each division, a jurisdiction within the gang's territory, and approves the crime specialties each is permitted to commit. This protocol prevents the various divisions and members from coming into conflict with each other. The only time gang members band together is when someone threatens or attacks one or more of their associates. On rare occasions a leader may issue a directive demanding violent acts to protect the interests of the gang or to avenge transgressions against the membership.

Dewey successfully prosecuted Luciano by asserting that he headed all New York City crime. Similarly Turkus had Reles fulfill his multiple-murder plea deal by testifying that his little local gang was the most powerful criminal threat in America. To make this sound plausible Reles claimed that the large, dominant Mafia gangs had ceased to exist at the end of Prohibition. Turkus backed him up and later wrote "As a factor of power in national crime, Mafia has been virtually extinct for two decades." While informant Reles never explained why the Mafia disappeared, Turkus nonetheless steadfastly maintained that Reles' entire myth was factual. It is incredulous that a New York prosecutor did not know about the Mafia's continued strong influence in that city.

The story the Prosecutor and informer invented could not have been more contrary to gangland reality. After Prohibition was repealed the available crime revenue in New York City no longer supported as many gangs. The Sicilian gangs survived because they were the largest, tightest-knit, and most-loyal organizations; they had well-entrenched territories where they continued their many traditional criminal activities; and they expanded into labor racketeering. The other ethnic Prohibition gangs were not big enough to challenge the Sicilian gangs, so they disappeared from the city within a few years. Some opened illegal casinos in criminally unorganized areas of the country, several were killed off during conflicts with other non-Sicilian ethnic gangs, a number went to prison, and the rest retired from organized crime (although many committed crimes as individuals).

Reles' revisionist history replaced the reality of individual territorial Sicilian Mafia gangs with a fantasy national, multi-ethnic *syndicate* or *cartel,* allegedly formed by Johnny Torrio in 1934 and composed of every major criminal gang in the country. Assistant DA Turkus repeated this ridiculous story later in his book, but neither the Prosecutor nor the informer ever offered even a hint as to why, or how, every gang turned its management over to a minor, powerless hood in another part of the country. Neither ever offered a scrap of evidence that such an organization ever existed.

The pair's fiction claimed that Torrio created "The Syndicate" and forged a mythical nationwide centralized murder squad known to the underworld as "Murder, Inc." It was responsible for every gang killing in the country. Reles' little local gang was the headquarters and directorship for this vast national murder-for-hire organization. In reality the nation's gangs did not pay anyone to do their killings. The leaders simply ordered subordinates to commit them gratis, as part of their membership obligation.

Even though Murder, Inc. existed only in Turkus' and Reles' wild imaginations, their story generated sensational publicity. Assistant DA Turkus shocked the nation when he wrote that Murder, Inc. had committed 1,000 killings across the country from 1934 to 1943. He admitted that he derived this number by simply adding up all the unsolved murders in major cities for this period. Neither Turkus nor Reles had any evidence linking a single one of these 1,000 murders to Reles' small Brooklyn gang.

Turkus claimed that Reles knew minute details about every murder he discussed, but neither man could name a single infamous Mafia figure murdered during their 1934-1943 time frame. Those 10 years were early in the nation's major gangs' long peaceful-coexistence hammered out by Luciano and the Young Turks, a peace that was perpetuated even while Charlie Lucky languished in prison. Thus, few gangland leaders were killed during this time.

This means Assistant DA Turkus lied when he wrote that he had painstakingly verified each of Reles' absurd allegations. While Turkus claimed to have an informant who could bust every hood in the country who had committed a murder, he was never called upon to explain why he withheld such significant evidence from the nation's DAs and police departments; the U.S. Senate's Kefauver Committee, which investigated organized crime; and his own book. Consider the sales potential of a book revealing the identity of the perpetrator of every unsolved murder in the country.

Eight members of Reles' gang testified as witnesses for the prosecution in one or more of the Murder, Inc. killings, and all eight contradicted Reles. During cross-examination all eight admitted that they had never heard of a national crime syndicate or Murder, Inc. Even Turkus' boss, Brooklyn DA O'Dwyer, later testified to the Kefauver Committee that information about organized crime operations presented in the three Murder, Inc. trials came exclusively from Reles. O'Dwyer added, "Although he [Reles] did mention the Mafia, I never felt that Reles knew too much about the Mafia, as such. He knew it was in there [organized crime]."[182]

Turkus wrote in his book *Murder Inc.* "The organization we broke open in 1940 is the same one that required a Kefauver investigation in 1950." His book was published in 1951 just as the Kefauver investigation was winding down. However, the Committee's conclusions, published in August 1951, shredded Turkus' credibility. The Committee had been holding hearings for a year and a half. Its large staff investigated every major gang in the country, and many high-ranking large-city law-enforcement officials testified. The Committee concluded that the structure of organized crime was totally different from that fabricated by Assistant DA Turkus and gangster Reles. Not only did the Committee report that it was unable to find any evidence that an organization such as Murder, Inc. ever existed, but on the contrary it found every gang did its own killing.

The country's most power underworld leaders, Luciano and Costello, never met Torrio, the supposed organizer of the syndicate of Reles' imagination. Costello testified that he had never met Torrio, even though he admitted knowing a couple dozen of the biggest Prohibition gang leaders, including Torrio associate Al Capone. Jimmy Blue Eyes told me that he never met Torrio, knew nothing about him, and never heard his name mentioned by any of his associates.[183]

The continued existence of Mafia gangs across the country is proof enough that everything Reles and Turkus claimed was untrue. Since not a single Mafia gang disappeared in 1934 or after that time, there has never been any place for, or need for, a national crime organization, nor any purpose for a Murder, Inc. (See Addendum N)

Reles' most preposterous assertions during his Murder, Inc. trial testimonies were repeated by Turkus in his book in the chapter entitled *Ladies' Night in Murder, Inc.* The informant and the Assistant DA claimed that Mafia wives bragged to the world about their husbands' criminal activities, and the Mafiosi in this gang and their women held an annual Miss Murder, Inc. contest that they proudly publicized to the public. Of course the reality about any publicity by this gangs' members is exactly the opposite from these ridiculously false assertions.

As Brooklyn Assistant DA Turkus and Manhattan DA Dewey both emphasized in their books, the gangsters of the Prohibition and the illegal-casino eras could not have been more secretive. They never talked about their criminal activities to anyone except with their cohorts and then only about the crimes they had committed together. In addition, these gangsters were extremely chauvinistic. The wife's place was taking care of the home and children, and the man's life was none of her business. When these men left their house they never told their wives where they were going, who they were meeting, or what their plans were.

In addition to their penchant for secrecy and their chauvinism, these gangsters had another strong reason to keep their wives totally ignorant about their business affairs. They had just one underworld code they lived by - never tell anyone you love about your criminal activities or associates. This protected organized-crime wives of this era from their husband's killers. When a criminal was murdered, it was to be expected that the wife would despise her husband's killer and want to exact vengeance. If she had any criminal information she could either testify against the killer, or if she was afraid to go public she could supply it to the prosecutor secretly. A gangster in this era knew he protected his wife by never talking to her about his activities or associates, thereby protecting his wife from ever being considered a threat by anyone in gangland. This is the reason virtually no organized-crime wife was killed along with her husband during this era. Thus, the Reles' and Turkus' contentions about braggadocio wives and *Ladies' Night in Murder, Inc.* contests are beyond absurd.

A gangster had another reason to keep his wife in the dark about his criminal activities. If she became angry with him and wanted to exact revenge against him, she could secretly inform to a prosecutor about his criminal activities, and even become a star state's witness against him if an exception to the spousal privilege against testifying applied in the case. Given all the reasons the hoods of this era had for maintaining total silence, it is not surprising that when one of them was knocked off gangland style, the teary-eyed wife invariably told newspaper reporters two things. She truthfully claimed to know nothing about her husband's business activities, and then she falsely described what a good man he was.

THE MURDER, INC. TRIALS & INFORMANT ABE RELES

Reles admitted in the first two Murder, Inc. trials that he made his living by running floating crap games, bookmaking, bootlegging, operating a loan-shark ring, and supplying strong-arm squads in labor disputes "for either side that would pay enough." Reles confessed, "In fact, I did anything in which I could make a few dollars." On the witness stand he admitted taking part in 11 slayings, describing the shootings, stabbings, and strangulations in gruesome detail. In one trial the presiding Judge abruptly adjourned the testimony by stating, "I need a rest."[184]

When Abe Reles agreed to become a state's witness and testify against his gang associates, Assistant DA Turkus moved quickly so he could obtain convictions prior to the beginning of the upcoming election campaigns. The first two defendants were Frank "The Dasher" Abbundando and Harry "Happy" Maione who were charged with killing Whitney Rudnick. Just two months after Reles agreed to talk, Turkus got them convicted. When the verdict was announced, both proclaimed their innocence and denied having ever met Reles. They were sentenced to death.

Criminals that began plying their trade after World War II routinely swore they were innocent, but the earlier Prohibition violators and illegal casino operators did not bother with such futility. I interviewed many of these men over the years, and their attitude to a man was "You do the crime, you pay the time." While I did not condone their crimes, I sympathized with those I had gotten to know who were convicted and headed to prison. They dismissed my concern, accepting their punishment as a price they had to pay for the lifestyle they had chosen. I never knew or heard of one of these men to complain about prison time for a crime they had committed - they only objected to being framed for a crime they did not do.

Remember, none of the Murder, Inc. defendants spoke publicly during their lives, so their statements were an indication that the legal system had gone awry. The defendants' immediate objections to the informants' veracity is a good indication that DA O'Dwyer made a deal with the state's witnesses to go free for murders they admitted to in exchange for perjured testimony that framed others.

Eight months later the New York Court of Appeals found a serious flaw in the Abbundando and Maione convictions and reversed them. The justices ruled that Reles' corroborating witnesses did not connect the two defendants to the murders. The court wrote, "Evidence which merely shows the crime was committed as described by an accomplice is not corroboration [of participation] as required by law."

Two months after this reversal, Assistant DA Turkus rushed for judgment by retrying the two defendants. This time Turkus produced another gang member who was willing to testify that the pair was connected to the murder in return for freedom from prosecution for a serious crime. This corroboration was all that was required by law, so Abbundando and Maione were again found guilty, and this time they were executed in Sing Sing's electric chair.

The second pair of defendants was Martin "Buggsy" Goldstein and Harry "Pittsburgh Phil" Strauss. They were found guilty of the first-degree murder of Irving "Puggy" Feinstein. The conviction carried a mandatory death sentence. Before the execution was carried out, Goldstein told the warden, "I never killed nobody." All four of these convicted men knew there was no escape from the prosecutor's trap, because DA Dewey publicly supported Assistant DA Turkus' ridiculous national syndicate and Murder Inc. fictions. The defendants spoke out only to set the record straight about being framed on perjured testimony.[185]

"LEPKE" & "GURRAH" INDUSTRIAL RACKETEERS

After Brooklyn Assistant DA Turkus convicted four Brownsville district gang underlings in the first two Murder, Inc. trials, he targeted the gang's co-leaders Louis "Lepke" Buchalter and Jake "Gurrah" Shapiro. Lepke was born on New York's lower East Side on February 6, 1897. His nickname Lepke is a shortened version of "Lepkeleh" meaning "Little Louis" in Yiddish. Lepke's Russian Jewish father died when he was 12, and his family moved to Brooklyn. Between the ages of 18 to 30, Lepke was in and out of prison for burglary, armed robbery, grand larceny, and consorting with criminals. During this time, he and Gurrah also became co-leaders of their notorious gang. Little is known about the scope of Gurrah's criminal activities beyond a couple of serious criminal charges and Reles' imaginative but fake Murder, Inc. tale. (See Addendum O)

Lepke and Gurrah became their gang's co-leaders in the middle of Prohibition following the murder of Lower East Side gang chieftain Jacob "Little Augie" Orgen. His killing was never solved, but his specialty had been offering muscle in union/management disputes to the party who would pay the most. The two co-leaders expanded the gang's muscle rackets by focusing on extorting both unions and businesses. Late in the Roaring '20s, Lepke and Gurrah threatened violence and ordered a number of killings to take over control of union locals in New York City that represented workers in several manufacturing industries and also the truckers who transported these companies' products. The nation's fashion hub was in the Big Apple, and Lepke and Gurrah had a stranglehold on the city's huge garment and fur businesses and also its bakery goods and flour.

Upon taking control of these unions, Lepke and Gurrah plundered the treasuries; sold out the memberships by negotiating *sweetheart* contracts that reduced worker pay, benefits, and work rules in return for payoffs from their employers; took kickbacks from companies and individuals who wanted to handle the employees' health and pension plans; and extorted bribes from unionized companies through threats of strikes. The pair even extorted non-unionized businesses by creating sham trade associations that demanded monthly "protection" payments to deter vicious beatings of owners, managers, and truck drivers, and also bombings consisting of stink, acid, or explosives against their plants' large valuable clothing or bakery inventories. The duo's trade associations demanded all member businesses to adopt price schedules with exorbitant increases of 50% to 100% of the existing rates, with the gangsters getting the lion's share. By eliminating pricing competition in these industries they forced the buying public to pay the brunt of their widespread extortions. Lepke and Gurrah achieved these objectives by becoming some of the most murderous organized-crime leaders of their time.

A FBI Internal Memo credits Lepke and Gurrah with having "organized the first large-scale kickback and shakedown rackets in legitimate business and industry." Companies that did not pay "protection" money were inflicted with bombings, assaults which sometimes involved the use of lead pipes, strong-arm robberies, and murder. The gang also threatened truck drivers in order to delay deliveries and disrupt business.[186]

For the decade following Orgen's murder, the vicious racketeering empire of Lepke and Gurrah seemed beyond the reach of the law. But half way through that decade Franklin Roosevelt was elected president, and he appointed Homer Cummings as attorney general. The administration was in its fourth month when the most shocking crime of that era occurred, the Kansas City Massacre. Three machinegun-toting men hid in ambush and without warning opened fire on seven lawmen, killing four and wounding two. Of the six who were hit, three were FBI agents. This led AG Cummings to create the first national war on crime against the wave of kidnappings and machinegun bank robberies in the Midwest that regularly made the headlines. He enlisted Congress to transform the FBI from an accounting agency of government funds into a secret national police force. This broadened the administration's focus with an achievable New Deal agenda victory, since FDR was elected by pledging to overcome the Great Depression economic calamity, and it was clear it would be a long struggle to overcome this.

Thus, one of U.S. AG Cummings' first criminal targets was the labor racketeering gang of Lepke and Gurrah. This was three years before Reles agreed to turn state's witness in Brooklyn, but this gang's two leaders found themselves in the center of what would develop into the most bizarre law-enforcement jurisdictional competition in American jurisprudence. AG Cummings went after the gang for violation of the Sherman Antitrust Act by interfering with interstate commerce through creating monopoly and price fixing in certain industries, while Manhattan DA Dewey went after the gangsters for violent extortion of the individual businesses within these industries. The AG issued the first indictment in these cases. It was against the pair of leaders and 156 other gang members for labor racketeering in the fur industry, but both prosecutors eventually charged both gangsters in multiple cases for different crimes. Then the AG issued a second indictment, this one for narcotics. This caused the pair to fail to appear at trial to face the first charge by jumping bail and going into hiding at separate locations. Four months later a determined AG Cummings offered a reward for the pair of fugitives' capture, and had his FBI Director, J. Edgar Hoover, sign the $5,000 wanted poster.

After six months, Gurrah grew tired of being on the run and voluntarily turned himself into the FBI, but Lepke remained in hiding. The U.S. Attorney prosecuted Gurrah for conspiracy and extortion. He was found guilty and sentenced to 15 years to life. Three years into his sentence at Sing Sing Prison he died of natural causes at age 47.[187]

Lepke continued his fugitive flight for another year and a half, when Manhattan DA Dewey also became desperate to capture him. From hiding, Lepke had ordered the murders of potential trial witnesses against him, and three of the five shooting victims had died. This was terrifying other witnesses and weakening the pending cases. At that time Lepke's gang members were searching for a union official who had turned informer, but when they encountered a legitimate music-publishing-house executive who resembled their target, they mistakenly shot him to death. Three days later DA Dewey asked New York City to offer a very large $25,000 reward for the fleeing gangster, and upon receiving city approval, the DA had the NYPD distribute one million "dead or alive" circulars to law enforcement agencies nationwide.

AG Cummings had initiated the War on Crime, and he expected his FBI Director to capture remaining fugitive Lepke, but J. Edgar Hoover was ill-suited for the task. He put himself through law school by working at the Library of Congress. Then America entered World War I and a month later the Selective Service Act became effective. It required all men aged 21 to 30 to register for the draft. Hoover searched for a way out of military service for his country, and he learned that Justice Department employees were exempted, so he obtained a job as a clerk. He quickly rose through the ranks, and he was appointed the head of the FBI government money accounting agency at age 29.

Hoover had never exhibited an interest in police work, and he spent his 48-year FBI Directorship trying not to be a cop. After the Kansas City Massacre, AG Cummings presented Congress a massive anticrime package, and Hoover lobbied heavily behind the scenes to remove his bookkeeping Bureau from assuming responsibility for bank robberies and being given the authority to make arrests. Hoover's efforts failed, and he was made America's top cop, heading the nation's new secret police force. For the rest of his very long tenure he quietly manipulated individual Congressmen to attempt to thwart every federal legislative proposal that would expand the FBI's authority to enforce more criminal acts.

Hoover also had a bizarre attitude about his responsibilities. He believed his job was to make citizens feel safe in bed at night rather than to actually ensure their safety from criminals. He focused on creating the appearance of successful crime-busting rather than doing it, except in high-profile cases in which the public expected to hear about results. Like many police, prosecutors, and judges, Hoover understood that the public wants the peace of mind that comes from knowing that criminals are caught, convicted, and punished, while innocent suspects are freed. Law enforcement officials know that the public is relieved and satisfied when someone is convicted of a crime and locked up. This awareness has too often led unscrupulously law enforcers to focus on creating the image of these goals, rather than working towards their reality. They are more concerned with making someone look guilty than finding the actual perpetrator.

In Hoover's case he bombarded Congressional hearings with reams of statistics about what a great job he was doing, but no one was ever allowed to confirm any of these numbers. Hoover's way of combating organized crime was to simply deny there was such a thing. He swore throughout his half-century of directing the FBI that no Mafia criminal organization existed in the U.S. He reiterated this lie to eight Presidents and 17 Attorneys General who were his bosses, to Congress which funded his agency, and to the American people who entrusted their safety and security to him.

Organized crime developed and flourished in America's big cities from the beginning of Prohibition, but Hoover prohibited his agents from investigating the country's biggest gangsters for four decades until AG Bobby Kennedy ordered him to finally do his job. This is illustrated by Moe Dalitz who headed the third largest liquor importing operation during Prohibition and was one of the most influential men in the history of American organized crime. Later in Moe's life he said to me in an interview, "Wasn't J. Edgar Hoover a wonderful man!", as the old gangster sat there with a huge smile from ear to ear over his fond memories of America's top cop. I just sat there trying to process this troubling incongruity.[188]

The primary job of Hoover's investigative detectives was looking for dirt on politicians, their supporters, bureaucrats, celebrities, personal enemies, activists, dissenters, and the rich and powerful. Hoover used this damaging information to silence and control these targets with threats of exposing the raw material maintained in official but inappropriate files. This anti-American, anti-democracy, un-Constitutional domestic surveillance was first revealed to the public and Congress early in Hoover's career in an August 19, 1933 *Collier's Magazine* article by Ray Tucker. Then a year after Director Hoover's death, former Assistant Director William Sullivan, who had been third in the FBI's chain of command, stated in a newspaper interview that Hoover "was a master blackmailer." He went on to describe how the Director's system worked. "The moment he would get something on a senator he'd send one of the errand boys up and advise the senator that we're in the course of an investigation and we by chance happened to come up with this data on your daughter. But we wanted you to know this; we realize you'd want to know it. But don't have any concern; no one will learn about it. Well, Jesus, what does that tell the senator? From that time on the senator's right in his pocket."[189]

Agents had to submit every derogatory rumor in a written report. These voluminous blackmail files were stored in filing cabinets in several secure areas of the FBI Building. Upon the Director's death, Richard Nixon demanded the secret files, but Hoover's career-long secretary Helen Gandy and his lieutenants lied to the President of the United States by claiming they did not exist. Then for the next two months they diligently but illegally shredded most of these blackmail files all financed by the taxpayer. None of these top FBI officials were criminally prosecuted.

The FBI Director got in a conflict with Democratic U.S. Senator Kenneth McKellar, and Hoover fired without cause three agents in McKellar's home state of Tennessee. The Senator chaired the Appropriations Committee and soon Hoover had to go before him for the FBI's annual funding. In two days of private hearings McKellar attacked Hoover about every negative thing he had heard about the FBI. A week later the highlights of Hoover's chastising were released in the Committee's scathing written report. One of the issues McKellar hit hard was that rather than crime busting, Hoover's FBI was a massive public relations machine. His PR division kept tight control over the FBI's publicity in press releases, interviews with reporters, speeches to various groups, and books about him and the agency. It also wrote and approved dramatic FBI agent stories for movies, detective magazines, radio shows, and comic books. Hoover replied to Senator McKellar that the FBI had no publicity people on its payroll, but he failed to tell the truth that they existed and were paid by the parent Justice Department. His answers were perjured lies because he claimed he was not involved with these activities, when these PR men indeed worked for him inside his agency.

Senator McKellar embarrassed Hoover for taking credit for solving so many kidnappings when these crimes were mostly broken from tips by local police; concerned citizens such as taxi drivers, filling station attendants, and store clerks; and inside informants. Then Senator McKellar humiliated Hoover's sense of manhood by accusing him of being unqualified because of no law-enforcement schooling, training, or experience. Then he emphasized the Director had never even made an arrest himself. This so rankled Hoover that he soon led three major arrests himself, and the details of how he cowardly hid away protected from the action until each suspect was in handcuffs is detailed in "All *Against* The Law" (by Bill Friedman). Hoover was determined to make his fourth and final personal arrest be labor racketeer Lepke because he was America's most famous fugitive, having been fleeing major federal and New York state charges for two years.

Senator McKellar's public insults of unprofessionalism finally put the FBI Director on board with his AG, who had introduced crime fighting into the national political agenda. Hoover was now hard at work establishing his image as America's top cop. These two federal officials were competing for Lepke's capture with Manhattan DA Dewey, who had his sights set on the Governor's Mansion in Albany, New York and then the White House in Washington. Dewey planned to win both positions by becoming the nation's formidable racket-busting prosecutor. In this competition Hoover and Dewey vied with each other to win the conservative Republican crown as the nation's toughest law-and-order enforcer by stridently espousing harsh anti-crime rhetoric. These two publicity hounds used exaggerated, self-aggrandizing publicity releases, press conferences, and books. In contrast, Democrat AG Cummings pursued Lepke through steady prosecutorial actions, while avoiding the other two officials' pompous hyperbole.

Dewey wanted Lepke bad enough to finally offer a huge $50,000 reward, and he announced to the press that he had enough racketeering evidence to put Lepke away for "500 years." The threat of a life sentence from New York State made the Fed's narcotics charge with its 2- to 15-year sentence Lepke's preferred option, especially since the underworld was well aware that DA Dewey had framed Luciano. Lepke's legal dilemma was explained to the FBI by Newark, New Jersey gangster Abner "Longie" Zwillman. He accurately predicted the outcome nine months before Lepke would decide on this course of action. Zwillman told agents in an interview that he believed Lepke was suffering a greater punishment by being a fugitive than if he were in jail where he would have more freedom. Zwillman said that he had personal knowledge that the only reason Lepke would not surrender was because Dewey framed Luciano and "numerous others for his own political glory." Zwillman stated emphatically that every one in the underworld knew Luciano never dealt in women and was framed. Days before the FBI's interview of Zwillman, DA Dewey had lost New York's gubernatorial election and this sent fear through New York's underworld. It meant Dewey would continue on as Manhattan DA, and gangdom expected him to help Brooklyn develop murder charges to improve his chances in the next election, which is exactly what he did. Zwillman stated emphatically that every one who knew fugitive Lepke was aware that he would surrender immediately on the federal charges, but he remained a fugitive "to evade frame-up charges by Dewey." Zwillman told agents he was thus "most positive" that when Lepke surrendered it would be to the FBI.[190]

As Zwillman had predicted in his FBI interview, nine months later Lepke sent word to Frank Costello that he wanted to turn himself in to the FBI, but he demanded Hoover guarantee two conditions. Lepke would be tried only for the narcotics indictment (not the fur-industry Antitrust charges), and Lepke would remain in federal custody for the length of his prison term and be protected from prosecution by Manhattan DA Dewey. Lepke knew he could only go free again if he served his federal time, and he hoped in the intervening years the New York charges would be forgotten.

However, Lepke did not trust a verbal deal with Hoover. Every one in organized crime knew that the Director three years earlier had broken the FBI's promise to arrange residency to alien brothel madam Anna Sage for fingering John Dillinger and walking him into the FBI's assassination in front of Chicago's Biograph Theater. Thus, Lepke selected an intermediary to approach Hoover, and he counted on the resulting publicity to make the Director keep his word this time.

Lepke chose Costello to forge the deal because he was America's most influential underworld figure, representing the imprisoned Boss of Bosses Luciano. Costello was as respected and trusted in the underworld as Luciano, and Costello was the only major hood with a somewhat clean image. He was popularly believed to be a legitimate businessman, operated elegant high-end illegal casinos fronted by first-rate restaurants in New York and New Orleans, and he enjoyed enormous political influence at Tammany Hall. No one in law enforcement or the press realized Costello was a Mafioso except for those cops who were on his payroll, mainly because he associated with many Irish in the power structure and had many Jewish friends.

Costello knew the best contact with Hoover was America's gossip king whose *Walter Winchell on Broadway* was the most read syndicated newspaper column, and his Sunday evening national radio show made him the number one broadcaster. In almost every production Winchell praised the FBI Director with folk hero status, and most Saturday evenings Hoover dined at Winchell's permanently-reserved table at the Stork Club in midtown Manhattan. It would later come out that Hoover was Winchell's chief source of dirt about the rich and famous. The FBI Director targeted the law-abiding citizens he disliked by taking information from his confidential FBI blackmail files, all of it collected and shared illegally by America's secret police chief.[191] (See also Addendum P)

Winchell and Costello knew each other well. They patronized the same restaurants and nightclubs, and Costello owned the famous Copacabana nightclub where he held the table of Winchell's choice for any show. One evening Costello privately asked Winchell to approach Hoover about a deal for Lepke's surrender. Winchell was receptive, but only if he could announce to his radio audience that he was in on the bust. It can only be assumed that the egotistical, self-serving Hoover choked when he heard he would have to share the capture of a public enemy with Winchell, but having come up empty handed after two years of searching, Hoover needed the arrest on any terms, especially with DA Dewey aggressively hunting the fugitive too.

Hoover had his own condition for a deal. There would be no voluntary surrender at the New York FBI Office, but instead he would write a dramatically-staged one-man "bust" of Lepke. Hoover's description of the agreement in his internal Summarization about the case said, "Mr. Winchell was authorized by the Director of the FBI, to publicly state that Buchalter's civil rights would be respected and maintained should he surrender." Don Whitehead, who wrote for the FBI, penned, "As the FBI closed in on Buchalter, Walter Winchell broadcast a radio appeal for the gang leader to surrender, with the promise that his civil rights would be respected by the FBI. … The FBI got Buchalter, and Winchell got an exclusive story." With the "capture" date approaching, Winchell in his usual brash, egotistical manner berated the gangster on his radio program - "Are you listening, Lepke? Are you listening? Come out, come out, wherever you are!"[192] (See Addendum Q)

It took just two-and-a-half weeks after DA Dewey issued the large wanted dead-or-alive reward for fugitive Lepke, Costello, Winchell, and Hoover to meet in pairs and finalize the fugitive's voluntary surrender deal. That evening Lepke showed up on time at the appointed site selected by Hoover. Afterwards the Director called a press conference at the New York City FBI Office. Hoover bragged to the assembled reporters that he had single-handedly captured the fugitive. Except for acknowledging the suspect was unarmed which sucked the drama out of his action, Hoover uncharacteristically refused to give a single detail about this seemingly amazing happening. All this secrecy puzzled the reporters. The Director lied by claiming he got Lepke through "FBI resources" and in denying there was a deal with the fugitive. He had no choice but to acknowledge his pal Winchell had made the successful contact with the gangster. Hoover did pointedly note that the NYPD and his nemesis Manhattan DA Dewey had no part in the capture. This led Brooklyn

Assistant DA Turkus to reveal that the two law enforcement agencies had agreed to notify each other about the search for Lepke, and then Hoover iced out the NYPD.

Later the Director wrote the FBI's official version. It states Hoover was walking New York City's streets by himself in the evening darkness when he encountered America's most-wanted fugitive and apprehended him without assistance. It sounded contrived because it did not explain why he was walking empty business streets alone, or why the country's most wanted man was wandering alone towards him.

Winchell later revealed how Lepke really surrendered that night, according to their deal. The gossip columnist stood unarmed at the specified sidewalk location. Then Lepke's car pulled up, and the fugitive casually stepped out. Winchell had to make sure the gangster was also unarmed so he frisked the cooperative man. Then the pair walked the sidewalk to an encampment of two-dozen FBI agents, guns in hand, surrounding Hoover's parked armor-plated limousine. The agents again frisked the suspect before cuffing him. Only when the prisoner was encircled by all these heavily-armed agents did America's action hero unlock the door and come out of hiding. Hoover's pathetic cowardice was beyond reason because Lepke desperately needed the Director's help to avoid the lifetime sentence DA Dewey had planned for him. Not only had Winchell just met alone and unarmed with the gangster, but he reported to his radio audience that it was a jolly good adventure.[193]

Just as the Director had fictionalized Lepke's so-called "capture," his official version of the FBI's two-year worldwide search for the fugitive is dramatic but equally as phony. "A manhunt that encircled the continental United States and extended into Mexico, Costa Rica, Cuba, England, Canada, France, Puerto Rico and Carlsbad, Germany. Summary reports alone succinctly setting forth contacts of Shapiro and Lepke, number over a thousand pages, to say nothing of the thousands of reports of Special Agents of the Federal Bureau of Investigation working in every section of the United States." In reality this major gangster's file is small at 184 pages, instead of Hoover's claim of "thousands of reports of Special Agents." In addition, Hoover left out the only significant fact about his fugitive run.[194]

The whole two years that FBI agents searched for fugitive Lepke the world over without ever picking up a clue as to his whereabouts, he remained close to his family home and Brooklyn Police Headquarters in a rented furnished single room. Hoover preached to his agents that a woman was often a criminal's weakness and trailing her could lead to him. He called such a hunt a *cherchez la femme* meaning *find the woman*. If the Director had assigned a single agent to tail the fugitive's wife, he would have followed her once a week to her husband's rented room where she handed over $250 cash for his living expenses from their two clothes-manufacturing companies. Later she was convicted of harboring her husband and sentenced to a year in federal prison.[195]

LEPKE THE POLITICAL PAWN FOR A PRESIDENCY

Lepke was in federal custody awaiting trial, but Manhattan DA Dewey had his sights set on convicting an alleged leader of the mythical Murder, Inc. gang to boost his next campaign for governor. Thus, just two days after Lepke's voluntarily surrender to the FBI, Dewey sent an Assistant DA to visit him. Director Hoover kept his deal with Lepke by blocking admittance to the prisoner except for FBI agents, defense attorneys, and family members. Dewey rebuffed several more attempted visits by Dewey's Assistant DA. The friction from this custody standoff increased the already intense rivalry between Hoover and DA Dewey to become the country's top crime buster, but both hid their mutual loathing when talking to the press. Since the two competitors were astute political animals, both made sure leaks about their animosity towards the other was attributed to anonymous sources.

Four months after surrendering, Lepke was tried in federal court and convicted of narcotic smuggling. He then pled guilty to avoid retrial of the rabbit-fur extortion charges. The federal judge gave him a combined sentence in Leavenworth of 14 years. DA Dewey had been waiting for this decision and immediately applied for custody in federal court, so he could try the gangster on a bakery-and-flour-trucking labor-racketeering indictment. Hoover was obligated to appear at the court hearing to explain his surrender promise to Lepke, but the FBI Director broke his solemn word by remaining silent. Hoover also hid this vital information from his Justice Department bosses, so a week later the U.S. Circuit Court of Appeals ruled that Lepke had to be transferred forthwith from federal prison to stand trial in Manhattan's General Sessions Court.

Two months after Dewey obtained the right to try Lepke, the Manhattan DA's blue-ribbon jury convicted him of bakery-and-flour-industry extortion. Lepke was given a 30-years-to-life sentence in state prison that was to begin after he finished his 14 years with the feds, meaning he would remain in prison until at least age 87.

While DA Dewey was convicting Lepke in Manhattan, Brooklyn's Murder, Inc. cases began developing after killer Abe Reles unexpectedly agreed to turn state's witness against his gang's members. Then DA Bill O'Dwyer cut deals with other gang members, who were charged with different felonies, to also turn state's witness. Three months after Lepke was convicted and pled guilty in Manhattan, Brooklyn DA O'Dwyer obtained a first-degree murder indictment against gang leader Lepke and two subordinates. They faced an automatic death penalty if convicted for ordering the killing of Joe Rosen four years earlier. He had been an independent garment trucker until the gang's illegal monopolistic practices had put him out of business. Lepke compensated Rosen by financing a candy shop for him. Then Manhattan DA Dewey got Rosen to become a potential informant against Lepke. One day Rosen was entering his candy store when assailants shot him dead.

Four months after DA O'Dwyer obtained the Lepke indictment, he began fighting to get the convict transferred from the federal Leavenworth Prison to be tried in Brooklyn for the murder of Rosen in a death penalty case. This would again be a violation of Hoover's surrender deal with Lepke that he would never be released from federal custody until he had completed his sentence. But the Director continued his silence, dishonoring himself and the country's justice system for which there would be enormous repercussions for the American people. For more than seven months, DA O'Dwyer continued to wrangle for custody of Lepke until U.S. Deputy Marshals brought the convict into a Brooklyn courtroom for arraignment.

DA O'Dwyer turned the third Murder, Inc. case over to his Assistant DA Turkus. Seven months later Turkus took the trio to trial for the Rosen murder. The three defendants were all Brownsville gang members – leader Lepke, lieutenant Emanuel "Mendy" Weiss, and Louis Capone. Turkus portrayed Lepke as ringleader of the fictitious Murder, Inc. and the other two as the shooters of

Rosen. All three of Turkus' Murder, Inc. prosecutions were presented to carefully selected blue-ribbon juries and were based solely on accomplice eyewitness testimony. Every one of these informers was given immunity from prosecution for serious crimes as the reward for testifying.

In Lepke's trial five of the eight state's witnesses testified they had participated in the murder with defendants Weiss and Capone. The other three state's witnesses claimed Lepke had talked about the murder in their presence. The prosecution witnesses described the seven-man murder team. A wheelman drove the car, a finger man identified the target, a hit man did the shooting, and four men kept the shooter company. They claimed it took seven accomplices to murder an unarmed man who was alone in his tiny shop to stock sweets on the shelves. Of this seven-member murder team, five were set free in return for being state's witnesses to convict the two who were defendants.

These state's witnesses described the motive behind the murder of Joe Rosen. He had been a truck operator, whom the Brownsville union-racketeering gang had extorted until he was forced to close his business. Then the gang paid him off to keep his mouth shut and to get him to move out of town and away from the jurisdiction of Brooklyn law enforcement. But Rosen kept returning, so they had to pay him several times to get him to leave again. Since the gang members admitted knowing the victim well, there was no need for them to have a designated finger man. It is inconceivable that a seven-man hit team was used to kill a single unarmed man alone without bodyguards, as alleged. It greatly increased the likelihood that an accomplice would turn state's witness, which is exactly what happened. Instead of Murder, Inc., these pug-uglies' testimony should have led to them being dubbed the "hold-my-hand gang."

Particularly difficult to believe in this case are Lepke's alleged conversations in front of so many underlings. Assistant DA Turkus said repeatedly in his book that no one could ever pin a murder rap on Lepke because he was so secretive. Like every other hood of that era, he gave orders to only one man, and it was always in private, so no corroborating accomplice witness would ever exist. Turkus himself wrote about Lepke, "That was part of his genius - that remarkable talent at covering himself. ... Always he had thought out these murder patterns with reasoned controlled cunning."

New York City Mafia leader Joe Bonanno wrote about organized crime communications that "Other than the top men, no one knew what was going on in the highest circle of power. Because of this grapevine system of passing information, rumor and innuendo often traded places with truth." It was a secret world filled with intrigue and treachery, and it is likely that some members have killed their bosses, or became state's witnesses, because they falsely assumed the boss was planning to have them killed.[196]

Assistant DA Turkus' prosecution of Rosen's murder had other problems. Three years before the trial, state's witness Max Rubin testified to a grand jury that he knew nothing about that murder. Then when he was offered a walk for his own serious crimes, he suddenly remembered Lepke planned the murder in front of him. In rebuttal, seven defense witnesses testified that state's-witnesses Rubin and Allie were not in Lepke's office on that fateful day. Lepke's defense attorney summarized the case to the jury as a diabolical frame-up. A blue-ribbon jury convicted the three defendants of first-degree murder, which carried an automatic death sentence. Lepke is the first and only organized crime leader in U.S. history to receive the death sentence.[197]

Assistant DA Turkus told the blue-ribbon jury that Lepke was a depraved murderer who headed Murder, Inc. and commanded 250 professional murderers across the nation. Turkus portrayed him as a man who quickly killed anyone who might testify against him. But Lepke's known actions did not resemble this portrait. For example, Turkus' own state's witnesses told how Lepke had repeatedly paid off the victim Joe Rosen to leave town and live elsewhere before he finally ordered him killed. Turkus gave eight of Lepke's associates immunity from major crimes for sending Lepke to the electric chair, almost certainly with perjured testimony. Yet Lepke and his so-called nationwide killing cartel never exacted any type of retribution against any of the state's witnesses.

An interesting footnote to the Lepke saga is that both DA Dewey and Assistant DA Turkus claimed for years that Lepke and Gurrah headed the fictitious Murder, Inc., a huge national crime organization that specialized in murder for hire and in protecting criminal fugitives on the run. Yet with all these alleged effective criminal hideaways around the country available at their fingertips, fugitives Lepke and Gurrah sought harbor from the law solely through their family members. (See Addendum R)

DEWEY'S POLITICAL MACHINATIONS

As soon as Lepke was convicted in Brooklyn on the first-degree murder charge, he appealed the conviction in state and federal courts. Brooklyn returned him to Leavenworth Prison to continue his federal sentence. DA O'Dwyer also immediately began lobbying President Franklin Roosevelt to commute Lepke's federal sentence and turn custody of him over to the state for execution in the electric chair. But FDR quickly replied that until all of Lepke's appeals had been exhausted and his guilt affirmed, the convict would not be turned over.

Brooklyn Assistant DA Turkus and Manhattan DA Dewey used their three trial successes during 1940 and 1941 against the local Brooklyn gang they called Murder, Inc. to enhance their planned political campaigns in 1942. Turkus was the Republican nominee for Kings County Judge in Brooklyn, and the centerpiece of his campaign was his nine first-degree murder, death-penalty convictions, seven from the three Murder, Inc. trials. However, in that election Turkus was easily defeated by Democratic Governor Lehman's legal counsel Nathan Sobel.

In regards to the political history of Special Prosecutor Dewey, he was elected Manhattan DA in 1937 but was defeated the next year in New York's gubernatorial election. Then in 1942 he ran for governor again, using his successful racketeering prosecution of Lepke's alleged Murder, Inc. as the cornerstone of his campaign. This tactic was credited by political analysis at the time with his victory. Then just months after becoming governor, Dewey broke his campaign promise not to run for president.

As the 1944 presidential primary campaign was gearing up, Governor Dewey publicly demanded that President Roosevelt pardon Murder, Inc. leader Lepke from federal prison so that New York State could execute him. Dewey's demand served no legitimate legal purpose, as Lepke was destined for execution upon completing his federal sentence. But Dewey wanted to expand his political base and garner votes by speeding up the execution process because it made more sensational press to have put him to death rather than just sentencing him to it, a rather macabre use of the *justice* system.

Lepke's final murder conviction appeal was to the U.S. Supreme Court, and it ruled unanimously he was to die after the state court fixed a new execution date. Brooklyn DA O'Dwyer began three months of fruitless wrangling with U.S. AG Francis Biddle to turn over custody of the Leavenworth convict. Then Governor Dewey formally demanded the surrender of Lepke to the state. It was a year before FDR was going to face voters for a fourth term as President, and Dewey was months away from the Republican presidential primaries. Dewey wanted the death of Lepke to enhance his tough law-and-order reputation, while FDR wanted to delay this political plum until after the results for the general election were tabulated. With Lepke's life a pawn in the upcoming primary and general presidential elections, both the Governor and the President presented disingenuous arguments to justify their possession of the convict.

The first of Governor Dewey's three fallacious arguments in his crusade for custody was that justice was being denied despite the guarantee that he would be executed upon completion of his federal sentence. The Governor's second argument was that the three codefendants had to be executed on the same day, but he never explained why because he had no reason. He refused to set execution dates for the other two just to be able to falsely wail about lack of justice. Dewey's third argument was that the law required he hold a clemency hearing before conducting an execution, but then he lied that the convict had to be in custody for the hearing. This was absolutely untrue. Not only was the convict's presence at the hearing not required, but convicts never appeared before the clemency panel as these pleas were always made by their attorneys.

President Roosevelt had AG Biddle falsely counter that the convict could not be pardoned until all the appeals and clemency hearing were concluded because the convict might end up going free. However, in similar cases before previous presidents, convicts had been released to states with the condition that the U.S. AG could revoke this action and order them returned to federal custody if any appeal rejected the execution penalty.

FBI Director Hoover had the perfect legitimate reason to hold on to the custody of Lepke because of the surrender deal he had made with the fugitive. In addition, Hoover could be terminated at will by either of his bosses, the President of the United States and the Attorney General. But sadly the Director had neither the integrity to live by his word, nor the loyalty to his bosses to step forward and assist their cause by telling the truth.[198]

Because Governor Dewey had no legitimate legal arguments, he escalated his attacks in the press for political gain. Thus, U.S. AG Biddle sent a letter to the Governor accusing him of doing exactly that, and the AG also released it to the press. In it he said, "It is surprising to me that you should choose to communicate with the President or with me in this important matter through the medium of the press. The statements and implications in your public announcements that we are openly restricting your efforts to have Lepke's death sentence executed are totally unwarranted." Governor Dewey and his AG came back punching in the political arena by viciously accusing the President of protecting a convict in prison from punishment. For the next two months Dewey inflamed the electorate into a bloodletting passion, and as public pressure grew, FDR decided this was a fight best not fought. The President turned Lepke over to New York just prior to the presidential primary campaigns but retained federal custody.

Once Dewey had Lepke in custody, he accelerated his execution date to the first day after all the appeal impediments were removed. This date fell in the midst of primary voting across the country and just four months before the Republican nominating convention. On that date Dewey had the trio executed in the Sing Sing electric chair one right after the other. His rush to kill as the GOP Presidential primary campaigns were beginning was rather ghoulish politics indeed.[199]

Unfortunately, serious doubt remains about the guilt of Lepke and the other six Murder, Inc. defendants who were convicted and executed for these murders. Like the four defendants in the first two trials, Lepke's co-defendant Weiss maintained, "I'm innocent. I'm here on a frame-up case." During the trial Lepke's attorney charged that Lepke was the victim of a frame-up in which admitted murderer Max Rubin "motivated by revenge and hatred" was given freedom for turning state's witness. In trial testimony Rubin was proven to have lied before the grand jury. Lepke appealed to the U.S. Supreme Court over the "poisoned atmosphere" created by the prosecution, but the court unanimously declined to consider the case. The day of Lepke's execution his wife gave the media his last statement that she had transcribed for him with a pencil in which he said he would "willingly go to the chair" if an independent commission would examine the facts and determine him to be guilty. He was seeking anyone who would look to see if the trial was as flawed, and the evidence as untrue, as he knew it to be.[200]

Lepke and the other six defendants in these three Murder, Inc. trials were career criminals and each most likely had been involved in some fashion with one or more murders. However, these trials were such a travesty of justice that four disquieting concerns about the defendants' guilt in these three specific cases lingers. The only certainty that came out of these three trials is that every one of the dozen or so total state's witness were freed even though each one admitted to being guilty of at least one of these murders. (See Addendum S)

The surrender of Lepke established a number of FBI records. Lepke was the first major organized-crime leader ever executed in the U.S., and he remains the only one. His voluntary surrender was Director Hoover's fourth and final personal "arrest," and this was the first major organized-crime arrest for the Bureau. Sadly, this was the FBI's only major organized-crime arrest for the next quarter of a century because of Hoover's failure to keep his word to Lepke not to deliver him to New York prosecutors. America's underworld was just as aware that the Director had previously failed to back up his Special-Agent-in-Charge Melvin Purvis' promise to prevent the deportation of the Lady in Red brothel madam for fingering and delivering John Dillinger to his death. That highly-publicized case was the first to lay bare to the underworld that Hoover was a dishonorable cop who did not keep his word. With no criminal willing to cut a deal with the FBI to turn state's witness, it became impossible for the Justice Department to prosecute organized-crime leaders who remained so insulated from their members who carried out their illegal orders. Compounding this woeful lack of integrity, the Director ordered his agents to continue to turn a blind eye to organized-crime offenses as this terrible criminal scourge expanded unabated across the nation.

The first gangster to attempt to turn state's witness was New York Mafioso Joe Valachi because he was afraid his gang was going to kill him in prison. However, Valachi bypassed Hoover and reached out to his boss U.S. AG Robert Kennedy for a deal he could rely on. With RFK's promise of protection, Valachi testified in nationally-televised Senate hearings about his eyewitness knowledge of the existence of the powerful Mafia gangs in many major cities, and he revealed to the American people for the first time the blood oath Mafia gang members take during their initiation ceremony. Despite Valachi's revelations, the Director continued to espouse his long-term lie that the Mafia did not exist in the U.S. While Bobby Kennedy was U.S. AG, he made Hoover do his crime-fighting job against organized crime for the first time, but after Kennedy resigned, the Director again ordered his agents to sit on the sideline as organized crime ravaged many of America's large cities.[201]

The Murder, Inc. myth about a national crime syndicate would never have been plausible if it relied solely on these three Brooklyn neighborhood murders which were committed by a local gang unknown to the rest of the country. Brooklyn DA O'Dwyer overcame these limitations by throwing in the homicide of a fourth gang member, Harry "Big Greenie" Greenberg. He was killed while he was on the run from the gang and hiding at the other end of the country in Hollywood. DA O'Dwyer claimed Big Greenie's slaying was spearheaded by high-profile gangster Ben Siegel because he was the perfect patsy to link with the small Brownsville street gang. Siegel had grown up in Brooklyn where the gang was based, and at the time of the killing he was also residing in Hollywood. To support the supposition of Siegel's guilt, DA O'Dwyer loaned his usual cast of perjuring state's witnesses, including Abe Reles with his rehearsed fictional Murder, Inc. testimony, to the Los Angeles County DA. It was Brooklyn DA O'Dwyer's intention to build the magnitude of the Murder, Inc. myth by adding Siegel's execution to it, and thus increase his own crime-fighting resume to bolster his upcoming campaign for New York mayor (details in Chapters 9 and 16).

DEWEY'S POLITICAL AMBITIONS & SARATOGA SPRINGS

Assistant DA Turkus' book *Murder, Inc.* was published in 1951 during the Kefauver Committee racket-investigating hearings. Kefauver was using the hearings to develop his own presidential campaign, and Dewey seems to have been gearing up for a third run at the White House. Turkus' crime book is highly political, supporting his Republican ally Governor Dewey, while attacking his Democratic enemies – his former boss Brooklyn DA and then New York Mayor Bill O'Dwyer and U.S. Senator Kefauver. Turkus' book attacks many legitimate weaknesses in the Kefauver Committee's conclusions, but both Turkus and the Committee lacked the slightest grasp of the structure of organized crime. However, as flawed as the Committee's conclusions were, they were closer to reality than Turkus'. Most significantly, the Committee found no evidence that Lepke Buchalter was a major organized-crime leader. Turkus may have written his book to support Dewey's third presidential nomination, or because he was afraid the Kefauver Committee findings would raise questions about the illegal and unjust way he sent seven men to the electric chair with his fictional Murder, Inc. myth.

If Dewey was gearing up for a third run at the presidency in the 1952 election, his racket-busting image was badly damaged by the Kefauver Committee's investigation of gambling in Saratoga Springs, New York in early 1951. The city was the most wide-open gambling center in the northeast for the better part of a century. Its casino resorts catered to the wealthy during a long summer season, which included operation of the famed Saratoga racetrack every August.

Testimony from Saratoga Spring's policemen and three top New York State Police officials were shocking. Each witness admitted that he made no effort to enforce state gambling laws against the almost one dozen casinos that operated wide-open every summer season.

Saratoga Springs Detective Walter Ahearn testified that during the gambling season he received $10 a night from the *Piping Rock Club,* and $50 a week from the *Arrowhead Inn* to carry cash safely to and from a local bank in a police car. However, he swore he had never been beyond the front door of either place. Both supposedly had gambling in the back room, but he claimed he had no personal knowledge either was a casino. Asked why he had made no gambling arrests, he replied, "I had no orders to go in. I still want to work." He said he would have been fired by Saratoga's Police Chief Patrick Rox or Commissioner of Public Safety Dr. Arthur Leonard. The detective made it clear that the gambling was under tight political control. If anyone wanted to run a gambling establishment, he said they would have to have "the right connections" with "the political leaders."

New York State Police Inspector Charles LaForge said that Saratoga Springs Police Chief Rox was cooperative in other phases of the law, but would not discuss gambling. Inspector LaForge believed the casinos had to have political influence to stay open. He said the Saratoga police were politically controlled and agreed with Senate Committee member Tobey's assessment that the police at all levels were "a sickening, a disgusting picture of incompetency."

The State Police officials' testimony matched that of the Saratoga police. Troopers were assigned to investigate the Saratoga gambling places in late July 1947. They wrote a report that gambling was operating "wide open" that summer, but it was passed up the chain of command and filed away.

All three State Police officials said that they could not bring the matter to Governor Dewey's attention because of the necessity of going "through channels." While they hoped the State Police would be called in, they agreed with State Police Superintendent John Gaffney, who explained that it was State Police policy to operate only in rural areas and not to investigate conditions in a city, except at the request of the mayor, the county DA, the governor, or in response to a citizen's complaint. Superintendent Gaffney said the Saratoga gambling report was ordered so that the State Police would have the information about the city if a complaint were made. However, Senator Tobey pointed out that Gaffney could have gotten a complaint from any citizen on the street. Chief Inspector Francis McGarvey added, "This, in police terms, would have been a pushover to suppress. This was all in one place. It was very easy to suppress. Any police organization could have suppressed that."

While Superintendent Gaffney testified that he knew of local and out-of-state racketeers running casinos, policy prevented him from taking action in policed cities. An outraged Senator Tobey said, "What you did was to bury the report, conceal it from the public, treasure it in your heart, save it, and mark it 'confidential.' You did nothing. You were a zero. ... You say it wasn't your duty. If I were the Governor of this state, I would give you just five minutes to get out of the place, or I would kick you out."[202]

Inspector LaForge testified that confidential sources told him that Meyer Lansky and Joe Adonis had an interest in the Arrowhead Inn. Senator Kefauver added that it was proven in closed session - and admitted by Frank Costello himself - that Costello had an interest in the Piping Rock. During Dewey's first gubernatorial campaign, he called Adonis "Public Enemy No. 1 of Brooklyn" and later applied the label to Costello. Yet despite priding himself on racket-busting, Dewey let the three big-time gangsters operate wide-open illegal casinos just 32 miles from the governor's mansion in

Albany while he occupied it from 1943 until 1950 when the Kefauver Committee inquiry focused a national spotlight on them. Only when they became a front-page headline scandal did Dewey exercise his authority and order the State Police to close the Saratoga casinos.

The Kefauver Committee tried to blame Governor Dewey for failing to close the gambling places in Saratoga Springs. The Committee combined the State Police witnesses' testimony that they could not act upon serious criminal ownership of the casinos without the direction of the Governor. But the Committee lacked a smoking gun connecting Dewey to the gambling, even though it was obvious the Governor had to know about the casino center operating openly under his nose, as did every other resident of the State of New York.

Senator Kefauver acknowledged that the Committee had never called a governor to testify, before pointedly announcing "but they are always welcome" to appear. Dewey feigned sickness at Kefauver's request. Governor Dewey also issued a statement that the State Police had no authority to close the casino, avoiding acknowledging that the law gave the governor precisely that authority and responsibility which he failed to exercise until headlines blared the news. He also ignored the fact that his administration gave the "Public Enemies" he had repeatedly publicly sworn to prosecute a free pass for this criminal activity. The Democrats on the Committee clearly enjoyed exposing racket-buster Dewey's hypocritical and transparent protection of the notorious hoods involved with Saratoga's illegal gambling.

Even Senator Tobey took off after his fellow Republican Governor Dewey, asking the press, "What is the reason the police don't raid them and what is the reason the Governor and state don't come down like a ton of bricks? Why is it we don't get action on things pronto? Why are they allowed to exist for 24 hours? … Those are the very things that, allowed to go on, make people lose faith in their form of government. Laugh if you will. These are rats in the meal of democracy." Any plans Dewey had for a third run at the presidency evaporated under the withering attacks upon his hypocritical racket-busting image. But there was much more to the Murder, Inc. saga.[203]

CHAPTER 9

BILL O'DWYER, ABE RELES, & ALBERT ANASTASIA

ABE RELES WENT WHERE?

When a criminal prosecutor is accused of corruption it is typically for accepting a bribe to let a guilty suspect go free. But this and the preceding two chapters explain how Manhattan DA Tom Dewey, Brooklyn DA Bill O'Dwyer, and O'Dwyer's Assistant DA Burton Turkus meticulously framed gang members despite knowing they were innocent of the crimes for which they charged them. These powerful prosecutors colluded to frame innocent men with false testimony, fictitious claims about a nonexistent large criminal conspiracy, and rigged juries. The goal of each of these three was to build his law-and-order crime-busting reputations to boost a pending political campaign.

First, Manhattan DA Dewey got a lifetime sentence against Charlie Luciano for a crime he had no involvement with, and even if he had, the trivial misdemeanor offense of voluntary prostitution booking warranted at most a $300 fine, not a lifetime sentence. Then, Manhattan DA Dewey taught Brooklyn DA O'Dwyer and his Assistant DA Turkus how to create the sensational Murder, Inc. cases and ultimately go after the death penalty for Luciano's Prohibition partner Ben Siegel. To understand what this nefarious trio had planned for Siegel, we return to the third Murder, Inc. trial against Brownsville district gang leader Lepke Buchalter for the murder of trucker Joe Rosen.

While Assistant DA Turkus was systematically presenting his case in Lepke's trial, star prosecution witness Abe Reles waited to be called to present his Murder, Inc. fiction to the jury. DA O'Dwyer kept the informant secluded and secure in protective custody in a closed-off section of the sixth floor at the Half Moon Hotel on the Coney Island boardwalk. Reles shared a large living-room suite with three of the gang's other informant witnesses, and each of the four men had his own attached private sleeping room.

One morning these informants' living arrangement changed abruptly. At 7:45 a.m. an executive arrived at his office on the second floor of the Half Moon Hotel and looked out his window below onto the one-story roof covering the attached kitchen extension to the hotel. Lying on the concrete roof he saw a motionless body. The executive quickly notified NYPD detectives on the sixth floor, and they rushed down to the executive's office and lowered themselves out his window onto the roof. The body was the trial's key prosecution witness Abe Reles, age 35. The thug's 5-feet-4-inch body was laying stretched full length with his head furthest from the building. Reles had fallen 60 feet from his bedroom window above and had landed on his back, breaking his spine to kill him instantly.

The police and the reporters said the body lay "about 25 feet from the wall." This long distance from the building made the stretched-out corpse look like a missile that had been propelled or catapulted out his window. This created a double mystery as everybody had two immediate questions. How did he end up in this location and position? How could this have happened amidst overwhelming police protection?

In the few minutes the detectives were alone with the body before the press arrived, they concocted an odd and convoluted explanation of how Reles met his death sprawled out on his back like that. Lying on his body were a couple of twisted bed sheets, and in his room they had found a strand of radio electrical-cord wire four-feet long with one end wrapped around his radiator steam valve and the other end dangling out the window. No other evidence was found and no one witnessed the plunge, but the detectives guarding Reles quickly contrived the following detailed explanation of the events outside his window that morning.

Detectives told the *New York Times*, "He let himself down, on the sheets, to the fifth floor. One hand desperately clung to the sheet. With the other, Reles tugged at the screen and at the windows of the vacant fifth-floor room. He worked them up six inches. He tugged again with his full 160-pound weight. The strain was too much for the amateur wire-cord knot on the valve. Little by little, it came undone. Reles tried to save himself. He kicked toward the fifth-floor window ledge with his left foot, but merely bruised the shoe leather from toe to heel. Then he plunged to the hotel's kitchen roof."[204]

Not only were the details of the detectives' statements wildly speculative, the investigation that followed was a travesty. NYPD detectives who were supposed to be protecting Reles in the suite were the first to arrive at his body, giving them an unfettered opportunity to alter the crime scene or destroy evidence. They did not bother to question any of the 70 hotel employees who were on duty at the time of his death. In effect, the detectives on duty investigated their own failed performance, and then the NYPD permanently sealed the file.

The NYPD medical examiner's report was likewise botched. There was no examination for injuries on Reles' body, or for damage to his clothing, to support the police hypothesis of an accidental fall. Every photograph was of Reles' fully-clothed body, so no bullet holes, stab wounds, or blunt-force trauma were visible. If someone had knocked him out, dressed him, and tossed him out the window, the photos would have covered up the murder, not uncovered it. In addition, the medical examiner did not run a drug screen to determine if Reles was rendered unconscious, although he did determine that Reles had not consumed alcohol, ruling out inebriation as a factor in the death.

Then the case laid dormant for a decade before the first extensive investigation of the circumstances surrounding Reles' death was conducted. The Kings County Grand Jury issued scathing conclusions about the limited, superficial, five-hour police inquiry that followed Reles' inexplicable demise. "We deplore the lack of proper investigation and the loose manner in which this important occurrence was investigated by the responsible agencies concerned."[205]

Not only did the NYPD fail to investigate the death of an important protected witness, the department arrogantly circulated its own unsubstantiated and improbable hypothesis - Reles was trying to escape from custody. Yet for Reles to attempt to escape by breaking through the screen and window on the floor below would have been extremely risky. Cops were stationed at every hotel entrance/exit, and they all knew what he looked like. Reles had no way of knowing whether the room below his was occupied that morning. If the room were occupied, consider the reaction of the guest when a stranger suddenly crashed through the fifth-story window, stood up, wiped off the broken glass and metal screening, and bolted out the door. As horribly shocking as this event would have been, the guest would have almost certainly called hotel security immediately, and they would have quickly sealed every exit and joined the NYPD in conducting a floor-by-floor search.

The limited NYPD photographs actually challenge the official account. These pictures display the flimsiness of the alleged sheet-and-electrical-wire-cord "rope." It is inconceivable anyone would have climbed out a hotel window holding onto a sheet held by only a thin wire twisted around it. One slight tug and the sheet would have slid out of the wire ring. Even though the sheet and wire props had to have been staged after the fact by the detectives on duty, the NYPD and Brooklyn DA O'Dwyer maintained that Reles' death was an accident caused by his own foolish behavior. However, they never offered a motive for his wanting to depart his comfortable secure suite.

Several of the 18 detectives assigned to guard Reles around the clock were called to testify at hearings into the incident, and every one of them contradicted the official escape hypothesis. They testified that during the 20 months Reles was an informer under protective custody he lived in fear that one of his murderous gang members would pop up and shoot him. He had never shown any inclination to escape, instead reacting with extreme terror to the outside world. When the suite's doorbell rang he always jumped, ran to his inner bedroom, and hid until the caller was gone. Even when his guards simply moved out of earshot he became fearful. When he went to Los Angeles to testify at Ben Siegel's murder arraignment, Reles would not board an airplane or enter a room unless a policeman was covering him front and back.

All the detectives who testified argued that Reles had everything to lose by escaping. There was no place else where he could be protected from the guns of the enraged gang members who were not under arrest. One of the gangsters Reles had agreed to testify against was Brooklyn/Manhattan Mafia gang lieutenant Albert Anastasia. When Anastasia thought he might be indicted he had gone into hiding, but he remained the gangster who most terrified Reles.

The level of fear that Anastasia's reputation provoked in the underworld was illustrated by one of Reles' tough associates, Vito Gurino. When he heard that fugitive Anastasia was looking for him, Gurino fled from his hiding place and raced into the Roman Catholic Shrine of the Sea in Manhattan. He shrieked hysterically to a priest that he was about to be killed and begged to be taken to Brooklyn DA O'Dwyer. The priest escorted him to the DA's office. During the late night questioning, the gibbering, fearful Gurino was in such dread that he repeatedly broke into terrified cries. He readily confessed to three gangland contract murders, and six months later he pled guilty to three charges of second-degree murder. To avoid ever facing Anastasia, Gurino gladly accepted a plea deal of consecutive sentences for a total minimum of 80 years.[206]

Once Reles became an informant against Anastasia, it is inconceivable that he would have attempted to escape police protection. Besides, Reles repeatedly claimed to the prosecutors and in trial testimony that he was safe only in protective custody because the "national syndicate" was gunning for him for testifying against them in the Murder, Inc. trials.

Suicide can also be ruled out. He would not have needed a sheet and telephone wire cord if he were aiming to kill himself. Besides, Reles' guardians described him as unconcerned about hygiene and appearance, which means it is unlikely he would have prepared for his own death that morning by changing from pajamas into full evening attire.

The evening before Reles' death his wife joined him alone in his hotel bedroom for a three-hour conjugal visit lasting until 11 o'clock. When the DA's staff informed her of his death, she said he had seemed perfectly normal during her visits. She could offer no reason why he might try to escape saying, "You boys were always nice to him."[207]

Reles' upbeat mood was substantiated by the three other gang informants sharing the suite. Even the detectives and the DA's personnel guarding the suite said he had been happy, and they never speculated about suicide because he had no reason to kill himself. In fact he was leading a criminal's dream life. The view from his window in the Half Moon Hotel looked eastward from the boardwalk over the beach to the surf breaking against the jetties and the ocean sprawling to the horizon. He was freed of any responsibility and no one controlled his behavior. He slept and napped whenever he felt like it and spent every day doing what he enjoyed. He exercised, read, listened to the radio, and did hobbies. Whatever he felt like eating was available from room service at any hour. Housekeepers cleaned his room and did his laundry. He had discovered villain heaven.

The mysterious long-distance fall gave "The Kid" Reles a posthumous nickname. He was forever remembered by the underworld as "the canary who could sing but couldn't fly." His baffling death had a chilling impact on American law enforcement - for the next two decades no organized-crime member dared turn state's witness to local police or sheriffs.[208]

RESTRICTED & SECURELY-PROTECTED ACCESS

The NYPD detectives who guarded Reles made it clear to the first reporters who arrived on the roof at his body that they were not sorry to see him dead. They described him as arrogant, surly, and hygienically challenged. He suffered from copious flatulence, which he did not bother to control or conceal, heightening the detectives' disgust for him. Detectives bantered sardonically at his death scene and concluded, "The only law that ever got him was Newton's law of gravity."[209]

The 24-hour detail of 18 NYPD detectives guarding the four witnesses at the Half Moon Hotel suite was divided into three shifts. The detectives who guarded him and the surviving three informants agreed that it would have been impossible for any outsider to penetrate into the suite because at least one guard watched the single entrance door around the clock. Thus, if Reles were murdered, the only possible perpetrators were his guards. However, no detectives were ever considered suspects because all the government investigations failed to determine why or how Reles went out that window. Nor did any of the many authors fascinated about early organized crime uncover anything new about the circumstances of this bizarre underworld death.

I evaluated Reles' death anew and by assembling every fact related to the case, I was finally able to solve what happened and why. I initially determined that there were only two possible scenarios. Either Reles jumped to his death for reasons no one who knew him could fathom, or the detectives charged with his protection murdered him.

Unfortunately the NYPD investigation was grossly inadequate, so every known fact led to a dead end but one - the significance of Reles' 25-foot vault *away* from the building. It is surprising that no one who studied the case explored this angle, because I was struck by the obvious fact that he should have been pulled straight down by sheer gravity, not away from the building toward the horizon. I compared the distance of Reles' flight to that of the greatest leaper of his era, U.S. track star Jesse Owens, whose 1935 world long-jump record of 26 feet 8 ¼ inches stood for a quarter century.

To reach sprinting speed long-jumpers jog at least 10 to 20 yards, and then sprint at least 10 more yards to attain launch speed at the take-off line. To achieve maximum distance, they fly through the air feet first with their body extended horizontally. Reles could not employ such a technique in his hotel bedroom. The edge of the bed was less than two yards from the window, so the best he could have done was take a couple of steps before leaning forward to dive headfirst through the relatively-small window opening. Even Owens at his peak could not have managed a 25-foot leap from that short navigating distance.

Reles' body position also negates the NYPD version of events supported by DA O'Dwyer. Remember, the official story was that Reles had tied sheets and a wire to the radiator, but they came undone so he fell. But if that were the case, he would have fallen straight down, landing within a couple feet of the building. Even if he had shoved himself out of the window frame, he could not have pushed more than a few feet from the hotel-room tower.

Since the facts prove Reles could not have caused his own death, the only plausible scenario is that he was murdered. It would have taken two strong men to hurl a man from a window to land 25 feet away. They would have had to hold his prone body headfirst and swing him in unison with a powerful heave.

Testimony by the three surviving gang informant witnesses reveals that two detectives could have flung him without anyone else in the suite being aware of it. A guard sat in a chair in each of the four sleeping informant's rooms and the fifth was in the living room. The detective sitting alone in the living room probably waited until he heard no sound from the other three bedrooms, and then joined the detective in Reles' bedroom. The detectives could have easily rendered the sleeping victim unconscious with chloroform or a whack on the head. No one in the other rooms would have heard anything. Even if Reles were still semi-conscious and tried to struggle, his radio, which detectives described as "blaring" that night, would have covered up any sound. Tossing the unconscious Reles out the window would not have created any noise, and he would not have yelled on the way down, which is why his body was not discovered immediately. (See Addendum T)

The blustery gangster once blurted out in open court, "All cops are yellow, and I'll fight any single one with guns, knives, or broken glass." But Reles could not overcome two guards he trusted from subduing him as he slept.[210]

NULLIFYING A MURDER INVESTIGATION

I began my inquiry into Reles' death to figure out how he ended up on that hotel kitchen roof top. Once I determined it was murder, I focused on the mystery of who did it and why. First, I identified several persons of interest who might have wanted him dead and amassed numerous details about them. But it became clear that the only people who had the opportunity to hurl Reles out the window that morning were two of the five detective guards on duty. More importantly, the only way a protected witness could have been so obviously murdered and yet the detective guards responsible never be held accountable was if Brooklyn's two top lawmen worked in tandem to cover up the crime. By examining a web of interrelated facts and relationships, it became clear that Brooklyn DA Bill O'Dwyer and his hand-picked NYPD Captain, Frank Bals, carried out this nefarious scheme to kill their own state's witness.

O'Dwyer was Irish, and as a young man he went to Spain to study for the priesthood before emigrating to New York City in 1910. He found work as a plasterer's helper and a longshoreman before becoming a policeman. As a rookie O'Dwyer was a comrade of Bals who joined the NYPD in 1916. While O'Dwyer worked for the NYPD, he studied law at night school. After becoming an attorney he practiced law for eight years before being appointed Brooklyn magistrate. Six years later he was appointed county judge and then was elected Brooklyn DA in 1939. Within months after taking office he began the Murder, Inc. prosecutions.

When O'Dwyer took over the DA's office, his prosecutorial staff was made up of attorneys along with a large 65-man NYPD Detective Bureau attached to it. O'Dwyer quickly placed his buddy Captain Bals in charge of this detective staff. The law-enforcement organizational structure in New York City was for each of the five boroughs in separate counties to have their own DA, but all five boroughs were under the jurisdiction of the mayor and the NYPD, with the police commissioner serving at the pleasure of the mayor. However, the manipulative O'Dwyer soon achieved a radical realignment of this command. He convinced NYPD Police Commissioner Lewis Valentine to have Captain Bals report to, and be accountable solely to, himself as DA. O'Dwyer and his lackey Bals now controlled all law enforcement in Brooklyn by bypassing the city's entire legal system. This rendered Brooklyn's internal police-investigation procedures non-functional.

I focused my investigation on Captain Bals because I believed the person who arranged Reles' death would almost certainly have had to have inside knowledge about the members of the protective detective squad. It would have been extremely risky for an outsider to approach just any guard. If an outsider had approached a honest detective, or even one who was corrupt but not capable of murder, the detective would have reported the approach and exposed the murder plan. It is important to recognize that even though many city police departments have suffered from widespread long-term bribery corruption that allowed wide-open illegal vice operations, the number of American policemen who have ever been suspected of a contract killing is infinitesimal. This makes it incredibly unlikely that two NYPD cops, who were capable of committing cold-blooded murder, would have ended up together on a five-man shift. This statistical anomaly makes it all but a certainty that Captain Bals identified two such murderous men on the force and assigned them to work beside each other for this premeditated duty.

Captain Bals had absolute authority over the detective squad that protected the informants, and according to his own testimony to the U.S. Senate Kefauver Committee organized crime investigation, he had indeed "carefully selected each member." In addition, the morning of the murder, Bals deviated from his own long-standing policy about the number of guards on duty. Both his own detectives and the three other informants testified that not having six guards on duty was highly irregular. Yet that morning a guard had reported ill and Captain Bals alone decided not to replace him. If he had assigned a replacement, it would have disrupted the murder scheme, because there would have been a guard in each of the four bedrooms and two in the living room. If the second detective in the living room was not part of the plot, he would have testified how two cops were in Reles' bedroom at the time he took flight. If Captain Bals had involved a third participant, he would have had to find another murderous detective and face the risk of having another accomplice who could have later turned state's witness against him. Since the two killer cops had no expectation their shift would ever be short a man, Captain Bals had to have been the leader.[211]

One fact in this murder strategy was most perplexing. The two killer cops did nothing to cover their trail even though they had to know that a legitimate police investigation would easily lead to their conviction. They knew the three detectives guarding the other informants would declare their innocence. The detective in Reles' bedroom would have had to be involved, and the DA would have been expected to easily cut a deal with him to nail the detective who was supposed to be sitting in the living room. Captain Bals lacked the authority to shield either his men or himself from a legitimate police investigation. He was just an opportunistic grafter, a cop with an open hand to any shady deal including murder. Captain Bals had no political connections beyond his boss O'Dwyer. But the DA had complete control of Brooklyn's criminal investigation and prosecution process. He had absolute authority over who would and would not be scrutinized, arrested, and tried. He also directed the methodology, cost, and diligence of every investigation and prosecution. Furthermore, he was connected to powerful political and underworld figures who might want Reles dead.

Because of DA O'Dwyer's absolute control, no murder investigation of Reles' death was ever conducted. Instead, the detectives personally selected by Captain Bals for the Reles detail flung him out the window and then planted false evidence at the scene before anyone else appeared. As soon as the press arrived minutes after Reles' body was discovered, the killer detectives told them their bizarre escape hypothesis. DA O'Dwyer and Captain Bals reinforced the detectives' statements by creating a false but confusing cover-up debate. Then O'Dwyer quietly quashed the inquiry while directing the medical examiner to list the official cause of death as an *accidental fall* while trying to escape.

For more than a decade, DA O'Dwyer and NYPD Captain Bals more or less stuck to their stories, although the details changed over time, becoming weirder and less consistent with the evidence planted at the scene. In later city and federal investigations, both men changed their hypothesis from failed escape attempt to fun prank gone wrong. With straight faces they maintained that Reles intended to shimmy down to the fifth floor, kick in the screen and window below his room, take either the elevator or the fire escape back up to the sixth floor, and knock at his suite door to shock his police protectors with his clever escape ploy.

Despite Reles' grubby, casual dress style, that cold mid-November morning he was fully dressed for escape. He was wearing a coat and sweater, and while his hat was left in the room, a checkered cap folded the long way was found in his left coat pocket. It could have been used to cover part of his facial features in the alleged escape attempt. Clearly, the detectives who flung Reles out the window first dressed him to support the escape story. Later, DA O'Dwyer and Captain Bals changed their supposition about Reles' motive, but they never explained why a sloppy thug would bother to fully dress for the cold outdoors and take a cap for a simple prank. Furthermore, no one ever accused this gruff, psychopathic killer of having a sense of humor or loving trivial pranks especially enough to risk his life dangling from a flimsy telephone wire cord stretched out from a sixth-floor windowsill.

At the Kefauver Committee hearings, the Chief Counsel told O'Dwyer, "Bals made a spectacle of himself before the Committee, and he gave the flimsiest excuse possible about the death of Reles." The Committee's disbelief about Bals' position, as well as their own stated belief that the detectives in the suite were the only ones with the opportunity to toss Reles out the window, seemed to shake up O'Dwyer because under the Senators' challenges he kept changing his position. O'Dwyer's testimony ultimately offered four contradictory explanations for Reles' death, but he steadfastly defended the police guards who failed to protect the informant witness. (See Addendum U)

Once DA O'Dwyer and Captain Bals had officially agreed upon a cause of death, New York Mayor Fiorello LaGuardia jumped in by announcing he had ordered "a very thorough investigation" into the police conduct that allowed a witness to fall to his death in an "attempted escape." This was typical LaGuardia hyperbole as he was the master of tough-talking rhetoric, buttressed by little substance. While LaGuardia ordered Bals to investigate himself, a futile gesture in itself, the Mayor dismissed the possibility of murder by endorsing the Bals and O'Dwyer escape hypothesis before the investigation began. Thus, Bals ignored the Mayor's order to investigate and the case died.

Next, NYPD Police Commissioner Valentine announced that he had demoted the five detectives on duty the morning of Reles' dive to uniformed street-patrol duty, but he did not reduce their pay. The demotion was a trivial penalty for two men who had carried out a well-paid contract murder. Two weeks after the death of the key witness in O'Dwyer's most important trial, the five detectives faced a public NYPD departmental trial at Brooklyn Police Headquarters charged with neglect of duty. Yet in his later testimony to the Kefauver Committee, O'Dwyer excused the detectives' sorry performance by testifying "I was prepared to defend them for carelessness."[212]

At the detective's departmental trial, DA O'Dwyer's performance was theatrical. He claimed that the detectives were heroes in protecting the informants from monstrous threats. O'Dwyer asserted the detectives had broken up a gangland plot to kill all four informants. In another dramatic incident one detective had thrown his body in front of an informant to prevent a sniper from shooting him on the sidewalk outside the hotel. Yet the DA declined to offer any facts or details. He refused to explain why no one was shot, how the gunmen in the two incidents escaped, why no APB (all points bulletin) was issued to apprehend the attempted murderers, why no police reports were filed, why no commendations for bravery were awarded to the detectives, and why the biggest law-enforcement story of the year was hidden from the press. He would not identify the perpetrators or the detectives allegedly involved. It was obvious the incidents were fictitious, but the DA was not properly cross-examined, and he left the room before reporters could ask for details.

At the conclusion of the NYPD trial, none of the guards was suspended, not even the one who allegedly fell asleep on the job in Reles' bedroom. Captain Bals did not receive as much as a reprimand.

THE CONSEQUENCES FOR MURDER

A great deal of evidence makes it clear who killed Reles and why. It all fits together as a coherent whole by first understanding the rest of the careers of DA O'Dwyer and Police Captain Bals, including their gross corruption along with their strong commitment to protect each other. It began with a very odd sequence of political events that surrounded Reles' murder. Six days before Reles died, Mayor LaGuardia had challenged DA O'Dwyer's independent NYPD empire by ordering him in writing to make the Brooklyn DA's confidential police records available to NYPD's Manhattan headquarters. This intrusion into Captain Bals' autonomy motivated him to announce his resignation, and he made it clear he was only loyal to O'Dwyer by telling the world he was his boy. He said, "In order to comply with the instructions that I received [from the Police Commissioner], it would have been necessary for me to betray the confidence that District Attorney William O'Dwyer placed in me. If I had failed to reveal this confidential information, I would have been subject to disciplinary action. I wouldn't sell out District Attorney O'Dwyer for any job and that is why I resigned." How bizarre that a top NYPD official thought his information was confidential from his Department. Captain Bals' written resignation delayed its effective date for one month, which gave him time to direct his two detectives to kill Reles and then manipulate the inquiry he knew would inevitably follow this shocking event.[213]

Four days after Captain Bals left the NYPD, Pearl Harbor was attacked, and Mayor LaGuardia put aside his domestic conflict over NYPD control. Actually, LaGuardia completely capitulated by giving in to DA O'Dwyer's demand to create a new confidential investigating squad responsible only to him. Less than two months after Bals failed to protect Reles, DA O'Dwyer appointed him to head the new secret squad of investigators. O'Dwyer even sweetened Bals' reward by arranging for him to double dip from the public trough by appointing him as a civilian chief investigator, so he could draw both his new salary and his NYPD pension.

Then World War II interrupted DA O'Dwyer's political career. He took a leave of absence to enter the Army as a major, and seven months later Bals resigned from the DA's office for a second time. This separation from the DA's office did not end this crooked duo's corrupt ways. After O'Dwyer completed his Army hitch, he returned to his position as Brooklyn DA, and he used this position to win election as New York mayor in 1945. Before O'Dwyer took office, Police Commissioner Lewis Valentine retired to enter private business, and outgoing Mayor LaGuardia named Valentine's successor as Deputy Chief Inspector Arthur Wallander. LaGuardia repeatedly stated that he selected Wallander because there was no way mayor-elect O'Dwyer could fault and override this appointment, intimating that he was well aware of O'Dwyer's corrupt past. LaGuardia's pronouncement was prophetic because Mayor O'Dwyer was unable to find a politically-acceptable justification for firing the respected Wallander.

Mayor O'Dwyer did force Wallander to accept the retired Bals as Deputy Police Commissioner, heading an independent NYPD unit with no accountability. O'Dwyer announced that Bals would maintain constant vigilance over the activities of the NYPD and would liaison with the Mayor's office.

Deputy Commissioner Bals handpicked 20 detectives for his secret unit. Then he opened a post office box, and he notified New York City's illegal gamblers to send their bribe payments for police protection to his address. The city's bookmakers quickly ran to their political protectors, complaining vociferously about monthly "big-money shakedowns." When a Broadway columnist published these rumors, Mayor O'Dwyer was forced to order an investigation but his actual goal was to cover up Bals' activities. O'Dwyer had already undermined the independence of police investigations, just as he had as Brooklyn DA, by appointing a political henchmen, John Murtagh, as Commissioner of Investigation. The Mayor later rewarded Murtagh with an appointment as Chief City Magistrate, but after O'Dwyer left this office, Murtagh was criminally prosecuted for "neglect of duty" and destroying records while he was Commissioner of Investigation. Murtagh had in his files the phone number of every bookmaker in the Big Apple, but he never conducted an investigation of any of them. He was obviously the ringleader in Deputy Commissioner Bals' bookmaker extortion scheme, but the jury did not understand his misdeeds so they acquitted him.

When the stink over Bals' illegal activities arose, Mayor O'Dwyer tried to appoint his corrupt Commissioner of Investigation to head the bookmaker-bribery investigation, but Police Commissioner Wallander adroitly blocked the move, announcing that the NYPD had begun investigating the "most cynical grafting spree in New York history." This was a charge the police department hierarchy could not tolerate because Bals was pocketing the graft that had previous gone to NYPD district officials.

Police Commissioner Wallander disbanded Bals' unit two months into its existence, but this move did not end Mayor O'Dwyer's payoffs to Bals, who kept his high-paid position, even though he no longer had any responsibility or authority. Publicly the two men were no longer close, but two months after Bals retired, Mayor O'Dwyer directed the Board of Trustees of the Police Pension Fund to take an unprecedented action. For the first time in the City's history, a retired cop's pension was increased, guaranteeing Bals lifelong payments that were three times higher than they should have been.[214]

Bals later testified to the Kefauver Committee that he organized the Mayor's NYPD squad to find connections between organized crime and the rackets. He was forced to admit, "I made no investigations. My squad was strictly information." He failed to explain how he acquired his information without investigating. He claimed that all the records from his command were stolen from police headquarters by unknown persons after he retired. Near the end of his vacuous presentation, Bals also admitted that O'Dwyer had arranged for his ridiculously excessive pension. Then O'Dwyer testified to Kefauver that Bals produced no reports about police corruption, even though he was responsible for investigating it.[215]

During a Brooklyn Grand Jury investigation of police links to organized gamblers in early 1951, five veteran detectives, all former members of Bals' confidential mayoral squad in 1946, suddenly retired and refused to sign waivers of immunity from prosecution. Bals did testify, but he also refused to sign a waiver. It is inconceivable that innocent men, who spent their careers pledged to enforce the law, would refuse to cooperate with a Grand Jury investigation unless they were first granted immunity from prosecution.

The record is clear. O'Dwyer and Bals were co-conspirators in graft, extortion, and murder. O'Dwyer rewarded Bals loyalty with ever increasing salaries and an unconscionably large pension. Their conspiracy was a vital piece in the puzzle of Abe Reles' death. It pointed me toward whoever was responsible for setting the assassination in motion, but I still was far from unmasking the individual who had paid off O'Dwyer to direct the murder. To get there, I had to determine who benefited most from Reles' death and establish a connection to DA O'Dwyer. My first task was to figure out whether Frank Costello could possibly be involved. He was a political campaign adviser to O'Dwyer, and he knew every major gangster who wanted Reles dead.

O'DWYER'S RELATIONSHIP WITH COSTELLO & TAMMANY

Solving Reles' murder was complicated because a number of violent hoodlums wanted to either silence him or get even. At the time he took his plunge, Reles' testimony had put four thugs on death row and he had a deal with prosecutors to testify against a leader in each of New York City's three major gangs in separate capital-punishment trials.

Before examining which gangster benefited most from Reles' death, it is important to understand O'Dwyer's ties and loyalty to his political sponsor Frank Costello. The public and press knew Costello as a political powerhouse at Tammany Hall, as a big-time bookmaker, and as a legitimate businessman. It would not be until after Costello retired that the NYPD, the FBI, the press, and the public would learn that he had been the Mafia Boss of Bosses for two decades.

Costello was O'Dwyer's most obvious contact to the underworld, especially since Costello was associated with all three major hoods Reles was to testify against. Costello was very tight with both Ben Siegel and Albert Anastasia, and he knew Lepke Buchalter well. This made him a viable candidate to be the intermediary who made the deal with DA O'Dwyer for a contract murder and slipped him the money from the hood responsible.

While O'Dwyer was serving in the Army during World War II, his association with Costello first became public. O'Dwyer and his political operative James Moran attended a cocktail party in Costello's suite, along with top Tammany officials including leader Michael Kennedy. O'Dwyer asked Costello for his support with Tammany Hall's leaders to be the Democratic candidate for New York Mayor in the 1945 election three years hence.[216]

In later appearances before the Kefauver Committee, O'Dwyer, Moran , and Costello denied that any political talk had occurred at that cocktail party by putting a patriotic spin on the meeting. O'Dwyer said he had been investigating possible corruption in Army contracts with garment businesses and wanted to find out what Costello knew about people involved in the contracts. O'Dwyer admitted he was accompanied not by other Army officials, but by his political fixer Moran, who was not in the military. O'Dwyer testified that Moran had joined him on the alleged Army business because he "was a friend of mine, and still is." And O'Dwyer asserted that at the time he only knew of Costello's reputation as "an outstanding bookmaker, a big one," not as "the prime minister of the underworld."[217] (See Addendum V)

O'Dwyer claimed he was helped in his Army investigation effort by garment manufacturer Irving Sherman, who just happened to be a good friend of both Costello and Joe Adonis. During O'Dwyer's 1945 mayoral campaign, Sherman made many long distance calls to the candidate. At that point in the campaign the earlier 1942 meeting of O'Dwyer with Costello and their relationship became a major issue, so Costello wanted Sherman out of sight. Just before the election, O'Dwyer asked Sherman to leave town, presumably so the press could not question him about his connection to the mayoral campaign. This worked, as murdering DA O'Dwyer was elected mayor of New York.

The Kefauver hearings clearly exposed the close link between O'Dwyer, Sherman, and Costello. When O'Dwyer was DA, and later Mayor, he communicated covertly but easily with his hoodlum pal Costello through Sherman and Moran. The May 1, 1951 Committee Report presented several negative conclusions about O'Dwyer's abuse and misuse of power, including the damning observation that "Despite Mr. O'Dwyer's frequent public castigations of Tammany Hall, and his acknowledgement that Frank Costello was a sinister influence therein, he has been on terms of intimate friendship with persons who were close friends of Costello. Many of his intimate friends were also close friends of racketeer Joe Adonis. He has appointed friends of both Costello and Adonis to high public office." (See Addendum W)

WHO WAS BEHIND RELES' MURDER?

The evidence proves Reles' murder could only have been orchestrated and covered up by DA O'Dwyer, implemented by Police Captain Bals, and carried out by two NYPD detectives. Informant Reles' death benefited three major gangsters, each of whom was facing the death penalty for a different murder. The question is - which one benefited the most?

Reles flew out the window three days before he was to testify as the key witness against Lepke Buchalter in the third Murder, Inc. trial. Prosecutor Burton Turkus insisted to the press that Reles' death would not seriously affect the evidence, and he was right. Turkus had eight other Lepke associates waiting in the wings to perjure themselves and a stacked blue-ribbon jury committed to accepting the prosecution's arguments. Even without Reles' testimony, getting a conviction proved to be relatively easy. Reles' timely murder did not benefit Lepke, who was convicted and then executed in Sing Sing.

Grand Juries, the U.S. Senate, and crime writers tried unsuccessfully to ascertain who might have wanted Reles flung out his hotel bedroom window. The date of the event was not a clue because two outside influences determined when Reles would die. DA O'Dwyer set the plot in motion when Mayor LaGuardia required Bals' rogue Brooklyn police squad to become accountable to the Manhattan NYPD leadership. This made Bals feel compelled to resign, so he had to implement O'Dwyer's scheme before he left the police force. Thus, the date had to be the first night one member of the protective squad's graveyard shift called in sick.

While the murder plot was set in motion just days before Reles took his flight out the window, it is clear that DA O'Dwyer planned it months earlier to have it available as an option if needed. This is why he changed the prosecution strategy in the third Murder, Inc. trial in case he decided to make Reles unavailable to testify. In the first two Murder, Inc. trials, Reles and his Murder, Inc. fiction had been the star witness and he was corroborated by a couple other gang members who testified the defendants had been the killers. Even though these convictions had been easy, O'Dwyer greatly changed the prosecution scenario for the third Murder, Inc. trial of Lepke by adding six additional state's witnesses with different testifying goals. In this trial three informant gang members claimed Lepke had talked about Rosen's murder in their presence, while five other gang members testified they were participants with the remaining two defendants in the trucker's murder. Since the trial began two months before Reles flew out the window, DA O'Dwyer had to have designed the murderous plot much earlier to eliminate the need for having Reles' testify.[218]

At the time of his demise Reles was set to testify in three separate murder cases. In addition to Lepke, he had agreed to testify against two leaders of much larger gangs. They were Ben Siegel who was in custody in a Hollywood jail awaiting trial (see Chapter 16), and Albert Anastasia who was believed to be hiding in anticipation of charges being filed in Brooklyn. Both California and New York had state laws requiring a prosecution witness who was an accomplice to the crime charged have a corroborating state's witness. Reles was the corroborator in both the Siegel and Anastasia cases, so his death weakened both prosecutions.

At the time Reles flew out his hotel window, Siegel's case was more urgent because he was in custody awaiting trial. But Siegel could not have contacted DA O'Dwyer directly because not only was he in jail, he had never met O'Dwyer. The hood had moved from Manhattan to Hollywood four years before O'Dwyer became the Brooklyn DA. Even if they had crossed paths, O'Dwyer could not have communicated directly with Siegel because it would have raised troubling questions about the Brooklyn DA's propriety and fitness.

In contrast Costello, who was closely associated with both DA O'Dwyer and Siegel, could meet privately with either the prosecutor or the hood without creating suspicion or embarrassment. As it will be seen (in Chapter 16), it is obvious that Costello did intercede on behalf of his pal Siegel. However Costello's goal was never to harm Reles, but rather to keep the informant from being available to testify at Siegel's trial. Since Costello successfully persuaded DA O'Dwyer to keep Reles in protective custody in his Coney Island hotel instead of letting him travel to Hollywood to testify, Reles had ceased to be a threat to Siegel, so he gained nothing from the informant's death.

Previously, DA O'Dwyer had flown Reles and another informant under heavy NYPD guard to Los Angeles to testify before a grand jury which indicted Siegel for murder. But before the case came to trial, DA O'Dwyer decided it was no longer appropriate to transfer Reles from protective custody in Brooklyn. Danger to the witness was not the issue because O'Dwyer let the other Brooklyn-gang informant appear at Siegel's trial. However, DA O'Dwyer gave no rationale for reversing his actions to cooperate with the Los Angeles DA. With no corroborating witness, the judge in Siegel's trial had to dismiss the murder charge against him for failure to present evidence of guilt.

Joe Adonis backed up Costello at the meeting at which he intervened with DA O'Dwyer on behalf of Siegel. Adonis was a political leader in Brooklyn, had been Siegel's partner during Prohibition, and was a close associate of Costello when the Young Turks campaigned to end underworld violence. With Siegel freed by this legal ploy, and Lepke not able to benefit from Reles' murder because six additional informant witnesses had agreed to testify against him, only one gangster had anything to gain from the informant's assassination. This was Albert Anastasia.

ANASTASIA WAS DOMINANT IN BROOKLYN

Albert Anastasia's criminal career ranged from the depraved depths of organized crime to the sordid underbelly of American politics, where the two worlds merge into a cesspool of greed, corruption, and human sacrifice. The following in-depth examination of Anastasia's villainous empire illustrates how his tentacles reached into Brooklyn DA O'Dwyer's innermost sanctum.[219]

Even though Anastasia and his crimes were repugnant to Luciano and the Young Turks, they needed his underworld political support to ensure their survival on the mean streets. Anastasia was a loyal ally and essential contributor during the gang's darkest days. Thus, it is important to understand Anastasia's background, even though he did not participate with the Young Turks' later development of the fledgling Las Vegas Strip casino industry.

Albert Anastasia was born Umberto Anastasio on September 26, 1902, in the fishing village of Tropea in Calabria, along the southwestern tip of Italy, where Costello also came from. At age 12, he shipped out as a deckhand on a tramp steamer and then knocked about the toughest ports in the world. Three years later he jumped ship, swam illegally to the U.S. shore, and blended in with the mass of longshoremen on the docks. Four of his seven brothers entered the country the same way. Albert's brother Tony later explained to the press, "We wanted to go to America. Who knew about passports in those days? Anyway, I bet 60,000 longshoremen got there by jumping ship."[220]

The original spelling of "Anastasio" was used by some branches of the family clan in America. Albert adopted the name "Anastasia" at his first arrest and bounced between the two spellings in various arrests over many years so that anyone checking either name came up with only part of his arrest record. He soon became involved with the criminal societies of Sicilian Mafiosi and of Calabrians in his Brooklyn-dock neighborhood. While some Prohibition hoods developed their reputations because the police harassed them with spurious arrests, Anastasia earned his record through his own vicious deeds. He was arrested 10 times between the ages of 18 and 52. Five of these arrests were for murders he very likely committed.

His first arrest was at age 18. He and Joseph Florino were convicted of murdering George Turrelo, a fellow longshoreman from Italy, during a quarrel. The pair of thugs sat in the death house at Sing Sing for 18 months until their lawyers won a retrial on a technicality. By that time Anastasia's Mafia associates had arranged for four key prosecution witnesses to go missing, at least one having been frightened back to Italy. At retrial the two defendants were acquitted.

This close brush with the electric chair did not temper Anastasia's penchant for violence. He was arrested for assault a year later, but he won discharge by again intimidating witnesses. Later that year he and Florino were charged with possession of a gun that was complicated by carrying a bogus revolver permit, so they were sentenced to two years for gun toting. Anastasia was later charged with four more murders, but he was tried for only one. He was acquitted because of the chilling disappearances of prosecution witnesses, and by testimony that changed from previous statements after witnesses were contacted by his associates.[221]

Anastasia became the lieutenant in the country's second largest gang, which was headed by Vincent Mangano. Rival Manhattan/Brooklyn Mafia leader Joe Bonanno later wrote about Mangano's situation, "He was older, and younger men in his Family coveted his position. He had to be especially wary of Anastasia, who probably had the most fearsome reputation in our world. I used to call Albert 'il terremoto' – the earthquake. Albert's ambition did not sit well with Mangano." Mangano disappeared in February 1951 and his body was never found. Anastasia immediately assumed leadership of Mangano's large gang.

In describing Anastasia's defiant appearance before the New York State Crime Commission, the *New York Times* reporter said, "His demeanor on the stand had the deceptive languor of a jungle cat." He was "generally considered the most feared figure in the underworld."[222]

Even though Anastasia was an ally throughout his criminal career to Luciano and Costello, when I brought up his name in an interview with Jimmy Blue Eyes, his face contorted into a painful grimace and he breathed heavily before saying, "Anastasia was the worst son-of-a-bitch I ever met." While Luciano and the Young Turks maintained peace between the five New York City Mafia gangs and the other Mafia gangs around the country for a quarter of a century because they were highly respected, it helped that the underworld was well aware that Luciano's gang enjoyed the steadfast support of both the psychopathic Anastasia and the murderous Al Capone.

Luciano and Costello headed the nation's largest gang, and Mangano/Anastasia and Capone headed the second and third respectively. Capone did not reach this stature until late in his rule, after he had wiped out most of the competing Chicago gang leaders and absorbed their surviving members. With the enormous firepower supporting the few policies Luciano and Costello imposed on the underworld, no one dared challenge them.

Even though Anastasia's and Capone's policies, values, and temperament were different from those of Luciano and the Young Turks, these men always maintained close personal ties. For example, Anastasia was extremely loyal to Costello, deeply respectful of Luciano, and a good friend of Adonis, who lived just around the corner from Anastasia's Fort Lee, New Jersey estate. Anastasia's abode overlooked the Hudson River and was surrounded by a seven-feet steel and barbed-wire fence and guarded at night by two roaming Doberman Pinschers.

Anastasia's extortion of New York-New Jersey dockworkers by the unions under his control was fictionalized in the 1954 Academy Award winning movie *On The Waterfront,* in which Marlon Brando's character, longshoreman Terry Malloy, single-handedly defeats the movie's powerful union gangsters. But on the real-life waterfront, organized-crime exploitation of workers and shippers continues to this day.

Six Brooklyn dock unions were locals of the powerful International Longshoremen's Association (I.L.A.) of the A.F.L., and they were known as the "Italian locals" because they were made up mostly of Italian immigrants. For many years they were controlled by a close-knit group of union officials headed by Emil Camarda, and they took their orders directly from Mafia chieftain Vincent Mangano and his lieutenant Anastasia. These gangsters turned the unions into their private poaching preserves as they extorted the working members and also the importers and exporters who shipped goods through the ports.

Brooklyn DA George Beldock described the situation to the press, "The gangsters and racketeers and the Camarda family dominated these locals. The Camardas were a clan of union officials headed by Emil Camarda, founder and general factotum of the [Red Hook] City Democratic Club. In this hideout, union officials played pinochle with Albert Anastasia, boss of the Red Hook [waterfront] underworld. In this club, Anastasia met his henchmen, his board of directors."[223]

Attorney Vincent Mannino testified before the Kefauver Committee that he was counsel to the six Brooklyn local longshoreman's unions. Over time he learned that Mangano called the shots in all six locals. Mangano told him, "Vincent, don't you know if it hadn't been for me you would never be the attorney for the locals?" Mannino also testified that a local union secretary confirmed this by telling him "Of course, it's true. Without Vincent Mangano Sr.'s okay, nobody could work here."

Mannino further testified about his role as board chairman of Brooklyn's City Democratic Club and about Mangano's dominance in Brooklyn politics. Mangano owned the club's building and had a great deal to say about running it. Attorney Mannino said, "The City Democratic Club was supposed to represent the Americans of Italian extraction, and naturalized Italians." "They often said the organization existed merely to help many deserving Americans of Italian extraction find their rightful place in the sun of our city. I felt that the reason why they were interested in this organization was to help and promote their own personal interests politically." Mannino also testified that Mangano and Anastasia "were frequently together in the City Democratic Club," that Mangano served on several of the club's committees, and that he saw DA O'Dwyer at the Club a number of times, primarily during major political rallies.[224]

Anastasia's physical aggressiveness got him promoted from longshoreman worker to pier superintendent, a position he used to elevate himself up to Mangano's Mafia lieutenant and muscle, making Anastasia the undisputed "boss" of the waterfront racketeers. His Italian was not much better than his English (his schooling ended at age 11), so he spoke seldom, and then in a hoarse, guttural voice. As awful as the sinister Anastasia was, at times he could seem pleasant, genial, and generous. He was a liberal tipper. However, even when he was at his best it is doubtful anyone considered him more than remote, dark, and menacing.

The attorney for a defunct worker reformist insurgent committee that tried to oppose the union rule of Camarda and his henchmen officials also testified before the Kefauver Committee. Attorney Marcy Protter said "Hiring on the waterfront was through the shape-up. Men shaped up for jobs once or twice a day, and they were selected for the jobs on the basis of their knowing certain individuals, and on the basis of certain contributions which they were required to make." Protter added, "In order to obtain work on a certain pier, you had to enter into a form of contract to have all your haircuts at a certain barbershop, and you paid in advance, each month, for those haircuts. But, if you showed up to get those haircuts, why, you no longer were eligible for a job on the waterfront." "Another method was that in the fall you were required to purchase all of the grapes to make your wine from a certain dealer. You had to pay exorbitant prices for these grapes, and if you paid in the proper amount, why, you could be employed when you appeared at the shape-up." Wine grapes were an essential part of the traditional life for Italian and Sicilian immigrants.

Protter went on to say that the Union also used the Columbus Day Ball to extort kickbacks from all dockworkers. They sold 10,000 tickets, but it was understood that no one was to show up unless they received an invitation because "the ballroom that was engaged couldn't hold more than four or five hundred people." He testified that the worker insurgents' group estimated "Between 40 and 50 percent of the longshoremen's wages had to be paid back."[225]

If a worker who paid these burdensome extortion demands had problems making ends meet, assistance was readily offered by the unions' omnipresent representatives dangling available loans at usurious interest rates. Nonpayment resulted in hounding and threats, followed by body realignment.

The officials of these six Brooklyn longshoreman's unions made the following admissions before the New York State Crime Commission. One local's books had never been audited by an accountant. Some of the locals' officials unabashedly claimed their unions' financial records of dues payments "must have gotten lost when moving." Other union officials testified that their unions did not keep accounting books and that their leaders took cash from the dues payments for personal purposes, whatever they wanted, without signing for or ever repaying the money.

An international vice-president of the I.L.A. maintained that four years' worth of large financial contributions from stevedoring companies were just Christmas gifts, which he claimed he immediately donated to other people he failed to identify. While this was tacit admission that he had committed a federal felony (union officials are prohibited from accepting money from unionized companies), no charges were brought against him.

One union local's financial secretary testified he knew Anastasia. This secretary said he never questioned the conduct of his local's affairs. He even remained silent when the members rejected Anastasia's brother Gerardo in an election, and then over the members' objections, the brother was appointed a delegate of the local. Regular visitors to the Red Hook City Democratic Club included most dock union officials, Anastasia, and others of similar repute. Witnesses testified straight-faced that the thugs would come to the club to "talk, play cards, and discuss politics and the weather."

DA O'DWYER SHIELDED ANASTASIA

DA O'Dwyer refused to enforce the laws he took an oath to uphold, according to Kefauver Committee testimony by union worker insurgent committee attorney Marcy Protter. He revealed he went to DA O'Dwyer's lackey James Moran to complain that the books kept by the individual I.L.A. unions contained receipt stamps for dues payments that did not appear on the union's books. Moran told Protter he would take no action on behalf of the rank and file unless I.L.A. International President Joe Ryan approved it, which he had not. In other words DA O'Dwyer's lackey said he was not going to enforce the laws of New York unless a criminal brought a complaint against himself.[226]

A disturbing picture of life on the docks was painted in testimony by union officials, attorneys for both the union locals and the reform workers, and disgruntled union members. In stark contrast, O'Dwyer's testimony was muted. The Kefauver Committee did force him to admit that complaints about conditions on the waterfront came mostly from longshoremen (regarding kickbacks to union bosses for access to work on the docks) and from companies (about extortionist rates they were charged to get goods loaded and unloaded, especially for perishable items), and that inventories suffered from a high pilferage rate. When Senator Charles Tobey asserted that the facts demonstrated Anastasia and other gangsters had stolen hundreds of thousands of dollars from waterfront unions, O'Dwyer was unable to offer an alternative conclusion.

A courageous young longshoreman, Peter Panto, became fed up with the extortionist union leaders, so he organized a workers' revolt against hoodlum control of the locals. He led a rank and file movement of insurgent I.L.A. members against gangster domination and kickback and extortion rackets along the Brooklyn waterfront. Six years later during a Brooklyn Grand Jury investigation, DA Beldock explained, "Peter Panto's revolt was getting somewhere. One night, he had 1,200 followers at a meeting. Soon thereafter, Emil Camarda [who controlled all six Brooklyn longshoremen locals] called in Panto for a fatherly talk. 'Peter,' he said, 'I wish you'd stop what you're doing. The boys don't like it.' Panto knew what that meant. 'The boys' was neighborhood language for 'the mob.'"

Panto's friends warned him not to leave home unprotected, especially if he was called to a meeting. DA Beldock continued to the Grand Jury, "Two weeks later, Panto told his sweetheart and her kid brother that he was going to meet some men he didn't trust, and asked them to notify the police if he did not appear the next morning." He did not appear, and they reported him missing.[227]

Panto had been warned that his life was in danger by worker insurgent attorney Protter, according to his later testimony to the Kefauver Committee. Attorney Protter reported Panto's mysterious disappearance to DA O'Dwyer, but the DA brushed Protter's concerns aside. Fearing that Panto had been murdered, Protter returned to DA O'Dwyer accompanied by the Brooklyn-Queens Labor and Citizens Committee to urge an investigation. But Attorney Protter recalled, "[O'Dwyer] accused the committee of seeking publicity. He stated that all the information we were giving him was fiddle-faddle, that he wasn't going to be forced into any position by any such actions."[228]

Nevertheless, DA O'Dwyer was forced to reverse his position because Mannino, the former attorney for the six Camarda unions, brought witnesses to the Commissioner of Investigation and to the DA. Attorney Mannino later testified at the Kefauver hearings, "[O'Dwyer] said he had almost an unbeatable case except that one additional piece of proof was needed. He asked if I would again help to get that additional information. I told him that it was rather surprising that he should be asking me to help. I had no means other than the most indirect means to try to get the information, that I thought that it was his task to do so."

O'Dwyer made clear to Attorney Mannino that if the American Labor Party would support him instead of incumbent Fiorello LaGuardia in the 1941 New York mayoral campaign that "I'm ready to call in the reporters next Monday afternoon and tell them that I am ready to break the Panto case." It was clear that the price for prosecutorial action in a murder case by the DA was political endorsement. Attorney Mannino explained he did not have that authority. Besides, the Party had already committed its backing to LaGuardia.[229]

Since the DA remained complacent about the murder case, Panto's followers raised a commotion that induced the New York City Department of Investigation to delve into the disappearance. The investigation quickly confirmed that widespread rackets were operating along the Brooklyn waterfront. This finding convinced Special Prosecutor John Harlan Amen to take charge. Amen had been appointed by Governor Lehman to look into political corruption in Brooklyn, and he launched a full-scale investigation into the affairs of the six racketeering waterfront unions that were dominated by Camarda and controlled by Anastasia.

The moment that Amen's Grand Jury subpoenaed the books of the six looted longshoreman union locals, attorney Paul O'Dwyer, the DA's brother, intervened to block Amen's efforts. The six locals had hired Paul O'Dwyer as their legal counsel soon after brother Bill was elected DA. Although no one ever made any public allegations of impropriety, the arrangement certainly gave Paul O'Dwyer an opportunity to meet with Brooklyn's most notorious hoods in legitimate-appearing circumstances, where he could have collected bribe money and bagged it to his brother. Paul O'Dwyer did not want to challenge a special prosecutor publicly in court, so he recommended to Camarda that the unions hire a specific attorney to get the subpoenas vacated.

Attorney Paul O'Dwyer's legal strategy resulted in a stay of the proceedings, but the court ultimately directed the six unions to produce their books to Amen's Grand Jury. The next day before the Judge signed his formal order, DA O'Dwyer suddenly initiated his own investigation of the Brooklyn waterfront. Camarda's six locals immediately delivered to the DA's office the books and records they had resisted turning over to Amen.

When DA O'Dwyer finally swung into action, he hit fast and hard. He began with a big publicity-generating raid. The police descended on the waterfront, rounded up more than 100 witnesses, including union officials of the six Camarda locals, and herded them into the DA's offices for questioning. The grilling went on all night, and it produced confessions of extortion, theft of union funds, destruction of union books, falsification of substitute books, and worker kickbacks of wages to mobsters. Chief Assistant DA Joseph Hanley announced that the racketeers had stolen more than $600,000 in dues alone. DA O'Dwyer added that the extortion was "terrific." His staff had broken the waterfront case wide open with pressure interrogations. Witnesses were jailed, and Assistant DA Ed Heffernan quickly brought the case before the Grand Jury.

DA O'Dwyer's aggressive investigation convinced Amen that the DA's office would do an effective job. Thus Amen, who had ultimate authority over the case, suspended his investigation and transferred all the files in his possession to O'Dwyer. As soon as the DA had all the union locals' records safely under lock and key, he promptly and quietly ordered his staff to abandon their inquiry. Five years later Assistant DA Heffernan testified to the 1945 Brooklyn Grand Jury that in the longshoremen's unions case he was developing before the Grand Jury he had obtained only partial testimony from one lone witness before DA O'Dwyer directed him to drop it. The jailed witnesses were released and stenographic notes of information from 100 witnesses were never transcribed. The DA's staff never read the union records turned over by Amen. O'Dwyer's lackey Moran handled the Grand Jury records and omitted all references to the case from the Grand Jury Docket Book. The permanent Grand Jury Trial Commencement Sheet also disappeared from Moran's "safekeeping."

DA O'Dwyer quickly stopped all investigative efforts, except for letting Assistant DA Heffernan complete and submit his summary report to the DA, so there would be some record of official action. The report found that the locals were "dominated by known racketeers ... and not serving the worthy purpose of labor unions." He warned that some union officials were criminals, the locals' financial records had been falsified, and the unions lacked democracy. Yet O'Dwyer never prosecuted any of these gangsters or union officials for the crimes listed in the report or for any other crimes. When O'Dwyer received the report, he officially conferred with the main target Camarda. From that moment on no one in the DAs' office looked at the case files again, as the DA let the statute of limitations for the many major crimes quietly run out.[230]

DA O'Dwyer not only ignored incriminating information about serious union abuses, he countered with a cover-up of these criminals. It was brother Paul who again came to the rescue by devising a scheme to create the illusion of reform. Under attorney Paul O'Dwyer's guidance, the DA conferred with I.L.A. International President Joe Ryan about the criminal element in Brooklyn, and Ryan in turn revoked the charters of the accused locals and ordered new elections. However, he realigned and forcibly installed the same officials into different locals, and they continued reporting to the same hoodlum directorate. DA O'Dwyer told Assistant DA Heffernan that this sham window-dressing resolved the locals' problems and ordered him to write a report closing his investigation.

The New York Crime Commission chairman later asked Assistant DA Heffernan, "Now isn't it actually a fact that you came to the conclusion that this reform wasn't very much of a reform, and so testified in your private hearings before us?" he replied, "Yes, that's quite true." The Commission counsel then presented charts showing that the officers of the six unions were reelected and still headed their respective locals 12 years later.[231]

Under DA O'Dwyer's protection, Mafioso Anastasia remained totally immune from criminal prosecution. However, before O'Dwyer snatched control of Amen's short-lived investigation, Amen had announced he was seeking Anastasia for questioning in the disappearance of union reformer Peter Panto. This drove the thug into hiding. Even after DA O'Dwyer wrested control of the case from Amen, Anastasia was frequently mentioned in the press as a suspect in both Panto's disappearance and the three Murder, Inc. trials, so he continued to remain out of sight.

While O'Dwyer quickly shelved the union corruption case, he had to maintain a pretense that he was working on the politically-charged Panto disappearance investigation. He satisfied reporters' questions for new developments by saying he wanted to question Anastasia. However, public pressure finally forced the DA to announce that if he found Panto's body, he was prepared to prosecute the murderers because he knew their identities and he had information linking Anastasia to the crime.

Then a year and half after Panto disappeared, DA O'Dwyer suddenly announced he had learned the whereabouts of his body. A squad of the DA's NYPD detectives went to the location in the desolate meadows near Lyndhurst, New Jersey. For three weeks they excavated through frozen earth and a casing of lime until they finally uncovered Panto's strangled body trussed with ropes.

Later that year murder-victim Panto posthumously received some measure of justice, but it did not came from DA O'Dwyer. Reformer Panto had been killed because he opposed Emil Camarda, the corrupt union official who was general vice president for the Atlantic Coast District of the I.L.A. Camarda went to a meeting at the office of a stevedore company official who did business with the unions. The Italian official was intoxicated and got upset when Camarda asked him to hire an Irish friend. The official then accused Camarda of being too interested in "getting jobs for the Irish," pulled a gun from his desk, and shot Camarda in the head and neck, killing him. Two months later the official pled guilty to the first-degree manslaughter of the 56-year-old union leader and received a five-to-ten-year Sing Sing prison term.[232]

Meanwhile DA O'Dwyer claimed he was still searching for Anastasia but had not been able to locate the Mafia lieutenant. O'Dwyer never did bring charges against Anastasia despite having two strong murder cases. DA O'Dwyer had the murder of 53-year-old Morris "Moishe" Diamond, the business manager of Teamsters Local 138. Diamond had been questioned by Manhattan DA Dewey about truck racketeering and then was subpoenaed. Soon afterwards Diamond was walking to work when he was fatally shot by a lone gunman. Seven weeks later Panto disappeared.[233]

Even though DA O'Dwyer's Assistant DA Turkus had successfully prosecuted the three Murder, Inc. trials, O'Dwyer announced he would personally handle the Diamond and Panto murder cases. However, after asserting sole control he let them languish, while continuing to brag to the press, "I have a perfect murder case against Anastasia, and I will prosecute him as soon as he is captured."

Assistant DA Turkus had relied primarily on the testimony of star witness Abe Reles in the first two Murder, Inc. trials. Turkus planned to feature Reles in the third trial too, but Reles was murdered three days before he was to appear in court. Reles was also to be DA O'Dwyer's key witness against Anastasia in the Diamond and Panto cases. When Reles was found dead on the kitchen roof of the Half Moon Hotel, O'Dwyer lamented, "the perfect case went out the window with Reles."[234]

A serious problem was that none of DA O'Dwyer's public statements were truthful about the strengths of the Diamond and Panto murder cases and about his case against perpetrator Anastasia. DA O'Dwyer's lies were exposed by four official investigations of his misconduct in office. This included two Brooklyn grand juries, the New York Crime Commission, and the U.S. Senate's Kefauver Committee.[235]

Lie # 1 by DA O'Dwyer was his claim of a "perfect murder case against Anastasia." The truth was O'Dwyer did absolutely nothing to develop a case against Anastasia for either the Panto or Diamond murders. During the 20 months Reles was a state's witness, O'Dwyer never bothered to question the talkative informant about Anastasia's involvement. Nor did the DA ever seek an indictment by presenting his corroborating witnesses before a Brooklyn grand jury. Yet O'Dwyer did allow Reles and a corroborating witness to travel to far-off Hollywood to testify before a grand jury against Ben Siegel.

Lie # 2 by DA O'Dwyer was "the perfect case went out the window with Reles." The first Brooklyn Grand Jury investigation concluded that DA O'Dwyer's strong collaborating witnesses were "sufficient to warrant Anastasia's indictment and conviction, but Anastasia was neither prosecuted, indicted, nor convicted." Incidentally, Assistant DA Turkus had developed the strong Diamond and Panto cases from the revelations of his Murder, Inc. informants.

The second Brooklyn Grand Jury analyzed the Diamond murder case and came to a more damning conclusion: "This is the murder which former District Attorney O'Dwyer characterized as 'the perfect case' which went out the window with Reles. Our investigation has disclosed that Abe Reles was not a corroborating witness in that killing. On the contrary, as a matter of law, he was only one of several accomplices. In view of the availability of the other accomplices, it follows that Reles was not even an essential witness."[236]

Lie # 3 by DA O'Dwyer was the repeated assertions that Anastasia was hiding from the law. The hood had actually been drafted and was fulfilling his World War II hitch as a technical sergeant, training Army longshoremen at Indiantown Gap, Pennsylvania, not too far from his old

Brooklyn haunts. While "hiding" in the military, he took advantage of a wartime law that granted quick citizenship to servicemen and then was honorably discharged as over age. NYPD Captain Bals, DA O'Dwyer's evasive Chief Investigator, was forced by the Kefauver Committee to admit that he made no effort to apprehend Anastasia as the chief suspect in two murders. Bals could have easily found Anastasia because his draft board knew where he was stationed at all times, and he gave his home address when he obtained a social security number after becoming a naturalized citizen.

It is inconceivable that DA O'Dwyer and Mafioso Anastasia were not in contact the whole time the gangster was allegedly in hiding. The two men had to plan strategy to protect Anastasia's criminal empire, and the DA needed to be paid for his protective services. Of course, most of their communication could have gone through the DA's brother Paul, who was attorney to the longshoremen unions under Anastasia's control. Furthermore, before DA O'Dwyer took a leave of office to go into the Army, he had all of his office's records related to Anastasia destroyed. His clerk Moran did the dirty work and admitted to the Kefauver Committee having pulled the NYPD "wanted card" files seeking the arrest of Anastasia and other waterfront criminals. This effectively eliminated any further prosecutorial action. Moran was also in charge of the records about Anastasia's criminal activities that similarly disappeared. Then, when new Acting DA Tom Hughes took over the office, O'Dwyer, lackey Moran, and Captain Bals conspired to keep secret from him the strong evidence and witnesses assembled against Anastasia because no statute of limitations against prosecution existed for murder.

The most important case of DA O'Dwyer's career was the Panto murder, but during O'Dwyer's three years in the Army he never once inquired about how it was progressing, despite being stationed near his old office in Brooklyn. Upon leaving the service, O'Dwyer reassumed his post as DA but continued to ignore the case. Soon after returning to the DA's office, O'Dwyer resigned to run for New York mayor.[237]

When Democratic DA O'Dwyer resigned to run for mayor, Republican Governor Dewey appointed Republican George Beldock as the interim replacement until the upcoming election. Beldock had a fine reputation as a judge; he had been elected by impressively obtaining the endorsement of both major parties; and he planned to run for DA in the next election. This is where the plot thickened. When Dewey had been Manhattan DA he had taught Brooklyn Assistant DA Turkus how to win the Murder, Inc. cases using extralegal means. In their interactions, Republican Turkus kept Dewey informed about the serious criminal violations being perpetrated by his Democratic boss DA O'Dwyer. Upon assuming office, DA Beldock promptly impaneled a special Additional Kings County Grand Jury and utilized Turkus' information to investigate the operation of the Brooklyn DA's office under O'Dwyer and specifically his conduct in the Anastasia case. Beldock planned to use the Grand Jury's findings to depict the type of DA he would not be in the pending election, and to also assist the Republican mayoral candidate running against Democrat O'Dwyer.

The Additional Kings County Grand Jury findings were accurate and damaging. The jurors' presentment of facts accused O'Dwyer and three assistants with "gross laxity, inefficiency, and maladministration" by failing to prosecute Anastasia for murder when he had "a perfect case." The Grand Jury stated that the DA's office abandoned prosecution of waterfront rackets and other serious crimes until the statute of limitations ran out, despite O'Dwyer's admissions that he had sufficient evidence to gain convictions. DA Beldock chimed in with a public announcement, "The killing of the waterfront investigation gave a free hand to organized murderers to prey upon the workers of the waterfront." Despite these disturbing revelations, New York City elected O'Dwyer mayor.[238]

Even more amazing, the Mayor-elect soon testified before the Grand Jury that the facts in its presentment were accurate, but he laid the blame on his staff. He said it was all the fault of his key associates, Captain Bals and lackey Moran. However, he never reprimanded them, and he continued to employ and reward them with choice political appointments. The Grand Jury panel came out with a second presentment with the same facts but included O'Dwyer's own testimony before the Grand Jury as proof that his staff had failed to prosecute Anastasia for murder when it had "a perfect case."

A Judge ordered both Additional Kings County Grand Jury presentments condemning DA O'Dwyer "stricken and expunged" from the record. While a grand jury may state its findings of fact, both presentments violated the law by identifying the names of witnesses and their actual testimony, which is confidential. The Judge also pointed out that the presentments were politically inspired because the first was issued a week before the election and written and signed by DA Beldock, a highly-unusual action since this was always done by the jurors in layman's language. In addition, at the very moment that DA Beldock had copies delivered to the court, he was distributing copies to the press. Finally, Beldock used the presentment in radio broadcasts both to boost his election campaign for DA, and to defeat former DA O'Dwyer in his campaign for mayor of New York City. Ironically, O'Dwyer won anyway, while Beldock lost his campaign to his Democratic opponent.[239]

While the Judge enforced the law, he did point out that the facts and charges contained in both presentments against O'Dwyer as DA were correct. For democracy to function, accurate information about elected and appointed officials and candidates must be transparent and readily disseminated, but DA Beldock did not go about disseminating this information the right way. O'Dwyer's criminal behavior as DA certainly warranted an in-depth investigation and prosecution because he was thoroughly corrupt, protected the most vicious gangsters, worked against the public interest, and directed the murder of his own star prosecution witness.

It was DA O'Dwyer's protection from prosecution of Anastasia and the other waterfront racketeers that allowed them to obtain and maintain complete control over the waterfront unions. As the Kefauver Report noted, "The racketeers are firmly entrenched along New York City's waterfront with the resulting extortions, shake downs, kickbacks from wages, payroll padding, gangster infiltration of unions, and large scale gambling. Most significant to the Committee is that the gangster who still appears to be the key to waterfront racketeering in New York is the same Albert Anastasia."

The Kefauver Report leveled many criticisms against O'Dwyer and concluded that "During Mr. O'Dwyer's term of office as District Attorney of Kings County, between 1940 and 1942, and his occupancy of the mayoralty from 1946 to 1950, neither he nor his appointees took any effective action against the top echelons of the gambling, narcotics, waterfront, murder, or bookmaking rackets. In fact, his actions impeded promoting investigations of such rackets. His defense of public officials who were derelict in their duties, and his actions in investigations of corruption, and his failure to follow up concrete evidence of organized crime, particularly in the case of Murder, Inc., and the waterfront, have contributed to the growth of organized crime, racketeering and gangsterism in New York City."[240]

In *On The Waterfront*, Marlon Brando's gutsy, determined character Terry Malloy survives a savage beating by hoods and, with all the longshoremen falling behind him in solidarity, victoriously walks the length of the dock past the vile union leaders to work. In real life, the idealistic and courageous union reformer Peter Panto ended up in a shallow, solitary, unmarked grave, followed by a visit to a sterile autopsy slab. His murder crushed the aspirations and bravery of his band of oppressed workers for the rest of their longshoreman careers. All of this was the direct result of Brooklyn DA and New York City Mayor O'Dwyer and FBI Director J. Edgar Hoover keeping their forces out of action while organized crime expanded its evil power throughout major U.S. cities.

THE PANTO MURDER BOMBSHELL

DA O'Dwyer's public statements about Anastasia played both sides of a precarious balancing act. On the one hand, the DA railed against the thug as a dangerous, high-ranking criminal and claimed to have a perfect murder case awaiting the gangster's capture. All the while, O'Dwyer was shielding Anastasia's pervasive, exploitive, violent criminal empire by failing to investigate, charge, or arrest him.

Three official investigations found O'Dwyer criminally malfeasant for failing to prosecute Anastasia for murder and for lying about his reasons for doing so. Unfortunately, a judge expunged the first action, and the statute of limitations for misconduct by DA O'Dwyer ran out prior to the next two investigations six years later. The following year a fourth investigation by the New York Crime Commission produced a stunning breakthrough in the Panto murder case.

At the Crime Commission hearing, former Brooklyn Assistant DA Heffernan testified to the identify of Panto's three murderers, and one of the suspects was Anastasia. This information had been given to Heffernan a decade earlier by Murder, Inc. prosecution-witness Albert Tannenbaum, and Assistant DA Heffernan had turned it over to his boss. But DA O'Dwyer had kept Tannenbaum's statement under wraps by telling NYPD Captain Bals to ignore the information, and by directing his clerk Moran to hide the informant's statement in a separate transcript file, under a heading that did not relate to either Panto or Anastasia.

The moment former Brooklyn Assistant DA Heffernan's testimony made headlines, the unpredictable O'Dwyer quickly produced another surprise by publicly validating Heffernan's accuracy. O'Dwyer telephoned from Mexico City to the New York City press, and he transformed the damning misconduct testimony into a defense. He claimed he could not have prosecuted Anastasia in Brooklyn, New York because Panto was murdered in the Lyndhurst, New Jersey home of one of the three killers. Former DA O'Dwyer explained that he had confirmed Tannenbaum's information when his office led the search that found Panto's buried frozen body outside Lyndhurst.[241]

The shocking revelations outraged former Bergen County, New Jersey Prosecutor John Breslin, who immediately responded that he had not taken action in the Panto case because of O'Dwyer's repeated assurances that he had solid evidence the victim was murdered in Brooklyn and merely dumped in Lyndhurst. O'Dwyer claimed he had lied to the New Jersey DA about the murder being in Brooklyn to get Panto's body transferred to use as evidence in his "perfect murder case." O'Dwyer's two statements were contradictory by first claiming he could not have used Panto's out-of-state murder against Anastasia, and then the next day saying he needed his body to build a murder case. O'Dwyer was actually stealing the key murder evidence to protect Anastasia from prosecution in Bergen County. New Jersey's Deputy Attorney General Harry Towe announced, "If it should turn out that the killing took place in Bergen County, my office is interested in going to work on it."[242]

The implications of this new information were an astounding indictment of O'Dwyer. It was already known O'Dwyer was guilty of gross malfeasance in covering up evidence and refusing to prosecute "the perfect [Diamond] murder case" against Anastasia. Former Assistant DA Heffernan's new facts about the Panto murder implied that O'Dwyer had an even more sinister role by hiding, hijacking, and destroying evidence, while also supplying false information to the Bergen Country Prosecutor that misdirected and led him to halt his legitimate murder investigation.

Tannenbaum had identified Panto's murderers as Anastasia, Emanuel "Mendy" Weiss, and James "Dizzy" Ferraco, whose house was where Panto was murdered. They killed him because the unions' intimidating threats had failed to deter his reform activities. This information would have laid the basis for a solid case in New Jersey. It would have given the Bergen County Prosecutor both motive and the two accomplice witnesses needed to convict Anastasia in a death-penalty case. In addition to Tannenbaum, the New Jersey Prosecutor could have easily turned accomplice Weiss into a corroborating state's witness by offering him a deal. Weiss was in custody in Brooklyn awaiting trial in the third Murder, Inc. case for which he would be convicted and sentenced to death. Since Weiss was the essential corroborating-accomplice witness against Anastasia, the Panto murder case died with his execution.

When DA O'Dwyer and Governor Dewey chose to execute Weiss, who was a subordinate in a small neighborhood gang, O'Dwyer let loose the country's most vicious, fearsome gangster. Anastasia was the independent lieutenant of the nation's second biggest gang and a commanding force in major interstate organized crime. When O'Dwyer's malfeasance in the Panto murder cover-up was exposed, he countered by offering political spin. He made it appear that the execution of Weiss was a public service by stating, "We convicted Weiss on another Brooklyn murder, and he was executed. You can't execute a man more than once, can you?" In doing so O'Dwyer completely ignored the cover-up of the Panto murder, his protection of Anastasia, and his execution of Weiss, who was the key witness in the case against the far more dangerous criminal.[243]

The reaction to the Tannenbaum revelations was explosive. New Jersey's top law enforcers weighed in with tough talk about O'Dwyer's gross misconduct, and the Bergen County Prosecutor and New Jersey Attorney General implied they would launch investigations. Sadly, these were the last public statements made by anyone in authority, and also the last questions raised by the press. The day after O'Dwyer's horrible miscarriage of justice was exposed, it literally was yesterday's news. New Jersey law enforcers made no effort to prosecute O'Dwyer, just as he had failed to prosecute Anastasia.

From early in my exhaustive cold-case investigation, it seemed likely to me that Anastasia was the biggest beneficiary of informant-witness Reles' murder. After I had compiled and examined the mass of information about DA O'Dwyer's malfeasance and Mafia leader Anastasia's criminal empire, I was astonished to realize that Anastasia derived no direct benefit from Reles' murder. Anastasia's legal protection was wholly dependent on DA O'Dwyer's refusing to prosecute. Thus, what had appeared to be a classic case of corruption turned out to be a standard murder case because it is now clear that DA O'Dwyer was the only person who benefited from Reles' death.

DA O'Dwyer masterminded the murder of his star witness because his conflicting public statements had backed him into a corner. His public positions about the strength of the Panto and Diamond murder cases were inconsistent with his statements about taking no action against Anastasia. DA O'Dwyer, Assistant DA Turkus, and Manhattan Special Prosecutor Dewey all portrayed Anastasia as America's arch criminal and the leader of Murder, Inc., their fictional nationwide crime syndicate. Additionally, DA O'Dwyer had repeatedly announced that he had built an airtight murder case against Anastasia and would charge him as soon as he could find him.

While all of O'Dwyer's inflammatory rhetoric made Anastasia a must-get prosecution target, the DA never made any effort to indict the Mafioso during the year and a half prior to Reles' death. DA O'Dwyer's lack of prosecutorial effort was raising political questions for which he had no legitimate response. Continued avoidance to act could have potentially exposed his misconduct in office. Facing disgrace and charges of criminal malfeasance, he was running out of options. He could save face politically by prosecuting Anastasia, but he dared not turn on his terribly dangerous patron and co-conspirator. The only alternative DA O'Dwyer could find was to destroy the public story he had built about having a strong case. This required he murder his star witness and then claim that he now lacked a corroborating witness so the case was over. O'Dwyer knew this strategy would work because he had never revealed that he had an abundance of corroborating witnesses against Anastasia without Reles.

DA O'Dwyer and his loyal lieutenant Captain Bals had absolute control over the police unit guarding all the informants including star witness Reles. Perhaps O'Dwyer had Captain Bals pay the two murdering detective guards out of some of the huge bribe money Anastasia had paid over the years. Whatever the relationship between the DA and the vicious Mafioso, it is finally clear that Anastasia had no reason to be concerned about either his public imagery or criminal prosecution as long as DA O'Dwyer remained loyal to him. Instead, it was DA O'Dwyer who was caught up in an impossible predicament because his own public deceptive statements about Anastasia were trapping him - he was simultaneously condemning the gangster while promising nonexistent prosecutorial action. The only beneficiary from Reles' murder was DA O'Dwyer, and thus Anastasia was as likely as surprised as anyone else to hear about the informant's fatal dive. All these factual pieces about O'Dwyer and Anastasia fit in this very detailed and tight context.

DA O'Dwyer's Assistant DA Burton Turkus went on to write his book about the fictional *Murder, Inc.* as fact. He would have done a greater service for society by writing the real-life drama of his criminal boss and entitling it *The Murdering DA*.

Not only did O'Dwyer get away with the cold-blooded murder of his own witness, but his political career continued to shine brightly. While he lost the 1941 New York City mayoral election to incumbent LaGuardia, he rebounded to win the office in 1945 and was re-elected in 1949.

However, in the first year of his second term, Mayor O'Dwyer was forced to resign on the eve of an NYPD scandal set off by the arrest of Harry Gross after he testified about his huge bookmaking operation centered in Brooklyn. Gross had accused Mayor O'Dwyer's five key political appointees and long-time close personal friends of taking bribes to protect his gambling operations. They were Police Commissioner Bill O'Brien, Deputy Police Commissioner Bals, James Moran, John Murtagh, and Chief of Detectives Bill Whalen. At trials Gross testified against 120 dishonest cops at all levels and gave the amount of his substantial payoffs to each one. (See Addendum X)

Even though O'Dwyer left the Mayor's office in shame, President Harry Truman quickly submitted his name to be U.S. ambassador to Mexico. The U. S. Senate was presented O'Dwyer's poor prosecution record against major crime figures while DA, but it took this esteemed body just a few days to confirm the appointment. Soon the five Kefauver Committee members questioned Ambassador O'Dwyer, and they were scathing in their criticism. But while they expressed shock and dismay at the revelations brought out by their investigation, all five senators on the Committee had been fully apprised about the facts from written reports six months earlier before they voted to approve O'Dwyer as Ambassador.

The Kefauver revelations were just one element of the perfect storm that was about to finally extinguish O'Dwyer's political career. As New York's Mayor, O'Dwyer had appointed his lackey Moran as Deputy Fire Commissioner. The president of the city's firemen's union testified that he gave $55,000 in union funds to Moran to get a better city contract for his members. Then Moran was convicted of leading a massive extortion scheme by requiring Fire Department inspectors to charge residents an illegal fee for oil-burner installation permits. (See Addendum Y)

This combination of exposés against his cronies, allegations about his malfeasance as DA and misconduct as Mayor, and the Kefauver revelations forced O'Dwyer to resign as Ambassador. He quickly emigrated to Mexico to avoid potential prosecution for his cover-up of the Panto killing and the corruption scams he directed, not to mention the fear someone might discover he orchestrated the murder of Abe Reles. O'Dwyer's wife parted company with him and moved to Spain.[244]

O'Dwyer is relevant here because he came close to arranging the execution of Ben Siegel for a murder he knew nothing about. And as DA, O'Dwyer forever tarnished the image of Luciano and the Young Turks by labeling them ringleaders of the fictitious Murder Inc. myth he and his assistant DA Turkus concocted with informant Abe Reles.

As for Anastasia, practically everything known about him is hideous. He is relevant here because he was a loyal ally to Luciano and the Young Turks, and he was a major supporter of them during the dark days of the Mafia wars with Joe "The Duck" Masseria and Salvatore Maranzano.

Charlie Luciano was still languishing in a prison cell, framed for life on a trivial, fineable misdemeanor of voluntary prostitution booking. But sometimes even the most dire of circumstances are changed when fate steps in.

CHAPTER 10

LUCIANO IN PRISON

LUCIANO & THE WAR

While Brooklyn DA Bill O'Dwyer was directing the Murder, Inc. cases and shielding Albert Anastasia's extensive dock criminal enterprises from prosecution, Charlie Luciano was serving out his long prison sentence year after year. Everyone thought Luciano would remain imprisoned for life, but early in World War II rumors started floating around New York City that he was contributing to the nation's War effort. For years after the Allies achieved victory, this gossip about Luciano's patriotism persisted, and it included mention of Governor Tom Dewey as the prosecutor who convicted him for life.

Dewey was disturbed to have his gang-busting name connected with that of the hoodlum. Thus, he decided to flush out the truth to determine what, if any, contribution Luciano had made during his adopted country's time of great peril. A decade after the conclusion of the War in 1954, Governor Dewey established a state commission to investigate Luciano's role. The U.S. Navy agreed to cooperate only after Dewey guaranteed that the investigative record would be permanently sealed. Thus, the hearings were held behind closed doors. Questions were asked of the Naval officers involved, the civilian prosecutors of Luciano, and even some high-ranking hoodlums and their attorneys who voluntarily testified to set the record straight. At the conclusion of these hearings, the Herlands Report was prepared and sealed, and the issue disappeared from public discourse.

Governor Dewey kept the sole copy of the report in his private records, and years later the family made it public. Information was also revealed by some of the key participants in what had been a top-secret wartime espionage and invasion strategy, when they testified at other hearings or spoke out publicly. All the information from these various sources was consistent, and it revealed an astonishing tale of mobsters giving great assistance to the Allies' War effort against Hitler's Nazi military machine. (See Addendum Z)

It all began early in World War II. In the four months following the attack on Pearl Harbor, prowling German U-boat submarines in the Atlantic Ocean sank an average of almost one and a half Allied merchant troop and supply ships daily, killing hundreds of sailors. In contrast, the Allies failed to sink a single U-boat, even though victory in Europe clearly depended on protecting Allied shipping in the Atlantic sea-lanes.

Since most of the sunk ships had departed from New York harbor, the Navy focused its security efforts on the Port of New York operations. It needed accurate intelligence sources to find out how the U-boats operating near the east coast were being refueled and re-supplied without returning to their European bases. The Navy also wanted to prevent espionage activities by port workers who might be providing German agents with ship convoy sailing times and routes, and it wanted to inhibit possible sabotage by embedded Nazi agents.

Two months after the outbreak of the War, these port problems became an urgent priority. The *S.S. Normandie* was docked at a New York pier being retrofitted to carry large groups of troops over long distances faster than any German submarine. It burst into flames and capsized, and the cause of the fire was never determined. Although no other major act of sabotage occurred on U.S. soil during the War, at that time officials feared that Axis saboteurs had set the fire. The *Normandie* loss was a terrible strategic blow, and it stimulated Naval Intelligence to take decisive action.[245]

Navy officials were especially worried that Italian-American and German-American criminals operating on the waterfront might be involved. The Navy suspected that German submarine packs operating off the Atlantic Coast were being re-supplied by fishing boats, but Naval Intelligence had been unable to obtain the cooperation of any entities or individuals operating along the port. Naval Intel had failed to penetrate the businesses operating on the port, the dockworker unions, or the fleets of fishermen. The Navy believed the roadblock was the absolute control that New York's organized crime gangs had over every entity associated with work on the piers, but in reality the barrier was cultural. Many of the fishermen, longshoremen, and other port workers and officials were clannish Italians or Sicilians, who innately distrusted authority and considered politicians and police their natural enemies.

To infiltrate the waterfront, the head of the U.S. Naval Intelligence investigative section known as *B-3,* Lieutenant Commander Charles Radcliffe "Red" Haffenden, proposed a radical top-secret counter-intelligence strategy. He recommended enlisting underworld leaders to prevent espionage and sabotage by the fishing fleets and waterfront workers.

One month after the *Normandie* fire, newly-elected Manhattan DA Frank Hogan, Dewey's successor, introduced Navy officials to Joseph "Socks" Lanza. He was the powerful rackets overlord of the Fulton Street Fish Market, the nation's largest wholesale fish market, covering three blocks of lower Manhattan. Lanza was born near the Market and started carrying the heavy crates of fish at age 15. When he was 20 he joined with other dockworkers to found both the Seafood Workers Union Local and the Fulton Market Watchmen and Patrol Association. This was almost a century after the Market had opened. His union controlled all loading and unloading of fish. Lanza's watchmen patrol was a squad of Mafia goons who protected and enforced his criminal enterprises even though his contract officially directed him to keep order for the city-owned Market.

Attorney Moses Polakoff contrasted the personality of his always-considerate client Luciano with Lanza. "Socks was a rough guy. He controlled the fish markets on the Lower East Side. He was a power. Nobody could sell fish without his approval. He probably shook them down, or he got paid off for protection or whatever. That's the kind of guy he was."[246]

During his career, Lanza was charged with several violent crimes, including homicide, but all were dismissed. Lanza used the dockworkers' union local and his security-badge-carrying patrol to introduce all-encompassing racketeering into the market with brutal force. In several trials, many witnesses testified to numerous crimes in the market. Lanza's union kept workers' wages low, gave the large fish companies sweetheart labor contracts for cash payments, and gave a few loading companies, all owned by Mafia associates, a monopoly to charge small fish companies extremely high hourly rates for this cheap labor. Lanza's cronies leased the Market's wholesale spaces from the city, and then they sublet each space to multiple wholesalers at higher rates. Lanza established a license fee for every type of business operating in the market. Ship captains were charged a fee for each catch they delivered to the wholesalers, stall wholesalers were assessed a fee to do business, and truckers paid fees that determined the order and speed with which their perishable inventory was loaded.

Lanza's Patrol also sold *protection* to wholesalers against trouble to protect their stalls, and to truckers to safeguard their vehicles parked on the surrounding city streets. Wholesalers who did not pay would find the electricity to their freezers cut off, their fish damaged, and stench bombs thrown into their stalls. Truckers who did not pay found tires slashed, trucks vandalized, and fish stolen. Even when protection was paid, theft was rampant and many workers and their families were beaten.

Lanza's patrol prohibited his union workers from loading for anyone who also bought or sold fish at other fish exchanges in or out of New York City. Additionally, the patrol kept wholesalers from transacting business with retailers who bought elsewhere, effectively eliminating the competing fish exchanges. Once Lanza had established this monopoly, he had a financial stranglehold over much of the Northeast's fish business. He then forced the stall wholesalers to pay uniform low prices to the boat captains and charge fixed high prices to the retailers and restaurateurs. He got a cut of every one of his illegal transactions. All these crimes greatly increased the price of retail and restaurant fish for residents in several Northeastern states.

Eleven years after Lanza had taken over absolute control of this huge city-owned industry, law-enforcement first investigated his extortion and protection rackets. Two years later Lanza and other union officials were charged with creating a monopoly and restraint of interstate trade. However, the charges were not about the Fulton Fish Market's salt-water-fish industry, but rather the fresh-water-fish business handled by the less well-known Peck Slip wholesaling center. Of all the domestic fish sold in New York, 95 percent was caught outside the state and sent to Peck Slip by railway express from Ohio, Michigan, Illinois, Wisconsin, Minnesota, Iowa, and Canada.

Unbelievably, Lanza had established similar union and patrol power over Peck Slip. He was called the *czar* of Peck Slip because he was accused of committing the same pervasive crimes as at the Fulton Fish Market. It was in the midst of the Great Depression, when the economy was crippled and 25 percent of Americans were unemployed. At the worst of the country's miserable financial collapse, he viciously extorted working men and small businessmen and gouged consumers.

When the judge acquitted Lanza and two other union officials for lack of evidence, he lamented that the frightened state's witnesses did not tell the same facts under oath that they had previously told the DA. But a federal grand jury had also charged Lanza, along with numerous co-defendants, for violating the Sherman Anti-Trust Act by monopolizing and restraining trade in a reign of terror at Peck Slip. In a series of trials a total of 55 defendants were convicted for conspiracy, and Lanza was handed a two-year sentence. While in prison, he was tried on similar federal charges involving the Fulton Fish Market. He and his two brothers pled guilty, and he received an additional six-month term.

Lanza continued to direct his racketeering activities from prison through an associate until he was released and resumed his position as undisputed czar of the Northeast fishing industry. Before being imprisoned, Lanza extorted Teamsters Union Local 202 officials. He threatened that he would prohibit their members from transporting fish at the two markets he controlled unless he was paid a salary of $120 a week while he occupied a cell. At one meeting Lanza slugged the Local's president, and then he returned with three goons waving guns at him. For Lanza's extortion of another union, DA Dewey indicted him and his four strong-arm associates, and two years later all five would receive long prison sentences.[247]

The pending long-term prison sentence gave Manhattan DA Hogan tremendous leverage to offer Lanza a plea bargain to elicit his cooperation with Naval Intelligence. But DA Hogan and Assistant DA Murray Gurfein were concerned with preserving their tough-on-crime, racket-busting image rather than protecting their country during a time of war. They took the hard position, "No deals for criminals." As Assistant DAs, Hogan and Gurfein had demonstrated their hard-line perverse dispositions a decade earlier, when they helped DA Dewey frame Luciano by pressuring witnesses to commit perjury. At the time Dewey told the press, "Frank Hogan took general charge of all the women" who were treated so badly while being held as material witnesses.[248]

The War news was grim. U-boat packs were sinking merchant ships in record numbers, and victory over Hitler and his Nazi regime hung in the balance. Naval Intelligence desperately needed help, and a few gangsters seemed to be the key to developing an effective counter-espionage program. Yet the DA's office, which regularly gave hoodlums and murderers a pass, would cut no deals with these gangsters to protect the nation and its fighting forces. The fate of the nation now depended on whether the Navy could find hoodlums to assist the war effort without being able to offer them any consideration at all in return. In other words, the Navy had to pray that, unlike these two prosecutors, a few gangsters who were in a position to assist were patriotic and willing to totally and unconditionally commit to helping their country.

The only assistance Manhattan DA Hogan would give Naval Intelligence was to ask Lanza if he would meet with the officials. Four months after the attack on Pearl Harbor, the Navy's underworld project began with a secret midnight meeting. Lieutenant Commander Haffenden asked Mafioso Lanza for his assistance in determining how the marauding U-boats were being re-supplied and getting convoy information. Lanza gave "100 percent" assurance of his collaboration. He followed their instructions and told every one involved with the fishing fleets, piers, and downtown plants to look for and report any unusual or suspicious behavior that might be related to sabotage, espionage, or assistance to enemy submarines. It was later learned by the Navy that Germany received no domestic help on the eastern coastline. By then the enemy was operating longer range, lighter U-boats that were refueled and re-supplied at sea or upon returning to base.

Lanza successfully enlisted the cooperation of every one in the fishing industry, most of whom were Italian and trusted him. But he hit an impenetrable wall with company officials, union leaders, and workers in the large shipping industry that stretched along many miles of waterfront. These people did not know Lanza, and they came from diverse ethnic groups. They feared that instead of assisting Navy Intelligence, Lanza might trade information about their activities to the DA in return for a plea bargain on his pending case. Even underworld powerhouses like Frank Costello and Joe Adonis were suspicious of the government's real motives, so they also shied away from Lanza's requests.

Lanza explained to Lieutenant Commander Haffenden that only one man commanded enough respect to enlist the aid of every ethnic group tied to the piers, the imprisoned-for-life Charlie Luciano. Lanza told Haffenden the truth that he had no influence with Luciano, but he left out why. Lanza's Fulton Fish Market enclave was located in the gang territory Luciano inherited in his battle for survival against the Duck Masseria. However, when Luciano became leader, he directed that every gang member be on his own, and he never hobnobbed with thugs who victimized people. Thus, Luciano never had any association with Lanza nor any of his extortion or violence.

During the fifth month of the war, U-boat sinkings of Allied merchant ships increased to more than three a day, and thousands of sailors drowned in the icy Atlantic. Rear Admiral Carl Espe described the military conditions that led the Navy to solicit Luciano's help. Espe wrote a few years later to the Herlands' investigation, "At this time, the nation was suffering heavy losses to its shipping from submarine attacks along the Atlantic Coast and the outcome of the War appeared extremely grave." This toll had to be diminished if the U.S. was going to win, so Navy brass approved seeking the aid of the country's most powerful gangland leader.[249]

DA Hogan and Assistant DA Gurfein asked Luciano's attorney Moses Polakoff to meet with Lieutenant Commander Haffenden. However, these two assistant prosecutors had helped Dewey frame Luciano, and they remained emphatic that the innocent Luciano not receive early parole. These two prosecutors were consumed with ambition and self-image, so patriotism and justice were concepts beyond their grasp. Polakoff had represented Luciano in the pair of prosecutors' framing case against him, but the attorney had barely gotten to know his hoodlum client. Thus, Polakoff brought his long-time client Meyer Lansky to dinner with Haffenden. The attorney knew Lansky was a close friend of Luciano and also both patriotic and fervently anti-Nazi.

Next, Governor Herbert Lehman granted the Navy's request to allow Intelligence officers and underworld leaders to meet with Luciano in a private room at the prison. Two months after Lanza had joined the War effort, Lieutenant Commander Haffenden sent Polakoff and Lansky to represent the Navy and request Luciano's assist. After listening to the proposal, the innocent convict responded in his soft-spoken but firm style with an unequivocal "No."[250]

Attorney Polakoff and Lansky later testified that Luciano's negative response was not due to lack of patriotism, but rather concern about his own survival. Luciano told them it is was still unclear which side was going to win the War, and if he was ever released he faced deportation. He knew that if he helped the Allies and was deported, the moment he landed in Italy dictator Benito Mussolini would have had him killed.

Luciano made it clear that unless he could be assured that his involvement would be kept totally secret, he would not help. Every one readily agreed. The Navy desperately needed his help, and none of the military and law enforcement officials involved wanted their name associated with Luciano's.

Lieutenant Commander Haffenden permitted attorney Polakoff to bring anyone Luciano requested to Great Meadow Prison. The warden kept a list of every underworld figure's name, which was made public by the 1954 New York State Legislature. The names of the infamous hoods who visited made headlines. In contrast, the prison listed the Naval officers as "unidentified" visitors. The official prison records noted the purpose of the meetings that were held in the warden's home by using the phrase "so that the inmate might render assistance to the war effort." Polakoff accompanied the hoods to 19 meetings to attribute a faux lawyer-client legitimacy to the gatherings, but he always sat alone on the other side of the room to avoid hearing what the gangland leaders discussed.[251]

Lansky liaisoned between Lieutenant Commander Haffenden at his office and Luciano in prison. He took Haffenden's concerns to the prison meetings, and from there he carried Luciano's directives to the relevant gangland leaders. Luciano also involved other key associates to carry out selected parts of the plans. For example, Lansky asked Costello and Adonis to meet with their loyal but psychopathic friend Albert Anastasia, the czar of the shipping piers. The thug pledged total support from the I.L.A. locals and every one else associated with the docks. This put Anastasia in the position of juggling convoluted roles on both sides of the law. He continued to enforce his massive criminal extortionist and violent rackets. But he still stayed out of public view because of a pending murder charge that Brooklyn DA O'Dwyer was trying to stall from Special Prosecutor Amen. At the same time, Anastasia was working full time as a technical sergeant in the Army training soldiers to be longshoremen. Finally, he made sure his surrogate union leaders and every one along the docks carried out Luciano's counterespionage and counter-sabotage directives.

These associates of Luciano quickly transmitted his statement that the homeland's war effort needed the help of every one on the docks. With the word coming from Charlie Lucky, everybody connected with the New York Harbor made an absolute commitment to protect it. Luciano also endorsed Lanza's intelligence activities and this expanded his role, especially with the other ethnic groups in the fishing industry. Anastasia's shipping and dock workers' unions gave Haffenden's agents false officials' credentials, and the union members gave the agents unfettered infiltration to the piers, warehouses, ships, and waterfront bars. The goal was to prevent sabotage, not to apprehend culprits after the damage had been done, so every one vigilantly watched for suspicious behavior. The dock workers stopped speaking about shipping activities because enemy agents were trying to find out convoy sailing times and their cargoes. Anyone who mentioned a word about their work in any bar in the area was told by the other drinkers to dummy up. If they persisted, customers took them out to the alley to instruct them in the virtue of silence.

Anastasia's unions controlled the Brooklyn stevedores, and they conducted waterfront strikes and interfered with wartime shipping. Lieutenant Commander Haffenden later testified he knew Naval Intelligence policy prohibited him from getting involved with labor disputes, so he advised attorney Polakoff about the disruptions. "Practically immediately the annoyance subsided," and Polakoff let him know, "Mission accomplished." When the words came down from Luciano, they had absolute finality. This was unlike their premature usage by President George W. Bush, who a half century later used the phrase at the very beginning of what was about to become America's longest war.[252]

Several Navy Intelligence agents later testified to the William Herlands Committee that once Luciano's associates went to work, the entire waterfront was bottled up. One agent said, "There was no active sabotage, no labor disturbances, no disruptions, nor delays of shipping out of the Port of New York." Another said, "We had everything sewed up tight: unions, docks, trucks, everything coming and going out of New York." By the end of the first year of the war the efforts of the Young Turks led to a decline in sinkings despite a great increase in the number of ships carrying troops, weapons, and supplies across the Atlantic.[253]

DA Hogan wanted to verify that the hoodlums were indeed giving the Navy proper support. He installed court-authorized wiretaps on the meeting-room phones used by Lansky, Lanza, and even Navy Intelligence. He turned his wiretap transcripts over to the Herlands Committee to confirm that the underworld cooperated fully in the War effort and that the Navy was clearly pleased with their successes.

Lanza had to withdraw from the Navy Intelligence effort a year into the War, when he and four strong-arm associates went on trial for a two-year old indictment of extorting $120 a week from the Teamsters local. After the prosecutor finished presenting his evidence, all five men pled guilty. The judge gave Lanza 7 ½ to 15 years and recommended the dangerous thug spend his entire maximum 15-year sentence in prison. But Governor Dewey inexplicably paroled Lanza halfway through his sentence. Even though Dewey had based his presidential ambitions on his tough-on-crime, racket-busting image, he released early and without explanation the most vicious criminal imprisoned in New York during his governorship.

Lanza's release should have become a major political scandal, but the Democrats were in no position to criticize. Lanza was closely tied to the top leaders of Tammany Hall. His extensive rackets in the city-owned Fulton Fish Market were protected by politicians who shared in the extorted plunder, making them ultimately responsible for allowing the violence that enforced it. Upon release from prison, Lanza was given a job in a hardware store owned by the former Democratic co-leader of his district. A year earlier Lanza's brother-in-law, a well-known racketeer, was appointed secretary to a New York Supreme Court Justice.

Seven years into Lanza's parole, an undercover NYPD detective was investigating a woman, and she invited him to her apartment. He looked at all the pictures on display, and when she was not looking he pocketed one of her with Lanza in a nightclub. The detective turned this photo over to Lanza's Parole Board agent, who soon arrested the Mafioso for violating parole by associating with a known criminal and for spending far beyond his hardware clerk's income. Two weeks later Parole Board member James Stone, a recent appointee of Democratic Governor Averell Harriman, restored Lanza's parole instead of re-imprisoning him. Stone's action set off a hailstorm of criticism from the Republican-controlled Legislature, which had ignored Governor Dewey's far more egregious act of paroling Lanza at the earliest date. Democratic Stone quickly resigned, but it was Republican Governor Dewey who had made his freedom possible.

The Joint Legislative "Watchdog" Committee set off intense investigations of Parole Board member Stone that made headlines every few days until the gubernatorial election. This biased long-time political witch-hunt failed in its mission to find evidence that Stone had been politically influenced in his decision. Even so, Governor Harriman was defeated in the election by Republican Nelson Rockefeller. Meanwhile, the rest of the Parole Board ruled that Lanza had to serve the remaining two and a half years of his original maximum sentence, and then they denied his parole requests, making him serve the whole term until he was 60 years old. The same political system the Mafioso had manipulated for so long finally turned against him - being associated with him or assisting him had become a liability.[254]

The racketeering and violence that Lanza introduced into the Fulton Fish Market continued unabated for three quarters of a century until the mid 1990s, when federal and city law-enforcement efforts reined in some of the abuses. One prosecutor said that everyone knew that two "governments" ruled over the market, and that the Mafia was the more powerful. Another said, "The result is a frontier atmosphere in which the prevailing attitude is that the Market is a sovereign entity, where the laws of economic power and physical coercion, not the laws of New York, prevail."

When Lanza pled guilty a year into the War, a much higher percentage of troop and supply ships were getting across the Atlantic, and the Allies were winning in North Africa. Once the Allies achieved victory in Africa, the Allied leaders gathered in Casablanca to plan their next moves. They decided to invade Southern Europe by using the island of Sicily as a stepping stone to Italy. The Allies had yet to amass sufficient forces to cross the English Channel from England into France and attack Hitler's massive defenses in Western Europe. Besides, they wanted to reduce the Nazi forces facing them in France by opening a front to the south through Italy to complement the Russian front to the east.

Invading Italy was ambitious and risky. The island was heavily defended by hundreds of thousands of Italian and German troops. It would be the largest amphibious assault in history, second only to the later planned invasion of Normandy in France. Yet the U.S. knew little about Sicily and its coastline. The Navy and Army desperately needed information about the island's sea and land minefields, port and beach facilities, shoreline gun emplacements and fortifications, and inland military installations. They also needed to know the island's political and economic situation and the identities of German and Italian agents. The new assignment for Lieutenant Commander Haffenden's B3 Naval Section was to obtain this critical intelligence. Time was of the essence because the invasion was to begin soon after the German and Italian armies in North Africa surrendered, and that turned out to be just three months hence.

Again just one man was able to rally Sicilian-Americans to the intelligence-gathering cause. Lieutenant Commander Haffenden had Lansky visit Luciano in prison one more time and had Lansky ask his dear friend to modify his information command structure to meet the new objectives. Lansky brought the information requests from Haffenden to Luciano, and then he passed Luciano's instructions to Joey Adonis. Luciano reached out to native Sicilians and Italians who had arrived in New York within the previous few years and thus had recent knowledge of the island and mainland. Adonis dealt with the fishing and shipping industries by continuing to call on the contacts of Lanza and Anastasia.

From the day after Lansky visited Luciano, hundreds of immigrants, many probably in the U.S. illegally, showed up at Lieutenant Commander Haffenden's office saying, "I'm here because of Charlie Lucky." They turned over thousands of personal photographs, which the Navy returned at the conclusion of the War, and they drew detailed maps of the current channels, ports, and land infrastructure.

Haffenden was especially interested in immigrants who had relatives in Sicily, because the Allies needed informants to help in planning the assault, local guides during the invasion, and residents to help stabilize and lead the conquered territory. Haffenden's boss told the Herlands Committee, "It was felt that since Mussolini had been responsible for the expulsion of many Sicilians, persons of Sicilian origin might be willing to aid Naval Intelligence," especially the Mafiosi who had dominated many towns and villages until Mussolini's persecution drove them into the hills. The assessment was correct - the Sicilians felt hatred and contempt for Mussolini.[255]

U.S. Naval Intelligence Officer Anthony Marsloe was asked, "Don't you imagine that some of the people you were meeting in America were Mafiosi and that their relatives would be Mafiosi back in Sicily?" He replied, "I couldn't care less what they were, if they could supply any information that would help the War effort."[256]

Mussolini was made Prime Minister by the King of Italy in 1922, and in the election two years later his Fascist Party won control of the Parliament by using violence and intimidation. Mussolini then barred all political parties but the Fascists, as he installed his totalitarian regime with a secret police force and press censorship. To unify all of Italy, including Sicily, he had thousands of Mafiosi imprisoned and forced others to flee to America. Many hid or became insurgents. Two decades later these partisans would welcome and assist the invading Allied army. But ironically and sadly ,their alliance with the U.S. military would bring the Mafia back to power after the War, politically stronger than before.

Luciano's point man for intel from inside Sicily was Vito Genovese. He had been Luciano's Mafia gang lieutenant until he had fled New York in 1934 to avoid a murder charge. Genovese was hiding in his native Sicily from the Fascist government's Mafia crackdown, but Luciano was able to get word to him. Genovese smuggled information back to the U.S. about Italian and German military preparedness and vulnerabilities, and he also prepared the Mafia resistance to join the invasion. When the Allies arrived in Sicily, Genovese became an interpreter for the U.S. military.[257]

Landing with the first amphibious wave to attack the fortifications along the shores of Sicily were Lieutenant Commander Haffenden and three other top Naval Intel officers. They were armed with information collected by Luciano, Lansky, and Adonis to help direct the troops inland. Beyond the beachheads, the waiting Sicilian Mafiosi ran out to greet the advancing American forces and quickly led them through the minefields and booby-traps to the Italian Naval Command's camouflaged headquarters. Because of their speedy advance they were able to capture the sensitive plans and maps, including the position of Italian and German Mediterranean naval forces and the safe routes through the minefields.

From the beginning of the beach assault, it took just five weeks for the Allies to drive the Germans out of Sicily. The incredible speed of General George Patton's blitzkrieg through Sicily amazed General Dwight Eisenhower and his planning staff who commanded the combined Allied forces. The Naval Intelligence agents who were in the forefront of the two invasions told the Herlands Committee that Luciano's informants had given them valuable topographical maps and up-to-date accurate descriptions of many key targets.

Around the time Sicily was being liberated, the King of Italy removed Mussolini from power, surrendered Italy to the Allies, and declared war on Germany. The speed of the Sicilian invasion and occupation of the well-fortified island is impressive when compared to other invasions and with the taking of the Italian mainland. In comparison to the rapid taking of Sicily, it took the Allies two years of bitter fighting to defeat the Germans in mainland Italy. And the enemy troops did not surrender until the partisans captured and hung Mussolini, and then two days later Adolph Hitler committed suicide.[258]

Luciano's efforts in taking Sicily saved hundreds, possibly thousands, of soldiers' lives. The Allies' unexpected quick victory to successfully establish a Mediterranean front in Sicily shortened the War. It also forced Germany to pull substantial troops from both its Eastern and Western European fronts to counter the Allied advance into the Italian mainland. Hitler's removal of so many troops from France made possible the Allies' successful D-Day invasion landing that continued its advance directly into the heart of Germany and victory in the European War.

Unfortunately, Genovese and the Sicilian Mafiosi were a very different breed from Luciano and the Young Turks. They stole U.S. gasoline and other war supplies and sold them in the high-priced black market. Following the invasion of Sicily, the Army Counter-Intelligence Corps made a pragmatic decision that negatively impacted both Italy and the U.S., and this problem continues to this day. They emptied the Sicilian prisons and freed all the Mafiosi. Then they appointed Mafiosi to key city administrative positions to gain quick control over Sicilian and some Italian cities so that the Allied troops could continue their advance without waiting to pacify each population area.

The Sicilian Mafia now had more political power over city governments than before the War, and they quickly became a main conduit of narcotics to the U.S., even processing Turkish opium into heroin. Their drug trafficking into the U.S. greatly increased illegal drug supplies and lowered prices, fueling a huge rise in addiction that forever changed America from an alcohol-oriented culture to one also heavily dependent on illegal narcotics.

For the Sicilian people, this new freedom from fascism meant total repression and exploitation by the Mafia. These criminals quickly and ruthlessly killed any political opposition. For the next half century they assassinated any political leaders, judges, prosecutors, and police who tried to exert some control. The Italian government did not launch a major offensive against the Mafia until 1992, and while it had some success, the problems persist to this day.

LUCIANO'S LEGAL MANEUVERS

Two years into the War, Luciano's attorney Moses Polakoff appealed to the trial judge to suspend two of the three consecutive sentences against his client so he would be eligible for parole after serving 10 years. Polakoff stated in open court that Luciano was cooperating with "high military authorities" and rendering a "definite service to the war effort," but he had to admit the details were a military secret. Polakoff emphasized to the judge that Luciano had cooperated without "any thought of consideration or hope of consideration."[259]

Navy Lieutenant Commander Haffenden and Manhattan Assistant DA Gurfein testified privately to Luciano's trial judge in chambers, although they could give no details because the military was at that moment using the information provided by Luciano's efforts to plan its invasion of Sicily. Both officials praised Luciano's contribution, but offered nothing substantive. Haffenden wrote his supervisor, "As we were at the time involved in war with Germany, no information was given in my testimony, other than generalities, as to the assistance rendered by Charles Luciano, no case, no facts, or anything that could be inferred as jeopardizing Naval interest was brought forth." New York's Commissioner of Corrections' letter to the judge commended Luciano for his conduct in prison as a "model prisoner," not surprising given Luciano's accommodating, considerate nature.[260]

The Judge denied Luciano's application but offered a distant ray of hope by saying, "The authorities have been interviewed, privately, in the public interest. As a result, the court is able to conclude that the defendant probably attempted to assist them, and possibly with some success. If the defendant is assisting the authorities and he continues to do so, and remains a model prisoner, executive clemency may become appropriate at some future date." New York City's newspapers reported the court hearing, but with no substantive information, the nature of Luciano's clandestine war activities became grist for the rumor mill.[261]

Two years later on V-E Day (Victory in Europe), attorney Polakoff petitioned Governor Dewey for executive clemency on behalf of Luciano. With the War in Europe ended, Polakoff felt at liberty to present in his plea Luciano's vital two-year contribution to the Allies' triumphant victory over Nazi Germany.

Luciano had offered crucial assistance to his beloved adopted homeland, during what the Navy's highest ranking leaders had called an "extremely grave" period of the War, but they conspired to repay him by keeping him in prison for 40 more years. Navy leaders wanted their name severed from the rampant rumors about his cooperation, so they officially denied any association with him, shredded documents, and used disciplinary threats to silence all Intelligence officers who had any knowledge of the underworld's war contribution. A court-martial notice was placed in every Intelligence officer's personnel file, and all were warned that proceedings would commence if they ever told the truth.

No one took Luciano's petition for executive clemency seriously. It was assumed that he was doomed to a lifetime sentence, especially under Governor Dewey. It was just over a year since Dewey engineered and rushed Lepke's highly-publicized execution, and Lepke was a small time gangster compared to Luciano. No one could conceive of Dewey jeopardizing his lifelong crime-fighter image by letting the hood go. After all as DA, Dewey had vilified Luciano as the most dangerous public enemy in America and then gone to extraordinary efforts to frame him to get him the long prison sentence. Given this background, Dewey stunned the nation when he freed Luciano from prison less than 10 years into the 50-year sentence. He ordered him to be deported back to his native Italy forthwith.[262]

Dewey's decision was inexplicable to everyone. His written announcement offered little justification, and he refused to offer further explanation. Since Dewey was an astute political animal, his timing in deporting Luciano was especially perplexing. Dewey was just gearing up for a third gubernatorial campaign for the election in nine months, and the presidency he craved was an achievable goal two years after that.

Dewey's most ardent political supporters and critics alike tried to make sense out of his pardoning of Public Enemy Number 1. Brothel madam Polly Adler voiced the question on New Yorkers' minds, when she wrote, "If [Luciano] was indeed 'ninety times guilty,' then why was he sprung?" The FBI agents who investigated Dewey's motive injected doubt about Luciano's guilt in their internal reports: "The New York Division advises xxxxx described as a witness for the prosecution in the trial of Lucky Luciano, personally admitted xxxxx he had perjured himself when he testified against Lucky Luciano. Xxxxx states that considerable opinion exists to the affect that Luciano was not guilty of the charges for which he was convicted and that Governor Dewey's parole of Luciano was motivated partially as an easing of Dewey's conscience."[263]

Reporters and authors mulled over Dewey's contradictory actions. As DA he had denounced Luciano, and then as Governor he set him loose. Many speculated that Meyer Lansky had paid Dewey for the pardon. Some journalists believed the rumors that Luciano had become some kind of World War II hero, and they wanted to believe Dewey had simply treated a patriot fairly and honorably.

It would be nice to believe that Dewey had a conscience and that his motive was above reproach. Unfortunately there was nothing virtuous or noble about his decision. He pardoned Luciano for the same reason he had framed him, a lust for power. The reason Dewey pardoned Luciano was revealed for the first time during my interviews with Jimmy Blue Eyes. He said his close friend Lansky had spent a great deal of time and money collecting affidavits from the state's key witnesses against Luciano, and all swore that Dewey had improperly pressured them to lie at his trial. Lansky and his associates had also participated in Luciano's stellar war efforts, even though Naval Intelligence adamantly denied the underworld's contribution. Jimmy explained, "Meyer [Lansky] told Governor Dewey that he would expose this gross miscarriage of justice [framing Luciano] perpetrated by himself and other government officials unless Charlie Lucky's sentence was commuted. Dewey acquiesced and deported him to Italy."

Dewey hoped the hit to his political image would be short-lived, but it was not. It was the first commutation granted in New York for the purpose of deportation. Freeing Luciano led to years of speculation and stinging Democratic political attacks about the Governor's motive. To extricate himself from the contradiction between his inflammatory prosecutorial statements and his pardon action, Dewey established the Herlands Committee to investigate Luciano's contribution to the war effort to try to justify his action. But the Navy blocked Dewey's plan to publicize the results by refusing to cooperate without a guarantee of secrecy. Dewey's vow of silence was not broken until after his death, when his estate gave the Herlands Report to author Rodney Campbell. The truth was also exposed by other sources. The FBI interviews of Naval officials was made public after passage of the Freedom of Information Act. Several New York State agencies maintained parts of the records and open legislative inquiries were conducted. In addition, key Naval officers gave press interviews despite official warnings to keep quiet. (See Addendum Z)

Luciano was not a U.S. citizen. He never qualified for automatic approval as the son of a citizen because his father was not naturalized until Charlie Lucky was an adult, and Charlie's teenage arrest record kept him from applying. Therefore, five months after he went to prison the Immigration and Naturalization Service (INS) filed a deportation order that was to become effective if he was ever released. One month after he was pardoned but before he was released the order was enforced. INS guards transported the prisoner from Sing Sing to the Ellis Island Ferry Depot. Waiting for a ferry to Ellis Island, 20 reporters tried to interview Luciano, but they were blocked from the pier by a line of resolute stevedores. Irate at being held at bay, these reporters manufactured stories about Luciano partying aboard the freighter with hoodlums, broads, and booze.

These allegations peaked the interest of FBI Director J. Edgar Hoover. He was not interested in the behavior of Luciano, who was now banned to Italy for life. He instead investigated whether public officials had handled his departure properly, and his agents found that every one involved had indeed acted with propriety. The main focus for Hoover's inquiry was to find out the reason why Governor and presidential candidate Dewey pardoned Luciano after having prosecuted him so vigorously. But except to find that Luciano was likely framed, this FBI investigation went nowhere. (See Addendum AA)

The INS had no jurisdiction over entry to the pier, which was private property, and Ellis Island had always been out of bounds for reporters. The pier superintendent tried to accommodate the reporters by asking Luciano if he wanted to grant interviews, but he said the press had not treated him well, so he had no desire to talk with them.

INS policy allowed lawyers and relatives to visit, so Luciano's attorney brought along Costello and Lansky, the two men who had done the most to free him, for a hour farewell meet. His old friends brought clothing. Luciano gave $400 in cash to Costello because the law allowed only $60 in currency be taken out of the country. Since there was no limitation on traveler's checks, they gave him $2,500.

At a Brooklyn pier Luciano went on board the freighter *S.S. Laura Keene* alone. No one visited him in his cabin, and no food or beverage was brought to him. Nine months after Luciano had filed his petition for clemency with Governor Dewey, Luciano walked out of his prison cell that had been his home for a decade to walk up the ramp of the freighter as its sole human cargo. Then the *S.S. Laura Keene* sailed off to Italy with its one-way passenger.[264]

A WINTER IN THE CARIBBEAN

Luciano settled in Rome, but he was lonely, without friends, and unhappy. Five months after his deportation, he obtained an Italian passport to emigrate to Argentina. At the same time, he submitted a six-month visa request to Cuba, where he had vacationed for long periods during and after Prohibition. Havana was a wonderful adult playground especially during the frigid northeast U.S. winters. He had developed friendships with many prominent Cubans, and he would be less than 100 miles from America, so his family and old friends could visit regularly.

Luciano led an inconspicuous life, but the Cuban Secret Police monitored him because of his notoriety. Neighbors living near his fashionable home were unaware of who he was. FBI agents reported, "According to these inquiries, women were never noted to have entered subject's residence. … The only unusual thing noted was the fact that groups of men called at subject's home frequently." The visiting men were a who's who of U.S. gangland leadership, coming to express their respect and friendship.[265]

Every one in Havana, even his servants, called him "Mr. Charlie." He lived quietly, unnoticed, and unbothered by the authorities. He accompanied friends to the races in the afternoon, and he and his pals enjoyed nightclubs and cabarets in the evening. He entertained lavishly. His entourages were always unassuming and polite so as not to draw any attention.[266]

Cuba's only legal casinos were the elegant Gran Casino Nacional and a low-wagering-limit facility, both at Havana's Oriental Park Racetrack. The Nacional featured dining, dancing, and gambling "after the races." Luciano and his pals spent many evenings at the glamour spot, and he was friendly with the casino's U.S. operators. His close friend Meyer Lansky had operated both casinos at the Oriental Park Racetrack in 1939, and a decade earlier near the end of Prohibition,

Lansky had set up massive molasses purchases from the Caribbean island. Since Lansky now lived in Florida during the winter, he often visited Luciano in Havana.

Luciano told the Cuban Secret Police, the FBI, and the Cuba press that he planned to remain for some time. He had intended to purchase an interest in the two casinos, but he said the deal was not consummated because the operations were deeply mired in politics. He gave no details, but since top Cuban politicians held interests in the casinos this answer seems to have been more polite than true. The two casinos were notoriously crooked. Cheating was so blatant that local reporters wrote stories about it, eyewitnesses informed the FBI, and Luciano saw it firsthand. Since Luciano had built a reputation for integrity in the gambling operations he ran before and after Prohibition, he did not want to be involved with such dishonest operators.

For more than three months Luciano enjoyed the warm weather, nightlife, and camaraderie of his many Cuban and U.S. friends. Then a reporter recognized him in the Jockey Club at Oriental Park as he socialized with some tourists and Cuban residents. It was a chance encounter that changed his life. The reporter wrote a story about Luciano's presence for the local weekly magazine *Tiempo En Cuba,* which featured his picture on the cover. Charlie Lucky's pals quickly bought up every copy they could find to stifle the publicity, but the magazine immediately printed a second run.

Four days later, Luciano's presence so near U.S. shores became a national scandal in America. A syndicated column in the New York City *World-Telegram* entitled *Wrong Friends* by Robert C. Ruark tore into Frank Sinatra for nightclubbing with the hoodlum Luciano in Havana. He lambasted the bobby-soxers' favorite singer for being a dreadful role model to America's youth. The columnist wrote, "Mr. Sinatra, the self-confessed savior of the country's small fry, by virtue of his lectures on clean living and love-thy-neighbor, his movie shorts on tolerance, and his frequent dabblings into the do-good department of politics, seems to be setting a most peculiar example for his hordes of [adoring fans]." It continued, "The friendship was beautiful: They were seen together at the race track, the gambling casino, and at special parties."[267]

Later that day Federal Bureau of Narcotics (FBN) Commissioner Harry Anslinger announced that legal pharmaceutical narcotics shipments from the U.S. to Cuba would cease until Luciano was taken into custody and expelled. Anslinger expressed fear that Luciano's conviction for a single illegal sale of a tiny dose of opium as a teenager three decades earlier made him a dangerous threat to redirect pharmaceuticals that were legal in Cuba to the U.S. for illegal sale. Anslinger's action set off a political hailstorm in Cuba. The Cuban government publicly and officially protested the sudden, heavy-handed ban and the U.S. government's "unjustified failure" to use accepted diplomacy to get action against Luciano. The Cubans also took offense at the unverified implication that Luciano or anyone else could illegally obtain the medical drugs entering their country.

The next day, a *Havana Post* reporter approached Luciano sipping coffee at a Vedado Café to tell him that he was back in the news spotlight. Luciano lamented, "This is terrible. I came here to live quietly, and now, all this blows up in my face." The Cuban Secret Police walked in, arrested Luciano, and took him to the alien holdover until the immigration department could settle his case.[268]

Despite Cuba's public indignation, it was not strong enough to stand up to U.S. government bullying. A Havana FBI report explained, "On February 27, 1947, Cuban President Dr. Ramon Grau San Martin signed a decree classifying Luciano as an undesirable alien in Cuba in view of his past criminal activities and ordering his deportation to Italy by the earliest possible means. The American Embassy in Havana was advised of this decision on the same day, and in turn advised the Cuban Ministry of State that no actual embargo had been placed on shipments of narcotics to Cuba, despite the statements to the contrary made by United States Narcotic Bureau officials."[269]

From the moment Luciano was taken into custody, he expressed sadness at the prospect of being tossed out of Cuba. After New York, Havana was his favorite city. Not wanting to challenge Cuban authorities, he offered to return to Italy immediately rather than await deportation proceedings. Three weeks later Luciano was placed on the Turkish merchant ship *SSW Banker* destined for Genoa, Italy.

Luciano told the Cuban Secret Police Chief that he would have departed from Cuba voluntarily if anyone had just asked. He said that his intent in moving to Cuba was to be near friends and relatives who resided in the U.S. While resigned to returning to Italy, he complained bitterly about the immense publicity his case had received. He also seemed to have anticipated U.S. objection to his presence, because he maintained a low profile, never sought Cuban citizenship, and his Italian passport contained additional visas issued by Venezuela, Bolivia, and Columbia, so he could stay in the Americas.

Luciano told the Chief of the Cuban Secret Police that he intended to return to the Western Hemisphere if proper arrangements could be made in Italy. He could not consider going to New York because his clemency stipulated 41 more years in prison if he were ever found on U.S. soil. He mentioned Venezuela and Mexico as possible destinations because of their proximity to the U.S. and his friends and family.

Despite finding no evidence of wrongdoing, Cuban officials acquiesced to U.S. pressure and turned down Luciano's repeated offers to leave voluntarily. By forcibly expelling Luciano, the government both prohibited him from ever reentering Cuba and prevented him from using his visas to other countries. Finally U.S. officials demanded that Italy permanently revoke Luciano's passport so that he could never travel again.

Once again Luciano found himself in the crosshairs of a U.S. public official acting for personal political gain. To understand why the retired hood became a major pawn in America's war on illegal narcotics requires a little background on the role Italy played in the U.S. drug problem. After World War II the Mafia in Sicily, more politically powerful than ever courtesy of the U.S. military, flooded America with illegal drugs and addiction skyrocketed. Prior to this post-war deluge only a small hard-core group of addicts used drugs, and suppliers were an isolated criminal breed far more violent than today's pushers. Even though the suppliers multiplied, they remained an insular group. Thus, FBN Commissioner Anslinger's frequent investigations never found a single major hood associating with known drug pushers.

From its inception the government's enforcement of illegal or controlled drugs had failed as miserably as its enforcement of Prohibition. But drug usage was not as visible or obvious to the typical citizen. Drinkers indulged publicly in popular speakeasies and nightclubs during Prohibition, while dopers shot up individually or in small groups, in private and behind closed doors. By the late 1940s any drug of choice could be found easily anywhere in the U.S.

Anslinger tried to cover his embarrassment at the mounting tide of illegally imported drugs by claiming that the FBN was up against an international organization of super-villains. Over time he accused every major U.S. gangster of being involved in drug trafficking. He singled out those involved with illicit casinos because they were famous with the public, but he never produced a grain of evidence against a single one of them.

Drug busts in this era did not involve American Mafiosi because Boss of Bosses Luciano and Frank Costello enforced a "no drugs" policy, prohibiting anyone associated with a Mafia gang from using or selling drugs. Despite their position, big-time gamblers became Anslinger's scapegoats for the FBN's failure to impede the rapidly expanding illegal drug trade.

When the press reported that major U.S. gang leaders were partying in Cuba with Luciano, Anslinger saw a great opportunity to improve his agency's drug-busting image. He claimed the gang-lord meetings were all about drugs, which was false. Anslinger publicly and aggressively attacked Luciano's presence in Cuba and banned the shipment of all legitimate narcotics to Cuba under the pretense that Luciano might obtain possession of them and sell them illegally in the U.S. It was a ludicrous position to go after a retired hood who was banned from entering the country while ignoring all the other American hoods who traveled back and forth to Cuba at will. Like every other U.S. citizen, they could carry all the illicit contraband their baggage would hold because airline and ship companies never inspected it in that era.

Anslinger and J. Edgar Hoover believed that the job of law enforcement was not to *ensure* the citizenry was safe, but to make them *feel* safe. As organized crime grew rapidly across the country, both the FBN and the FBI were more devoted to their public relations efforts than crime busting. In their world, substance was irrelevant, appearances were everything.

The dozen FBN agents that Anslinger dispatched to Havana reported that Luciano and the other hoods spent most of their time gambling at the racetrack, enjoying fine restaurants and nightclubs, and frequenting a couple high-class brothels. Five years later, several of the top hoods who visited Luciano would start building luxury casino resorts in Havana. Every executive I knew who had worked in a Havana casino fondly remembered it as the world's most fun party town until Fidel Castro's communist regime shut it all down.

It was Anslinger who supplied all the information for the U.S. Senate Kefauver Committee hearings. Information in the Federal Bureau of Narcotic's files led to the Committee issuing subpoenas primarily to gamblers, while ignoring many dangerous gangsters and virtually all of the nation's drug pushers, whom the FNB had yet to identify because they were so segregated from the rest of the underworld. Historian Arthur M. Schlesinger, Jr., commenting on the agency's ineffectiveness, observed wryly that when the Kefauver Committee said there was a national crime syndicate, "the Federal Narcotics Bureau, which was having troubles of its own in stopping the smuggling of heroin, welcomed the alibi of an international criminal cartel."[270]

J. Edgar Hoover refused to cooperate with the Kefauver Committee. Hoover developed little information about the country's major criminals during the 1920s through the 1940s, as the FBI's own files demonstrate. He got away with his refusal to assist the U.S. Senate's huge crime investigation without a whimper of a complaint because of the true nature of his agency. Hoover's FBI agents focused on collecting negative information about politicians, celebrities, and the rich and powerful. No Washington politician dared criticize or stand up to Hoover. He died after 48 years in office without one president or congressman ever having publicly challenged him or his flagrant illegal and Unconstitutional abuses of power (see "All *Against* The Law" by Bill Friedman).

The Cuban police, the Italian police, and three U.S. agencies – the FBN, the FBI, and the Treasury Department - repeatedly investigated Luciano from the time of his deportation from America until his death. These agencies said either publicly or in documents released later that they never found any evidence or reason to believe Luciano was involved in illegal activity, specifically narcotic trafficking, as Anslinger had repeatedly claimed despite no evidence whatsoever.

LUCIANO IN EXILE

Charlie Lucky lived the remaining years of his life quietly in Italy. Despite "the sun and sea and the sky of Naples," he was bored. He longed to walk the congested New York City sidewalks he loved. Luciano knew he could never return, but he always planned to be buried in his adopted homeland. He had even purchased an expensive New York City vault housing 16 coffins for him and his family.[271]

The Italian magazine *L'Europe* wrote Luciano's "greatest desire is to forget and be forgotten. He is a tight-lipped individual who is in the habit of answering the most searching questions with a stony-faced silence." He never confirmed or denied any of the countless articles, books, and other stories written about his American past. He always denied he was involved with prostitution, and he only broke his silence to call the prosecutors, "Stinkers."[272]

The series of magazine articles continued: "Who would blame him for feeling bitter? Since 1945 his life has been one of continuous harassment, persecution and provocation." The moment he landed in Italy, the police jailed him for three weeks and then let him move into a Rome apartment. The Italian authorities were bothered that he did not work most of the time, even though his lifestyle was modest and his expenditures small. He was able to retire at a simple level because he had been Prohibition's most successful violator and was a partner in casinos after that. The police were also concerned that Luciano occasionally socialized with other Italians who had been expelled from the U.S. However, having lived in America from the age of 9, he no longer had anything in common with anyone he met in Italy. Typical of old men, he preferred to commiserate with life-long friends and acquaintances who shared the allure of New York City's frenzied hubbub.

"However, Lucky's worst enemy, the Federal Bureau of Narcotics, under the direction of Harry J. Anslinger, was not satisfied that his days as the king of vice were over. From Italy, they believed, Lucky was still manipulating the strings of international dope traffic. It was at this time that an anonymous letter was sent to the President of the Italian Republic accusing Lucky of white slavery, forging of passports, opium and cocaine traffic, homicide, moonshining and burglary. Coincidentally enough, the American press started a big anti-Lucky campaign and the Narcotics Bureau brought pressure to bear on the Italian authorities 'to do something about him.'"

Every time the FBN made a major bust of drugs originating from Italy or transported by Italians, Anslinger accused Luciano in the media. He would pressure Italy to jail Luciano on suspicion, and to toss everything in his apartment into a pile like trash. Anslinger never uncovered any evidence against Luciano or connection with any crime, and none of the Italian interrogations yielded any results. Luciano "later complained that those nine days in the Roman jail were worse than the nine years in Sing Sing. … To avoid continuing pressure from the U.S., the police ordered him back to Palermo, a city which he did not like. Finally he obtained permission to settle in Naples."

Five years after Luciano's deportation to Italy, FBN Special Envoy Charles Siragusa, who had the power to investigate narcotics trafficking to the U.S. from Europe, arrived in Naples and focused on Luciano. "His reports reveal that he firmly believed, and, perhaps, still does, Lucky to be the mastermind behind every single shipment of narcotics. … However, no direct connection was proved with Lucky Luciano" with any narcotic shipment or any suspected smuggler.

Three years later the new head of the Italian regional police in Naples, Dr. Giorgio Florita, took steps to get Luciano expelled from Naples to his native village of Lercara Friddi in the Province of Palermo, Sicily. When Rome rejected Florita's request, he got the Provincial Commission of Public Order and Safety to restrict Luciano's activities. His driver's license and new passport were confiscated. He was given an 8 p.m. curfew, and his home was subject to police raids at any time. The Italian police and the appeals court that denied Luciano's claim were influenced by the U.S. FNB's Siragusa.

These restrictions on Luciano's life lasted for three years until a Neapolitan court found no evidence to justify continuing them. The court ordered the police to remove their curfew and allow Luciano to leave Naples without special permission. Four months later the Naples Prosecuting Attorney questioned Luciano for two hours in front of the Appellate Court about whether he was involved with a meeting of U.S. Mafia leaders in Apalachin, New York. "He emerged nervous and sweating from a closed hearing in an Appellate Court. Insisting he was leading a straight life and dealing with honest people, he charged, 'They're still trying to frame me.'" Luciano said, "Until I read all that trash in the papers, I never even heard of Apalachin. I still don't know where it is – and don't care. I'm clean. I even pay my income tax. They got nothing on me and never will have."

Next the Prosecutor requested the Appellate Court allow the police to put Luciano back under close surveillance for two more years. But "The Appellate Court confirmed an earlier decision by the Naples Court to the effect that the police had no authority to conduct surveillance on Luciano or control his movements, inasmuch as insufficient evidence had been produced to indicate that Luciano is engaged in illegal activities or activities inimical to the best interest of the Republic of Italy." The FBI agents who prepared the detailed report about Luciano for Director Hoover concluded, "In the eyes of the Italian law Lucky is an honest citizen. His FBI record is long and thick with notations, but after each one of them we read 'fine paid' and 'discharged' or 'released.'" The FNB's Siragusa finally left Italy after eight years of persecuting the retired aging hood.[273]

When a reporter once asked Luciano why he never married, he replied, "I've got enough troubles." All of his associates said that he was too shy to establish a relationship with a woman, but in Italy he developed the first romantic attachment of his life with Igea Lissoni. She was a former ballerina with the La Scala, Italy's most famous ballet company. Igea and Charlie married three years after his arrival. They lived an inconspicuous life in Naples. After she had surgery for breast cancer, he nursed her during her long terminal illness. At the same time, he was trying to fend off Siragusa's persecution. After celebrating their 10th anniversary, Igea died at age 37. At her funeral his old American-deportee friends told reporters that it was the first time they saw Charlie Lucky cry.[274]

THE LAST TESTAMENT OF LUCKY LUCIANO

Late in his life, Luciano was approached by Martin Gosch to do a movie about his life. Gosch worked for American and Spanish film producers. Luciano told old associates in Italy and a few U.S. relatives that he did not trust Gosch, and he wanted nothing to do with him. When it appeared that Gosch was going ahead with a fictitious movie that he falsely claimed was autobiographical, Luciano became very upset. Accompanied by friends, Luciano went to Naples' Capodichino Airport to meet with Gosch, set things straight, and get the writer out of his life. A short time before Gosch's plane landed, the agitated Luciano suffered a fatal heart attack at age 64.

FBI agents reported to Director Hoover that at Luciano's funeral in Italy there were more police than mourners. In addition to the FBI agents, there were U.S. FBN agents who were disappointed to find no criminals among the mourners. Two U.S. INS agents stationed in Italy showed up to confirm that Luciano really was dead. Even though the Navy had officially denied its association with Luciano for three decades, three Office of Naval Intelligence officials attended to pay their final respects with a salute to America's war collaborator and strategist.[275]

Luciano's lifelong friend and former partner Joe Adonis lived in Avelino, only 25 miles from Naples, but the two were never allowed to visit or communicate. Italian authorities denied Adonis permission to attend the funeral, but he sent a floral display with the inscription, "So long, pal."[276]

The U.S. Consulate in Naples got approval from Washington to allow Luciano's family to return his body to America by explaining, "A dead body is without nationality." Sixteen years after he was deported, Luciano was buried alongside his mother, father, aunt, and uncle in the family vault in St. John's Cathedral Cemetery, Middle Village, Queens, New York. A reporter watching the service asked Luciano's brother Bartolo if he knew the identity of the saint depicted in the vault's small stained-glass window, and Bartolo replied, "I don't know. I'm not acquainted with saints."[277]

With Luciano dead, Gosch immediately began fabricating stories about his near-encounter with the famous gangster. He claimed that Luciano had dramatically collapsed dead in his arms at the airport, even though Luciano's associates, airport officials, and the police all knew that Luciano died before Gosch's plane ever landed. Then Gosch told reporters that he was there to discuss a planned motion picture, but he never mentioned a book. He later claimed he had interviewed Luciano repeatedly prior to his death, but this was debunked by *New York Times'* organized crime investigative reporter Nicholas Cage when *The Last Testament of Lucky Luciano* was about to be released. Cage exposed it as a fraud in a long, scathing analysis on the paper's front page. Despite the publisher's attempts to defend the book, they never produced any evidence that Gosch had ever interviewed Luciano nor that Luciano had approved the project. Cage's newspaper exposé was devastating. He compared the text with other books about organized crime, official documents, newspaper reports, and his own interviews with 20 experts who concluded it was riddled with contradictions, discrepancies, and inaccuracies.[278] (This fraud is detailed in Addendum BB.)

Luciano officially died of a heart attack, but no autopsy was performed. His associates believed his distress over Gosch's fraudulent movie "autobiography" plans aggravated his ulcers, causing severe bleeding. They harbored an anger toward Gosch as if he had intentionally killed Charlie Lucky, but they honored their fallen buddy's memory by foreswearing vengeance. Fortunately, Luciano never saw the Gosch travesty published in his name. In contrast, it was unfortunate that he died 15 years before another book, *The Luciano Project: The Secret Wartime Collaboration of the Mafia & the U. S. Navy,* by Rodney Campbell revealed his invaluable contribution to America's War effort.

The U.S. deported Luciano almost a year before Ben Siegel opened the *Flamingo Hotel* on the emerging Las Vegas Strip. Except for Prohibition rumrunning, Luciano was a casino operator and bookmaker his whole life, as were all the people close to him. It would be his Prohibition gang's leaders and his close New York and New Jersey associates who would follow Siegel's lead and build 80% of the resorts in the two decades of the Las Vegas Strip's Golden Era that began with the opening of the fabulous *Flamingo*.

Next is the career of Luciano's Prohibition partner and World War II collaborator Joe Adonis. This is when he operated fine restaurants and elegant high-limit, but illegal, casinos.

CHAPTER 11

THE ACTION CROSSED THE HUDSON RIVER

JOE ADONIS IN BROOKLYN

Joe Adonis was born Giuseppe Antonio Doto in Montemarano, Italy on November 22, 1902. His father immigrated to the south section of a Brooklyn waterfront slum, and when he had saved enough money for the trip he brought his wife and their four children to join him. Joe was then 6. After grammar school, Adonis worked around the waterfront until he partnered at age 17 with Charlie Luciano, Meyer Lansky, and Ben Siegel in Prohibition's most successful fine-liquor importing operation. Adonis was arrested five times from the middle to late Prohibition, receiving small fines for liquor smuggling and a street fight.[279]

Adonis dressed conservatively and immaculately in tailor-made suits. He became the political power of Brooklyn because he liked to help people. He readily contributed to charitable causes and was especially generous with the residents in the poorer sections he knew so well from his background. He opened his upscale *Joe's Italian Kitchen* early in Prohibition in an out-of-the-way, run-down neighborhood. He offered good food, a large variety of fine foreign liquors, and gracious hosting. He spoke softly, smiled often, and joked easily. This winning combination made his speakeasy a popular hangout with prominent politicians, borough officials, businessmen, and stage personalities. Adonis spent his time cultivating the bigwigs of the city's various political parties, so leading politicos felt comfortable meeting not only with their allies but also their opponents at *Joe's*. Hoods made it their hangout because Adonis negotiated on their behalf with the judges, prosecutors, and police who also frequented *Joe's*. In addition, Adonis tried to mediate gang disputes to peaceful conclusions.

While Albert Anastasia controlled the waterfront-workers' vote through union leader Camarda's Red Hook City Democratic Club, Adonis represented Brooklyn's large populations of fellow Italians and Jewish compatriots who merged into a single commingled society. He was their spokesman and advocate. Politicians turned to him for advice about how his constituency would vote and for financial support. The Kefauver Committee depicted Adonis as the dominant influence with Brooklyn's leading politicians. Its investigation found that Manhattan's political kingmaker Frank Costello did not venture into Adonis' domain, but an in-depth magazine investigation concluded Adonis "is Costello's principal political henchman in Brooklyn."[280]

Brooklyn's predominantly Italian and Jewish populations backed the Democrats, as did the Joe Adonis Social Club because the party supported the interests of his workingmen constituency. However, Adonis used his close contacts with leaders of every party to endorse the agenda he thought was in their best interest. He even broke with tradition by openly giving large financial support and voter endorsement to Republican-Fusion mayoral candidate Fiorello LaGuardia in 1933. Adonis was tired of Irish politicians failing to address the problems of his fellow Italians and his many Jewish neighbors except on Election Day. LaGuardia had both Italian and Jewish heritage, and Adonis concluded that it was sensible for both groups to support LaGuardia. Adonis' political machine was powerful enough to swing a district election the way he wanted, and the press revealed that he had personally contributed $25,000 to the reform mayoral candidate. Nevertheless, Adonis remained loyal to the Brooklyn Democratic municipal candidates, working for their election based on the issues they supported and the frequency of their visits to his speakeasy.

Adonis invested his Prohibition profits in local businesses. His Kings County Cigarette Service operated cigarette vending machines in stores, bars, restaurants, and poolrooms around Brooklyn. He also owned three used-car lots in Brooklyn. After the repeal of Prohibition, Adonis moved out of his old neighborhood and opened a high-class restaurant on Pineapple Street in the quiet Brooklyn Heights section. It became the gathering place for older Brooklyn families, artists, and authors. It also drew some politicians, but Adonis let the city's hoodlums know these diners would not appreciate their company. Adonis continued to operate his *Joe's Italian Kitchen* because it was profitable and furthered his political objectives.

As the 1937 election campaigns geared up, Adonis reevaluated the political landscape. He was dissatisfied with Mayor LaGuardia, who had neither helped nor hurt his Italian and Jewish constituencies, so he switched his support from the incumbent to the challenger, U. S. Senator Royal Copeland, who was a candidate in both the Republican and Democratic mayoral primaries. LaGuardia had built his political image on bombastic law-and-order rhetoric, but all his attacks were directed solely at those hoods who contributed money or votes to opposing candidates. For example LaGuardia had destroyed Costello's slot-machine business after the 1933 election, but he never mentioned Adonis' name during his four-year term because of his financial and political support. This all changed the moment Adonis endorsed the opposition in the 1937 campaign. Mayor LaGuardia retaliated against Adonis in his Brooklyn speeches by suddenly calling his former supporter "a gangster and the leader of the underworld." Incumbent Republican politicians followed with frequent verbal assaults and facetious criminal charges that began the slide of Adonis' political and social standing in Brooklyn.

One year after Manhattan DA Dewey had framed Luciano to prison for life, DA Dewey arrested Adonis for assault and robbery in a truck hijacking of crude rubber. The victim appeared at Adonis' arraignment expecting to identify his assailant, but he was disappointed to tell the judge that he had never ever seen Adonis. If Adonis had really been a suspect, Dewey would have first put him in a lineup to verify for the jury the victim's ability to recognize his assailant. Instead, this false charge was brought in time for it to be added to Adonis' police record in Dewey's report to Governor Herbert Lehman about Tammany Hall Democratic leader Albert Marinelli and his criminal associates. DA Dewey then began an early gubernatorial campaign speech by accusing Adonis of being "Public Enemy Number 1 of Brooklyn" and "a gangster and the leader of the underworld."[281]

DA Dewey's ongoing public hostility drove Adonis to move his business operations west across the Hudson River to New Jersey, where he kept a lower profile. Adonis sold his interest in his upscale Pineapple Street restaurant, but he kept his Brooklyn home address. Adonis already owned the Automotive Conveying Company in Cliffside, New Jersey. It had an exclusive contract with America's dominant car company to transport all new cars, trucks, and parts from Ford's Edgewater, New Jersey plant to dealerships in many Northeastern states.

Three years later Mayor LaGuardia and DA Dewey escalated their attacks on Adonis' reputation with phony legal persecutions. The Mayor directed Commissioner of Investigation William Herlands to refuse to renew Adonis' three used-car-lot licenses because he had not submitted to be fingerprinted and checked. This was a false attack because the law required only the person making the application for a corporation to be fingerprinted. In addition to unlawfully revoking his three car-lot licenses, the dirty political duo had the Federal Alcohol Administration (FAA) initiate a formal complaint to determine if Adonis was a hidden owner of Thomas J. Molloy & Co. It was one of the largest wholesale liquor distributors in the U. S., but the FAA uncovered no such evidence.

If the illegal tactics Mayor LaGuardia and Manhattan DA Dewey used to harass and destroy Adonis' businesses were not offensive enough, these two Republicans decided to manipulate a legitimate investigation by Democratic Governor Lehman. He assigned John Harlan Amen as Special Prosecutor to supersede Brooklyn DA William Geoghan and make a proper inquiry into government corruption. Mayor LaGuardia and Manhattan DA Dewey wanted to deflect attention from their own misdeeds and to also further bully a political opposition supporter. Thus, the Mayor and DA influenced the Special Prosecutor to ignore the Governor's directive to inquire into political corruption and instead institute two bogus criminal charges against Adonis. As the election campaigns of Mayor LaGuardia and DA Dewey were gearing up, Amen prosecuted Adonis in the two following cases for kidnapping, extortion, and assault. It is amazing that Amen could keep a straight face before the juries with the bizarre gobbledygook he presented.

According to Special Prosecutor Amen, Isidore Juffe and Isidore Wapinsky had failed to pay money they owed Adonis, so he had them kidnapped and held until a ransom of $5,000 was paid on their behalf. Juffe was the only victim to testify to the event because the other alleged victim had died naturally of angina pectoris. Juffe claimed both he and Wapinsky were tortured, injured, and bloodied, but Prosecutor Amen had no corroborating evidence whatsoever that a kidnapping had even occurred. Neither of the two alleged victims had filed a police report, sought medical treatment, took photos of his abused body, or ever told a single person about such an incident. Juffe, who had a long arrest record and three felony convictions including swindling, had waited eight years after the alleged kidnappings supposedly occurred to make his first report to the NYPD. He was facing serious criminal charges, and he asked for immunity by offering to manufacture a case against major mobsters.

Make-believe victim Juffe's testimony exposed the blatant dishonesty, corruption, and hypocrisy of New York Mayor LaGuardia, Manhattan DA Dewey, and Special Prosecutor Amen by pursuing the case against Adonis. Juffe testified Albert Anastasia stood and watched him be beaten, and Juffe claimed he heard Adonis' voice talking to someone in another room but never saw him. Thus the case was much stronger against Anastasia because the defendant saw his face. In addition Anastasia was being vilified in the press at that time as a top leader of the frightening but imaginary Murder, Inc. as he hid out from pending murder charges. Yet Amen, LaGuardia, and Dewey gave a complete walk to the most dangerous, scary, and exploitive criminal of his time. Instead they went after the benign Adonis, who had only been involved with Prohibition smuggling and gambling, and was at that time solely involved in legitimate businesses and politics. Anastasia was given a pass from prosecution because he contributed to their campaigns and his club gave them political support.

Adonis' real crime was that had dared to support the workingman's concerns against the interests of the wealthy and their Republican political machine. This was at the time when Brooklyn Assistant DA Turkus, under the guidance of Dewey, was fabricating the testimony in the three Murder, Inc. trials. Thus, DA Dewey instructed Prosecutor Amen how to have alleged-victim Juffe interject some of the Murder, Inc. fiction into his prepared testimony. Then Juffe added a new wrinkle to the case by telling the jury his abductors had dragged him before an underworld three-judge "kangaroo court." Of course, nothing like his conjured-up court ever existed in crimedom. Adonis' defense attorney correctly charged in his opening address to the jury that alleged-victim Juffe accused Adonis "because it would please Mayor LaGuardia" and get him a pass for his serious crimes which were all too real.[282]

The jury acquitted Adonis and alleged accomplice Sam Gasberg from the bogus kidnapping charges, but the jury could not agree on the equally fallacious extortion and assault charges. Amen first retried Gasberg on these two charges, but the moment Amen concluded presenting his frivolous case, the judge acquitted him for lack of evidence. With the flimsiness of his case exposed, six days later Amen withdrew the extortion and assault charges against Adonis.[283]

In the kidnapping trial, alleged-victim Juffe testified that he did not complain to the police about the kidnapping for eight years after it supposedly occurred because "I would have been bumped off." However, Juffe clearly had no fear even after lying to frame Adonis for kidnappings and extortions that never happened, because after the trial the "victim" opened a small restaurant in Adonis' Brooklyn neighborhood. Juffe hosted his dinner guests nightly, which made him an easy target for revenge, but he ran his restaurant un-pestered until he died naturally of a heart attack.[284]

Despite enduring five years of prosecutorial and media persecution by the three Republican officials – New York Mayor LaGuardia, Manhattan DA Dewey, and Brooklyn Special Prosecutor Amen – Adonis proudly joined Meyer Lansky early in World War II to lead the implementation of Charlie Luciano's counterespionage and invasion strategies for Naval Intelligence to protect and defend his beloved adopted homeland.

BEN MARDEN'S *RIVIERA*, & WILLIE MORETTI IN NEW JERSEY

Major wide-open illegal casinos were typically located in a small town near a large city that was separated by a county line or state border. The local residents condoned these illegal casinos because they produced good-paying jobs, business for local vendors, large charitable donations, and augmented income for the police and politicians without increased taxation.

One of the country's most famous was Ben Marden's *Riviera*. He advertised in New York newspapers that his nightclub was "Just across the George Washington Bridge, 15 minutes from B'way (Broadway)." It sat at the cliff edge of the Palisades in Fort Lee, New Jersey. The *Riviera's* windows commanded a magnificent view of the necklace of lights along the Bridge and the entire length of Upper West Manhattan one mile distant.

Marden opened his original *Riviera* building early in the Depression, but it burned to the ground on Thanksgiving Day four years later. It took eight months for him to reopen his swank new building as an 800-seat nightclub, featuring the top saloon entertainers and fine food. The *New York*

Times described the structure: "Built on the brink of the Palisades overlooking the Hudson River, the resort features a huge circular room enclosed entirely by glass windows which may be lowered, and is covered by a domed roof which may be drawn back to expose the entire room to the open air."[285]

Above all, the *Riviera* was known for its gambling. The casino's limousines and a succession of cabs shuttled players back and forth across the bridge from a reserved stop on Broadway. Table games were featured on the second floor in the Marine Room. The players' games of choice in that era, in order, were craps, roulette, and chemin-de-fer. Guards at the bottom of the stairs allowed only known players to walk up, restricting every one else to the dining and entertainment rooms. The guards specifically turned away the town's local residents to avoid them becoming resentful over gambling losses at the tables.

Ben Marden's *Riviera* was the forerunner of a series of casinos on the New Jersey side of the George Washington Bridge. A key figure in this gambling proliferation was Guarino "Willie" Moretti, born in New York in 1894. The humorous, wisecracking Moretti later charmed the Kefauver Committee, as he answered all their questions while telling them nothing of substance. For a time he was a featherweight prizefighter weighing between 97 and 121 pounds. He explained that he was convicted of second-degree assault at age 19 and was sentenced to five years at Elmira Reformatory, but he was paroled after one year for "exemplary behavior." Upon release the NYPD picked him up twice on harassment charges, so he moved to Philadelphia, where he was arrested seven more times but never jailed. From that time on, most of his income came from gambling, mostly at horses, but also prizefights and crap games. To Chairman Kefauver's question about his horse system, he explained, "Bet 'em to place and show. You've got three ways of winning. Come out to the track some time, and I'll show you."[286]

Moretti married and settled in East Paterson, N. J. He joined a local Prohibition ring, and then he became a gambler, which was the chief source of income listed on his yearly tax returns. He was politically active, establishing close associations with New Jersey police officials, prosecutors, and politicians in Bergen, Passaic, and Essex Counties. His reply to Senator Kefauver's question about his political power in New Jersey was, "Everybody thinks I have (power)." He explained his wide acquaintanceship included several officials, but "I am bipartisan. I don't belong to any party."[287]

Moretti would later establish a politically-friendly gambling beachhead for Luciano and the Young Turks on the New Jersey side of the New York border. Moretti was close friends with Luciano, Costello, Adonis, bookmaker Frank Erickson, and Vito Genovese from his teenage years. These relationships never waned. Costello was best man at Willie's wedding, and Costello and Adonis were each godfathers to one of his three daughters. Moretti visited Luciano in prison to assist in the World War II effort, and Moretti later visited his exiled "intimate friend" in Havana to commiserate. To Senator Kefauver's question as to how he knew so many hoods, Moretti answered, "People of character don't need introductions. They know each other automatically." Moretti testified that he never owned a gambling game nor shared in financing one. But Willie's brother Salvatore, known as "Solly," would become a partner in casinos, mostly with Adonis. Willie's role was clearly larger than he stated.[288]

The burgeoning New Jersey illicit gambling industry erupted into political scandal late in World War II. State Attorney General Walter Van Riper was running for governor on a reform crusade platform, and he directed raids against casinos in Union City, and then indicted a local police captain and a patrolman. Their defense attorney sent letters to the AG and Governor Walter Edge, both Republicans, claiming this was the height of hypocrisy because they only raided casinos in Hudson County which had a high Democratic voter registration. No raids were conducted in Republican Counties even though he listed the addresses of 18 illegal casinos in Bergen, 13 in Passaic, and 12 in Atlantic. The letter was copied to newspapers, so the AG ordered the three county prosecutors to immediately investigate, but all reported visiting these sites to find little or no gambling going on. The defense attorney's letter stated that Adonis and Costello, both targets of New York City Mayor LaGuardia, were "in command" of the dice games and horserace wagering in Bergen County. The AG charged that the pair had operated one of the nation's largest casinos in Cliffside until forced to close two months earlier. Adonis and Frank Erickson, who was Costello's bookmaking partner, had indeed moved their gambling headquarters to Bergen County on the other side of the George Washington Bridge to avoid the harassment of New York Mayor LaGuardia.[289]

FRANK ERICKSON: FROM NEW YORK TO NEW JERSEY

Norwegian-Irish Bookmaker Frank Erickson was born in New York in 1895. He admitted dropping out of school "about the fourth grade." It was popularly believed, but impossible to confirm, that he was committed to an orphanage where he met a girl who later became his life-long wife. During his teens he worked as a busboy in Feltman's restaurant at Coney Island, but by the age of 20 he moved on to small-time bookmaking. He developed a close friendship with Frank Costello, who shared his passion for gambling on the ponies and sports.

Costello made a good living by taking big wagers at racetracks from bettors who did not want to lower the pari-mutuel odds by betting at track windows. He then placed the same bets with bookies who took a 5% commission. Later, when the McFarland U.S. Senate Subcommittee asked him how Congress could stop bookies, he smiled and testified, "Stop horseracing. … You can't operate unless you get the green light from somewhere."[290]

Very early in the Roaring '20s, Costello branched out from the local betters and paying the commission bookies by partnering with Frank Erickson as the bookmaker. Costello supplied a large bankroll, contacts with big-time bettors in both the under and overworlds, and protection with politicians and the police. Erickson capitalized on this opportunity to become one of America's premier bookmakers. Several legislative investigations and criminal trials publicly scrutinized Erickson's bookmaking operations. Major bookies in that era only handled horseraces, which were by far the most popular form of gambling in America, but Erickson also took prizefight, baseball, basketball, and hockey wagers by telephone from big bettors in all 48 states.

Erickson's chief business was as a *layoff*, or *commission*, bookmaker. He took large bets from bookmakers, when they were overloaded with wagers on one horse compared with the other horses in a race. These bookies reduced their vulnerability in case such a horse won by passing off the excess amount, known as their *exposure*, to one or more layoff bookies, making them in effect bookies' bookies. The press crowned Erickson the biggest of the nearly two dozen commission bookmakers in the country because prosecutors had hyped up his image to demonstrate they were going after a master criminal. In reality bookmakers did not know the size of each others' secretive businesses, and law enforcement knew much less. It was clear Erickson was very successful. He wore expensive clothes, but he was not physically impressive. He was short, plump, and balding, and he was known for his blank expression.

Costello did not get involved in Erickson's bookmaking operation. He was known as a silent partner, but Costello was certainly not a secret partner. Their association was well known, and this would cause serious problems for Erickson after LaGuardia became Mayor in 1934. The vengeful LaGuardia made Costello the first target of his tough-on-crime crusade because he had supported the opposition candidate. After LaGuardia very publicly smashed Costello's slot machines and dumped them in the river, the Mayor continued to focus his wrath upon Costello by making his bookmaking friend Erickson the principal target of his anti-crime rhetoric for the remainder of his first term.

Two years into Republican LaGuardia's vendetta, he turned his fury into action when a political scandal swirled around Democratic Brooklyn DA William F. X. Geoghan. LaGuardia's diatribes distracted public attention away from the DA's serious failure to prosecute criminals and dishonest public officials into a focus on possible political corruption involving the DA's close social relationship with bookmaker Erickson. The mounting clamor forced Governor Lehman to hold a public hearing against a fellow Democrat, but the Governor blatantly sidestepped the overwhelming evidence of DA Geoghan's personal relationship with the bookmaker by untruthfully ruling that his transgressions were not serious.

Three years later a scandal erupted over DA Geoghan's selection of his close friend NYPD Lieutenant Detective Martin Cannon to be chief of the DA Office's investigators. In Mayor LaGuardia's continuing campaign against Erickson, he let go with a rambling public harangue. The Mayor bellowed, "I personally had ordered the police to keep an eye on this man Erickson, a notorious gambler whom we do not want in this city. ... I think it has been established [that Detective Cannon], assigned to the District Attorney, has been gambling with Erickson, a man I ordered arrested by the police every time he enters the city. ... I'll see that Adonis, [slot operator] Byk and Erickson give Brooklyn a wide berth – the dead line for all three of them is the boundary line of the City of New York. I don't care who their friends are." By this time Adonis had also fallen into disfavor with the Mayor for switching his support to the opposition candidate. The evidence that was developed against NYPD official Cannon was conclusive. The Police Commissioner suspended him, and the Herlands Report to the Mayor recommended he be fired. Then Mayor LaGuardia, whose political career was based on his frequent tough-on-crime rhetoric, inexplicably instituted no disciplinary action against Cannon, who later retired in good standing and drew a full pension.[291]

After this the Governor was forced to supersede Brooklyn DA Geoghan twice with a special prosecutor because of scandals over his failure to properly handle major cases including murder. The finale to the DA's nine-year reign came when the Brooklyn Democratic organization turned him down for endorsement in December 1939 and instead selected Judge Bill O'Dwyer for this position. As we have already seen, O'Dwyer brought his friends into the DA's office and their actions were far more atrocious than Geoghan's. O'Dwyer was the patron arch friend who protected Albert Anastasia's vicious dock extortions and violence, and who directed the murder of prosecution witness Reles. This is a painful example of the old saying, "Don't ever think things are so bad they can't get worse."

During Lieutenant Detective Cannon's scandal, the Police Commissioner discovered that Erickson obtained a police pistol permit and renewed it five years later. He immediately sent detectives to Erickson's expensive Forest Hills, Queens home to confiscate the weapon and the permit. In response Erickson voluntarily appeared in Commissioner of Investigation Herlands' office to find out why the Mayor wanted to chase him out of town. At that moment, newspapermen were reminding Mayor LaGuardia that he had threatened three days before to have Erickson arrested on sight as soon as he appeared in New York. The bombastic-talking Mayor weakly tried to cover up his bluffed threat by saying, "Erickson appeared voluntarily without being summoned." So, one reporter asked, "Why didn't you stop him from returning from Florida?" The Mayor snapped: "I think he ought to go back to Florida. We don't want that bum here at all, and we don't want other punks like him here either."[292]

A month later Erickson again voluntarily surrendered in Queens County to be arraigned on a perjury charge for having stated on both pistol-permit applications that he had never been arrested. In reality he had been arrested for bookmaking five times during Prohibition, and he had been convicted once but received a suspended sentence. Erickson told Commissioner Herlands that he needed the pistol because his brother-in-law had been kidnapped, and he had received kidnapping threats, but he had never reported these serous crimes to the police.[293]

In addition to the perjury charge, the pompous and hypocritical LaGuardia had ordered the Police Commissioner to also arrest Erickson for vagrancy because he had no visible occupation and appeared to maintain himself only by gambling. In grandiose style the Mayor had announced to the media, "Public officials are of just two kinds; those who want to put punks, tin horns, gangsters, and pimps in jail and to keep them out of the city. That is the kind I am. The other kind are those who want to keep them out of jail and in the city. … Erickson is no good and we don't want him around." As usual, LaGuardia's hyperbole went for naught, as the newspapers reported that an indignant Erickson dumped $125,000 worth of securities on the Judge's bench, forcing him to dismiss the silly vagrancy charge.[294]

A month after the dismissal of the vagrancy charge, Erickson went on trail for pistol-application perjury and faced a maximum of 15 years. However, the notary publics who handled the two pistol-permit applications testified they could not remember whether they had formally sworn Erickson. The judge immediately directed acquittal for lack of any evidence, and then he criticized Mayor LaGuardia for bringing the vacuous case to court. The judge told the Assistant DA prosecuting the case, "This is not your fault if someone in a fit of excitement wants to throw matters such as this into court. I am not going to let this case go to the Appellate Division and get scolded for incompetency because I am afraid of someone. You cannot guess a man into prison."[295]

DA Dewey later wrote about the leadership style of his law-and-order ally Mayor LaGuardia. "He was petulant, and sometimes he was cruel. … LaGuardia was explosive and unpredictable. He concentrated all attention on himself. He could be utterly irresponsible in his statements and indulge in demagoguery of the most unbelievable character." This was the best Dewey could say about his crony LaGuardia despite saying they had a "very important political relationship." Yet LaGuardia's name is honored to this day at the nation's most important international airport in New York City despite a career of trashing Constitutional rights, subverting justice for all, and crushing the freedom to politically disagree that are such important components of democracy.[296]

In the middle of Prohibition, Erickson moved his bookmaking operation into a swank Broadway office. Seven years later he moved the "wire room" in which operators took telephone bets to Bergen County, New Jersey. This was shortly after LaGuardia took office and went after Erickson's pal Costello's slot machines. Erickson continued to collect from losers and pay off winners from his Times Square headquarters until LaGuardia went after him for gun-permit perjury, and he also moved that office across the George Washington Bridge. The Mayor's apparent victory forcing Erickson to move backfired because he continued to be the favorite bookie of New Yorkers, but he now was safely ensconced away from the prosecutorial authority of LaGuardia's city and state law enforcers.[297]

Erickson had other problems at the same time these prosecutors and politicians were hounding him. One day he went to the New York Athletic Club for a meeting with some associates. They were talking in a private room, when three gunmen burst in to rob the bookie of the $100,000 he was reportedly carrying. An unbelievably brave chambermaid changed this dynamic. She instinctively hit one man who reacted by knocking her down, and as she laid beneath this monster she let loose with blood curdling screams. Her hysterical volume made the men flee. In the escape one of the would-be robbers was trapped and killed himself. The other two were captured and sent to prison. This little woman single-handedly thwarted the robbery attempt. The *New York Times* reported, "It was said that Erickson gave the chambermaid a $1,000 reward and arranged for her to receive $25 a month for the rest of her life ($365 in today's dollars)."[298]

Erickson's other business interests included a partnership in the Club Boheme casino in Hollywood, Florida with Lansky's group, and an investment in a Manhattan nightclub. Erickson and several partners ran a lottery through the mail but stopped operating it after the U.S. Postmaster General started investigating their illegal business. The only good thing that could be said about it was that it was not rigged and paid fairly. Erickson invested $250,000 in Miami's Tropical Park Racetrack that was arranged by Chicago gang member John Patton, Sr. The pair sold their interests six years later, and then Erickson financed his Miami attorney Abe Allenberg in the operation of the Wofford Hotel. The new partnership included Mafiosi Anthony "Little Angie Pisano" Carfano of New York and "Johnny King" Angersola of Cleveland, so the Wofford Hotel became the winter vacation spot and meeting place for notorious underworld figures from the Northeast and Midwest states. The Wofford also became the headquarters for Erickson's extensive illegal bookmaking operations inside Florida's racetracks and at three Miami Beach resort hotels - the Roney Plaza, Boca Raton, and Hollywood Beach. Erickson's agents took bets directly from customers at the tracks and from guests enjoying the three resorts' beaches, and then the agents telephoned them into his headquarters at the Wofford. Erickson used the hotel's banking system to cash players' checks and to transmit to his New Jersey offices the money won from the players' losing horserace wagers.[299]

THE MORETTIS WORKED FOR ERICKSON & ADONIS

When Erickson moved his telephone bookmaking operation to New Jersey, he reached out to the top local bookies for contacts and legal protection. Brothers Willie and Salvatore "Solly" Moretti had contracted with at least one worker in every major Bergen County factory to book the other employees' bets for them. Erickson incorporated the brothers' booking operation and paid them to handle the support services for his national operation. They chose the locations, arranged deals for telephone wire rooms, and handled legal protection with the local police, prosecutors, and key politicians. Five hundred Bergen County homeowners and shopkeepers rented their telephones to bookies for use a few hours each day, according to testimony by the New Jersey Bell Telephone Company attorney in a bookmaking case. He said his company had disconnected 1,077 telephones in the county during the previous two years because of suspected bookmaking activities, almost all of it on the company's volition rather than orders from law enforcement.

Erickson became the consummate bookie in Bergen County, and Joe Adonis soon became the County's leading casino operator. When New York City Mayor LaGuardia and Manhattan DA Dewey began their scornful and strident radio and press tirades and prosecutorial harassment against Adonis during the 1937 election, he slipped into obscurity in Manhattan. He likely opened his first New Jersey casino the next year, but later legislative and prosecution investigations only uncovered casino records back to 1944, so Adonis always maintained he began his illegal operations then. That was the year Adonis sold his fine Brooklyn home and moved his wife and four children into a mansion in Fort Lee, New Jersey high on the Palisades, towering 300 feet above the Hudson River.

Bergen County's two big gambling operators were closely tied to Frank Costello. He was Erickson's bookmaking partner, and he was also Adonis' political ally and gang leader. Thus, it was natural for Adonis and Erickson to cooperate, especially since they were in different types of gambling, so they were not competitive. Adonis and Erickson shared the Moretti brothers' management services and their political and law-enforcement protection contacts. In addition, Solly Moretti was one of Adonis' five partners in his New Jersey casino operations.

Ben Marden closed his *Riviera* casino late in World War II. It was an unusual illegal operation for that era because the building was situated in a conspicuous location, and the nightclub's big-name entertainers were widely advertised. In contrast, when Adonis succeeded Marden as Bergen County's top casino operator, Adonis had Willie and Solly Moretti select isolated locations for casinos, and he promoted them only through word of mouth between serious players. Adonis specialized in high-stakes, or *carpet,* casinos that were plushy decorated in rambling old mansions. The Morettis picked abandoned or rundown estates that were secluded far off main roads with no neighbors who might object to bright car lights and slamming doors waking their families throughout the night. In contrast, Adonis' low-limit joints, known for the *sawdust* on the floor, were typically placed in old garages, barns, and factories distant from residential neighborhoods so as also not to disturb anybody.

These remote locations were always within city limits, so state troopers could not conduct a raid without first obtaining a court order through the local police department. Whenever the state submitted an application for a court order to the local police, they gave advanced warning to the operators. During the 1940s, casinos operated in 18 little municipalities in Bergen County that were within a few minutes of the New Jersey side of the George Washington Bridge.

These casinos depended primarily on regular players who lived in New York City, but Adonis' casinos also paid commissions to bellmen, bartenders, and front-desk clerks in the better New York City hotels for steering wealthy room guests. His casinos offered free chauffeur-driven Cadillac-limousine service from midtown Manhattan hotels and nightspots and from the homes of the bigger players. The drivers, known as *luggers,* and the steady stream of cabbies, always turned off their lights, when they got within a football field or so of the casino's doorway. After dropping off their passengers, they parked away from the mansion in the darkness awaiting a flashlight signal to pick up waiting players. At about 9 p.m. every night the casino started to get busy, and the action continued until a little before the break of dawn, when the remaining waiting vehicles pulled out. The whole day the isolated old mansion sat abandoned and quiet, but after darkness set in, it magically came alive again filled with activity and excitement. This procedure allowed the players to testify honestly before the Kefauver Committee and other investigative bodies that they never knew what building they had visited because they always approached and left in darkness. Dealers swore they never knew who the owners were because only the game supervisors gave them orders.

Upon arriving at Adonis' finest carpet casino, extremely polite guards carefully frisked both the men and women for possible weapons. They vigilantly protected the players because a robbery or any violence would destroy a place's reputation with its cash-carrying clientele. Patrons were then ushered into the luxuriously appointed dining room, supervised by a sophisticated maitre d'hotel. Beyond the dining room was the gaming room. Players said they were never concerned about being arrested in these illicit casinos. Just like the NYPD, the local police ignored the gamblers except when politicians cried for reform to energize an upcoming election campaign.

Despite national gas and tire rationing during World War II, the limousines and cabs rolled every night and kept the casinos busy. Even though meat, sugar, and butter were restricted and in short supply, Adonis' carpet casinos offered players free of charge the best steak dinners, choice liquors, rare wines, rich desserts, and faultless service in elegant surroundings.

Adonis also had a sawdust joint two miles from the George Washington Bridge. It was in the township of Palisades near the Palisades Amusement Park, which is now the Six Flags Great Adventure. The large joint had more than twice the tables of Adonis' carpet casinos, and it was jammed by men only. It offered these smaller bettors the same free amenities but with less costly products. Food and beverage was available in a lunch bar. A fleet of sixteen less-expensive limousines transported players from a midtown Manhattan parking lot. Two *dispatchers* screened would-be players before loading them into a vehicle to be taken directly to the games. As an aside, on Palisades Avenue opposite Palisades Park, memorialized in Freddy Cannon's 1962 hit single *Palisades Park*, was Duke's Tavern where the gambling operators met socially.

Adonis' main operation was *Costa's Barn* in Lodi, which was the largest and most famous in the state. He later testified that it was "a plush spot" for several years until a New York gambling investigation "got hot." Then he converted it into a "sawdust place," so it could be closed down quickly. In its heyday, its exterior looked like a garage, but players described its interior as "plush, comfortable, and solid."[300]

An FBI evaluation concluded, "Various accounts in New York City newspapers during the year 1944, reported that Costello and Joe Adonis, the well-known racketeer, ran the 'Big Hall,' a gambling establishment in Cliffside Park, New Jersey, until the day before it was raided by representatives from the Bergen County, New Jersey Prosecutor's Office, and that the night before the raid, the paraphernalia was moved, indicating a 'tip off' had been given in advance of the raid. It was further alleged that Costello and Adonis make Bergen County Headquarters for their gambling activities."[301]

The financial and bank records for Adonis' Bergen County casinos during the late 1940s were presented in the Kefauver Committee's Report. It noted that the casinos listed maximum profits of $250,000 a year for income tax purposes, but they banked $1 million in checks a month in New York City alone, so it was obvious that the profits must have run to millions of dollars a year (when the dollar was worth nine times more than it is today). The Committee's analysis did not consider that the unreported cash take was much larger than the checks they deposited. The cashier who deposited the checks at the bank daily also exchanged many thousands of dollars in old $50 and $100 bills for crisp new ones to snappily pay off to winners that evening.

While Adonis was operating in New Jersey, he was an investor in several high-limit elegant casinos operated by his former rumrunning partner Meyer Lansky. Adonis invested in the Piping Rock and Arrowhead in Saratoga Springs, New York, and the Colonial Inn, Club Boheme, and Green Acres Club in Hollywood, Florida. The books showed Adonis had 15% interest in Lansky's Colonial Inn nightclub and casino in Dade County, Florida, and Erickson held 5%, probably fronting part of it for Costello. Adonis also was a partner with Costello and Lansky in an early television-supply business.

The casino operations of Adonis and the other gamblers were a financial benefit to the small New Jersey cities where they were located, so voters defeated reform candidates and ignored the objections by newspapers in other counties. The locals also disregarded complaints by New York reformers about the safe haven that Bergen County offered for illegal gambling less than a mile from their city. But the Kefauver Committee exposed the nature of the county's casinos to national scrutiny during its August 1950 hearings. It announced that New Jersey gamblers operated with impunity, particularly in Bergen County. This compelled New Jersey and New York authorities to take action. Anticipating the developing reform movement, Adonis closed his casinos in early 1950.

ERICKSON HELPED THE GOVERNMENT - OOPS!

Erickson moved his bookmaking headquarters to Bergen County to sidestep Mayor LaGuardia's harassment. This allowed him to operate undisturbed for 16 years until he became enmeshed in a new round of political and legal problems because of the U.S. Senate Interstate Commerce Subcommittee under Senator McFarland. It was studying a bill to forbid the interstate transmission of information about the horses in a race just prior to its start. The bill was intended to deny important wagering information to bookmakers and handicappers (bettors) at off-track locations.

Erickson appeared before the Committee, and he should have invoked the Fifth Amendment for his own protection. Instead he testified frankly as an expert and a public-spirited citizen to assist the government in writing an effective law. Erickson established his expertise by readily admitting that he had engaged in illegal bookmaking on a nationwide scale for three decades, and that he made more than $100,000 annually. He acknowledged paying his brother $20,000 a year ($180,000 now) just to carry the cash to the banks. The New York papers printed his income testimony, and five days after he testified, Manhattan DA Frank Hogan ordered NYPD detectives assigned to his office to seize the gambling records in Erickson's Park Avenue office. Detectives confiscated a truckload of his business records covering the previous 15 years that exposed some of his other gambling activities. For example, his 1949 tax return listed partnerships in two Dade County, Florida casinos. One was in the Boca Raton casino, and the other was with Meyer Lansky's group in the *Colonial*

Inn. Frank Costello's name did not appear in any of Erickson's gambling business records, not even in his large bookmaking enterprise. Just as Erickson fronted for his pal Costello's interest in their bookmaking partnership, Erickson likely fronted for Costello's share in the casinos. Erickson did make Costello a partner in five profitable oil leases in Texas and Oklahoma, and he also loaned Costello $50,000 as the down payment to buy three buildings in Manhattan's financial district.

The contents of the business papers seized by the Manhattan DA tweaked the interest of U.S. Senate Subcommittee Chairman McFarland, who asked the U.S. Attorney to determine whether Erickson committed perjury. In his testimony Erickson had not indicated a close business relationship with Costello, and Erickson denied any interest in a gambling casino.

Five days later Manhattan DA Hogan indicted Erickson on 60 counts of bookmaking. He pled innocent, but DA Hogan alleged that Erickson, Adonis, and Costello made up the "big three" of gambling in the U.S. Eighteen days after being charged, Erickson pled guilty to the 60 counts of bookmaking. This was just seven weeks after he testified before the McFarland Committee studying racing-information dissemination.

The three-judge panel sentenced Erickson to two years and suspended three more years "on condition that Erickson never engage in bookmaking or in gambling again." This condition prohibited him from bookmaking for at least five years unless he wanted to risk serving the entire five-year sentence. Erickson was the first top bookie who had ever been convicted in New York. The bosses of bookmaking operations had always been insulated from the law by their collectors and runners, who were paid to take their arrests and serve their sentences. This was the first time financial records were used to convict a bookmaker by having the betting clients, who could be identified from the records, ready to testify at the trial. Erickson had 10 previous arrests, all for bookmaking or vagrancy, but none had led to any jail time.

While Erickson was in prison, the U.S. Senate Kefauver Committee subpoenaed him to testify. At the hearing, his attorney first explained his client's legal dilemma by reading the following statement on his behalf. "I am presently serving a jail sentence in connection with bookmaking charges in the State of New York; I am under other charges in the State of New Jersey; the Federal Government has filed income tax fraud charges against me going back many years. My name has also been included in publicity emanating from this Committee and referring to alleged nationwide racketeering syndicates. In view of these facts, I feel called upon for my own protection to refuse to answer any questions concerning my activities, since I have every reason to apprehend that any information given by me will be used against me in support of criminal charges, both of a federal and of a local nature."

Having learned his lesson with the McFarland Committee, Erickson refused to testify about his business, criminal record, or background, except to tell the Kefauver Committee, "My business? I have no business. I am in jail." He did admit to being a member of the National Democratic Club, but he denied ever making a political contribution or taking an active part in any political campaign. He did not mention that politics were his partner Costello's domain. Erickson was returned to the New York prison, and the U. S. Senate proceeded to indict him for contempt by refusing to answer questions. Two-and-a-half years later, the federal government dropped the pending 74-count contempt indictment, because the U.S. Attorney explained that recent U.S. Supreme Court decisions "broadened the scope of the privilege against self incrimination under the Fifth Amendment accorded to witnesses appearing before Congressional committees. Under these decisions, the courts have generally found that the very nature of the hearings conducted by the Kefauver Committee, which was a special committee to investigate crime, was such as to create a setting adverse to the witness."[302]

Because of good behavior Erickson served the minimum 16 months for bookmaking, but as he walked through New York's Rikers Island jail gates to freedom, New Jersey officials were waiting to handcuff and escort him to Bergen County on another bookmaking charge. Erickson pled no defense to a charge of operating a telephone-betting network and served almost 11 months of a 12-to-14-month term in New Jersey State Prison. The charges piled up. Two months later he was given a 6-month sentence for evading $146,000 in federal income taxes in 1945 and 1946. Erickson was also hit heavily for payment of U.S. and New York State back income taxes.

While Erickson was in federal prison, New York's Moreland Act Commission opened public hearings on the state's scandal-ridden raceways. The investigations found that politicians, and persons with underworld backgrounds or friendships, had been hidden owners of close to a million dollar's worth of stock in several New York harness racing tracks. Among those who were found to have secretly struck it rich on the trotting tracks were Erickson's son and son-in-law, Irving Sherman, who was a close friend of Costello and a political intimate of former Mayor Bill O'Dwyer, and several Republican political leaders and close associates of Governor Dewey. The tracks were required to purchase the interests of these people.

After Erickson's string of imprisonments and scandals, he sought respectability and took to describing himself as a real-estate dealer, as did his friend Costello. Erickson maintained a real-estate office on Park Avenue. He was about to undergo surgery for bleeding ulcers when his heart stopped. Erickson died at age 72.[303]

EVERYTHING UNRAVELED FOR ADONIS

For a decade Adonis kept a low profile while he operated illegal casinos in Bergen County. Then he was suddenly thrust back into the headlines when it was reported that he was a victim in a get-quick-rich scheme. He was swindled out of a $105,000 investment. This fraud came to light because a U.S. Senator, Postmaster General Jess Donaldson, and a U.S. Attorney brought the wrongdoing of a government official to light in embarrassing detail during refreshingly candid press conferences.

The culprit was Harold Ambrose, who was Public Relations Assistant to the Postmaster General. He was a postal employee for 15 years before he ran into financial difficulties and concocted a pyramid scam. Ambrose contacted individuals, most prominently-known gamblers, and offered them an investment opportunity to combine their money with his high-ranking position to corner the market on scarce commemorative U. S. stamps by causing a shortage and driving up collectors' prices. He created fraudulent catalogues that listed allegedly rare stamps at inflated prices, when these stamps were actually offered for sale by post offices at face value to collectors. Ambrose used the money of the first investors to buy a few scarce stamps to show potential investors he possessed them. Then he paid the original investors a tidy profit with the money from those who followed. His pyramid scheme collapsed when he could not get enough new investors to keep making payments to existing investors. The last speculators, including Adonis, lost their investments.

Ambrose had gotten into this position because early in the Great Depression he had married the niece of Wyoming Democratic Senator Joe O'Mahoney. Work was scarce so the Senator arranged a low-level Post Office Department job for his nephew. Over the years Ambrose rose through the hierarchy to his high-ranking position. When Ambrose's wife learned about her husband's troubles, she went to her uncle, and the Senator told his niece that her husband had to come clean with the Postmaster General. He immediately fired him and began a criminal investigation. Ambrose pled guilty to fraud and served the minimum of a 2- to 7-year prison term.[304]

The newspaper articles about Ambrose's case falsely implied that Adonis was somehow involved with the fraud. In reality he had violated no law and was a victim who was swindled out of $900,000 in today's money. However, Adonis never threatened Ambrose to get his money back and even refused to testify against the thief before the Federal Grand Jury. Adonis stood silent because of his gang's opposition to violence and vendetta, and because of a popular attitude that remained prevalent in the Las Vegas gambling fraternity until the 1980s: "If you are going to be a sucker, at least be a quiet one." Whining was considered demeaning.

Two years after Adonis was swindled, the Kefauver Committee publicity about his illegal casino operations forced him to close them, and it also hurt his legitimate business interests. The Committee's hearings in Detroit focused on Ford Motor Company's large work-release program for serious felons exiting prison. Ford executives claimed that this was an important social rehabilitation plan for ex-convicts in order to reduce gang killings, and to assure the company protection from outside gang pressure. Other witnesses countered that these hard-core gangsters were employed solely to threaten and to violently attack company employees who wanted to improve their working conditions by legally unionizing and striking.

This convict-work-release program was so important to Henry Ford that he made the man who ran it - Personnel Director Harry Bennett - the most powerful official in the company. Bennett was known as Ford's *strong man,* but he later indignantly denied to the Kefauver Committee that his so-called *trouble squads* were dangerous thugs. He testified, "The newspapers might call them hoodlums, but I don't." Bennett's star example was Chester La Mare, a felon who was paroled into the custody of the Ford Motor Company and given a half-interest in the fruit concession at the Dearborn plant. His parole was arranged through the U. S. Secret Service, after the previous fruit concessionaire had been shot. Bennett testified, "Chet didn't know a banana from an orange, but we wanted the people to stop being shot for delivering us fruit." The success of Ford's experiment was somewhat blemished early in La Mare's new fruit-business career, when Castellammarese gangsters murdered the high-ranking Mafioso in his home during the national Sicilian gang war. Bennett was replaced upon Ford's death as soon as Ford's grandson, Henry Ford II, became president.[305]

Adonis benefited from Henry Ford's penchant for hiring hoods. Adonis was a major shareholder in Automotive Conveying Company, which hauled all cars, trucks, and parts from the Ford assembly plant at Edgewater, New Jersey to many Northeastern states for 13 years prior to the hearings. Bennett denied to the Kefauver Committee any knowledge of Adonis' involvement, despite his successor's testimony that Bennett had negotiated the contract with Adonis. The company issued statements of surprise and dismay that Adonis was a major shareholder in a company that held an exclusive contract, even though the *New York Post* had revealed this relationship a decade earlier. Ford Motor Company then requested the Interstate Commerce Commission hold a hearing to drop the exclusive services of Automotive Conveying Company. This pressure led four months later to the company reporting by telegram to the Kefauver Committee that Adonis had sold all his stock in the conveying company. Everybody seemed content with the transportation company's cleaned-up image, until the purchaser, Charles Chiri, was arrested six years later at the national meeting of America's Mafia leaders in Apalachin, New York.[306]

During this period, criminal charges piled up against Adonis. Manhattan DA Hogan was the first by charging Adonis, Solly Moretti, and three associates with two misdemeanor gambling counts. They were accused of the crime of *persuading* for having transported New Yorkers to gamble at a New Jersey casino. Manhattan DA Hogan said several law-enforcement agencies agreed with his view that the Adonis group "for more than a decade have operated a chain of the largest and most active gambling houses east of the Mississippi River." These charges about activities in New Jersey had no basis under New York law, but it is unclear whether it was the DA or the Judge who finally dropped them.[307]

Two and a half months after the charge in Manhattan, a Special Bergen County Grand Jury indicted Adonis and four associates for operating three gambling houses. At the opening of their trial, the five partners pleaded *non vult*, or no defense. New Jersey Attorney General Theodore Parsons recommended a minimum sentence of 18 months for Adonis' first prison term. The judge said he accepted the plea bargain, but then he imposed a longer sentence of two to three years. A shocked Adonis stood silently, but his face reddened, as he realized the State Attorney General had lied to him by giving the judge different instructions than in their plea deal. Even so, the *New York World-Telegram* still referred to the good-natured Mr. A. as "the laughing boy of the underworld."[308]

Shortly after Adonis entered Trenton State Prison on the gambling charges, he was indicted for contempt of the U. S. Senate by refusing to answer Kefauver Committee questions about several issues including his campaign contributions. The press noted that Adonis was the best-dressed man at the trial despite having to dress and groom himself in his cramped prison cell. Both sides conceded all relevant facts, and Adonis accepted a trial by judge to hear the debate over the legal points. The Federal Judge dismissed 15 of the 16 counts and sentenced him to three months in prison on the final count for refusing to testify about his political contributions because "It is not a crime generally to make a campaign contribution." His federal contempt sentence was to begin as soon as he was released from state prison on gambling charges.[309]

But four months later the U. S. Court of Appeals acquitted Adonis on that single count. It applied the U.S. Supreme Court's principle of the right to refuse self-incrimination with the descriptive words "the chase" had gotten "too hot" and "the scent, too fresh." "The Kefauver Committee had committed itself to trying to discover a tie-up between organized crime and politics and government; and Adonis had been coupled with Frank Costello as ring-leaders of such crimes. The Committee's objective, together with its characterization of Adonis, was reiterated in various public statements." The Court ruled that admission by Adonis of making political contributions would have proven half the crime, and all that would have been needed for conviction was to identify the purpose of the contributions.[310]

Adonis was soon indicted for immigration perjury by two levels of government. He was charged for testifying he was born in the U.S. to the Bergen County Rackets Grand Jury, and he was charged two months later for lying by claiming he was a U.S. citizen before the Senate Kefauver Committee.

Adonis' immigration status was jeopardized by two clauses in the 1953 amendment to the McCarran Act that made it easier to deport alien criminals. One clause required an alien to have an immigration visa on entering the U.S., and Adonis had failed to get a re-entry permit in Miami after vacationing in Cuba in the winter of 1948. Another clause removed immunity for having spent three years in the U.S. following an illegal entry. This wiped away the benefit Adonis previously held from having resided in the country continuously for the five years since his Cuba visit.

Within months of the new law becoming effective, AG Herbert Brownell, Jr. slated 50 top foreign-born crime kings for one-way tickets home. The AG said about his hoodlum drive, "Another great help has been foreign-born groups who have gotten behind this drive [to rid their neighborhoods of gangs]. Actually less than one percent of the crime in the U.S. was committed by the foreign-born. But a surprising number of them worked their way to the top in the rackets."[311]

The Department of Justice used the evidence in the first perjury indictment in Bergen County to issue three days later a warrant for Adonis' deportation. The Immigration and Naturalization Service (INS) held hearings inside prison walls to determine if Adonis could be deported to Italy as an undesirable alien for re-entering the U.S. illegally. When he was asked if he understood the nature of the charges against him, he grinned broadly and replied: "I don't know. There're so many of them." Adonis claimed he was born in Passaic, New Jersey, and then his mother took him back to Italy for a few years until they returned to the U.S. permanently. However, investigators produced Italian birth certificate photostats for Joey and his entire family.[312]

On the Bergen County gambling-house charges, Adonis served two years and two months with time off for good behavior because he was a *model* inmate at Trenton State Prison. Three weeks after his release the U.S. AG issued a deportation order. The Italian Foreign Office spokesman said his country did not want racketeers who were born there but lived most of their lives in the U S. like Adonis and Luciano. He explained, "It's not blood that makes a man delinquent. It's society." He conveniently ignored the salient fact that the Mafia culture these men had been part of in the U.S. had been imported from Sicily where the syndicate originated. The U.S. government refrained from deporting him because they were hoping he would testify against other racketeers or corrupt New Jersey politicians.[313]

During his deportation battle, Adonis was convicted on both perjury charges. In a non-jury trial the County Judge found him guilty of lying to the Bergen County Grand Jury by testifying he was born in the U.S. The Judge sentenced him to 2 to 3 years in prison, but he suspended this pending the outcome of the INS deportation proceedings. The Judge said, "I wouldn't want to delay your deportation by as much as one hour." He emphasized that if by any chance a final order for deportation of Adonis was not issued, he would be cast into jail at once.[314]

Less than three months later, Adonis was given an 8-month to 2-year sentence for falsely swearing he was a U.S. Citizen at a Kefauver Committee appearance. Ironically, he invoked the Fifth Amendment more than 100 times that day, but he did not exercise this right for the only answer that could cost him his beloved adopted homeland's domicile.

After the U.S. Supreme Court refused to review his case, Adonis was facing both the county and federal perjury sentences followed by an inevitable order for deportation to Italy. He proposed to voluntarily retire to his native Italy and live there permanently in lieu of serving the two prison sentences. The government accepted. As Adonis departed New York City six years after the Kefauver Committee publicity began unraveling his world, he told the press that he did not want to go, but "it's a must." He said he was not bitter at having to leave his wife, son, and three daughters behind in their accustomed life, just "sorry that they have to take this shock." In the midst of all his criminal cases, the IRS had brought income tax liens of $413,964. A month after arriving in Italy, Adonis settled by paying $67,000 in back taxes.[315]

REFORM CAUGHT UP WITH WILLIE & SOLLY MORETTI

The Kefauver Committee exposures led to the closing of gambling in New Jersey, and the jailing of Adonis and Solly Moretti for operating a casino for Adonis and bookmaking for Erickson. Solly's brother Willie was not criminally prosecuted and lived a quiet life socializing with old friends. As Willie liked to do, one day he planned to join four acquaintances for lunch at Joe's Restaurant in Cliffside Park, New Jersey. The others arrived at 11 a.m. and sat at a front table in the empty restaurant. When Willie pulled up in his cream-colored convertible, one associate walked out to greet him with a friendly slap on the back. Then the five men sat, laughed, and joked in Italian.

When the woman proprietor walked to the kitchen in the back of the long, narrow restaurant, two of the men instantly pulled out .38-caliber revolvers and opened fire, shattering the silence of the vacant place. At the same moment the other two stood up in front of the windows blocking the view inside from the city's main street. One shot pierced Willie's left ear and exited his mouth through his right cheek. As he dropped to the floor, a second shot caught him on top of the head. Another bullet was found in a hole in the south wall of the restaurant, and three spent cartridges lay near his body. The proprietor and the waitress ran from the kitchen to the scene, but the assassins had fled. Upon viewing the body, the woman proprietor became hysterical and fainted.

The killers left two expensive felt hats bearing the name of a Brooklyn tailor on a wall rack. These and the fingerprints from the drinking glasses the killers used were taken by the State Police. None of the weapons were found, unusual in an organized-crime hit. The forensic evidence led the police nowhere. It was clearly not a robbery because Willie had $2,000 cash in his pocket. Marked in the newspaper on the seat of his car was his intention to make a $500 bet in Belmont Park's third race. He wrote "show," but the horse Auditing ran fourth out of the money.

Shortly after Willie Moretti's murder, Kefauver Committee Counsel Rudolph Halley commented in a hearing about 130 telephone calls Willie had made to Frank Costello. These calls were made eight years before his murder while Willie was recuperating from an illness in California. Halley speculated that Costello had banished Willie from New Jersey because he was talking too much about criminal activities, and the calls to Costello were pleas to be allowed to return. However, Costello countered in his testimony that the calls were evidence of friendship, not a boss-underling relationship. These calls were never connected to any aspect of Willie's life by Counsel Halley, New Jersey's AG Theodore Parsons, Manhattan DA Hogan, or writers about early organized crime. However, all perpetuated the supposition that this was the reason he was killed. All of them supported this unfounded conclusion even though it ran counter to Willie's lifelong silence about his own and every body else's criminal activities. Every time Willie testified at a government inquiry, he charmed the interrogators and answered every question without saying anything substantive about his own or his associates' activities. This included the gambling investigations by the Kefauver Committee and the Bergen County Grand Jury, before which he avoided mentioning anyone in the underworld, but implicated government officials he had bribed.[316]

More than five years after the killing of Willie Moretti, a murder attempt was made against Costello. This led some writers about early organized crime to try to tie these two homicidal events together by also including the close business and personal relationship between these two men that was revealed by the Kefauver hearings. Using these three elements they wove a fantastic but convoluted tale of long-term gangland intrigue.

The only thing these authors say that is relevant is that Willie had become irrelevant to gangland after reform closed illegal gambling. However, if Willie had indeed been the ill fated, symbolic opening pawn in a conflict to send a message to Costello, it would not only have been a highly unusual strategic tactic but also a total failure. Not only did the Boss of Bosses change nothing in his career or lifestyle, but he did not utilize his massive firepower either for bodyguards or to stop this supposed threat. In reality Costello was not shot until he was released from prison, and a conflict had developed when he attempted to take back control of his Mafia gang. If the conflict had begun years earlier when Willie was murdered before Costello was confined in the prison, when he entered he would have been a trapped, stationary, defenseless target who would have been easily taken out by fellow convicts loyal to the opposing enemy. As an aside, this quarrel over power impacted the development of the *Tropicana* resort on the Las Vegas Strip.[317]

Moe Dalitz used to warn the legitimate people whom he liked to steer clear of dealing with organized crime with the statement, "Everything in the underworld is not as it seems." He told me this statement the first time I interviewed him, and it applies here because the truth in this case might well amaze us, just like the facts about the Arnold Rothstein' shooting and Abe Reles' murder. In Willie's case, public officials are the most likely suspects but previous authors did not research this blatant aspect of the case.[318]

At the time of Willie's murder, he was scheduled to be a witness in the trials of high-ranking New Jersey public officials who were indicted for misconduct in office. This included four mayors, five chiefs of police, a former Bergen County chief of detectives, an ex-assistant prosecutor, and three county detectives. New Jersey AG Theodore Parsons' staff downplayed Willie's testimony in the upcoming trials as not vital, but the retired gambling operator was far from a peripheral witness. He was the bagman for bribe money from Adonis, Erickson, and possibly others, so he possessed incriminating testimony that would have helped end many or all of their careers and sent them to prison.

Not only did New Jersey AG Parsons lie in downplaying informant Willie's relevance, but he said he believed racket leaders silenced Willie, even though his office never uncovered any business or criminal activity or conflict to support this. Surprisingly, the AG's investigation never considered that New Jersey officials might have contracted for the murder, especially considering that the day before Willie was killed, Fort Lee Police Chief Fred Stengel was indicted for failure to take action against the casinos run by Adonis and the Morettis. Upon receiving the news, Chief Stengel drove to a patch of woods at the Fort Lee-Leonia boundary and ate his .38 caliber service pistol via his temple. It is not difficult to imagine that some of the many other indicted politicians or law enforcers might have been just as violent, but one or more employed gangsters to point a gun at the witness instead of themselves.

The indicted public officials were taking bribes from New York hoodlums operating gambling in their communities, so one might have turned to his benefactors to eliminate the affable gambler who had become a threat to him. This scenario explains the hats found at the murder scene being made in Brooklyn, and these public officials may have also had the power or influence to impede the AG's investigation of Willie's murder, which went nowhere despite having fingerprints and two eyewitnesses who could testify what the four killers looked like. In addition to all the county officials who were indicted, some of New Jersey's top state officials also had reason to silence Willie, because the reputation of Republican Governor Alfred Driscoll, who appointed Republican AG Parsons, was sullied during the illegal-gambling bribery investigations that resulted in indictments against more than 100 top Bergen County law enforcers and politicians and many more in other counties. The most unusual part of this case is New Jersey AG Parsons' steadfast denial that any of this multitude of public officials whom Willie was a key state's witness against was even a person of interest in this well-planned assassination.

Underworld friends did not attend Willie's funeral out of respect to his family's image. His brother Solly and Adonis were both serving time for gambling in State Prison at Trenton, where Solly soon died of a cerebral hemorrhage. At the funeral parlor a garden of floral offerings was stacked up to the ceiling, as more than 5,000 people from every type of background attended Willie's funeral. Throngs ringed the church, and the crowds followed the caravan to the funeral home and inundated his gravesite. These were friends and neighbors from the many little hamlets in Bergen County who said they were remembering Willie's "small kindnesses."

A year before Willie Moretti was killed, all forms of gambling, except policy-numbers lottery, were closed down in New Jersey and New York. Had the 57-year-old lived, he would have likely joined some of his many life-long friends among Luciano's key associates, who were at that time building gambling resorts along the Las Vegas Strip. If so he would have undoubtedly become one of the most amusing, colorful, and beloved characters to populate the Strip's most special era.

ADONIS IN EXILE

Adonis was deported to Milan, Italy, where he lived quietly and alone in a luxurious seventh-floor apartment downtown, as his wife remained in America living near their four adult children. However, Adonis' hoodlum notoriety accompanied him, and three months after his arrival a priest refused to accept him as a child's godfather at a baptism. For the next 15 years he lived obscurely and without incident. The once dapper Joe Adonis had become Giuseppe Doto, an aged and tired man, ailing from heart trouble. He walked slowly, and even the police acknowledged that he was in obvious pain.

Then the daytime slaying of the Chief Prosecutor of Palermo, capital of Sicily, embroiled Adonis in Italian politics. As part of the government's largest postwar Mafia crackdown, Adonis was arrested in a nationwide police sweep on a "custody prevention" warrant used to limit the activities of known criminals. A special anti-Mafia tribunal suspected Adonis of having gangland connections. These supposed ties appear to have resulted from his occasionally reminiscing with other old, retired, deported New York and New Jersey underworld buddies; but the court exiled Adonis for four years, a common practice in Italy. He was banished to enforced residence in the small Adriatic Coast hill town of Serra Dei Conti with 3,000 people. Adonis' wife came to Italy to help him settle in his new home two miles outside of town, and then she returned to their family in the U.S.

Adonis' activities were highly restricted. He was not allowed a telephone to talk to his wife, children, or grandchildren in the U.S. He had to stay in his home from 10 p.m. to 7 a.m. He was banned from leaving the little town, even to go to the seacoast 15 miles away, but he was required to take a cab every week to report to the police. The local police chief said, "He doesn't like to live in the countryside. He keeps saying how different New York is," just like his pal Luciano.

Before the tribunal exiled him, Adonis wailed, "I'm just a poor old man. I don't understand what you've got against me." He pleaded, "I'm a sick man. If you send me to exile, it'll kill me." He was prophetic. Five months later he died in lonely exile in the hospital at age 69 from heart and lung complications following a bout with pneumonia.[319]

His wife and two of his four children arrived from the U.S. to see him a few minutes before his death, and they flew his body back to New York for burial in the family plot in Fort Lee, New Jersey. Joining his family at the burial were 20 other mourners, but none of his former colleagues. One mourner who came to remember him said, "He helped a lot of people. He did a lot of good."[320]

Long-time pals Adonis and Luciano were buried on opposite sides of the Hudson River, where they had spent their young adulthoods and careers. Their two gravesites were along the route they drove their illicit liquid cargos into Manhattan, after racing them across the open sea and through the countryside. Bergen County on the New Jersey side, and Manhattan in New York, were where they dealt with, and fended off, the most dangerous villains of their time. This is where they gambled big at the races and dice tables; loved the many memorable women of their lives; and cheered on the greatest entertainers during the pinnacle of popularity of the American nightclub and Broadway show. This is also where both tried to elude the most ambitious, unscrupulous, and ruthless politicians of their time. Adonis and Luciano ultimately lost. Both were driven into exile from their beloved adopted homeland, the country they had worked so hard and so effectively to protect in its moment of most desperate menace during World War II.

During the eight-year period between the deportations of Luciano and Adonis back to their native Italy, the other three partners from Prohibition's biggest fine-liquor importing operation, and the other two Young Turks, were developing the marvelous Las Vegas Strip. Luciano and Adonis may never have visited Las Vegas, but their values of discouraging violence, keeping their word, and negotiating fairly were exemplified and preached by the other five Young Turks and their close associates that became the mob who built the Strip. Thus, the code of conduct of Luciano, Adonis, and the other Young Turks was adopted by the early Strip resort leaders.

Adonis' influence on the development of the Strip was led by two New Jersey associates. Joseph "Doc" Stacher was a close friend of Adonis and was also an illegal casino operator but in another county. Stacher would go on to build and become the unlicensed behind-the-scenes operating partner of the *Sands*. It would become a top Strip high-rolling casino during the glamorous 1950s era. It featured the Rat Pack, making it the hip place to be. The Young Turks and their close associates would turn the Las Vegas Strip into the world's high-end gambling capital, and America's center of superstar nightclub entertainment in their casino showrooms and star-studded lounges.

In absentia, Adonis's values were also felt in the development of the Nevada casino industry through the involvement of one of his New Jersey casino partners. Gerardo "Jerry" Catena would go on to become a key figure in Bally's slot manufacturing company that for many years dominated the flourishing Nevada casino and slot-route markets, and he surreptitiously sold his mechanical Santas to illegal as well as legal slot operations in a number of cities around the country.

Back when Adonis was still riding high as New Jersey's top illegal casino operator, Frank Costello was operating elegant casinos and slot routes in the northeast and in the south. And now we follow the path that the Boss of Bosses took on his journey to the Las Vegas Strip.

CHAPTER 12

THE ACTION MOVED INTO CAJUN COUNTRY

COSTELLO FROM YOUTH THROUGH PROHIBITION

Frank Costello was born Francesco Castiglia on January 26, 1891 in Cosenza in southwestern Italy. His family immigrated and settled in Harlem when he was 4. He dropped out of elementary school, but little else is known about his youth beyond his police record. He became a stick-up man who robbed working people of the cash they were carrying. This resulted in assault and robbery arrests at the ages of 17 and 21. Both were dismissed, although he was undoubtedly guilty. He listed his occupation with the NYPD as plumber or pipefitter.[321]

At age 24, Costello was arrested for carrying a concealed revolver and the charge was plea-bargained down from a felony to a misdemeanor. The Judge accepted the DA's bargain but at sentencing considered Costello's two prior robbery arrests by saying, "One case was he assaulted and robbed a woman going to the bank with $1,600. ... I have looked him up, and I find his reputation is not good. On the contrary, it is bad. ... I have got it right from his [Greenwich Village] neighbors that he has the reputation of being a gunman, and in this particular case he certainly was a gunman. ... Now, I commit him to the penitentiary for [the maximum of] one year." The 10 months he served in Welfare Island Penitentiary made an impression. Costello came to realize carrying a gun gave the cops an easy way to incarcerate him. He later told his pal Jimmy Blue Eyes and his attorney separately, "I made up my mind I would never pack a gun again. And I never did."[322]

Charlie Luciano and his Prohibition partners also developed a no-weapons policy. They only carried guns when riding shotgun over liquor shipments or when dealing with ominous enemies. This policy was part of their penchant for peaceful resolution of conflict, and early in Prohibition, they converted former street-heist man Costello into an advocate for their non-violence initiative. Costello was already moving towards non-violence because he had a great talent for negotiation and compromise with both competitors and adversaries. Since Costello shared these key values with Luciano and his partners, he became an integral member of the group's inner circle, even though he was their biggest liquor-importing competitor.

Criminals who use guns in the commission of their crimes select weapons that cannot be connected to them. Organized-crime shooters typically steal and do not register their hit guns because the ownership records would assist the police to quickly identify them as the likely culprits. In contrast to violent criminals who prey on innocent people, Luciano and his associates used guns only for self defense, so they registered them with the police. They warned other criminals that the jail sentences for carrying an unregistered gun was much longer than for Prohibition violations. Thus, the Young Turks often carried concealed weapon permits alongside their gun-registration cards in their wallets. At that time concealed weapon permits were extremely difficult to obtain by law-abiding citizens, but police chiefs and sheriffs usually had the authority to issue them. They typically provided them to political supporters, and some gave them to known criminals for large campaign contributions or cash bribes.

Ben Siegel is an example. He obtained a concealed weapon permit to legally protect his group's illegal liquor runs from the freighters off the shores of New Jersey to their warehouses in the heart of Manhattan. An FBI internal report stated, "It was disclosed that Nick Delmore, using his influence with Chief of Police Frank Brennan of Elizabeth, New Jersey, obtained revolver permits for the following individuals: Benjamin "Bugs" Siegel [and two others]. The reason furnished for the issuing of the above gun permits was for the protection of the Rising Sun Brewery payroll, which it will be noted, was an illegal operation during prohibition."[323]

As the gangland stature of Luciano, his partners, and Costello grew, their admonishment against carrying weapons was accepted by most organized-crime hoodlums. After the Young Turks reached the zenith of their power in 1931, practically no murdered gangster was found to be carrying a gun. This unarmed policy made hoods defenseless against the violent enemies who attacked them, but a concealed gun would have rarely helped because mobsters invariably attack without warning.

Organized crime is a world of secrecy, intrigue, and treachery. Its killers are masterful at luring an unsuspecting victim into a secluded place for a bogus meeting of friendship, business, or reconciliation. The shooters also hide along the path of an intended victim who follows a daily routine. They wait until the target is within a few feet and open fire without warning. Because the victim is invariably unarmed, the killer can miss the first few shots and still take out his shocked, trapped, defenseless quarry.

Since organized-crime killers take out victims easily without a fight, crime book and movie authors attribute this effectiveness to competence, but these perpetrators' abilities are highly overrated. They are thugs who are not trained in stalking or surveillance techniques, and rarely spend time on firing ranges developing marksmanship. Some organized-crime shooters have used shotguns or machine guns to spread a wide array of bullets on a relatively nearby target, but not one has ever used a rifle from a long distance.

Organized-crime killers lack the knowledge and skills that the CIA and military special forces use to penetrate the location of a protected target and assassinate him. Even so, the CIA employed multiple Mafia leaders to attempt to kill Fidel Castro of Cuba. As the government decision makers should have anticipated, the Mafia attempts were a fiasco that failed miserably.[324]

Several tell-tale signs at a murder scene indicate it was committed by an organized-crime gang. The victim is unarmed but usually has a police record. The gun is tossed at the scene, so the murderer is not carrying incriminating evidence if stopped by the police while getting away. Finally, a small caliber .22 or .25 weapon is used. While larger caliber bullets like .38's and .45's have greater velocity, they pass through the brain and out the other side of the skull. A number of people are walking around who had one of these larger bullets zip through their brain without apparent impact on any vital aspect of their physical functioning or personality. They seem perfectly normal after the skin punctures heal, the headache subsides, and the ringing in their ears dissipates. In comparison, a .22- or .25-caliber bullet penetrates the skull but lacks the velocity to exit the other side. Thus, it ricochets inside the skull, tearing up the brain a number of times and causing instant death.

Costello not only rejected gun carrying, but he also scoffed at the use of bodyguards. He knew they would be the first shooters his enemies would offer big money to for doing him in. His attorney

George Wolf later wrote, "Frank Costello was the Boss of Bosses, but never carried a gun, nor employed a bodyguard. He always said, 'If someone wants to score, the bodyguards are the first ones they buy off.'"[325]

During the four years between Costello's release from prison on the weapon charge and the beginning of Prohibition, he always claimed that he was employed as a salesman for the Horowitz Novelty Company. Since this company was formed just five months before Prohibition began, Costello never revealed his activities during the first three-and-one-half years following prison. Then he became a partner in Henry Horowitz's Novelty Company that sold fountain pens, razor blades, and other sundry items. But it also manufactured *kewpie* dolls, which were offered as one kind of prize in illegal punchboard gambling devices that were popular with bar patrons. Players paid a fee to punch a peg into one of the board's many holes to push out a tiny piece of rolled up paper that listed the prize, if any. If the player won a kewpie doll, he could surreptitiously turn it into the bartender for the cash prize. The Henry Horowitz partners' small investment produced good revenues, but the company went bankrupt in a year. The accounts payable exceeded the outstanding debt, but the indebtedness was explained to the U.S. Bankruptcy Referee as, "The debts which are due the company cannot be collected by the bankrupts as they are all East Side gangsters."[326]

When Horowitz's bankruptcy occurred six months into Prohibition, Costello joined Big Bill Dwyer's Prohibition gang and rose to become his lieutenant. When Dwyer went to prison, Costello bought the nation's second biggest rumrunning operation from him (see Chapter 1). Late in Prohibition, Costello financed Frank Erickson to make him one of America's premier bookies (see Chapter 11).

Costello developed another major gambling operation with "Dandy Phil" Kastel. He was born on New York's Lower East Side in 1886, and he became a con man. During the Roaring '20s stock-market boom, he ran a "bucket-shop" operation, selling phony securities in storefronts and over the telephone. He was criminally charged several times but all were dismissed, until he was convicted in federal court of mail fraud for fraudulently selling stock through the mails. After Kastel served his three-year sentence, Costello made him the managing partner of his new slot-machine business. Jimmy Blue Eyes said, "I didn't know Kastel, but he was very close to Frank [Costello]. We [the men in his group] lived in separate worlds." This was true of all organized-crime gangs in that era. No one talked about their criminal activities, nor their legitimate business operations either, to even their closest associates except for the events or businesses in which both were involved.

Mills Novelty Company was the country's largest manufacturer of slot machines. It was based in Chicago, with a plant in Long Island. The machines were illegal in every state since this was before Nevada legalized gambling. Costello cut a deal for the exclusive right to buy slots in New York City and also placed them in Connecticut. His Tru-Mint Company had a dozen subsidiaries throughout the city, each fitting within a political division boundary or a police station command jurisdiction. Costello had obviously cut a deal with the politician or precinct commander in each.

Costello developed a clever marketing ploy to circumvent the anti-gambling laws. The 5¢ machines dispensed a candy mint with every handle pull, so his attorneys could argue before friendly judges that these were legal candy-vending machines. His machines were easily modified to also dispense metal slugs for winning-reel combinations, and the retail stores redeemed the slugs for replays or cash. The machines paid out 80% to 82% return on the money inserted.

Costello placed his slot machines in speakeasies, nightclubs, drug stores, cigar shops, and even candy stores where he placed short ladders nearby, so young children could reach the handle and play the mechanical Santas. He owned the machines and paid each location owner 40 percent of the win. By 1931, the year Nevada legalized casinos, Costello had 5,186 machines on his route. It would be 1990 before a Nevada slot-route operator, United Gaming, would have that many machines in various locations throughout the state. Costello's Tru-Mint office had 14 telephone operators, who dispatched mechanics to quickly repair malfunctioning machines at the many locations needing service. Costello also sold machines to other hoods to place in their territories.[327]

Costello's slots were protected from political criticism by his powerful influence with Tammany Hall, and he received immunity from prosecution by high-ranking police officials. A beat cop would occasionally question a store about the legality of the machines, and the storeowner would point out the little sticker on every machine listing the company's name and phone number. Upon receiving a call from a curious cop, one of Costello's agents quickly showed up and rewarded the law enforcer's diligence with a little bonus.

One of Costello's subsidiaries brought suit against harassment by the police, and a Federal Judge ruled in 1931 the purpose of the machines was to vend mints, so he issued an injunction prohibiting the police from seizing them. This protection from police interference lasted for two years until the city's appeal to the U.S. Circuit Court of Appeals led to revocation of the injunction. For the most part, Costello's machines continued to enjoy immunity through political and police protection.

A year later Fiorello LaGuardia became Mayor, and he wanted a big publicity event to back up his bombastic tough-on-crime rhetoric. The easiest and most obvious target to hit was the very public slots, especially since Costello had supported the Mayor's campaign opponent. Public ire had been provoked against the slots by the conspicuous ladders that assisted children to gamble. Thus, LaGuardia ordered the NYPD to seize the machines. While the police were confiscating 1,000 machines, Costello's employees quickly rounded up and stored the other 4,000. LaGuardia also invoked an old, never used law giving the mayor the right to act as judge in certain criminal proceedings. He switched into the role of magistrate and held slot hearings in the police station, where he sentenced the operators on the spot. Next, the Mayor stood on a boat deck, smashed the seized slots with a sledgehammer, and dumped the pieces into the East River. He made sure he was surrounded by newspaper cameramen to photograph his judicial session and slot smashing. During and after his slot crusade, LaGuardia issued frequent statements denouncing Costello as "a bum."[328]

The slots were quickly replaced with pinball machines that also paid off in slugs redeemable for cash. However, Mayor LaGuardia ignored these similar illegal gambling devices because the criminal operators were his political supporters. Throughout his 12-year tenure as mayor, reformer LaGuardia franchised a crap game operation openly in the lobby of his political organization. The Horace Harding Republican Club was the Republican's counterpart to Tammany Hall. Jimmy Blue Eyes recalled, "The Republican Club crap game was operated by Cockeyed Nicky and Fat the Bush." LaGuardia only went after gamblers and gangsters if they backed the political opposition.

COSTELLO & PHIL KASTEL IN LOUISIANA

A year after Costello placed his New York City slots in storage, an opportunity arose for him to place them back into service in politically-volatile Louisiana. The seeds were sown seven years earlier in 1928, when Huey "Kingfish" Long became governor. Upon assuming power, he began to single-handedly reverse the democratic ideals achieved by the American Revolution. The leaders of that war had come from monarchies, so they offered the kingdom of America to their successful field general George Washington. It was his amazing rejection of sovereign power that led the founding fathers to institute democratic elections and to create three independent branches of government, with each one responsible for preventing the other two from abusing their power.

A century and a half later, the Great Depression rendered one-quarter of the country's families unemployed. These people were desperate, and even many of the employed were morbidly fearful about the future. Governor Long exploited this tragic situation by claiming a stronger governorship could solve these problems in Louisiana. What he actually did was wipe out the separation of powers and civil-rights protections embodied in the Constitution, and plunged his state back into authoritarian rule.

Long made the governor totally dominant over the legislature, solely in control of all parish (county) and municipal agencies, and completely shielded from interference by the courts. His laws made it a crime for a judge to question his activities, and during the 1934 election, the campaign platforms of four of the seven elected State Supreme Court justices supported his absolute power grab. Long refused to endorse any politician's campaign unless the candidate submitted to Long an undated but signed resignation to ensure unquestioned loyalty. Thus, Long acquired sole authority to make, interpret, and enforce state and local laws.

Long established this power by rewarding every one who jumped to his commands, and by harshly punishing every person and community who stood in his way. He appointed loyal administration officials, and then directed them to exceed their authority under the existing law to whip the legislators into obedience. Next he ordered the legislature to pass hundreds of laws to eliminate democracy and replace it with a military/police state. His power was so great that newspaper reports typically referred to Long as the *dictator* of Louisiana. Most compared him to Hitler and Mussolini, who in the early 1930s were consolidating the authority of their fascist-Nazi regimes in Germany and Italy, as they planned their alliance to militarily conquer the whole world.

The authorities the Legislature granted the governor would take pages to list, so just a few of the most important powers he had to command allegiance and to damage opponents follow. The state National Guard and a newly-created secret-police force became known as the governor's *Storm Troopers* to enforce martial law in cities that bucked his demands. The governor controlled local sheriff and police department policy and hiring, while the Attorney General was empowered to supersede any DA who failed to do his bidding. The governor controlled local voter registration, and his minions knocked 35,000 legitimate citizens off the voting lists in a single day. The governor took control of local property assessors, so he could lower taxes for supporters and raise them for foes, and the state Bank Examiner was given the authority to indefinitely postpone bank debt payments for those who capitulated to his demands. The governor controlled all state, and most local, government contracts, so he paid off business friends with excessive contracts that raised the state debt by ten fold in a few years. While he conspired with big businesses to rip off the taxpayers, "the Hitler of the Bayous" (the marshes of Southern Louisiana) political agenda focused on repeated public attacks on the evils of these same businesses and also "the lying press," just as dictators on the rise have always done. He frequently quoted the Jewish and Christian testaments to his constituents, as he built a modern version of the tyrannical Roman Empire to oppress them.

Two years after becoming Governor, Long was elected to the U.S. Senate, but he waited 17 months to go to Washington to accept this office because he had to continue to be governor until he was able to get a puppet elected to run the state. His mouthpiece governor was Oscar K. Allen, whose initials were appropriately *O. K.,* and were popularly interpreted to mean *anything Long wanted.*

Long became a national political figure by winning over the nation's unemployed, the many still employed workers and farmers who were scared about the future, rural residents, and the devoutly religious by making them outrageously grandiose promises that were financially impossible for the country to keep. At the height of the Great Depression, his goal was to redistribute the nation's wealth to make "every man a king," so millions across the country joined his "Share-the-Wealth Clubs." He proposed to limit everyone's income to $1 million a year [that is $16 million buying power today], and to restrict everyone's capital worth to $3 million total, so everyone would have a much more equal economic opportunity. He promised to eliminate poverty by giving every American an annual share of the wealth of at least $5,000. At today's value, this would be $80,000 a year, an amount multiples higher than the nation's gross national product could possibly produce.

Long's political rhetoric was about social progress, compassion for the underdog, and the people's needs, but he actually did precious little for them. He had the power as dictator to pass any bill, but he never proposed bills related to long work hours, the minimum wage, child labor, or women's problems in the workplace. His followers considered him a modern-day Robin Hood because he introduced or expanded a few construction and social programs, but Louisiana still languished far behind most other states. He ranted about poverty and the state's backwardness, but he did nothing meaningful to reduce either, as Louisiana remained one of the world's most impoverished locales. As one critic stated, "Huey P. Long gives the people the headlines, and the corporations the profits." He also profited handsomely by earning $100,000 per year as special legal representative of the state boards he controlled (a $1.6 million government salary today). Behind his snake-oil good-guy public oratory, Long was consumed by selfishness and motivated by a lust for power.[329]

Long began his military conquest of the state during his first year as Governor in 1929. He sent the National Guard into Jefferson and St. Bernard Parishes, which flank the city of New Orleans. These raiders attacked the illegal casinos and brothels, seized and destroyed their property, confiscated money and placed it in state coffers, and searched patrons over their objections, all without the slightest legal authority. After this Gestapo-crushing of civil liberties, he forced the underworld, the politicians, and the voters in these two parishes to become solid supporters to avoid further assaults by the state. Then the illegal casinos and brothels were allowed to reopen and operate without hindrance, as long as they paid off the appropriate fixers who worked for Long.

The combination of martial-law raids against cities that did not capitulate to his demands, and the numerous reward/punishment policies imposed upon businessmen, politicians, and government employees, resulted in the whole state paying homage to the Kingfish. Just one man steadfastly refused to back down - New Orleans Mayor T. Semmes Walmsley. He was suave and quiet, in marked contrast to his uncouth and bellicose political nemesis. However, the Mayor's gentlemanliness belied great political savvy, and a determination to defend the political independence and autonomy of his city, with arms if need be, against the man he said was seeking to become the "Louisiana Hitler."

Walmsley fought a strong multi-year war to maintain city home rule, even though the Legislature continued to transfer most of his authority to the governor and drove the city to the edge of bankruptcy. Walmsley's political supporters continued their defiance by running their own slate of candidates against Long's in the 1934 election, so Long launched what he thought would be the final battle against the last remaining obstacle to his complete domination of the state.

Long began his attack in a radio broadcast against "the cesspool of iniquity in New Orleans," and Governor O. K. followed with a letter to the Mayor, Chief of Police, and DA, threatening them with "removal and prosecution" for failing to clean up the wide-open illegal brothels and casinos. Two weeks later Senator Long directed his Governor to order 2,500 machine-gun brandishing state National Guardsmen to take control of the city. A hoard of Guardsmen stormed the City Hall Annex and took command of the voter-registration office. The Mayor quickly countered by moving a force of about 100 policemen into City Hall across a narrow street from the Annex. The two armed battalions, with guns ready, faced off at each other through their windows. At the same time Mayor Walmsley had 400 cops surround police headquarters to resist a reported attempt by Long to seize the whole department. The Mayor announced, "New Orleans is fighting for her municipal independence now. We'll go as far as this political pirate wants." Business and civic organizations opposed the troop occupation because it hurt business, and parents of the soldiers asked President Roosevelt to "end the outrage" in which someone could be unnecessarily hurt. But Long continued to ignore both the will and the needs of the people.[330]

Senator Long's real goal was to control voter registration and the voting machinery for the upcoming election. In addition to blocking new registrations, he had tens of thousands of legitimate citizens removed from the voting rolls. However, he sanctimoniously claimed imposition of martial law was to remove vice and sin from the city. The Governor backed up this contention by ordering the militiamen to investigate whether the casino and brothel operators were paying graft to public officials. Senator Long self-righteously fulminated to the Legislature against the red-light district, gambling, and late spots of New Orleans, while the adjoining parishes of St. Bernard and Jefferson, which the Senator politically controlled, featured "much more wicked attractions for visitors."[331]

In the September 1934 election, Long won handily statewide, but he ran very close in New Orleans. Thus, he could not risk calling for a municipal election to oust the Mayor that might fail, so he had to live with His Honor's defiance. The Governor withdrew the Guardsmen immediately after the election, and the St. Bernard and Jefferson Parish's gambling resorts started the dice rolling and the roulette wheels spinning again. However, Senator Long's charges of vice and gambling in New Orleans, and Governor O.K.'s threat of state intervention, forced the Mayor to wipe out vice in the city. He ordered the police to shut down the brothels and casinos with vacating notices. As a result of the most drastic cleanup effort in New Orleans history, the vice lords quickly moved on to more hospitable localities, so the police raiders arrived to find most buildings deserted and displaying "for rent" signs.

This created a problem for the scripture-quoting hillbilly-tyrant. He surreptitiously encouraged vice operations in the cities he controlled, but he had taken a highly-visible position against them in New Orleans, including during the two-month imposition of martial law. His populist image would have been damaged if he had allowed the brothels and casinos to reopen, so he developed new operations, which he could distance himself from politically by blaming them on new operators who entered the business since his crackdown.

In search for new vice operators, Long contacted Costello about the availability of his New York City slot machines that had been closed down a year earlier. Costello later testified to grand juries and legislative inquiries that the Kingfish introduced himself by telephone and then came to New York to meet. Costello testified that he was "the lucky one" who was picked to run machines in New Orleans, with Long guaranteeing police protection. Costello never explained why or how Long personally handled the transportation of the slots to New Orleans.[332]

The Bayou Novelty Company was formed by six partners made up of Costello, his associate Phil Kastel, two managers, a lawyer/CPA, and a political insider/bagman who represented Long and took care of the local politicians and police. Kastel headed the new slot-route operation and owned 40%, fronting half this interest for Costello.

Costello told a *New York Post* reporter confidentially that he and Kastel paid Long to take over exclusive slot operations in New Orleans. The reporter kept his word and did not print the story, but he quietly informed the FBI. Following up on this lead, agents found "Throughout the city of New Orleans, in practically every barroom, restaurant and drug store, there are slot machines." Agents also learned that not only were the slots a Kingfish-Costello monopoly, but police prohibited other pinball vendors from placing more than one machine in a location.[333]

As part of the deal, Costello determined the number of locations suitable for slots in New Orleans, so Long could pass appropriate legislation to tax the slots for an old-age pension. Long's alleged concern for widows, orphans, the aged, and the blind was well established, and Bayou Novelty was chartered for charitable enterprises. When the Kefauver Committee told Costello that his slots were never legalized, he replied, "Well, they probably would, if he had lived." Long's word was law.[334]

At that time, the country was still in the depths of the Great Depression, and President Roosevelt was just getting his federal public-works programs fully operational to create jobs for unemployed workers and inject consumer-buying power back into the economy. As an alternative presidential candidate, Senator Long continued the nationwide promotion of his radical social platform of redistributing America's wealth more equitably. This made the backcountry hillbilly the most prominent politician in the country after Roosevelt, and a serious challenger to him in the 1936 presidential primary elections. It was clear that in those financially-chaotic times the Democratic candidate would win the presidency in 1936, just as in 1932. Not only was Long about to publish a book brashly titled *My First Year In The White House,* but he brazenly told his associates and the press that he could solve all of the country's problems if the American people would follow the lead of Louisianans and agree to make him dictator of the nation.

A month after cutting the slot machine deal with Costello, Senator Long spent the evening ramrodding more power-consolidating bills through the Louisiana House of Representatives. As he walked out of the chamber, a man walked through the State Police bodyguards surrounding Long, pressed a 32-caliber automatic pistol against his ribs, and shot him once. That single bullet entered the upper right side of Long's abdomen, punctured his colon in two places, pierced his kidney, and exited from his back. Long's so-called *protectors* knocked the assailant down, and while he was lying on the ground, they executed him with a massive volley of firepower. His body had 61 bullet holes. Long died in the hospital a day and a half later at age 42.[335]

The dead man who the bodyguards filled with lead was a respected 29-year-old eye, ear, nose, and throat specialist in Baton Rouge, Dr. Carl Weiss. Except for being an anti-Long supporter, no motive was ever discovered. The young doctor had spent the whole Sunday of the shooting with his wife, 3-month-old baby boy, and parents at mass and at family and recreational activities. Then he prepared for his patient's surgery the next morning. The eyewitness testimony that attempted to establish the doctor as the shooter, rather than the bodyguards, was contradictory and confusing.

The State Bureau of Criminal Investigation Chief conducted a one-man investigation of his fellow officers that was a travesty, avoiding every serious issue. More than a half century after the shooting a professional forensics investigation was conducted. This time an autopsy was performed on the doctor's exhumed body. It was found that most of the bullets were shot into his back. State authorities again concluded that the doctor was the shooter primarily because they could not prove he was not. However, the lead investigator gave the most objective conclusion ever made about the case at a meeting of the Academy of Forensic Scientists: "It is submitted that there is significant scientific evidence to establish grave and persuasive doubts that Carl Austin Weiss was the person who killed Senator Huey P. Long."[336]

The important question is not who killed Long - the doctor, another bystander, or a bodyguard. It is who instigated and directed the murder, paid the shooter and his bodyguards to cover it up, and what was their motive? Was it a real patriot who saved the country from a domestic Hitler planning to install his brand of oppressive Nazism nationwide, a close subordinate who coveted to be king, someone with a personal grudge, or an isolated nut? It must be noted that virtually all solved U.S. political assassinations have been perpetrated by isolated crazies with bizarre rationales. However, in this case it appears Long's bodyguards participated in at least covering it up.

After Long's death, his political machine maintained its dictatorial rule over Louisiana, although its leaders jockeyed for position. Nine months after the assassination, the political machine finally met Mayor Walmsley's demands to restore local self-government to New Orleans, and he kept his promise to then resign. The Long political machine retained control over the independent city by appointing a strong Long supporter as Mayor, former State Commissioner of Conservation Robert Maestri. The new Mayor announced that slots would be closed, but his appointment perpetuated the Long machine's domination of the city and control over the law enforcers. The Mayor soon vacationed in Hot Springs, where Costello met with him to adjust his slot deal to His Honor's satisfaction, and it was again business as usual.

The Long political machine's corruption and unfavorable economic policies have continued to this day. America became aware of how impoverished the State of Louisiana still was, when Hurricane Katrina flooded New Orleans in August 2005. At that time it was publicized that one-third of the city's residents lived below the poverty line, more than twice the national average.[337]

The six Bayou Novelty Company partners were indicted in 1939 for evading $530,000 in federal taxes, making it the second largest IRS case to that time. Interestingly, the government did not challenge the $1.25 million in revenue they reported yearly ($19 million today), but instead charged the six with falsifying the amount of income allocated to each partner, so as a group, they could collective pay at the lowest tax brackets possible. A month later the IRS sent 15 deputies around the city sealing the cash boxes on the slot and pinball machines to start collection of the government's alleged share from the take, but the Judge ordered the jury to return a verdict of acquittal. While the partners escaped the criminal charge, Costello had to pay a total of $550,000 in personal back income taxes and penalties to the federal and New York governments.[338]

After the IRS case, the tainted Bayou Novelty was replaced with a new company, Pelican Novelty. Then the Louisiana Mint Company was formed in 1942. Costello was apparently having trouble with law enforcement, because he introduced his New York City deception of having his slots pay off in mints and slugs that the store converted into cash for players. This company had the same six partners but with the addition of Jake Lansky, who fronted his brother Meyer's interest.

During Mayor Maestri's 10 years in office, Costello's slot operations were pretty much left alone, but in 1946 deLesseps S. "Chep" Morrison was elected. He ran on a reform platform, and shortly after entering office he closed down all wide-open slot-machine operations, specifically Costello's. In the process the police confiscated 600 machines of the Louisiana Mint Company, and the company instituted a long litigation fight against the city that appears to have been futile. According to Metropolitan Crime Commission head Aaron Kohn, Mayor Morrison then did what crusaders invariably do: "He kicked out one group of racketeers to bring in his own group." Former FBI Agent Kohn went on to say that Mayor Morrison lacked integrity.[339]

Costello continued to operate slots in Jefferson and St. Bernard Parishes during Morrison's first term. However, he had to withdraw his slots from New Orleans, which had housed three-quarters of his 8,000 machines. Costello kept them in storage, hoping to defeat the Mayor's reelection bid with a friendlier candidate.

During the 1950 reelection campaign, the FBI found "Other news releases in this connection indicated that Mayor Morrison is running for re-election as Mayor of New Orleans and at the recent meeting of the American Municipal Association he made charges that the Costello machine which is allegedly represented locally in New Orleans by Costello's Lieutenant Phil Kastel is attempting to prevent his re-election." "Recent news releases relating to the meeting of the members of the America Municipal Association at Chicago last week have contained statements attributed to Mayor Morrison of New Orleans and Mayor Bowron of Los Angeles to the effect that Frank Costello, the notorious underworld character, heads nationwide gambling syndicates which dominate rackets in Los Angeles, New York, New Orleans and Miami." The two mayors said "Morrison had asked the FBI to investigate the Frank Costello Gambling Syndicate," but "No record can be located in the Bureau files of a request from Mayor Morrison for investigation of Frank Costello by the FBI." These statements illustrate the FBI's reliance on newspaper articles collected from cities throughout the country. Morrison's reelection finished Costello's New Orleans' slot dreams.[340]

Upon entering the New Orleans slot business, Costello and Kastel formed two companies in the city in their wives' names. The Crescent Music Corporation and the One-Stop Coin Machine Company were route operations that placed jukeboxes and vending machines in retail outlets. Local

Mafia leader Carlos Marcello was a partner in these vending machine businesses. The partners liquidated both companies 13 years later.

Right after the end of World War II, a year before reform-candidate Morrison would be elected Mayor for the first time, Costello and Kastel opened a luxurious high-limit roadhouse casino just inside the border of Jefferson Parish. Its splendid location was only a 15-minute trolley ride from downtown New Orleans. They renovated and lavishly-furnished their Beverly Club in the former Suburban Gardens nightclub. Its showroom featured the top headliners of the day, its restaurant was one of New Orleans' finest, with top-name bands for dinner dancing, and its plush casino offered high-limit crap and roulette games for the upper crust. Fine evening attire was required. It was one of the country's most lavish nightclubs and casinos, and it became the place to go in that section of the South. Kastel said in an interview years later, "At the Beverly, it was no sneak operation. We had the doors wide open. If it hadn't been [classy], I wouldn't have operated it."[341]

The Beverly Club's five partners were Costello, associates Kastel and Lansky, local Mafioso Marcello, and the ever-present Louisiana political insider/bagman. Kastel was the operator. Costello testified to the Kefauver Committee that he was paid $1,500 a month to recommend acts, since he owned America's most famous nightclub the Copacabana, and to solicit business of people planning to visit New Orleans. Costello later admitted that he and Marcello each owned 20% of the Beverly Club. Costello claimed that he first learned of his Mafia partner Marcello's criminal record when the Kefauver Committee made it public. Marcello had convictions for marijuana peddling, robbery, and assault. Kefauver described Marcello as "one of the principal criminals in the United States" and "as one of the United States' worst criminals."[342]

Jefferson's political boss and sheriff was Frank "King" Clancy, so locals frequently referred to the parish as "Clancy's Kingdom." He allowed casinos to operate openly, but he proudly testified before Kefauver that for the 22 years he had been in office he had treated the illegal casinos and horse-bookmaking parlors as relief projects for the unemployed, requiring each one to hire a specific number of local jobless residents. He also warned the operators that he would close them if the neighbors complained. However, he refused to answer many of the Committee's questions, and Kefauver expressed disbelief that a sheriff would resort to hiding behind the Fifth Amendment.

Kefauver said he would seek Senate contempt citations against the Beverly partners and Sheriff Clancy for refusing to answer questions. Thus, 10 days later, a repentant Clancy appeared again and readily yielded to the Committee's demands to close down gambling in Jefferson Parish to get out from under the pending contempt charge. In fact to show good faith, the Sheriff had already shut down all gambling preceding his second appearance. This included the swank Beverly Club. Hundreds of casino workers had already applied for unemployment insurance. The Sheriff's candid testimony and full disclosure led the Committee to drop contempt charges against him.[343]

COSTELLO AS LEADER

When Luciano received the long prison term on the framed prostitution-booking charges in 1936, he promoted Costello from his lieutenant to acting leader of the nation's largest criminal organization and Boss of Bosses. A decade later when Luciano was about to be deported to Italy, he officially promoted Costello to leader of the nation's largest gang and as il primo Mafioso.

Costello was a creature of habit who followed a daily routine, and these activities were well scrutinized by the NYPD and the press. As the city's business offices came alive, he rose at his luxurious seven-room Central Park West apartment and began receiving calls on his private, unlisted telephone. After showering and putting on a silken dressing gown, he ate breakfast in his dining room, often joined by people important to him. No one dared visit his apartment without an invitation or first obtaining permission. He hosted business partners, trusted henchmen, gamblers, Tammany Hall leaders and politicians, business leaders, financiers, union leaders, friendly city officials, judges, prosecutors, entertainers, and socialites, all seeking his advice or assistance. His most frequent guest was bookmaking partner Frank Erickson, followed by political ally Adonis, and the other Young Turks - Jimmy Blue Eyes, Meyer and Jake Lansky, and Siegel when he visited town from his Los Angeles base.

As noon approached, he had a chauffeur take him to the Waldorf-Astoria, where he had lived in a suite before moving to his apartment. He stopped first at the barbershop for a shave, manicure, shoe polish, and massage. Then he proceeded to the hotel's grill to meet associates for lunch. He began with a whisky sour, but he had tomato juice instead if he had stopped first at the bar to meet someone and had a cocktail there. He was a good but not extravagant tipper.

In the afternoon, he attended the horseraces during the seasonal meets. Otherwise, he either sweated in the 25-seat steamroom of the Biltmore Turkish Baths; played golf in the 80s as a member of the Pomonok Country Club in Flushing, Long Island; drank moderately at his reserved corner end of the Waldorf's men's bar; or kept appointments. At all these activities, he typically conferenced with one or more friends or associates.

The FBI noted internally that following these afternoon activities "at approximately 6:00 p.m. each day he visits the Copacabana Nightclub, where he conducts more business." FBI surveillance observed Costello discussing business quietly over drinks at a table in the empty showroom as the staff readied for the dinner crowd. Typically Costello would talk in whispers at one table, while men waited at up to six other tables for their turn to be summoned to an audience. "It was also noted that young men in the place were frequently making phone calls and reporting to him."[344]

From the Copacabana, Costello would telephone his wife Bobbie with the time to meet him for dinner at the Waldorf. Also, during every super star's engagement at the Copa, the couple attended a dinner show. She would show up for dinner and the show bedecked in jewelry and a fur, and he wore expensive conservative suits. To these dinner performances, he usually invited associates and their wives, and at the conclusion he escorted his guests backstage to meet the celebrated entertainer.

Costello's voice had a gritty quality because his vocal cords had been scorched while having polyps removed as a young man. Costello later said, "I went with the wrong doctor." A lifetime of smoking exacerbated the situation. His voice became a rough whisper with age, and it sometimes disappeared entirely in mid-sentence. Marlon Brando listened to his voice from Kefauver-hearing tapes for his role as the *Godfather* (1972). Despite the gravelly sound of his voice, Costello had a quiet, gentle speaking style. He was charming and gracious, and very well liked by people from every level of society. People usually described him as being a *real gentleman* or a *fine man*.[345]

Few people ever pushed Costello hard enough to see the emotion behind the calm. While he never raised his voice, he had a commanding presence that let him put someone in their place with a few soft-spoken but well-aimed words. He never talked tough or threatened. He would smile and offer a cautionary admonishment within a factual assessment like, "You know. That's not nice what you did." His intensity left the listener with no doubt that Costello had reached the end of his patience, and every one present could feel the rapidly escalating tension under his cool façade.

Jimmy Blue Eyes said, "Frank was considered more like a businessman [than a hood]." He did not look like a hood and never acted like one. The world knew him as a gambler, successful businessman, and political kingmaker. Even the NYPD would not learn that he was a Mafioso, let alone the Boss of Bosses, until after he retired. He was always the height of propriety and fit in easily with respectable and polite society and politicians. He and Luciano were the first gangsters to go uptown and blend in seamlessly and be accepted by all strata of the overworld. But in Luciano's case, DA Dewey's bogus public criminal invectives against Luciano made most people falsely assume that a dangerous tough guy lurked beneath his pleasant, accommodating persona.

The Jewish Los Angeles bookmaker Mickey Cohen raved about Costello as "a wonderful, fine gentleman" in his autobiography and in a TV interview. He had nothing but admiration for Costello, even though the Mafia gang in Los Angeles had fought a prolonged violent war against Cohen. "There was nobody in the world [even] your presidents, your kings, or whatever - nobody compared with Frank Costello. He was a dignified man; class just leaked out of him." "Frank Costello, who I admired with every bit of might that I could possibly respect a man." In case you are wondering, English was actually Cohen's native language.[346]

Costello was the country's most visible and best-known gambler. He was the second hood to have his face glare from *Time Magazine's* cover, accompanied by the article *I Never Sold No Bibles*. The 1949 Costello edition was 20 years after Capone's cover. Costello was dubbed *the Prime Minister of the Underworld*. Late in his life, he talked to author Peter Maas for two months about a possible autobiography. After one discussion, Maas escorted the 81-year-old Costello to his apartment building's front door. On his way back inside, the author was stopped by the Italian doorman, who quietly exclaimed, "Hey, that's the real godfather!"[347]

Costello had money, power, a family, a fine apartment on Central Park West, and a two-acre summer country estate at exclusive Sands Point, Long Island. But the secretive Boss of Bosses sought a psychiatrist when he was in his 50s. Various authors have written folklore as fact about his private sessions. They claim that he had depression, insomnia, or some unsatisfied emotional need, so the doctor allegedly advised him that he craved social acceptance by people besides hoodlums and corrupt politicians. Supposedly the doctor counseled, "Get out and meet some nice people." The flaw with all these suppositions was that Costello spent most of his adult life associating on a daily basis with people from every walk of life. Whatever his malaise or its solution, no one but his psychiatrist ever knew.[348]

Jimmy Blue Eyes said, "Costello was a nice guy, but he had a big ego." He was impressed with his own importance to the point of arrogance, but several other qualities made him "a well-liked guy" and effective leader. He was personable, absolutely kept his word, and was loyal to friends, so people instinctively trusted him.

Costello had spent his youth as a street robber, but his close friendship with Luciano and his partners during Prohibition transformed his punk values. By the time he aligned with their gang, he had rejected violence and vengeance, as strongly as Luciano, Adonis, Jimmy Blue Eyes, Lansky, and Siegel. He supported their attitudes with his own observations that killing each other just made a lot of people dead, which he had seen led to more antagonism, fear, and reprisals. He understood that violence did not make their world safer, but much more foreboding and dangerous. Jimmy Blue Eyes emphatically told me, "Frank didn't like violence. He didn't believe it was the solution to any problem."

Costello was committed to negotiation, compromise, cooperation, and fairness. Jimmy Blue Eyes said to me, "He liked to bring people together." Ever ready to arrive at a compromise, he always tried to reach consensus. He not only preached nonviolence, but he dealt with everyone as if he expected a non-violent, mutually-agreeable outcome. It was only after every alternative to make peace with a threatening enemy failed that he would consider as the last resort violent pre-emptive self-defense. Author Peter Mass got to know Costello during two months of interviews and he concluded, "He was a man who would go way out of his way to avoid violence. He believed that, with serious effort, there are few things that can't be worked out peacefully."[349]

New York City Mafia Leader Joe Bonanno wrote, "Costello was a suave and diplomatic man. ... He preferred to settle arguments at the conference table rather than in the streets. Despite his moderate ways, Costello knew that to survive in our world a man had to be versatile, and thus Costello was not without his 'muscle.'" Like Luciano, Costello was supported by the psychopathic Anastasia and the violent successors of the murderous Capone. With their implied threat in the background, he was able to keep the peace between discordant factions of the five New York City Mafia families for almost a quarter of a century. However, his rule of the underworld was absolute primarily because he had earned the profound trust and deep-rooted respect of all American criminals of every nationality, and he never utilized fear tactics, except during extreme clashes when survival demanded it.[350]

Costello was so openly vocal against violence that a national magazine revealed this at the height of his power in 1947. "Although in his younger days Costello had something of a reputation as a gunman, in his maturer years he has consistently deplored the use of violence. He became convinced more than twenty years ago that more could be accomplished by persuasion and by the judicious handling of politicians and officials than by the use of guns and bombs."[351]

Later in his life, a shooter's bullet missed killing Costello by a fraction of an inch. At the shooter's trial, Costello denied having seen the perpetrator, even though forensics proved he was looking directly in his face when shot. Although the Boss of Bosses had been the target of murderous ambition, he ended the conflict by negotiating a peaceful resolution without retaliation against either the shooter or the instigator. Then he made an unprecedented overture of reconciliation by inviting the attacker to his home for dinner with his family.

Years afterward, the man who had instigated and ordered Costello's assassination was in prison, where fellow inmates plotted to murder the trapped and helpless convict. These felons had never met Costello but all revered his life's work and intended to avenge him. The warden concluded that Costello, who was then retired from gangland activity, was the only person who commanded enough respect in the underworld to rescue his intended assassin from this fate. The warden asked

Costello to travel to the prison and intercede to save the life of the man who had failed by a hair's width of having had him killed. Costello went to the prison, and under the warden's auspices he met with his attempted murderer to demonstrate that he harbored no animosity. Upon seeing Costello's offer of mercy, everyone of the inmates stopped plotting revenge against their fellow convict who had instigated and directed the attempted assassination of Costello.[352]

Luciano and his associates spent their lives promoting non-violence and opposing vengeance. They had a passionate dedication to peace and accommodation that is rarely encountered even in the overworld. These comrades' philosophy served them well in their dangerous world. All eventually retired from their illegal businesses, relinquished their positions of gang power, and withdrew from gang involvement. Retirement is something the media claims organized crime, especially the Mafia, never permits, but all the Young Turks, with the exception of Ben Siegel, lived long lives and died of natural causes.

Costello, as Boss of Bosses, also enforced Luciano's other major policy of banning any Mafioso from using or peddling illegal drugs. This crime was much more likely to lead to conviction and a member turning state's witness. Violation was punishable by execution. As Jimmy Blue Eyes said, "Our group was utterly opposed to drugs. We were only in liquor and gambling. We made more money after Repeal, when we all went into gambling."

Even though the Mafia had the country's biggest, strongest, and most loyal gangs, their criminal prospects were limited by a serious shortcoming. They were highly insular and isolated from the larger society, as they wanted to deal strictly with Sicilians. Their crime territories and their associations were essentially restricted by the geographical boundaries of Sicilian and Italian neighborhoods and businesses. In marked contrast, Luciano and his associates were ecumenical or all inclusive. They liked, respected, dealt with, and reached out to hoods, politicians, and businessmen of all nationalities, and they encouraged every one to cooperate with each other.

Costello epitomized the values of Luciano's group. He always tried to expand and enlarge his social and political world. He met regularly, and became friends, with people from all walks of life, including Tammany Hall political leaders, city officials, judges, lawyers, union officials, businessmen, financiers, socialites, nightclub entertainers, movie stars, Hollywood producers and agents, favored newspapermen, gamblers, racketeers, killers, and every one else who influenced the New York scene.

Costello related to all nationalities but socialized more with the Jews and the Irish. For example, his rumrunning associate Dwyer and his bookmaking partner Erickson were Irish. His partner Kastel in slots and casinos, and his casino partner and close gangland advisor Lansky, were both Jewish. This was also true of Arnold Rothstein, with whom Costello frequently loaned money back and forth. His wife Loretta, who went by the nickname Bobbie, was Jewish. His attorney George Wolf wrote, "He once told me, 'When I met Bobbie, it was like meeting one of my own people [culturally]'" even though she had grown up on the wealthy side of Park Avenue, while he was from the Harlem-slum side.[353]

Author Peter Mass said that during their conversations, it was clear that Costello was not ethnically oriented like the old Sicilian Mafia bosses. "He certainly didn't hold in awe some of the

Mafia leaders of the past who are revered by everybody else in the organization, yet he spoke with great regard about Meyer Lansky."[354]

A NYPD detective-lieutenant who kept Costello under surveillance said later, "In those early years when I knew and worked on him, all of his close associates were Jewish or Irish. You'd never see him with Italians. We had no idea he was involved with them." In reality, he also had a number of very close Italian associates like Luciano, Adonis, Jimmy Blue Eyes, and Albert Anastasia.[355]

Costello's ethnic values were representative of much of New York City society. The Italian and Jewish cultures were extremely compatible and congruent. Both groups also related easily with the Irish culture. Thus, Jews and Italians were frequently associated in friendship and business, and many were close to the Irish. It was the similarities and closeness of the large Italian and Jewish populations in Brooklyn that led Adonis to politically represent and speak for his Jewish neighbors as readily as his Italian countrymen.

In contrast, virtually every street gang in the U.S. was ethnically based, even though some accepted members of two or three nationalities. Only three major Prohibition gangs were ecumenical and reached out to competent individuals of every background. These were Luciano and his comrades, Costello/Dwyer, and Cleveland's Jewish Navy. The diverse contacts they established opened up the opportunities for these three groups to become the biggest importers of fine liquor during Prohibition, to operate the largest number of illegal casinos across the country during the 1930s and 1940s, and to build most of the Las Vegas Strip resorts from the mid 1940s through the 1960s.

Capone and his successors headed the only other major Prohibition gang that dealt with all nationalities, and it was unique in absorbing diverse membership. For example, Capone's key lieutenant was the Jewish Jake Guzik, who managed the group's businesses and finances. Thus, the Chicago gang participated to a lesser degree with the big three groups in the early development of the Strip. In later years they grew to become major players in the Strip gambling resorts.

THE FBI HAUNTS COSTELLO

Costello supplied the capital for several illegal casinos to be operated by his managing partner and front man Al Contanto, whom the world knew as Al Howard. Each summer Howard ran the *Brook Club* and the *Piping Rock* casinos in Saratoga Springs in upstate New York, and during the winter he operated the *Embassy Club* casino in Miami, Florida. He also had the on-again off-again *Embassy Club* and *Royal Box Club* casinos in the heart of Broadway's Great White Way of sparkling theater marquees.

In 1935 two dealers who worked Howard's seasonal circuit of casinos made the trek from their Brooklyn home to Miami to be ready to go to work at the *Embassy Club* casino when it opened soon for the winter season. They were flat broke so they decided to rob some wealthy tourists visiting Miami. At the racetrack each afternoon, they observed a vacationing New York City socialite, who "habitually wore jewelry of great value." The pair went to her hotel and got her room number by posing as flower deliverymen. Then the armed pair burst into her hotel suite and tied up both the woman and her escort. They stole her fine jewelry valued at $185,000 and his watch, cigarette case, and wallet.[356]

One robber took the gems to their New York base to sell to a fence for cash. The other robber remained in Miami, but he needed eating money so he decided to steal a couple bicycles. As he was grabbing them, he was arrested by Miami police. Officers found in his room the robbed man's stolen property, and they got the thief to confess to the gem robbery and implicate his partner. Miami detectives notified the NYPD, and they arrested the partner and obtained his confession. He was extradited back to Miami, where the pair was convicted and each sentenced to 25 years.

Since the woman's stolen jewelry had been transported across state lines, the FBI entered the case. When agents found that the country's two biggest jewelry fences were involved in handling the gems, they intensified their investigation. Agents learned that robber Nicholas Montone had taken his loot to New York City and met with Robert Nelson. He was known as the *Walking Pawnshop* because he offered quality jewelry at wholesale prices to the wealthy patrons of the city's racetracks. The NYPD claimed Montone was America's most influential stolen-jewelry fence.

Montone had then met with private detective Noel Scaffa. He was renowned for having returned stolen jewels to insurance companies during the previous 10 years valued at $10 million [$140 million today]. Scaffa got away with negotiating on behalf of gem robbers by denying he represented them. He claimed "recovering" of the stolen jewels by falsely stating that he traced their possession to fences he never identified during his investigations he never conducted. Scaffa got the insurance companies to offer rewards of 30% to 45% of the radiant baubles' insured value for their return, along with requiring the companies to request sentence leniency if the robber were caught.

Early in the FBI's investigation, agents assumed a major underworld figure had to be behind such a large interstate conspiracy. They targeted Costello as the mastermind because the robbery pair had been dealers at his illegal casino operations and he knew them. When Montone had returned to New York to fence the jewels, he was broke so he had telephoned his former employer Costello to ask for an advance on his upcoming dealing job in Miami. Costello invited him to meet in the public 25-chair Biltmore Turkish Baths steamroom, where his casino partner Howard and their floor supervisor "Broadway Charlie" Stern showed up. The pair often met with financier Costello there.

Montone told the three casino leaders that he was penniless. Costello later stated to the FBI, "He just said he had come back from Miami and was broke and wanted a few dollars. He did not mention this jewel robbery. I knew about it because I had read the newspapers." Costello gave him a little money to live, Broadway Charlie hired him a New York attorney, and Howard gave him money to employ a Miami attorney against the serious local charges. Costello also said to the FBI, "I want to tell you something. Here's the position I am in. I was born in New York. I am here all my life and I know everybody, and I am inclined to help almost everyone, if possible, with no interest, personal, financial, or otherwise. When they're in trouble, sick or need rent and I got it, I help them and I believe it's my reputation. It is my only interest in this whole situation."[357]

Not only had Costello employed the two robbers as dealers, but a month before the jewels were heisted at the Miami-Biltmore Hotel in Coral Gables, Costello had vacationed there with his wife, bookmaking partner Erickson, and friends. This was a mere coincidence because Costello spent part of every winter at this hotel visiting his close friends Meyer Lansky and Jimmy Blue Eyes and their nearby Miami casinos in which he was a partner. Costello also escaped the winter snow by visiting his New Orleans casino and vacationing in Hot Springs, Arkansas. Concerning his most recent visit to the Hot Springs baths, he told the FBI, "I met some friends down there, a few judges, a few district attorneys, and a few senators. They all go down there. I had no particular plan to meet anyone." "I did not go to Hot Springs for business."[358]

In this case the FBI's detective work was exemplary. By conducting extensive interviews with every one connected to this case, agents effectively filled in the details not uncovered in the Miami Police and NYPD investigations to produce a detailed summation of the entire crime. The FBI documented that every aspect of the crime was committed by the two bumbling robbers and the country's two biggest fences. This left no role for Costello or anyone else to be participants.

The FBI found Costello's only relationship with the robbery pair was as a casino employer. Costello and his three casino operators had no association with the two fences, and both fences denied ever hearing about any of these four gamblers being involved in the crime. Even though the FBI had proved that the four gamblers had not been participants in nor benefited from the crime, the FBI charged them along with the two fences in one indictment for having somehow mystically conspired to transport the stolen jewelry across state lines.

FBI Director Hoover brought these unfounded charges because of his penchant for crime-busting publicity to establish his image as America's top cop. By including Costello and his three interstate illegal casino operators in the charges, he elevated a local robbery into a major underworld conspiracy. Within his agency Hoover operated a vast internal publicity machine to extol the exploits of his FBI. Hoover's publicity machine, bizarre decision making, and political agenda goals are presented in several historical books that document from the FBI's official internal records the Director's frequent administrative indiscretions.[359]

Hoover had a second motive for including Costello and his casino operators in the robbery charges. The Director had a personal grievance against insurance fence and private detective Scaffa, and including the casino group to expand the scope of the crime helped Hoover carry out his vendetta. Scaffa had inadvertently offended Hoover's crafted public image, when the fence had lied to FBI agents that he had never handled the stolen gems in this case. This led the Director to issue a press release to the nation correctly announcing that the FBI played a leading role in cracking the major Miami jewel robbery, but in this release Hoover also mistakenly credited Scaffa with *arranging* the return of the gems. Just as the Director's press release was being distributed, Hoover's error was exposed by the Miami Police Chief of Detectives in his testimony in the robbers' trial. He testified Scaffa was actually an illegal fence who *personally* turned the stolen jewels over to him.

Embarrassed by the revelation that Hoover had publicly praised a perpetrator, the FBI quickly built a case to nail Scaffa. Within a month agents apprehended him on charges of perjury to the Grand Jury for having falsely denied his fencing role, and he was convicted. The judge sentenced him leniently to six months, rather than the maximum 15 years, because Scaffa had confessed to the FBI and had implicated notorious fence Walking Pawnshop Nelson for having kept the stolen jewels in safekeeping.

In addition to the perjury conviction, the FBI already had charges pending against both fences, Costello, and his three casino operators for transporting the stolen jewelry. Upon their arrests, Hoover issued his second press release announcing his agents were attempting to break up a group of jewel thieves engaged in the "most extensive racket my men have turned up in recent years."[360]

According to internal FBI memos, its own officials and the prosecuting U.S. Attorneys had different opinions about the strength of the case against Costello and his three casino operators from "very weak" to "a 50-50 chance to convict." They held this judgment even though America's secret-police force had nothing linking these four casino operators to the crime but unrelated associations. After doing nothing about this frivolous case for two years, the Justice Department, with Hoover's approval, requested the Judge to finally dismiss the charges against all six defendants including Costello and his three casino associates.

If Costello and his three casino operators had been successfully prosecuted for simply talking to and financially assisting a criminal defendant with living money and legal fees after the fact, as some U.S. Attorneys believed might have been possible, it would have set a frightening legal precedent and created a chilling, possibly catastrophic, assault on civil liberties. Any accused lawbreaker's relatives, friends, co-workers, or good Samaritans would have faced potential accomplice arrest in the fundamental crime for merely offering words of encouragement or supplying basic assistance after the fact.

In this peculiar case, FBI Director Hoover betrayed the public trust in multiple ways. He lumped two unrelated groups of defendants into a single indictment. Then, he left Costello and his three casino operators in prosecutorial limbo for two years, even though an in-depth FBI investigation had proven them innocent. Finally, he incomprehensibly dropped the charges against all the defendants, despite possessing strong evidence against the country's two biggest fences. Dismissing the case against the fences violated Hoover's oath of office, and it turned his public promise to protect the American people into a lie.

The Director's third press release in this case, issued at the time this group of six defendants was arrested, promised a nationwide FBI campaign to determine if insurance companies were instigating robberies by offering thieves large rewards for returning jewelry stolen from people they insured and by also supporting immunity from prosecution for the thieves. Hoover's press release contained his usual political-reformers' tough-law-and-order rhetoric, laced with official legalese, making his inexplicable refusal to follow through and incarcerate the nation's biggest jewel-theft criminal ring bizarre. FBI agents had solved every aspect of this case, and they possessed overwhelming evidence. Yet Hoover declined to prosecute. Unfortunately, this case was typical of Hoover's 48-year feeble and spotty leadership in fighting organized crime.

Hoover's claim about Scaffa being a dominant fence was confirmed during his six months in prison for perjury because no major gem robberies were attempted on the East Coast. Scaffa's fencing to insurance companies was ultimately ended when New York State revoked his private-detective business license. This took away any legitimate claim Scaffa could have for possessing stolen jewelry. However, Pawnshop Nelson kept plying his discounted fine jewelry trade at racetracks.[361]

The FBI file on Costello is a paradox. The FBI took no notice of Costello during Prohibition, despite his being the nation's second-largest violator. After Repeal the FBI ignored Costello's illegal casino operations in four states and his nationwide illegal bookmaking operation. When Hoover finally did take an interest in Costello, it was for a bogus robbery charge. In the middle of the FBI's jewelry-robbery investigation, Costello became Acting Boss of Bosses for the imprisoned Luciano, but agents ignored Costello's activities for the next decade. Then Hoover investigated him in several cases only because of orders from his Justice Department superiors, but the FBI unbelievably never learned Costello was even a Mafioso, despite his being Boss of Bosses.[362]

During Hoover's half-century directing the FBI, he repeatedly swore no Mafia criminal organization existed in the U.S. He spewed this falsehood to eight Presidents and 17 Attorneys General who were his bosses, to Congress which funded his agency, and to the American people who entrusted their safety and security to him. As organized crime developed and flourished in America's big cities with the advent of Prohibition, Hoover relegated his national secret-police force to the sidelines, where they remained missing from action.[363]

When the FBI needed information on an organized-crime figure, agents often produced a summary of the documents already in the criminal's file, rather than scrutinize his current activities. As an agent explained in Costello's file, "The purpose of this report is to assemble all information immediately available regarding Frank Costello, who is generally considered as the most influential underworld character in New York City, in order that the Bureau and the New York City Office might have readily available information regarding his background should an investigation be conducted at any time in the future." "The information contained in this report was obtained from review of the files of the New York Office," all of which had been filed at least eight years earlier.[364]

The only thing the FBI's two-year gem-theft investigation produced about Costello was some personal lifestyle information. FBI agents sat in a room down the hall from his Waldorf-Astoria suite monitoring an extension phone with no mouthpiece, so their surreptitious activity could not be overheard by the subject. The FBI wrote down Costello's conversations, plans, and activities. After 12 days of listening, it became obvious to agents that their wiretaps had been compromised because Costello called someone about how phone taps worked and also stopped talking on his home phone. The FBI immediately discontinued the home tap. FBI agents assumed their rather public surveillance had been exposed by hotel employees who liked Frank and his wife Bobbie.[365]

During this fruitless 12-day tap of Costello's suite, the FBI picked up no discussion of criminal activity. However, agents did learn his suite contained six rooms, and the couple had a butler and a maid, who called the grocery store to order food deliveries. Frank called his tailor regularly for shirts or suits. One day Frank told an associate he won several hundred dollars at the horseraces, after his wife had earlier told a friend she played 50¢ on a number-racket lottery ticket. Frank told one caller he would have no cash for a week, and he needed that for something. Costello occasionally told callers to meet him at a designated time at the Waldorf's bar or restaurants, the Biltmore Turkish Baths, his golf country club, racetracks, baseball games, or various business offices.

COSTELLO'S BUSINESSES

Costello spent much of his career competing illegally with the racetracks for their clienteles' potential wagering revenue. Earlier in life he had personally taken big wagers at the tracks from other players, and then he financed Erickson's large nationwide bookmaking operation. Despite Costello's illegal rivalry, he had ties to the track managements, especially at Roosevelt Raceway in Westbury, Long Island. Manhattan DA Frank Hogan first discovered this when he began investigating Costello's possible criminal activities in 1943 and ordered wiretaps of his telephone conversations. The Kefauver Committee and New York State investigated this relationship during hearings. Unfortunately, the testimony of the two key witnesses, Costello and Raceway Counsel George Morton Levy, was contradictory and confusing, especially their interpretations of their wiretapped statements. The reasons each gave for their dealings was clearly untrue. Whatever their actual relationship, only the following facts about Costello and the track are known.

During World War II, the Raceway hired Pinkerton's detectives to rid the park of bookmakers because they were in direct competition with the track for wagers from its biggest bettors. Raceway Counsel Levy tried to persuade the track management and Pinkerton's to allow the Costello/Erickson bookmakers continued access, but his reasoning was never made clear. The next year management did not renew its costly contract with Pinkerton. This allowed the bookies to operate openly again. The bookmaking became so blatant that the New York State Harness Racing Commission Chairman threatened to revoke the Raceway license unless it was stopped.

Raceway Counsel Levy's solution was to have the track employ Costello at $15,000 a year ($150,000 now) to keep bookmakers away from the track. From two days after Costello was hired as a consultant and throughout the four years of his employment, the track inspectors made no more complaints about bookmakers. Costello may have told his bookmaking combine to act less conspicuously because the heat was on, he may have used the Raceway's payments as bribes to silence the inspectors about the bookies' activities, or he may have told the underworld that the Raceway was under his protection and they had to stay away. In any event, Costello reported his legal consulting income on his tax returns. The Raceway finally stopped paying him because the IRS ruled the track could not deduct the payments as a necessary or ordinary business expense, even though Costello offered the same service as Pinkerton, which the IRS accepted as legitimate.

Three years later the Moreland Act Commission began hearings on New York City's scandal-ridden raceways. The testimony exposed some high-ranking politicians, and some of Costello's close associates, of being hidden owners of $1 million worth of stock in several trotting tracks. The shareholders included bookmaker Frank Erickson's son and son-in-law, and former Republican state assemblyman, Irving Sherman, who was a close friend of Costello and a political intimate of Mayor Bill O'Dwyer. All owned stock under other peoples' names, and probably fronted interests by Costello. Governor Dewey expressed outrage at revelations about the Democrats' sordid involvement, but when the highest echelons of the Republican Party were also exposed, he withheld any comment for the same infractions. The Commission ordered the raceways to buy back the stock from the people who were found to be fronting for others, and cracked down on the tracks' managements.[366]

Costello owned one of the country's largest legal Scotch importing companies under his associates' names for almost two decades. As repeal of Prohibition was to begin, Costello arranged the deal for his company Alliance Distributors with one of his major Prohibition suppliers, William Whitely Liquor Company of London. Costello explained to the Scotch provider that he enjoyed a close-working relationship with his former liquor sellers in every state, and they now needed to buy the same products from a legitimate distributor, making him the logical wholesaler.

Costello arranged for New Orleans oil and horseracing investor Bill Helis to loan the money to create Alliance, and he acquired exclusive U.S. distribution of Whitely brands, including the two most popular Scotches in America - Kings Ransom and House of Lords. Kastel officially owned the company for a year until he sold it to Costello's old Prohibition friend Irving Haim, so Kastel could focus on Costello's burgeoning Louisiana slot route.

Costello received two shillings, sixpence (about 50 cents) on every case of King's Ransom and House of Lords imported into the United States. When the NYPD picked up this connection in its 1943 Costello wiretaps, the company told the Police Commissioner that it had reorganized and discontinued his commissions. The firm did not reveal Costello's commissions were replaced with a $35,000 monthly stipend, which was the average amount of his former commissions.[367]

Costello rarely visited the company's offices, according to Grand Jury testimony by Alliance's Assistant Treasurer and Office Manager Lilen Sanger. She was the sister-in-law of Company President Haim. Since three other employees told the Jury he was often there, DA Dewey prosecuted her for perjury, but at her trial, no one could put her in an office at the times they had seen Costello. Three Special Sessions Judges acquitted her. One Justice announced the decision by saying, "The facts presented here raised a grave suspicion as to whether this defendant did not know Costello, but it is the opinion of the court Miss Sanger's guilt has not been proved beyond a reasonable doubt."[368]

A decade after Sanger's perjury trial, the State Liquor Authority refused to renew Haim's liquor license because he had *close* business and social relations with Costello. The Liquor Authority let Haim's liquor license expire, and Alliance Distributors, then named International Distributors, went out of business.[369]

Costello made just one legitimate investment in his own name. He created the 79 Wall Street Corporation as the sole stockholder in 1944. He made a $55,000 investment and assumed the $250,000 mortgage for three office buildings in New York City's financial district. They were four to 13 stories tall. After his purchases the city reduced the buildings' combined assessed value by 8%, even though land costs were rising. He sold them in 1950 for $500,000. This investment allowed him to describe his profession as *real estate dealer.*

The FBI and other investigators always found, "Costello's name never appeared on record in any of his enterprises. When he had to admit an interest, he always explained that he had a 'piece' of an owner's interest and received a percentage of his share of the profits." Costello did everything else on a strictly cash basis including investments, many business and all personal purchases, political and charitable contributions, and bribes. He even offered to pay at least part of his business-building rentals in cash to reduce taxes for both himself and the property owner. He owned everything else in the name of a front man or a close relative. For example Costello rented his Central Park West apartment, and he bought his twelve-room two-acre summer Sands Point residence, in his wife's name. Sands Point was an exclusive residential section on Long Island.[370]

This lack of transaction records made it very difficult to trace any business or gangland connections to him, as was learned by multiple federal agencies, the NYPD, and the DA's office during numerous investigations of Costello's activities. An excellent investigative magazine article at the height of his power reported, "They still have no very clear idea how he operates his many enterprises. Nor can they define with exactness his position in the underworld hierarchy." It correctly identified his key associates because of their frequent meetings, but it remained uncertain if he was the top man as they suspected or how the others lined up under him. The NYPD assumed "Costello dominates gambling in New York, New Jersey and down the Atlantic coast to Florida" based solely on his long-term close association with these operators.[371]

Costello told a closed hearing of the Kefauver Committee that he kept $40,000 to $50,000 cash in a home safe. However, in a subsequent public hearing, he refused to repeat that he stashed as much as $450,000 in today's dollars at his home because he feared the resulting publicity would endanger his family's safety. Even though the purpose of Congressional hearings is to gather facts to develop effective bills, Kefauver wanted drama for the nation's first televised prime-time legislative hearings to advance his campaign for the Democratic presidential nomination. Thus, the Senator threatened Costello with contempt charges to compel him to testify, even though the information was already available to his Committee from its private hearing and it had no relevance to any possible legislation.

Ten days after Costello was forced to testify, three men in their early 20s entered the lobby of Costello's fashionable Central Park West apartment building in the late afternoon. One poked a pistol against the doorman, and the trio forced him into a waiting elevator, where they ordered the operator to take them to the 18th floor. They demanded the doorman and elevator operator take them to Costello's penthouse apartment. They rang his door bell for five minutes, but getting no response, they departed in a car driven by a fourth accomplice.[372]

The thugs arrived with no knowledge about Costello's apartment, not its number, floor, or location in the hallway. This means that they had never been there, nor had they obtained the information about the safe full of cash from anyone who had. Besides, every Costello acquaintance knew that he held business meetings at the Waldorf or the Copa every afternoon and would not be home at that time. These hooligans had obviously learned about this easy and valuable target from the testimony that Costello had so strenuously objected to presenting on television a little over a week earlier. Costello never told his family, or even his closest associates, anything about his business, including the contents of, and the combination to, his safe. Thus, if his wife Bobbie, their adult children, and grand children had been home, the armed intruders might have tortured and murdered them futilely seeking the combination. Costello warned Kefauver about the serious threat such personal and irrelevant testimony posed to his family, but the Senator irresponsibly and ruthlessly forced him to present it to the American people to use the hearings as a political showcase to advance his political ambitions.

The Hollywood film industry and much of the U.S. public have glamorized and greatly exaggerated the power and connections of the Mafia with the larger society, but this incident illustrates that even the Boss of Bosses and his family are vulnerable to basic crimes, such as this home invasion by gun-toting street punks. If Hollywood put this story in a movie, they would have the godfather put out the word, and the perpetrators would be quickly identified and summarily killed. In reality, the Boss of Bosses did not have a clue how to track them down to protect his family from more armed robbery attempts, and neither did the NYPD.

COSTELLO'S POLITICAL SCANDALS & LEGAL ENTANGLEMENTS

Costello was the most commanding political kingmaker in American history. In the nation's biggest city that housed its financial center, Costello was the most influential figure by far, and he ruled during the era of the powerful big-city Republican and Democratic political machines (Chapter 5). Regarding New York City politics, Jimmy Blue Eyes said, "Frank was politically knowledgeable, and he liked foolin' around with it. He wanted to be known as the *boss* of politics. He controlled most of the political leaders, but what good was it? No one ever benefited [referring to his group]."

Costello dominated not only the political world, but as the Boss of Bosses also the underworld. Yet every one who dealt with him was impressed by how adroitly he managed his extraordinary power. Those who watched his maneuverings said he knew both the uses and limitations of power. He seemed to always search for consensus rather than to achieve victory at anyone's expense. He avoided abusing his power and creating conflicts. He was the epitome of give and take negotiations – give the other person something he considered of equal or more value in return for what he wanted to take. Thus he developed practically no enemies during his long career. He was respected by virtually every one who dealt with him, or who was affected by his decisions or actions.

Costello was the most revered American criminal by both the underworld and the overworld, except for the quiet, calm Luciano, who was in a league of his own. Only three men earned the respect of the entire underworld - Luciano, Costello, and Moe Dalitz. These three headed the three largest Prohibition groups, and operated the county's largest high-end illegal-casino chains during the 1930s and 1940s. In addition, they or their associates went on to lead the building of the Las Vegas Strip.

Luciano and Costello dominated politics in New York City, and they commanded the allegiance of the nation's underworld. Right behind them was Moe Dalitz of Cleveland's Jewish Navy. Unlike Luciano and Costello, who were successive Boss of Bosses, Dalitz had no power in the underworld, but he developed extraordinary influence because of close personal ties with more Mafia leaders than any Italian-American. He was also the only person who was ever able to rally every Las Vegas casino operator behind common goals. Dalitz became the most influential man in Nevada history. Yet all three men wielded their tremendous power judiciously and with consideration of their impact on others, so each one developed many admirers and caused virtually no one to say a bad thing about them.

Four other men shared the values of Luciano, Costello, and Dalitz, but they never achieved their lofty stature throughout the underworld and the overworld. Adonis, Lansky, Siegel, and Jimmy Blue Eyes were as highly respected and trusted, but they never held major underworld decision-making positions nor attained the great political clout. Still, these four achieved a reverence from every one they dealt with that no else in the underworld came near. Siegel is important because he laid the groundwork and proselytized the potential of the Las Vegas Strip with his partners and their close associates. As they went on to build and dominate the Las Vegas casino industry and ingratiated themselves with the political scene, Lansky and Jimmy developed great local influence.

Costello's New York City political power base was the Democratic leaders at Tammany Hall. He and many Tammany officials testified over the years about their close associations with each other. About Costello's Hot Springs visits, he testified "I go down there to take baths." He met friends like "a few judges, a few district attorneys, and a few senators. They all go down there." Former Brooklyn DA and New York Mayor O'Dwyer admitted to the Kefauver Committee that Costello was the biggest influence in Tammany Hall, but O'Dwyer added there were other important people.[373]

The *New York Times* frequently ran articles about Costello's influence with both Tammany Hall and specific politicians. The newspaper typically referred to Costello as *the slot-machine king,* and sometimes as *a casino operator* in New Orleans and New York and *a former bootlegger*. The newspaper criticized Costello at times for associating with underworld figures, but never mentioned the Mafia, a connection the NYPD did not even realize at the time.

Costello's powerful influence over Tammany Hall's leadership was attacked annually during election campaigns by the Republican candidates, but they rarely substantiated their allegations. The press began to refer to these predictable Republican political harangues against their designated whipping-boy racketeer as *Costelloisms*. For example, a 1950 article began, "Gov. Thomas E. Dewey carried his charges of *Costelloism* against his Democratic opponents into Western New York tonight." Remember that while Governor Dewey used bombastic rhetoric about Costello, he also allowed his illegal *Piping Rock* casino to operate in Saratoga Springs undisturbed by the state police over which the Governor had ultimate authority. Mayor LaGuardia delighted in terming him *bum,* and Costello complained in a 1946 press conference, "It has become popular to link my name with any type of story to fit any investigation."[374]

A few of the accusations were validated. As an example, Manhattan DA Hogan used information obtained from a 1943 wiretap of Costello's unlisted home phone to create a political scandal. This was the first revelation the voting public heard about Costello's strong influence over Tammany Hall. Hogan issued a long formal statement that Costello, "ex-convict and underworld leader, allied with certain leaders in the Democratic Party, brought about the nomination of Magistrate Thomas A. Aurelio as a candidate for Justice of the Supreme Court [which is the name for a city-court judge, as the Court of Appeals is New York State's highest court]." In the transcription Costello congratulated the candidate for his nomination and also said, "It went over perfect. When I tell you something is in the bag, you can rest assured." Aurelio's shocking reply was, "I want to assure you of my loyalty for all you have done. It's undying."[375]

DA Hogan continued, "Costello had been busy on Magistrate Aurelio's behalf for some time. He was in daily touch, personally and by telephone" with top city Democratic leaders. Hogan turned this political bombshell about the hood and the Magistrate into an attack on the Democratic Party, but this was his typical hypocritical, phony reformer rhetoric. DA Hogan left out that not only had the Republican Party also nominated Aurelio to be Justice, but Republican Mayor LaGuardia had reappointed him Magistrate eight years earlier.

The Magistrate disavowed knowledge of Costello's alleged criminal background, and refused both parties' demands he withdraw his candidacy. The American Labor Party quickly substituted another candidate, who was supported by the Mayor and the Bar association, but the Republican and Democratic Parties could not agree on another candidate. While both parties said they wanted a honest man, each one's unspoken definition of a honest judge actually meant one that would make decisions recommended by their party's leaders in *cases of interest*.

A number of legal actions in the following weeks failed to remove the parties' endorsements from the ballots or to prevent Aurelio from running. As one Judge ruled, "Ethics are up to the voters." Even though Aurelio resigned as City Magistrate to avoid removal hearings, the Bar Association brought disbarment proceedings. A Buffalo Judge dismissed them by finding it "not proven" that Aurelio had any direct knowledge about Costello's bad reputation or character. The Appellate Division concluded, "The record is such as to arouse suspicion. …Suspicion, however, is not proof."[376]

Costello and city Democratic leaders testified in the disbarment proceeding and in an October Grand Jury investigation of Aurelio's nomination. All openly acknowledged the hood's powerful influence over the appointment of Tammany Hall's top leadership. They revealed that Costello met occasionally with top Democratic politicians at the racetracks, fashionable restaurants, and expensive nightclubs. Costello readily admitted that he never had held a position in a political party, and he never had registered to vote.

The Democrats officially joined the Republicans in naming an independent candidate and supporting a write-in campaign. Aurelio won because his was the only name printed on both parties' ballots, and Tammany Hall covertly supported him. The combined total for the two other candidates was much larger, but they split the opposition vote. Republican Mayor LaGuardia summed up the election, "Aurelio was elected because of the insistence of the Republican Party in putting up a third candidate," rather than supporting American Labor's choice. Despite all the tough-on-crime rhetoric by Democratic DA Hogan and Republican leaders Mayor LaGuardia and Governor Dewey during Aurelio's scandal-plagued first election campaign, no candidate opposed the Judge for reelection 14 years later. He had the endorsements of the Republican, Democratic, and American Labor Parties. Thirty years after the scandal, he was still a sitting judge when he died at age 81. Even though Republican leaders laid off Judge Aurelio after his first election, they continued to portray Costello as the Democratic political fixer and to exploit this image in future campaigns by depicting him as the sinister racketeer power behind Tammany Hall.[377]

DA Hogan appealed to voters in both parties by registering with the Democrat Party and spouting Republican anti-crime talk. He created a false reputation for bipartisanship because as a self-proclaimed Democrat he prosecuted top Democratic politicians, and the hoods who supported them. But this was only when Democrat politicians and hoods opposed the campaigns of Republican Governor Dewey, Mayor LaGuardia, and their cronies. For example, DA Hogan called the Judge Aurelio case a Democratic scandal, when the Republicans were equal supporters of the candidate.

Although Hogan was a Democrat, he was always aligned with Republican Dewey. During the Depression, Hogan could not make a living as an attorney, so he asked Special Prosecutor Dewey for a job in 1935. The next year he helped Dewey frame Luciano by directing the torture of the brothel women, and for this Dewey made Hogan his assistant. When Republican Dewey ran for Governor of New York in 1941, he recommended "Democrat" Hogan replace him as Manhattan DA. Hogan was DA for 32 years until he had to resign because of deteriorating health. He enjoyed a good reputation, but serious questions linger over many of his choices about whether to prosecute or not. He alone made the decision not to make any plea bargains with the criminals who could potentially save the lives of thousands of U.S. soldiers during World War II in the Navy-Luciano anti-Nazi effort.

Mayor LaGuardia took every opportunity to personally bedevil Costello under the cover of law for his support of opposition candidates. Late in World War II LaGuardia ordered the NYPD to begin a capricious harassment of the hood. This situation began when Costello took a taxicab from the Hotel New Yorker. Minutes after Costello exited the cab, the driver noticed two envelopes lying on the back seat. They contained a total of $27,200 in cash, and this honest man took them to the police station. Three days later Costello showed up at the NYPD Property Clerk's Office to claim his wad of $100 bills. Accompanying him were the cab driver and the Hotel New Yorker's Assistant Manager. Both witnesses identified Costello as the man who took that cab. Shortly afterward Mayor LaGuardia pressured the hotel to fire its Assistant Manager of 13 years, whose only comment to the press was, "I guess it's a crime to tell the truth." The Mayor destroyed an innocent man's career solely to punish him for testifying conscientiously to the truth. LaGuardia had no interest in truth, justice, or the U.S. Constitutional right to dissent. He was all about rewarding his supporters and vindictively crushing his opposition, and any one else who happened to inadvertently get in his way. Politicians who campaign as reformers like LaGuardia spout great ideals, but they are often more mean-spirited and dishonest than the criminal element they thrive on castigating.[378]

LaGuardia and NYPD officials acknowledged the money belonged to Costello, but despite having no evidence whatsoever, they claimed it was "outlaw money," meaning it was acquired through some illegal activity or illegitimate transaction. Thus, they sought to turn it over to the police pension fund. Mayor LaGuardia said, "What I am interested in is where did the bum get it, and where was he taking it?" Two days later Costello brought a civil suit, and the next day a surprising ally intervened on Costello's behalf. The federal government supported the hood's claim for the money because the IRS wanted to collect a $33,000 income tax lien against Costello's Louisiana slot income, which he was paying off at $1,000 a month.[379]

Over the next two-and-a-half years the case went through several state courts with conflicting decisions. Mayor LaGuardia's position, which some court rulings leaned toward, was in effect that Costello had to prove his money had not committed any crime, rather than the city having to prove it was the product of illegal activity. In the final trial the city focused on the legality of the source of the money, while the IRS ignored such niceties. It was only concerned with money collection, not its antecedents. Costello testified one envelope of cash was from his Louisiana slot and casino partner Kastel, and the other was a loan from his brother-in-law Dudley Geigerman, who worked for his slot company. Just before Costello got into that taxi, Geigerman handed him both envelopes at the Hotel New Yorker. The jury ruled in a ten-to-two verdict that Costello was the rightful owner of what would be $330,000 in today's money. As Costello was handed the $27,200, an IRS agent seized $24,300 to satisfy the outstanding amount of its lien. Costello had rewarded the cabbie with $500 cash and a $3,500 War Bond, totaling 15% of the total he had returned. Costello's IRS liability was paid, but he had to absorb the substantial attorney expenses. His only comment to reporters, "Give me a break for a change and write a nice story about me."[380]

Mayor LaGuardia may have been an ever-present thorn in Costello's side, but his undoing came from facing the Kefauver Committee hearings head on. Jimmy Blue Eyes told me, "Costello loved publicity and wanted a lot of it. ... He thought he was half legitimate or something. ... All of us agreed we would take the Fifth Amendment on everything before the Kefauver Committee. Costello had a lot of ego and thought he could outwit the Committee members. He was the only one of us who talked, and his answers made the whole hearing. This interested the public, generated tremendous publicity, and this fueled many of the reform movements that hurt all of us."

Jimmy was right that Costello attracted the public's attention, but the many local reform movements were caused by the testimony of the local law enforcers and politicians who admitted to taking bribes to allow the illegal casinos to remain open. Most of these illegal casinos were in a small town, and each attracted the wealthy residents from a large nearby city. The voters wanted the prosperity these casinos brought to their town, but they could not stomach hearing about the depth of corruption of their officials, so they voted them out across the country except in Hot Springs, Arkansas, where the casinos kept right on going wide-open.

The Kefauver hearings were held in 1950 and 1951 when many Americans were buying their first black and white television sets. The networks presented many of these hearings live to large daytime audiences. This was the first time America had been able to watch its government in action, or to observe the nation's most infamous hoods either talk about their illicit activities or else repeatedly take the Fifth Amendment to avoid incriminating themselves. The hearings became a sensation, and the highlight was the appearance of the nation's most notorious gambler, Costello. He refused to testify unless the cameras were taken off him, so the lenses focused strictly on his hands. It made for riveting viewing to hear the Senators bark questions and the gangster reply defiantly while the audience stared at the nervous agitation of his hands. This changed the American culture as families stayed indoors, gathered in the eerie half-light of their living rooms, completely transfixed on a single matter.

Costello had one special enterprise that was completely legit. He owned the Copacabana, the most famous and glamorous nightclub in the country. Its resounding success was created by one extraordinary entertainer whose name is all but forgotten today, Joe E. Lewis. Yet this man set the standard for live entertainment in America's nightclubs and in the showrooms of the nation's illegal casinos and along the Las Vegas Strip for the half century that all enjoyed such great popularity, the 1940s through the 1980s. The chronicle of the Copacabana and this entertainer who was so highly revered by his fellow performers during that era of spectacular nightlife follows.

CHAPTER 13

JOE E. LEWIS & COSTELLO'S COPACABANA

JOE E. LEWIS, MACHINEGUN McGURN, & THE COPA

For a glorious half century, America's big cities were home to superlative live entertainment in magnificent nightclubs and casino showrooms, both legal and illegal. The stellar saloon entertainers of the 1940s through the 1980s were usually preceded by superb dining to create a thoroughly memorable evening. The standard for live performing in this era was established by a comedian, who became the most honored entertainer of his time. Few Americans today know the name of Joe Lewis. Even in his heyday, only nightclub and casino showroom goers had heard of him, but he was the nation's biggest draw in both venues.

When Joe entered the entertainment scene, it seemed almost hopeless that he could become successful. He suffered from overwhelming physical, mental, and emotional impediments, and he faced a long difficult struggle trying to develop the many necessary skills to overcome these infirmities. A humble man, he had no interest in fame or stardom. His inexhaustible determination came from his burning passion to make people laugh, because making others happy was his greatest satisfaction.

A beautiful human being, he was always pleasant and kind with everybody, and he was never known to say a mean thing about anyone. His former wife later said of him, "Joe never learned how to be small." This made him one of those rare individuals about whom nobody ever said a bad word. An exceptionally generous man, he gave to those in need, but he respected their dignity by never mentioning his bountiful good deeds. Joe's career is relevant to this history, because he not only became the biggest draw in the Young Turks' illegal casino showrooms, but when they later built the Las Vegas Strip, he became that town's most popular attraction. Joe Lewis was America's superlative entertainer when the Young Turks reigned supreme.[381]

During Prohibition, Joe Lewis became a Chicago nightclub singer. He developed a big following as the singing-comedic Master of Ceremonies for the revue at the Green Mill speakeasy. After performing there for almost a year, he agreed to move for more money to the soon to open Rendezvous Café. Joe's decision infuriated the Mill's silent partner, Machinegun Jack McGurn. This was more than a year before McGurn would direct the St. Valentine's Day Massacre, but he had already earned a fearsome reputation as Al Capone's top gunner. After Joe finished one of his last Green Mill performances, he walked back to his hotel room. A car pulled up alongside, McGurn leaped out and warned Joe not to leave the Mill, because "You'll never live to open [at the Rendezvous]."[382]

Joe bravely defied the killer by going ahead with the planned opening of the new speakeasy. Joe's fans moved with him to the Rendezvous, causing business at the Mill to quickly plummet. McGurn's response would dramatically alter the course of Joe's career, and with it, the development of entertainment at the illegal casinos and legal Las Vegas Strip gambling resorts owned by Charlie Luciano's associates.

A week after opening, Joe was awakened in the morning by a knock at his hotel door. As he opened it, three armed thugs shoved him back into the room and maimed him almost fatally. He was knocked unconscious and his skull was fractured by crushing gun-butt blows to the head. One of the thugs then used a hunting knife to viciously slash him a dozen times, slitting Joe's throat and vocal cords and narrowly missing his jugular vein. The brute gashed open his left cheek from ear to chin, and he all but cut his tongue off. The three thugs severely injured both legs and an arm, and left him for dead in a spreading pool of blood.

Joe awoke dazed in the empty room. Both legs and his right arm seemed paralyzed, and he was unable to talk. He could not call for help on the phone or to other room guests along the hallway. In a Herculean effort, he somehow dragged himself to the door and crawled up against it to a standing position. Finally he somehow turned the knob with his blood-soaked hand, and then leaning against the wall, he used his left arm to pull each leg inches at a time toward the elevator bank. There he pressed the button and collapsed into unconsciousness. The elevator operator arrived to find the badly-mutilated man slumped on the floor covered in blood.

Amazingly Joe survived, but he was left with terrible disabilities. His tongue had to be reconnected, the dangling flap of skin that had been his cheek had to be sewn into place, and two legs and one arm had to heal. The worst problem was permanent brain damage. He no longer remembered many words, and he did not recognize the letters of the alphabet. Fortunately, a Notre Dame English professor met with him every day during his six-week hospital stay to teach him to speak, read, and write again. He began with a kindergarten-level alphabet book. This Catholic Priest professor not only gave the Jewish Lewis the basic skills to become an independently-living man again, but inspired the wholly-demoralized victim with a will to live.

Joe got into this terrible predicament because he was determined to live life his way, and he had even defied death to do it because he cherished his independence. Now, despite his devastating physical and mental handicaps, he knew he had to entertain again. It was the only way he could again experience his only joy in living, his only passion - making others smile. He knew the only way to reach his objective was through a long, tenacious struggle to fully recover physically, and then he would have to build all new talents to entertain from scratch. These almost insurmountable obstacles blocked his arduous path to being able to live life his way again.

Unbelievably, just three months after the brutal attack and the callous impairment, Joe returned triumphantly to the Rendezvous stage to reaffirm his defiance of McGurn. The sold-out audience anticipated seeing an inspiring comeback by the gutsy survivor. Tragically, his beautiful singing voice was gone forever, so he stuck to jokes, but he had also lost his comedic-delivery abilities. Even worse, no one could understand one word because of his serious speech impediments. His dream to perform was no longer backed up with the ability, his shows became empty, and he was soon out of work.[383]

The country's top speakeasy stars gave benefits to pay Joe's hospital bills and enough cash for him to live for awhile. At the home of Al Jolson, Joe recuperated for the next year. A few times Hollywood stars took him out to speakeasies and got him up on stage, but nobody laughed because of his slow recovery. Despite the excruciatingly slow improvement in his physical and comedic skills, he was determined to become an effective performer again because he so cherished making people smile with delight. His agent respected his desire and determination and continued to get him sporadic work as a comic. He was a fill-in for clubs' open dates when no big names were available, or to replace a sick star. With each engagement Joe improved his walk, facial expressions, speech, and timing, but his performances remained amateurish and his audiences meager. Club owners who had been his friends tried to help him by offering handouts but gave him no jobs.

After three years of perseverance and self-rehabilitation, his agent landed him the role as second banana in a Broadway show, but it closed in less than two weeks because of a weak storyline. The nightclub jobs remained infrequent. He wrote different types of humor for his nightclub act, but they did not work for him, not even the obvious Jewish dialect of his background, or the old standby of playing a drunk. Nothing impassioned him but making people amused and cheerful, yet every determined effort was stopped by a roadblock. To numb his frustration, he sadly grabbed for a glass of Scotch upon waking and sipped frequently the rest of the day until he turned out the bed lamp the next morning. Fortunately the booze did not divert his single-minded determination to perform well again, even if this seemed to be an impossible dream to the rest of the world.

Six years into his attempted comeback, he replaced his once beautiful Irish ballads with clever parodies of popular songs. This would become a staple in his act. It started with the $25 purchase of a song written to the notes of a hymn, and soon his small audiences screamed out at every performance for him to sing *Sam, you made the pants too long*.

Willie Wilkerson, publisher of the powerful trade paper *Hollywood Reporter,* was talked into giving Joe a week's gig at his Trocadero, the Sunset Strip's leading nightclub. At the end of his first performance, Wilkerson, whom no one ever accused of being a decent man, gave Joe a withering lambasting for ineptitude and cancelled the rest of his engagement. Wilkerson then told his agent that Joe's problem was not a lack of ability but a demoralized attitude. He believed the aspiring comic was afraid and convinced he was washed up. He concluded that Joe needed to rebuild his confidence and comedic skills, beginning with learning what to do with his hands on stage.

Wilkerson's assessment may have been harsh, but he then explained to the agent that he had the perfect venue for Joe to reconstruct himself with minimal pressure. He hired him to MC the Sunday evening *Undiscovered Stars of Hollywood* shows, which exposed unknown talent to the movie industry's producers, directors, and casters. His one-day-a-week performances seemed like a step down, but they gave Joe time the rest of the week to work on his physical and talent difficulties, while at the same receiving a livable wage that kept him stocked with booze. In addition, women once again became interested in the company of the jovial, kind, sexually un-aggressive entertainer.

When Joe became the Trocadero's MC, he had less talent than the most unseasoned novices he introduced. However, he improved during his 14-month record run at the club, and he decided to take on the nightclubs of New York City once again. Unfortunately, he was still not ready, so he settled back into his well-established routine of intermittent low-paying gigs, which never landed him another engagement.

McGURN AFTER CAPONE

While Joe was recovering from the vicious beating, he refused to identify his three assailants to police. However, he did tell a close friend who was a Chicago Police Captain about McGurn's menacing threats prior to the beating. Later, he told those who closely guided his career about his simmering hatred for McGurn. Joe knew the gangster was responsible for the attack, even though he was not one of the three goons who actually did it. For the decade following Joe's horrific maiming, the comic's career was in shambles, and then he heard that McGurn had also fallen on hard times.

During the six years McGurn had led Capone's entourage of protectors, he had lived high. It should be noted that the police and press often call the most frequent companions of top mobsters *bodyguards,* but very few hoods actually utilized them except during extreme gangland conflict. Capone was the rare exception because his rampant ambition for monopoly and expansion created many dangerous omnipresent enemies.

The day Capone was convicted of tax evasion, McGurn lost his large bodyguard/hit-man salary. While the other gang members continued to work at their various illicit business interests, there was no longer a position for McGurn. When he complained about his financial plight, the gang's new leaders turned a deaf ear. McGurn became half owner in a few gambling enterprises, but they never seemed to last long. For example, soon after the 225 Club nightclub-casino opened, it had a small fire and then the police prevented it from reopening. McGurn was no longer listed by the Chicago Police as a Public Enemy on its major criminal roster. McGurn remained in great physical shape and golfed frequently in the 70s, but he was now unemployed. He lost his home and car because he could not make mortgage and loan payments. Penniless, he depended on living money from his mother.

McGurn's routine included bowling on Friday nights after midnight. One night two companions joined him at the alley. Three other men came in shortly after they did. McGurn removed his overcoat and suit coat and was about to pick up his bowling ball, as the three strangers formed a tight semicircle behind him. One screamed, "Everybody stand still. Move and you die!", as all three pulled out pistols and shot him in the head and back, killing the 32-year old instantly. The shooters stuffed their weapons into their overcoat pockets and fled down the stairway to the first floor exit. McGurn's two companions picked up their coats and the score sheet with their initials on it, and ran out with a dozen customers following. Only the owner, his porter, and his pin setter remained, and the proprietor said, "I crawled under a pool table. When I came out, all were gone except the dead man on the floor." The other two witnesses, the porter and the pin setter, were no more helpful.[384]

The shooting took place one hour after the seventh anniversary of the St. Valentine's Day Massacre, for which McGurn was still a suspect. However, no one believed any gangster waited that long to exact vengeance. McGurn had recently made many enemies. An Oak Park Police Lieutenant testified at the Coroner's Inquest, "A dozen times McGurn has called us to say that his life was in danger. Last October, we went to the house on a call and found him locked in a clothes closet. He wouldn't come out until he was sure we were policemen. He couldn't have been very prosperous, as a finance company took away his big automobile only a few months ago." When threatened, the vicious, sadistic bully was terror-stricken and hid like a coward.[385]

After Capone had gone to prison, McGurn had brought his 24-year-old brother into his various business ventures. Two weeks after McGurn was killed in the bowling alley, his brother was shot to death in a pool hall. The modus operandi of the two killings were identical, and the lead murderer in the pool hall even cried out, "This is a stickup" before opening fire. As the shooters ran, a block away they dropped their guns. One was traced to the same Indiana pawn shop as a gun used in the murder of State Representative Albert J. Prignano. This politician had frustrated the attempts of Capone gangsters to entrench themselves in 20th Ward politics and rackets. This is the closest Chicago Police got to solving these three murders of the McGurn brothers and Prignano.[386]

McGurn was killed just over four years after leaving Capone's employ. During that period he had become a fearful coward who hid in his closet, no longer capable of trying to defend himself. Compare this behavior with what he been during his Capone years when he not only killed cold-bloodedly, but showed exceptional survival skills in the face of severe attack. This disparity is illustrated by three other attempts on his life. All three times the shooters were the Gusenberg brothers, Peter and Frank, and George "Bugs" Moran's brother-in-law James Clark. These serious attempts motivated McGurn to seek vengeance against these North Side enemies. McGurn pushed Capone for authority to eliminate this threat, and 10 months after the third attack, McGurn directed what would become known as the St. Valentine's Massacre.

In the first attempt, McGurn was leaving his mother-in-law's home by the back door. As he was walking through the alley, four men leapt from hiding. McGurn was surprised but instinctively took off running as they opened fire. The bullets whizzed all around him, with several passing through his hat, but none touched him. The police heard about the attack and located him, but he dummied up.

Four months after McGurn had ordered the almost fatal stabbing of comedian Joe Lewis, McGurn decided to go out late one evening. He lived at Capone's headquarters at the McCormick Hotel. When he walked out to get in his car, he failed to notice that a parked car contained three men who were waiting for him to come out. When he drove away in his car, they followed and slowly caught up with him. The three men pulled up along the driver's side of McGurn's car and then tried to crowd him to the curb. McGurn floored his accelerator, pulled ahead, and the race was on. A high-speed chase zigzagged in different directions around the area until McGurn pulled up in front of his hotel. He ran inside McCormick's Smoke Shop lounge and into the phone booth to call for reinforcements from upstairs. The assailants in hot pursuit quickly stopped outside and two men ran in with one carrying a machinegun. The machinegunner strafed a dozen bullets at him in the phone booth, but the moment McGurn heard the first shot he crumpled to the floor. The attackers assumed their bullets floored and killed McGurn, so the shooter ran out as the second man covered his retreat by walking backwards with his automatic pistol aimed at the people inside. Both assailants jumped into the car and the driver sped away. McGurn and a real estate agent sitting in the lounge were seriously shot. The agent was bleeding from shots in the right lung and the left arm, while McGurn was bleeding worse from wounds in the chest and both arms. Ambulances rushed both to the hospital. When police arrived and tried to question him, McGurn swore at them and demanded to see a lawyer. The indignant police charged him with disorderly conduct for being shot at his hotel.

A month later the Judge dismissed the facetious disorderly conduct case. McGurn walked out of the court building a free man and got into his car without realizing the same trio of shooters was parked in wait. At first the assailants trailed him, but then they turned on a crossing street, sped up, drove to the first parallel street to McGurn, and turned in the same direction to get ahead of him. Finally they turned to get back to his street, and came in the opposite direction towards him. In an intersection they passed beside McGurn's car and opened up with the machinegun. McGurn slammed on his brakes, jumped out, and ran into a building doorway with the machinegun blazing at him. They sped away, leaving his car and the doorway riddled by the hail of gunfire, but his speedy running kept him from being hit.

Two years later police stopped McGurn and arrested him for carrying a machinegun in his automobile, but he was freed on a technicality. Two weeks later police raided his apartment in the Guyon Hotel to find shotguns and pistols. He told the police, "A man can keep arms at home," and smiling, he added, "I have to keep an arsenal to protect myself." What a difference between this man and the one who would hide in fear while waiting for police protection six years later.[387]

JOE E. LEWIS PERSEVERED

McGurn's death may not have helped Joe Lewis with his agonizingly slow improving abilities, but it allowed the aspiring comic to stop suffering from a picture behind his eyes of the vicious attacker roaming the streets, an image that clearly haunted him. Whenever he was asked about his facial scar, he described a fictional car accident. When friends asked him why he lied about the cause of his disfigurement, he replied "What's the use telling the truth and making 'em have bad dreams? Bad dreams are bad. I know. I used to have 'em regular."[388]

Joe was able to wisecrack about his painful and traumatic experience. At a press conference, he named the many Chicago nightclubs he had played, and in mentioning the Rendezvous he said, "I was cut short there," referring to the slashing. Joe, always the fall guy in his humor, in this case joked lightly about horrifying adversity.[389]

Joe continued working on his career. He changed his stage name by adding the initial *E.* to end confusion with World Heavyweight Champion Joe Louis. He knew some of the people who came to his shows were disappointed to find out they were not going to meet the famous boxer. Besides, many people called him *Joey.*

He was billed as *Joe E. Lewis* for the Broadway show *Right This Way.* Because of a weak plot it quickly closed, but a few years later during World War II a song from the show, *I'll Be Seeing You (In All The Old Familiar Places),* became a favorite with separated spouses and lovers.

Joe E.'s style and abilities continued to improve, and he became a moderate attraction on the national nightclub circuit during the next four years. However, by then this shtick had become passé with his regular audiences, so his agent William Morris Agency could no longer get him bookings. When his comeback seemed finished, an opening became available for the late show at a third-rate New York City nightclub. The Copacabana had been open a year, and its minor revue was doing poorly. It had never used name acts and could not afford one, so Joe E.'s agent agreed to a low salary for midnight shows only. But Joe E. needed a livable income, so the agent also booked him into a new Broadway show, *The Lady Comes Across.* This was the only time the easy-going comic argued with his agent because it would be a grueling performance schedule to follow *The Lady* with the Copa show every night. In addition, screaming loud enough so people in the Broadway show balcony could hear every word would strain his repaired voice. Worst of all would be the extreme disruption the 1 p.m. Broadway matinees would cause to his lifestyle. Joe never woke until mid afternoon, and then he had to recover from his hangover. On matinee days he would start on Broadway at 1 p.m. and finish at the Copa at 1:30 a.m. This was a 12-hour-plus performing day. While these drawbacks seemed overwhelming to Joe E., the only way he could still perform in a nightclub was to accept this deal so cleverly-assembled by his agent.

The show's Boston pre-Broadway tune-up received bad revues because it had poor dialog, and Joe E. knew from the crowd's weak reaction at the curtain calls that it was doomed. One month after the bombing of Pearl Harbor, *The Lady* opened on Broadway. The next morning *Lady's* devastating New York revues hit the newspaper stands, and that night following its third performance the producers announced to the cast that the show was closed. For Joe E. it had been a long, rough day, beginning with facing the morning's bad reviews, performing the show at the matinee and both evening performances, and then hearing the closing announcement that it was a failure.

Joe E. headed for the Copa, where his engagement had started the night before *The Lady* opened. The first two nights his nightclub act had sparse midnight audiences, and he had no reason to believe the third night would be any better. He later told close associates that waiting in the wings to go on with the late-night show at the Copa was the worst moments of his life, except for the slashing. He had just struck out a third time on Broadway, and he feared he was about to establish a dubious show-business record that would never be equaled - being closed by a Broadway show and canceled in a nightclub engagement the same night. As he stood backstage, he was sure *The Lady's* bad reviews would wreck his late-night Copa run and finish his career. He was afraid he would never again be able to do the one thing he truly loved, make people laugh with joy.

As Joe E. stood waiting for what he thought was going to be his introduction to oblivion, the production manager in the control booth prepared the orchestra leader and the sound, light, and stage crews for the opening beat by barking the count-down into their head sets. "Five. Four. Three. Two. One. Showtime!" The house lights on both sides of the curtain dimmed. The drum roll began as the announcer boomed through the darkness, "The Copacabana is proud to present Joe E. Lewis." The orchestra broke into his trademark introduction, *Chicago, That Toddlin' Town,* as the spotlights swirled around the parting curtains. That is when he walked onto the stage to face his destiny.

As Joe E. approached the front of the stage, he tried to understand what he was seeing. When he had read *The Lady's* dreadful revues, he had been totally disheartened because his livelihood depended on the show's survival. His disillusionment about the show's future had kept him from being uplifted by every New York City reviewer going gaga over his dazzling performance in this bad vehicle. He had no idea these reviews about his personal performance had made him the city's number-one entertainment attraction. He looked out to see every seat filled. He also accomplished something that never happened in American nightclubs - he had standing room only. Patrons were wedged shoulder to shoulder along the back wall and both side walls, standing with drinks in hand.

The crowd was waiting with great anticipation, and he was finally ready to become a star. Every performing element he had been improving during 14 years of self-directed physical rehabilitation, relearning, and evolving came together that magical night. He walked and held his hands naturally to portray an array of moods. He expressed his intense reactions visually with hand bumps against his head, jumps leading to heel kicks in mid-air, and odd personalized dance steps, like flat-wheeled pirouettes, mambo moves, and a running stagger. He spoke clearly, and complemented his words with a full range of facial expressions that conveyed the appropriate attitudes and feelings. He had finally attained perfect comedic timing. After long experimentation of various comic styles he had found the one that suited him. He simply played himself, a somewhat inebriated gambler who appreciated womanhood. He had transformed himself into the consummate stand-up comic.

Joe E. walked on stage and grabbed the whisky tumbler sitting on the piano, and held it up while calling out *Post time!* He took a long swig of undiluted Scotch. From that moment he owned that audience, just as he would every audience for the next quarter century.

The next afternoon Frank Costello's Copa renegotiated his contract for three shows nightly. The club extended his three-week contract three times, but at the end of his 12-week run, he was already committed to a year of nightclub performances across the country. Before the Copa engagement, he had appeared in revues, in which he introduced four or five other acts as the Master of Ceremonies before giving his monologue. Now he was the headliner, backed by a female singer to open his shows. The *New York Mirror* awarded Joe E. Lewis the Gold Medal for "The Outstanding Nightclub Performer Of 1942." That year he became America's most highly-paid nightclub entertainer, a position he held for two decades.

When Joe E. opened at the Copacabana, it was an obscure, dying night spot. The excitement generated by his engagement catapulted it into the most famous nightclub in America, and every great entertainer sought to play in Joe E's house as the pinnacle of their career. Sammy Davis, Jr. wrote that it had "the best performers in the business. That's where they played, the Copa." Sammy set the Copa's all-time attendance record and biggest revenue during his engagement a half year after the assassination of President John Kennedy. This engagement of Sammy's was also near the time President Lyndon Johnson signed the Civil Rights Act making Africans equal citizens and giving them admittance to any public facility. Another star, Bobby Darin, became the final member of an incredible series of superlative American saloon entertainers who spanned the half-century of the nightclub. Earlier in his career, at a time when he was turning out rock-and-roll hits in his youth, he confided to close associates, "I will know I am a star the night I walk out on the Copa's stage."[390]

The Copacabana booked stars at the peak of their careers, when they had a hit recording, a smash movie, a sensational TV appearance, or were otherwise basking, or being pillared, in publicity limelight. America's leading entertainers moved into and out of the Copa's roster of stars. But every one who loved New York nightlife knew that come September, Joe E. would kick off every star-studded fall-season reopening of the Copa before he went on to play his circuit of the country's other preeminent nightclubs. He remained the Copa's headliner-in-chief for the next unbelievably record-breaking 25 years, until a stroke reined in America's master entertainer while he was still at the top.

Joe E.'s transformation as a performer during his initial Copa appearance was summed up by three of the nation's top entertainment reviewers. A review before he appeared at the Copa stated, "Joe E. Lewis went along for seasons as a fair-to-middlin' performer and then suddenly hit his stride and became a topliner." After his engagement another said, "The word genius is a sadly battered one, but brush it off, shine it up, and hang it on Joe E. Lewis. It is the one way you can describe this very funny man. I knew a day when genius would have been the last word I'd have applied to Joe, but that was a day before Joe really had found himself, when the well of humor within him ran unevenly. Long since, however, he has hit the stride of which he always has been potentially capable." The third wrote, "If there was a better entertainer in the nightclubs than Joe E. Lewis, I missed him, and I wouldn't believe it, anyway. … After all, you can be just so good, and that ends it."[391]

Newspaper reporter and author Damon Runyon wrote about his favorite comedian and gin-rummy opponent, "Lewis has no competition." Joe E. cracked back, "And if Runyon knew how to break up his kings, he wouldn't have to write for a living."[392]

Joe E.'s name was almost unknown with the general public, but he was the undisputed king with America's nightclub audiences. He played the finest places, including a personally triumphant return to Hollywood at Wilkerson's newest nightclub, Ciro's, where he was a smash. This club became a centerpiece in Joe E.'s annual circuit, and the many movie stars who had encouraged him during his long, difficult rehabilitation poured in to enjoy his personalized kibitzing ad-libs. Joe E.'s crowds were a who's who of the rich and powerful in each city he appeared. The top civic leaders, socialites, celebrities, businessmen, hoods, and racetrack personalities came to howl.

Joe E. played the premier illegal high-limit casino nightclubs around the country every year, especially those owned by Luciano's closest friends. He appeared at Meyer Lansky's *Colonial Inn* near Miami during the winter season, and at Costello's *Piping Rock* in Saratoga Springs during the summer season. During Joe E.'s *Piping Rock* engagements, silent partner Joe Adonis dined in the restaurant every night before joining the star between performances to play high-stakes gin rummy. The other casinos on Joe E.'s circuit were Costello's *Beverly Club* outside New Orleans, and Moe Dalitz's *Mounds* in Cleveland and his *Beverly Hills Country Club* near Newport, Kentucky, the country's most elegant and largest nightclub.

Luciano's buddy Ben Siegel introduced Joe E. to Las Vegas showroom audiences at his new *Flamingo* in 1947. Upon Siegel's death a couple months later, Joe E. moved to the *El Rancho Vegas* where he became a fixture for about half of each year. No other star commanded more than a three-to-four-week engagement in Las Vegas. Lewis was the town's biggest star during the 1950s, the city's greatest boom era, when 10 major Strip casino resorts opened. For the rest of his career, Joe E. worked exclusively at casino showrooms, legal and illegal, and the nation's premier freestanding nightclubs.

Joe E. was in a class by himself. He was the high-limit gamblers' favorite Las Vegas entertainer by a long shot. High-rollers came in droves because Joe E. was one of them. He wagered at racetracks during the afternoon when horseracing was America's biggest sport; he played $5-a-point gin rummy with friends between performances; and he bet in casinos from the close of his late show until the sun rose. All the gambling in Las Vegas was legal, and wide-open illegal casinos were readily available in the big cities where he appeared. When joking about the turf, tote, and tout, Joe E. showered audiences with his losing afternoon racetrack pari-mutuel betting tickets while explaining, "I spent my whole life following horses that followed other horses."

This was the era of the *rounder* - men who liked to drink, gamble, and chase women. Joe E.'s lifestyle, stage character, and humor epitomized the rounder. He joked about wagering, drinking, and sexual innuendo. He was the master of double entendre.

Joe E. was the poster boy for self-indulgence, parlaying his considerable faults into a highly successful career. He drank and gambled heavily, and he was a chain smoker. This did not help his gravel voice that rasped like sandpaper rubbed together because of the horrible knife slicing. He scrupulously avoided moderation, exercise, and other healthy choices that were counter to instant gratification. He lived the adult escapism that Las Vegas was all about during its Golden Era.

His fun-loving enjoyment of his own act was contagious with the audience. Just before each punch line, his wizened face got a mischievous twinkle like a little boy about to say or do something naughty. Joe E. was usually described as *charming,* but rather than being sophisticated or suave, his slashed, nerve-damaged face, blended with his gentle warmth and sincere humility, gave him a rugged charm. He was one of the great ad-libbers. The spontaneous and witty Joe E. took delight in chewing up hecklers who insisted on trying to take up the floor. His clever squelchings of the offensive manners of the rude became the highlights of his shows.

Joe E. made a great impression on me in my youth. My parents took me on their summer-vacation drives across the country. They stopped a few days in Las Vegas in 1954 and 1956, and I was privileged to see Joe E. at the *El Rancho* on both trips. I was the only youth in those showroom audiences at America's adult playground. I wore a suit like all the men, while the women wore elegant, stylish cocktail dresses and minks. I was 12-years old the first year, so I did not understand some of Joe E.'s double-entendre jokes, but his timing was so impeccable and his expressions so precious that I howled with glee along with every adult there. The next trip I had gone through puberty, and I understood every one of his jokes. I have been fortunate to have seen practically every great comedian of my lifetime in live performance, and I have admired and laughed wholeheartedly with each of them. However, I wish just one more time, I could see Joe E. walk out to the front of the stage and call out *Post time!*

In talking about drinking, Joe E. always referred to Prohibition as *The Great Drought.* He tied appropriate topical political humor into his routine. For example, he opined about the alcohol-drink sales tax passed to help finance World War II. "The 30% Federal tax is a wonderful thing. Buying a drink is now patriotic!" Imbibing from his glass on stage, he quipped, "I drink to quiet my nerves. My doctor keeps asking me, 'How noisy can your nerves be?'"

Joe E. Lewis publicly squandered every paycheck on gambling and drinking, but he indulged these passions only after he first privately gave money to every one he knew, or encountered, who was in need. He tried to keep his charities secret, but many people saw him routinely extend his generosity to those who were having financial difficulties or were down and out. It was obvious to every one who knew him that he gave away a huge fortune over his life. None of the hard adversities, impediments, or frustrations of his life, nor the horror of any gangster or homeland terrorist, no matter how vicious and cruel, ever dimmed his spirit, caring, or helpfulness. He was dedicated to making every one around him feel better with a smile, a quip, a pat on the back, or a handout.

In addition to three performances seven nights a week, he typically ran out between shows one night or afternoon a week to headline a charitable benefit for the needy. He was ready to help everyone, but he appeared most often for the nation's fighting men and their families, war-bond sales, destitute old entertainers, ill or handicapped children, Europe's Jewish war refugees, and impoverished segregated African-American neighborhoods. These charitable benefits drew audiences of up to 20,000, with everyone attending making a contribution to the cause.

A year and a half after his initial Copa success, he put his booming career on hold without pay for almost three months. He devoted himself to entertaining the fighting men in the South Pacific. He hopped 30,000 miles from island to island to give up to four one-hour shows a day at different Army camps and makeshift jungle stages for the United Service Organization-Camp Shows (USO). He often ended his nightclub shows with, "May the good Lord take a liking to you, but not too soon." This thought never touched any of his audiences more than these soldiers, who were preparing to again enter fierce battles.

Joe E.'s special long-term cause was paying the living expenses for Bill Robinson, the great tap dancer who became destitute after his legs wore out and he could no longer perform. The African-American Robinson had an illustrious career and opened new opportunities by becoming the first African performer to appear in vaudeville and in Florenz Ziegfeld's *Follies* on Broadway. He starred in a dozen movies, including playing and dancing opposite child phenomenon Shirley Temple in four that were released during the four years she was Hollywood's biggest box-office draw. He went on to become a premier New York City headliner in Broadway revues and at the famed Cotton Club. Like Joe E., he was a gambler and a drinker, but unlike Joe E., Robinson was unpleasant company when inebriated. The rest of the time he was a delightful personality with an infectious smile and a sparkling wit. Whenever he was asked how he was doing, he jubilantly replied, "Everything's copasetic," meaning first-rate. He may not have coined the word, but his exuberance certainly popularized it. Orphaned at a young age, Robinson was renowned for generously giving most of his income to the needy of all races, especially to schools and orphanages. He additionally averaged more than one charitable benefit daily throughout his long career, often relinquishing professional dates to help others. When Robinson retired broke, Joe E. took care of him in comfort for the rest of his life.

Four years after World War II ended, Robinson died of a heart ailment at age 71. Even though racial segregation was engrained in the culture and the civil-rights movement had yet to make press headlines, his funeral transcended this racial divide, as the greatest European-American entertainers and athletes came to pay their final respects. Irish Mayor Bill O'Dwyer gave only one eulogy while in office, and no one could remember another New York mayor ever giving one. O'Dwyer spoke directly to Robinson's casket, "The affection and joy you gave is measured by the sorrow of seeing you go."[393]

The city gave this tap dancer and humanitarian a hero's send off. The NYPD cordoned off the cross streets along his beloved Broadway the whole eight-mile procession route from his Harlem Baptist church to the Brooklyn cemetery. His flag-draped hearse and entourage of flower-bedecked cars was slowly led by a row of mounted police in dress uniforms. The silent mourners lining the sidewalks on both sides were wedged 10 deep behind barricades manned by 500 officers. The city's schools were closed that day so the children to whom he had contributed so much could say goodbye. On that cold winter day, men and boys removed their hats and placed them over their hearts as the hearse passed. Before pausing for a short time in the middle of the enormous silent throng packed into Times Square, the mounted honor guard and hearse stopped in front of the Palace Theater where Robinson had enjoyed great success in the heyday of vaudeville. The stars, choruses, and orchestras of Broadway's musicals had gathered en mass to give him a roaring rendition of *Give My Regards to Broadway.* The NYPD said 500,000 quietly lined the route that morning to pay tribute. On that busy business morning, New Yorkers joked that "the only way you could get to the West Side or the East Side was to be born there."

When Robinson died, the Irish Ed Sullivan called the Jewish Joe E. and told the comic that he did not want to write in his syndicated column *Looking at Hollywood* that the African dancer was a great man. Instead, Sullivan said he wanted to write that Robinson was such a great man that he would pay for all his funeral expenses. Sullivan acknowledged that Joe E. had covered Robinson's living expenses for years and had earned the right to pay for his funeral. But Sullivan said he would consider it a special favor to be allowed to do this. Sullivan also pointed out that he had always treated Joe E. well in his column, even during his rough struggling periods. Joe E., in his usual unassuming manner, was happy to let Sullivan take all the public credit for the cost of the funeral.

Six months after the funeral, Ed Sullivan again stood at Robinson's gravesite. This time there were no reporters, cameras, or crowds as Sullivan directed the laying of the tombstone he had made for him. Then a rabbi and a priest each gave their respective blessings while a choir sang. Standing at attention throughout these services was a color guard representing the Army, Marines, Air Force, Navy, and Coast Guard with their respective service flags and the American flag waving in respect. After every one else departed, Sullivan said his private goodbye. Robinson had been raised by his grandmother who had been freed from slavery by Abraham Lincoln. Thus, inscribed on his tombstone is a quote by the President, "With malice towards none, with charity for all.[394]

Robinson had been nicknamed Bojangles, a stylized pronunciation of the name Boujasson, the hat maker from whom he admitted pilfering a beaver cap when he was just eight years old. Ironic that a man who carried the nickname for a childhood theft would devote his adulthood to giving millions upon millions of dollars to the most needy. Although nicknamed Bojangles, Robinson's life was nothing like the 1968 hit song *Mr. Bojangles.* Written 20 years after Robinson's death by Jerry Jeff Walker, the song depicts a forlorn old alcoholic dancer, who could still show great flashes of his special talent. It was likely patterned about the life of one of the many Robinson imitators who danced for tips in small bars and honky tonks.[395]

Whatever this hit's origin, Sammy Davis, Jr. told his nightclub and showroom audiences, "This song is very special to me." At rare moments he added that he always feared his free-spending lifestyle would end him up like the song's Bojangles, an over-the-hill hoofer having to work honky tonks. Sammy began his brilliant tap-dancing career in the 1933 Hollywood movie *Rufus Jones for President,* in which the adorable 7-year old was dressed in a stylish suit and cap to sing and dance the tough-talking song *Ill Be Glad When You're Dead You Rascal You.*

Sammy demonstrated his potential with a commanding stage presence, and it would have been a beautiful moment of Hollywood cinema, except his debut film drove home the segregationist attitudes of the time. Sammy was surrounded in the *Rascal* scene by an African-American ensemble in a town-hall recital setting. The chorus was dressed in fine suits and gowns, but each held a chicken breast in his or her hand from which each took bites to demean them with a racially stereotypical image. The director made Sammy end his routine with a close up of a big munch on the piece of chicken he held throughout his performance.

For Sammy, *Mr. Bojangles* may have represented many sad memories. He made it his signature song and dance routine in his live performances. At each concert Sammy would wait until the applause from his next to last song died down, and then he would set off his finale with a resounding cheer from the audience as he carefully positioned his trademark derby hat in a dashing pose and transformed his posture into that of the old but still spirited tap dancer. As in life, Bojangles was honored long after his death with the symbol of a hat.

The press remained unaware of Joe E.'s great generosity to Robinson, and so many others, because the humble comedian never talked about his bigheartedness. Likewise, the press never caught on that Joe E. was the most honored comedian of his lifetime by America's funniest men and women, along with all the great singers and actors. The Friars Club, an organization of the nation's most famous comedians, voted him *Abbot,* the official name of its CEO. They honored him by keeping him in this position as long as he lived, and even after a stroke kept him from performing during the last five years of his life.

The top stars of show business gave Joe E. countless testimonials to raise money for charities. These combination uproarious-roasts and reverent-tributes set records for the number of leading entertainers attending and the amount donated. At one of the many Joe E. love fests, he responded at the conclusion, "If I had known you were going to talk about me this way, I would have done the decent thing and died first."

Joe E.'s favorite hangout, the Friars Club, is where today's top comedians typically meet when they visit New York City. It is interesting that a half century after Joe E. gave his last performance on stage that the room in which he used to play gin rummy with cronies is still named the *Joe E. Lewis Card Room.* In addition, the Lucille Ball Room for dining still has the *Joe E. Lewis Bar*, where it is always "Post time!" I recently asked a Friars official why, with the many great and famous comedians since his passing, has his name been kept on two rooms by a membership that never even saw him perform. He replied, "You have to understand, here he's a legend."[396]

Joe E.'s profound impact on the development of Las Vegas showroom entertainment continued after his death for another generation because of his weighty influence on young singer Dean Martin's career. Dino was a minor nightclub singer in 1946 when he partnered with Jerry Lewis, whose act was silent pantomimes done to 78 rpm musical recordings. The pair quickly became the hottest nightclub, movie, and television comedy duo in the country. They were the country's comedy sensation, and they sold out the Copa for eight years. They were at their peak when they gave their emotional last performance there before breaking up in 1956.

Jerry Lewis was the comedic goof-ball, while Martin was the straight man who interspersed their comedy shows with a few ballads. Along with many others, Dean wondered what would become of his career without Jerry. To avoid the frenzied onslaught of the press over the breakup, Dean sequestered himself in a suite at the *Sands Hotel*, the pair's Las Vegas Strip home.

Sands Managing Director Archie Loveland went up to Dean's suite to offer sympathy and support. Loveland told me, "Dean was extremely depressed. He didn't know what was going to happen to him. No one thought he could do anything without Jerry. The *Sands* partners, including [Frank] Sinatra, got together and gave him a chance. They gave Dean his first appearance as a single in a two-week engagement. Sinatra joined him on stage. Many Hollywood celebrities came to his performances to cheer him on. Dean sang, but it wasn't much of a show because he had no act. He had no format or individual image. I met with Dean again when his engagement closed and advised him to go study the master, Joe E. Lewis, to learn how to add some humor to his singing act."[397]

Dino spent time studying Joe E.'s performing mannerisms and humor. Dino then began standing at the microphone holding a tumbler of Scotch from which he indulged liberally. He walked with a slightly-woozy stagger, and when Dino began songs he slurred *Uhhhhh Yaaaa* in fluctuating pitches, as if struggling to find the opening notes.

Dino became the only big-time nightclub star besides Joe E. to feature parodies of popular songs throughout his act. Dino changed the lyrics and cut each short with a Joe E.-style double entendre quip line. He interspersed his songs with jokes and wisecracking about drinking and chasing women, even though married, and he soon became known as much for his comedic talent as his hit recordings.

Like Joe E., Dean was a genuinely easy-going, considerate gentleman, with natural charm. Just before each punch line, he had a twinkle in his eyes, but it was one of being pleased with himself rather than naughty like Joe E.'s gleam. Dean, too, was amused by his own jokes, and laughed as he tossed off each quip with carefree ease. Later in his TV career, Dino was toast master for many specials based on the Friars Club's roasts turned into an art form and popularized by Joe E.

Sands Manager Loveland concluded his interview with me by saying, "Dean stole Joe's material and drunken image and that took him to stardom. Dean took a lot of his material from Joe for a long time. He became a singing Joe E. Lewis." Dino confirmed the influence of Joe E.'s style on his career in a reflective newspaper interview at age 70. He said he had to reinvent himself for a new career just like Joe E. did. Dino explained, "It took me about a year to develop my own style. I got Sammy Cahn to write a few special lyrics for me [parodies], and I started doing this Joe E. Lewis-type thing."[398]

For the next decade, Joe E. did his act at one end of the Strip, and Dino did Joe E.'s act at the other end. They were the only two superstars who held a glass of whiskey in their hand during their performances. Instead of complaining about Dean's imitation, Joe E. began quipping in his act, "I don't drink any more than the man next to me, and the man next to me is Dean Martin." However, when a reporter asked if Dean drank as much as he did, Joe E. quipped, "I've spilled more than he's drunk." Joe E.'s philosophy was "A man is never too drunk to drink if he can lay on the floor without holding on."

Dean Martin came back at Joe E. Lewis in his act with, "Joe E. and I were together at my home about two weeks ago. We were in my den one morning...swimming! He mixed himself a peculiar drink, and I asked [Dino would lean over looking down at the floor], 'What are you drinking down there?' He looked down at me...and said, 'Scotch and carrot juice.' I asked, 'Why?' He said, "I get drunk but I see good." Dean continued with a Joe E. line he would use the rest of his nightclub career. "But I want to say one thing in all seriousness. I feel sorry for you people who don't drink. I mean it. Because when you wake up in the morning, that is as good as you're going to feel all day."

After Joe E.'s stroke, Dino replaced him as the number-one attraction in Las Vegas by continuing to combine Joe E.'s stage persona and humor with his fine vibrato-laced crooner's voice. In this popularity category, Dino would be overtaken by just one other entertainer, Elvis Presley in 1969, when he became Las Vegas' most phenomenal draw ever. However, Dino's position as the Strip's most popular entertainer with high-rolling gamblers was never challenged by anyone. This was an interesting career transposition for Dino because the comedy duo of Martin and Lewis had drawn large mass audiences rather than casino players.[399]

Joe E.'s impact on nightclub and casino-showroom entertainment during the half-century era of the great saloon entertainers from the beginning of the 1940's through the 1980's was astonishing. No other entertainer may ever overcome more career impediments and disappointments attempting to make a decent living, and then totally dominate his chosen field for more than two decades. In addition, it is doubtful any other entertainer will put such a gracious imitator on top for more than another two decades.

Interestingly, both Joe E.'s and Dino's careers as entertainers took off in casinos owned by Luciano's close friends. Joe E. and Dino were the ultimate entertainers for two generations of nightclub rounders, and the biggest Strip attraction for America's high-rollers when Las Vegas was a gambling town, with the resorts driven primarily by casino revenues. In contrast, today's Strip megaresorts derive most of their revenue from high-priced non-gambling facilities, rather than their casinos that have been reduced to minor side attractions or amenity facilities.

COSTELLO'S *PIPING ROCK* CASINO & COPACABANA NIGHTCLUBS

Costello owned the *Piping Rock Club* on Saratoga Lake in Saratoga Springs in upper state New York from the late 1930s through the 1940s. Operating the club were three department directors responsible for entertainment, food and beverage, and the casino. The *Piping Rock* offered fine dining and nightclub shows, and a casino was in a separate building behind. Near the restaurant door that exited onto the passageway leading to the gambling building, three *spotters* stood greeting and approving players for admittance to the gambling. Each spotter specialized in a different group of players - the Copacabana-crowd regulars, the locals and other New Yorkers, and out-of-state tourists including those who had visited Florida casinos Costello had an interest in. These specialized spotters were an early type of hosting by player-geographical origin that would be developed into an art form a few years later by the Las Vegas Strip gambling resorts. The spotters let recognized players go past them by signaling to the two armed former policemen who blocked the casino doorway. The gambling room offered craps, roulette, chemin-de-fer, and birdcage dice games.

Costello's partners in the *Piping Rock Club* were Joe Adonis and Meyer Lansky, who was fronted by his brother Jake not only there but also at the *Beverly Club* and slot route in Louisiana. These three close-knit friends invested in each other's casinos. Costello had a piece of Adonis' Bergen County casinos, and both were partners in Lansky's *Arrowhead* in Saratoga and his Florida casinos.

Frank Costello operated the *Piping Rock Club* each summer, and he closed it every year at the end of the August horseracing season. He decided to have his casino's entertainment and food managers keep their staffs together the rest of the year to operate a nightclub in the heart of Manhattan near the southeast corner of Central Park.

Costello opened the Copa in a remodeled restaurant in late 1940. Its location and entrance were not impressive. It was in the basement of the 13-story Hotel Fourteen with a separate entrance that became known as *three steps up and one flight down.* At the top of the three steps was the club's lobby with the choice of the Copa lounge to the right or a stairway down to the showroom to the left. Stars could go from their hotel room in the Hotel Fourteen down into the Copa's kitchen and backstage. During one of Martin and Lewis' engagements, comedian and TV-series star Phil Silvers was staying in the hotel. During the middle of their performance, he walked out on stage impromptu and unannounced in his pajamas and loudly objected to their making too much noise for the people sleeping upstairs.[400]

The Copacabana's main room was ill-suited for stage entertainment because it had four large structural columns that interfered with the audiences' view. These posts were covered up with tall round white tree trunks with huge white palm branches extending out from the post trunks at ceiling level over the tables and chairs surrounding them. The first time comedian and TV-series star Morey Amsterdam played the room, he looked around the audience and announced, "This joint's got more posts than the American Legion." The showroom opened with a seating capacity of 400, but soon after Joe E. Lewis' act became the town's biggest attraction, the room was expanded out to seat 670 at the tables and another 50 at the bar, making it one of the biggest nightclubs in New York City. Joe E. kept them filled nightly for the rest of his career, as he was the club's top draw until a stroke sidelined him, and Sammy Davis Jr. took over as the Copa's biggest attraction.[401]

Following Joe E. Lewis' initial engagement, the Copa became the nation's most celebrated nightclub headlining the top saloon entertainers. The shows opened with the famed Copa Girls, the beautiful, alluring, and leggy chorus line. Since the country's greatest showplace was named after a Rio de Janeiro hotel, it featured alternating Latin and American bands for dancing with dinner and between the shows. However, it offered French cuisine and Chinese dishes prepared by two separate staffs of specialty chefs. It was the only nightclub in New York City whose food was reputed to rival the city's finest restaurants. What an experience the Copa offered that was unlike anything that exists today. The greatest performers, top big-band music and dancing, exceptional food, the world's finest beverages, and the spontaneous thrills. The Copa was the height of glamour, elegance, and sophistication, the ultimate fun and enjoyable evening out.

Costello had three key operating executives at his Saratoga Springs *Piping Rock Casino,* but he did not need his casino manager at the Copacabana in Manhattan. There he brought in his entertainment director Monte Proser and his food and beverage manager Jules Podell. Costello never kept anything in his name, so he made Proser and Podell his front men as the owners of record. Jimmy Blue Eyes related, "Everyone knew Frank was behind the Copa." Most late afternoons Costello held business conferences and was in total charge at the empty showroom tables before the dinner crowd started arriving.[402]

Proser assembled the greatest line-ups of entertainment stars ever. He was a quiet, creative, and effective force. He had previous experience with Broadway shows, a string of Beachcomber nightclubs, and the *Piping Rock Casino* showroom. Proser directed the Copa's entertainers, musicians, chorus line, stage and light crew, and the staff in the showroom that dealt with the public. When Costello went on to open the *Tropicana* resort on the Las Vegas Strip, he brought Proser in as his entertainment director.

Podell was a long-time restaurant man who ran the kitchen and waiter staff, but he functioned like a domineering street bully, a totally different attitude from anyone else Costello did business with. He was a tyrant who had a growling voice, shouted strings of obscenities, was verbally abusive, and even slapped waiters.

Despite Podell's awful treatment of the food preparation staff, they produced exceptional food and provided excellent service because Podell monitored every meal that left his kitchen. The servers had to stop for his inspection. He lifted the cover on each plate and checked the portion size and its appearance. Anything that dissatisfied him had to be done over. Once a waiter passed Podell's eyeballing, another checker waited at the door leading into the showroom for a second examination. Podell was obsessed with cleanliness. If he saw a small piece of food on the floor, he would stop everything until it was properly cleaned up, and if there was the slightest spot on a waiter's white jacket with it crimson collar, he made them stop and immediately change into a new one.

Podell adopted the racial-discrimination policy of Manhattan's earlier Cotton Club nightclub. He accepted African-American stars to perform, but he refused admittance to African customers. As a teenager, before Harry Belafonte would decide on a career as an actor and singer, he quit high school to join the U.S. Navy to fight late in World War II. While on leave in New York City, he took a date to see the Ink Spots at the Copacabana. He and his date joined the line waiting to get into the Copa, and when they reached the doorman, he was told every one else in line had reservations and the show was sold out. He wrote years later, "The humiliation for us was severe. ... Our night was destroyed, and all I could do was slink off, humiliated and with my rage in check. Little did I know that I would one day have my payback with the Copacabana." It happened a decade later while Belafonte was riding high on movie and recording successes. He stood waiting backstage in the wings listening as the announcer barked, "the Copacabana is proud to present Harry Belafonte." That night the crowd cheered him on as his chant of *Day-O* flurried through the room's white palm tree branches.[403]

In the early 1950s Podell ended the Copacabana's discrimination policy. Possibly either the ecumenical Costello, who grew up in Harlem, or Joe E. finally were able to influence Podell with their broader worldview of respecting all humanity and individual dignity. Over time the music of the Copa's superstars changed along with the culture. Diana Ross and the Supremes were the first of several Motown groups to perform there. Then Podell brought in the Four Tops to attract graduation parties as summer was approaching and the adults were starting their vacations. On opening night the Four Tops got into an argument in their dressing room about some internal dispute, and two refused to go on with the other two. When Podell heard about this intensifying conflict, he went directly to their dressing room, and barked in his tough movie-gangster style: "I paid for four Tops. I don't want no two Tops! Either I get four Tops, or there'll be no Tops!" All four opened side by side.

Jack Entratter started his career as a New York cab driver and became the bouncer at the Copa, or as Jimmy Blue Eyes told me, he was "a door bender" who let people in at the entrance. He later took over the entertainment when Proser moved on to another location. What a leadership combination Entratter was with food manager Podell. Entratter was described by several executives who worked with him in Las Vegas as arrogant, domineering, and abusive, much like Podell. But Entratter treated the entertainers well, so they liked him. When the *Sands Hotel* opened on the Las Vegas Strip, Entratter was licensed as its director of entertainment, and he soon stole from the five existing Strip hotels a number of top stars who had worked for him at the Copa. Years later he became the *Sands* resort president.

The Copacabana was clearly an underworld joint where gangsters were treated like royalty. Jerry Lewis wrote, "At ringside, was the galaxy of the heads of the New York families. ... And after the show, when you were summoned to the table, you went so that they could introduce you to their children and their wives." New York hood Jimmy Hill (Ray Liotta's main character in the movie *Goodfellas* 1990) explained, "Friday nights at the Copa were for the gangsters and their girlfriends, and Saturday nights were for the same men with their wives." Over the years self-proclaimed organized-crime writers have claimed the underworld had many rules, but most of this is nonsense. Yet one rule was absolute - girlfriends only on Friday nights at the Copa. These gangsters' wives associated primarily with each other, and if one of these wiseguys had brought his wife on a Friday night, the word about these husbands' girlfriends would have been related to their wives. Pity the poor hood who ever violated this rule by turning the gangsters' wives against them.[404]

In the middle of World War II, the NYPD License Bureau investigated New York nightclubs to determine whether they were paying sales and business taxes, when Mayor LaGuardia stepped in and ordered the NYPD to investigate the Copacabana ownership. The NYPD Detective assigned to investigate testified he wanted to determine "if there were known racketeers or gangsters frequenting the club," specifically Adonis, whom DA Dewey had labeled as Brooklyn's Public Enemy Number 1. He also wanted to find out "if a Frankie Costello was connected in any way." While the Mayor never explained why he initiated this police inquiry, the timing indicates it was to harass and embarrass his two prime political nemeses. LaGuardia instigated it right after Supreme Court Justice Aurelio was elected over his opposition because of Costello's political support.[405]

The inquiry remained dormant for almost a year, and then the NYPD's Division of Licenses held a cabaret-license revocation hearing over possible Copa hidden ownership. This was less than three months after Costello took the Mayor to court to retrieve his misplaced $27,200 cash, and the New Jersey Governor accused Adonis of operating one of the nation's largest illegal casinos in Cliffside, to which he was openly transporting New York players right under LaGuardia's nose.

The subpoenaed Costello refused to testify, and at his contempt hearing, his attorney charged that his client was a victim of Mayor LaGuardia's "unsated feeling of intense hatred. ... The purpose of this examination is to harass and annoy my client and to prejudice his lawful rights to satisfy a desire for revenge on the part of the Mayor of this city and his Police Commissioner. ... As evidence of the hostility of these two men, [he presented the Commissioner's statement:] Costello is not a local bum but an international thug. I don't know where he will go when he dies, or if there is a hell deep enough."[406]

Despite Costello's pleas, the judge ordered him to testify in the license-revocation hearings to avoid the contempt charge. Instead the Copa reached a compromise with the city. While management did not admit a connection with Costello, it stipulated that any interest "is completely terminated and severed." The seven individuals whom the city had connected to the operation of the illegal *Piping Rock Casino* sold their interests and were terminated, including Jules Podell. The agreement said of the sole remaining official owner, "In so far as Monte Proser is concerned, he states that so far as he knows Costello has not and never had any interest in Copacabana, Inc." However, the following year, Costello's political ally O'Dwyer was elected Mayor, and under him, manager Podell was allowed to continue running the Copa and was referred to as its owner. Three years into O'Dwyer's administration the showroom was almost doubled in size.[407]

Five years after he allegedly severed ties, Costello's name would be again linked with the Copacabana because he was a chief promotor of charities. The Salvation Army asked New York City's 123 biggest contributors to serve as vice-chairmen to its fund-raising campaign. Costello took the honorary appointment seriously and started raising funds from potential large donors. He had the Copa closed to the public one evening to throw a $100 per person dinner party (equivalent to $900 today). Costello had the meals served without charge to the charity, so all the money could go to help the city's neediest. The party was attended by 150 Tammany Hall officials, politicians, Supreme Court Justices, and socialites. When Costello's involvement was publicized, all the contributors were embarrassed that their names were connected with the host, except for Dr. Richard H. Hoffmann, a psychiatrist who had treated Costello. Thus, the Salvation Army quickly announced that Costello had withdrawn from further fund-raising efforts. However, the Salvation Army compassionately kept Costello's large contribution to assist the poor. Republican Party leaders exposed the dinner host's name to the press to embarrass Tammany Hall, but they backed away from their initial calls to investigate the gathering because they did not want to be seen as attacking the Salvation Army's important work. The Copa issued the following statement, "There are only two partners who have all the stock – Jules Podell and Monte Prosser. Costello never had anything to do with it." During future elections Republicans used this dinner to refer to Tammany's leaders as the *Copacabana cabinet.* When Podell closed the Copa in 1973, it was the end of the big New York nightclubs because the discothèque scene was flourishing.[408]

Costello was officially made head of his Mafia gang and the Boss of Bosses by Luciano while their friend Siegel was becoming involved with the *Flamingo* resort project in early 1946. Then in the 1950s Costello, like his pal Adonis, faced multiple prosecutions. Separate government agencies went after Costello criminally, and denaturalization proceedings were launched to strip his U.S. citizenship and return him to Italy to join his exiled buddies Adonis and Luciano. Despite Costello's long-term legal problems, his reign as America's crime leader remained secure during the Las Vegas Strip's early glory years, as he oversaw his closest associates create most of the great gambling resorts. Costello assisted in raising the financing of several of his pal's resorts. Once the criminal and denaturalization problems were behind Costello, he personally built the *Tropicana* on the Strip. He had his long-time casino and slot partner Phil Kastel act as the resort owner and manager while fronting Costello's interest on the Nevada gaming license.

While Costello was busy with his casino and slot route in New Orleans, his casino in Saratoga Springs, his national bookmaking operation, and the Copacabana, his pals Meyer Lansky and Jimmy Blue Eyes were busy with their own gambling operations. Their adventure under the palms follows.

CHAPTER 14

THE ACTION SETTLED UNDER THE PALMS

"JIMMY BLUE EYES'" EARLY CAREER

Vincent "Jimmy Blue Eyes" Alo was the close friend and lifelong partner of Meyer Lansky, but Jimmy kept a low profile and is practically unknown to the public. Jimmy was born in the Bronx in 1904. After completing grade school at 15, he became a runner for a big Wall Street firm. He thought he would spend his career with this firm, but after four years, his boss disillusioned him. Jimmy explained at my first interview with him, "I did a good job, and got a few promotions. Two guys, who were much newer with the company, were promoted ahead of me. I complained to my boss that I deserved the promotion. 'I have been here longer, I'm doing a good job, and I'm even going to business school at night to better myself.' My boss said, 'Leave the business end to me.' I was the only Italian, so I stood out among all the Irish and Germans. I knew it was discrimination against my Italian heritage, so I quit the next day; and I never worked again the rest of my life."

Prejudice against the growing population of Italian immigrants was pervasive in the early part of the 1900s, and his boss' bigotry deeply impacted him. "I decided the only way I could avoid discrimination was to become my own man. The only opportunity open to me to become an independent entrepreneur at 19 was to enter the underworld." This was three years into Prohibition, and Jimmy joined a couple partners in the illegal lottery numbers business in Harlem. It was popular with the poor, just as state lotteries are today.

"I committed a robbery with three other boys, but they got away. I served six months in Sing Sing. I had my record expunged thirty years later. After that, I was only involved with illegal liquor and gambling."

Jimmy Blue Eyes next went to work for New York Prohibition beer baron Owney Madden, and then Jimmy joined the fine-liquor-importing partnership of Charlie Luciano, Meyer Lansky, Ben Siegel, and Joe Adonis in 1929. These five partners developed close, life-long personal friendships, and Jimmy became a trusted adviser to Mafia-gang leader Luciano and his successor Frank Costello.

In discussing his life, Jimmy Blue Eyes related a personal story from his Prohibition career. "One time, I took a boat out to a ship to pick up whiskey and convoy it into New York City. When I got home late, my wife was upset because she'd cooked dinner, and it was still waiting for me. She wanted to know why I hadn't at least called. I told her I'd been out on the ocean and then in the countryside, and there were no phones along the way. She told me, 'I'm never going to cook dinner again,' and she never did. For the rest of our lives, we went out a lot, and we had someone come in and do the cookin'."

After Prohibition, Jimmy Blue Eyes had a most unusual lifestyle for a hoodlum, or for that matter a legitimate businessman. "I had no interest in managing anything, not even my own businesses," both of which were illegal. One group of partners operated lottery numbers, and the other managed the casinos. He had no specific responsibilities, but he was always a valuable advisor and a strong backup who supported his associates.

This freedom allowed Jimmy Blue Eyes to devote himself to do just those things he enjoyed. From the time he entered the underworld at 19, he played golf every afternoon, and went nightclubbing and dancing every evening. He and his family later resided in Las Vegas. In addition to golf every afternoon, he and his wife regularly enjoyed the fine gourmet rooms, the country's greatest showroom and lounge performers, and dancing to big bands at the top of the *Desert Inn* and the *Dunes.* "It was a fun town then, with great entertainment and serious (casino) players." He continued to play golf into his 80s and to dance evenings into his early 90s.

One day on the golf course, Jimmy Blue Eyes had a run-in with the law. In the middle of the game, two FBI agents playing in the foursome following his started walking towards him. Jimmy seethed inside. The agents knew where he lived, so the FBI had no reason to embarrass him by arresting him in front of his country club friends. As they approached, his inner voice screamed out, "You low-life, uncivilized, unprofessional bastards." As they got close, one of the agents stuck out his hand to shake. He said, "I'm agent *so-and-so*. I've been playing golf behind you every day for the last 20 years. Tomorrow I'm retiring. This is agent *so-and-so*. He will be playing golf behind you every day for the next 20 years." After this courtesy introduction, the agents turned, walked back to their group, and continued their surveillance.

Jimmy Blue Eyes slept late every morning to prepare for his afternoon of golf and late evening out. "I was an avid book reader all my life just like my friend Meyer (Lansky)." "I just wanted to make a few dollars and live good." He was extraordinarily successful in these life goals. "I had fun, made some money, and formed wonderful friendships. That's the most important thing a person can do."

During one of my interviews with Jimmy, his adult grandson asked him, "Why didn't you buy some of the cheap, undeveloped land along the Florida coast (where he operated casinos) during the Depression?" Jimmy replied, "We were making so much money in the '30s, we never thought about making investments for the future."

Senior citizens typically curtail their youthful drinking habits, but Jimmy Blue Eyes could still consume prodigious amounts at age 91. For my first interview with him, his grandson drove me to his house, and he complained both ways about a bad hangover. In contrast, Jimmy had drunk far more alcohol the night before, and he mentioned how good he felt. He was highly animated and articulate during the interview.

Author and screenwriter Nick Pileggi told me, "Jimmy had the most unusual life of anyone in the underworld. After he got out of prison at the age of 19, he never worked again a day in his life. All the other hoods worked in some business." Pileggi had lunch weekly with Jimmy for five years. Pileggi wanted to write his life story, but Jimmy talked to me instead because he wanted to reminisce at the end of his life with someone who had also known the gamblers, hoods, and values of the illegal Prohibition and casino world in which he had spent his life. He lamented, "I'm talking to you because everybody I know is dead."[409]

Jimmy Blue Eyes was the only one among his tight-knit associates to grant an interview with an author, and he waited until late in his life to finally meet with me. The first interview caught me up in a legal brouhaha and potential scandal as a Nevada gaming licensee for interviewing a man at 91 who was still listed by the FBI as "a semi-retired capo in the Genovese crime family."[410] (See Addendum CC)

JIMMY BLUE EYES JOINED "POTATOES" KAUFMAN

At the same time Frank Costello was moving his stored New York City slots to New Orleans, Jimmy Blue Eyes joined an illegal Miami casino venture. This opportunity arose because of Jimmy's penchant for helping people. His sage practical advice was sought by criminals at all levels, making him gangland's highly-respected peacekeeper and intermediary along the Eastern seaboard and in Las Vegas for a half century. He was able to make peace between antagonists, and to reassure people who were innately wary of each other. His abilities were valued by businessmen as well. Jimmy was exceptionally perceptive, a skillful negotiator, and trustworthy. In addition he was well known for being polite, considerate, and helpful. Jimmy made a comment that explained his well-known attitude, "I always went out of my way to be nice to the porters and other workers at the bottom of the status rung and to help people who were down and out. Every one in my group did. We considered everyone worthwhile, no matter what their job or standing in the social order."

One of the people Jimmy helped was Chicago casino operator Jules Kaufman, who was born in that city in 1899. When he was 12, his parents went out one evening. As the couple was walking back and got close to their house, four armed men drove up and attempted to rob them. In this botched robbery, they shot his mother to death. His eight-year-old sister told reporters at the scene, which was a few doors from their home, "Papa and mamma were happy when they went away tonight to the theater. They haven't had a quarrel since I don't know when."[411]

The shooter was turned into the police by his cousin for the reward, and the four men were convicted of murder. The shooter got life, and the other three 25 years. This meant little to young Julian's family who had to move. His father told friends he could not go near the home without feeling the horrific force of the tragedy. The victim's husband refused to pay the shooter's cousin the reward because the robbers pled guilty, rather than being convicted as stated in the reward offer. The shooter, and his mother, repeatedly asked for his parole, arguing the victim was partly responsible for the shooting because she screamed, but authorities did not buy this.

Julian Kaufman was nicknamed "Potatoes" because his father was a major produce commission merchant. Potatoes spent his career managing casinos for the North-Side gang leaders. He was very close to Dion O'Banion, Hymie Weiss, Schemer Drucci, and Terry Druggan. Kaufman was a prominent figure at each of their funerals, and he was frequently seen hanging out with top North-Side gunmen at speakeasies and sporting events.

At age 24, Potatoes was arrested as an accessory to a murder that he had nothing to do with. The case involved Chicago gangster John Duffy, who was in a drunken rage one evening. When his live-in girlfriend, Maybelle Exley, talked back to him, he murdered her. Shortly after killing his girlfriend, Duffy went to Potatoes and asked to borrow his car to "pull off some jobs," but Duffy actually wanted to dispose of her body. Potatoes wanted no part of his alleged planned crimes and refused to loan his car, so Duffy stole it. Next, the intoxicated Duffy decided to go out and kill a hood he was mad at. The vocal Duffy talked about his plans, and his intended victim's friends heard about them. They grabbed Duffy, took him for a ride, and dumped his body along a road used by rumrunners. They hoped their murder would be written off as another Prohibition slaying. Instead, Potatoes became an early suspect in the case because Duffy had been driving his stolen car, and police arrested him. The police finally understood that Potatoes was also a victim, rather than an accomplice, so they dropped the murder charge before he was indicted.

Duffy turned to Potatoes for use of his car because he was well known in the Chicago underworld as a *good fellow,* who often loaned money to people who asked for a favor. Potatoes was respected because he always talked straight and dealt honestly, and he kept his mouth shut about other peoples' business.

This case created other problems for Potatoes. While he was being held on the murder charge, his wife, Marian, visited him. The observant Chief of Detectives recognized that she was sporting a bejeweled ring stolen in an armed robbery of another woman. The victim had been waiting at a red light with her two small children in the car when she was robbed at gunpoint. When the Chief of Detectives asked Marian where she got the ring, she admitted her husband had bought the ring and other jewelry from well-known fence Joseph "Yankee" Schwartz, whom she referred to as a *diamond broker.* The Chief of Detectives arrested the couple for possessing stolen property, but this case appears to have been dropped by the prosecution.

Potatoes bought the stolen ring even though he knew firsthand the type of fear armed-robbery victims experience. A year before, he had complained to police that two men had pulled up next to his car at an intersection and robbed him of $150. This made Potatoes one of the few hoods to file a police-victim report against other criminals, a rather futile gesture since he had no idea who the robbers were.

A couple of months after the Maybelle Exley murder charge was dropped, Potatoes was involved in another violent incident. He almost ran down two police officers who were crossing a street intersection. When one protested about his reckless driving, Potatoes began smashing him over the head with a revolver. Just as Potatoes was preparing to shoot him in the chest, the other policeman pulled Potatoes off. The beaten officer was hospitalized in serious condition with a possible skull fracture and severe lacerations on the head and face. At the police station, Potatoes showed his concealed-weapon permit from a Justice of the Peace. He also said he was a personal friend of the cop's captain and threatened *to get* both officers' jobs. The police planned to arrest him for assault with intent to commit murder, but this case does not seem to have been pursued. This inaction likely resulted from Potatoes' close friendships with the North-Side gang leaders and their influence with bribed political leaders, the Cook County prosecutor, and police officials.[412]

Following the vicious beating of the officer, police added Potatoes to their list of the usual suspects routinely taken into custody for questioning about major crimes. However, he was always released without arrest. The officers who were angry over the beating of their fellow cop picked up Potatoes so often that he complained to Chief of Detectives Stege in front of the press, "Can [Policemen] Drury and Howe arrest me every time they see me?" Stege replied he guessed they could. Potatoes asserted, "There's got to be a stop to this so far as I'm concerned. I'm no ex-convict or bootlegger. My father left me my money. My kids are getting so big now that I don't want them to be always hearing that their father was picked up as a suspect in this or that." Despite Kaufman's vicious, unprovoked beating of the officer and all the harassment pickups, Potatoes never developed a reputation as a violent hood. As Jimmy Blue Eyes said, "Potatoes was a soft fellow [meaning not a tough guy], who looked like a delicatessen owner. He was smart."[413]

Potatoes was best known for running Chicago's ritziest casino, the palatial *Sheridan Wave*, named for its location on Waveland Avenue near Sheridan Road. Customers knocked at the front door, and the doorman peered through the slot in the door. He admitted only known players that he recognized but they had to be in formal dress. The gambling room was ornately-furnished. Heavy drapes covered the windows and cascaded down to the richly-carpeted floor. Tuxedo-attired waiters served complimentary trays of food and beverage to players at the high-limit gambling tables. The waiters offered the world's most expensive liquors, with champagne the most popular drink, along with trays of fine food, including caviar. The games were roulette, craps, blackjack, and bird cage dice.

Potatoes operated the *Sheridan Wave* for three years until the election of Cook County State's Attorney Swanson in 1928. Then a dozen cops broke through the door, pushed back the guards, herded the guests outside and dispersed them, arrested the operators, and smashed the tables with axes. Several days later Potatoes got a Circuit Court Judge to enjoin the police and the State's Attorney from "trespassing" or interfering with the members of "an orderly private athletic club." The next day crowds filled the newly-installed tables, and the place ran without police hindrance.[414]

Ten months later, a newspaper exposé forced Police Commissioner Russell to announce a police campaign against the 29 casinos operating under court injunctions that prevented police raids. He sent undercover detectives into each of them to collect evidence of gambling. At the end of the two-month investigation, he got the court to dissolve the injunction, and he permanently closed the *Sheridan Wave*. This was four months after the St. Valentine's Day Massacre, when the gang of Potatoes' North-Side silent-partner, Bugs Moran, had been seriously diminished. Potatoes avoided the ongoing warfare by hiding out in New York City, and then his next move was a surprise. He opened two casinos - the *Dell's Roadhouse* and the *Dell's Winter Club* - but they were in the heart of the suburban territory of his life-long South-Side enemy, Al Capone. He typically absorbed the members of competing gangs when he wiped out their leaders, and Potatoes obviously cut a deal for Capone to be his new silent-partner, or he would not have been allowed to operate.[415]

Potatoes and his wife divorced, and Marian settled in Hollywood, Florida. Potatoes took a trip there to visit their son, Edward, and Marian introduced her former husband to her friend, Broward County Sheriff Walter Clark. Miami was in the adjacent Dade County, and that city was where the wealthy residents and tourists were. Potatoes never considered opening a casino in Miami or Dade County because the local law enforcers prohibited illegal casinos from operating if they were large or remained open beyond the tourist season. However, Hollywood had an ideal setting. It was near Dade County's northern border and 20 miles from Miami. Potatoes cut a deal with Sheriff Clark to open an illegal casino in Hollywood.

Potatoes always had one or two working junior partners in his illegal Chicago casino operations. As he organized his new Florida casino venture, he asked Jimmy Blue Eyes to be his partner. Jimmy told me, "Potatoes asked me to join him because I'd done him a couple favors in New York." When I asked Jimmy what he had done to help Potatoes, he stared at me without altering his expression. I faced his rigid gaze until I interpreted his message that the interview was not proceeding until I moved on to another topic. The favors might have been for many reasons, but Potatoes was never involved in business in New York. Thus, Jimmy most likely placed his large gang's protective shield around Potatoes while he hid out in New York City to avoid Capone gunsils who were systematically wiping out Moran's gang after the St. Valentine's Day Massacre. Then Jimmy may have asked a personal favor of his gang's ally, Capone, to absorb Potatoes into his gang, as he had other North-Side lieutenants who offered to switch loyalties.

The partners opened their new Florida casino inside the *Hollywood Country Club,* and months later they moved their operation two miles closer to Miami in the tiny fruit-and-vegetable farming community of Hallandale Beach. This was a poor area dependent on itinerant seasonal workers, but it was the closest place to Miami's lucrative resident and tourist markets just across the county border that was safe from police interference.[416]

One or two small casinos had operated in Hallandale two years earlier. Jimmy Blue Eyes mentioned, "Capone was rumored to have operated a casino before going to prison, but I wasn't there. No one [who was there] told me one way or the other." At that time, Capone used his regal Miami home for *vacations.* This was his term for avoiding visibility during political campaigns, police and prosecutorial heat, and Chicago's winters. This is where he later died from syphilis after his release from Alcatraz.

Potatoes and Jimmy built their Hallandale operation inside a huge wooden one-story circular produce-packing shed, which they named the *Plantation.* A horsebook filled a large room during the afternoon. It was crammed with tables for players to read their *Racing Forms,* and the walls were lined with boards listing the horses in each race. Miami already had a major bookmaking combine known as the S&G Syndicate, but the *Plantation* was more exciting because it featured the area's only horserace announcer. He added fanciful dramatic color to the tickertape reports of the horse's positions at each furlong, or quarter mile, along the track.

The rest of the building housed 11 roulette, eight crap, and two chuck-a-luck bird cage tables. A supervisor sat high up on a stepladder next to each table to closely watch every move, especially those by the dealers. Jimmy said, "We opened up like we were legal" because they had the blessing of Sheriff Clark, who was known by every one in the area as "the boss of Broward County."

At the conclusion of the day's horseracing cards, bingo-calling equipment was placed in the room for games in the early evening. The room was already packed with long convention-room tables to hold the players' bingo cards. The selected numbers were broadcast on loudspeakers throughout. At the end of the last bingo game, the table games opened and about half the bingo players moved over to that room. The partners treated bingo as a loss-leader to fill the casino. They paid back all the bingo-card purchase money as winning pots and absorbed the room's operating expenses.

Most of the year, the *Plantation's* gambling crowd was primarily Miami residents and the rest were vacationers. Miami's tourist season was the three months from January through March, when the hotels were jammed by affluent vacationers escaping the worst of the winter cold in New York and other Northeastern cities. During the season, Potatoes' *Plantation* became the most popular place in Southern Florida. A steady stream of cars from Miami to Hallandale began nightly at 6 p.m. to quickly fill the 1,000-seat bingo parlor as soon as it opened at 7 p.m. Another 1,000 people lined the walls holding their cards horizontally flat in their hands so the chits did not slip off.

The crowd dressed casually like in small mid-western towns. Every one removed their coats and dripped sweat under the brilliant, hot lights hanging from the rafters. A tiny bar in one corner sold low-priced beer, soft drinks, and sandwiches.

To cater to Miami's wealthy vacationers, Potatoes and Jimmy opened the *Colonial Inn,* an upscale carpet joint across the street from the Plantation, at the beginning of their second winter tourist season. Jimmy said, "While the Plantation was a big bingo hall, with games at night, the Colonial Inn was like a nightclub, with a class casino." The nightclub offered fine dining and top entertainment to attract the affluent to the gambling. Just like Adonis' casinos in northwest New Jersey, the combined places of Potatoes and Jimmy catered to every income group.

Jimmy Blue Eyes told me, "I let Potatoes run the casinos" in the *Hollywood Country Club* and then the *Plantation* and *Colonial* in Hallandale, just like he let his Harlem lottery numbers partners run that business. Jimmy continued to be physically active in Florida just like he was in New York. "I played golf every afternoon and went dancing every night." He also took his wife out to dinner frequently because of her lifelong ban on cooking in the evening. Miami resident Harry Katzen told me that at age 92, "Jimmy Blue Eyes is alive, and still goes out every night. He goes dancing." He added, "Jimmy was very nice, always a gentleman. Like Lansky, he was behind the scenes."[417]

MEYER LANSKY'S EARLY CAREER

Meyer Lansky was born Meyer Suchowljansky in Grodno, Poland in 1902. Because of that country's anti-Semitic Pogroms, which were violent mob massacres that killed many Jews, his father immigrated to the U.S. ahead of his family. At Ellis Island officials gave him the new surname of Lansky based on the last letters of his long real name. His father saved money for two years to pay for the trip so his wife and sons Jake and Meyer, who was 9, could join him in Brooklyn in 1911. Immigration officials assigned Meyer the birth date of July 4, 1902, and the family always celebrated his birthday on Independence Day even though he was likely born later that year. Three years after arriving in Brooklyn the family moved to the Lower East Side of Manhattan in 1914.

Prior to Meyer becoming a major Prohibition importer, little is known about his life. Books, movies, and television portray his younger years according to two books - *The Last Testament of Lucky Luciano* and *Meyer Lansky: Mogul of the Mob.* Both have been totally discredited as hoaxes. (See Addendum DD.) To show how little was known about Meyer Lansky even six years after Prohibition was repealed, he was incorrectly listed as *Meyer 'Charley the Bug' Lansky* in a *Los Angeles Times* article, despite the names Charley and Bug never having been associated with him.[418]

At age 16, Meyer was arrested the first two times three weeks apart. Felonious assault was dismissed, but he was found guilty and fined $2 for misdemeanor disorderly conduct for annoyance. The charges were brought by two different women, who both lived on Madison Street, but NYPD records of old cases contain only arrest dates, charges, and dispositions. With no factual details whatsoever about the felonious-assault and misdemeanor-disorderly-conduct arrests, some authors about early organized crime leapt to the conclusion that both complainants were prostitutes, and guessed that Lansky was trying to force them into slavery as their pimp. They misleadingly presented wild speculation as fact.

While nothing is known about Meyer as a teenager, this would be a total contradiction of the man every one knew as an adult. He never pushed anyone around, and he was always extremely protective, respectful, and chivalrous towards women. Every one who knew or dealt with Meyer spoke about him just like his life-long friend and partner Jimmy Blue Eyes, who said thoughtfully to me, "I don't know what he was like when he was younger, but I can't imagine the man I knew was ever capable of such a thing." Jimmy also said about their small, close-knit crime partnership, "We were utterly opposed to anything involving women, specifically pimping. We were only in liquor and gambling." This was demonstrated by their contempt for Al Capone because he was a brothel operator, even though he was a close underworld political ally of their gang.

Every one who was close to Meyer believed there were three much more likely reasons for the two arrests, if the complainants were indeed prostitutes. He may have cussed at a hooker because she either would not stop hustling him, or she repeatedly chided the 16-year old with, "Let me make a man out of you." He was also capable of putting a pimp in line physically, if necessary, for mistreating a woman in his presence. He was a short 5-feet, 4-inches but tough enough to survive a lifetime on the mean streets. Another possibility is a cop may have had a personal vendetta against Lansky and he may have let the women go in return for falsely arresting the 16-year old to embarrass him with his family.

These two youthful arrests occurred a year before Prohibition began. Meyer also had three minor arrests late in Prohibition. He was charged with Ben Siegel under the Public Health Act, which was dismissed. Then Meyer paid a $100 fine for violating the Volstead Act. Finally Meyer and Ben were rousted in a hotel suite for meeting with other ranking underworld figures, but this unconstitutional arrest was quashed in court.

In another case, gangster John Barrett accused Meyer of being with the two men who shot him in 1928, but victim Barrett refused to sign a complaint or to testify, so the Long Island arrest was dismissed. Thirty years later this felonious-assault arrest was resurrected at Meyer's Immigration and Naturalization Service (INS) deportation hearing. Convict Daniel Ahearn, serving a 30-year sentence, testified he was trying to increase his chances for parole by claiming Meyer had admitted to him his role in the old shooting. Ahearn's hearsay testimony is dubious for multiple reasons. Not only did Meyer vehemently dispute the accuracy of Ahearn's statements, but Meyer's attorney demonstrated serious inconsistencies in them. Ahearn's explanation about the motive being a Prohibition deal conflict was sketchy, exactly the same as the victim's had been, as if he had been prepped from the old statement. Since Meyer never told anyone, not even his closest associates, about his background or criminal activity, it would have been bizarre for him to tell a stranger about a crime he always denied being involved in. In addition, Meyer was the underworld's staunch critic of unprovoked violence, so Ahearn's testimony that Meyer bragged he cruelly used the victim for target practice was totally out of character, especially considering the two accusers at this hearing later died of old age without the man who they alleged was *cruel and vindictive* exacting any retribution for their false accusations that came close to costing him his citizenship.[419]

Every book about early organized crime ascribes different jobs for Meyer during the three years after he finished grammar school and before Prohibition began. The only documented information available about him from age 15 through 17 is the dubious testimony of the two former associates in Meyer's INS deportation hearing. The pair's combined testimony said Lansky was an auto mechanic by day, a crap-game bouncer at night, and occasionally a union thug during strikes, breaking up businesses. Ahearn even testified that Meyer was involved with these small-time activities a year after he had become Prohibition's largest importer. If there is any truth about Meyer being involved in criminal activities, it is surprising that the small fries in the underworld and the union movement never bragged about knowing him, so they could connect themselves personally to one of the most infamous and powerful hoodlums. Meyer always told his children about the hard work in being a car mechanic during his youth, and they never doubted the veracity of his stories.

LANSKY JOINED JIMMY BLUE EYES

While Potatoes Kaufman and Jimmy Blue Eyes were planning their elegant new *Colonial Inn* in Hallandale, Jimmy's closest buddy, Charlie Luciano, was being framed by Manhattan DA Tom Dewey into what appeared to be a life-sentence. Thus, Jimmy invited his second best friend, Meyer Lansky, and his other close associates, Frank Costello and Joe Adonis, to join their Hallandale partnership in the *Plantation* and *Colonial* casinos.

The additional partners brought in needed financing for the *Colonial* development, and they also distributed their personal risk by investing in multiple illegal casinos. Meyer, Costello, and Adonis spread their total investments among small partnerships in each other's operations around the country, so when the law or reform politicians closed one down, they did not lose everything. For example, Meyer was an investor in Costello's *Beverly Club*, and Meyer's brother, Jake, fronted his interest in Costello's New Orleans slot operation and *Piping Rock* in Saratoga Springs. Similarly, Costello and Adonis were partners in Meyer's *Arrowhead* in Saratoga as well as the *Colonial* and *Plantation* in Hallandale.

Potatoes admired Jimmy's independent lifestyle of spending all day every day enjoying himself, so Potatoes soon turned over management of the two Hallandale casinos to Meyer. Even though Potatoes was the principal partner, he moved to New York City, where he had once hidden out from Capone, to enjoy himself every day. Three years later, he died of a heart attack at age 40.

Authors about early organized crime invariably explain in detail how Meyer learned the gambling business as a young boy. This puzzled me, since my research found Meyer always employed, and gave a partnership interest to, an established expert manager to run each one of his casino operations. I questioned why such a supposedly knowledgeable operator would employ and give an interest to an expensive unnecessary backup. I always posed my questions during interviews in a way to conceal where my assembled facts led, and what hypotheses I was developing, to avoid influencing the answers. Thus, I said to Jimmy, "I understand that Meyer was a great casino manager," which caused him to go into fits of prolonged hysterical laughter. When he finally regained his composure, he replied, "Meyer didn't have the slightest idea how the games were played. He never dealt any of 'em. Forget about protecting from cheating." He then laughed some more.

My next two questions were whether Meyer was a good host, and whether he was an effective credit authorizer. To both questions Jimmy's answer was, "I don't know." He then concluded, "I played golf everyday and danced every night." Based on interviews with executives who worked for Lansky's casinos, it appears he set policy but stayed distant from the operations.

Jimmy volunteered to me proudly, "We ran the first legit games. The rest of the country was mostly bust-out joints. Up and up casino gambling was something new." It was the height of the Depression, so "we kept out the locals who couldn't afford to lose. We donated to the local hospital and many others for good will."

When Manhattan DA Hogan seized the business records of Costello's bookmaking partner Frank Erickson in the 1950 raid, the *Colonial Inn* financial records for 1946 showed the partners donated 6% of their $686,000 ($7.5 million today) profits to "charities." The partnership at that time included Meyer, his brother Jake, gambling operator George Sadlo, Jimmy, Adonis, Erickson fronting for Costello, three local men, and the casino managers from Detroit. Jake Lansky was the group's front man with the community and with charities to shield his notorious brother Meyer and his close associates from publicity. Jake soon moved his family permanently to Hollywood, Florida, near their Hallandale casino operations. Jimmy and Adonis also bought homes, but Jimmy returned to his New York home at the end of the tourist season each year.

Costello spent part of each winter season visiting his Hallandale investments. He bought some lots in his wife's name and began building a home in 1951, but after unfavorable publicity about their casinos by the Kefauver Committee, he permanently discontinued construction.[420]

Meyer was Costello's closest advisor, and Costello arranged a political favor for his son, Paul Lansky. He obtained an appointment for Paul to West Point through New York Congressman Michael Kennedy, whom Costello later successfully backed to become head of Tammany Hall.

The *Colonial Inn* was the plushest casino along the Gold Coast, a 60-mile stretch of Florida's eastern seaboard from Miami extending north to West Palm Beach, with Fort Lauderdale in the middle. The *Colonial Inn's* casino became that area's most famous high-end operation, and its night-club-style dinner showroom featured America's top saloon entertainers.

The *Colonial Inn's* winter-season opening each January headlined comedian Joe E. Lewis. His audiences of rounders and players loved the many jokes about the lifestyle of the heavy drinker and degenerate gambler. A horseplayer, one of Joe E.'s most famous lines was, "I bet a horse at 10 to 1, and it came in at a quarter to two." When Lewis appeared, Adonis, who was based in New Jersey, would join him between performances to continue their high-stakes, cross-country, gin rummy games.

Then Pearl Harbor was attacked, and America went to war weeks before the 1942 winter season was to begin. Rubber tires and gasoline were severely rationed, reducing vacationers to Miami and day-tripper travel from Miami. Meyer's partnership shut the *Colonial Inn* for the duration of the war, but the *Plantation* remained a popular gambling spot with locals.

With the ending of the War, Florida's population grew because of its year-round mild climate. It had been a major training center for soldiers, sailors, and aviators, and afterwards many returned to become permanent residents. They often encouraged their family and friends to join them in this beautiful state. Tourism flourished, as Florida became the Northeast's winter playground. Hotels had been built in Miami during the 1930s despite the Depression. Then the nation's post-war economic boom spurred fresh hotel construction, along with fine motels, featuring ocean views, stretching between Miami and Hallandale.

Gulfstream Park Racetrack had opened within a city block of the *Colonial Inn* before the War, but the owners ran out of money on the fourth day of racing. The Park remained unused except for occasional music events and various racing contests until new owners resumed horseraces near the end of the War. It was soon drawing large numbers of Miamians and tourists during racing seasons.

One year after the racetrack reopening, Meyer refurbished the *Colonial* and reopened it, and he upgraded the *Plantation* and added a showroom. A number of other casinos and many horse parlors opened along the Gold Coast, but Meyer understood that the casino with the nearest location to player markets had a strong competitive advantage. Thus, Meyer and his partners opened two new casinos after the War - the *Boheme Club* and *Greenacres*. Both were along major roads from Miami on the closest pieces of available land to its county line.

Their upscale *Boheme Club* was the first casino from Miami across the Broward county line along the coast road to Hallandale. Affluent tourists in formal evening dress arrived for an evening out. It was an elegant nightclub featuring dining, dancing, and a floor show. It featured a Paris-style production show with a bevy of showgirls in various elaborate, exotic, and romantic scenes that were interspersed by outstanding specialty acts like jugglers and magicians.

A year after the *Colonial* reopening, they opened the swanky roadhouse *Greenacres* casino. It was even closer to the county line than the *Boheme* along the slightly inland U.S. 1. While the *Colonial Inn* had the glitz and glamour, *Greenacres* was larger, featured a restaurant popular with Miamians, and became the top casino for serious gamblers. It offered *New York Craps*, in which the high rollers wagered against each other, and the House took a commission out of every wager won. The only action the House banked, or *faded,* was the excess amounts no players would or could cover. With New York Craps, the casino's potential win was much less than if it had banked the action, but it never lost, except for its gamble on the excess wagers. It drew beaucoup high-end action because it was the favorite of many of the area's most devoted gamblers.[421]

Detroit casino owners Mert Wertheimer and Ruby Mathis were driven out of that city by the law at the end of the War, so they joined Meyer to manage the reopened *Colonial Inn* for the 1946 winter season and got a one-third interest. They had some kind of falling out because Jimmy refused to discuss anything about them. From then on, Dino Cellini managed Meyer's casinos. Jimmy said, "Dino was responsible for the total operation," even though crime authors invariably refer to him as just the credit manager. Since he was salaried, the Wertheimer/Mathis one-third interest was distributed among the remaining partners, increasing their holdings an average of 50% each.

Cellini had been part of the dealing crew that cheated the partners' casino so badly in the second year of operation that they did not make money during their busiest month (see Chapter 4). I asked Jimmy how he could trust Dino after he ripped them off. His only answer was, "We continued to employ Dino because he knew the business. That's the way it was." Through the 1970s, a casino manager's primary responsibility was to be an expert on cheating, or thieves would quickly bankrupt the operation. A substantial percentage of the country's illegal casino employees knew how to cheat for or against the House, and a multitude of slight-of-hand crooks applied their trickery from the other side of the tables.

Casino operators learned that the best way to catch a thief is to use another thief. The problem is, "How can you trust them?" The answer is, "You can't," even though most casino operators employed them just like I did in my Las Vegas Strip operations, when so many employees and players were proficient at stealing. Jimmy and Meyer survived their maneuverings on the dangerous mean streets because they had outstanding perception of people and relied on their instincts, which stood them well. They trusted Dino, and he remained their capable manager for many years. Jimmy said, "Dino was the nicest guy in the world, and he was a close friend."

Dino Cellini came out of the Steubenville, Ohio illegal casinos, which were a prolific training ground for capable dealers who ended up working around the country. It was a small town with three major industries - a huge steel mill, lots of brothels, and some tiny gambling joints, with a few tables each. The city bordered Pennsylvania and Virginia, which restricted alcohol sales and banned gambling and prostitution. The casinos had major crap business and good wheel (roulette) play. Casino executive Freddie Ayoub and other Steubenville graduates told me, "The chips were piled high on the tables, and the dealers really pushed them." The best way for a dealer to learn is to face big, fast action from knowledgeable players. Steubenville produced the finest wheel dealers I ever encountered.

Freddie Ayoub told me, "Dino (Cellini) was the most knowledgeable man about the business I ever met. He was a top marketer. No one could cheat him. He had a lot of respect by anyone who knew him. When he walked in a room, he impressed people because he commanded respect." "Dino was always a gentleman. He helped a lot of people and always looked out for the small guy [in a tough, often impersonal business]." Freddie stated emphatically, "Dino later went on his own, but he openly expressed his loyalty to Meyer. He was Lansky's man." Cellini was known for his dedication to working out complicated mathematical equations in long hand with pencil and paper. He would sit by himself in the casino and calculate, usually to get his mind off an argument with his wife, a former Miss America runner up. This was his version of worry beads absorbing the frustration or stress.[422]

MIAMI'S S&G BOOKMAKERS & ILLEGAL CASINOS

Meyer Lansky placed casinos just beyond the Dade County line because a majority of Miami residents strongly opposed their existence. Despite this strong voter antagonism, owners of the posh hotels along Miami Beach's Collins Avenue resort strip were forever optimistic they would one day be allowed casinos. Every Miami hotel built from the 1920s on featured a large lobby intended to house gambling tables in the future. During the rest of the century, hotel owners sporadically lobbied for legalization, but Floridians decisively rejected every attempt, even when casinos proliferated across much of the rest of the country. In contrast, licensed horse and dog tracks and jai alai frontons were very popular in Miami, and illegal bookmaking operated wide open.

Two years before World War II, a group of independent Miami bookies united to create a large combine. They obtained a city business license as *S. and G. Investment Company*, so they became known as the *S&G Bookmaking Syndicate*. The partners said the initials stood for nothing, but locals assumed it meant "Stop and Go." A few years into its operation, a federal war-economy measure closed most of the nation's racetracks, causing this venture to almost go under. But at the conclusion of the War, the wealthy tourists poured into Miami Beach, and their business allowed S&G to develop into the nation's most sophisticated illegal off-track bookmaking organization.[423]

The five S&G partners invested their profits in valuable real estate fronting the ocean and in other legitimate investments, courted influential political friends, and contributed generously to local charities to create goodwill throughout the community. Honest politicians feared that calling for criminal prosecution of this group would cause the S&G partnership to respond with overwhelming financial contributions to rival candidates, ensuring defeat in the next election. This threat also intimidated city judges when sentencing S&G bookmakers, because more than one judge was defeated by their enormous contributions to opponents. In the five years following the War, no bookie was given a jail sentence. S&G accepted frequent arrests of its bookies, who generally paid a $200 fine that was considered an unofficial licensing fee to help fund city government.

Once the five Jewish S&G partners had acquired the political clout to protect bookmaking in Miami, they were able to organize the city's bookies of every nationality. S&G supplied independent bookmakers a shield from law enforcement, protection from competition in each designated territory, legal counsel and bondsmen if arrested, and the essential wire service race information. In return, bookies paid the group an up-front fee based on the potential business at each location, half their winnings, and fees for bribes to the police and for the wire service.

Horseracing was the dominant form of sports betting in the country. Many residents bet the horses at strategically-placed S&G tobacco-stand operations, and wealthy winter tourists wagered while sunbathing on the beach. Each large seafront hotel leased a beach cabana and an exclusive concession to a bookie at up to $45,000 for the three-month winter season. The cabana boys ran the sunbathers' horse wagers to the bookies who reported them on direct phone lines to S&G's main office. The hotel bookies often operated in the gift shop too.

A former S&G employee Sy Freedman told me, "They also had a big phone bank that took calls from anywhere in the country as long as they knew the caller. It was on the second floor over a nightclub and restaurant named Gray's Inn. They took high-rolling tourists to the track and took their large bets so it wouldn't impact the totalizer odds. When they got overloaded on *chalk* (a long shot), they would go to the track window and lay off the amount to the track they didn't want to fade. This brought the odds down on what they had left."[424]

Miami Police Chief Luke Short complained to City Councilman Melvin Richard that he had been told to "lay off" bookmaking by the unidentified city councilman to whom he reported. This corrupt councilman had a number of very lucrative business dealings with a S&G partner. Councilman Richard made a tape recording of his conversation with Chief Short and played it at the Kefauver hearings. In it Chief Short admitted, "The city could be closed up in a matter of hours," but he shut the bookies down twice and was ordered to allow them to reopen. Police Chief Short was professionally offended by the Miami City Council's secret, unwritten directive to ignore S&G bookmaking, but he had to go along with it to keep his job. To distance himself from this repugnant policy, he delegated total authority over bookmakers to Detective Pat Perdue, and the two police officials never talked about gambling again. Detective Perdue's independence led to his becoming referred to as the "one-man vice squad."[425]

S&G vigorously protected its established territories from encroachment by competition, but there was never a hint of violence by them. They had Detective Purdue shut down all competitors. In effect, S&G licensed illegal bookmakers, and those who were unlicensed by them were arrested. For example, when New York and New Jersey bookmaking-partners Frank Erickson and Costello invested in Lansky's Broward County casinos, Erickson extended their horse-wagering business into Miami by taking away the bookmaking concessions from S&G at three oceanfront resorts - the Roney Plaza, Boca Raton, and Hollywood Beach. S&G paid Police Detective Perdue to advise the three hotel owners not to turn their bookmaking concessions over to Erickson. When his warning failed, Detective Perdue exercised his police authority. The Kefauver Report summarized, "Shortly after Erickson obtained the concession, the Roney Plaza was raided by Perdue and the concession was forced to discontinue. Great publicity was given to this raid as contrasted to raids on other hotels which were not widely publicized and which usually resulted in a fine with the gambling allowed to be resumed."[426]

Erickson had political clout with Florida Governor Millard Caldwell, but he lacked authority to tell the local police to lay off. Detective Purdue's actions illustrate the great dependency that organized crime gangs like the Mafia, even Boss of Bosses Costello, have for support from the local police and usually the district's politicians, judges, and prosecutors. These crime gangs cannot effectively open up illegal gambling and brothels in a neighborhood without the backing of the local political and legal authorities, because so many customers, neighbors, and others know about their existence.

S&G and Detective Perdue may have closed Erickson's hotel concessions, but they never bothered Erickson's bookie agents who plied their trade inside Florida's racetracks competing for the fans' wagers. Interestingly, bookie Erickson was a partner in Miami's Tropical Park Racetrack, just as Costello had interests in several New York tracks.

Two years later, Chicago-gang chief Tony "Big Tuna" Accardo devised an unusual scheme to muscle a takeover of S&G by going over the heads of the local police and politicians. He utilized the services of long-time Chicago-gang representative William Johnston. He was a principal in the operation of a number of horse and dog tracks in the Chicago area and in Florida. Johnston cut a deal with Florida gubernatorial-candidate Fuller Warren.[427]

Johnston became one of the three huge contributors to Warren's campaign. In return, Warren promised if elected governor to carry out Accardo's plan to have Chicago gangster Harry Russell take control of the highly-successful but illegal S&G bookie operation. In Chicago, Russell owned the Silver Bar and Grill on State Street, managed the gang's bookmaking operations, and had formerly operated a casino for partner Accardo. When gangster Russell made his initial offer to S&G to become the managing partner, the owners rejected it. They did not want an additional partner interfering with their highly successful business or slicing up their profits. Then Governor Warren set out to change the owners' minds by appointing his own Special Gambling Investigator, and by telling him to follow the orders of Chicago gang associates Johnston and Russell about which S&G bookies to raid. The Governor's Investigator relayed these orders to Dade County Sheriff Jimmy Sullivan, who had his deputies carry out the gangsters' orders.

To intensify the pressure, the Chicago gang took advantage of its close link with the owners of the Continental Press Service, the powerful nationwide racing news wire service monopoly. Its information was essential for bookies to quickly determine horserace winners and pay off winners. Thus, the Chicago owners had Continental's regional distributor shut off its service to S&G bookies. This did not stop them. They countered by using long-distance telephone calls to obtain the Continental wire service results from other Florida users. Continental retaliated against all this opposition by cutting off its wire service to the entire state. Ten days later S&G capitulated to the demands of the Chicago gang. The moment S&G made Russell its sixth equal partner, the raids and arrests of its bookies ceased.

A pair of transactions show Russell received his S&G partnership without any investment. While Russell officially paid $20,000 for his one-sixth interest, a year later the S&G partners returned this money when they bought Accardo's yacht Clari-Jo for $20,000. This purchase was on paper only, as Accardo retained possession and exclusive use of the yacht at its Fort Lauderdale moorings. Accardo and his gang-lieutenant Jake Guzik did not try to hide their ownership of Russell's interest. They reported an S&G operating loss on their 1949 business-partnership income-tax return. A year later S&G dissolved because under Russell's management the highly-successful operation was no longer profitable. It is important to note that S&G closed during the Kefauver investigation, but these hearings launched local casino reform movements around the country that did not disrupt many bookmaking operations. Thus, Russell destroyed a very profitable business that could have continued to operate for years under the protection of local politicians if it had not been for Chicago's forced takeover and his destructive leadership.[428]

Earlier that year, Tony Accardo had his brother Martin make a $100,000 cash investment in the fledgling *Miami Beach Morning Mail* newspaper to counter the bad publicity emanating about S&G. The paper operated just 48 days before it went under. The paper gave Accardo the opportunity to reaffirm the Chicago gang's loyalty and respect for Costello with an editorial praising the New Yorker.

"Whistling Jimmy" Sullivan was a smiling, cigar-smoking, Irish Miami traffic cop, who was nicknamed for using a distinctive whistle to direct drivers and pedestrians at a busy downtown intersection. His enjoyable style got him elected Dade County Sheriff late in World War II. Local newspapers reported that illegal casino operators from around the country soon sent emissaries to meet with Sullivan about opening up just outside the Miami city limits in his county jurisdiction. The Sheriff permitted a few illegal casinos to operate closer to Miami than Lansky's casinos did, as tourism boomed during the post-war winter season. Most of these operations were low end, except for the upscale *Brook* in Surfside that catered to gamblers in white tie and white tailcoat tuxedos, but Meyer's casinos offered finer service, dining, and entertainment. His casinos may have been a longer drive, but they were a better product in a growing tourism market, so their win increased every year after the War. These were Meyer's most successful years, despite the added competition closer to the primary market.

A week after Sheriff Sullivan allowed the first two casinos to open in the county, a *Miami Herald* reporter charged into the places with a photographer to prove the clubs had illegal gambling in a major exposé. Sheriff Sullivan refused to pursue the *Herald* reports by arrogantly explaining, "We are so busy with more serious criminal activities involving rape, robbery, murder, manslaughter, and the like that we don't have time to assign deputies to run down everybody's tips or rumors of gambling, whether from anonymous telephone calls or unsupported newspaper gossip." But the *Herald* series attracted the attention of U.S. Attorney General Tom Clark, who called for a crusade against organized crime. This publicity finally forced Sullivan to act. His deputies raided some of the more notorious clubs, but he waited until the lucrative winter season was over before cracking down. His on-again off-again enforcement allowed them to reopen the next winter.[429]

As the U.S. AG's crusade was pressuring Sheriff Sullivan to close the illegal casinos in Dade County, the U.S. Attorney for Florida obtained an injunction against Lansky's *Colonial Inn* in Broward County to abate the nuisance of gambling. This injunction was issued in the middle of the three-month 1948 winter-tourist season, but a considerate Judge did not make the injunction effective until the club's normal closing date. That night the *Colonial Inn* offered dining and dancing but no gambling. At the final show, Joe E. Lewis pointed to the casino room's locked doors and complained to the audience, "Everything happens to me. I was just about to get even."[430]

Lansky did not challenge the injunction that closed the jewel among his clubs because the resulting publicity might have prompted closure of his remaining casinos. Instead, he moved the *Colonial* gambling tables and continued to operate them at his *Greenacres, Boheme,* and *Plantation* casinos.

LANSKY'S HIGH-END SARATOGA CASINO & OTHER BUSINESSES

Saratoga Springs was a quiet town resting in the foothills of the Adirondack Mountain range in northeastern New York. The therapeutic qualities of its sulfur water and baths made it an exclusive summer resort. To its south was Manhattan, 190 miles, and the state capitol in Albany, 32 miles; to the east was Connecticut, with Hartford, 148 miles, and New Haven, 185 miles; and to the north was Montreal, Quebec, Canada, 188 miles.

The tiny spa town featured several large hotels and anywhere from one to a handful of elegant casinos for the better part of a century. These illegal operations offered action every evening to wealthy summer visitors. Casino gambling became a much greater tradition than the sulfur bath parlors during Saratoga's August horseracing season, something like mint juleps in Louisville on Kentucky Derby Day.

Three factors protected the casinos all those years. The locals elected politicians who shielded the casinos from interference because they depended on the tourists for business, jobs, and tips. The state's politicians did not dare to offend the affluent and influential clientele. The gambling rooms remained inconspicuous from the spa's non-gaming visitors and reporters, because they were denied entry and a view of what went on behind closed doors.

The city's first casino was opened by Dick Canfield at the same time as the soon to be famous Saratoga racetrack during the Civil War in 1864. The casino operation was within walking distance of the racetrack and allowed race fans to continue gambling late into the evening. The old brick edifice of the original casino in Congress Park today houses a historic museum.

The 1907 national reform movement closed the casino, but within a few years gambler Arnold Rothstein had a high-end casino going full blast. His operation included an expensive restaurant that was complimentary to players. Rothstein also went to extraordinary lengths to collect his players' gambling debts. He sent his employees every weekday morning to stand in line at the doors of his players' home-city banks. As soon as they opened, his staff quickly converted the players' large gambling-loss checks into cash before anyone could stop payment.[431]

In the middle of Prohibition, Charlie Luciano, who had worked in illegal casinos and operated crap games in his early career, invested rumrunning profits in the popular *Chicago Club* casino in Saratoga Springs. Over time he developed contacts with the country's best casino managers, and his experiences allowed him to assist his associates enter the casino field after the repeal of Prohibition. Luciano sold his decade-long interest in the *Chicago Club* when Manhattan Prosecutor Tom Dewey framed him, but three of his closest associates – Frank Costello, Joe Adonis, and Meyer Lansky – followed his lead in Saratoga Springs.

Meyer headed the casino partnership at the *Arrowhead Inn,* while Costello had the *Piping Rock.* Meyer was seen around his casino, but Costello stayed near his Manhattan base, as he had Joe Stein manage and front his casino. Interestingly, the president of Lansky's *Arrowhead* operation was Costello's dentist, Dr. Charles Singer of New York City. Meyer's brother, Jake, fronted for him on most documents at the *Arrowhead Inn* and in Costello's Louisiana operations. Meyer and Costello were partners in each other's Saratoga Springs casinos, and Adonis was an investor in both. These three dear friends also partnered in Meyer's Florida casinos, Costello's Louisiana casino and slot route, and Adonis' New Jersey casinos.[432]

The *Arrowhead Inn* and the *Piping Rock* were high-end casinos with nightclubs that featured the country's leading saloon entertainers. A show's headliner and the supporting act were usually a combination of a singer and a comedian, with an opening novelty act, such as a juggler, magician, trained animals, ventriloquist, acrobat, dancer, dancing couple, or ice skater. The show followed a dinner of superb food and fine wine, interspersed with dancing to a big-band orchestra.

Jimmy Blue Eyes was proud that he and Meyer ran some of the few legit games in the nation, but the short racing season put pressure on them to win during this period. Even though they were open for more than three months from mid-May to Labor Day, the month of horseracing was what drew most of the affluent players. Jimmy told me, "Saratoga had just August each year during the racing season, and we had to win." The year's potential profits depended on the outcome of that one month. These were true gambling men.

Meyer and Jimmy operated with the same crew during the summer in Saratoga and for the three winter months in Hallandale. The owners and their casino and restaurant staffs followed the sun and the ponies.

Racing stopped during World War II, and most Saratoga casinos closed for the duration. Jimmy said, "During WWII, Meyer had the dog track in Council Bluffs, Iowa, but he didn't have any casino games. He was with Bill Syms. He had the dog track in Hollywood, Florida, and was the operator in Council Bluffs. I wasn't involved, and I don't know why he was." Council Bluffs was across the Missouri River from Omaha, Nebraska. Paul Bryant, son of Alabama's famous football coach Bear Bryant, operated slots at the dog track in the mid 1990s. He told me then, "Council

Bluffs is still looked down on by the people of Omaha because historically it had the brothels and illegal gambling, even Meyer Lansky. It was the tough town bordering Omaha."[433]

Syms and Meyer signed a contract to operate greyhound racing during the war years, which they appear to have done successfully, but the track was closed after the War. If their goal was to put gambling tables in it, the political situation never materialized. However, during the country's post-war economic boom, Lansky's *Arrowhead* and the other Saratoga Springs casino resorts flourished again.

During World War II, jukebox music became popular bar and coffee-shop entertainment. Vendors developed jukebox routes to supply these establishments with machines, repair service, and new 78-rpm records to keep up with the weekly hit parade. Wurlitzer was one of the four major jukebox manufacturers, but it had difficulty selling them in Chicago because the coin-machine operators were strongly entrenched with most of the bars and coffee shops, according to testimony by the company Sales Manager to the U.S. Senate McClellan Committee. The situation changed, when the Sales Manager met gang leader Tony Accardo and his lieutenant Greasy Thumb Guzik. They bought 2,700 machines because Wurlitzer was the first company to offer lease-purchase deals with no upfront investment. Wurlitzer received a sizeable percentage of each juke's earnings until the purchase price and the high-interest rate were paid in full. This arrangement turned jukes into a big business in Chicago.[434]

Another tough city for Wurlitzer to crack was New York, until the Sales Manager met Lansky and gave him the distributorship for the Northeast Coast. Wurlitzer made the same arrangement with major underworld leaders in other cities, but when its Cleveland office was bombed, the company strategically withdrew from that town.

The Chicago mob and the other criminal gangs established and enforced monopolies for their lucrative territorial jukebox routes by using the threat of union strikes or violence, and when this was not heeded, they violently attacked businesses and owners. In contrast, Lansky adopted professional operating and marketing business standards for his Emby Distributing Corporation. He introduced lease-purchase financing for jukeboxes by passing on Wurlitzer's deal to each location, which paid the principal and interest out of weekly revenues, along with his repair and record-replacement costs and his profit. This was a much better deal than his competitors offered with their large weekly fee that did not include a machine-purchase payment. Meyer's lease-purchase financing scheme was later adapted by an associate of Adonis to build Bally's into the dominant slot-machine producer for Nevada.

Lansky brought two partners into Emby. They were experienced Wurlitzer salesmen, and they were outstanding jukebox marketers. They bought unproductive routes, built up their volume with more-current and regularly-updated record selections, and then sold the routes at a profit. In addition to successfully operating his best routes with superior business tactics, Meyer also aggressively offered Wurlitzers for sale to every one who wanted them, even to competing route operators from both the under and over worlds.

Lansky formed Emby while he was leading the war-intel offensive for Luciano and Navy Intelligence Commander Haffenden. Meyer hired away Haffenden's high-ranked and respected associate, Ben Espy, as a key executive in his new lawful enterprise. Meyer clearly had nothing to hide; and no one in this elite Navy unit, the Manhattan DA's office, or the NYPD ever heard the slightest rumor of Lansky, Costello, or Adonis being involved in violence or underhandedness of any kind. Several legislative investigations found the same spotless non-violent record for them. Lansky was well-known for two qualities that made him very successful in business. He always dealt fairly, and he always kept his word. He was the epitome of trustworthiness.

Lansky and his associates rejected the two main tactics of gangsterism - monopoly and violence. Meyer never interfered with competitors' activities, and he never pressured potential or existing clients for their business. Every one in Meyer's lucrative Manhattan marketplace was insulated from threats of violence and extortion because all knew he was chief advisor to Costello, head of the nation's largest gang. Meyer never pushed any one around, but if any one had threatened violence against him, his associates, or his businesses, he would have defended quickly and decisively.

Meyer's approach to both legal and illegal business was the exact opposite of monopoly. He was well known to welcome, encourage, and assist competitors. His advice was sought by underworld and overworld investors, even those in competing ventures, because of his business acumen, his knowledge of the political and gang scenes, and his willingness to assist others.

Lansky and his close Jewish and Italian associates had very different values from America's two-dozen Mafia gangs that brutally enforced monopolistic control over all crime in their geographical territories. These were referred to as *closed cities* by the FBI because outsiders were not allowed in without some kind of accommodation. These gang leaders charged flat payments or took a piece of the action to allow other gangs to operate casinos and other activities within their boundaries.

In contrast, the Mafia gang headed by Luciano and later Costello, who were backed up by Adonis, Jimmy Blue Eyes, Siegel, and Lansky, never claimed territorial prerogatives or interfered with competition. They simply offered a better casino product in Bergen County, New Jersey; Saratoga Springs, New York; Hallandale, Florida; Las Vegas, Nevada; and Havana, Cuba. These cities and Los Angeles, along with Tucson and Phoenix, Arizona, where Siegel was involved with the horserace wire service, were declared *open cities* by this group, and these were the only cities that all U.S. Mafia gangs, and later organized crime syndicates of other nationalities, recognized as being open to all comers. These open designations lasted during Lansky's and Siegel's lifetimes and continue still to this day almost three-quarters of a century later.

Lansky operated Emby until Wurlitzer, who had invited him to become a distributor, asked him to sell it over embarrassment about the criminal-mastermind myth that the press had manufactured for this legitimate businessman and illegal casino operator. Lansky, Costello, Adonis, and the two Emby partners then created Consolidated Television to put TVs in bars and clubs. However their one-time sales of TVs produced little profit compared to jukeboxes, which required the latest hit records, regular maintenance, and coin removal. In addition, their adjunct Tele-King company manufactured a poor quality TV set, so neither business lasted long. It is unclear what their business plan might have been. These men were highly successful in many legal businesses, and they were the top Prohibition rumrunners, led the largest expansion of illegal casinos across the nation, spearheaded the legitimate development of the Las Vegas Strip, and directed the greatest war-intel coup in history, as agents of the U.S. military. They accomplished all this, while competing with the country's most violent and dangerous criminals, and while facing off against this nation's most Machiavellian and adversarial political figures and law enforcers. However, they obviously miscalculated the potential of the fledgling TV business and produced a resounding dud with this one.[435]

KEFAUVER TOOK ON FLORIDA LAW ENFORCEMENT

The Kefauver Committee's shocking revelations about extensive Florida sheriff and police corruption collapsed a drive to legalize casinos that was launched a few months earlier by the Miami Beach hotel owners and other businessmen. These exposures forced Governor Warren to send personally-signed letters to each of the state's 67 sheriffs and 185 police chiefs to close illegal casinos within 30 days or face summary suspension. A letter from the Governor 15 days later asked for progress reports, and every sheriff and police chief reported that gambling had ended, even though no gambling arrests had been made anywhere in the state. Those officials who allowed gambling simply lied while doing nothing.

State Attorney General Richard Ervin conceded to the Kefauver Committee that state officials had not previously interfered in local law enforcement. He left out that Governor Warren had ordered police raids against the S&G Syndicate to pressure his Chicago gangland representative into their partnership.

The Governor's anti-gambling edict to local law enforcement interestingly avoided mentioning bookmaking, especially the large S&G Syndicate. But this group voluntarily disbanded about a month before the issuance of the Kefauver Interim Report, and both the Committee and the Syndicate credited its demise to the widespread coverage about the revelations by the press and radio. In reality the highly-successful S&G inexplicably became a money loser from the time Russell became a partner 16 months earlier, and this lack of profitability led to its closure.

A month later Chairman Kefauver said that organized crime is corrupting law enforcement officers in many cities "on a scale that makes the corruption of Prohibition days look like kindergarten play. So widespread are organized criminal operations and the conditions under which they are permitted to continue that they threaten to make a shambles of law enforcement and to create such a universal disrespect for law that our entire system of government may be endangered." Despite the extensiveness and gravity of this problem, J. Edgar Hoover prohibited the FBI from investigating organized crime, and he refused to supply any information from its files to assist Kefauver's U.S. Senate Crime Investigating Committee.[436]

The Kefauver revelations set off a series of legal actions against the S&G leaders, law enforcers, and the governor that did little more than sully their reputations. Felony illegal gambling indictments were served on the six S&G's leaders, including Chicago-interloper Harry Russell, and the IRS filed liens of up to $1 million each against the original five partners nine months later. Unfortunately, the results of both prosecutions were not available.

The Kefauver Committee obtained enough testimony about Dade County Sheriff Jimmy Sullivan's corruption from current and former deputies to force him to file amended income tax returns with the IRS increasing his revenue by $50,000 ($480,000 today) for the first four years he was in office. Sheriff Sullivan admitted firing two deputies over instigating bookmaking cases, but he bogusly argued his deputies should have been too busy with serious crime to waste time with bookmakers in their grasp. The Kefauver Report summarized, "In Dade County, which adjoins Broward County, Sheriff Jimmy Sullivan also testified, incredibly, that he was not aware of law violations. Here, as in Broward County, the testimony is uncontradicted that bookmaking and other forms of gambling are on a wide-open and notorious basis. Complaints were made to the sheriff by the Grand Jury, the Crime Commission, and others, but the sheriff took no effective action." And it concluded, "Much of Sullivan's testimony was vague and evasive and the Committee does not consider it credible."[437]

A majority of the Miami City Council supported wide-open illegal gambling, and they fired City Manager Richard G. Danner, former FBI agent in charge of the Florida office, after he supported Sheriff Sullivan's law-and-order opponent in the run-off primary. Sullivan won reelection by claiming gambling was rampant inside the city, where he left enforcement of the laws to city police.

Three weeks after Kefauver's Miami hearings, Governor Warren sent his third letter to every police chief and sheriff to close all gambling within 30 days, or he would summarily suspend them without a hearing for neglect of duty. One of the first to go was Broward County Sheriff Walter Clark, protector of the casinos of Meyer Lansky and Jimmy Blue Eyes.

Sheriff Clark was Broward County's elected law enforcer for two decades when he testified before the Kefauver Committee. He defended his long-term hands-off-gambling administration in various ways. He testified, "I was elected on the liberal ticket, and the people want it. I let them have what they want for the tourists down here." He said he knew that Meyer Lansky's *Colonial Inn, Greenacres,* and *Boheme Club* had gambling, but as long as none of his constituents complained about them, so be it. Actually the residents benefited from their existence. The casinos' massive kitchens bought the small farming community's products, and casinos provided high-paying and -tipping jobs for hundreds of locals, many of whom were recommended for employment, in writing, by Hallandale's mayor.[438]

The Committee forced Sheriff Clark to admit he assisted the casino operations. His three-man Hallandale Sheriff's force directed traffic in front of the casinos. The Sheriff protected their bankrolls by deputizing the Rolfe Armored Car drivers and by having his uniformed deputies escort the nightly cash deposits. Clark admitted amassing a large amount of money, as well as extensive real estate and business holdings during his tenure in office.

Sheriff Clark received payoffs from the casinos and bookmakers, but his primary income came from his own illegal gambling enterprise. He was a one-third partner in Broward Novelty, which operated a major "bolita," or policy numbers racket. The company also held federal licenses for slot and pinball machines, even though all three activities were illegal in Florida. "It is obvious that a law-enforcement official who is himself engaged in gambling operations can have no special desire to enforce gambling statutes," pointed out the Kefauver Preliminary Report.[439]

Governor Warren ordered Sheriff Clark's suspension immediately following his Kefauver gambling-violation acknowledgements. This ended Meyer Lansky's illegal casino operations in Florida. Sheriff Clark was finally removed from office almost a year later by the Florida Senate.

Dade County Sheriff Jimmy Sullivan was as great an offender as Broward's Sheriff Clark, and his answers to the Kefauver Committee were equally unacceptable. But Sullivan had followed the direction of Governor Warren's Special Investigator W. O. "Bing" Crosby in the pressured takeover of the S&G Syndicate, so the Governor was forced to protect his collaborator with transparent political manipulations. Warren rebuffed every removal demand by saying he would act if the Dade County Grand Jury did. When the Jury finally indicted Sullivan based on his Kefauver testimony of allowing gambling and accepting bribery, the Jury directed the matter to the Governor for faster action than the DA could accomplish through criminal prosecution. Before nightfall, Warren kept his promise and suspended Sullivan from office. The indictment also alleged that the Sheriff used the power of his office to permit Harry Russell to penetrate the giant S&G. Unfortunately, the Jury did not realize that the Governor was the real villain behind this case.

The racket-busting Jury next indicted Sullivan and five of his deputies for taking bribes from Russell's S&G Syndicate and casino owners to allow them to operate and to warn them of pending raids. The five immediately resigned and submitted to arrest. Interestingly, the casinos paid larger bribes to the law enforcers when their biggest players visited town because they could not risk having them arrested and publicly humiliated.

Six months after Sheriff Sullivan was indicted, the Florida Supreme Court ruled the indictment was "void and ineffective," with tortured reasoning. The Court said it was lawful for him to allow criminal activity to go on if he refused to enforce, selectively enforced, or favored personal relationships, rather than taking direct payoffs. Governor Warren quickly backed the Court's argument, claiming his own study of the Grand Jury's evidence had revealed no violation of state law, and he restored him to office. Responding to public indignation, Miami's two newspapers - the *Herald* and the *Daily News* - immediately came out with front-page editorials demanding the Governor's impeachment.

The Florida House of Representatives responded three days later by unanimously adopting a resolution appointing a committee to investigate public officials for reinstating Sullivan. The Governor was not named, but the resolution recognized that "there have been recent demands by the public and the press for impeachment of public officials." The Kefauver Committee announced in its Final Report that it could not understand, and strongly condemned, the Governor's reinstatement of Dade County Sheriff Sullivan "without a full and public investigation of all the facts brought out by this Committee and by the Dade County Grand Jury."[440]

The day before the Report was issued, the newly-enfranchised Sullivan added insult to injury by reappointing three of the deputies who were under indictment for bribery charges. This embarrassed the Florida Supreme Court, which ordered an immediate show cause hearing as to why Sullivan should keep his badge, but the Justices again capitulated.

The Florida House-of-Representative's action was an intra-party fight between the 92 Democrats among the 95 members. Governor Warren's former supporters introduced articles of impeachment, charging 11 counts of misconduct in office. The four major ones were helping Chicago gangster Russell gain partial control of the S&G bookmakers, reappointing State Racing Commissioners guilty of failing to enforce racing laws and allowing bookmakers in racetracks, reinstating three ousted sheriffs who were guilty of protecting gamblers, and failing to list the three biggest contributors in his successful campaign. The House Democrats then dismissed all charges by voice vote as somehow "not legally sufficient" for impeachment.[441]

In contrast, the Kefauver Committee, under Democratic control, took a sane and aggressive stance towards Sheriff Sullivan. The Governor publicly defended his reinstatement with the twisted conclusion that both the Florida Supreme Court and House of Representatives had upheld his actions. Despite repeated demands to appear before the U.S. Senate, Warren sent a letter stating, "I do not consider myself accountable to your Committee, to the United States Senate or to any official or agency of the federal government for the discharge of my constitutional duty in this matter." The Kefauver Committee had invited many Governors to testify, but Warren was the first to refuse a polite request and also the Committee's follow-up firm demands that stopped short of an official subpoena. However, the U.S. Senate's mounting investigative and political pressure was too great, and Sheriff Sullivan immediately resigned the very day the Governor told Congress to shove it. The next day Warren ended the controversy by appointing the Assistant City Manager of Miami as Sheriff of Dade County.[442]

Warren served two terms as Governor through 1952, when he was barred from seeking a third successive term. He ran again in the next Democratic gubernatorial primary in 1956 on a segregation platform, but he did not come close to defeating incumbent Leroy Collins, who had succeeded him.

EVERYTHING CAME UNDONE FOR LANSKY & HIS PALS

At about the time Broward County Sheriff Walter Clark was indicted, a Broward County Grand Jury charged Meyer Lansky and some of his associates, including his brother Jake and Jimmy Blue Eyes, with gambling. They pled guilty, paid fines of $1,000 to $3,000, and moved from Florida to New York, where Lansky faced additional prosecution.

When Democratic Senator Kefauver first proposed the creation of his Crime Investigating Committee, GOP Senators believed they had the political clout to block its authorization. They wanted to shield Republican politicians across the country from being exposed and embarrassed by the planned Committee's three-to-two Democratic membership advantage, including the chairman, who would set the agenda. When political momentum for creation of the Committee became inevitable, New York Governor Dewey realized the ensuing reform mania could damage his carefully-crafted racket-busting image. For seven years in office, Governor Dewey had protected Saratoga's illegal casinos behind the scenes. However, now he ordered the state police to close the casinos on Labor Day, the final day of operation for the 1949 season, to prevent their reopening for the 1950 summer season, when the Kefauver Committee would be investigating in earnest.

Dewey acted in order to resurrect his law and order image for a third run at the presidency, but his dream was destroyed by the Kefauver Committee's New York City hearings, which lambasted the Governor's failure to close Saratoga Springs from 1943 through 1949. These hearings showed Dewey's anti-crime rhetoric to be the height of hypocrisy, when it came out that Saratoga Springs' key casino operators were his political adversaries he had vilified so viciously as DA - Costello, Adonis, and Lansky. Dewey tried to counter this devastating publicity by ordering a Special Blue Ribbon Grand Jury in the Republican-dominated Saratoga County seat in Ballston Spa. He mistakenly thought he could control these jurors to favorably investigate gambling and corruption in his interest, but they too wanted to protect the Saratoga Springs politicians and casino operators. His action was way too little and far too late.

The casino closures greatly reduced Saratoga's 1950 summer tourism, badly weakening its economy. The throngs of tourists no longer packed the sidewalks, nor sat in rocking chairs on the hotel porches. The lucrative casino and restaurant jobs were gone. Tipping was way down in the hotels, restaurants, and taxis. Expenditures in the town's small shops dropped dramatically. The locals felt the economic repercussions, and none considered this progress.

The residents understood that their strong economy depended on casino-generated tourism, so they always voted in local politicians and law enforcers who protected these illegal operations. Thus, these Saratoga Springs' officials dragged their feet in cooperating with Governor Dewey's loyal prosecutors and Special Blue Ribbon Grand Jurors. These delays embarrassed Dewey's ambition for resurrecting his presidential candidacy. It was almost two years after the casinos were closed before the Special Grand Jury investigating gambling and corruption issued indictments, and this was just within the deadline imposed by the statute of limitations for misdemeanors. By then, Republican candidate Dwight Eisenhower's campaign was already in full gear for the 1952 presidential nomination. Governor Dewey had been the GOP's losing standard-bearer in the previous two presidential elections, but the sordid Saratoga revelations meant he could no longer mount a credible racket-busting candidacy against the General who had successfully directed the Allies' World War II European theater against Hitler's Nazi Empire.

The Saratoga Special Grand Jury indicted seven men involved with the *Arrowhead Inn* nightspot for gambling, conspiracy, and forgery. The three key figures were Lansky, Joseph "Doc" Stacher of New Jersey, and James "Piggy" Lynch, who was serving time with Adonis in New Jersey for operating his Bergen County casinos. Lansky and Stacher were identified as founders of the L. & L. Company, formed to operate the *Arrowhead Casino.* At the time of the indictment, Stacher was the hidden unlicensed operating principal building the *Sands* on the Las Vegas Strip, one of the leading Golden Era high-rolling resorts.

The forgery indictment was bogus. It was brought because the local partners in the *Arrowhead* had signed the liquor license without mentioning the names of either Lansky or Lynch. At most this was an administrative case for the Business Division, which had already voided their license. Thus, Meyer's attorney had an easy time getting the judge to dismiss this charge before it came to trial.

The rest of the indictment was also weak. The Grand Jury's investigation could link Lansky only to the restaurant but not to the illegal casino room. Thus, his attorney Moses Polakoff was confident he would win. However, Meyer did not want to risk a trial. He told his attorney that he was afraid the trial testimony might incriminate others, but this was virtually impossible unless he took the witness stand, which he did not need to do to win. What the considerate Lansky really feared was having his friends tarred and feathered by the press during their coverage of his trial, since the media was already well on its way to demonizing him as a dangerous public enemy.

Lansky's only criminal activities during the 1940s were his illegal casino interests, but reporters fed on each other's reports of his occasional meetings with many of the East Coast's most infamous crime leaders. The press used these meetings to create a shadowy image that Lanky was some sort of behind-the-scenes powerful criminal mastermind. In reality he attended these meetings to sell his Wurlitzer jukeboxes because all these crime leaders or their close associates operated bars. In addition, he was there to help bring people together in various legitimate business deals, when the two parties did not trust or were wary of each other. He was the one man everyone in the underworld trusted. The media hype about his supposed exalted criminal stature culminated with a *New York Times* story about Meyer and his wife sailing in the Italia's five-room royal suite for an Italian vacation and a social visit with his deported friend and former partner, Charlie Lucky. So enthralled was the *Times'* society page with Meyer's supposed gangland status, it contained a complete description of the couple's fine boarding attire along with a photo of them.

Then the Kefauver Committee's Interim Report #3 contained a conclusion that was factually accurate, but the nation's press over-interpreted it concerning Lansky. What the conclusion actually said was, "3. Crime is on a syndicated basis to a substantial extent in many cities. The two major crime syndicates in this country are the Accardo-Guzik-Fischetti syndicate, whose headquarters are Chicago; and the Costello-Adonis-Lansky syndicate based in New York. Evidence of the operations of the Accardo-Guzik-Fischetti syndicate was found by the Committee in such places as Chicago, Kansas City, Dallas, Miami, Las Vegas, Nev., and the west coast. Evidence of the Costello-Adonis-Lansky operations was found in New York City, Saratoga, Bergen County, N. J., New Orleans, Miami, Las Vegas, the west coast, and Havana, Cuba. These syndicates, as well as other criminal gangs throughout the country, enter profitable relationships with each other. There is also a close personal, financial, and social relationship between top-level mobsters in different areas of the country." The press and law enforcement exaggerated the import of this conclusion to mean that two nationwide gangs operated most organized crime in the country, and they were headed by a total of six men. For the next three decades, they depicted Meyer as Public Enemy Number 1 and the mastermind behind virtually all major crime in America, even though he had never been a gang leader. In a world of large Sicilian gangs, he was a Jewish nonmember. Thus, he was never a man of power, but a man of influence because of the personal respect he generated from his trustworthiness and the sensible advice he offered. Because of these qualities, he would go on to become a silent and hidden partner in a number of Las Vegas Strip gambling resorts, never as a principal but always as the man who brought everyone together and mediated their inevitable disagreements. Because of the persuasive myth that Lansky was a criminal mastermind, the press jumped on every rumor that he might be involved in a Las Vegas casino, but at the most he helped bring the operators together or was a passive investor.[443]

Meyer and his associates always resented those politicians, law enforcement officials, and newspapers who repeatedly berated them as dangerous hoods, when their only crimes were for Prohibition smuggling and illegal casinos that were victimless crimes. After Prohibition ended, they were barred from the liquor business. They chaffed because the men who sold them the legitimate booze were allowed to build liquor empires and to become wealthy scions and socialites in their countries. For example, Samuel Bronfman built Canada's worldwide whiskey conglomerate Joseph E. Seagrams & Sons, which made several of his family members billionaires. Lewis Rosenstiel created Schenley Distilleries, which became America's largest. Joe Kennedy's Prohibition profits made him one of America's wealthiest men, and he used his fortune to form a family political dynasty, with three sons becoming U.S. Senators and one reaching the presidency.

At the time Lansky pled guilty to five counts of *Arrowhead Inn* gambling and conspiracy charges, one former partner in the *Arrowhead,* Adonis, was serving two-to-three years in a New

Jersey prison on Bergen County gambling charges; and another former partner, Costello, was serving 18 months in a federal prison for Kefauver Committee contempt. Three months after Meyer plead guilty, he was sentenced to three months in the Saratoga County jail, fined $2,500, and given three-years probation. Polite as always, he got a month off for good behavior. It was Lansky's first and last jail sentence, despite extensive, long-term investigative and prosecutorial efforts by a number of federal agencies against their concocted Public Enemy #1. Upon his release from jail, he moved from New York City to Florida. All six of his *Arrowhead Inn* partners, and virtually all of the other Saratoga gamblers and politicians who were charged, received fines with no jail time. Unlike Lansky, none had been falsely branded as a Public Enemy.

Saratoga jurors would have almost certainly found Lansky innocent. The residents supported the wide-open casinos for almost a century, and they voted for the novel dual political structure that unofficially licensed the gamblers. All the casinos appear to have been located within the city limits, but they were divided into two different tax zones. Those in the city's center tax zone, or inner-circle, were under the authority of the Democratic City officials, and the bigger places were in the county's outer-circle tax zone under the Republican County politicians. The two competing political parties, two separate government jurisdictions, and two independent law enforcement agencies worked in tandem to control which operators were allowed to open casinos in the city and how they were allowed to operate.

Dr. Arthur Leonard was Saratoga's Commissioner of Public Safety and Democratic leader, who had direct authority over the city's police force. State police officials testified to the Kefauver Committee that Police Chief Patrick Rox was cooperative in all phases of the law, except gambling, which he never discussed with anyone. He silently followed his marching orders from the Democratic politicians, while the County Sheriff was under the thumb of Republican leader James Leary, who never held elected office.

The residents understood that what the reformers called *corruption* was in their best economic interest, and they kept reelecting the same pro-casino officials year after year. Governor Dewey used his Special Blue Ribbon Jury to try to place all the blame on these local officials. He wanted to cover-up the fact that as Governor he was ultimately responsible for the existence of the casinos, and he could have immediately and permanently closed them with a one-sentence executive order to the state police, which he finally did after six years in office.

Typical of Dewey injustice, his specially selected Special Blue Ribbon Jurors and the Ballston Spa City Republican officials he controlled blamed the conscientious whistleblowers about the illegal casinos and not the Governor as the ultimate culprit in their rigged investigation. For example, Saratoga County Sheriff Frank Hathorn resigned three weeks after the Special Grand Jury recommended that Dewey remove him despite his longevity. Sheriff Hathorn had told the Kefauver Committee truthfully that illegal casinos had operated in Saratoga Springs "ever since they ran the horses there."[444]

They pushed State Police Inspector Charles LaForge to resign, even though he had filed a detailed report about wide-open gambling to his superiors two years earlier, and under orders of their boss Governor Dewey, they filed it away. Dewey's Jurors also pressured Saratoga Springs Police Detective Walter Ahearn to resign because these two law enforcers most helped expose the gambling corruption to the U.S. Kefauver Committee investigations. Strong law-and-order politician and former prosecutor Governor Dewey in reality crushed the careers of those who actually enforced the law and testified truthfully.

Republican Leader James Leary was recognized as the Saratoga County Republican political boss for half a century, although he never held public or party office. The Special Grand Jury indicted him for perjury and conspiracy to obstruct justice. The prosecution presented to the jury that a bank Leary was involved with rendered special services for gamblers, and that he owned stock in the bank under a "dummy" name of another individual. Leary's attorney told the Jury in his summation that Governor Dewey ordered the Saratoga gambling investigation in order to get Saratoga County "Republican leader James Leary" for circulating a negative letter at a political convention, which the Prosecutor of course denied.

Dewey's whole career, as a Special Prosecutor, DA, Mayor, and Governor, involved prosecutorial misconduct. He ran the gambit from framing innocent suspects, retaliating against legitimate citizens exercising their Constitutional right and civic duty to protect their fellow Americans from bad government officials, destroying the reputation of legitimate people who supported opposition candidates, and covering up his own malfeasance in office.

The trial jury that tried Republican leader Leary was made up of Saratoga Springs residents, who almost universally disagreed with the state's anti-casino law, so they did their duty to their fellow townspeople and nullified the law by finding the 73-year old innocent. They used the jury box to protect their popular local officials, just as they continued to reelect them despite the on-going gambling and corruption investigations that blasted them. After the jury's innocent decision was rendered, the judge castigated the members in open court because their verdict "stuns justice," was a "gross miscarriage of justice," and that "the court whole-heartedly disapproves of the jury's verdict." Against the mountain of evidence, he declared the jurors had rendered "a distinct disservice to the people." Fellow locals cheered the verdict.[445]

Physician Arthur Leonard was reelected Saratoga Springs Commissioner of Safety for a quarter of a century. Following a court order requiring him to testify before the Grand Jury, he resigned at age 72. This was the day after he was reelected in the primary for another two-year term. When asked if he planned to withdraw his name from the general election, he replied: "Of course not. Why should I? That's something for the people to decide. It's a chance for vindication." In the general election the city's voters reinstated Dr. Leonard to office. But three weeks after taking office, he again resigned when Governor Dewey's Special Blue Ribbon Jury ordered him to waive immunity, as a public official. The Jury's manipulative political ploy to simply oust him became transparent, when they failed to follow through and question him.[446]

The Special Grand Jury then returned a 17-count indictment against Dr. Leonard for accepting bribes. The misdemeanor indictment charged that Leonard used his quarter-of-a-century tenure as City Public Safety Commissioner as part of a conspiracy to "see to it that the gambling operations of the [*Piping Rock*] casino were not interrupted, interfered with or molested by the Saratoga Springs city police." The New York Supreme Court dismissed all counts on the ground that he was too old and too ill at 75 to stand trial.[447]

Of the 54 indicted gamblers and politicians, only Lansky and one other casino operator received jail time, and they shared the same County cell. Many of the indicted pled guilty and were fined. There were no jury convictions.

Meyer was highly respected and admired by every one who encountered him. He was a hero to the Saratoga Springs townspeople for bolstering the local economy and the residents' average income. Even if the County's criminal case against him had not been so weak, those who sat as jurors would have undoubtedly found him innocent, just like Leary, the politician who protected Meyer's fine high-end casino operation those many years.

Kefauver's investigations were a major blow to Lansky financially. The Committee spawned numerous local reform movements across the country, and they shut Lansky's illegal casinos in Hallandale, Florida and Saratoga, New York. They also wiped out his investments in Adonis' Bergen County, New Jersey casinos, and Costello's Saratoga and Louisiana casinos and slot route. All these losses occurred in 1950.

Meyer had fortuitously begun investing in legal casinos on the Las Vegas Strip four years earlier. He was a hidden and silent unlicensed partner in the third Strip hotel-casino, Siegel's Fabulous *Flamingo,* which opened in late 1946. Lansky also was an investor and partner under his brother's name in the next Strip resort-casino, the *Thunderbird,* which opened a year and a half before Kefauver's Committee reform impetus really got rolling across the country.

Meyer continued to live in Florida, but Siegel had sold him about his great vision for the future of a marvelous gambling and entertainment Strip in the southwest desert. Lansky would go on to implement Siegel's dream by spearheading his close northeastern gambling associates in developing legally-licensed Las Vegas casinos. All the other major illegal casino operators across the country were also closed down by the local reform mania aroused by the Kefauver hearings, and Las Vegas offered them the opportunity to go into legitimate businesses and become respected members of the community. In addition, Meyer was already exploring the possibility of legalizing casino resorts in Havana, Cuba.

Ironically, Kefauver's investigations benefited Meyer's legitimate Las Vegas and Havana gambling resort investments. By closing practically every illegal casino in the country, Kefauver created a huge pent-up demand by the nation's players for destination casino resorts like Las Vegas in Nevada and Havana in Cuba. Kefauver destroyed what Lansky possessed, while simultaneously creating even greater opportunities for the enterprising businessman.

Joining the Young Turks and their associates in the development of the Las Vegas Strip was the Chicago gang. For the two decades after Al Capone went to prison, this gang had three successive leaders before the fourth participated in the gambling resorts along the Strip. The growth and transformation of the Chicago gang under these three successive leaders comes next.

CHAPTER 15

CHICAGO - PROHIBITION TO UNION TAKEOVERS

CAPONE TURNED TO UNION RACKETEERING

The Chicago gang was a dominant force on the Las Vegas Strip in the 1970s and 1980s, but these gangsters' power was acquired decades earlier during the Roaring '20s through labor-racketeering activities begun under Al Capone. Back then the rising stock market was accompanied by a construction and manufacturing boom, and the beginning of skyrocketing union membership nationwide as workers wanted a bigger piece of the pie. During the Great Depression union growth continued, as the employed tried to protect their jobs from the mass of unemployed, who were willing to work for less money. As union treasuries swelled from the monthly dues paid by millions of members, extortionist bullies started plundering these funds through threats of violence against, and a number of murders of, union leaders.

Labor racketeering developed into a big-time crime because of actions in Chicago's laundry industry. Two union locals specialized in laundry employees, with one representing the plant workers and the other the truck drivers. The heads of both locals had violent criminal pasts, and they joined forces to control the laundry business by forming the Master Cleaners and Dyers' Association. It charged independent laundries a monthly membership fee in return for peace from union strikes and hooligan violence. The Association also forced its member establishments to gouge Chicago consumers with exorbitantly high fixed prices from which it took a substantial cut. Non-member laundries were attacked by Association thugs. They smashed windows, planted acid and dye bombs in loads of customers' clothes, overturned trucks, and slugged employees.

The city's laundry owners got no help from the police department because Mayor Bill Thompson and Cook County State's Attorney Robert Crowe were in league with these terrorist union leaders. Many laundry owners protected their businesses and workers by hiring their own brutes. One large group of independent laundry owners created a central cleaning plant - the Central Cleaner and Dyers - and brought major gangsters into their union-business relations. The plant was operated by Bugs Moran and his North Siders, and they also protected the owners' shops.

Seeing this new business model work, Morris Becker, who had sold his large dyer and cleaner business because of 10 years of union violence, was prompted to make South Sider Al Capone a principal partner in his new chain - the Sanitary Cleaning Shops. The gunsils of Capone and Moran who guarded these plants scared off the union thugs. This created wide-open laundry competition that led to a price war benefiting the city's consumers. Becker later testified against leaders of the Union and the Master Cleaners and Dyers at trial. "Our shops had been bombed 40 times, and the union had bled us to call off the strike. The police, the State's Attorney (Crowe), and the United States Attorney would, or could, do nothing, so we called in a man that could protect us, Al Capone. He did it well."[448]

Capone learned about the great profit potential of union exploitation from the Sanitary Cleaning Shops venture, and from the moonlighting activities of one of his gang's low-level beer workers, Murray "The Camel" Humphreys. He was born in Wales in 1899 and grew up in Chicago. He and his assistant, Machinegun McGurn, supplied the muscle for a few of the city's early independent labor racketeers. Their success led Capone to promote Humphreys to head a new labor-racketeering division for the gang. Its income grew rapidly because of Humphreys' readiness to terrify and to kill. Humphreys initial targets were the treasuries of big unions. He threatened the leaders and their families with physical harm if they did not turn over their unions' cash reserves.

Humphreys kidnapped a few union leaders and demanded ransom payments from their subordinates for their safe return. The most publicized kidnapping was that of Milk Wagon Drivers' Union President Bob Fitchie. It occurred as he arrived home one night and stepped out of his car. He reported, "I was kidnapped at 5 p.m. I was on my way to my home. As I turned my car into the alley, there I saw a car parked diagonally across it. Four men stepped out as I approached. They put guns in my belly. They told me to get in their car. I was ordered to put my head down and keep it down. One man told me if I raised my eyes he would blow my head off. The car ride was an hour to an hour and a half. I was blindfolded in the car and when we got out, it was dark. I was taken into a house and placed on a couch. All the time I was there, I was blindfolded." They made him write three letters urging his Union to pay a $50,000 ransom ($750,000 today) for his safe return. The Union's Treasurer and Business Manager Steve Sumner drove the cash to a school and placed it on the steps, but instead of leaving as directed, he testified "I left the money there and then hid close by to see what happened. The men who came to get it were Murray Humphreys and George 'Red' Barker." A blindfolded Fitchie was released from captivity at an intersection, but the two-day kidnapping ordeal weakened him physically and emotionally. Within a few months he died.[449]

The police did not learn about the kidnapping until after the criminal statute of limitations had run out, but the IRS filed a civil claim against Humphreys for the taxes he owed on the ransom payment and other income. The gangster argued that the IRS only had Sumner's claim that he delivered the money to anyone, let alone to Humphreys. However, the U.S. Circuit Court of Appeals ruled that the Union official's testimony, along with the victim's quick release upon payment, proved the case. Humphreys delayed paying the tax claim for a decade. His $25,000 settlement was $10,000 less than the original amount, and just one-third of the current bill with accrued penalties and interest.[450]

Humphreys and his associates escalated from violent robberies of union treasuries and kidnappings to forcible takeover of union leaderships. They paid off some leaders and threatened others either to become their pawns or to resign and be replaced by the gang's associates. The gangsters murdered some leaders. Once in control of a union, the gang siphoned off a percentage of each month's total membership dues, appointed henchmen as phantom union officials at high pay, and plundered health insurance and pension plans with exorbitant administrative fees by gang representatives who at the same time reduced members' medical care. In addition, the gang's members and associates were offered pension fund loans at low interest rates to finance legal businesses. Some of these businesses quickly declared bankruptcy to avoid any repayment of the loans. Adding insult to injury, the gang used some of the stolen union funds to bribe crooked politicians for protecting their illegal exploitation and oppression of the workers. Finally, the gang's union leaders demanded their memberships vote in a large unified block under the watchful eyes of their gunsils to keep these politicians in line.

The gang also threatened unionized businesses with strikes to extort cash bribes. Such strikes cost both the establishments and the workers dearly. Threatened strikes were also used to make unionized businesses buy specific goods or services from gang-allied companies at inflated prices, and also to participate in monopolistic-pricing practices to rip off consumers living within the gang's territorial control. Moreover, the gang sold out the memberships it was supposed to represent by signing sweetheart contracts with some employers. In these deals union leaders negotiated wage-and-benefit packages below union scale in return for cash kickbacks.

But the gang's exploitation did not stop with unionized businesses. The gang victimized various non-union industries by creating sham trade associations. These groups ostensibly represented the interests of the member businesses, but these nonexistent shells really fronted a terrorist extortion known as *protection* from damage and harm. The only benefit businesses received from membership was assurance they would not face arsons, bombings, beatings, kidnappings, or murders.

Business owners and union bosses had nowhere to turn for law enforcement protection from these domestic terrorists. The Republican political machine, mayors, prosecutors, and police in Chicago; the sheriffs in Cook County; and some Illinois governors and attorneys general were corrupt tools of the gangsters. The gang bribed the politicians; controlled large voting blocks of union members; and directed employees at their many taverns, nightclubs, and brothels to work during elections as precinct workers to get out the vote either for or against targeted politicians.

A few union leaders refused to capitulate to these terrorists' demands. Some were killed. North Side Gangster Roger Touhy later wrote, "The unionists in the suburbs around me lined up armies of bodyguards. One of the hired gun fighters was Lester Gillis. He built up quite a reputation as 'Baby Face Nelson.'" One major national union leader resisted the gang's overtures for years, but it was a costly and frightening battle for the Musician's Union's James "Caesar" Petrillo. He traveled around town with bodyguards sitting around him in his car, as the gunmen in the car behind watched these guards in case they were tempted by the gang's offer of more money to kill him.[451]

Capone next targeted government agencies for takeover. He contrived a sinister master plan to seize control of the City's building and safety departments. He then conspired with Mayor Thompson to get his henchmen appointed to head these agencies so they could impose financially-prohibitive regulations on contractors and building owners. The goal was for the appointees to routinely ignore building and safety violations for businesses in return for cash kickbacks. Capone achieved the first two steps of his plan by getting Mayor Thompson to appoint his political lackey City Sealer Daniel Serritella as Superintendent of Streets, and by having an ordinance creating a Bureau of Plumbing introduced before the City Council. Next, Capone's gangsters threatened to bomb the homes and kill the families of those Aldermen (City Councilmen) who failed to vote in favor of his bill. Some of the frightened but honest Aldermen anonymously whispered these draconian plans to reporters who put them on the front pages. This shocking publicity effectively blocked Capone's scheme before it could be launched.

Previous authors about early organized crime have guessed incorrectly as to who were the first three successor gang leaders who followed Capone when he was sentenced to the long tax-evasion prison term. This information was documented in extensive and detailed reporting by Chicago's dedicated investigative reporters, and it is reported here for the first time. Before Capone was sentenced, practically all his lieutenants had been ensnared by the IRS's determined drive against them. They were either facing trial, serving time, or released on parole and prohibited from associating with known criminals. Capone's two key men and head accountants - brothel-operator Jake Guzik and gambling-operator Frank Nitti - were both serving tax evasion sentences. Capone was incarcerated when the country was mired in the Great Depression, and it was obvious Prohibition would be ending. This made him look to the future income of the gang that he futilely hoped to take over after being released years later. Thus, Capone selected his aggressive labor racketeer Murray Humphreys. This was an effort to make up for some of the gang's soon-to-disappear illicit booze profits by expanding Humphreys' vicious takeovers of Chicago union locals. Sadly, Capone's plan to transform the gang's business model worked.

Humphreys had McGurn systematically use force, including more than a half dozen murders, to assume control of Chicago's laundry industry's two union locals and two owners' associations. The manager of the independent International Cleaners and Dyers plant, Benjamin Rosenberg, conducted a courageous battle to rid his business of Humphreys' gangsters, even after thugs kidnapped and threatened him and his wife. Then one evening Rosenberg was walking toward his home to have dinner with his wife and three children, when three men in a car drove up from behind him, pulled beside him, and shot him to death with six bullets. Public and press indignation over the violence forced the Prosecutor to bring charges against 17 union and trade association leaders, attorneys, and gangsters for fomenting terrorism, violent extortion, and conducting illegal strikes and boycotts against the laundry industry.

During the four-month extortion trial, Humphreys remained a fugitive from both the extortion and IRS charges. One of the many Chicago businessmen who testified against Humphreys was NFL pioneer George Halas, owner of the Chicago Bears football team and the White Bear Laundry. The amount of eye-witness testimony seemed overwhelming, but Humphreys had the Prosecutor in his pocket confusing the issues, so the jury acquitted. This courtroom defeat made law enforcement look impotent against Humphreys, who was emboldened to become even more aggressive and violent. This led to the first city-wide laundry-union contract, which was renewed for decades. The last Laundry Workers' Union boss to be murdered gangland style was in 1959, a quarter century after Humphreys started his move to take control of the industry.[452]

Even though writers about early organized crime have created an image of Capone being all-powerful in Chicago, he never achieved gangland control over the whole city. When he joined the Colosimo gang, Torrio dominated most of the south half of the city. During the first four years of Prohibition, Torrio and Capone wiped out most of the small gangs that had enclaves in this territory. Dion O'Banion had a major gang in the northeast third of the city, and several other large gangs had segments within it. During the next six years Capone wiped out or absorbed all of them, but he never challenged "Terrible" Roger Touhy, who controlled the western two-thirds of the North Side (one-third of the entire city) and part of the western suburbs.

While copious investigations, hearings, and trials document Chicago's many violent Prohibition gang conflicts, no one at the time ever examined how Touhy maintained unbroken peace with all the city's ambitious, murderous gangs, including the ever-expanding Capone and his successors. Prior to Prohibition, Touhy's key gang members had reputations as bank robbers, but Touhy had been a union organizer, knew the union leaders, and was sympathetic with the workingman. He safeguarded the cash treasuries for a number of unions, and he warned Capone and his successors to leave these unions' leaders alone if their gang wanted to maintain peace with him. They all did.

Touhy hated Capone for a number of reasons. Touhy did not trust Scarface because he made gangland truces to create quiet periods during which he planned sneak attacks. Touhy held Capone in contempt because he was a pimp whose brothels the Irish Touhy, like the Irish O'Banion, prohibited in his territory. And Touhy was incensed by Capone' violence against the workingman. Touhy later wrote, "For years Al Capone was in the business of providing thugs and scabs to break strikes for employers. In breaking a strike, Capone would weaken the image of the union's leadership and then put his own thieving men into the organization."[453]

Touhy maintained his long, stable peace with the city's other gangs until late in Prohibition. Then he supported the International Brotherhood of Teamsters in its violent conflict with a breakaway group of Chicago locals known as the *Outlaw Locals* that were under the control of Humphreys' associates. As hostilities escalated, Touhy had gang members burst into the Outlaws' headquarters to kill Humphreys, but he was not there. Humphreys did not retaliate because, like Capone, he was afraid to confront the Terrible Touhy Gang in mortal combat.

Then John Factor, the brother of cosmetics king Max Factor, soon proposed a Machiavellian scheme that would both eliminate Touhy's gang for Humphreys, and simultaneously block Factor's pending extradition to England for having engineered a massive swindle of his native countrymen. Humphreys agreed, and Factor set the scheme in motion by disappearing in a fake kidnapping. He reappeared 12 days after the alleged kidnapping began, and claimed to have been set free because the ransom had been paid.

During that period the rest of the plot unfolded. The day after he vanished, Humphreys had his henchman, Prosecutor Thomas Courtney, announce to the press that Touhy's gang was behind the kidnapping. British officials quickly branded the kidnapping a fake, and the Chicago police strongly doubted Touhy's gang was involved based on lifelong experience with the Touhy brothers' criminal activities. This did not deter the Prosecutor who simply bypassed the Police Department and manufactured his case directly with Factor and the phony backup witnesses Humphreys had agreed to supply.

Touhy's gang made a second attempt to kill Humphreys at the Outlaw Locals' headquarters, but they missed him again. Prosecutor Courtney charged Touhy and his gang leaders with kidnapping and implored the Federal Government to stop extradition proceedings against supposed kidnap-victim Factor until he finished testifying against his alleged captors at trial and also against the villains' inevitable appeals. Courtney successfully used his fraudulent witnesses to frame the Touhy gang leaders to life sentences for kidnapping pretend-victim Factor in a crime that never occurred. This wiped out Touhy's gang and gave Humphreys total domination of organized crime in Chicago and its suburbs. Two-decades later, a Federal Judge reviewed Touhy's well-reasoned appeal and ruled the kidnapping was a "hoax" that was based on perjured testimony.

The IRS indicted Humphreys, and he fled to a hideout in Mexico. Before running he turned leadership of the gang over to Frank Nitti. After a long search for Humphreys, a frustrated IRS Agent threatened new leader Nitti with prosecution for harboring the fugitive. Soon Humphreys telephoned the Agent to arrange his surrender in Indiana. Within four hours after turning himself in, he had pled guilty to tax evasion and received an 18-month prison sentence. Humphreys may have relinquished gang leadership when he went into hiding south of the border, but he remained a key lieutenant for the rest of his life. A decade after going to prison Humphreys continued to share in the gang's gambling profits with Nitti and Guzik.

The Chicago gang's leadership structure was inadvertently exposed by Guzik. He maintained the gang's financial records, and he stored the books containing all their gambling results in a place where few would consider looking, his hotel-suite stove. When he ended his lease on the suite, he accidentally left his books in the oven. Then new tenants moved in, and the first time the wife was going to bake she discovered them. Realizing their significance, the couple turned the books over to the anti-Caponite *Chicago Tribune* rather than to the corrupt police department that likely would have handed them back to Guzik. The next day the *Tribune* published an analysis of one month's results of the gang's Cook County gambling operations including the percentage of the profits distributed to each leader.

But times change. At age 60 Humphreys appeared before a Federal Grand Jury. He looked to be a pathetic has-been, badly crippled from arthritis. He had difficultly walking with a cane and told reporters he wore a patch over one eye because of a nervous disorder brought on by the arthritis. He complained, "I haven't enough life left in me to do anything." The once foreboding gangster was an isolated recluse, living alone in a Chicago apartment, where he shunned his neighbors and frustrated his landlord, who once threatened him with eviction for nonpayment of rent. The IRS pursuit of this decrepit, penniless man seemed pointless and even mean-spirited.

But agents had discovered that Humphreys led a double life, and in the other one he was healthy, wealthy, friendly, and charitable. Using the false identity of retired oilman Lewis Hart in Key Biscayne, Florida, Humphreys kept trim by bicycling daily in his neighborhood with his blonde twentyish wife. He continued to be a dapper dresser and an affluent, friendly socialite, residing in a mansion surrounded by a nine-foot stone wall. During the IRS's investigation of the amount of money he had spent maintaining two residences and two identities, he was charged with lying to a Federal Grand Jury investigating organized crime.

Three months later the FBI went to his Chicago apartment to arrest him. He refused to open the door, so the agents kicked it in to find themselves facing the gangster pointing a gun at them. It was a tense situation. Instead of shooting the gangster, the agents charged him and wrestled the weapon from him. They took the handcuffed offender to the Federal Building. He quickly bailed out, and no longer feigning illness or poverty, he told reporters that he never felt better. The gangster returned alone to his apartment, and within hours the 66-year-old suffered a fatal heart attack.[454]

Future Chicago gang leaders would become major powers in the development of the Las Vegas Strip casino resort industry largely because of Humphreys labor-racketeering activities two to three decades earlier. His impact was felt in three ways. First, the international hotel, restaurant, and bar workers' unions and their Las Vegas locals would represent the majority of resort employees along the Strip, and the Chicago gang leaders had absolute control over all these unions' leaders and their negotiations.

Second, John Factor remained beholden to the gang for faking his kidnapping and framing Touhy. Later gang leaders Tony Accardo and Sam Giancana would direct Factor to buy the bankrupt *Stardust* project in the middle of the Strip in the 1950s, finance completion of the hotel and casino, and lease it to their chosen licensed operator, Moe Dalitz. He had maintained strong business and underworld political ties with every Chicago gang leader from early in Prohibition. This would make Giancana the hidden unlicensed owner of the world's largest resort hotel and biggest casino.

Third, the Chicago gang's control over the huge Teamsters Union Pension Fund would allow future leaders to become the biggest financing force in the Nevada casino industry. An early Pension Fund loan to a Las Vegas recipient would go to Dalitz's Sunrise Hospital, followed by loans to both of his Strip casino-resorts, the *Desert Inn* and the *Stardust*. The Pension Fund would later totally finance the building of *Caesars Palace,* which would become the world's most famous resort, greatest high-rolling casino, and foremost star-studded entertainment center for three decades.

The gang leaders would okay Pension Fund loans to Strip resort owners in return for cash kickbacks. The gang leaders final coup was to begin secretly purchasing casino resorts for themselves through licensed front men. The Pension Fund, under the gang's direction, invested more money in the Strip gambling-resort industry than any other source during the 1970s and 1980s. This was the era when industrialist Howard Hughes owned the most Nevada casinos, including three he bought that already had Pension Fund loans - the *Desert Inn,* the *Frontier,* and the *Landmark.*

THE RISE OF FRANK NITTI

Around the time Humphreys went to prison for tax evasion, he had Frank Nitti succeed him as leader of the Chicago gang. Nitti continued to head the gambling operations, and he took over Humphreys' direction of the major labor-racketeering operations. Upon Humphreys' release from prison, Nitti gave him back leadership of the labor-racketeering division, but Nitti continued to set policy and maintain the direction of labor racketeering.

Nitti also started spreading the gang's influence into other areas of the country. For example, he absorbed a small Southern California Mafia gang in a subordinate role by offering it protection by the large Chicago gang. Nitti continued Chicago's long-time strong ties with Charlie Luciano and the Young Turks in New York and with Moe Dalitz in Cleveland. As Ben Siegel, Dalitz, and Chicago expanded into the Southwestern states, Nitti agreed with the others to give Siegel absolute power to mediate any territorial disputes in the Southwest to prevent conflicts between the three group's representatives.

Nitti was born Francesco Nitto near Salerno, Italy in 1886. He immigrated with his widowed mother and sister to Brooklyn when he was 7. He adopted his American alias Frank Nitti as his official name the day he became a U.S. citizen. Nothing is known about his youth. While writers about early organized crime always assume he was part of Brooklyn's street gangs, he was never arrested nor mentioned in any newspaper article or book about New York City gangs. The 5-feet 6-inches Nitti later told the IRS that he held various "ordinary jobs" in Brooklyn until he moved from home to unknown whereabouts. A decade later when Prohibition was beginning, Nitti surfaced in Chicago, but he did not go to work for the Capone gang until a few years into the Noble

Experiment. How Nitti got this key job is not known, but his family had lived a few houses from the Capone family in Brooklyn. This seemingly obvious connection may not have been relevant because Capone was only 11 when the 24-year-older Nitti left Brooklyn, and it is doubtful a close bond developed between a young man and a neighbor child.

Jake Guzik made Nitti a bookkeeper who did the accounting for the gang's Cicero casinos and metropolitan Chicago liquor distribution. Nitti was never involved with Capone's violent security division except to threaten delinquent liquor purchasers with Machinegun McGurn's collection squad. These threats are likely how Nitti got the nickname "The Enforcer," but others always did the enforcing. His avoidance of violent confrontation is illustrated by an incident that took place in Lake County, Illinois. Two Deputy Sheriffs tried to pull his car over near Antioch because it resembled one used in recent robberies, and Nitti and his two associates sped away with the police firing shots in hot pursuit. Instead of returning fire, the fleeing trio tossed two sawed-off shotguns and a pistol into a ditch and then pulled over and submitted to arrest.

Nitti was the designated fall guy to take a prison sentence for Capone, who never signed any document. Nitti was responsible for turning the checks from regional alcohol distributors and casino players into cash at outlying banks. When the IRS went after Capone, they first focused on his lieutenants with the hope of tying their violations to him. Thus, the IRS indicted Nitti for failing to pay income taxes on all the funds he handled because these banks had no records of who received the cash he converted from the checks. Nitti quickly went into hiding. Agents searched futilely for seven months until they began trailing one of Nitti's associates. They eventually trailed this man to Nitti's richly-furnished apartment hideout. IRS agents raided the apartment and captured the accountant in bed with his wife. Nitti pled guilty and accepted an 18-month sentence in Leavenworth "to avoid months of worry and uncertainty." He was released after 14 months with time off for good behavior. Since he served his full sentence without parole, he was free to associate with other gangsters again. The Federal Board of Tax Appeals compromised the IRS civil tax claim of $286,000 gross income for just the $15,000 Nitti asserted was his net income for which he owed taxes. No investigation was ever conducted over this shockingly lenient Appeals decision.

While Nitti was in prison, an important mayoral election was held. Chicago voters wanted the right to drink, but they abhorred the gangsterism that supplied it. When Prohibition had begun, Republican Bill Thompson was the Mayor, and he completely sold out his office and his appointed Police Department to every gang leader willing to grease his palms. Three years into Prohibition the city's gang violence was so bad, and Thompson's reputation so tarnished, that he decided not to run for reelection at the end of his second term. That is the year Democrat William Dever was elected Mayor, and he and his handpicked Police Chief quickly and completely shut down all vice inside the city limits and drove Al Capone into a Cicero home base. Under Dever's administration all brothels, casinos, racebooks, speakeasies, and alcohol production in Chicago were shut down and kept closed (see Chapter 6).

After four years of running a clean city, Dever ran for reelection on his honest and impressive record, but the public continued to yearn for the right to drink. By then Thompson's corruption and the lawless terrorism that came with it had faded from the voter's memory. Thompson ran against incumbent Dever on a platform of wide-open booze and saloons. He even painted Mayor Dever as the bad guy. At one public appearance, the flamboyant campaigner debated two live rats that he claimed portrayed his opponents. The Windy City's thirst made Thompson victorious.

When Republican Thompson came up for reelection in 1931, the public was conflicted. The citizenry was disgusted with the most horribly corrupt mayor in American history, and with all the domestic gang terrorism he protected which had included the St. Valentine's Day Massacre. But voters still wanted the freedom to drink. This time his opponent was Democrat Anton Cermak, who was another reformer in the mold of earlier Mayor Dever, but Cermak was a clever campaigner who took into account the voters' two inconsistent positions. He ran on a reform ticket that rejected support from all gangsters, but he also featured the glaring contradiction of supporting wide-open illegal booze. This was a winning pledge combination to beat incumbent Mayor Thompson. Cermak waited until he assumed office to announce that in addition to reforming corruption in government, he was ordering every gangster to clear out of town before the opening of the city's upcoming *A Century of Progress Exposition.*

New Mayor Cermak soon realized that a member of his reform ticket, County Prosecutor Thomas Courtney, talked like a tough law-and-order enforcer but was a complete sellout to the gang led, in order, by Capone, Humphreys, and Nitti. Prosecutor Courtney was committed to protecting the gang's plundering of the citizens of Chicago. To fight these gangsters, the Mayor created a special police detective unit to work under his office's exclusive control. He announced that he had ordered his special Hoodlum Squad to break up all gangster meetings and to drive the hoodlums from the city. He targeted 39 Public Enemies on an updated list of the Windy City's worst criminals that he had ordered compiled by the police command. Almost all these gangsters immediately went on vacation or into hiding. One week after the Squad was formed, a policeman was shot to death in a North-Side speakeasy, and the enraged Mayor publicly suggested the police fire first in their dealings with gangsters.[455]

A week later, operating in this emotionally-charged atmosphere, four of the Mayor's Hoodlum Squad Detectives raided the Loop headquarters of Nitti, who was then a gang division leader under Humphreys. The raiding Detectives reported that Nitti inexplicably fired a gun at them, and he hit the arm of lead Detective Harry Lang. He returned fire with shots to Nitti's neck, chest, and back near his spinal cord. Close to death in the emergency room, Nitti requested a priest administer the last rites for the dying, as he cried out, "O, God, save me this time!" The next day police charged the gravely-wounded gangster in his hospital bed with assault to commit murder against the Detective. And the public lauded these Detectives as heroes.[456]

The press did not believe Nitti's complaint that he was the victim of a police assassination attempt. The reporters even ignored Nitti's six associates who were with him, and who all swore the only guns in the building were brought in by the police. At the time no one even questioned why Nitti had been shot in the back. In addition, no one took notice of Detective Lang's highly irregular actions after the shooting. Even though he was a cop experienced in protecting others and defending himself, he insisted on a 24-hour police bodyguard, not only for his home, but also for himself while he was on and off the job.

Nitti's recuperation was slow and painful, and he was still suffering three months later when he went on trial for shooting the lead Detective. The first state's witness called by the Prosecutor was Detective Lang, and he boringly affirmed every point in his initial report about being the victim. Then the Defense Attorney stood up and asked his first question, "Who shot you?" Detective Lang answered, "I don't know who shot me." This contradicted his official report that it was Nitti who shot him. Detective Lang's statement created bedlam in the courtroom as several interested parties instantly leapt toward the Judge's bench shouting at once in disbelief. The two Prosecutors demanded a perjury charge, Lang's attorney admonished his client not to answer any more questions, and police officials expressed disgust at Lang's admission. A recess was called, and Detective Harry Miller excitedly told his fellow officers that his partner Lang was "a dirty son-of-a-bitch" and was afraid of hoodlums. Nitti sat at the defense table quietly observing and smiling at all the uproar going on in front of him.[457]

The Prosecutor should have recognized early on that there was a problem with this case. On the day Nitti's office was raided, one of the four members of the Mayor's Hoodlum Squad had not been available to accompany the group, so Detective Chris Callahan was called in from another unit. After the raid, Detective Callahan had consistently refused to testify before the Cook County Grand Jury or at Nitti's trial because he was not about to lie to cover up another cop's actions. But the day after Detective Lang's explosive admission in court, Detective Callahan testified in court what had actually happened in Nitti's office. Detective Callahan explained he had been instructed by Detective Lang to take Nitti into a separate office to search him, and he found Nitti was not carrying a gun. Detective Callahan held Nitti's hands behind his back during the search, and Detective Lang suddenly drew his gun and fired two shots into Nitti. Detective Callahan jumped away from the flying bullets, letting Nitti fall on his stomach, and Lang fired again into the wounded victim's back. Detective Callahan testified, "There was only one gun fired up there. Lang must have shot himself," so he could lend justification to his attempted assassination. The testimony by Detectives Lang and Callahan forced the Judge to immediately free Nitti with a directed verdict of not guilty.[458]

The Prosecutor immediately walked Lang's partner Detective Miller from the courtroom directly into the Grand Jury. Miller testified that he had heard rumors that Lang had accepted a $15,000 payment from North Side gang-leader Ted Newberry to kill Nitti, a lieutenant in the rival South Side gang. Detective Miller had heard that Detective Lang talked to gang-leader Newberry just before Lang asked for a raid to be conducted. Detective Lang's request to raid was unusual because this was Detective Miller's case, since he had gathered all the evidence about the illegal activities at the building. Following Miller's testimony, the Grand Jury charged Detective Lang with assault to commit murder and also perjury for repudiating his Grand Jury testimony about who shot him. The disgraced Detective Lang was still sitting in the courtroom after his shocking testimony when the police arrested him. It is clear that Nitti also knew who had ordered his shooting, because three weeks afterwards gang-leader Newberry's body was found on a lonely road near Gary, Indiana.

Nitti was asked to cooperate with the prosecution of his assailant, but he said, "I would just as leave drop the whole thing and go some place to recover my health." Nitti never filed a complaint against the Detective, refused to testify until he was subpoenaed, and then failed to show up as a State's Witness, which caused the Judge to drop the case. Detectives Lang and his partner Miller were fired and were required to return the commendations the Police Department had earlier issued for shooting the defenseless Nitti.[459]

Detective Lang never talked about why he destroyed his police career by testifying truthfully in court to destroy the false attempted-murder case he instigated against Nitti. But it seems certain Lang cut a deal to save his life. Detective Lang exhibited great fear after his assassination attempt against Nitti. Lang then saw how fast Nitti dispatched Newberry, and he was aware of Nitti's long and painful recovery. In return for Lang's honesty in court, Nitti refused to assist in the prosecution of his assailant, and then Lang was appointed as a business agent for the Hebrew Butchers Association. This organization just happened to be the creation of one of Nitti's labor racketeers.

CHICAGO'S MAYORS CERMAK & KELLY

Two months after Nitti was shot, an assassin shot at President-elect Franklin Delano Roosevelt (FDR), and some wondered if Nitti was behind it. It occurred soon after FDR won the 1932 election, while he was enjoying a leisurely 12-day Bahaman fishing vacation with friends. Upon the yacht's return to its Miami dock under the setting sun, he was driven to nearby Biscayne Bay Park to greet 25,000 waiting supporters. Associates hoisted the polio-crippled Electee from the back seat of his open convertible and sat him atop the car's trunk with his feet dangling on the seat. He spoke to the crowd over a microphone for less than a minute, and then he was helped back down to his seat, so he could talk to the dignitaries who had walked over from their chairs on the amphitheater stage to congratulate him. As the police motorcycles revved up to lead his car slowly out of the large gathering, FDR asked Chicago Mayor Cermak to hold off their talk until they boarded the train together for New York. FDR waved to the crowd as Cermak turned and walked to the back of the car. He was unintentionally heading right towards a man in the fifth or sixth row of spectators about 25 feet from FDR. At that moment, this short man stood up on the wooden box he had carried in with him and fired a gun five times. The first shot struck Mayor Cermak. As the woman next to the shooter tried to run away, she accidentally kicked his box, ruining his aim on the second shot. The man behind was finally able to grab the shooter's arm to deflect his aim on the final three shots. These last four shots hit four other people standing near the convertible, and all four were within two feet of the firing line between the shooter and FDR.

As Mayor Cermak fell, he cried out, "The President - get him away!" Every one around the car waved their arms in the air urging the driver to take FDR out of danger, but the President-elect ordered his driver to stop as the hail of gunfire continued. He directed two men standing nearby to place the fallen Mayor in the back seat beside him. As FDR's car sped amid screaming police sirens to the hospital, he held the badly-wounded Mayor, who gallantly exclaimed, "I'm glad it was me instead of you." The press reported the courageous and heroic actions of FDR who was just 17 days from taking over leadership of the financially-troubled Depression-era nation.[460]

The shooter's first bullet hit Mayor Cermak in the abdomen. He improved daily. Then he suddenly took a turn for the worse and declined rapidly, dying in the hospital three weeks after the shooting. The doctors never released the autopsy, but a group of modern doctors concluded the only explanation for his symptoms and decline was septicemia, or fecal fluid leaking into the abdominal cavity from a punctured intestine. If doctors had conducted an early exploratory surgery, like the one they did to save one of the other victims, this would have been discovered and repaired.[461]

As the shots rang out at the assassination scene, the spectators quickly surrounded the shooter, threw him to the ground, and beat him mercilessly. The nearby police struggled to pull them off while bystanders were yelling, "Kill Him!" Police finally rushed the subdued man to jail, where multiple agencies, especially the Secret Service, undertook extensive interrogation about his life and motive. He quietly and calmly cooperated with each interrogator's rehashing of the same questions about his background and political views, and his answers were always consistent.

Assassin Giuseppi Zangara had emigrated from Italy nine years earlier. He described himself as an isolated loner with no attachments, and this was supported by fellow workers and other apartment tenants in the cities in which he had resided. The first time he ever talked to anyone about his political views was during the interrogators' interviews. In venting his anger over the oppression of the working man, the bitterness he had about his life, illness, and economic plight emerged.

Zangara talked mostly about searing abdominal pain, and he incessantly rubbed his belly with his hand. His chronic pain began with his father's merciless beatings at six years old whenever he failed to work at adult labor jobs or expressed a longing to go to school. As an adult he displaced his hostility from his father to remote authority figures, blaming presidents, kings, greedy rich men, and capitalism for forcing him into child labor and denying him an education and a good life. Limited medical tests during his life and an autopsy after his death never identified the cause of his pain. No one doubted he was truly suffering, but it could have been psychosomatically induced from his early beatings and the resulting deep resentment toward his father and the rich and powerful. When his pain peaked, it triggered a desire to kill a leader "who oppress the working man." "As a man, I like Mister Roosevelt. As a president, I want to kill him. I want to kill all presidents." Despite Zangara's idealistic rhetoric about the miserable oppression of the masses, he was actually concerned only with his own suffering. Regarding his five innocent victims he said, "They had no business getting in way of bullet." He had never heard of Cermak, but when he found out he was a mayor, he said proudly, "I'm glad I got Cermak." He exhibited no remorse, no regret.[462]

As always happens with political assassinations, questions about a possible conspiracy arose. Since Cermak was the only one of the five shooting victims to die, some Chicagoans speculated he was the intended target. They totally ignored the fact that he survived the shooting and died from inadequate doctoring. These conspiracists hypothesized that Zangara was the tool of gangster Nitti to avenge his shooting and attempted-murder framing by Mayor Cermak's Hoodlum Squad two months earlier. This possibility was soon forgotten, until it was resurrected a quarter century later by John Lyle. He had been the only city judge to aggressively harass Capone and his associates. He had made it more difficult for them to get bail bond money whenever they were charged with a crime. He used his highly-publicized nuisance actions to campaign for and lose the 1931 Republican mayoral primary to incumbent Thompson, who then lost the election to Cermak. When Lyle wrote his 1960 book about the Capone Era, he hyped it by claiming Nitti was behind Cermak's killing, a charge he had peculiarly never made until the dollar signs of potential book sales arose. Unfortunately, Lyle reshaped the facts to support his allegation, and future self-promoting crime authors continued his deceptions.

These self-styled crime authors proposed two motives for Zangara intentionally killing Cermak, but neither had any basis. Their primary supposition was that Nitti promised to take care of the assassin's ill mother in Italy, but this was not a possibility since she had died when he was two. Their second conjecture was simply ridiculous. They speculated that Nitti's enforcers pointed out to Zangara that it was preferable to settle his large outstanding gambling debts by dying from electrocution than at their hands. However, no gangland gambling operation would have loaned any money to Zangara, who had been an unemployed bricklayer for the previous three years. Besides, the assassin would simply have fled from such an outlandish threat and disappeared into another state under an alias.

In addition, Nitti would not have used Zangara and his wacky assassination strategy that had little chance for success and absolute certainty of capture. Not only did he fail at his only opportunity to kill FDR, but Zangara had been much closer to Cermak earlier that afternoon. While the Mayor waited for FDR's car to arrive, Cermak sat patiently in the front row on the bandstand. Zangara could have walked up very close to him and have had an unimpeded target.

Given the way the shooting came down, if Mayor Cermak had indeed been the target, Zangara would have stopped firing after the first shot, because Cermak instantly collapsed to the ground and was safely protected from the line of fire by the whole body of the car. After the first shot Zangara, who stood only five-feet one-inch tall, would have tried to immediately get lost in the large crowd. As White House Secret Service Chief Michael Reilly concluded, "Cermak always went unarmed, unescorted, and unharmed because no one to my knowledge wished to attack him. … They would have mowed Cermak down either in Chicago or Miami (where he was staying unguarded at his winter-vacation home) with their customary cold blooded efficiency."[463]

These crime authors published their conspiratorial conjectures despite being unable to connect Zangara to either Nitti or Chicago. More importantly, their fundamental assumption was untrue. Nitti had no vendetta for Zangara to carry out. Nitti knew Mayor Cermak had nothing to do with his shooting because Nitti had already killed the man responsible, rival gang-leader Newberry, who had paid Detective Lang to shoot Nitti. Not only did Nitti not want revenge against the Mayor, but Nitti even ended his personal conflict with the disgraced former Detective who almost killed him with three bullets by refusing to testify against him and by obtaining him a union-official job. The Secret Service, the FBI, the Chicago police, police agencies in every city in which Zangara had resided, and many newspapers did intensive interviews with every one who had come into contact with the shooter. The Secret Service investigation report alone filled three volumes. Nothing tied Zangara to Chicago.

These various investigators searched intently for a more sinister motive than Zangara's explanation, because his political views seemed superficial and bizarre, but none was found. The two possible motives that follow were not considered by the investigators, but the available evidence makes them likely. Interestingly, Zangara's presidential assassination attempt accomplished the goals of both motives. Consider the first possible motive. He complained in every interview about his dismal hopeless life. His savings were depleted; he had no hope of finding work in the depths of the Depression; his pain was becoming unbearable; and he was clearly depressed. "My work has been a failure. My life is ended." He was a man bent on suicide, something he had earlier admitted to a Miami acquaintance. He told the judge and interrogators he had expected the police to gun him down in the park because there was no escape with all those people surrounding him. When Zangara's suicide by cop failed, he refused attorneys, a trial, and an appeal. At his guilty plea, he justified his actions to the judge without remorse, guaranteeing his electrocution. His decisions combined to cause a quick rush to judgment. Two weeks after Cermak died, his killer was executed.[464]

Zangara's second possible motive arose from his exaggerated sense of self-importance. This was exemplified by his defiant, disrespectful contempt toward every one he came into contact with. In his distorted thinking, shooting the President-elect freed him from his pathetic existence, while also making him the infamous champion of the downtrodden. The witnesses at his execution were astonished at his matter-of-fact determined walk to his death, especially without showing any bravado. Strapped in the chair, Zangara vehemently complained, "Lousy capitalists. No picture. No one here take my picture. All capitalists lousy bunch of crooks." His final words through the hood were dramatic, "Goodbye to all poor people everywhere!" A moment later, he ordered his executioner, "Push the button! Go ahead, push the button!" He only had one complaint that day - no record was made of his heroic death just before 2,300 volts coursed through his body.[465]

In a tragic irony, this assassin who hated the wealthy and powerful had killed Chicago's first foreign-born mayor, a Czechoslovakian who had grown up in poverty in America, developed successful businesses, and had an effective administration to help the citizenry. The Republican *Chicago Daily Tribune* editorialized about the Democratic Cermak's two-year leadership of the city. "Mr. Cermak's predecessor [Thompson] had made a ruin of every function of government upon which he could lay his hands." Cermak was "facing problems more difficult than any in the city's annals. A regime of unprecedented recklessness and almost unequaled corruption had left municipal finance and administration in a state of demoralization, funds exhausted, credit destroyed. Mayor Cermak took up what seemed an almost hopeless task of rehabilitation with courage and vigor. His choice of key men in his cabinet was of first rate material. ... Contrasting the deplorable situation of government when he took office with the progress made since, gives a measure of honorable accomplishment which places his mayoralty high in the annals of the city."[466]

The killing of Mayor Cermak was a catastrophic loss for the city of Chicago because he was the last hope for crushing gangsters Humphreys, Nitti, and their gang. He was assassinated almost three months before the opening of *A Century of Progress Exposition*, the date on which he had ordered every gangster to be gone from Chicago. Just weeks after this crime-fighter's death, Ed Kelly was elected mayor, and he quickly sold out his administration to gang-leaders Humphreys, who already had Prosecutor Courtney under his control. Kelly's takeover of city government gave Nitti enough time to install upscale illegal casinos in prominent locations near the *Exposition's* entrance-exit. Mayor Kelly's Police Department failed to investigate Humphreys' many violent extortions of merchants, union leaders, and workers; turned a blind eye to Nitti's casinos, bookie parlors, and slot operations; and ignored Guzik's brothels. Kelly appointed many unqualified relatives of gang members to good-paying city jobs, and the Mayor sent his unemployed political supporters to Nitti's illegal casinos for lucrative jobs.

County Prosecutor Courtney assisted gang-leader Humphreys' extortions by telling citizens who complained to him that their eye-witness victimization did not warrant prosecution. In the weeks before elections, Prosecutor Courtney ordered Nitti's gambling operations closed, and then he made grandiose proclamations to the press that he had driven the gang out of business or greatly weakened it. But these illegal places always reopened the day after elections. At least Courtney's prosecution record against the large gang was consistent. During his 14-year tenure, he never convicted a single gang member of any crime. The Mayor and the Prosecutor joined forces to turn the city's law enforcement system into an arm of the Mafia gang, assisting these mobsters' domestic terrorist exploitation of the community.[467]

NITTI'S POLITICAL POWER & UNION TAKEOVERS

When Murray Humphreys went into hiding in Mexico to avoid going to trial on the laundry-extortion and the IRS charges, he relinquished gang leadership to Frank Nitti. The Enforcer was a cold, distant introvert, and his precise diction put people off. Corrupt union leader Willie Bioff later described his boss Nitti's terseness in testimony, "He was very frank and to the point. He never went into long, lengthy conversation." Nitti kept to himself in public and drank little, so he generated little publicity. He spent much of his time in Miami, where he had a large home, just like an earlier predecessor, Al Capone.[468]

Five years into Prosecutor Courtney's reign, Courtney publicly criticized the police because wide-open casinos and bookies were as prolific under Nitti as they had been under Capone. Courtney used law-and-order rhetoric to express his indignation at this lawlessness, while directing the police to raid and close dozens of specific bookies. In reality, all these operations had refused to subscribe to the General News Bureau's horseracing information service controlled by Nitti. As a result of Courtney's actions, a U.S. Attorney's investigation found that more than 1,000 illegal bookmaking parlors were operating wide open in the Chicago area, and all subscribed to Nitti's race service to avoid police interference.

Humphreys had finally wiped out every other organized-crime gang in Chicago before turning over power to Nitti. With no other criminal competition protecting any part of the city, Nitti became a more demanding and vicious political manipulator. He ordered the murders of two elected Democratic State Representatives who would not do his bidding. As Albert Prignano walked up to his home porch steps one evening, men with revolvers sprang from bushes, shooting him to death. A year-and-a-half later, John Bolton drove through an intersection, and the men in the car that pulled alongside fired shotgun sprays, killing him.

For 30 years Alderman Mike "Hinky Dink" Kenna was called the boss of the rich and wicked 1st Ward. Here he made politically possible the brothel empire of Colosimo, Torrio, and Capone and then Torrio's and Capone's first major Prohibition speakeasy district. However late in his time in office, the once powerful and shrewd politician became old, feeble, and mentally incompetent. Nitti, and the gang leader who succeeded him, both repaid Hinky Dink for his great contribution to the gang all those years by holding him a captive prisoner in his home for at least the last 13 years of his life. He was surrounded by a police bodyguard and a hood, paid by the gang, to keep him from speaking to anyone and to make him sign whatever they put in front of him. Since Hink never showed up at city hall, former brothel-keeper Jake Guzik telephoned city officials to inform them of Hink's supposed orders. Hink was re-elected because Capone's puppet - 1st Ward Republican Committeeman Dan Serritella - failed to run opposition candidates against the senile old man. Hinky Dink left a huge estate, and his most fervent wish was to have a small mausoleum built to house his wife and him together forever. However, his greedy relatives, who inherited all the money, blocked the executor from carrying this out. Instead, both their graves ended up with cheap headstones.[469]

Nitti ran the gang's gambling operations, and he actively directed Humphreys' takeovers of Chicago union locals. Nitti began using the power of some locals to control and monopolize whole industries within the city. For example, he had a grand scheme to control post-Prohibition legal alcohol sales, but just one man stood in his way, George McLane. He was the long-term Chicago Bartender's Union Business Agent, who had single-handedly kept the organization alive during Prohibition, when illegal speakeasy operators prohibited employees from joining unions. After Repeal he had rebuilt the Local's membership to 4,500.

One day McLane was walking along the sidewalk, when Nitti's plug uglies drove up beside him, stopped and jumped out of the car, shoved him in, and took him to a hotel room to face threats by Nitti and 20 menacing goons. After three such kidnappings to different hotels failed to force McLane to cooperate, Humphreys and two hooligans walked into his office, pointed guns at him, and Humphreys threatened, "This is absolutely your last chance. We take over, or we'll blow your mother fuckin' head off!'" McLane later testified, "In fear of my life and my men's lives, I consented." He was allowed to keep his job as long as he turned a blind eye to their activities and kept his mouth shut.[470]

Nitti looted the Bartender's Union $150,000 treasury, stole a percentage of every month's total membership dues, and assessed members an annual fee for hospital care that only gave coverage to Nitti's gang members and their families. Nitti also initiated his scheme to control all beverage sales by the city's bars and cafés. He had the Bartender's Union Local create a liquor-sales department that forced unionized liquor establishments to buy certain brands to maintain labor peace. The Local also started a *bartenders' school* to teach each member which brands to push on their customers. Goons, passing themselves off as instructors, ordered them to promote brands of beer produced by Nitti's breweries, soft drinks from his bottling companies, and liquor brands handled by wholesalers who paid Nitti a substantial promotional fee. His brutes, acting as organizational agents, threatened owners of the city's taverns and cafés to join the Union.

McLane was too fearful to question Nitti's activities for almost a year. Then his swelling anger overflowed in a courageous exposé to the press. He also filed criminal charges against Nitti with County Prosecutor Courtney, and petitioned a Federal Judge to replace Nitti's Union forces with a court-appointed receiver. Then he quickly and wisely went into hiding until three policemen were assigned to protect him and his Bartender's Local's offices.

At a Federal Court hearing to make the temporary receiver permanent, the two warring factions presented a surprise compromise. Under this *harmony pact,* the Judge would approve an election with Nitti's Union Secretary running for the presidency and control of the Local, with McLane seeking reelection as Business Agent. The Judge rejected this gangster-sponsored plan, and supervised the election of a new slate of officers that completely removed Nitti's criminals from power.

McLane followed the announcement of this pact with another surprise. Even though he had revealed all of Nitti's awful criminal activities before the Cook County Grand Jury and the Federal Judge, McLane suddenly reversed course by refusing to repeat these testimonies at gangster Nitti's trial unless he was granted immunity from prosecution. County Prosecutor Courtney should have readily granted this request because McLane was a victim and not a participant, but the corrupt Prosecutor's goal was to throw this trial against Nitti. He therefore denied McLane's request for immunity knowing it would keep his star witness from testifying, and thus give the Judge no option but to direct a verdict of not guilty. Upon Nitti's acquittal, Humphreys beamed on the union official who had been expected to crush his gangster boss, and McLane told a bailiff, "Now I can campaign for reelection as Union Business Agent. Peace is wonderful."[471]

McLane's actions seemed inexplicable. He accepted the gangster's harmony pact that maintained the status quo he had risked his life to overthrow, and he also suddenly refused to testify without immunity even though he had already placed this information into two court records that could be used against him if the Prosecutor so decided. One fact might explain McLane's peculiar behavior. His brother-in-law was his corroborating witness, and he disappeared for some time prior to the trial without any explanation. The following interpretation of this incident makes sense out of McLane suddenly agreeing to the peace pact and refusing to testify, but it must be emphasized that this explanation is pure speculation that lacks any supporting evidence. What if Nitti's union-leader kidnap squad had snatched the missing brother-in-law and told McLane, "We can win this case two ways - by killing your brother-in-law because your testimony would lack corroboration, or by your refusing to testify without immunity. Your choice!" The gang was certainly motivated to go to such extremes – three of the defendants were the gang's leaders who succeeded Capone - Humphreys, Nitti, and Paul Ricca.[472]

McLane's history with the union was stellar. He had single-handedly held it together, conducted a heroic one-man resistance against Nitti, and successfully cleaned up the Union's leadership. Despite all this, he was defeated for reelection as Business Agent because the membership could not forgive his harmony pact with Nitti that the Judge rejected. He finished his career where he started, bartending.

Nitti's ambition for union power stretched far beyond the Windy City's boundaries. He allied with labor-racketeering gang leaders across the country to assemble enough votes at national union conventions to have his henchmen elected as their heads. One of these was the International Alliance of Theatrical Stage Employees Unions (IATSE), and it would become his most lucrative takeover. This plot started out as a small-time hustle by two minor union officials. George Browne was the business Agent of the IATSE Chicago Local for stagehands, and he was organizing an association of chicken dealers on the side. He decided to have his Local assist his 250 unemployed stagehand union members with a soup kitchen during the height of the Great Depression. Browne's cohort in this venture was Willie Bioff. The soup kitchen had the unemployed members eat for free, the 150 working members eat for a moderate price, and politicians and theatrical folk made larger contributions on their occasional visits to have a meal. Rather than giving all the soup kitchen's cash above the food and labor costs to the unemployed men's families as the two union leaders claimed, they pocketed it. When they started the kitchen, Bioff was organizing the city's kosher butchers (the group that would later hire disgraced Police Detective Lang after he admitted in court that Nitti had not shot him.)

A year later Browne and Bioff entered Union negotiations with Barney Balaban of the large Balaban & Katz movie theater chain. The pair wanted to restore the pay of IATSE projectionists that the firm had cut five years earlier at the beginning of the Depression. However, Balaban explained that he would have to give the other unions the same deal, which he could not afford. Balaban countered with an offer to make a $7,500 contribution to IATSE's free-meal program for unemployed members that would cover an entire year's operational expenses. Bioff instead negotiated a $20,000 cash bribe ($320,000 today) by agreeing IATSE would never again mention restoring the pay cut. Since Browne and Bioff no longer needed the income from IATSE's soup kitchen for needy members, they announced it went bankrupt. On the night the pair received the cash bribe, they celebrated their ill-gotten gains with a party at the *Yacht Club* nightclub and illegal casino. It was owned by Nick Circella, alias Nick Dean, and they foolishly told Circella about their profitable extortion. He in turn relayed their success to fellow gang-member Frank Rio, the former bodyguard who had taken the year's fall in a Pennsylvania prison with Al Capone. Rio soon met with the two union officials in a car and told them, "We want 50%, or else." Browne began to refuse, but a worried Bioff warned him, "I think it would be prudent to avoid the 'or else.'"[473]

Nitti next had his four labor-racketeering lieutenants notify gang leaders across the nation that Browne was his candidate for President at the upcoming IATSE national convention. IATSE's local representatives from across the nation elected Browne without opposition. The Chicago gangsters immediately cautioned Browne and Bioff, "Don't get caught wrong by us." President Browne soothed his nerves throughout his tenure by consuming copious amounts of beer daily. Browne quickly appointed Bioff and gangster Circella his personal representatives with fat salaries and princely expense allowances. Browne and Bioff stepped in to conduct those local negotiations that could benefit Nitti's pocketbook, but all their actions needed the approval of Circella, their gang boss.[474]

Nitti's first target for his national IATSE leaders was the Chicago Local of the Moving Picture Operators' Union. Tom Maloy started the Local a dozen years before movies talked, and he became an early labor racketeer. At 5 feet 5, he ran his union with an iron hand, stole from the workers he represented, and murdered at least two complaining members. To win contract concessions during union strikes, Maloy stink-bombed theaters. After winning these expensive clauses from the theaters, he did not enforce them as long as theaters gave him kickbacks. When the IRS charged Maloy for taxes on income he stole from the membership, Nitti turned on him. One day Maloy had lunch at home and then drove back to his office. Along the route a car sped up beside Maloy's car and terminated his 20-year leadership of the Union with 10 shotgun slugs and one pistol bullet in the head. He was 42.

Five days later, President Browne personally took over control of the "scandal-plagued" Moving Picture Operators' Local in order to "purify" it. He not only ousted all officials, but he rescinded Maloy's special work permits. These permits had kept older members unemployed in favor of newbies who paid 10% of their salaries to the Union treasury. Browne made his gangster boss Circella his personal representative with the Local at a high salary. This set up the gang's absolute control over the Local for decades to come. Circella began issuing his own work-permit system, and he also ordered the Local to finance him a second nightclub and illegal casino, the *Colony Club*.[475]

As temporary leaders of the Moving Picture Operators' Local, Browne and Bioff soon entered contract negotiations with the Chicago theater owners. These owners had selected Balaban as their representative because of his earlier successful bribery deal with the pair. During private meetings, Bioff accepted a $100,000 payment to let this IATSE local be the only one in the country that did not require two men in projection booths, saving the theater operators $.5 million in salaries a year. A Prosecutor later asked Bioff whether a second projectionist was necessary, and Bioff testified, "To be honest with you, I never was inside a booth. I wouldn't know." In recognition of their successful negotiations, Nitti and his four labor-racketeering lieutenants called Browne and Bioff to a meeting in a Chicago hotel room. The gangsters congratulated the pair. Then they forced a new deal on them. They upped their demands from a one-half to a two-thirds share of this bribe and all future ill-gotten loot. Browne and Bioff, facing the gang's massive and murderous firepower, docilely accepted this new division of spoils.[476]

JOHNNY ROSSELLI WAS THE MAN ABOUT TOWN

The gang's union-racketeering leaders soon planned a much bigger score, and for this, Nitti enlisted gang-member Johnny Rosselli because of his special connections. His background is relevant because he was a good friend of Ben Siegel in Los Angeles and Las Vegas, and he would later have an important influence on the development of the Las Vegas Strip. He was born Filippo Sacco in the small Italian village of Esperia on July 4, 1905. When he was 6, his family immigrated to Boston. They called him Johnny, and he later chose the alias Rosselli because he saw this signature on some Italian paintings he liked. He obtained a forged U.S. birth certificate under this name to be able to claim citizenship and avoid having his true alien identity traced from his new name.

After his parents died in his mid teens, he moved to Chicago, but a year later persistent tuberculosis drove him to the warmer climate of Los Angeles. Arriving early in Prohibition, he rode shotgun for the rumrunning operation of Tony Cornero, who would later own two of the earliest casinos in downtown Las Vegas and then build the *Stardust* resort on the Strip. Rosselli switched over to the booze-smuggling operation of Jack Dragna and his tiny Mafia gang. Dragna was a crude man who, as a traditional Sicilian Mustache Pete, remained distant from the surrounding community. In contrast, Rosselli was sophisticated, suave, and related easily with people. Moe Dalitz' primary enforcer all the years he lived in Las Vegas was Mark Swain, and he told me, "Johnny came closer to being real class than anyone in the rackets, with the exception of Moe." Everybody trusted Rosselli because he always lived by his word, and he quickly became Dragna's closest associate, handling the gang leader's dealings with the huge surrounding non-Sicilian culture.

In a visit to Chicago, Rosselli met Capone at the Dempsey-Tunney championship fight, and the two developed a close relationship. Three years later Capone visited Los Angeles, and Rosselli escorted Scarface and associate Charles Fischetti during their stay at the Biltmore Hotel. This visit cemented Rosselli's position as a one-man outpost for the Chicago gang. Rosselli started criminal and business enterprises for Capone and later Nitti, and he represented their interests in the Southwest. Rosselli even convinced Dragna to subordinate his tiny gang to Chicago's leadership. This gave Dragna a large powerful ally and a continuing tie to Rosselli's non-Sicilian negotiating services, while the Chicago gang gained a small group of readily-available soldiers in Southern California.

When Rosselli thought he or his Chicago bosses might need the local protection of Dragna's muscle, Rosselli brought the Mafia leader in on their business deals. Rosselli also received a piece of the action in the deals he negotiated for Dragna. For example, Rosselli arranged a partnership for Dragna in a gambling ship that operated in international waters just outside of the three-mile U.S. territorial ocean limit. It sat anchored in a line of casino ships along the Long Beach coast known as *Gambler's Row* that was not bound by any nation's laws. Strings of bright bulbs lit each ship's outside superstructure, making the long line of ships glow across the night horizon.

The old wooden schooner Monfalcone featured a large casino and a ballroom with dining and big-band dancing. Open water taxis with canvas roofs ran gamblers between the ship and shore. As part of the LAPD's gangster-harassment program, they once arrested Rosselli, Dragna, and Chicago gang member Charles Fischetti as they drove away from the ship's water-taxi beach dock. Fischetti was Capone's cousin, and a conduit between Chicago and Rosselli when he was representing their interests. That night Dragna was carrying the casino's cash win, and he was charged with possessing several revolvers. A month later the Monfalcone accidentally burned at anchor, and the partners replaced it with a surplus Navy steamer called the Rose Isle that housed a larger casino.

Rosselli never talked about his criminal activities or underworld connections, but he dropped vague comments to let everyone know he represented the interests of major gang leaders because he was tough. He cultivated an image that he could be valuable to legitimate people who needed help on the other side of the law, and he developed a wide-acquaintance of powerful associates in both the under and over worlds. These connections often allowed him to help people who were facing intimidating opposition by powerful men, government agencies, or unions. Rosselli later volunteered to the FBI, "I was practically a bum until 1935." In the previous seven years, he had been arrested five times for robbery by the LAPD. These appear to have been harassment busts because he was always released the next day, even though he possessed unregistered revolvers, sawed-off shotguns, or knives on his person or in his car. He was with Cornero on an early roust, and later with Dragna, when he was carrying the Monfalcone's win.

Rosselli was a master at handling contentious situations. Dalitz primary enforcer Mark Swain told me, "Johnny never lost his cool. He was the ultimate diplomat, mediator, negotiator. He represented all the families. He was at home on everyone's turf, and could not be touched anywhere, because they all needed him. He was the one they called upon to negotiate settlements when they had disputes with other groups." This gave Rosselli great influence in the underworld, even though he was never a gang leader or decision maker.

Rosselli was the peacekeeper representing the Chicago gang and all the gangs to the west and south, while Luciano's best friend Jimmy Blue Eyes was the man of reason along the entire East Coast. Both men tried to help any person who approached them with a problem, and they later represented their own gang's interests in Las Vegas.

In conducting negotiations between hostile gangsters, Rosselli faced tough, enraged, and stubborn leaders. He diffused the threats they spat out against their enemies with reactions of astonishment, disbelief, and amazed humor. His favorite ploy was to laugh in shocked response, "Aw, come on! Ya can't mean it." By seemingly not taking the angry threats of pending violence seriously, the mobster's steaming rage soon evaporated, and this allowed rational discussion to commence about goals, options, and consequences. Rosselli's easy laughter worked effectively, but this was reinforced by an underlying serious intensity that made the antagonist aware that if an agreeable settlement was not reached, Rosselli was prepared to return unannounced to kill him for continuing the conflict.

Rosselli may have been a likeable fellow, but he was a dangerous gangster in the mold of the Torrio-Capone-Humphreys-Nitti gang, rather than the anti-violence adherents of Luciano, the other Young Turks, and Moe Dalitz. Rosselli was a professional killer who worked for a number of gangs in eliminating problems within and between gangs. He was never suspected of a specific killing because he was not associated with any of his gangster victims. Therefore, no one had any idea whether he killed a few or several men. Decades later the CIA would enlist Rosselli to direct the attempted murder of Cuba's Fidel Castro. Rosselli brought in the Mafia chiefs from Chicago, New Orleans, and Tampa Bay, but the well-entrenched Cuban leader was safely outside their reach.

Whenever a conflict festered in a Las Vegas Strip casino between the in-house representative of a Chicago-gang hidden interest and the licensed managing partner, everyone knew Rosselli would soon arrive for tête-à-têtes to make nice between them. Dalitz' primary enforcer Mark Swain said, "Johnny was the outside man who kept every one from Chicago in line, but he never threatened anyone. He would grin you to death. Johnny would smile if everything was all right, but if he was mad, he would quietly make a phone call and either hurt or kill you. Everyone knew how easily he could kill."[477]

Rosselli and Ben Siegel were close friends. Siegel had more underworld power in both Southern California and Las Vegas than Rosselli because he was associated with the biggest gang in the country, and because he was the official mediator to keep the New York, Chicago, and Cleveland gangs from having conflicts in the Southwest. Conversely, Siegel's only business interests in Los Angeles were minor rooting partnerships in illegal casinos, while Rosselli was very active criminally in LA. Rosselli was in and out of numerous ventures. Late in Prohibition he invested in a speakeasy restaurant and nightclub on Hollywood Boulevard that was owned by two brothers. Rosselli's presence made the *New Yorker* a popular hangout for gamblers and hoods, and the LAPD was frequently called to quell problems. It was in this period that Rosselli became very sick from tuberculosis and was confined for long periods of rest in a sanitarium to let his body overcome the disease. The rest of his life he took care of his health and drank little alcohol.

Rosselli became a favorite in Hollywood society. Many studio chiefs were fascinated with gangsters, and those who were serious gamblers encountered Rosselli sharing their deep passion at the town's illegal casinos. Johnny cultivated the company of studio owners, producers, and stars at the racetracks in the afternoon, the most popular nightclubs during the evening, and the casino at the Agua Caliente race track at Tijuana on weekends.

Rosselli had a big smile, and could converse on any subject. He was known to talk about anything but himself, so he devoted a good portion of his time with dates listening rather than talking. Affable, debonair, ominous, and flush with cash, he was always on the lookout for attractive women. He dated a number of famous actresses, and his close connections with the film industry made him pursued by young girls filled with dreams of becoming starlets. Many of Las Vegas' casino owners and executives and their big players during the 1940s through 1960s were philanderers or womanizers. But Rosselli, who regularly visited the Strip for three decades, consistently escorted the most appealing companionship of any man ever associated with the town.

IATSE'S HOLLYWOOD-MOVIE-INDUSTRY EXTORTION

Johnny Rosselli was assigned a key role in Frank Nitti's first big-time IATSE racketeering scheme that targeted the Hollywood film-production companies. The young movie industry's annual revenue graph resembled a roller-coaster ride. After Al Jolson's voice was added to *The Jazz Singer,* movies had exploded into America's number-one form of entertainment. But just five years later the Depression had driven several major studios into receivership. As box-office receipts dwindled the studios substantially reduced production-worker salaries. The IATSE President preceding George Browne responded with a strike. The studios quickly filled the strikers' jobs from the vast army of unemployed, but the replacements were afraid to cross the striking workers' violent picket lines. To end this intimidation, the studio leaders turned to their gangster-friend Rosselli to keep their entrances open by guarding them with goons. Within a week most striking members of the Union quit their membership and crossed the line, breaking the strike. This abortive strike meant the 27 Hollywood movie-industry Locals that Browne inherited upon becoming IATSE President a year later represented a minority of the production workers.

IATSE President Browne could only become a force in Hollywood if his Locals expanded their memberships to win major jurisdictional battles with other unions over who represented which studio-employee categories, and to do this, he needed a dramatic contract-negotiating success. He accomplished this by giving no warning before ordering his projectionist members to walk out of 400 theatres in Illinois that were showing Paramount movies. The walkout occurred during the middle of movies, forcing the theaters to refund the patrons' admission fees. The theater-owners complained vehemently to Browne that he was breaking the promise he had made in the earlier $100,000 bribe for immunity from "trouble" through the length of the contract, but he turned a deaf ear.

The Hollywood studios had refused to talk to President Browne about union-jurisdictional disputes, but they needed their theater-admission income to pay their current film-production expenses. With their financial survival threatened, the movie heads turned to gangster Rosselli for his sage underworld-insider advice. They trusted him because he had supplied goons to end union-employee-picketer threats against replacement workers during two strikes, and because he had worked as an undercover investigator for their labor representative. In addition, the studio leaders had close personal relationships with the socialite mobster, who frequently gambled, attended social events, and played tennis with them.

The studio chiefs never suspected that their loyal friend Rosselli and the IATSE leaders were working in tandem for Nitti, who was orchestrating the intricate extortion scheme. The studios were surprised when they later learned Nitti had ordered IATSE President Browne to pay a union-official's salary to Rosselli, under the false name "Chicago representative McCarthy." Rosselli recommended the studios reinstate the IATSE's former jurisdictional authority, so the studios would have friendly union leadership to deal with, meaning one they could bribe. At a quickly-arranged meeting, the film chiefs and the leaders of other Hollywood unions agreed to recognize the IATSE. The successful weekend projectionists' strike in Illinois caused membership in the IATSE's Hollywood Locals to quickly double to 12,000.

The next step in Nitti's convoluted plot was to stop the influential movie trade-journal *Daily Hollywood Reporter* from criticizing IATSE's planned sweetheart studio contracts. To accomplish this, Willie Bioff threatened publisher Willie Wilkerson with strikes by the food-servers union local at his Sunset Strip Trocadero and Vendome restaurant-nightclubs frequented by the film community. This scared the cash-strapped Wilkerson, because he gambled away everything he earned from his successful businesses and then some. Wilkerson responded to Bioff by telegram, "For whatever mistake I have made I stand willing to do anything you dictate." Wilkerson then turned to his longtime friend Rosselli and asked him to intercede. The gangster told Wilkerson he had negotiated a good deal with Bioff, which was the one Nitti sought. The *Reporter* agreed to omit stories about studio-union affairs in return for Bioff's promise to prevent restaurant strikes.[478]

Wilkerson would later influence the development of the Las Vegas Strip. He decided that the best way to deal with his gambling addiction was to occupy his time building and running a Las

Vegas Strip resort so he would no longer visit the other casinos. Wilkerson came up with imaginative names for his popular Sunset Strip nightclubs, and he selected *Flamingo* for his Las Vegas resort project. While the foundation was being laid, Wilkerson spent his evenings gambling at the two existing Strip resort casinos and blew his whole construction budget. This forced him to sell off most of his partially-developed project and controlling interest to Ben Siegel for him to complete and operate.

The revived Hollywood IATSE next turned its scare tactics against the studios. The short but muscular Bioff played tough guy with the moguls. He told them his Chicago gang bosses would order debilitating strikes or their murders, if they did not accede to extortionate demands or if they dared to report the threats to law enforcement. During the union-contract negotiations and in announcements to the public, President Browne stood up for the membership by demanding large wage increases and threatening costly strikes. However, between Browne's official negotiating sessions, Bioff held secret meetings with individual employers. He offered them sweetheart contracts that substantially reduced the union's demands and guaranteed no strikes at the studios and their theaters in return for bribes. Nitti gave Bioff absolute power over the final settlements, so he left each meeting with $50,000 to $100,000 cash. The total studio bribe taken by the gang over the two years during the Great Depression was $2.5 million ($38 million today). The companies benefited from these large payoffs to the union leaders because they reduced labor costs by many times the amount of the bribes. This was a co-conspiracy by two groups of crooks - the union leaders and the studio chiefs - to steal potential salary and benefit increases from the hardworking and trusting union members. This made the studios guilty of bribery, and the union leadership guilty of both bribery and extortion, because studio heads later testified they initially got involved in the payoffs because they feared for their lives from Nitti's Chicago gang.

This union/employer collusion was brought to light by Bioff's greed. He had directed Twentieth Century-Fox's Joseph Schenck, discoverer of Marilyn Monroe, to arrange a false $100,000 bank "loan" to Bioff. The Union official wanted to buy a piece of land with his share of the studio bribery cash without paying income taxes on it. An IRS audit uncovered that Schenck paid this so-called bank loan to Bioff with cash from a safe-deposit box filled with unreported casino gambling winnings. The IRS first convicted the movie mogul for tax evasion of his winnings. Then the Justice Department launched extortion investigations into the two IATSE leaders because this phony loan occurred right after the signing of the IATSE's contract. Schenck agreed to cooperate with the government for reduction of his prison sentence from three years to four months. This led to the conviction of Browne and Bioff for extorting $1 million from Schenck and the other movie producers and exhibitors. The two Union leaders received respective sentences of 10 and 8 years.[479]

While Bioff awaited trial for the other Hollywood studio extortions, his past caught up with him. At 21 he had been sentenced to six months in jail for being the manager and bouncer of a Chicago Prohibition speakeasy-brothel, but the sentence was never imposed because the brothel owner had influence with corrupt Mayor Bill Thompson. When Bioff's 17-year-old outstanding case was disclosed by newspaper columnist Westbrook Pegler, the Governor of Illinois ordered Bioff extradited from Hollywood and saw to it that this time he serve his full pimping sentence.

Upon release, Bioff was welcomed back into power by the IATSE despite being a convicted pimp and facing extortion charges. The IATSE was a member of the American Federation of Labor (AFL), which was a coalition of diverse nationwide unions whose only interest was in collecting dues from as many workers as possible. It did not care if its unions' leaders were dishonest or acted criminally toward their working members. The AFL even defended corrupt union leaders in court against suits by abused and disgruntled members. It also buried all complaints about union gangster intimidation in the office of its chief attorney, Joseph Padway, who drew up the charters for Nitti's gang-dominated unions and represented his union leaders.[480]

FDR was the first presidential candidate to rely on labor-union election support. As President, he had Congress create the National Labor Relations Board (NLRB) in 1935 giving unions more authority to organize new members, but it also gave union heads frightening power to dominate their members and extort their employers. The Federal Government asserted sole legal jurisdiction over unions and then failed to protect workers from abusive union leaders. Every government agency refused to drive labor racketeers, disreputable and abusive union leaders, and convicted pimps like Bioff out of union leadership by falsely arguing they lacked legal jurisdiction. This included the NLRB, the Labor Department, the Justice Department, and the FBI.

The FBI's claims of lack of jurisdiction were proven untrue during hearings by the U.S. Senate Committee on Racketeering. These hearings found that most of the 35 Chicago industries victimized by gangsters were engaged in interstate commerce, which gave the FBI and the Justice Department the authority to prosecute. The Racketeering Committee and President Roosevelt asked the FBI to move ahead against these gangsters, and Hoover's huge detective force could have crushed these domestic terrorist gangs.[481]

Unfortunately, Hoover was allowed to operate in total secrecy with no one having access to his files or auditing his actions. He focused his detectives' attention on his personal agenda of political espionage of legitimate influential people, and also a few high-profile kidnappings, to make it appear he ran a legitimate police agency. Not only did Hoover fail to fight these domestic-terrorist criminals, but he steadfastly maintained that organized crime did not exist. By holding his FBI forces on the sidelines, these large gangs were rapidly muscling control from many unions and plundering from massive numbers of workers, merchants, and consumers.

This is a tragic illustration of how the government's failure to regulate and enforce oversight of those in positions of power or fiduciary responsibility leads to the most manipulative, exploitive, and greedy criminals assuming control. The only dedicated effort against organized crime's first four decades of development was by the IRS, which diligently worked to put away union and gang leaders for not paying taxes on bribe and extortion payments and other illegal income uncovered during its audits.

Over the last half century, union membership nationwide has fallen dramatically for three reasons. Republican leaders have strived to stifle the existence of unions as part of their pro-business agenda, employers have developed more sophisticated legal tactics to combat union-organizing drives, and Democratic leaders have failed to amend the National Labor Relations Act to rein in bad union leaders, to require union leaders to act in the best interests of their memberships, and to demand truly democratic union elections. In reality, Democratic leaders have tried to strengthen the power of union bosses, rather than protect their memberships, because almost all these leaders endorse and support Democratic candidates. This too often makes the workers pawns in power plays between greedy and unscrupulous employers versus corrupt and abusive union leaders.

One statement during the Browne-Bioff extortion trial of Joseph Schenck captured the Prosecutors' interest. Harry Warner of Warner Brothers Pictures testified that Bioff told him "the boys in Chicago were expecting a Christmas present," so he gave Bioff an extra $25,000. This was the first time Prosecutors realized that gangsters were involved in the Hollywood union extortions. An indictment was issued a month later for the IATSE leaders' gang-member boss, Nick Circella. He pled guilty and was sentenced to 8 years in prison.[482]

Then Circella joined state's witnesses Browne and Bioff to build the Prosecutors' case against gang leader Nitti and his associates in return for reduced sentences. A year later the shocking murder of Circella's former longtime girlfriend Estelle Carey in her expensive North-Side apartment impacted the investigation. The 34-year old former model had been a dice dealer in Circella's nightclub-casinos for many years. The assailant viciously beat her, slashed her face, and then burned her to death. Everyone assumed Nitti ordered this hit to silence Circella, but there were a number of other possible motives and suspects. The attractive woman had many men in her life. She was the girlfriend of several hoods and was a "party girl," meaning a sexually available girl who enjoyed adoration and expensive gifts. Robbery could have also been the motive. The attacker ran out her back door carrying two expensive full-length fur coats, but a witness in another apartment saw only his back.

The evidence in the case was ambiguous, not affording a straight line to any motive. She knew her attacker. She was on the telephone when the doorbell rang, and she told her cousin, "Call me back in an hour." She was preparing two cups of cocoa in the kitchen when her visitor attacked her. The viciousness of the crime indicated a passionate hatred. The killer beat her with a blackjack, breaking her nose, smashing her lips, and leaving severe bruises on her face. He then slashed her face with a knife six times, including slashing her throat and left eye before setting her prostate body on fire. He left his 10-inch blackjack on the kitchen floor, along with her blood-spattered rolling pin and blood-stained bread knife. This did not seem to be the well-planned murder of a hit man. It could have been a robbery, but $2,500 in jewelry in her bedroom was not taken along with the two furs. No one was ever charged.

Near the time former girlfriend Carey was killed, Circella's wife was warned by some of Nitti's associates that her husband better stop cooperating with the gang's Prosecutors. His wife begged him to stop assisting, which he immediately did. Even with these actions against the wife, the overall pattern does not make Nitti the probable culprit behind former girlfriend Carey's murder. It was gruesome even by Nitti's standards, especially since she would have been an innocent pawn and not a traitor to the gang. Nitti would have made the same frightening impression on the State's Witnesses by having her more humanely shot in the head. Besides, Nitti's associates never bothered the wives of either Browne or Bioff, who both went on to testify against the gang. Then after completing his 8-year sentence, Circella walked the streets of Chicago unbothered by the gang.

Even without Circella's help, the Prosecutors indicted eight gangsters for extorting $2.5 million from the Hollywood movie-studio and theater-operators industry. Included were Rosselli of Los Angeles and six Chicago gang members. In addition to extorting bribes from the industry, they were charged with stealing from the union membership by pocketing their dues and assessing 2% of their salaries.

Five hours after these indictments were made public, Nitti took a walk beside the tracks of the Illinois Central Railroad. Less than a mile from his grand North Riverside home, a slow-moving freight train crept up slowly behind him. A conductor and two switchmen were looking forward from the caboose's protruding side windows, and watched him stagger along, turn toward the fence, sit down against it, and fire two bullets that passed through the brim of his brown-felt hat. They told police he next "put the gun to his head and pulled the trigger. There was a shot and an audible dying gasp, as the man fell" on his back, with his head against a fence post. This fatal shot entered his right temple, and the .32-caliber revolver remained in his right hand.[483]

Nitti's hat contained five bullet holes, including one at the top that had a bullet stuck in it along with a lock of hair. A total of six bullet holes were in his hat and head, but his revolver contained only three spent casings, so he had to have reloaded before the trainmen saw him fire three times. The simplest interpretation of this evidence is that he started with a loaded gun, and before they encountered him, he had fired these six bullets and reloaded, making a total of nine shots. Thus, it is likely he missed both his head and hat three times. This could have been caused by the bad aim of a drunk with a high blood-alcohol level of .23. It more likely resulted from the hesitancy of a man who wanted to live but felt he had run out of alternatives.

The Chicago gang's leadership never dealt with any outsider unless a member vouched for him, and the gang held that member accountable for the person's dealings with the gang. Because Nitti had vouched for Bioff's trustworthiness, his co-indictees warned him that he had to prevent Browne and Bioff from testifying before the Federal Grand Jury. However, Nitti could not get to them because they were protected in isolation at a Federal Prison. Nitti's failure to do this meant he soon faced a vicious beating death at the hands of his associates, and a single self-inflicted gunshot in a drunken stupor must have seemed preferable.

Nitti's widow's brother testified at the Coroner's Inquest that for months before his suicide Nitti appeared to be "nervous and ill tempered" and acting strangely. This was probably related to the lethal threat he faced, but Nitti had also been in poor health in recent years. He had been hospitalized for chronic stomach ulcers and for old injuries to his spine suffered when Detective Lang shot him in the back. It is ironic that the 58-year-old gang leader took his own life 10 years after calling out to God to let him survive the Detective's bullet wounds as he lay in the emergency room. Catholic funeral rites were denied Nitti because of his suicide, so his kin buried him in an unhallowed plot in a private ceremony. The IRS scooped up Nitti's assets to settle outstanding income tax claims on his share of the Hollywood extortion cash, leaving his wife and adopted son destitute.

THE IATSE RACKETEERING TRIAL & PARDONS

Imprisoned former IATSE leaders George Browne and Willie Bioff were the star prosecution witnesses at the Hollywood movie extortion trial of the remaining five Chicago gangsters, and Los-Angeles-based Johnny Rosselli. The two former IATSE leaders testified that the defendants had directed their illegal union activities. Bioff testified that the Hollywood film industry was so financially strapped and vulnerable to ruin from long strikes during the Depression that he had planned to use repeated strike threats to shake down 20% to 50% interest in the movie companies within five years.

The Prosecutor did not charge the movie officials with bribery, because he needed their state's-witness testimony to corroborate Browne and Bioff, and to let the jury see the fear on the victims' faces as they testified to convict the gangsters. The movie producers and studio officials testified that they were the victims of extortion. It was true that they had initially paid the IATSE leaders out of fear of strikes and physical harm, but all testified without any reprisal in the three Chicago-gang extortion trials. The three trials were of Union leaders Browne and Bioff, their gang boss Nick Circella, and the Chicago gang leaders. The gangsters' defense correctly argued the IATSE dealings became mutually-negotiated bribery settlements that cut the studios' wage expenses by many times the amount of the payoffs. Not only did the industry benefit handsomely, but the movie producers brazenly supported the IATSE leaders before the NLRB against complaints by aggrieved union members. The real victims in this case were the IATSE workers because the movie officials became co-conspirators in league with the gangsters. When the Judge announced the jury's guilty verdict, he castigated the gangsters for betraying their union members and, without waiting for sentencing recommendations, gave each one the maximum 10-years.

The great benefit the film studios received during Browne's IATSE leadership became apparent following his extortion conviction. The AFL and the unions he controlled slowly expelled him from membership, and a new IATSE president was elected. He diligently fought for the interests of his members in negotiating a five-year contract between his Hollywood Locals and the studios. He ended the Unions' illegal extortions and bribe-taking, but long, violent, and costly union-jurisdictional strikes against other established studio unions, such as the film-set carpenters, continued off and on for the next five years. The workers were paid much better when they were not out on strike, but the industry had been far healthier financially when it paid off the corrupt leadership of Browne and Bioff to ensure small wage increases and labor peace and stability.

As for the Chicago Movie Picture Operators Union Local, the gang maintained total dominance for decades under each successive leader. All used the same violent and exploitive practices, including murder, sale of Union memberships, sweetheart contracts with theaters and concessionaires, and stink bombs in theaters. Federal officials in 1942 described it as "the most corrupt of all the corrupt unions in America," and in 1960 they said, "It carries on its rolls more big-name hoodlums than any three other racket-run unions in the country." More than 40 members of the Local were brothers, sons, nephews, or cousins of gang leaders, and they voted as a block for the reelection of the corrupt Union leadership.[484]

After Nitti's suicide, Hollywood-extortion co-defendant Paul "The Waiter" Ricca was made the gang's leader. Ricca knew he and the other defendants would likely lose their pending conviction appeals, so before entering prison, he directed his lieutenant, Tony Accardo, to begin implementing a complex plan to gain the gangsters' freedom through early parole. The convoluted workings of Ricca's scheme were later exposed by an exhaustive nine-month Congressional investigation.

Step one was to transfer the convicts to a prison closer to Chicago. For this the gang turned to St. Louis, Missouri attorney Paul Dillon, who defended gangsters and was active in the city's Democratic politics. The 70-year-old attorney was well known to the Chicago gang because he had represented Movie Operators' Union head John "Big" Nick, and he was also a vice president in the Browne and Bioff IATSE Union. In defending Nick, Dillon had gotten a receiving-bribery case dismissed by a Circuit Court Judge, and he had arranged a parole from a federal extortion conviction, exactly what the Chicago gang leaders were looking for now.

In addition, Dillon had been a key political supporter of President Harry Truman in his home state. Truman's base was in Kansas City, and Dillon became his St. Louis campaign manager when Truman first ran for the U.S. Senate 13 years earlier. After Truman succeeded FDR as President, Dillon was a frequent White House visitor. Dillon was also friendly with the Federal Parole Board Chairman who quickly transferred the gangster prisoners to Leavenworth, Kansas to be nearer to their Chicago families, without specifying whether he was referring to their *blood* or *crime* families. The Chairman took this action despite a strong written complaint by the Atlanta Prison Warden to his Federal Bureau of Prisons bosses stating, "From information received, it is quite evident that money is being paid to obtain the transfer of these men to Leavenworth."[485]

Step two was to get the remaining extortion charges dismissed because their existence prohibited paroles. For this the gang hired Dallas lawyer Maury Hughes, who represented gangsters, was a Texas supporter of Truman, and was a close friend of fellow Texan Tom Clark, whom Truman had appointed U.S. Attorney General. Attorney Hughes had AG Clark make all the charges simply vanish, except for mail fraud that resulted from sending the stolen Hollywood union funds to Chicago. Clark's Assistant next asked a judge for dismissal of the mail charges by lying that the IATSE Union leaders were solely to blame for the crimes. He also violated accepted procedure by approaching a different judge than the one who did the harsh sentencing and knew the case, and by acting without the defense counsel making the request or being present.

Step three was needed because criminals typically go through cash fast, and the convicts had to raise money to pay off their outstanding IRS tax liens for their bribe income that also prohibited paroles. Even though the Cook County Sheriff had long prohibited slot machines, they were suddenly installed in the country-town taverns under his jurisdiction for two and a half months. Tavern owners told reporters, "We got the machines whether we wanted them or not."[486]

In a related action two months earlier, the Chicago gang had murdered James Ragen, owner of the Continental Press nationwide horserace information wire service, causing it to cease operation and ending its competition with the gang's recently-created Trans-American Publishing & News Service. The murder motive was clearly greed, and the Congressional Investigating Committee recognized Ragen's profits might have been needed to help pay the gangsters' pending IRS settlements, major lawyer fees, and huge cash bribes to President Truman's officials and their political bagmen friends.

Step four was to settle the prisoners' outstanding IRS tax liens, and the gang hired politically-influential Chicago lawyer Eugene Bernstein. He and the IRS remained silent on why the gangsters' tax claims first had the added penalties waived and then were settled for less than 20 cents on the dollar. Four years later the IRS made these gangsters pay another $44,000 in gift taxes, because attorney Bernstein paid their liens with fat bundles of cash, and because the gangsters refused to identify the source of their $190,000 settlement payments.

Step five was to throw elections in some Chicago wards to satisfy the Truman Democratic administration that wanted the Democrats to keep control of the House of Representatives. In that general election the Chicago Republican candidates were highly successful, except for the five wards won by Democratic candidates. Political observers were struck by the sudden switch in voter sentiment to Democratic candidates, and the mysterious failure of Republican leaders to campaign in those wards. Rumors circulated in these Italian neighborhoods that they delivered their votes "so the boys can get out on parole." As a *Chicago Tribune* Editorial said, "The Capone gang is known to control the Republican Committeemen in a number of Chicago wards, but these are the wards that piled up some of the biggest Democratic majorities." Truman's aids were said to be greatly gratified by the gangsters' results, but it was not enough to keep the Democrats from losing control of the House of Representatives.[487]

Step six was to file parole applications to free the gangsters at the earliest date, which was after serving one-third of their 10-year terms. Both the Prosecutor and the Judge in the case sent letters to the Federal Parole Board and to U.S. A.G. Clark strongly opposing their release. The Prosecutor stated, "The convicted defendants are notorious as the successors to the underworld power of Al Capone. They are vicious criminals who would stop at nothing to achieve their ends. The investigation and prosecutions were attended by murder, gunplay, threatening of witnesses, etc." He specifically recommended, "That the mail fraud indictment be kept open" to prevent the paroles. The Judge said the theft from the workers they were supposed to represent deserved "severe punishment," which is why he gave them the longest sentence possible under the law. At the sentencing, he pointed out that the pending mail charges meant they would serve the total time imposed, and his letter reinforced this by concluding, "I feel very strongly that the full sentences should be inflicted." Despite these admonitions by the Prosecutor and Judge, A.G. Clark had the pending mail-fraud charges dismissed.[488]

But with every essential element now in place, St. Louis Attorney Dillon met secretly with the two Parole Board members recently appointed by U.S. Attorney General Clark. They improperly approved the gangsters' releases without public notice, a written record, or the knowledge of the third member. Dillon then had Parole Board Chairman T. Webbe Wilson order parole officials at Leavenworth Prison and the Chicago office to expedite the paroles, so the prisoners could be freed in five days, waiving all procedures to achieve this "unholy speed." These two board members then assured the third that "the Capone gang was a fairy tale" and this case was about union leaders accepting bribes and not gangster extortion. The third member later testified no one had studied these convicts' cases. The three members unbelievably later claimed to have no awareness they were dealing with the nation's most notorious criminals, even though every American school boy knew their names. The three vicious Chicago gang leaders and Rosselli were released seven days after Dillon's secret meeting with the Parole Board Chairman, even though in that era the Board only released the least violent, and the least likely to re-offend, federal inmates.

The *Chicago Daily Tribune,* which single-handedly set off the IRS probe of Al Capone, immediately launched an investigation into these paroles of his successor gang leaders. The *Tribune's* revelations set off a storm of protest that led the U.S. House Committee On Expenditures to begin hearings to prove its contention that huge bribes had been paid to top administration officials. The Committee publicly berated and embarrassed the Attorney General and the Parole Board members for their many lies about their activities, and for placing the public at extreme risk from widespread domestic criminal terrorism. The Committee hammered these officials with proof the paroles were fraudulent because of four actions by the convicts - they failed to list all their arrests, they violated parole by having Accardo pose as an attorney to visit prisoners Ricca and Campagna, they refused to reveal the source of their IRS payments, and they associated with other convicts while on parole. This did not induce the Board to revoke the paroles until the exasperated Committee threatened to slash the agency's budget. Each gangster immediately appealed his parole rescission, even though convicts have negligible Constitutional rights and the Parole Board has broad enforcement discretion. Despite this awesome edge, the Prosecutors lost every parolees' appeal in U.S. A.G. Clark's final sellout to these vicious terrorists who spent almost no additional time in prison.

Despite these despicable actions by the administration's top officials, their political bagmen, and the gangsters, only Parole Board Chairman Wilson suffered punishment. He soon resigned, presumably a wealthy man. The corruption may have begun with these officials, but President Truman directed the cover-up of these gangster's premature prison release. All agencies under A.G. Clark and the IRS were ordered to remain silent by claiming Executive Privilege. This concept is invoked only by dishonest and corrupt administrations to cover up criminal acts, but it is not mentioned in the Constitution. And it is in total contradiction with the critical Constitutional mandate to Congress to protect the American people from an unscrupulous Executive Branch through checks and balances.

The Committee's final report about Democrat Truman's paroles was approved unanimously and without objection by any Democrat Representative. The report expressed conviction that attorneys Dillon and Hughes paid big bribes to the top government officials who acquiesced to the gangsters' wishes, but it found no evidence. Even though the Committee stated that A.G. Clark knew more than he was willing to divulge, the Senate rewarded him a year later by approving his lifetime appointment to the U.S. Supreme Court. The Democratic *New York Times* disgustingly called Clark "a personal and political friend [of Truman's] with no judicial experience and few demonstrated qualifications."

During the hearings, the U.S. House Committee requested the FBI's Hoover to investigate because "There are nasty rumors in Chicago that somebody got a lot of money to let these desperate gangsters out of prison." When Hoover's files were opened later under the Freedom of Information Act, they revealed the FBI was unable to find evidence anyone accepted a bribe until 17 years later through a microphone planted by agents in the gang's private meeting room in Celano's Tailor Shop. Agents overheard gang leader Murray Humphreys tell an associate how he had arranged bribe payments to former U.S. A.G. Clark and the Parole Board Chairman through attorneys Hughes and Dillon. The information was not legally admissible because no court had authorized the microphone, and the statute of limitations had long ago run out on the crime. As Humphreys was telling his tale, Clark, who had so callously sold out the justice system and the American people to the country's most dangerous domestic criminal terrorists, was celebrating his 15th year on the U.S. Supreme Court.[489]

BIOFF & RICCA AFTER PRISON

Not only did President Truman's Attorney General and Parole Board let the country's most dangerous gangsters go free, but these officials also carried out a vendetta for these criminals by refusing clemency for the Prosecutor's three state's witnesses who convicted them. Nick Circella had greatly assisted the Prosecutor before becoming afraid to testify, but the Parole Board made him serve his whole six years, twice the time they gave his gang leaders. Then the INS deported him as an illegal alien to Argentina. Because U.S. A.G. Clark's actions of punishing the informants were such an affront to the justice system, successor Francis Biddle requested the Judge intervene, and he quickly commuted the long sentences of George Browne and Willie Bioff to the three years they had served.

Both State's witnesses moved out of Chicago, legally changed their names, and created false background stories to tell every one in their new lives. Bioff lived quietly as William Nelson in a fashionable residential area in Phoenix, where he described himself as a retired businessman who dabbled in stocks and bonds. As Nelson, he befriended conservative Republican Arizona U.S. Senator Barry Goldwater, and became his "expert consultant on labor racketeering issues." The Goldwater family would later develop close ties with other Las Vegas and Arizona hoods.

One day Bioff said goodbye to his wife at the doorstep of their home, got into his truck to go fishing, and waved as he stepped on the gas peddle. A powerful dynamite explosion shredded the truck and Bioff's body. He was 54 years old. Everyone assumed Bioff was murdered in retaliation for testifying against the Chicago gang leaders. The chief suspect was the charismatic and well-liked Johnny Rosselli. This was because of his lethal aura, and because he was the lowest-ranking gang extortion co-defendant. However, the LAPD quickly eliminated him as a suspect by verifying he was in Los Angeles at the time of the Phoenix blast. Besides, Rosselli was not the type to hire someone else. He earned his deadly image by doing his own killings up close and personal. Finally, Rosselli was never resentful about his prison sentence. He told close friends that he loved his stretch in prison because he had no responsibilities, and he had so much time to read histories of major political figures, which he really enjoyed.

In addition, Rosselli and the Chicago gang leaders likely had learned Bioff's new name and location long before he was murdered. Not only had he become a high-profile figure in Phoenix, but he commuted to work every week on the Las Vegas Strip, where he was very visible as the *Riviera Hotel-Casino* Entertainment Director from the time of its opening more than six months before his murder. He dealt with entertainers from all over the country. He also often walked through the casino between the lounge, showroom, and his office, which meant that many hotel guests and casino players saw him.

The Las Vegas interests of the Chicago gang were represented by transplanted-resident Marshall Caifano, and by regular visitor Rosselli from Los Angeles. Both men made the rounds of the hotels nightly, and they hung out in the casinos and lounges. The four hotels Rosselli stopped at every night to talk to acquaintances were the *Riviera, Tropicana, Desert Inn,* and *Thunderbird.* It is all but certain that someone associated with the Chicago gang recognized Nelson was Bioff in Las Vegas or Phoenix well before that fateful morning. Bioff was not murdered until 11 years after being released from prison, but two days before he was bombed, he did seem to be afraid of someone when he placed his house up for sale. He had been involved in recent business deals, and his whole career had been involved in illegal larcenous activities.

Bioff's cohort and fellow state's witness Browne was never disturbed by the gang, but he had done a better job of maintaining his anonymity. He was known to have lived out his life in the Midwest, likely in Illinois for much of it.[490]

Because of the scandal over the release of these major criminals, Rosselli went back to prison for longer than any of the Chicago gangsters, serving five months of his remaining six years and eight months. Upon his release both times, he was employed by movie production companies that gave him ambiguous titles defining no specific role. He immediately regained his former Beverly Hills socialite status. His strong influence with the film industry was illustrated by the actions of producer Joseph Pasternak. He took a day out of his busy schedule to escort a 14-year-old girl around the Metro-Goldwyn-Meyer (MGM) studio facilities and introduce her to all the major stars who were filming. She was the daughter of rising Chicago gang leader Sam Giancana. He became the gang's operational leader because senior boss Tony Accardo preferred to stay in the background as the policy decider. Giancana would later become an unlicensed hidden interest in the building of the large *Stardust* casino-resort. The movie *Casino* (1995) relates to the operation of the *Stardust* two decades later by the successor of Giancana.

The parole of gang leader Ricca prohibited him from associating with anyone suspected of being part of the Chicago gang for the next seven years, so upon his release, he turned leadership over to Tony Accardo for having so effectively ramrodded his complicated release. Ricca remained very close to Accardo, and Chicago newspaper reporters at times questioned whether he had taken back leadership.

Ricca's Hollywood extortion conviction made him a target by the INS to revoke his citizenship and deport him back to his native Italy. The INS investigation went nowhere for three years until an anonymous phone caller revealed Ricca was in the country under a false identity. The caller supplied his real name and criminal record in Italy. Ricca was born Felice De Lucia on July 10, 1898. He grew up in a suburb of Naples surrounded by a blood-drenched vendetta that killed 14 members of his family and the other family. At age 17 he was convicted of one of these killings and served the three-year sentence. Upon his release he killed the man who was the witness against him at trial, and he fled to France. Italy tried him in absentia, and he was sentenced to 21 years in prison. Using an alias to avoid capture, he fled to Chicago and became a waiter in the Bella Napoli Café. The nickname "The Waiter" stuck with him. He worked his way into the gang, and Al Capone was best man at his wedding.

Ten years after the anonymous phone tip, the INS went to court to denaturalize Ricca for lying on his citizenship application by using a false name and failing to list his two murder convictions in Italy. The Judge invalidated his citizenship for fraud, and Ricca immediately began a succession of court challenges to avoid deportation to Italy where prison awaited him. Ricca's gang income was not enough to fund his enormous attorney fees to gain parole and then keep it from being rescinded, and to also fight denaturalization. Ricca turned to William Johnston, who had contributed large amounts to Florida Governor Warren in the gang's pressured takeover of the S&G bookmaking syndicate in Miami. Johnston collected a fund from the Florida dog-track owners he headed, and arranged strange loans from Chicago's Sportsman's Park Racetrack, an insurance company, and a bank that were almost certainly Ricca's profits from his hidden Racetrack interest. Ricca also had Jimmy Hoffa, a year before he became International Teamsters Union President, direct his two Detroit Teamsters Locals to buy Ricca's palatial four-acre Long Beach, Indiana summer estate for twice its appraised value. Later, while Bobby Kennedy was counsel to Senator McClellan's Rackets Committee, he showed how rotten this home purchase was for these two Union Locals. Still short of cash, Ricca opted to pay his attorneys instead of the IRS, which led to a tax evasion conviction. In an amazing irony, his effort to avoid serving the 39 months left of his Hollywood extortion sentence, assuming time off for good behavior, caused him to serve 27 months of a three-year IRS sentence.

As Ricca was to be released from prison for the IRS conviction, the INS ordered him deported, but Ricca did not want to return to Italy and the long murder sentence that awaited him there. The INS let Ricca submit applications for haven in 47 nations. Ricca filled them out truthfully, listing his entire criminal record including his murder convictions. He also attached copies of newspaper articles he kept in a scrapbook that described what a loathsome creature he was, and they depicted his Chicago-gang associates as even more disgusting parasites. It should come as no surprise that the entire world turned its back on him, even his native Italy. The INS District Director naively concluded, "Anyone who would write 47 letters is sincere in his efforts to satisfy the government," but Ricca's intent was to reinforce these countries' resolve to resist U.S. diplomatic pressure to accept him. An outraged U.S. Attorney General Bobby Kennedy demanded the State Department stop issuing visas for Italian emigrants until that country accept Ricca back, and Italy capitulated. However, Ricca continued to delay his deportation with successive creative appeals that took about one-and-a-half years each before the U.S. Supreme Court found it without merit to be heard.[491]

Two years after Ricca sent the letters to foreign countries, FBI agents curbed a car in which he was riding with Accardo and another gang leader. The agents arrested Ricca for lying under oath at INS hearings that his income was solely from horserace winnings. At his trial racetrack police testified he was never at the track, and Ricca's testimony was not credible. Ricca claimed he won $80,000 at the $10 windows of Chicago-area racetracks because "every horse I bet that year came in first and never placed second or showed third." The Jury unbelievably bought it and acquitted him.

The dispute over Ricca's citizenship between the U.S. and Italian governments went on for 28 years, until the INS gave up the deportation fight on his 74th birthday. At that time the head of the Chicago Police Department's Organized Crime Unit lamented, "The boys still go to him or Accardo on the overall decisions of how the Outfit operates." A year later Ricca, who remained a stateless person, died from heart disease in the hospital. At his funeral the priest said, "Paul De Lucia received the last rites of the church upon his death. What greater consolation can there be for a family than to know that their loved one died in the grace of God." No one asked his murdered victims' families if this priest's absolution of the killer gave them any solace.[492]

This history of early organized crime concludes with the life and career of the remaining Young Turk, Ben Siegel. He had the great vision for a Las Vegas Strip of gambling resorts. Thus the final chapter closes with the day he realized the tiny isolated Southwestern desert town had enormous untapped business potential.

CHAPTER 16

GO WEST YOUNG MAN

SIEGEL FOLLOWED THE STARS TO HOLLYWOOD

Just six days after newly-inaugurated Mayor Fiorello LaGuardia confiscated and smashed Frank Costello's slot machines, Ben Siegel checked out of his residence at the Waldorf-Astoria and moved his family to Los Angeles and stayed at his sister's home. Siegel later testified he moved because his two daughters were ill, but Jimmy Blue Eyes told me, "I suspect that Ben was concerned that his flamboyant, colorful lifestyle would lead LaGuardia to name him Public Enemy Number 1 and get him convicted." Siegel's relocation soon led Charlie Luciano's former partners and close friends to move their illegal enterprises out of New York City. Costello moved his slots to New Orleans, where he also opened a casino, and his bookmaking partner Frank Erickson moved his operation to New Jersey. At about the same time, Jimmy Blue Eyes and Meyer Lansky opened their casinos in Hallandale near Miami, and then Joe Adonis moved his casinos across the Hudson River to New Jersey.

Siegel moved two years before Special Prosecutor Tom Dewey began his frame of Luciano. Had Luciano joined any one of his friends in their migration, he would have avoided the dreadful persecution by Dewey, but he adored living in the Big Apple too much to leave until Prosecutor Dewey had targeted him for the framing. While DA Dewey and Mayor LaGuardia ruined the lives of the Young Turks supposedly over their illegal gambling operations, it was really because of their support of political opponents. In contrast, these two self-proclaimed law-and-order crime-busters practically ignored the criminal activities of New York City's five exploitive and violent Mafia gangs that plundered and hurt the legitimate citizens, because these gangsters did not challenge these leaders politically with contributions to their opponents or large neighborhood voting blocks.

A year after Siegel moved, he purchased a palatial residence in Holmby Hills, immediately west of Beverly Hills. Years later an FBI internal report concluded, "It is believed that with the exception of a few trips to New York City, Siegel maintained his permanent residence on the west coast."[493]

When Siegel made his move, he realized the great opportunity for illegal gambling in the Southwest because it had no large criminal organizations claiming exclusive territories. Besides Prohibition, the only crime Siegel considered participating in was gambling because it was the crime of choice for young Jewish men. This is because U.S. neighborhoods with large Jewish populations always featured two things - excellent social services, such as hospitals and social welfare, and wide-open gambling. In the Jewish religion, gambling and drinking in moderation are not sins, so wagering and Prohibition were the only profitable criminal enterprises that did not cause embarrassment for the participant's family nor invoke their condemnation.

Authors of early organized crime always describe Los Angeles gangsters Jack Dragna and Mickey Cohen as Siegel's lieutenants, but these writers fail to explain how these three men came together and never address the dissimilarities in their backgrounds. They came from different states, belonged to different gangs, and had separate business interests. They came together because Siegel sold his vision of expanding gambling to the gang bosses of Dragna and Cohen, and he invited them to participate with him in developing gambling businesses in the Southwest.

Siegel came from New York City, where he had been Luciano's Prohibition partner. Dragna's small gang was long entrenched in Los Angeles, and a few year's before Siegel arrived in Hollywood Dragna subordinated his gang to Chicago under Capone's reign. Cohen grew up in Los Angeles, and he became a boxer for Moe Dalitz's partnership in Cleveland before returning to Los Angeles to represent their interests. From early in Prohibition, Luciano, Siegel, and the other Young Turks had maintained strong ties with both Cleveland's Dalitz and the Chicago gang's successive leaders.

Siegel proposed to the heads of these three gangs that they cooperate to create the greatest expansion of illegal gambling. He envisioned the three gangs operating completely independently in Southern California. To avoid interference with each other's operations, Siegel offered to mediate between Dragna and Cohen to ensure that the interests of the three out-of-state leaderships never came into conflict. This made Siegel the arbitrator and peacekeeper for the three gangs' leaders and the dominant underworld personality in the Southwest. He was kind of like the Boss of Bosses of that section of the country. But while Dragna and Cohen were certainly ready to order their soldiers to do Siegel's bidding to protect his interests, their criminal activities were completely independent from him.

MICKEY COHEN REPRESENTED CLEVELAND

Meyer "Mickey" Cohen grew up in Los Angeles with his Russian-Jewish immigrant parents. He was a diminutive 5-foot-3, with built-up shoes raising him to 5-foot-5. In his autobiography *Mickey Cohen: In My Own Words* he explained the attitude he had about work from the time he was a teenager. "Of course, if there was any way to steal the money, I'd steal it, too." Cohen's published words demonstrate that he was not particularly intelligent, nor was he knowledgeable about the larger society around him. He bastardized the language throughout his oral-history tapes made for his book's writer. "I can't look things up in a dictionary because I don't know how the ABC's go in continuity." "I was an uneducated person and had a fear of opening my mouth that I would sound stupid because my vocabulary was very, very poor. Don't forget, I was just a plain vulgar heist man. I hadn't been around with a lot of good decent people, only a lot of plug-uglies."[494]

As a teenager Cohen was aggressive and quick-tempered, bullying himself to the top of a gang in Los Angeles. At the same time, the short, tough street fighter also tried making it as a featherweight boxer. This career took him to Cleveland, where he got to know Dalitz, and then to New York City, where he got to know some of the major hoods because they loved boxing. After he suffered a bad beating in the ring, he became a stickup man who robbed stores, and then he went to work for Capone's gang in Chicago. Cohen was arrested many times in Cleveland, Chicago, and Los Angeles, but he had few convictions. The principal charge was for embezzlement in Chicago. He then went to work for Dalitz's gang in Cleveland. Cohen wrote that the gang told him to return to Los Angeles and work with Siegel "to have somebody stand in for their end of the action."

Cohen wrote that Siegel gave him a whole new perspective on life, at least as much as he was capable of absorbing. "I didn't realize much of any other way of life than hustling until my last trip out to Los Angeles with Benny Siegel, when I was given the takeover with Benny, and I became involved in a higher element of people. Then I started to realize how crude and rough I was. My way of life was so bad." Siegel took him to elegant dinner parties with socialites and celebrities, where Cohen kept his mouth shut to hide that "I was stupid." Ben made him file his first income tax return, and Cohen had to have Ben show him how to fill it out. Cohen never got why he should "cut the government in" by paying taxes. After all, the government never helped him heist the money.

Mickey Cohen's primary business was a dozen bookmaking parlors, and he liked to bet on his own horse selections with other bookies. Miami Bookmaker John O'Rourke testified to the Kefauver Committee that in 1940 Cohen called him asking to accept his personal bets on races run at tracks outside of California. Cohen bet by long-distance telephone from Los Angeles to Florida as many as eight races a day. At the end of five months, O'Rourke settled their account. He paid Cohen total winnings of $60,000 ($920,000 today), conceded he was too good, and refused any further action.

JACK DRAGNA REPRESENTED CHICAGO

Gang leader Jack Dragna was also under Siegel's mediating authority. Dragna was born in 1891, and he immigrated to Southern California around 1908 at about age 17. He was convicted of extortion in 1915 and spent three years in San Quentin. Little more is known about his street-gang activities. During Prohibition he was a small-time smuggler on the West Coast, and shortly after it ended he was convicted for failing to pay the federal excise tax on alcohol produced at a distillery. Next he went into the legitimate importing of olive oil, and he was a partner in importing bananas from Central America on old, surplus military freighters. Then he got into bookmaking and occasionally ran small casino-game operations.

Even though Dragna's gang never totaled more than a dozen members, it still made him the top Mafioso on the West Coast. The underworld referred to them as "The Mickey Mouse Mafia." This name did not refer to their location near Hollywood, but rather signified their ineptness and lack of character. Every member sometime during his career informed to the FBI on the other members' activities.

Dragna wanted traditional Sicilian Mustache Pete isolation from the rest of the world and also complete control of his world, so he did not branch out with other gangs and did not work well with partners. Thus, he developed very limited criminal interests in the rapidly growing Southern California area. A Dragna gang member complained about this in his autobiography *The Last Mafioso: The Treacherous World of Jimmy Fratianno.* "Los Angeles was a rich city and they had starved in it. Las Vegas was just across the street and they had starved. The Los Angeles family never had a boss that knew how to maneuver, how to make real money. All Jack Dragna had ever cared about was to make enough money to keep himself in booze and broads."

Similar comments were made by bookmaker Jack Richards, who was close to Siegel and was his bookie. Richards told me, "Jack Dragna was nothing. Always small time. He was reputed to have some big money, but I never heard tell of him making any anywhere." Mark Swain, who operated Ben Siegel's Lake Mead yacht as a teenager and then became the primary enforcer for Dalitz, told me, "In the rackets, Dragna's gang was small time. They were bunglers. They were the Abbott and Costello of organized crime."[495]

In one area, Dragna and his gang stood out – they were quick to murder those in their way. During Dragna's angry, threat-filled confrontations with others, he liked to use the term *sudden death*. This was decades before the term was adopted by the National Football League for overtime games. Despite Dragna's criminality and violence, the Los Angeles County Sheriff's Department issued him a concealed-weapon permit.

An internal memo by the FBI's Los Angeles Office said, "Ignacio Dragna, alias Jack Dragna, is an uncouth individual, 56 years of age, 5' 5", dark, swarthy and speaks with a heavy accent." Mark Swain's assessment was more blunt, "The Dragna brothers [Jack and Tom] were two crude assholes. They were pigs in a trough." Since Swain was a very refined man who fit easily into all levels of society and always spoke politely, this nasty description indicated just how disgusting he found this pair of brothers.[496]

BEN SIEGEL'S EARLY LIFE & ARREST RECORD

Ben Siegel's murder made banner headlines across the country, and then a succession of fake *biographers* wrote fanciful fictions focusing on his nickname *Bugsy* to make him wacky beyond belief to stimulate sales. These sensationalized fantasies became an enduring myth about his life, even though not one of these authors researched documents or conducted interviews with a single person who knew anything about Siegel's criminal activities. These fabrications were the basis for movies like *Bugsy* (1991) and HBO's *Lansky* (1999) in which not one scene had any relationship to the reality of his life.

Siegel's life and career were extraordinarily different from this nutty myth. Few facts are available about his youth because he never spoke to even his closest associates about his background, personal life, criminal activities, or legitimate businesses. He was silent about himself, despite being a gregarious and fun-loving guy, who would readily discuss any other subject of common interest.

When Siegel was 40, a dozen years after the repeal of Prohibition, the FBI finally assembled an internal background summary about him. It was based solely on informants reporting hearsay and rumors that were told decades after the alleged incidents occurred, making its authenticity dubious. Its descriptions of his earlier criminal activities is contradicted by other documents, knowledgeable individuals, and even the FBI files about other mobsters. This flawed document is the only available attempt to research his early years. It states Benjamin Siegel was born on February 28, 1906 and lived with his parents in Brooklyn. It also says, "He claims to have an eighth-grade education." The report concludes that as an adult, "He stood 5' 9" tall, weighed 157 pounds, and was a dapper dresser."[497]

These fraudulent biographers' descriptions of Siegel's criminal activities are woefully lacking. Some name the crimes he supposedly committed simply by rattling off various categories of felonies. Others list specific crimes, but they fail to offer dates, police jurisdictions, specifics, names of victims, or identification of their sources. These authors create unsubstantiated accusations to sensationalize Siegel as a dangerous gangster, but their descriptions do not jibe with his benign New York City police record that none of these authors apparently bothered to examine.

Besides, Siegel was 13 when Prohibition began, so as to all the crimes and gang leaderships these writers attribute to him before then, he would have had to have committed them while he was a child in grammar school. These self-proclaimed biographers so fictionalized his life that they did not even bother to compare his birth date with the date Prohibition began to realize all their utterances were the rankest nonsense. They created and then perpetuated a fairy-tale, toughest-hombre-to-ever-come-down-the-pike, but in doing this they made Siegel into a baby bandito, or maybe more accurately an "enfant terrible."

In reality, Siegel's first three arrests did not occur until he was a leader of Prohibition's most successful liquor importing group, and all three arrests were for misdemeanors that involved no violence or victims. The first was a minor liquor violation of the Public Health Act that was dismissed. His only conviction occurred during a Miami Beach vacation. He was a player in a gambling den with "a huge roll of bills," when the police raided, and he paid a $100 fine. Finally, Siegel and Lansky were rousted in a hotel suite for meeting with other underworld figures, but courts quickly quashed this type of NYPD-harassment arrest as violating constitutional rights.[498]

Author Dean Jennings in *We Only Kill Each Other: The Life and Bad Times of Bugsy Siegel* wrote that Siegel beat a charge of carrying a concealed weapon in Philadelphia, Pennsylvania in the middle of Prohibition, but he offered no details about the incident, not even why it was dropped. The FBI never found any charge against Siegel in Philadelphia, but agents did discover that Siegel was issued a concealed-weapon permit by the Elizabeth, New Jersey, Chief of Police, making it legal for him to pack a gun to defend himself in a neighboring state he was known to visit.[499]

Author Jennings also claimed Siegel was arrested for rape, but he offered scant information in his single sentence description of the alleged case. He said, "Siegel was first arrested at the age of 20 in Brooklyn when one of the neighborhood girls whose name never made the police records charged him with rape, but the girl was persuaded to drop the charges before the case came to court."

Author Jennings' claim is not credible. The FBI completed its background investigation of Siegel two decades before Jennings' book was published, and nothing about rape or any other type of sexual crime was listed in his arrest summary by the NYPD in whose jurisdiction Siegel lived his whole life until after the repeal of Prohibition. Even without the FBI's validation that no such arrest occurred, it is clearly impossible for Jennings to have been the first and only writer to discover information about this alleged arrest. In that era reporters from a half dozen major New York City newspapers inspected the NYPD arrest summaries daily; and the NYPD, like other large city police departments, had a public information officer who was quickly informed by substations about arrests of famous people. He in turn immediately notified the press to avoid accusations of special treatment or cover-ups for the powerful. The arrest of Siegel for rape would have led to banner headline treatment because newspapers of that time thrived on exposing hoodlums and also placing titillating sex crimes on the front page, making his arrest for such a crime doubly newsworthy.

It is important to understand that the police must have three elements to arrest someone for a crime against a person - a specified crime, a suspect, and the name of the victim. Basic police procedure prohibited the arrest of Siegel without the victim's name, and the alleged victim could not have withdrawn the charge as author Jennings claimed. No woman could have proven she was the unidentified woman listed in the arrest record, rather than a prostitute hired by Siegel to expunge his name. Legitimate crime writers document from the police crime report the victim's name, the dates of the crime and the arrest, the location, the type of crime, details of how the crime was committed, and the date and reason for disposition. Even though Jennings did not write a single one of these elements about the crime, and the police had no power to arrest without the victim's name, it is incredible that every author who later wrote about Siegel was too ignorant about police procedure to realize Jennings' alleged rape arrest had to have been a hoax to sensationalize his book. Not only did every organized-crime writer repeat this false allegation, but most further spiced up Jennings' fiction by describing Siegel as having committed multiple rapes, all without offering any evidence or basic police-report information about any of these asserted crimes.

Unbelievably, Jennings' one-sentence fictional description of the alleged rape by Siegel contained another major factual error that he and later writers would have discovered had they properly cross-checked their sources and dates. Jennings' blurb had Siegel allegedly committing rape in his Brooklyn childhood neighborhood even though he had moved away seven years earlier to Manhattan to join his rumrunning partners. At the time of Jennings' fictitious crime, Siegel was actually an extremely wealthy entrepreneur and a generous tipper living in the world's most expensive hotel suite. Since this was at the height of the Roaring '20s high-spirited economic-boom atmosphere, New York City's most appealing party girls, gold diggers, and call girls would have been more than receptive to pleasing the glamorous hoods most intimate and personal desires.[500]

Every woman who was quoted about knowing Ben while she was either a teenager or an adult described him as a polite gentleman, innately respectful of women, and/or sexually non-aggressive. Not one person who knew or dealt with Siegel could imagine him ever having raped. As his Prohibition partner Jimmy Blue Eyes recalled, "Ben was real bashful in his 20s. The guys used to joke, 'He couldn't get laid in a whorehouse.'"

A typical description of Siegel concerning women is the following incident that occurred in Minnesota after he had settled in Hollywood, California. Dave Berman, who would later become a Las Vegas Strip casino manager, was dating his future wife Gladys. As a favor to Siegel, he asked Gladys and her girlfriend to stay at a local hotel to look like girlfriends of "a visitor from New York." The two men hoped this subterfuge would keep police from noticing Siegel's presence in town. Berman introduced them to "Mr. Cohn," who put them in a luxurious suite on his floor. The two women said he was "suave and exceedingly polite." All he asked of the pair was to occasionally escort his visitors between the lobby and his suite, which he never left to avoid being recognized. Cohn was alone in town for two weeks, but he told both single women he was married and made no overtures to either. Gladys' daughter Susan Berman later wrote in her autobiography, "Mr. Cohn left in a great hurry at the end of the two weeks. He didn't even take time to pack and his friends all seemed concerned that he should leave immediately. But before he left, he thanked Gladys and Ruth." A few weeks later, Gladys saw Mr. Cohn's picture in a *Collier's* magazine, but the name in the caption was about the infamous Bugsy Siegel.[501]

Siegel's strong moral and chivalrous values about the treatment of women are illustrated by his reaction to a request to open a laundry to clean towels for the madams operating illegal brothels in New York City apartments. These brothels used a large quantity of towels because each prostitute would wash and then wipe off each trick's parts both before and after use, and she did the same to herself afterwards. Thus, prosecutors had introduced laundry records about major towel deliveries at trials as corroborating evidence of prostitution. Jimmy Blue Eyes explained to me, "New York City's brothel madams approached Charlie [Luciano] to supply them towels and other supplies. The madams knew we didn't keep records and never testified about anybody else's business. The supply company was totally legit, but this deal really upset Ben. He felt it immorally put us on the business side of prostitution. He objected to taking money from women for any reason."

SIEGEL'S INFAMOUS TEMPER & HIS MONIKER "BUGSY"

The cornerstone of the Siegel myth is a ferocious insane temper, but the many people who witnessed his rage all told me it was within the normal range. While they placed his temper into a normal perspective, all emphasized they hoped to never see it again, because anger is always unpleasant to be around. Several of his close associates imitated his style of temper for me, and it is likely that every one has experienced worse.

What made Siegel's temper so memorable was its startling mercurial nature – fast up and fast down. His close associates told me, "Benny had an instant and explosive temper." He blew without warning and seemed to be almost out of control, but he still said what was on his mind without humiliating his target. After venting, he cooled off just as quickly. He typically returned within a hour to pat the person on the back to acknowledge the issue was over. No one could remember him blowing up without justification. And his explosions were infrequent. Few people witnessed him go off more than once, and no one saw his temper closer than at six months intervals.

Siegel rarely lost control in public, but executives observed a few exceptions that occurred in his *Flamingo Hotel-Casino* on the Las Vegas Strip. For example, Ben once mistook a patron who was wearing a white shirt in the restaurant for a dealer on break. Ben yelled forcefully enough at the shocked man for being in the wrong place in the hotel for a dealer that the customer never returned.

Only once did Siegel get upset at someone he knew was a customer. Several executives reported the following observation to me. "Ben was sitting at a *Flamingo* lounge table talking to a newspaperwoman, but he kept watching a player at the crap table repeatedly shake his cigar ashes on the rug. Ben was neat. Finally the player dropped his butt on the floor and squashed it into the rug with his foot. This was more than Ben could stand. He charged over to the man, tapped him on the shoulder, and read him off. He had security throw the man out. Ben returned to the newspaperwoman and apologized. 'I can't believe anyone can be a pig like that.' She was not impressed enough with his outburst to bother writing about it in her article."

Lou Hershenberg was a casino pit executive at the *Flamingo* when it opened, and he told me about one of the few other times that Siegel showed temper publicly. "One night, I accompanied Ben to the *Las Vegas Club* to play craps. He bet the $200 maximum on all the numbers. The dice sevened-out, and the stickman had a cutesy song about everyone losing all their money. I thought it was funny and so did the (two) dealers and boxman, until Ben thought he was being mocked over his losses. He started to get real upset, and we wiped the smiles off our faces fast, as we saw the anger quickly build on his. As soon as our shocked, frozen expressions registered on him, his face immediately changed. He started laughing and looked quite chagrined by the fear he realized he had caused. We all responded with halfhearted smiles in relief of having just escaped his wrath."[502]

Jack Richards was a major horserace bookie and later a Reno casino owner who worked for Siegel in LA. He told me, "The worst word in his very foul vocabulary was *rat*. To this day, I squirm when I hear it. Benny only used it when he was mad at somebody, and he said the word so insidiously foul that the hair stood up on every one around him. It terrified everyone. He occasionally said 'That fucking RAT!' about somebody who had wronged him, but it was the word *rat,* not the then less prevalent and more unacceptable *fucking* that got to everybody."

When the *Flamingo* opened, Jack Walsh was General Manager, and he told me, "For Ben, cleanliness was next to Godliness. He would personally go on routine inspections of all the [hotel] rooms himself. If he found anything not up to his standards, his temper would really blow. He would get double mad and read the people responsible the riot act." GM Walsh pointed out that Ben had an opposite side that came through the rest of the time. "Ben treated the employees well. I never heard of him mistreating any employee or resident [of Las Vegas]. This was a small close-knit community. With his reputation, any improper behavior would have circulated through the casino and town quickly." Siegel expected the employees to follow the rules, but he also had a warm personality and treated them well.[503]

The Las Vegas casino industry was built by former illegal casino operators who typically had a second-grade education and had spent their lives surviving in a rough world devoid of police to protect their bankroll or territorial right to exist. Many had poor people-handling skills. Many casino executives were aloof or abusive to the employees, ruling by intimidation. Siegel stood out as one of the most friendly, personable, and considerate casino owners in history.

The night Siegel was killed, his death was announced over the *Flamingo's* public address system. The shocked employees, especially the women, stood around crying and consoling each other for a long time. Based on national employee surveys, few of America's top business leaders today would evoke any real grief in the work place if their death were announced.

Siegel was typically described as a *businessman type.* No one found him aggressive, domineering, overbearing, or demanding, as implied by the myth. His Prohibition partner Jimmy Blue Eyes and other close associates said, "Ben never threw his weight around." Las Vegas restaurant and casino employees at other establishments never had any idea who the customer they were serving was until after he left and someone told them.

Authors about early organized crime created Siegel's mythical temper in an attempt to explain why he was nicknamed *Bugsy.* I asked Jimmy Blue Eyes where it came from. He met Siegel when he was 23-years old, and Jimmy told me, "The name *Bugsy* had to have come from his youth because no one in the underworld used it. I never heard anyone in New York say it while he was alive, not even behind his back. Ben had a great sense of humor and loved joking around. He might have said something crazy to other school kids, and a classmate could have used it in a funny retort. Somehow, the newspapers later picked it up." It is clear the nickname came from Ben's youth, but he never talked to anyone about its origin or anything else about his background. No author interviewed anyone who knew him in his youth or who had any knowledge about its origin.

Just like in New York, no one who knew Siegel later when he lived in Hollywood or Las Vegas ever heard the name *Bugsy* used by anyone at any time. The term was so foreign to people who had known him well that I intentionally used it while interviewing them to observe their reaction. To a man they would visibly snap their heads back like I had slapped them. He always introduced himself as *Ben*, but his employees called him *Mr. Siegel*.

During Siegel's Manhattan years he was able to maintain an amazingly low profile, despite being the country's leading Prohibition rumrunner and a top power in the underworld. In fact the *New York Times* mentioned him in just 13 articles during the 27 years between the onset of Prohibition and his murder. The first *Times'* article to mention Siegel did not appear until two years after the repeal of Prohibition. Siegel's name came out a week after Dutch Schultz was killed because the Dutchman's "business" papers tied him to police officials and politicians. This revelation caused Mayor LaGuardia to order the Police Commissioner to break up such corrupt connections with his department. The resulting *Times'* article contained a list of the usual notorious hoods' names issued by the Commissioner, and he was quoted as including "Charles (Bugs) Spiegel." Siegel was so unknown to the Police Commissioner and the *New York Times* reporter that both got all three of his names wrong. Ben was never associated with either the nickname *Bugs* or *Bug*, but *Bugsy* stuck after the Police Commissioner misspoke for this article. Seven of the remaining 12 *Times'* articles gave differing variations of his supposed nickname. In order they were *Bug, Bug, Buggsy, Bug, Bugsie, Buggsy*, and *Bugs*. One of these other articles also gave his first name as Charles, and an eighth did not include a first name, which the press always tries to include for correct identification of the subject. These newspapermen obviously had no clue about what he was called in real life.

When Siegel moved to Hollywood, the *Los Angeles Times* popularized his nickname by prominently inserting it early in almost every article concerning him. All but 20 of the paper's 566 articles referred to him as *Bugsy, Bugsie,* or *Buggsy*. A 1946 FBI internal report, written after Siegel had been a hoodlum for more than 25 years, illustrates law enforcement was still speculating about what, if any, nickname the underworld used for him. The report quotes an informant, who claimed to have great knowledge about Ben and Meyer Lansky, as calling them *Bug* Siegel and *Bugs* Meyer. Yet no one ever applied a nickname to Lansky, and no one in the underworld ever heard Siegel referred to as *Bug* or *Bugs*.[504]

A few underworld toughs possessed names like the *Blade* or *Killer,* which accurately described the bearer's vicious nature. These depraved hoods frightened every one who ever looked into their eyes. However, the nicknames of most criminals had curious origins. They were benign, just cute phrases that a friend or associate laid on them to describe a physical or personality characteristic, or as a joke.

A good example was Siegel's Prohibition partner Vincent Alo, who everybody knew by his nickname Jimmy Blue Eyes. A common American nickname for *Vincent* is *Jimmy.* He was called *Jimmy* by his family and friends from the time he was little, but I realized when I sat down at the dining-room table for my first interview with him that I was, surprisingly, looking at a man with brown eyes. I could not resist asking him to explain this eye-color discrepancy in his nickname, and he told me, "I had five female cousins who wanted to learn to dance, and I was their practice partner. So, in school, I was the only boy who danced well. One time, there was a dance at school, and the boys lined one wall, while the girls lined the other. I have brown eyes, and both were blackened from a [officially sponsored] boxing match the night before. When I started dancing with a girl, she sang out loud the lyrics of a popular song of the day - *Brown Eyes, Why Are You Blue?* When the other boys heard it, it stuck; and I have forever been known as *Jimmy Blue Eyes*."

In all likelihood, Siegel's nickname resulted from just such a childhood kibitz. The press popularized the name *Bugsy,* but during his life, everyone called him *Ben.*

Ben's nickname was altered and expanded by two Federal Prosecutors during a 1939 Grand Jury investigation. These Prosecutors based their inquiry on a known underworld pattern of some criminal-gang members avoiding law-enforcement heat in their home town by cooling off in other cities under the protection of a local gang. With no evidence, these Prosecutors took a giant leap to the erroneous conclusion that independent crime gangs in different cities were a single interconnected nationwide organization. The Federal Prosecutors' investigative arm was the FBI, but its records show at the time of this inquiry that it had no knowledge of the actual activities of Siegel and Lansky. This dearth of facts did not deter these zealous, over-reaching Prosecutors from contriving and attributing bogus criminal activities to Siegel and Lansky simply because the two were known to be good friends.

These Prosecutors announced to the press as fact that "Siegel, with his partner, Meyer Lansky, were the bosses of a gang known as the *Bug and Meyer Mob.* … As early as 1931 the Bug and Meyer gang began to extend its empire … the Bug and Meyer gang were extended to Philadelphia, Pittsburgh and Cleveland." These Prosecutors had everything all wrong. Siegel and Lansky never had legal or illegal business in any of the cities they claimed. In 1931 they were operating only in Manhattan, where they were the country's biggest rumrunners. The Prosecutors stated further, "Siegel and Lansky set themselves up in Los Angeles," but Siegel was living there off his Prohibition stash during their 1939 Grand Jury inquiry, while Meyer was running two casinos near Miami in Florida. These Prosecutors' fictional yarn did not deceive their handpicked Grand Jury, which refused to indict because of no evidence.[505]

The *New York Times* never again mentioned these U.S. Prosecutors' groundless allegations about the Bug and Meyer Mob, but self-proclaimed crime historians picked up the fictitious *Bug And Meyer Mob* name from one article and wrote about it as if it had really existed. These authors made up false stories about the pair's illegal activities that went far beyond the Prosecutors' fictions. For example, Dean Jennings' wrote the following fantasy that future authors embellished. "In the old days in New York, the mob called him 'Bugs' because he was a hothead. When he and Meyer Lansky formed their Jewish gang, the cops and the newspapers called it the Bug-Meyer mob." However, no such gang ever existed, and no such gang was ever mentioned by the newspapers. Further, all of Siegel's and Lansky's business partners and close associates were Italian or Sicilian rather than Jewish. This demonstrates just how easily enduring myths about nonexistent criminal activities and organizations can be concocted by ambitious and deceitful police, prosecutors, and authors.[506]

Since authors about early organized crime knew nothing about Lansky's and Siegel's youthful years before Prohibition, they latched on to these U.S. Prosecutors' made-up yarn about how the

Bug and Meyer Mob became powerful late in Prohibition, but they applied this sham gang name to the pair's earliest years. These fake biographers alleged that Siegel and Lansky ran this fabricated gang as much as three years prior to Prohibition, but not one of these authors named the pair's mob associates or underlings, or with whom they conducted business. Various books have alleged the pair participated in all kinds of vicious crimes, without ever once listing the victims, jurisdictions, dates, or details they pretend to be so knowledgeable about. In addition, these books often contradict each other, and none offers any sources for its information. These authors created a myth that the two became violent protectors of liquor truck convoys and possibly also truck hijackers. In actuality no one in the New York underworld ever heard of this imaginary Bug and Meyer Mob, and no one was aware of Siegel or Lansky being involved in any illegal activity in New York City besides rumrunning.

When Prohibition began, Siegel was a grammar school student of 13. A few months later after turning 14, he completed the eighth grade and quit school to join a partnership with Lansky, Luciano, and Adonis to take advantage of the tremendous opportunities offered by Prohibition. This quartet's rise in this new world was meteoric. By the time Siegel would have reached the 11th grade, he and his gang were well established as America's biggest rumrunners, and both the 17-year-old Siegel and Luciano lived in the luxury of the world's most expensive address, suites at the Waldorf-Astoria.

The authors about early organized crime later revived the Bug-and-Meyer myth that the U.S. Prosecutors fabricated late in Prohibition, but these writers changed the time frame to pretend they knew what Lansky had done during the three years prior to Prohibition between the ages of 15 and 17. Amazingly, none of these authors did enough research to realize Siegel was 13 at the beginning of Prohibition. Thus, these writers incredibly have an 11-year-old Siegel and 15-year-old Lansky leading a fictional Jewish gang of no more than a dozen members in Manhattan, even though this was the heartland of the country's two biggest Sicilian Mafia gangs, one with 600 shooters and the other 450. This means these kids would have had to have somehow pounded these huge gangs into submission. If this had been true, the monumental exploits of these child gangsters would have been glorified by the press to make them the most celebrated criminals in American history.

In reality, Luciano's youthful importing partnership expanded so rapidly in Manhattan early in Prohibition that The Duck Masseria, leader of the country's largest gang, pressured the Sicilian Luciano to take a blood oath to lead an independent division of his Mafia gang. In return for joining Masseria's gang and sharing their profits with him, Luciano's importing Sicilian-Italian-Jewish partnership received unfettered access to the nation's most valuable liquor marketplace. Luciano and his associates spent their careers making accommodations with established local gangs, not fighting them.

The U.S. Prosecutors in 1939 had no evidence to back up their phony assertions of a multi-city Bug and Meyer Mob, and their handpicked Grand Jury served justice by refusing to indict Siegel and Lansky. However the newspaper articles about these Prosecutors' fake allegations inspired Brooklyn gangster Abe Reles to create a grave injustice eight months later. Reles embellished the U.S. Prosecutors' national-gang hoax to concoct his Murder, Inc. fable and get immunity from a dozen murders by offering a sensational state's-witness story against members of his Brooklyn gang and also against Siegel. But before facing this murder charge, Siegel's actual youth follows.

THE LIFE-LONG PARTNERSHIP OF SIEGEL & LANSKY

Siegel and Lansky never mentioned to anyone how they met, but two separate times during their youths they lived in the same New York City borough. Siegel was born and grew up in Brooklyn, and Lansky lived there the first three years after his family arrived in this country until he was 12 years old. It seems unlikely they were already best friends at that time because 12- and 8-year olds do not usually share many common interests. When Lansky's family moved, it was to the Lower East Side of Manhattan, which is where Siegel started hanging out after completing grammar school four months into Prohibition. When the two teamed up to became empire builders in the liquor importing and wholesaling business, Lansky was 18 and Siegel 14.[507]

Movie Actor George Raft, who was a close friend of Siegel and one of the original investors in his *Flamingo Hotel-Casino,* told author Jennings, "I knew him [Siegel] when he was a tough kid on the Lower East Side in New York. He was gutsy and ambitious. He came out here [Hollywood] because he wanted to be somebody." Siegel certainly had guts. Close associates said he was always the first one to stand up and protect a threatened friend.

Authors about early organized crime invariably perpetuate a myth that the Lansky and Siegel friendship was a contrast in brain and brawn. Lansky is depicted as the great thinker and Siegel as the psychopathic murderer. In reality their only difference was in temperament. Lansky was a quiet, studious, conservatively-dressed introvert, while Siegel was a gregarious, expressive, flashily-clothed extrovert.

Those who dealt with both said they shared power equally and respected each other's opinion. Jimmy Blue Eyes explained to me, "Meyer and Ben were equal in their relationship, but they handled things different. It was a difference of personality, not ability. Meyer was more subdued. He was quiet and disappeared in a crowd. He never pushed. He was a most passive guy."

Los Angeles bookie Mickey Cohen wrote in his autobiography, "Meyer Lansky doesn't run around with glamorous broads. He's not a flamboyant man at all. He's a loner. Meyer can stay in a room with his wife or whoever he's with at the time. He don't go much for partying. He has his own way." "I have a great love and respect and a complete high regard for Meyer Lansky."

Jimmy Blue Eyes told me, "Meyer did not like publicity." Author Lacey wrote that Lansky told a friend of his son, Buddy, "You must never advertise your wealth." Lansky did not spend money on his lifestyle, but he was a meticulous dresser. Lansky lived in a small, modest home, while his close associates - Siegel, Luciano, and Costello – lived in elegant suites at the world's most expensive address, the Waldorf-Astoria.

In contrast to the always quiet and self-contained Lansky, who went unnoticed in a room full of people, the intense and dynamic Siegel made a commanding presence in any gathering. Mark Swain, who ran Siegel's yacht at Lake Mead and cooked for him and his guests, told me, "Ben was high-strung and always looking at everything going on around him, but he was always tuned into the conversation he was carrying on."

Siegel tended to react with strong emotion. Some people who encountered him on a superficial level misinterpreted his vitality and exuberance for impulsivity, even volatility, but he was a very deliberate, methodical, strategic decision maker and planner. His business endeavors and criminal activities both demonstrate this.

Lansky and Siegel shared four traits - intelligence, street smarts, physical toughness, and the guts to face any challenge or difficulty put in their way by America's most violent criminals. Lansky was the more abstract, theoretical, academic thinker. He read history and geography his whole life, and whiled away the hours in old age with friends challenging each other's knowledge. He would have been a strong competitor in today's TV trivia contests. In contrast, Siegel was the more practical, business-like, problem-solving thinker.

Jimmy Blue Eyes told me, "Meyer was the smartest of all the top guys (hoods). He was one of the main guys (in the Mafia), even though he was Jewish. He had no education, but he knew human nature. He had common sense. He knew how to talk to people. He knew who to talk to, and who not to talk to."

Author Jennings quotes Siegel, as once saying in Hollywood about Lansky, "There is a guy who has a brilliant mind and for my money is one of the great organizers of his time. I don't see him much any more, and that's too bad."

Lansky was an effective deal broker and negotiator. He put business combinations together for other investors who then ran them. Every one who knew Lansky trusted and respected him. Author Lacey summed up his interviewees' attitudes with, "No one who knew Meyer Lansky as a friend ever had a bad word to say about him. ... Meyer also had the ability, rare at any age, to mediate and settle differences through intelligence and reason."[508]

Siegel had a very different business style. He built, managed, and marketed his own successful companies. Jimmy Blue Eyes said, "Ben was a smart guy. He took care of the [huge national horserace] wire business" for their gang. Every one who dealt with Siegel in Las Vegas had high respect for his business acumen.

In different fashions, both put together successful large business deals throughout their lives, beginning in their teens. Both did this by always having business partners with whom they worked well, and making their word an absolute bond, better than any contract ever written.

Both Lansky and Siegel were extremely loyal to friends, but their social and personal interactive styles were very different. Lansky was quiet and distanced himself from people he did not know well, but the many people who developed personal relationships with him had great affection and admiration for him. Jimmy Blue Eyes described Meyer's treatment of friends to me. "Meyer only cared about one thing and that was friendship. He was always concerned with the welfare of other people's health and families. Whenever he encountered anyone he knew, he always wanted to know about the well being of his family members in order, starting with, 'How are you?' 'How's your wife?' and 'How are your kids?' He was truly interested. He listened and discussed the person's problems with them. This is what he liked to talk about most, and this is why people liked him so well. Meyer was a totally loyal person and always stood by his friends. He was one of the nicest human beings there ever was."

Jimmy Blue Eyes told me, "During Meyer's arrest for possession of a prescribed drug, the federal agent told him, 'We're going to charge you with drugs. What'll your friends think of you now?' Meyer replied, 'Look, everybody who I am close to knows better. If you've lived as long as I have and made as many wonderful friends as I have, I am a very lucky man.' His friends knowing better was all that was important for him."

As reticent as Lansky was in groups of people, Siegel was gregarious. He had honed his social skills to become the epitome of classy propriety by the time he moved into the Waldorf-Astoria. Later in his Hollywood period, he was the favorite on many top stars' and producers' party guest lists.

People who were close to Siegel, and those who dealt with him superficially, typically described his personality as *personable*. He possessed the rare ability to mix well with everyone, at all social levels. His close Las Vegas business associates and Lake Mead yacht staff were amazed at how seamlessly he moved between meetings with the roughest, most dangerous underworld gang leaders, the financial community, legitimate businessmen, local town's people, his executives and employees, and America's upper crust of wealth, power, celebrity, and/or snobbery.

In all my interviews, I never found one person who knew Siegel on any level who had a bad word to say about him personally, and none of these people had ever heard anyone else say they disliked him. This includes his mortal business enemy, Dave Stearns, who believed Siegel's horserace-wire-service monopoly in Las Vegas was overpriced. Thus, he felt justified in pirating the service's daily broadcasts for the six years Siegel did business in Las Vegas. The FBI feared Stearns' brazen informational theft would pressure Siegel to kill him, so an agent was stationed in the small town of 10,000 people just to monitor their activities. I asked Stearns in an interview, "Weren't you concerned Siegel would kill you for stealing from him?" He immediately became very angry that anyone writing about Siegel could ask such a naïve and outlandish question. He indignantly exclaimed, "Ben never would've killed anybody over money!"

At the end of my second two-hour interview with Stearns about his rivalry with Siegel, I asked, "What did you think of Siegel personally?" He replied, "My answer isn't what you expect. I totally objected to one of his business tactics, and I fiercely fought him over it the whole time he was here. It was the same tactic Howard Hughes uses, and I have no respect for him. But on a personal basis, I can't tell you that I didn't like Ben." That was the worst thing any of my many interviewees said about him.[509]

Siegel's Las Vegas attorney Lou Wiener told me, "The day after Ben's murder, Beverly Hills Police Chief C. H. Anderson came to Las Vegas for a couple of days and talked to local people, trying to develop leads. Before he left, he told me. 'I couldn't find anyone in town who didn't like him.'"[510]

Siegel and Lansky had contrasting personalities, but they shared strong personal values, such as keeping their word, fierce loyalty, and caring about other people. These catapulted them to the pinnacle of the underworld and the business world in every area of the country in which either conducted business during his lifetime.

THE MURDER, INC. CASE OF "BIG GREENIE"

When the NYPD made a harassment roust of Siegel and seven hoods in a hotel suite, the illegal bust was dismissed by a court, but this arrest would still embroil Siegel in the so-called Murder, Inc. trials a few years later. In attendance with Siegel were Lansky and another illegal casino operator, Joseph "Doc" Stacher of New Jersey, who would later build the *Sands* resort on the Las Vegas Strip. Also there were three gang members from the Brownsville district of Brooklyn - co-leaders Louis "Lepke" Buchalter and Jake "Gurrah" Shapiro, and their underling Harry Gottesmann, who everyone knew as Harry "Big Greenie" Greenberg. A mug shot of the eight was printed by New York newspapers, and this strong visual public record proving that Siegel knew Big Greenie would later haunt him.

Two years after this hotel roust, the INS deported Big Greenie to Poland following his third imprisoning for burglary. He reentered the U.S. by using his dead father-in-law's passport, but he and 14 other Brownsville gang members were soon charged with extortion. Big Greenie fled to Montreal, Canada, where he hid for two years before sending a note to gang-leader Lepke threatening to surrender on the charges against him and turn informer for DA Tom Dewey if he was not paid $5,000 living money. As a result of attempting to extort his gang, Big Greenie soon heard his fellow members had targeted him for death. He ran to avoid both his gang bent on retaliation and the police who were hunting him as a fugitive avoiding prosecution.

Big Greenie took up residence in Hollywood, where a Brownsville-gang associate recognized him and trailed him to his apartment. He lived there under the name George Schachter with his wife and sister-in-law. For the next few days the associate parked his car down the street and watched Big Greenie's comings and goings. The target only left his shelter each day near midnight. In that era few people shopped at night so he was much less likely to be spotted by anyone who knew him. He would drive for a newspaper and some food while the city slept. On Thanksgiving-eve night, he followed his usual routine. When he returned home and parked his car, an assailant ran up behind Big Greenie's car and shot him in the head five times killing him in the driver's seat.

Three months after Big Greenie's murder in Hollywood, Abe Reles turned state's witness in Brooklyn. He told Prosecutor Burton Turkus about four Brownsville-gang homicides that would become known as the Murder, Inc. cases. Reles fingered Al Tannenbaum as the getaway driver in the Big Greenie murder in Hollywood and an earlier Brooklyn gang murder. When Tannenbaum was indicted for the Brooklyn murder, he also turned state's witness in return for immunity and filled in the details about Big Greenie's murder.

Brooklyn DA Bill O'Dwyer quickly billed the Big Greenie case as a Murder, Inc. homicide because he was a member of Brooklyn's Brownsville gang. DA O'Dwyer specifically inserted Siegel in the Hollywood murder to bolster his fictitious story that the Brooklyn gang was a nationwide murder ring. Siegel's name was well-known to the public, unlike the gang's leaders, and his alleged leadership role placed Murder Inc. on the West Coast as well as in Brooklyn. DA O'Dwyer claimed Siegel's earlier Prohibition meeting in a Manhattan hotel suite roust was a conference of Murder, Inc. gang leaders called by Siegel to finance the flight of potential subpoenaed witnesses against the ring and to slay informers. (However, if the gang had been financing fleeing witnesses as DA O'Dwyer asserted, it would have sent Big Greenie living money, and he would not have had to resort to extortion demands.)

DA O'Dwyer's Assistant Prosecutor Turkus flew to deliver to Los Angeles County DA Buron Fitts the depositions of informants Reles and Tannenbaum. A few weeks later both informants were flown under heavy guard in a secretly chartered plane from Brooklyn to testify before the Los Angeles County Grand Jury. It indicted five men for murdering Big Greenie. The three in LA were Ben Siegel, Hollywood barbershop proprietor Harry "Champ" Segal, and New York and Seattle fight promoter Frank Carbo. The two in Brooklyn were Brownsville gang-leader Lepke and his lieutenant Mendy Weiss.

Five LAPD Detectives went to Siegel's Holmby Hills mansion to arrest him, and his butler let them in. They found his bed sheets still warm, but a hour and half of searching the home proved futile. Then one Detective found a broken shelf in a linen closest. He crawled through a trap door in the ceiling to the attic, calling out, "Come on down Ben." This he did without incidence. As he was led out of his home, Ben waved a handcuffed hand to an astonished neighbor and cheerily called out, "Hello Gene."[511]

Siegel told the Detectives, "All you had to do was telephone and tell me to come in." He explained he hid when he saw a bunch of men in street clothes running across his lawn toward his house. His hiding did not indicate he lived in fear because he was unarmed, and he kept the two pistols in his house locked in a safe hidden behind a sliding panel. Siegel did not keep a gun around for protection, even though he possessed a concealed weapon permit from the Los Angeles County Sheriff's Department. These were almost impossible for legitimate citizens to get, unless they had close ties to a sheriff, a police chief, or a high-ranking political leader, until many states, not including California, started greatly liberalizing their concealed-weapon laws around 1990.[512]

Following Siegel's arrest, LA DA Fitts quoted a letter from Manhattan DA Dewey, who had assisted Brooklyn Prosecutor Turkus in fabricating his Murder Inc. fiction. "Siegel is a big notorious gunman and racketeer. He is working with a combine throughout the country and receives a cut from the Lepke mob." LA Chief Deputy DA Eugene Williams supported Dewey's contention by saying Siegel, "admitted knowing Lepke and other big-time racketeers from the East" because they all grew up in Brooklyn. DA Fitts announced all the evidence against Siegel and the four others was supplied by Brooklyn DA O'Dwyer's Murder, Inc. investigation and by his state's witnesses, who were going to again present their sham history and structure of mobdom (see Chapter 8).[513]

At his arraignment Siegel told reporters, "I'll beat this thing if it takes everything I've got." He always maintained, "It's a bum beef," just like the seven Murder, Inc. defendants before their executions in the three Brooklyn trials. Siegel asked the Judge for bail because the evidence was so weak. Upon its denial, he was pale, perspiring, and distressed. He languished in jail waiting for trial because of delays caused by the election of a new LA DA.[514]

It is all but certain that Siegel had never met Brooklyn DA O'Dwyer. Siegel had left his Brooklyn roots for Manhattan and then moved on to Hollywood years before O'Dwyer became DA. This made Siegel just another hood available for framing to feed O'Dwyer's unbridled political ambition. DA O'Dwyer blasted Siegel in the press as a vicious hood and readily supplied two of his state's witnesses to the LA DA for the grand jury to charge him with murder. This spurred Siegel's three closest friends to swing into action, just as they would soon assist Naval Intelligence during World War II. Lansky flew from his Cuban vacation to visit his pal Siegel in jail, and he flew from there to New York to confer with Adonis and Costello. Both men paid visits to DA O'Dwyer. Adonis, the Democratic political leader of Brooklyn, had led O'Dwyer to victory as DA. Costello, the biggest Democratic political kingmaker in New York, would later back O'Dwyer for mayor of the nation's largest city. Adonis and Costello demanded DA O'Dwyer save their buddy, especially since both knew he had nothing to do with the Brownsville gang's activities or with Big Greenie's murder. Even though Brooklyn DA O'Dwyer had fashioned the case against Siegel for the LA DA, Adonis and Costello pressured him to now covertly destroy the case against their buddy.

DA O'Dwyer began his sabotage with a weekend train trip to LA accompanied by Acting Detective Captain Frank Bals (who would later direct the murder of witness Reles while in protective custody - see Chapter 9). Brooklyn DA O'Dwyer conferenced with newly-elected LA DA John Dockweiler, and then the two DAs told the Judge the case against Siegel was dead. DA O'Dwyer explained that his primary obligation was to the people of Brooklyn, and he did not want to risk having his pending cases discredited if his witnesses' testimony failed to convict Siegel in California. This argument had no validity. The cases were separated by a continent and had no bearing on each other. No matter how vacuous DA O'Dwyer's reasoning, LA DA Dockweiler now had no evidence and had to move for dismissal. After four months as the house guest of the county jailer, Siegel returned home a free man.

The dismissal of Siegel's murder charge was reported very differently in articles by the *Los Angeles Times* and the *New York Times,* as both DA's spun the story for their own benefit. DA O'Dwyer let LA DA Dockweiler cover his derriere by claiming state's witness Reles was critically ill in a Brooklyn hospital and was incapable of travel, but this should have done nothing more than postpone the trial. At the same time, a New York associate of DA O'Dwyer put out an unattributed rumor to the press that Reles was in the hospital, but *the New York Times* did not buy this information. Instead the paper investigated and revealed Reles was known to have a minor stomach ailment, but he was still seen visiting O'Dwyer's office on "official business" almost daily.

Because of this press criticism, DA O'Dwyer kept up a charade of continuing to go after Siegel by participating in a joint inquiry with the LA DA. This allowed DA O'Dwyer and Detective Captain Bals to take a first-class vacation in sunny Southern California during the February New York winter at taxpayer expense. DA O'Dwyer vacationed at his Imperial Valley *command center* for 10 days, while Bals *worked* out of a luxury Los Angeles hotel, searching for evidence against Siegel he knew did not exist. DA O'Dwyer soon shelved this pointless cover-up investigation.

Despite the dismissal of the Los Angeles murder charge, Reles' testimony in an unrelated case continued to bedevil Siegel. Before Reles became a Murder, Inc. state's witness for O'Dwyer, he had testified before a New York Federal Grand Jury investigating who had harbored fugitive Lepke during the two years he evaded New York indictments. In that case Reles also falsely accused others to save himself. Reles knew Siegel's name as a big-time hood would excite the U.S. Attorney. Thus Reles alone implicated Siegel by claiming he briefly visited Lepke at his home prior to his surrender to Federal authorities. Hearing this, the Grand Jury subpoenaed Siegel to testify, but he refused to answer the Jury's questions because he never talked about his or other people's business. A Judge jailed him indefinitely for contempt, and after six days of incarceration he agreed to testify. He told the Grand Jury the truth that he had no contact with Lepke during the two years he hid in a rented furnished room close to Brooklyn police headquarters. Later testimony by Lepke and every one who was involved in harboring the fugitive proved that he never returned to his home, making Reles' testimony that Siegel met Lepke there another one of his many confirmed perjuries as a state's witness.

A year and a half after Reles testified to the Grand Jury, the FBI finally arrested Siegel and 13 others for misdemeanor harboring of a fugitive. Siegel challenged his extradition to Brooklyn to face this charge because it was based solely on Reles' perjured testimony. At the hearing in Federal Court, Siegel testified he had never met or ever seen Reles until he entered the courtroom to appear at the hearing against him. He also testified he had not seen Lepke for six years, since before he had moved to Hollywood. Siegel also testified he was only in New York once during the two years Lepke hid out, and he produced travel receipts to prove he arrived at the airport with just enough time to board an Italian ocean liner for a Naples vacation. The travel service that sold him the tickets and two passengers on the ship testified he was indeed a passenger. All said Siegel had a good reputation. In contrast, a LAPD Detective Lieutenant testified he was acquainted with Reles and among police officers his reputation was bad. In making his ruling, the U.S. Commissioner said, "I am frank to say the witness Reles is entitled to little credence. Nevertheless, his testimony, together with the testimony of the defendant, convinced me that this defendant here is the person the Grand Jury intended to indict." He released Siegel on $25,000 bond pending appearance in New York.[515]

While this harboring charge was pending against Siegel nine months after the Big Greenie murder-charge against him had been dismissed, three citizens oddly decided to come forward for the first time as witnesses to the murder, leading the LA DA to reopen the case. Newspaper heat to prosecute Siegel forced DA O'Dwyer to fly Tannenbaum to Los Angeles to testify before the Grand Jury for a second time, but DA O'Dwyer somehow justified not sending Reles in order to satisfy his political backers, Adonis and Costello. Siegel was charged again with the Big Greenie murder, creating a dilemma for him with the two cases. If he surrendered in Hollywood for murder and was again jailed, he would forfeit the $25,000 bond [$380,000 today] he deposited in New York to appear in Federal Court for the harboring arraignment. Eventually the U.S. Attorney dropped the false fugitive harboring charges and took no further action. This allowed Siegel to voluntarily surrender to the LAPD, just like he had earlier told the Detectives he would do on the day they charged his home and sent him scurrying to the attic. Siegel was again denied bail, and he whiled away in jail as the prosecution delayed his trial date.

Reles had implicated Siegel in the Big Greenie murder by testifying to the Los Angeles County Grand Jury that he heard Siegel tell Lepke at his Brooklyn home, "If Big Greenie is there [Hollywood] when I get back, he won't leave Los Angeles." All of Reles testimony about the existence of a Murder, Inc. has already been exposed as untrue and perjured in the three Brooklyn trials (see Chapter 8). In addition, Siegel and Lepke were both well known for never talking about illegal activities in front of anyone but their closest associates. This was even admitted by Reles and Brooklyn Murder, Inc. Prosecutor Turkus during those trials. Both stated that Lepke never talked in front of anyone but his lieutenant Weiss. However, this single false sentence of testimony by Reles was enough to set in motion the first Big Greenie murder indictment against Siegel, even though all of Lepke's harborers testified that Lepke never visited his home while a fugitive to meet with Siegel or anyone else as Reles falsely claimed.[516]

DA O'Dwyer and Prosecutor Turkus used Reles' testimony that he overheard conversations between Lepke and Weiss to make Reles a corroborating witness to execute four men in the first two Brooklyn Murder, Inc. trials. To execute Siegel, DA O'Dwyer also needed Reles to overhear another conversation by Lepke to corroborate Tannenbaum's eye-witness testimony about the murder, but then DA O'Dwyer flip-flopped and started protecting Siegel on behalf of Adonis and Costello. Thus, DA O'Dwyer undermined the LA DA's case by refusing to allow Reles to travel to Hollywood to testify the second time Siegel was charged with Big Greenie's murder. Then, as Siegel sat waiting in jail, Reles flew out the window of his Coney Island hotel room.

Even though the LA DA lacked a corroborating witness for Tannenbaum, he still tried Siegel and Frank Carbo, whom he accused of being the shooter of Big Greenie. First, the LA Prosecutor's opening statement followed the pattern established in the Brooklyn Murder, Inc. trials by stressing the defendants' participation in the imaginary killing syndicate without offering any evidence or testimony of its existence during the trial. Then with Reles dead, the Prosecutor hoped Tannenbaum's eye-witness testimony would be supported by Big Greenie's widow's account of her husband's murder. She did testify to seeing Tannenbaum visit with her husband on at least six occasions, but she never heard Siegel's name mentioned by anyone.

When star-witness Tannenbaum testified, he admitted he was a New York labor racketeer. He headed "goon squads" specializing in sluggings and stink bombs to discourage labor unions from molesting those manufacturers who purchased the violent anti-strike services of Lepke's Brownsville gang.

Tannenbaum testified in detail about the planning and execution of Big Greenie's murder, but he became mixed up during cross examination, as both defense attorneys hammered away at him. He sweated, squirmed, and became flustered, as they forced him to admit inconsistencies in his story. They repeatedly made him go over one discrepancy. He had testified to both Grand Juries that co-defendant Carbo had stuck his hand inside the driver's window and shot Big Greenie dead, but at the trial, he said he did not see Carbo insert his hand inside the driver's window. Every one in the court must have wondered what difference it made whether his hand was, or was not, inside the window, but with each question the defense attorneys included the term *driver's door,* which the witness repeated in each answer. Then one of the defense attorneys finally hit the witness with the autopsy surgeons' findings. The five bullets had entered the right side of Big Greenie's head as he sat in the driver's seat, so they had to have been shot through the passenger's window, not the driver's window, as Tannenbaum testified time and again.

The defense attorneys then pressured Tannenbaum to explain his confusion about which side of the car the shooter was standing near. To get out of his contradictory testimonies, the witness claimed he intentionally gave false testimony under oath in both Grand Jury appearances, but his justification for doing this was nonsensical. He claimed unidentified people, who "you just can't refuse," ordered him to perjure himself. However, his lying about which window was shot through was of no benefit to the charged gang's members. Had his claim been true that the gang got to him, the gang's members would have threatened him not to testify at all, but this did not happen and could not have because Tannenbaum had been kept in protective custody incommunicado from the world since his arrest in Brooklyn. His grossly inaccurate and pathetic presentation proved beyond any doubt that he had not witnessed the murder that fateful night.[517]

The three new Los Angeles witnesses testified they had not seen Siegel near the crime scene that night. This meant no one could corroborate Tannenbaum's testimony, which was the only evidence against Siegel, so upon the Prosecutor's conclusion of his case, the Judge dismissed the charge. Siegel could never be tried again because he was placed in legal jeopardy by facing the prosecution's presentation. This ended Siegel's second four-month hospitality with the County Jailer. As he walked out, he joyfully responded to reporters' questions with, "I don't have to say anything. The judge said it all."[518]

In retrospect, it is obvious DA Dockweiler never had a legitimate case against Siegel. What is not clear is whether Dockweiler selected this as his first case in office and prosecuted it himself because he lacked experience in prosecution, or whether he thought this failure would somehow enhance his political-reform hyperbole. Dockweiler had been a Democratic U.S. Congressman from California, and he had lost his campaign for governor two years before winning as DA.

When Reles had turned state's witness to avoid the possibility of the electric chair, he had to incriminate higher echelon gangsters in his imaginary Murder, Inc. story. He went after his gang's leaders and former Brooklynite Siegel, who was the most notorious hood on the West Coast, even though Siegel had nothing to do with their gang. However, Siegel was the perfect patsy because he was famous while the Brownsville gang leaders were not; he lived on the opposite coast, so his involvement supported Reles' claim that Murder, Inc. killed for gangs across the country; Siegel knew Lepke while growing up in Brooklyn and had a meeting with him at a hotel that turned into a NYPD roust a decade earlier; and Reles had falsely testified five months earlier to a Federal Grand Jury in a different case that Siegel met with Lepke while he was a fugitive in hiding.

Tannenbaum had to make his testimony consistent with Reles' Murder, Inc. story by elevating Siegel's status in the underworld, so he falsely testified, "Ben Siegel was the supreme gangster in the United States. He had been the big boss for the last 10 years throughout the country." Tannenbaum also had to involve Siegel in Big Greenie's murder, which forced him to create absurd testimony about how the crime was committed. His testimony that Siegel joined the Big Greenie slaying squad has always perplexed organized-crime writers because the greatest benefit of being a gang leader is having the other members commit the crimes and shoulder all risk of jail time. This is why no other major gang leader was ever known to have participated in a killing.

Tannenbaum's claim that Siegel was along for the murder to drive one of the two cars defies reason, but he added even more unbelievable elements. He testified Siegel drove his own car to the killing, which would have exposed his license plate to any witness who wanted to jot it down. He also claimed Siegel drove the getaway car containing the shooter covered in gun-powder residue, which put him in jeopardy of facing the death penalty. At the most, the savvy Siegel would have driven the *crash car* behind the getaway car to risk only a reckless-driving ticket if he had to force a pursuing police cruiser off the road. Tannenbaum's testimony about Siegel was contradicted by his fellow gang informer's Grand Jury testimony in which Reles maintained that Tannenbaum was the getaway driver. Another Tannenbaum statement is doubtful. He testified he brought the two murder guns on the plane from New York, even though Siegel's close LA associates, Jack Dragna and Mickey Cohen, had been found by the LAPD to maintain large untraceable arsenals.[519]

It also does not make sense that Lepke would have used the defendants Carbo and Segal, who were known to be professional killers and whose faces were known in Los Angeles. Lepke almost certainly used his Brooklyn gang members because their faces had never been seen in Los Angeles, unlike Siegel, whose photo had been printed in local newspapers. In addition, Lepke's gang members were brutal thugs who did his bidding, and they were less likely to turn state's witness against him if they were ever charged with a serious crime.

Not only is the fictitious Murder, Inc. myth about a nonexistent nationwide gang, but Lepke shared no other criminal link with Siegel. Lepke was a vicious labor racketeer who used his power over union workers to extort businesses, while Siegel was only involved with Prohibition liquor and gambling. Siegel did not respect Lepke and had no loyalty to him. On the contrary, Siegel was incensed with Lepke at the time of Big Greenie's killing because two months earlier Lepke's gang member Reles presented perjured testimony to frame Siegel for the fugitive harboring charge. Lepke had not prohibited Reles from committing this treacherous act or made him recant. Siegel was angry at Lepke and distrustful of him. Even though authors about early organized crime have tried to make sense out of this bizarre case against Siegel by falsely claiming he was associated somehow with Lepke's gang, Siegel actually had no motive whatsoever to protect Lepke from extortion by one of his own gang members, especially Big Greenie who was already trying to frame Siegel in the Lepke harboring case.

Most important, it was impossible for Siegel and Lepke to have met to plan Big Greenie's killing as the Murder, Inc. fiction creator, Reles, testified he overheard. Big Greenie was spotted in Hollywood a week before he was murdered, but Lepke had voluntarily surrendered to the FBI's Hoover three months earlier and was being held incommunicado. Not only did Federal lock-ups prohibit known hoods like Siegel and Reles from visiting inmates, but Hoover blocked all guests including Manhattan DA Dewey from seeing the isolated Lepke. Besides, Reles testified they met at Lepke's home, which he had not visited in over two years because he had been holed up in his fugitive hideout before surrendering to the custody of Hoover.

Reles depicted Siegel as a dangerous hood to the Federal Grand Jury investigating the harboring of Lepke, but if Reles believed this, he would have gone into hiding after framing Siegel. Instead Reles openly walked the streets of Brooklyn and hung out at his regular haunts with no fear of Siegel retaliating because Reles knew the description of Siegel in his testimony was not true. He and every one in the underworld were well aware of Charlie Luciano's and the Young Turks' two-decade-long vocal advocacy of non-violence and no vengeance.

Siegel certainly had the necessary firepower readily available to take out Reles because Anastasia headed the vicious Brooklyn waterfront gang, the second largest gang in the country, and Anastasia had strong loyalty to both Costello and Adonis. In this situation, Siegel would have greatly benefited by eliminating Reles, but Siegel did not yet realize what a serious threat he was up against. Five months later, Reles entered DA O'Dwyer's protective custody to testify in the Brooklyn Murder, Inc. cases, and to again frame Siegel, this time for Big Greenie's slaying. As a result, Siegel languished in jail for two four-month stints, and Siegel only avoided the electric chair because his buddies Costello and Adonis were so politically close to DA O'Dwyer, who undermined the LA DA's phony case against Siegel.

Siegel's total police jacket contains just a handful of non-violent, victimless misdemeanors when the fallacious Big Greenie murder charge is appropriately removed. Police also pulled Siegel in a few times in routine roundups of the usual suspects for questioning about big-time gangland murders before promptly releasing. However, it is important to note that no police agency in the country ever suspected him of killing anyone and not even a person of interest in any slaying. At the end of Prohibition Siegel was 27 years old, and for the last 14 years of his life he lived in Hollywood and Las Vegas, where every one who knew him said not one person with whom he had a serious disagreement was later slain, beaten up, or threatened.

During Siegel's first four-month jail stint awaiting trial for the Big Greenie murder, a scandal erupted over his preferential treatment in the Los Angeles County Jail. The public was righteously incensed by this unequal justice, but the larger story never surfaced. The LAPD, prosecutors, and judges have always maintained a separate justice and incarceration system that gives the rich and powerful in Beverly Hills and Hollywood special privilege beginning with the arrest process. LAPD officials gave a signed business card and instruction letter on official stationery to their friends and the rich and powerful that directed any policeman picking them up to take them to the comfort of the Beverly Hills VIP Holding Tank without booking them. They were treated as untouchables until their high-ranking police patron arrived to personally handle the situation. This policy is still in effect today.

Siegel benefited from this well-established system, but his case was exposed in the papers only because he was a famous hood. Since the newspaper publishers and many of their prominent advertisers benefited from this LAPD system, the papers never reported when anyone but a gangster was treated this way to protect their unjust and unfair secret perks.

While Siegel's treatment was not exceptional for the rich and powerful, the specifics demonstrate how much the jailors trusted his word and had no fear of him despite his notorious reputation. During two months of detention, Siegel was permitted to leave the jail for 18 day trips. The Deputy Sheriff who escorted him violated safety procedures by removing Siegel's handcuffs and letting him change into civilian clothes. The Deputy gave the hood complete freedom in the passenger seat while his own hands and feet were occupied driving, and the Deputy left Siegel alone having lunch with film actress Wendy Barrie at a fashionable Hollywood café, while he went to the men's room. This Deputy placed his career and possibly his life in jeopardy by removing these safeguards to accommodate the prisoner, so he was clearly convinced Siegel was not dangerous and would keep his word not to try to escape or overpower him. The Deputy's supervisors obviously shared this opinion of Siegel because they violated the requirement of having two guards accompany prisoners outside the Jail. Even Sheriff Eugene Biscailuz trivialized such safety violations down to minor indiscretions in regards to Siegel by telling reporters his Deputy "made mistakes, but I still have faith in him as an officer."[520]

Instead, Sheriff Biscailuz made the jail physician, Dr. Benjamin Blank, the villain in this scandal. However, he was not the worst offender and for the most part was following established polices of special treatment for the rich and famous. Siegel's nine visits to his attorney and nine to his dentist were approved by a judge. While Dr. Blank issued the dental excuses, all were first requested by Siegel's dentist and then they were approved by the judge. The problem was not in the absences, although they were assumed to be contrived, but Siegel's outings lasted about seven hours due to long lunches rather than the four hours authorized by the judge. This was the fault of the Deputy escorting Siegel, not Dr. Blank.

Special treatment accorded Siegel inside the jail included wearing tailored sporting clothes and paying another prisoner to polish his shoes daily, but the Sheriff admitted that prisoners were allowed to pay other inmates to polish their shoes before court appearances. Siegel paid a guard to buy and refrigerate in the kitchen his grocery list that included choice steaks, pheasant, and partridge that was prepared by a jail chef as part of a diet prescribed by the Jail Physician. Doctor Blank also kept a stash of toothpaste, figs, and candy for Siegel in his private office, and he gave him free use of the hospital telephone. According to four Deputy Sheriffs during the various hearings over this scandal, Doctor Blank escorted an unidentified stranger into the Jail Hospital more than once and let him meet privately with Siegel in his office with the door closed. The stranger arrived at the jail two weeks after Siegel was arrested, but it never came out that this was Lansky who had flown in from a Havana, Cuba vacation to commiserate with his pal and help plan his defense.

The Sheriff punished three members of his jail staff. The Deputy who escorted Siegel was suspended for 30 days without pay and demoted to driving an LAPD radio car for a couple of years before being promoted to a top Sheriff's position. The Sheriff switched the Chief Jailer of 11 years with the Chief Criminal Deputy but did not demote either of their ranks. The Sheriff's only strong action was the firing of Doctor Blank.

Doctor Blank had been forthright in answering questions about his conduct by the Sheriff, the Civil Service Commission, and the Grand Jury. The Doctor declared Siegel was a good friend of his for a number of years, and they frequently attended the same dinner parties and movie premieres. The Doctor believed in Siegel's innocence based on a career of working with criminals. The Doctor easily explained the $32,000 in checks that Siegel made out to him, which the LAPD seized at Siegel's home when they arrested him in the attic. The checks were made out several years before the arrest to repay a personal loan the Doctor made to Siegel to finance a business venture (described below).

The Doctor had devoted his career to service, not greed. As the Jail Physician, he had the right to spend one-third of his time seeing private patients, but he often put in 10 to 12 hours a day at the Jail Hospital, as he built a reputation for excellent treatment of the prisoners. He held the position of County Jail Physician more than 17 years, and was 2 ½ years away from being able to retire with a pension, when he was fired. Doctor Blank then became an Army Medical Corps Captain and went overseas to treat War soldiers wounded on the battlefield.

The new Jail Doctor's evaluation of Siegel confirmed he had been sick with colitis and gastritis that rightfully required special medication and diet. While an inmate, Siegel had dropped 18 pounds before the treatment began to reverse the weight loss. The new Doctor kept Siegel in the hospital five days after taking over the position before considering him well enough to release back to his cell, indicating his stay in the hospital under Dr. Blank had been proper.

Dr. Blank's violations were minor compared to the standard preferential treatment of the wealthy and influential celebrities and businessmen of Beverly Hills and Hollywood. For example, Doctor Blank's indiscretions pale compared to the more recent 2007 celebrity scandal case in which the LA County Sheriff thumbed his nose at the Judge's sentencing orders by sending home a sobbing Paris Hilton because she cried out for her mommy from her cell. Despite this gross violation of the judicial branch's direct orders, this Sheriff was not punished for breaching the separation of powers.

Since Doctor Blank's favorable treatment of Siegel fit Hollywood's justice norm for the rich and powerful for the last century, it means his ouster might have been motivated by personal interests. Immediately after the Sheriff suspended Doctor Blank pending investigation, he announced a new temporary Jail Physician who just happened to be DA Dockweiler's brother-in-law. This relative had left another position, so it should not be surprising that upon the Sheriff's firing of Doctor Blank, he gave the DA's brother-in-law the permanent position. In fact, of all the officials involved in handling Siegel, only the seriously punished Doctor Blank seems to have made no more than minor transgressions.

The second time Siegel was incarcerated to await trial for the Big Greenie murder, the new County Jailer strictly enforced the rules. For example, guards confiscated $10 cash from Siegel for carrying more than $5 on his person and admonished him to reduce his candy intake to stop eating more than his share. Contrary to the myth authors have created about Siegel's criminal career, this candy-splurging caper is close to the worst charge in his police file that he actually committed.

Two and one half years after being exonerated in the Big Greenie murder, Siegel was again arrested in Hollywood, but this time it was for the non-violent, victimless crime of misdemeanor bookmaking. Ben was accompanied by his New York friend from adolescence, movie-star George Raft, when he visited the luxurious Sunset Towers apartment of his friend Allen Smiley, a self-styled movie producer. The trio was playing gin rummy, when Siegel decided to telephone in some personal $1,000-a-race horse wagers with his bookmaker Jack Richards. At that moment LA Sheriff's Deputies broke down the apartment door. Ben gently protested that the arrest was a bum rap because "until you guys busted in here, I had made five bets and lost four." In comparison a bookie would have had records of reams of wagers in order to make a living. The three men made it clear that the only illegal bookmaking was going on at the other end of the telephone.[521]

When the Deputies burst in, Siegel laid the telephone receiver on the table, and his bookie Jack Richards listened to the following interaction in the room. He told me that as the Deputies arrested all three for bookmaking, Raft panicked and began begging for mercy. In that era the public held movie stars to a high standard of conduct, and film fans, who could become offended by one indiscretion, finished the careers of several scandal-tainted stars by boycotting their movies. Raft knew this arrest had a real possibility of ending his livelihood. Richards said he could tell by Raft's statements that he had pulled out the crucifix he wore around his neck in desperation because "he swore on it that they had not been bookmaking, but only placing some bets of their own. They let him be." The Deputies did not arrest him along with the other two, even though they usually arrested everybody when a location was raided. They may have thought Raft's involvement would hurt their case because the jury might not believe a major Hollywood star would be bookmaking on the side.

By the time reporters caught up with Raft, he had regained his composure and played his tough-guy movie-character image with reporters by falsely claiming that he had asked Deputies to take him to jail with his friends. Executives at Raft's studio strongly admonished him to protect his career by being unavailable to testify a month later, when Siegel and Smiley were arraigned in court, but Raft instead put friendship ahead of his career by presenting a strong defense of Ben at the public hearing. Raft testified that personal horse-race wagering had occurred during the gin-rummy game at the apartment, and he admitted that a racing form and scratch sheet are "part of my standard equipment" as a player. Raft pointed out to the Prosecutor that he had found a scratch sheet at his home "when you came to question me about this. ... I've always played the horses, and I probably always will. ... The bookmaking charges against Ben are the most ridiculous thing I ever heard of."[522]

Raft told one untruth by testifying Ben made the horserace telephone call to Nevada, the only state where off-track betting was legal. Ben had established a major legal horserace betting operation in the tiny town of Las Vegas, but betting against himself would have been pointless, so Ben was placing bets in Los Angeles with independent bookie Richards, who was breaking that state's law. Ironically, Raft's well-publicized appearance for his pal Siegel improved his box office appeal because the public now thought they were watching a real-life gangster on the screen.

The defense attorney demanded a Deputy Sheriff produce a seven-page list he confiscated from Smiley's apartment containing the names and telephone numbers of bookies, not players. The Deputy Sheriff was also forced to admit that all the confiscated wagering slips from the apartment contained only notations of wins and losses, rather than the complete records that bookies maintain to identify the bettors in code.

Despite all this defense evidence, the Judge upgraded the crime to a felony and bound the pair over for trial. However, the prosecutor had practically no case. He offered Siegel and Smiley a $250-fine recommendation for a guilty bookmaking plea, which they accepted in lieu of facing a long sentence if convicted. It was Siegel's only felony conviction, which his FBI file says, "is a source of constant irritation to him." Associates said Ben was deeply bothered by his guilty plea because he was innocent. The stoic attitude of Siegel and his associates about prison sentences was, "You do the crime, you pay the time," but Ben objected to a conviction for a bum rap. His personal horserace wagers were legal.[523]

SIEGEL'S LOS ANGELES BUSINESS INTERESTS

Siegel invited crime leaders from New York City, Cleveland, and Chicago to join him in opening up illegal gambling in Los Angeles, but the Chicago gang had dramatically different values from the other two gangs. The Chicago gang, and its Los Angeles gang subsidiary under Jack Dragna, would participate in any type of crime that had the potential to show a profit, no matter how exploitive or heinous, and both gangs were murderous. In contrast, Siegel's associates and Moe Dalitz were involved solely with the crimes of gambling as well as liquor until the repeal of Prohibition, and they only used violence in self-defense.

The Chicago gang never made major inroads in Southern California crime because Dragna, the leader of the Mickey Mouse Mafia, had traditional Sicilian values of remaining isolated from other nationalities, and he lacked criminal ambition. Instead he focused on his small legitimate businesses. The police also stymied the gang. Despite the lily white, professional image of Detective Joe Friday in the 1950s' television series *Dragnet,* the LAPD was notoriously corrupt in the 1930s and 1940s, and many fictional Hollywood movies were made about the criminal propensities of this detective force. Siegel's advance man to Los Angeles, bookie Jack Richards, explained to me, "The LAPD offered all the same services as the Mafia, even a murder-for-hire unit. They weren't about to share their monopoly with outsiders."

Moe Dalitz sent Mickey Cohen to Los Angeles strictly to open up a chain of bookmaking parlors. Siegel wanted to open casinos and planned to expand the national horserace wire service throughout the growing Southwest. Jimmy Blue Eyes told me, "Ben came to Southern California to take over the racing news."

The national horserace wire was owned by Moses Annenberg. He started his career by handling the circulation wars in several cities for William Randolph Hearst's newspaper empire. Competing newspapers hired goons to violently take over prime sales locations and protect them from the other papers' thugs. Annenberg went on to build a large and influential newspaper chain and also the national horserace wire. It provided two critical services to bookies - historical performance information about each horse to help bettors trying to select which of the ponies to wager, and instant results at the starting bell, at each furlong (quarter mile), and at the completion of each race to protect bookies from mistakenly paying off on a loser.

Bookies stopped accepting bets at the starting bell to avoid being *past-posted,* a prevalent form of cheating by dishonest bettors. Bookies who did not use the wire service were subject to serious past-posting. A thief would have an accomplice at the track relay a race's result to a phone in a building or store near a bookie, so the thief could run in and make a large wager on a horse that had already won with a bookie who was unaware the race had not only started but had finished.[524]

A year after Siegel moved to Los Angeles, Moses Annenberg, whose *Nationwide News Service* was based in Chicago, cut a deal to give Capone's former gang 10% of the Los Angeles distributorship. It is possible that the gang muscled its way in, but the limited size of this interest in one city makes it much more likely that it was payback for something illegal the gang did on behalf of Annenberg. He told the owner of his LA distributorship, Gene Normile, who was the former manager of Boxing Champion Jack Dempsey, to give 10% of his revenue to gang member John Rosselli. Normile complained that he could not afford that size payout, but Annenberg told him to pay, "even if you have to take if off the top," meaning out of the fee Normile paid for the service from Annenberg. Rosselli claimed he got the 10% share as payment for his job of getting more illegal bookies to buy the service, but he said he was more concerned about talking them into not stealing the service by tapping into the phone wires. He testified to Kefauver that he persuaded bookies to stop tapping merely by talking to them, but admitted his reputation as a tough guy may have helped.[525]

Rosselli invested with Normile when he took control of the Agua Caliente Race Track outside Tijuana, Mexico, by paying off a labor lien against the Track. Normile ran successful meets for two years, but labor trouble caused Mexico to take the track away from Normile. During Rosselli's life, he became a partner in a number of legitimate, existing operations, but nothing became public about how these deals came about. These interests were probably for doing illegal favors for the owners.[526]

When Annenberg's *Nationwide News* was forced out of business by the combined action of the federal and Illinois governments, his manager, James Ragen, opened *Continental Press* to continue supplying the bookies of the U.S., Canada, and Cuba. At that time Ragen turned the Los Angeles distributorship over to his son-in-law Russell Brophy. Rosselli worked a few months for Brophy as a consultant, but when Brophy was severally beaten, Rosselli backed away from the wire service business.

Siegel clearly thought he could cut a deal to become a partner in the Los Angeles distributorship, but neither Normile nor Brophy would let him participate. Before Siegel moved to town, he sent bookmaker Jack Richards to Los Angeles to convince the illegal bookies that they should take this valuable service, but neither racing-news operator was interested in his ability to increase their business.

Siegel was more successful in Phoenix, Arizona. He became a partner with Gus Greenbaum, who was one of the nation's big commission bookmakers, meaning he took the risk on excessively large wagers on specific horses from bookies. Siegel also became a partner in the Phoenix wire-service distributorship owned by Tony Corica, and Greenbaum helped sell their service to many of the bookies whose excess action he took.

Greenbaum liked to bet the ponies, but he could not place large bets with Phoenix bookies because he was their layoff bookie. Thus, he placed his wagers by phone with Jack Richards in LA, or in whatever city he resided in at the time. It was betting from Greenbaum to Richards that was going on when Siegel was arrested in Smiley's apartment. Smiley had two telephones - a house phone connected through the apartment building's operator and a private direct line. Greenbaum called in his horse wagers on the house phone to Siegel, and Siegel repeated them on the private phone to Richards, who booked them. Siegel later paid off losses to Richards, or else Siegel collected winnings for Greenbaum. Overall, Greenbaum was a big winner. Richards said, "I believe Gus was the greatest horse player of all time, even though he bet a lot of *smart money,*" meaning on favorites. He clearly knew quality competitors when he observed their musculature and their spirited heart.

Fixed races were rare. If a horse was paying even money, the fixers might arrange to have another favorite pulled to increase the size of the winning payoffs. Richards, other bookies, and serious horse bettors I have known who took advantage of allegedly fixed or sure bets typically ended up with bad results. Richards admitted being involved in five fixed races during his career. "Something always went wrong. I lost on all of them. In one, a 14-year-old beat the favorite."

Siegel told people that most of his income came from big-money gambling on horses, baseball and football games, and an occasional election. When Santa Anita was racing, he placed large wagers on the horses every day at the track, and on the other tracks' races on the other days he phoned them in. But Ben's bookie Richards said he lost more than he won. The press referred to Siegel as a *sportsman* because it failed to uncover how he financed his high-end, celebrity-filled, fantasy-like lifestyle. No documents exist concerning Siegel's business interests during his Hollywood years, and he was as tight-lipped about his activities as any Prohibition gang leader.

Unidentified FBI informants and some crime writers have speculated that Siegel had 5% to 15% of various well-known illegal casino operations in the Los Angeles area, but none of these people had factual information about his activities. As one FBI summary reasonably concluded, "The informant said that Siegel actually has nothing in California that 'you can put your finger on.' Although he is the recognized leader on the West Coast of all activities of New York, Chicago, Detroit, and other major cities' gang activities, they do not control gambling in the Los Angeles area. Siegel liked California and has made it his home there for several years for that reason. He does not want to become too involved in illegal activities in California because he is attempting to enjoy a 'good' reputation there." Even Hoover's FBI recognized Siegel's bad-guy reputation was way overblown.

When LA DA Fitts investigated Siegel's Los Angeles activities in preparation for the Big Greenie murder trial, he only found that Siegel had invested as a silent partner in some illegal casinos and an offshore gambling boat. Chief Deputy DA Williams said, "Siegel told me that he began to get into the money as a bootlegger many years ago and made most of his money in various gambling ventures in the East."[527]

Siegel did have a small interest for a time in the *S.S. Rex* gambling ship that operated outside of territorial waters along the Long Beach coast. It was owned by Tony Cornero, who would later build the *Stardust* on the Las Vegas Strip. Cornero owed Siegel $50,000 for some reason, and he paid him with a 5% interest in the ship. Siegel decided he was not getting a proper cut of the cash count, and he wanted Cornero to buy out his share. Cornero refused, and Siegel started pressuring him. Siegel was supplying the race wire service to the boat through his Phoenix distributorship. The *S.S. Rex* race book was doing a terrific business, so Siegel raised the monthly service fee from $500 to $5,000. Cornero countered by canceling the service. Then he ran an underwater cable along the ocean floor three miles from the ship to shore, where he continued running the cable under the sandy beach and over telephone poles to the nearest bookie parlor, where he surreptitiously tapped into its phone line.

The conflict was resolved by three owners of the *Colony Club* casino, who bought out Siegel's interest. The *Colony* was a hot spot far out of the city on a county road that was the forerunner of what would later become known as the Sunset Strip. Two of the three purchasers - Farmer Page and Guy McAfee – would go on to build the two most popular downtown Las Vegas casinos, the *Pioneer* and the *Golden Nugget,* respectively. This was before Siegel would build the *Flamingo Hotel-Casino*. McAfee was a partner in both the *Colony* and the *S.S. Rex* while he was still a top LAPD Vice Squad official. Eddie Neallis was the third man who bought Siegel's interest in the *S.S. Rex,* and many years after Siegel's murder, he would build the *Aladdin* on the Las Vegas Strip.[528]

Siegel may have been a minor partner in other Los Angeles area casinos. He was highly respected by the criminal element, and he had an extensive political network through his nightly society functions. While he clearly had strong political connections, they obviously were not with those who controlled the approvals for illegal casinos in either the city or county. One FBI report quoted a redacted informant, who said that an unidentified representative of Siegel approached an unidentified official of the "Los Angeles [County] Sheriff's Office with a proposition to afford Siegel protection in the County for operating gambling. This deal was declined [redacted]. Siegel has allegedly had a difficult time obtaining police protection in this area because the local authorities were apprehensive of an infiltration of Eastern gangsters and hoodlums." Siegel's attempted bribery shows his interest in having casino operations. Just like Siegel, Rosselli was never able to get on the inside with the city's main gambling and political bosses despite attempting to join the main gang on several occasions.[529]

When Luciano's associates spread out across the country, each did everything as an individual, even if many invested in each other's enterprises. Jimmy Blue Eyes told me, "By the time Ben came to California, he was mostly on his own. He wasn't in with Meyer in the *Plantation* in Hallandale. Ben had little contact with Meyer by then."

During the years Siegel lived in Hollywood, his most profitable business interest was importing Scotch, but this time it was lawful. During World War II fine liquor was again in short supply. The U.S. entered the War only eight years after Prohibition ended, and the nation's alcohol manufacturers had not yet developed a large stock of quality, aged liquor. The primary source was from England, but shipments from there were threatened by German U-boats, and every other Western European country was under German control. American liquor wholesalers sold a case of Scotch for $50 to $60, but the right to buy each case included the purchase of several cases of U.S.-made junk booze, meaning cheap gin, vodka, and rum that bars serving high-end drinks did not offer. Siegel offered any brand desired in any quantity, without cheap-quality side transactions. He also had next-day delivery, but he charged $120 or more per case. Even at this much higher price, his was a better deal. None of his social or illegal gambling associates ever had any idea who provided him with this plentiful supply, but Ben returned home from a two-month European vacation a month before WWII broke out on that continent. It is likely he established his fine Scotch importing business with his gang's former English Prohibition suppliers while he visited there.

Siegel was always so secretive about his liquor activities, that even during Prohibition the press and FBI failed to notice his illicit activities. Thus, only one innovation he contributed to his Prohibition smuggling partnership ever came to light. All the garbage collected in New York City was loaded onto barges and dumped out in the ocean. Siegel bribed these barge crews. After each crew dumped its load of trash, they went to a spot in the ocean that was not known as a rum-smuggling path, so it was ignored by the Coast Guard, Navy, and liquor pirates. In the meantime, Siegel's high-speed boats were loading up at freighter ships beyond the territorial limit, and then they raced to the same compass reading as the empty garbage barges. There the liquid cargos were transferred from the speed boats to the slow-moving barges for delivery to the city's sanitation pier. From there, the gang's trucks convoyed them into their Manhattan warehouses. Law enforcement never considered the smelly, filthy, unsanitary rubbish barges and docks as potential smuggling conduits for the world's most expensive and finest beverages.

Siegel was a man of leisure in LA. He had employees manage his horserace wire-service and his premier Scotch importing during World War II, and he was a silent investor in a few casinos. This allowed him to take long sea-voyage vacations. He could not have risked being incommunicado for months at a time if he were operating his own illicit businesses. While he was away he could not have protected his interests from a coup by lieutenants or a takeover by other gangs, cut the necessary deals for protection from law enforcers, arranged to protect arrested employees, or negotiated to keep them from turning state's witness against him.

Siegel took one three-month sea expedition to search for buried treasure on the uninhabited Cocos Island 300 miles southwest of Costa Rica. He sailed a year before World War II broke out in Europe, and it turned into quite an adventure. Accompanying him were two dozen social-registry passengers and a crew of long-term inner-city buddies. He and his Hollywood socialite friend, Countess Dorothy di Frasso, financed the trip, but typical of Siegel's legitimate business deals, he had the terms negotiated and signed by a friend, Marino Bello. He was the stepfather of actress Jean Harlow, who was Siegel's close friend and godmother to one of his two daughters. Bello chartered the 200-foot, three-masted schooner, Metha Nelson, with the cover story it was for shark fishing in the warm waters off the Guadalupe Islands and Central America to research and market medicinal oil.

An English passenger later revealed why they went on the treasure hunt. "It is true, we were all intrigued by the gold hunt. It seems that a Canadian chap along [on the trip], Bill Bowbeer, knew a lot about a solid gold statue of the Madonna worth some fabulous sum such as $300 million. It was supposed to be encrusted with diamonds and rubies and rare stones and had been smuggled from Lima, Peru, by some priests and nuns. A Captain Thompson learned of the Madonna and reportedly murdered the religious people, stole the treasure, and then hid it on Cocos Island. Bowbeer claimed to have information about where it was hidden. We did a terrible lot of digging on the hot island and gleaned only a needed bit of exercise."[530]

The adventurers eventually tired of digging up the island only to unearth shovels left behind by earlier treasure expeditions. On their return voyage, Schooner Captain R. B. Hoffman bounced two of the crewmen in San Jose, Guatemala over an argument. The pair boarded the Italian passenger ship Cellina to return home, and Hoffman wired its Captain to have the pair arrested for mutiny. The Captain of the Cellina put the two fugitive mutineers in irons, and wired the FBI, who arrested the pair upon docking in San Pedro, California. The two Jewish crewmen denied the charges and countered they were victims of Captain Hoffman's anti-Semitic persecution. They claimed he made their life so unbearable aboard the Metha Nelson that they had to jump ship. Two days later Captain Hoffman sent a wire from Acapulco emphatically denying he had brought mutiny charges against the pair, probably because of the unfavorable publicity he received from the crewmen in the press, but the FBI, which possessed the Captain's original wire to the Cellina, continued its investigation.

The press reveled in the dramatically developing story about mutiny on the high seas, and the initial accusations placing racism or religious intolerance at the heart of the conflict between the German Captain and Siegel's Jewish cohorts. This saga seemed like a prelude to World War II that Nazi Germany would launch eight months later along with its gas-chamber concentration camps. However, a much different picture of their conflict soon emerged, as every one aboard related their experiences to the FBI, a Federal Grand Jury, and the press. These explanations sounded more like an epic clash of incompatible work ethics between two divergent cultures and generations. The Captain was a German martinet, who expected strict obedience from his subordinates, while Siegel's crew were U.S. street-punks, who considered it an obligation to defy and challenge all authority. What a volatile mix of extremes this was.

The Captain, crew, and passengers on board viewed this clash from very different vantage points. The Captain apparently realized that *mutiny* was too strong a term to apply to the misfit crew he had inherited, but he told the Grand Jury he found himself in command of a *hell ship* manned by rebellious, strong-willed men who flouted his authority at every opportunity. He complained the crew frequently brandished pistols, behaved more like gangsters than sailors, shirked their duties, and refused to obey orders. The Captain had to bail some out of Mexican jails, fight others, and use an iron fist to keep the ship running, including putting more than one man in chains. It was clear this group of armed thugs joined the cruise to have fun, and they had drinking bouts off and on the ship.

While the Captain viewed the crew as mutinous, Siegel and the crew interpreted his extremely brutal and punitive measures to maintain a semblance of discipline, such as chaining deck hands to stanchions for a week at a time, as hateful and assumed it to be racial and religious prejudice. The real problem was neither side had the slightest grasp of the other's culture or values.

Siegel tried to mediate the conflict between the Captain and his gangster crew, but he only succeeded in aggravating it. Siegel objected to Hoffman's brusque, dictatorial, almost demeaning attitude towards subordinates because Siegel was an outstanding leader. The employees of Siegel's various businesses were dedicated to him because of their admiration. He set high standards, but he lavished appreciation, which inspired them to want to please him. He was the master of dangling the carrot, but he made it clear the stick was available if necessary. Siegel and the Captain were at opposite extremes of people-handling skills, and they could not bridge their differences with any type of compromise. Therefore, Siegel chose to act as a buffer every time the skipper tried to knock some discipline into the men to keep the schooner running up to his usual standards. However, this only inflamed the conflict by undermining his authority and violating a primary law of the sea - a captain has absolute command on a ship.

In contrast to the Captain and the crew, the socialite passengers said they had a great adventure, and were unaware of any conflict. Siegel had invited along wealthy friends who originated from several countries and nationalities. The English passenger summed up what the others had to say by telling reporters, "Sure, sure old man, there was a bit of bickering here and there. A bit of Scotch and soda was had by all, but really there was no mutiny. A lot of balderdash, I calls it. We really had a ripping cruise. The moonlight in the South Seas was terribly romantic."[531]

The Grand Jury no-billed the mutiny case against the two crewmen, but the FBI continued its investigation in the belief Siegel's motive for the cruise was to harbor fugitive New York City labor racketeer Lepke Buchalter on the island and supply him money, food, and liquor. This incorrect impression resulted from Brooklyn gangster Abe Reles' false Federal Grand Jury testimony about Siegel and Lepke being involved in the non-existent Murder, Inc. During the entire schooner trip, Lepke was hiding in an apartment near a Brooklyn police station.

The Federal Bureau of Narcotics (FBN) and U.S. Customs Service suspected Siegel was planning to use the voyage to smuggle a cargo of contraband goods, such as drugs, furs, or jewels into Los Angeles. These authorities later told the press that this was definitely proven false, but not until Customs agents obtained a search warrant in secret and did an unannounced search of Siegel's home. They were trying to find smuggled perfume, but they apologized to Siegel as they left, "We acted on bad information." His file was closed with a "no evidence" notation.[532]

On the return home, as the nightmarish conflict between the Captain and crew reached its zenith, an unrelated disaster afflicted this ill-fated voyage. The adventurers were struck by a hellacious 72-mile-an-hour gale in the Bay of Tchuantepec off Acapulco, Mexico. This fierce storm split the main mast, shredded all the sails, and broke the crankshaft of the auxiliary diesel engine that was used when the wind was insufficient to sail the ship. As the terrifying storm subsided, every one aboard felt great relief over having survived it. But this was short lived because they realized they were helplessly adrift alone in the ocean, with no means of communication. Every one aboard stood on deck scanning the horizon in every direction desperately hoping to sight another ship. A whole day passed. That night no lights were seen in the distance. Then another day passed. Finally at nightfall, they sighted the lights of the Cellina in the distance and sent up flares. The Cellina shifted from her course to reach the disabled Metha Nelson, floundering helplessly in a rough sea. The Cellina towed the schooner to Acapulco for repair.

Siegel and his friends, the Countess Dorothy di Frasso and County Jail Physician Blank, jumped ship in Ensenada because it was faster to drive back to LA than ride on the schooner's repaired auxiliary engine without having any sails. More than three years after this expedition, Dr. Blank was fired as Jail Physician for minor favors to inmate Siegel. It is likely the temporary $32,000 loan from the Doctor was to provide Ben quick financing for this misadventure to achieve untold riches.

HOLLYWOOD'S HOODLUM SOCIALITES

Ben Siegel was handsome with black hair and dark eyes. His vanity made him fastidious about his appearance, and hyperconscious about any skin blemish. He had a pathological fear of losing his hair, which started thinning before he was 40. He frequently combed his hair in public to fluff it up.

Siegel worked out daily at an athletic club. His Las Vegas attorney Lou Wiener told me, "His stomach was flat as a table top. He was in some kind of shape." Professional boxer Jackie Fields occasionally put on boxing gloves with Siegel, and when Jackie was later a Strip casino host he reminisced with me, "Ben threw a hard punch and was a good street fighter." Ben was also good at handball, which he played daily. He finished his workouts in the steam room.[533]

Ben was personable and friendly. People described him as a classy or refined gentleman, and he was the epitome of propriety because he had mastered all the social graces. He never got out of line in public. Every one who dealt with him regularly was impressed with how easily he associated with people from every level of society. He moved seamlessly from one social group to another. In addition to being polite, he was generous to charities and a big tipper, so he was well liked by those who dealt with him. The *Los Angeles Times* reported that "Siegel was long one of Hollywood's best spenders in nightclub and gambling circles."[534]

Jimmy Blue Eyes said, "Ben was real bashful in his 20s. The guys used to say, 'He couldn't get laid in a whorehouse.' When he went to California, he lived a different life. He was a glamorous, debonair hoodlum, and the Hollywood starlets were fascinated by him. The interest from these beautiful women changed him" into the charming man and flirt who people in Los Angeles and Las Vegas encountered.

The captivating Siegel acquired four sponsors in Hollywood society. These two men and two women traveled in different social sets, so they collectively gave him a broad circle of acquaintances in that culture. The first was actor George Raft, who had become friends with Ben when they were teenagers in New York City. Raft said in press interviews that he was crazy about a lot of men who were labeled gangsters, especially the Young Turks like Siegel, Adonis, Costello, and Willie Moretti. Raft admitted that he studied their little mannerisms and gestures and then incorporated them into his film gangster characters.

Since these four hoods were always gentlemanly in their dealings, it means Raft's tough-guy acting style was based mostly on New York beer baron Owney Madden, who believed his press clippings and acted like the thug he was said to be. Mickey Cohen wrote in his autobiography, "George Raft is a real fine decent guy, the kind you couldn't help liking. … I think George prefers to be around people of the racket world. His idol was Owney Madden, who was a tough little Irishman with the guts of Carranza. He never backed down from nothing."

Entertainer Dean Martin was a close friend of actor George Raft and gangster Johnny Rosselli. Dino said in press interviews that he grew up doting on Raft's movie acting, and when he became a star, Dino was a regular at Raft's Coldwater Canyon home. Raft always had beautiful nude women hanging around his pool. He began these afternoon pool parties many years before the appearance of publications and movies containing nudity, so he enjoyed a novel lifestyle for that era.

Dino said to another author, "Shortly after I first arrived in Hollywood, I had a chance to go to George Raft's house. As a kid, I guess I'd seen every picture he ever made, and to me he was a super-star. I was awed by his place in Coldwater Canyon. It was like the temple of a brothel. The most gorgeous women in town would be there. It wasn't just sex. They would swim nude in the pool or we would sit around and talk. George would lounge all day in his silk robe at poolside. He never swam. In fact, the only exercise he ever had was with broads or shuffling a deck of cards."[535]

Raft and Siegel frequently palled around Hollywood together. Raft liked to act like he was one of the boys, but in the underworld, he was a hanger-on. He socialized with the gangsters, but he was segregated from their criminal discussions and activities. This made him a pretender in real life, just like in his acting roles. He tried to play the part of a hood when he was with them, but he lacked the stomach for their big-time horse wagering. He was just a $5 bettor. His card game of choice was bridge, not poker, and he belonged to a bridge club because he was a competitor rather than a gambler.

Siegel and Raft bet at Santa Anita Racetrack by day and escorted starlets to the nightclubs by night. Raft bought a small rooting interest in Siegel's *Flamingo Hotel-Casino* on the Las Vegas Strip, and later in his career, he worked as a host to big players in Lansky's high-end casinos.

Ben's second Hollywood social sponsor was mobster Johnny Rosselli. He became part of that Hollywood scene a number of years before Siegel arrived. Rosselli was a member of the Friars Club and an exclusive country club, but Ben was not permitted at the golf club because he was Jewish. Siegel also had a societal shortcoming - a lower-class New York City accent.

Many of the studio heads loved gambling and were enamored with gangsters. They also employed Rosselli to protect them from union picket violence. He socialized with the movie moguls, and he introduced Ben to them and the stars at the most exclusive restaurants and popular nightclubs in the evening, the Santa Anita and Hollywood Park Racetracks in the afternoon, and Tijuana's Agua Caliente racetrack casino on the weekends. The acceptance of hoodlums Siegel and Rosselli in private clubs and the social circles of important Beverly Hills businessmen and film celebrities was condemned by the California Governor's Commission on Organized Crime Report, which said "A revival of decent social and business ostracism for professional criminals in California undoubtedly would help to discourage them from coming to our State and from remaining here."[536]

Siegel and Rosselli dressed casually, but they were the two sportiest and flashiest dressers of their era. Rosselli was more suave, but Siegel had more underworld power. He was the mediator for the New York City, Chicago, and Cleveland gangs in Southern California and later in Las Vegas, while Rosselli was the Chicago gang's representative in both locales. Siegel was the epitome of Charlie Luciano's avoidance of violence and exploitation, while Rosselli was the quintessential hit man and dangerous gangster.

Rosselli and Siegel were appealing to women, but both turned to putty around them. People who were associated with both hoods said, "They made fools of themselves fawning over beautiful women."

Ben's third Hollywood social sponsor was socialite Countess Dorothy di Frasso. Her father was an American multimillionaire leather-goods manufacturer, and her second husband was the distinguished but broke Italian nobleman, Count Carlos di Frasso. The couple used her fortune to purchase the palatial Villa Nadama in Rome, which they turned into a gathering place for European celebrities. She later divorced him, sold the mansion to Italian dictator Benito Mussolini, and moved to Hollywood. She became the town's most lavish party giver during the 1920s and 1930s.

Countess Dorothy di Frasso was a regular item in the social columns, and her greatest publicity came "when she introduced Siegel into the swankiest circles of movieland society," according to author Jennings. Ben and the Countess were close friends, and he was her escort at the best social functions and at star-studded movie premiers. Ben had several close women friends during his life, so her being 18 years older was not relevant to their friendship.

When every one at an event was an entertainment celebrity, the dashing, daring hoodlum commanded the ultimate status, a unique celebrity among celebrities. A society columnist summed it up, "He tossed lavish dinner parties and because entertaining gangsters was a kick for the jaded Beverly Hills set, he was a frequent guest at other people's dinner parties." "The woman responsible for Bugsy Siegel's manners (and he did have beautiful manners) was the late Countess Dorothy di Frasso. She was his good friend for years." "When he made the crossing to Europe on luxury liners, he was always invited to sit at the same tables with members of the (World) Social Register." Despite his impeccable social graces, his lofty standing in societal circles was threatened by the Big Greenie murder charge because of the newspapers' description of him as a dangerous hoodlum. But this only seemed to make Ben more of a prized social catch and more appealing to single women.[537]

Ironically, it was Ben's friendship with the Countess and her social celebrity that brought him to the attention of J. Edgar Hoover's FBI. It was a bureaucracy far more concerned with what the rich, famous, and powerful were up to than the underworld. Until Ben began escorting her several years after the repeal of Prohibition, FBI files reveal the agency had remained unaware of his existence and criminal career. He had rarely been in the press and was publicly low profile until then.

Just five months after Ben and the Countess returned from their long treasure-hunting voyage in the South Pacific, they sailed for a two-month European vacation. The Countess told intimates that she and Ben visited her former husband in Italy less than three months before Germany set off World War II by invading Poland. Mussolini was hosting two of Hitler's top officials - Minister of Propaganda Joseph Goebbels and Air Force General Hermann Goering. Siegel devised a daring plot to dramatically shock Germany's burgeoning military machine. He planned to kill the two Nazi leaders and then, with the Countess in hand, courageously flee between Italy's large German and Italian troop emplacements to safety. Her former husband was not physically able to escape, and he would not have cooperated because he supported the two fascist regimes. The Countess knew that Mussolini would have been humiliated by the murders, and he would have viciously tortured her husband to death. Siegel was determined, but she finally got him to acquiesce for the safety of her former husband. Count di Frasso lived in Italy under Mussolini's rule during WWII, and out of respect for his position, she abandoned the U.S. for the duration, living in Acapulco, Mexico.[538]

When the Countess was questioned about her relationship with her hoodlum companion by author Jennings, she said, "I don't care what others think, but to me Ben is a kind of knight. If he had been living in the time of King Arthur, he would have been a gallant member of the Round Table."

Siegel's name was publicized one other time in relationship to the War. He signed in as a visitor to Great Meadows Prison and met with Charlie Luciano in a private room. New Jersey gambler Willie Moretti accompanied him. While Lansky was Luciano's chief lieutenant in the Navy's World War II counter espionage and Sicilian invasion intel efforts, it was never revealed what, if any, contribution Siegel made. He had been living in Hollywood for the previous decade, and he may have just been saying *hello* to his former Prohibition partner and dear friend.[539]

The Countess succumbed to heart failure at age 66 at the beginning of 1954. She died as she had lived, surrounded by celebrities and wealth. That night she had attended a party thrown in her honor at the *El Rancho Vegas* on the Las Vegas Strip, with actors Clifton Webb, Marlene Dietrich, and Van Johnson among the attendees. Cary Grant drove her to the Union Pacific passenger train to Los Angeles and helped her board for the 3 a.m. departure. She died in her roomette, apparently while asleep on the bed, with her full-length mink coat spread over her and wearing $250,000 in jewels.

She seemed to have led a charmed life. She was born into wealth, married into nobility, and made herself a leading international hostess and favorite darling of most of Hollywood's top-ranking stars and international café society in both the U.S. and Europe. It seemed like she had died at the peak of how she lived, but probate of her estate portrayed a very different picture of her finale. She had sold her Hollywood home, moved into a New York City hotel, and spent all of her possessions and money, except for the beloved jewels and furs she wore on this trip. She would have had to auction them to pay future living expenses. Her estate totaled $22,000 after her jewels were sold at auction for far less than their appraised value and her estate taxes and administrative expenses were paid. Her estate was worth just a portion of her primary $75,000 bequest to her housekeeper and companion. Impending poverty would have destroyed her image in society, and she would have been abandoned by practically all her plastic friends in her chosen superficial culture. The timing of her death was certainly fortuitous to save her from being exposed as no longer belonging in a world in which status and net worth are synonymous. But oddities about the circumstances soon surfaced.

The cause of death was listed as a heart attack because she had suffered from a coronary ailment for the last 10 years, and because she frequently complained during a week of evening parties at Strip resorts of intermittent heart spasms. She made it known to friends that week that she needed to take the nitroglycerin tablets she carried for relief. One night at the *Sands Hotel* Marlene Dietrich helped her in the ladies lounge during a sudden heart spasm. On another night, Tom Douglas, the *El Rancho Vegas* show producer, invited her to be a house guest and rest up in his Las Vegas home. But she replied, "I feel it's an awful imposition to stay at your house. … I think I'm going to die." She complained of another seizure the night of her death, and told friends she decided to call her heart doctor for an appointment and take the train back to Los Angeles to see him.[540]

In studying her final week of activities, her story has a questionable ring. Her burst of heart spasms was unusual, her premonition-of-death statement was odd, and she curiously told her friends she was making an appointment with her heart doctor, when she actually made plans to see her chiropractor. All this talk about her heart ensured no toxicology screen would be run to determine if she had or had not overdosed. Had her heart problems that week been a charade, so the world would never know what her final moments alone in that passenger-car roomette were really like?

Ben's fourth Hollywood social sponsor was Virginia Hill. She was one of 10 children in a poor Alabama family who left home at 16 to become a waitress at Chicago's 1933 World's Fair exhibition. While dating successful Chicago bookmaker Joe Epstein, she met many of the country's top Prohibition hoods. She became a party animal, drinking heavily and whooping it up with her entourage every evening at one nightclub after another.

Virginia moved to New York with aspirations of becoming a Broadway actress. Joe Adonis romanced her for a while, and he took her on a trip to Hollywood, where he introduced her to his old friend actor George Raft. She moved there with the hope of getting into the movies. She partied nightly at the best nightclubs where the stars, producers, and directors hung out.

While the Countess was born to wealth and married into nobility, Virginia came from extreme poverty. No one knew where she got her money, but everyone knew how she spent it. Virginia tossed the most extravagant parties that Hollywood has ever seen. Her nightly galas became legend in café society. Gossip columnist Hedda Hopper told author Jennings, "What I remember about this girl is that she had the swingingest parties in town, and had a purse so full of new hundred dollar bills." She always had new expensive clothes and lots of jewelry, and she gave expensive gifts to friends.

Virginia's functions were regular fodder for the society pages. She could have used her notoriety and Hollywood connections to become a movie star. She either did not realize the potential of her glamorous situation, or she was enjoying her lifestyle too much to consider building a career.

At a time when ladies never swore, and men did not swear in front of women, she had a *foul* mouth. Several underworld figures told me, "She was the first woman I ever heard say the word *Fuck!* And in public yet." Virginia's foul vocabulary could have made truck drivers blush.

Major Riddle (that was his first name, not a title) was a wealthy trucking and oil magnate, who would later own the *Dunes Hotel-Casino* on the Las Vegas Strip. He told me, "I dated Virginia for about a year in Chicago during the early 1930s. She was a very pleasant female. She called me one time in New York years later, and she came over. She was a different girl than I knew. She was very foul mouthed. Every other word was a four letter one. She was as bad as the most vulgar man. I wouldn't have dated her then." He never saw her again.[541]

The FBI recorded Ben and Virginia talking over an illegal bug that agents had planted in his *Last Frontier* suite on the Strip six months before his fabulous *Flamingo* opened. The FBI director was offended by profanity, so the agent who transcribed the conversation warned and prepared Hoover at the beginning of his memo that the pair had an *"OBSCENE CONVERSATION."*

FBI agents reported in their Siegel file, "The following is a description of Virginia Hill, comprised from information received from persons who have known her:" Virginia Hill was born in Bessemer, Alabama August 25, 1917. She was 5' 4", 116 to 130 pounds. She "wears daring clothes, smokes and drinks excessively, uses foul language and considerable makeup, spends money freely. … As caution on Hill's description, attention of Bureau called to fact Hill frequently dyes hair and changes hair style." This was to warn agents that her appearance could change dramatically if they ever had to search for her. Her reputation is "bad, promiscuous."[542]

Virginia met Ben in Hollywood. They could have been introduced by a mutual acquaintance, but they also could have encountered each other in any one of the top nightclubs they both frequented. The introduction would have been easy because both knew many of the filmland society who visited these clubs. Thus began the most famous romance in the history of organized crime.

On the surface, they did not seem like a match because Ben never swore in public. But except for this one unladylike quality, Virginia was very compatible with him socially because she, like Ben, was cordial, a big tipper, and charitable. She gave generously to every charity that approached her, and she picked up the bills of other groups whom she knew at the clubs. Both she and Ben treated the working and service people with respect. Her pleasantness and fast pocket book ingratiated her with Hollywood's nouveau riche.

Ben moved into Virginia's Beverly Hills home. The world knew her as his mistress. A few of the authors about early organized crime said that Ben named his Las Vegas hotel and casino *Flamingo* after the colorful birds, which inhabited the lake at Florida's Hialeah Race Track, but most writers tried to spice up the couple's romance for their fictitious books by claiming that this was Ben's pet name for Virginia. There are two problems with these creative fictions. Ben never called Virginia *Flamingo*, and he had nothing to do with naming the hotel.

Instead, it was Willie Wilkerson, publisher of the *Hollywood Reporter*, who conceived of the proposed hotel, bought the land, and recorded the name *Flamingo* on the original plans he submitted to Clark County before Siegel ever heard of the project or had any involvement with it. Wilkerson had already pioneered Sunset Strip clubs, and he had created distinctive names for his nightclub restaurants, including his three most successful - the *Trocadero, Ciro's,* and the *La Rue.*

Wilkerson was a gambling degenerate and bet big on something almost daily. The high-roller wagered at the illegal casinos in the Los Angeles area, on the off-shore gambling ships floating near the Long Beach coast, and in the Agua Caliente racetrack casino on the Mexican border. He frequently chartered a plane to play in Las Vegas. In addition to casino gambling, he was a regular at Southern California's racetracks, and he was welcome in the private no-limit poker games at the homes of Hollywood's movie-studio leaders. He was a *fish,* which in poker parlance means someone who wagers on a lot of hands, rather than just those few that have a reasonable probability of being the best at the table. Thus, it was easy for proficient players to devour his bankroll. Wilkerson was after action and excitement, and unconcerned with strategy or winning.

At some point, Wilkerson decided it would be better to own a casino than to gamble in them. He bought the land for the *Flamingo* and began building the foundation. However he could not visit his Las Vegas construction site without making a wager, or *lay-down* (which is putting chips or cash down on a table layout's betting areas), at the nearby casinos. He squandered his construction funds at these tables, and his project lay dormant until Siegel got interested in the insolvency-distressed sale price and bought majority interest of the project.

Wilkerson owned and operated some of the finest restaurant/nightclubs in the metropolitan Los Angeles area, but he regularly gambled away his money faster than his popular and profitable nightclubs could rake it in. His places were dutifully frequented by the many Hollywood leaders and stars, but for more reasons than the food and entertainment. Wilkerson may have been morbidly afraid of Bioff and organized crime, but like Bioff's IATSE Union and the Chicago gang, Wilkerson also blackmailed the movie industry. Instead of the threat of strikes, he used his *Hollywood Reporter* reviews and gossip to pressure the Hollywood studio leaders, directors, and stars to frequent his expensive clubs. They visited his clubs regularly to curry favorable comment, and more importantly to fend off derogatory mention in his influential paper. He practiced these extortionist tactics for more than two decades, and every one in the film colony capitulated to his demands rather than risk potential ruin by reporting his extortion to law enforcement. If anyone had exposed him, he would have retaliated with devastating attacks in his powerful publication.

While Wilkerson catered to the wealthy of Hollywood and Beverly Hills, his most valuable customer was Virginia Hill. His clubs were her main hangouts for throwing Hollywood's most expensive parties. She typically spent between $1,000 and $3,000 for an evening at a nightclub, which would equal $13,000 to $40,000 today. The society columnists called her Hollywood's *champion spender.*

Her frequent nightclub parties gave Ben the on-going opportunity to reciprocate with Hollywood society. When he was at peoples' homes, or talking with them at the racetrack, he could invite them to her next nightclub soiree. When he made the nightclub rounds and got into an interesting conversation, or he needed to talk to someone about something weighty, he would say, "Let's go over to Virginia's party. It's a lot grander than this." It always was.

Major Riddle told me that when he dated Virginia as a teenager in Chicago, "I never knew her to work, but she always had money. She never asked me for money, which I always liked." She never worked after her initial World's Fair stint, as she spent each day resting up, and preparing for, that evening's festivities. Thus, the source of her income was puzzling and rift with rumor.[543]

The FBI spent a great deal of time trying to discover where her large cache of money came from, and whether it was from violating laws within its jurisdiction. The FBI assumed she, and possibly Siegel, were in narcotics, but extensive investigation found no connections with either one of them to drug operations. At that time illegal drugs were used only by a small minority of the population, and the pushers remained isolated from other criminal gangs.

Virginia testified to the Kefauver Committee that she won most of her money betting on horses, and men gave her the rest. Senator Charles Tobey asked, "Young lady, what makes you the favorite of the underworld?" She mortified the Bible-quoting politician and stunned the nation by answering, "Because, Senator, I'm the best piece of ass in America!"[544]

Virginia further testified that bookmaker Joe Epstein of Chicago took care of her money and gave her funds as she needed them. Epstein eluded a subpoena issued by the Committee and never testified. She told the truth, but no one understood its significance. Her brother Chick Hill told author Jennings that Epstein put an ordinary shoe box filled with $10,000 in cash on a plane from Chicago to Los Angeles every week. The brother picked it up at the airport and handed it over to her. The offerings began in the depths of the Great Depression, and continued through the 1940s.

That is when $5,000 was a good annual income, and she was spending $10,000 a week on fun, without ever investing any of it.[545]

Epstein kept this up for more than two decades, even though Virginia rarely saw him and was constantly dating other men. He could never break his attachment after meeting her as a sweet, innocent ingénue. Maybe it was undying love, but he never expressed his feelings about her to people he was close to. They thought his support might have become a habit that he may not have been able to explain even to himself.

Writers about early organized crime usually describe Virginia as beautiful, as did some of the people who I interviewed. However, the consensus of most people I asked who knew her was, "She was average looking, with an average body," probably referring to her tendency to plumpness. You can judge by your own taste if you look at photos of her at the Kefauver hearings. She seems to have wrapped her earthy personality, high spirit, and fun-loving style into potent sex appeal.

I interviewed every one who spent much time with Siegel in Las Vegas, but their knowledge of Virginia was superficial because she only got into discussions with close friends. All the interviewees said that when they encountered her she was very pleasant, but she always let them lead the conversation.

Virginia usually accompanied Ben on his Las Vegas visits, but she never went to the site of the *Flamingo Hotel-Casino* while it was under construction. After it opened, she stayed in their suite or at the pool until the sun went down. Then she met Ben at the bar, restaurant, or showroom. She was always in his company, except when he stepped away from their table to talk business privately with someone, or she went to the casino tables to gamble.

The romance of Virginia and Ben was tumultuous. They each had great lust for, dependency on, and jealousy towards the other, but both were very independent personalities. Both wanted to have many friendships with the opposite sex and this raised each other's ire. This is probably what Jimmy Blue Eyes meant, when he told me, "Virginia was an aggravating bitch, but she could be a nice girl at the same time."

Jimmy also said to me, "Virginia was promiscuous." Her social life was high profile, and she was well known for often dating two or more men at the same time. Even when she was involved with one man, she dated on the side as the mood struck her. The former wife of Virginia's brother, Jerri Mason Hill, told author Jennings, "She slept with everybody, I guess. I don't think she missed one." She said Virginia interfered in her marriage and succeeded in breaking it up "because I would not go into gambling, drinking, and carousing and sleeping with other men."

Siegel had the largest yacht on Lake Mead, and he used it to entertain friends and business associates. Mark Swain operated the boat for him. He had been a Navy Seal in World War II, and he would later become Moe Dalitz's chief enforcer, business partner, and resort executive. Even though Swain was a tough man in a rough world, he admitted being intimidated by Virginia's brashness. At social functions, her eyes focused on individual men and she slowly looked them up and down.

Swain was 19 when he started working on the yacht. She would walk around the boat and sunbathe naked in front of Ben's underlings. Virginia would mention Swain's tight-fitting pants and come over and pat him on the butt. He told me, "She made me extremely nervous because she was obviously making eyes. If Ben had ever come around a corner and saw her ... the consequences frightened me." Swain always worked as far away from her as possible. He would see her eyes following him around the boat. He said to me, "She knew she had me treed, and she seemed to enjoy it." Swain did the cooking. She would sneak up quietly behind him and wait until he was lifting two sizzling frying pans off the stove. Then she would slip her hand between his legs and grab hold of his privates. He said, "I was lucky I never tipped boiling grease all over myself."

Ben was as blatant as Virginia. He was always looking for women and he was not discreet. He could be interested in a woman across the room, and every one there was aware that he was focused on her. He was often accompanied by two or more women, even when Virginia was with him. When he entertained local residents on his yacht or at the *Flamingo,* he often also had Virginia, actress Marie "The Body" McDonald, and other single women as guests.

Ben acted like a classic playboy, but every one who knew him said he had great respect for women and treated them as very special. Always the consummate gentleman, he never talked to anyone about a sexual conquest. Thus, no one ever knew which girls were friends and which were lovers. Surprisingly, all his executives, business associates, and male friends in Las Vegas felt that he just liked feminine companionship. The people surrounding Ben were aware of how jealous Virginia was, and they felt she was perceptive enough to have recognized if anything was going on with any of the women with whom the couple socialized. Not one person who knew Ben well in Las Vegas would hazard a guess on whether the other women in his life were romantic interests or platonic friends. His public friendships with women gave no cues about any intimate involvement.

NEVADA'S INVITATION TO A HOOD

A few weeks before the New York City murder of Boss of Bosses Duck Masseria, an unrelated event occurred at the opposite end of the country. Nevada became the only state to legalize casinos. This was of no significance at the time to Luciano and the Young Turks. They kept enjoying their great Prohibition success. It was not until Prohibition was repealed almost three years later that these partners had to replace their lost liquor importing income, and they searched out prospects in gambling. None considered Nevada at that time because every potential tourist market for the city had readily available wide-open illegal casinos, including Los Angeles and Palm Springs.

A decade after Nevada legalized casinos, it became the only state to allow off-track wagering. This law could have been entitled *An Invitation To A Hoodlum* because Siegel immediately moved his horserace-wire distribution and bookmaking headquarters to the small town of Las Vegas just weeks before the first resort opened on what would become the Strip - the *El Rancho Vegas Hotel-Casino.* Siegel sold his wire service to every legally-licensed bookie who opened in town.[546]

Siegel soon bought two existing small downtown casinos, and he studied the potential for tourism. It was limited at that time because Las Vegas had few hotel rooms, only 10,000 residents, and was an unheralded railroad-watering stop between Los Angeles and Salt Lake City, Utah for steam-driven locomotives. Even though the country had numerous illegal wide-open casinos operated by Siegel's associates and many other gamblers, Ben would single-handedly make Las Vegas a nationally-famous gambling center, with his fabulous *Flamingo* resort-casino. He planned an elegant high-end gambling resort like those in Saratoga Springs for affluent Southern Californians and wealthy Northeasterners desiring moderate climate for a winter escape.

Siegel developed a grand vision of a marvelous glowing gambling-resort corridor along the highway leading into Las Vegas from Southern California, and he enthralled some of his and the other Young Turks' close associates with this potential. Jimmy Blue Eyes told me, "After Siegel's murder New York built Las Vegas. They invested their own money, without financing." The Young Turks and their associates would build 80% of the hotels in Las Vegas during the two-decade period between 1946 and 1966, from the *Flamingo* to *Caesars Palace.* This included Prohibition partner Moe Dalitz and his Cleveland gang who would build the *Desert Inn,* the Strip's finest high-rolling resort, and complete the bankrupt *Stardust* project, turning it into the world's largest hotel and biggest casino. The Chicago gang also partnered with some of the Young Turks early on, and two decades later Chicago would become a major force in the Las Vegas casino industry.

The next volume in this historical series will cover the early years of the Nevada casino business and the delightful characters who made their mark in this unique culture. It all began with one man's vision of a great tourist economy, but he had to overcome a difficult political and moral climate to make Nevada the only state with legalized casinos. This was in 1931, early in the Great Depression's national economic collapse. To be successful, the casino operators had to innovate ingenious marketing techniques to attract those who could afford to gamble. Their casinos were jammed with table players, and a cacophony of coin payoffs clanged in the metal slot-machine trays. Then came World War II, and these successful operators were faced with domestic shortages and restrictions that had to be overcome. Finally, the post-war national economic boom swept the country, and a multitude of casinos were built in Las Vegas, Reno, and Lake Tahoe. These busy gambling halls felt like they were out of the wild west, and they exuded friendliness. They were run by many truly colorful operators. This was when the Las Vegas Strip saw its greatest growth of wonderful resorts, with most run by the key mobsters presented in this book. They offered star-studded entertainment headed by Joe E. Lewis, and they drew in their serious players from their closed casinos across the country to keep the action going around the clock. These hoods created the world's greatest adult playground.

This is when Siegel opened his fabulous *Flamingo,* as his blueprint for a ribbon of glittering casinos along a desert highway began to become a reality. The man who murdered Siegel and his motive will be revealed with an already completed cold-case investigation. (Contrary to all the organized-crime books, his partners were clearly not involved!) As a result of Siegel's murder and a nearly successful attempted takeover of the state's government by a criminal gang, a bitter political fight developed over Nevada's future. This resulted in the state establishing control over the operation of the industry, and every casino owner had to undergo a background investigation and be licensed in order to operate. The state asserted its authority late in the 1940s, just as this fantastic, intriguing, and colorful era of these early, staunchly independent, casino operators was winding down.

RELEVANT ISSUES THAT DIGRESS BEYOND THE TEXT

30 ADDENDUMS - A to Z and AA to DD

Some other issues are pertinent, but they digress from or elaborate on the main historical topics addressed in the text. These issues are explored in more depth in 30 Addendums for interested readers and historians. The Table of Contents contains the titles about the issue in each addendum.

ADDENDUM A – Chapter 1 – page 3

THE MORAL CRUSADERS' CAMPAIGNS THAT PRODUCED PROHIBITION

Even though the colony of Georgia's 1733 prohibition experiment failed, colonial moral crusaders determinedly developed local prohibition movements whose goal was the complete eradication of alcohol from the country. These groups' political influence grew over time, and during the four-year period beginning in 1851, they succeeded in having laws passed prohibiting the manufacture and sale of alcoholic spirits in 13 states starting with Maine. (Some of this information is from the state of Maine at Maine.gov and the Maine Almanac in MaineHistory.info.)

A quarter century later in November 1874, the first national prohibition group was created. The Women's Christian Temperance Union (WCTU) was formed in Cleveland, Ohio, by the first prohibition activists to picket bars and saloons and pray for the patrons' souls. They proclaimed that liquor abstinence would eradicate many major social ills. They knew from sad experience what social scientists would validate decades later - a substantial percentage of criminal activity, especially rape, wife beating, and physical and sexual abuse of children occurs under the influence of alcohol, and later it would become a leading cause of automobile accidents and resulting deaths. But while these zealous social reformers were preaching that America could be cured of its ills by wiping out the curse of alcohol, much of the country's population wanted the freedom to drink, creating a long-running political conflict. The WCTU proudly touted its religious basis and idealistic goals, but it was quiet about its racial discrimination which denied membership to immigrant women and even American-born women if they were Catholic, Jewish, or African-American. The WCTU grew, and at the time of World War I, it had 12,000 local affiliates with 350,000 members who were predominantly Protestant and evangelical middle-class women. (Some of this information is from the Women's Christian Temperance Union at WCTU.org, Fordham University at Fordham.edu, Ohio Historical Society's OhioHistoryCentral.org, Ohio's Westerville Public Library at wpl.Lib.Oh.US, Ohio State University at OSU.edu, NewWorldEncyclopedia.org, and *Rumrunners, Moonshiners And Bootleggers* The History Channel 2002.)

Two decades later on December 18, 1895, the National Anti-Saloon League was founded by the local chapters in Oberlin, Ohio and Washington, D.C. Composed primarily of Methodists and joined by other denominations whose churches and congregations financed and supported dry politicians, its motto was "The saloon must go." The two national religious organizations of the League and WCTU combined efforts and developed a potent political lobby. By 1900, more than half the States had gone dry, as had many counties in wet states.

World War I officially broke out in Europe on August 1, 1914, and the U.S. entered on April 6, 1917, to "make the world safe for democracy." With the advent of war, the temperance movement capitalized on the public's aroused patriotic spirit. Four months into the war on August 10, 1917, Congress passed the Food and Fuel Control Act, known as the Lever Act. It gave President Woodrow Wilson authority to create agencies to regulate the distribution, export, import, purchase, and storage of food, making him dictator over the food supply. Wilson proclaimed, "Food will win the war," as he promoted patriotic cooperation that was backed up by the power to coerce. He successfully encouraged the nation's housewives to voluntarily sign pledge cards for wheatless Mondays, meatless Tuesdays, and porkless Saturdays, and for school children to sign, "At the table I'll not leave a scrap of food upon my plate. And I'll not eat between meals." This allowed food exports to soar for the war effort.

Since the administration strived to curtail "non-essential" industries, the Drys campaigned against fermenting beer because most brewers were German-Americans. The Drys portrayed them as subversive by declaring beer to be the product of Kaiser-loving fifth-columnists. At the height of this crusade, the November 21, 1918 *New York Times* screamed a headline - *Enemy Propaganda Backed By Brewers* – because a majority of the U.S. Senators at a Justice Committee hearing, pandering to the temperance crowd, attacked the brewers as disloyal even though the facts showed the positions that the U. S. Brewers Association had taken were legitimate. Two years before entering the war, the Association had opposed supplying munitions to the Allies in order to protect America's official position of neutrality. The brewers also refused to purchase from companies helping finance prohibition groups determined to put them out of business, which was not only their right but a sensible response. Despite having no evidence that the beer industry was disloyal, the Drys' efforts led both the Food, Fuel, and Railroad Administration and the War Industries Board to announce on September 7, 1918, that beer manufacturing must cease on December 1, 1918, until further notice, and Wilson's order followed days later. This action was justified as being a wartime necessity to save grain needed for the troops, but it was not rescinded when the war ended with the armistice on November 11, 1918, three weeks before the beer ban became effective. The government still implemented it under President Wilson's executive order because it was a month before the Prohibition Amendment would be ratified.

Four months after passing the Lever Act, Congress proposed on December 18, 1917 ratification of the 18th Amendment to the U.S. Constitution outlawing "the manufacture, sale, or transportation of intoxicating liquors," based on a draft submitted by the Anti-Saloon League. It was ratified on January 16, 1919, following approval by the 36th state, Nebraska; and the ratification was certified on January 29, 1919. The National Prohibition Enforcement Act, called the Volstead Act, was passed late that year on October 28, 1919, to set penalties for violating the Amendment, and both the Amendment and Act took effect a year later on January 16, 1920. (Some of this information is from the National Archives at Archives.gov and the Maryland State Archives at MSA.Maryland.gov.)

ADDENDUM B – Chapter 1 – page 5

PRESIDENT WARREN HARDING TOTALLY CORRUPTED
PROHIBITION ENFORCEMENT EARLY ON

Democratic President Woodrow Wilson helped shepherd in Prohibition after achieving victory in World War I. A year after this ban on alcohol began, Wilson was succeeded as President by

Republican Warren Harding in 1921, and he appointed Roy Haynes as U.S. Director of Prohibition and Harry Daugherty as U.S. Attorney General (AG). These two men totally undermined Prohibition enforcement. The corrupting influences of the Harding Presidency can be seen in the following cases. Secret Service Special Agent Frank Wilson built a massive Prohibition fraud case against Pennsylvania Federal Prohibition Director Bill McConnell. As Agent Wilson wrote in his memoir, "Over one thousand permits for whiskey for medicinal purposes had been issued to legitimate drug companies in Pennsylvania which did not know their names were used. In this way the corrupt politicians delivered some two million gallons of liquor into the hands of racketeers." U.S. AG Daugherty did not allow Special Agent Wilson's strong case to be presented to a grand jury. This caused Assistant U.S. Attorney Henry Walnut to strenuously object to the AG's dereliction of duty, and the very next day, the AG fired his Assistant. Despite becoming an unemployed private citizen, Walnut remained a dedicated prosecutor, and he continued exposing the AG's malfeasance to the press. Within days of this public exposure, Daugherty ordered the case be placed immediately before the grand jury, which soon indicted 49 defendants. However, Assistant Walnut's replacement delayed the trial, and when it finally began, he sat silent as the defendants' attorney presented a motion to dismiss the charges, causing the judge to toss the case. A reporter polled the jury and all 12 were going to vote guilty. Media outcry forced the U.S. AG to indict Prohibition Director McConnell for the minor charge of misfeasance, but the corrupt AG then allowed that case to die without action. At the beginning of his tenure, AG Daugherty arranged for Harding to pardon the nation's most dangerous incarcerated gangster, Ignazio "Lupo the Wolf" Saietta (in Chapter 2). After leaving office, Daugherty was tried for corruption for his role as AG in the Teapot Dome Scandal that allowed oilmen close to Republican President Harding to steal from the government's huge oilfields in Wyoming. The jury acquitted him of defrauding the U.S. Government he was supposed to represent and the oil was never retrieved.

ADDENDUM C – Chapter 1 – page 6

MOONSHINING FROM EARLY AMERICA THROUGH PROHIBITION

Many 1920s Prohibition violators came from families who had been moonshiners since colonial times in the late 1700s. They turned to this business in response to a series of violent conflicts and taxation laws. The first event was the seven-year war from 1754 to 1763 that the British won against the French and their Native-American tribal allies, who partnered because they feared the large growing English settlements would expand westward and seize their lands. In this conflict's later years, it became the first worldwide war in a fight by major European powers to dominate colonial development. In addition to England and France, it involved Austria, Prussia, and Sweden with fighting in several countries and continents. Britain's great territorial victory gave it possession of all North America east of the Mississippi River, but it drove its government into heavy debt, leading Parliament to impose new taxes on the colonies to help pay for the protection they received. (Some of this information is from the Ohio Historical Society's OhioHistoryCentral.org and from the nonprofit Independence Hall Association's USHistory.org.)

The British and colonial governments had long imposed excise taxes, tariffs, and customs duties on importers and import sellers, who passed these taxes on to consumers by raising product prices. These are called indirect taxes because they go rather unnoticed by consumers, just as today's gasoline excise tax of 48¢ per gallon is unseen by most consumers. (The average U.S. gasoline tax for July 2010 was 47.7¢, with the federal tax at 18.4¢ and the average state tax at 29.3¢, ranging from 8¢ to 49¢, according to the American Petroleum Institute's API.org.) To pay the war debt, Britain imposed its first direct taxes on the colonists in 1765. These required sellers of a few products to list the tax on top of the purchase price so consumers paid it directly, something like today's sales tax. The Tea Act was passed early in 1773. Since this direct tax on tea affected many consumers, it became the symbol of British domination and the battle cry that led to the Revolutionary War. The famous Boston Tea Party was a protest by a group of colonial activists who disguised themselves as Mohawk Indians on the night of December 16, 1773, to board three ships of an English company in the Boston harbor and dump every container of tea into the water.

In reality, the heaviest tax burden for colonists was an indirect one placed on alcohol manufacturers. These taxes were less obvious, but they generated great opposition. Colonists vented their anger by quietly evading payment. Many immigrants brought the expertise to make whiskey from their homeland, and they started selling their cheaper untaxed home mix to neighbors. These stills were small, but so many colonists started commercial operations that avoiding liquor taxes was soon a major industry.

The colonies created the Continental Congress in order to have a combined and unified voice to present their grievances to London about exploitive British regulations and import and export restrictions. However the various colonies held different positions on how to deal with Great Britain, ranging from succession to various forms of greater independence. The First Continental Congress convened nine months after the Boston Tea Party on September 5, 1774; the American Revolution began on April 19, 1775; and the Second Continental Congress approved the Declaration of Independence on July 4, 1776. Eight years into the Revolutionary War, Britain and the U.S. separately declared hostilities at an end early in 1783; the last British troops left the colonies on November 25, 1783; and the Revolutionary War officially ended with the Treaty of Paris on January 14, 1784. (Some of this information is from the U.S. Treasury Department's USTreas.gov, the University of Minnesota Department of Sociology's Soc.UMN.edu, the National Park Service's NPS.gov, and *Taxation in Colonial America* by Alvin Rabushka.)

The U.S. Constitution was ratified on June 21, 1788 and went into effect on March 4, 1789, the day the first U.S. Congress held its initial meeting. George Washington, who had been the Continental Army Commander in Chief during the Revolution, was sworn in as President two months later on April 30, 1789. The colonists had fought the Revolutionary War to eliminate direct taxes, but the new federal government began operation deep in debt from the eight-year military conflict. The U.S. government inherited the cost of the Revolutionary Army from the Continental Congress that had been prohibited from raising taxes, and the federal government also assumed the War debts of the 13 states. To pay this huge obligation, an excise tax was placed on a few products in March 1791, with the heaviest burden again falling on the manufacturers of domestically distilled spirits. Congressmen justified this as a luxury tax and prohibitionists supported it as a tax on sin. Drinkers were infuriated that the War created the very tax problem that it was intended to eliminate, so the moonshine industry continued to boom. Drinkers, moonshiners, and citizens opposed to taxation were defiant to government authority - they wanted a strong army to protect them from colonial nations and Native Indians, but they objected to paying taxes to support the American troops just as they had for the British troops. This made hollow their Revolutionary rallying cry "taxation without representation is tyranny," since they objected just as strenuously to the same type of taxation by their democratically-elected representatives.

The large eastern whiskey distilleries passed this tax on to consumers, but the small farmers on the country's western frontier faced major obstacles trying to comply. The law charged small producers a discriminatorily three-times-higher tax per gallon and made it difficult for frontiersmen to make payment. For example, the farmers in the small frontier settlement of Pittsburgh had to travel by horse to Philadelphia 300 miles away to register their stills, and then after making each batch of hooch, they had to pay the tax in cash. Not only was the traveling difficult, but the farmers had little cash income because the frontier worked primarily on the barter system. These farmers distilled excess grain into alcohol to trade locally for the goods and services they needed. The farmers could not earn cash income by competing against the commercial distillers in the eastern markets because they had to pay a higher tax rate and had the cost of transporting their whiskey great distances through the mountains on poor dirt roads.

Frontier citizens had other major complaints against the distant inattentive federal government. It offered no protection from ongoing Indian attacks. It also failed to assist in having Spain end its blockade of the Mississippi River that prevented U.S. frontier citizens from trading with eastern cities and other countries. Spain controlled the New Orleans territory at the entrance to the mighty river, and President Washington was not able to consummate the Treaty of San Lorenzo with Spain, granting the U.S. unrestricted access to the Mississippi River and removing Spanish troops from American soil, until 1795, months after the mounting Whiskey Rebellion would end.

Many frontiersmen operated small stills, but most ignored the tax. As opposition grew, they held meetings and signed petitions before turning loose the violent individualism found on the wild frontier of the young country. Some moonshiners beat and even tarred and feathered federal revenue officers, and threatened or beat local residents who offered these officers office space or housing. Because this kind of violence occurred in the western counties of half the states, many western counties never had a resident revenue officer.

A year and a half after passage of the law, President George Washington issued a proclamation on September 15, 1792, condemning interference with collecting spirits taxes. But over the next two years, the violent opposition grew, especially in four southwestern Pennsylvania counties that contained a quarter of the nation's stills - the counties of Westmoreland, Allegheny, Fayette, and Washington. In Westmoreland, the situation flared into a vigilante mob riot against U.S. Marshal David Lenox on July 15, 1794. He was traversing western Pennsylvania serving papers on those who had not registered their stills. These papers required the accused to travel to the federal district court in Philadelphia and pay a large fine that many could not afford. A group of armed thugs in Westmoreland County forced the Marshal to flee to Pittsburgh. Their rage then turned against local Revenue Inspector John Neville, who had accompanied the Marshal. That night a mob of 35 armed men marched seven miles to the Inspector's plantation to demand his resignation. Expecting trouble, he and some friends barricaded themselves in his home, and in the ensuing gunfight wounded five of the insurgents. The community was enraged by this bloodshed in what they considered a stand for liberty against their new government. The next day on July 17, 1794, 500 insurgents marched toward the Inspector's plantation; but Neville, who had been a brigadier general under Commander in Chief Washington, prepared to again defend his home against an enemy force. He requested help from the local fort, and a U.S. Army contingent confronted the advancing vigilante mob. In the ensuing battle, the greatly outnumbered soldiers had to surrender and were permitted to retreat back to their fort before the horde burnt Neville's plantation buildings. In the battle with the Army, several men were wounded, and the rebel's leader, Revolutionary War hero Major James McFarland, was killed. Sorrow and rage over McFarland's death, combined with the exhilaration of victory over the U.S. Army, inflamed the community to again take up arms for liberty against perceived oppressive taxation. The following day a U.S. Army Major dispatched a letter dated July 18, 1794 to the White House, describing the mounting insurrection and cautioned about the possibility of another revolution.

A week later, 5,000 armed rebels demonstrated their defiance to taxation of whiskey at Braddock's Field near Pittsburgh. This burgeoning rebellion forced President Washington to issue a proclamation on August 7, 1794 directing the rebels to return home and to order state governors to mobilize 13,000 militiamen and artillery units by invoking the first use of the 1792 Militia Law. This contingent marched against the Whiskey Rebellion, and it was larger than was Washington's Continental Army most of the time during his defeat of the British. In the Revolutionary War, Washington had taken command of 14,500 men in 1775, but this fell to just 11,000 during the winter of 1777 at Valley Forge, when many of his starving and freezing soldiers died because the Continental Congress lacked authority to raise taxes and because the colonial governments failed to adequately feed and clothe their troops. Throughout the Revolutionary War, the total fighting force rarely rose over 20,000 and dropped down to 10,000 in 1780 because of casualties and enlistments being finished. President Washington placed this anti-insurgent militia under the command of Revolutionary War hero General Henry Lee. His son, Robert E. Lee, would later switch loyalty to lead the next armed insurrection against the U.S., the Civil War. (Some of this information is from the Smithsonian Institute's SI.edu, and from PBS.org by the Claremont Institute.)

After a month-long march, this large U.S. militia force neared the rebels' location, and the greatly-outnumbered insurgents fled home to their farms or hid. The Army arrested 150 rebels, but President Washington ended the criminal prosecutions by authorizing pardons on July 10, 1795, both for those who had not yet been tried and for the two who had already been convicted of treason and were scheduled to be executed. The large militia began heading home in mid-November 1794, while leaving a regiment in the area for several months to ensure the rebellion had evaporated. With federal authority restored, the large still operations near cities and towns started paying the tax or were shut down. Many of the mainly Scot and Irish western Pennsylvania farmers were diehard moonshiners or tax haters, so they moved to the rural, unsettled, and back wood areas of Kentucky and other mountain regions of the mid-Atlantic and Southeastern states to ply their illicit trade. This continues to be a major industry today in many pockets of this part of the country.

Although the violence of the Whiskey Rebellion had been limited to districts within certain states, many citizens across the country had objected to the excise tax on distilled spirits producers. They believed the only legitimate federal tax was tariffs imposed on importers of goods into the country. The zeal that had led some men to take up arms was soon directed into political activism. When George Washington decided against running for reelection after serving two terms, his Vice President, John Adams, succeeded him. But six years after the end of the Whiskey Rebellion, Adams' reelection was thwarted by Thomas Jefferson who campaigned against all internal federal taxes. Jefferson entered the White House on March 3, 1801, and in his first year in office, he repealed all federal domestic taxes including the 1791 distilled spirits excise tax. For most of the next half century, the U.S. Government relied solely on import tariffs, which grew quickly with the Nation' expanding foreign trade.

(Some of this information is from the Department of Treasury's Alcohol and Tobacco Tax and Trade Bureau's TTB.gov, the George Mason University Center for History and New Media's WarDepartmentPapers.org, George Washington's papers at the University of Virginia's GWPapers.Virginia.edu, the National Endowment for the Humanities' Edsitement.NEH.gov, and the *History of Washington County from Its First Settlement to the Present Time* by Alfred Creigh.)

The moonshining operations that developed in this early period of the country's history became family affairs and were passed on from father to son. Generations later, some of their offspring managed the Prohibition gangsters' distilleries or taught them their craft. They simply enlarged the size of their recipes because their family stills contained a few hundred to many hundred gallons, while the major Prohibition stills held thousands of gallons.

The colonial and early U.S. periods would establish the forces that would lead to both the creation and the violation of Prohibition in 1920. One group of settlers developed a strong prohibition movement, while another politically pressured the reduction of taxes on distilled spirits, and a third developed the expertise to manufacture moonshine and the ability to outwit federal revenuers to avoid all taxation.

ADDENDUM D – Chapter 1 – page 6

PROHIBITION MOONSHINER CAR RACES LED THE WAY FOR NASCAR

During Prohibition, moonshiners developed the fastest cars on the road. They stripped down cars to carry a load of moonshine from the hills to distribution points and modified the engines so they could outrun the Prohis and police along the route. During the two decades prior to Prohibition, world-record automobile speed trials became important events, and France and Belgium were the top race locations. With the advent of Prohibition, the premier site became the hard packed sand between Daytona and Ormond Beaches in Florida where the southern moonshiners liked to test their stripped-down revved-up cars against the swiftest. These races resulted in one world mark after another falling until speeds approached 300 miles per hour at the end of Prohibition. Motor sport racing stopped during World War II, and two years after the war ended in December 1947, NASCAR (National Association for Stock Car Auto Racing) was created in Daytona Beach by Bill France Sr., who started racing there after the end of Prohibition. Its early races used standard stock sedans that were only modified by tweaking and tuning the engines, and many of the early legendary drivers that built NASCAR were moonshiners. (Some of this information is from NASCAR.com, DecadesOfRacing.net, and the University of Minnesota Department of Sociology's Soc.UMN.edu.)

ADDENDUM E – Chapter 1 – page 6

THE MOONSHINE FERMENTING AND DISTILLING PROCESS

The moonshiner's craft is a fascinating process that is described here for those interested in it or in how closely it relates to baking bread at home. Moonshine alcohol is made from a mash of four ingredients - water, grain, sugar, and yeast. First the grain is ground into a meal and then cooked with water to extract the sugars from the grain's starch. After the mix cools, yeast - a microscopic single-celled fungus – is added to feed on the other nutrients in the grain. As long as the still or vat is open to the air, the yeast breathes oxygen and the thriving colony multiplies. As soon as the still is sealed from air, the yeast can only survive by extracting oxygen atoms from the sugar. To do this, yeast enzymes convert or break down glucose sugar ($C_6H_{12}O_6$) into two carbon dioxide gas (CO_2) molecules and two ethyl alcohol (CH_3CH_2OH) molecules. The yeast excretes both new chemicals, and fermentation ends when the yeast cells die in their own excrement, unless the fermenter intentionally stops the process to achieve a specific lower alcohol percentage.

Beer, wine, and bread are fermented with a species known as baker's yeast, or Saccharomyces cerevisiae. Bread makers use it because the yeast's tiny carbon dioxide bubbles cause the bread to rise and create a light fluffy texture. When the bread is baked, the alcohol molecules evaporate, which is why the dough may fall a bit when cooking. Beer and champagne makers capture the carbon dioxide bubbles along with the alcohol to create their sparkling beverages.

Fermentation produces beer with a maximum alcohol content of about 8%, wine at about 14%, and whiskey at 20% to 21%, although whiskey manufacturers usually stop the process at around 8.5% to achieve the best quality. Hard-liquor fermenters use different strains of the same species of baker's yeast, because they produce a better beverage during distillation. This is the process by which moonshiners increase the alcohol content of the fermented mash by cooking it in a still or boiler.

This distillation process separates the alcohol from the mash because alcohol boils at 173 degrees Fahrenheit, which is 39-degrees below the boiling point of water at 212 degrees, and a still's cooking temperature is kept near the lower point. The vaporizing alcohol is lighter than air, so it escapes through the tube at the top of the still. This tube bends through a pool of cold water to condense the alcohol steam back into a liquid, which drips from the end of the tube into a storage container that is airtight to prevent evaporation. Higher alcohol concentrations are produced through redistillations. After the clear and colorless moonshine is strained to eliminate impurities, it is bottled and ready for immediate consumption.

In contrast to moonshiners, legal whiskey manufacturers employ a more sophisticated distillation process, and they also mellow the harsh raw distilled product by aging it in newly charred oak barrels for years to give it an amber color, a fine aroma, and a tasty smooth flavor. The process of aging whiskey was unintentionally discovered by a Bourbon County, Kentucky farmer who sealed his favorite brew in a toasted barrel in 1789, the year the newly-elected U.S. government was inaugurated.

ADDENDUM F – Chapter 1 – page 12

COSTELLO'S RUMRUNNING OPERATIONS AND
THE GOVERNMENT'S INVESTIGATION AND TRIAL

The prosecution's federal Prohibition cases against Bill Dwyer in July 1926 and Frank Costello in January 1927 were based on the testimony of several of their gang leaders, many boat crew members, and a number of corrupted Coast Guardsmen, all of whom had pled guilty. Some NYPD police officers admitted other cops assisted Costello's rumrunning. Their combined testimonies reveal far more about Costello's operation and corrupting influence than was learned about any other Prohibition gang. Several of the Costello-trial jurors said they did not convict him because of the poor caliber of the prosecution's witnesses and the shocking government "undercover" work, which the defense exposed during the trial to the jury and the public for the first time. The investigation involved the kidnapping of defendants, the denial of their Constitutional right to contact an attorney, and torture to force confessions and their agreement to testify against the other defendants. Public condemnation of these dreadful investigative techniques grew to such a pitch that U.S. Representative Fiorello LaGuardia, who would later run for New York City Mayor on a reform platform, issued a statement on August 2, 1926 claiming that the man responsible, Bruce Bielaski, was not an employee of the government but a paid informant. But LaGuardia's lie was quickly contradicted by top Treasury Department officials who confirmed Bielaski's status - he headed all federal undercover operations, as the personal representative for General Lincoln Andrews, the man in charge of Prohibition enforcement.

Most of Costello's associates who turned state's witness revealed that Bielaski released them on bail, paid them high salaries for many months prior to the trial, and promised to drop the charges against them after they testified. Then during the trial preparation, if one of these witnesses gave an unscripted answer to a prosecution question, Bielaski threatened him with stoppage of income, revocation of bail, and prosecution. At trial, the most appalling testimony about federal official Bielaski's actions was from the Coast Guard crew who let Costello's speedboats whisk by unmolested in the middle of the night. Former Coast Guard Captain Nicholas Brown testified on January 7, 1927 that he had been arrested but freed on bail, until Bielaski's agents kidnapped him and three of his Coast Guard subordinates and carried them aboard the Cutter Seneca. The four kidnappees were confined in irons in the ship's brig for a week of torture, as the ship meandered aimlessly at sea. Brown testified, "The place was like a madhouse. I was almost out of my head. We were shackled with double irons and kept in confinement the whole week. The hatches were battened down, and the air was foul. They fed us rotten meat and gave us rotten water. Sometimes someone would look in to see if we were active. We were not allowed to communicate with our friends." At the end of the week, Bielaski sent a radio message to the cutter asking kidnappee Captain Brown whether he would confess his rumrunning activities and testify against Costello, and Brown said he was in a state in which he readily "came through."

Despite the bribery, intimidation, and torture of potential witnesses by Bielaski, the government was amazingly unsuccessful in its prosecution of Prohibition violators during 1925 and 1926. Of the 94 "higher-ups" indicted across the country, only Dwyer and his associate were convicted even though Bielaski's undercover agents had pressured one or more indicted co-conspirators in every case to plead guilty and enter the government's employment. When the Costello-ring trial ended in January 1927 with no convictions, legal observers generally accepted that it was a severe blow to the government's methods of prosecuting liquor conspiracy cases. Other prosecutors later decided to retry Costello, but the endless delays had caused their case to evaporate, as witnesses had moved without leaving forwarding addresses and the records and evidence had unexplainably disappeared.

ADDENDUM G – Chapter 2 – page 25

U.S. IMMIGRATION PATTERNS DETERMINED
THE ETHNICITY OF PROHIBITION'S GANG LEADERS

America's immigration patterns determined the ethnicities that would be most common among the major Prohibition leaders. These same gang leaders then went on to operate high-end illegal casinos across the country for two decades before building the early Las Vegas Strip. The ethnicities of the various gangs can be understood with the following analysis of the detailed historical figures of the Immigration and Naturalization Service and the Bureau of Census. Europeans from specific countries emigrated to the U.S. for the century-long period beginning in the early 1800s to the early 1900s. New European arrivals were often too poor to move inland more than a few miles from the Manhattan shore entry port at Castle Garden that was transferred to Ellis Island in 1892. These ethnic groups were treated with little respect, so they banded together in their own low-income ethnic residential areas where neighbors shared their cultural and linguistic heritage along with their difficult financial struggle in this new land. Teenagers of some of the newer arrivals created or joined street gangs in their neighborhoods. These immigrant families remained in these neighborhoods unless the father or the sons found higher paying jobs that allowed them to move into better neighborhoods and assimilate into the larger culture. Many of these immigrant families' sons became cops and politicians to police the newest group of immigrants and their wayward boys.

Pervasive changes in the immigration pattern dramatically altered the ethnic balance and culture of New York City every few years. From the 1840s to the 1920s, between one third (34%) and one half (47%) of all residents were foreign-born, and the ratio in the borough of Manhattan was always slightly higher (by 3 to 7 points) than the city as a whole. The first large wave of migration to America began in 1840, and a few European countries supplied most immigrants for the next half-century. Until 1890, the largest source country was Germany, followed in order by Ireland, England, and the Scandinavian nations.

Although large in numbers, the German immigrants had little impact on America's "English" culture because most moved to small Midwest farming communities, where their long work hours kept them from being politically active, and their sons were not exposed to inner-city gang life. The Irish came because of unemployment and starvation resulting from the 1845 potato crop famine, and oppressive British rule and landlords. By 1850 the Irish were by far the largest ethnic group in New York City. Thus, they had the toughest street gangs, but later in the century, this large population group would make up more than half the police department and dominate much of the city's political structure.

Beginning in 1890, the ethnic immigration pattern changed dramatically. Jews from several East European countries became the largest immigrant group. They were escaping from Russia's political abuses, including stifling discriminatory laws and violent government-sanctioned Pogroms, and they also came from Polish, Austrian, and Hungarian Christian-inspired anti-Semitism and religious persecution. With the advent of Italy's 1887 agricultural depression, Italians seeking work became the second largest group of immigrants. They settled in large cities like New York, Chicago, Cleveland, Buffalo, Detroit, and Milwaukee. In these slum communities, the youthful Sicilian immigrants who joined street gangs introduced the Mafia criminal tradition they had grown up with. Thus, New York City's expanding Italian and Jewish ghettos produced many of the top Prohibition gang leaders. Most of the ambitious street-gang leaders at the beginning of Prohibition were born between the late 1890s and the beginning of the 1900s, putting them in their early 20s at the advent of the Roaring 20s when the great profit opportunities from liquor violations opened up.

ADDENDUM H – Chapter 3 – page 30

NYPD'S BEATING OF LUCIANO, AND THE
FRAUDULENT AUTOBIOGRAPHIES ABOUT LUCIANO AND LANSKY

Luciano told his partners that NYPD detectives beat him, and he told the investigating patrolman that he did not recognize his assailants. This did not stop biographies about organized-crime from fabricating that the leader of another New York City Mafia gang, Salvatore Maranzano, ordered Luciano's beating. When I told Jimmy Blue Eyes this, he roared with shocked laughter for a long time because he thought such an idea was so stupid. He said, "Other mobsters wouldn't have beaten him that bad and then let him live for fear of the certain retaliation to follow. They would have murdered him." If Maranzano were that imminent a threat and that dangerously vicious, Luciano's gang would have definitely made sure with a pre-emptive strike that he never had the opportunity to do anything like that to one of them again. This Maranzano-beating fiction was created by two phony "autobiographies," but neither subject of these two books supplied any information about their lives to these or any other authors. The first fraud is *The Last Testament of Lucky Luciano* by Martin A. Gosch and Richard Hammer, which was completely discredited by the press and ensuing authors. This book's fantasy about Maranzano ordering Charlie beaten was repeated in the equally false and ridiculous *Meyer Lansky: Mogul of the Mob* by Dennis Eisenberg, Uri Dan, and Eli Landau. (Many details about these two fraudulent autobiographies are in Addendum L for Chapter 5 about Rothstein, in Addendum M for Chapter 7 about Luciano, in Addendum BB for Chapter 10 about Luciano, and in Addendum DD for Chapter 14 about Lansky.) Other biographies about organized crime, including *Frank Costello: Prime Minister of the Underworld* by his attorney Wolf, said cops beat Luciano because he would not reveal the hiding place of gangster Legs Diamond. Jimmy no longer remembered why his pal was beaten, but he said emphatically it was not about Diamond.

ADDENDUM I – Chapter 3 – page 33

JOE BONANNO'S SELF-SERVING AUTOBIOGRAPHY

Joe "Bananas" Bonanno became head of the Salvatore Maranzano Manhattan/Brooklyn crime gang at the end of the Sicilian-American War. Late in life he wrote *A Man of Honor: The Autobiography of Joseph Bonanno*. It is a self-serving book that ludicrously describes his Mafia organization to be little more than a benign fraternal organization, while falsely denying his gang participated in many serious, exploitive, and vicious crimes. He wrote about the Sicilian-American War from the point of view of the Castellammarese, who he presents as aggrieved, innocent victims. Thus, I only quote from his book concerning those events at which he was personally present and that are also substantiated by reliable sources. I ignored the incidents he described based on information he obtained from other sources because they are fraught with the error typical of second-hand reports. Every quote by and paraphrase of Bonanno in this book comes from his book.

ADDENDUM J – Chapter 5 – page 63

ARNOLD ROTHSTEIN'S CRIMINAL IMAGE WAS A MYTH CREATED BY AUTHORS

Writers about early organized crime have falsely portrayed Rothstein as the mastermind of crime in New York City, but they have associated him primarily with two types of crime. One was financing *bucket shop* brokerages, which specialized in selling securities in the booming stock market of the Roaring 20s and then declaring bankruptcy before delivering the shares purchased by investors. The other was the fencing of securities that were stolen at gunpoint from messenger boys delivering them to brokerage houses and banks. Rumors about Rothstein's involvement in these two activities grew out of testimony presented in one bankruptcy and one criminal case in which he was not a defendant nor suspected of having done anything wrong. In fact, the DA and the NYPD publicly exonerated him of any improper conduct in both cases.

The only known link between Rothstein and a bucket-shop brokerage was with E. M. Fuller & Co. The company's accounting records showed that the gambler borrowed money several times by pledging securities as collateral, and he repaid his loans in a timely manner. When the company dissipated all the investors' money, Rothstein became a witness on multiple occasions in the company's extended 1923 bankruptcy hearings. Rothstein was always depicted by every creditor and the judge as a legitimate borrower because the company's books proved the company's principals looted all the investors' cash. Not one penny ended up in Rothstein's hands.

While Rothstein did nothing wrong, his testimony was interesting. He refused to answer questions about where he got some of his stocks and $60,000 in government bonds on the grounds of self incrimination. He did explain that they could be bought anywhere at the time he obtained them. "Why you could buy them from a truck in those days. You could buy them at the racetrack or anywhere. I bought $150,000 worth there." When the creditors' attorney commented, "Maybe they were paying bets that way," Rothstein could not refrain from adding, "That's a fact, too." (Rothstein's two quotes are from the December 8, 1923 *New York Times*.)

Rothstein claimed his visits to the home of E. M. Fuller & Co. partner Frank McGee were social in nature. He denied he made any profit from the visits, and he could not remember the names of anybody he met there. When an attorney asked whether several were present on those occasions, he answered: "I usually walked into a full house." At which point the bankruptcy referee interjected, "What did the others have?" Rothstein explained that he was speaking of the number of people present and not a poker hand. With that, the referee adjourned that session. (The quotes by the referee and Rothstein are from the December 8, 1923 *New York Times*.)

Rothstein was linked just once to handling stolen securities. Testimony in that criminal trial portrayed him as the good guy who mediated to get them back to their rightful owner. The testimony came from a criminal defendant who used it to bolster his denial that he was the real thief. His testimony was nonsensical and his accomplice denied that Rothstein was involved. In addition the DA and the NYPD were convinced that Rothstein had no involvement with these securities, even though his role as depicted by the defendant would have been as a legitimate, public-spirited citizen.

The two defendants in that trial were Eugene McGee, brother of Frank McGee in the E. M. Fuller bankruptcy case above, and a former assistant federal prosecutor. Both were charged with possessing $137,000 worth of securities stolen in mid 1927 from Broadway brokers Taylor, Bates & Co.. McGee testified in his defense on May 13, 1929 that he wanted to obtain the securities, so he could return them to the company from which they were stolen. He hoped that this good deed would aid in his effort to be reinstated by the bar association. McKee said he begged Rothstein to ask his underworld contacts to put out word that a reward would be paid for the securities' return. Within days McGee said Rothstein handed him the securities in return for $13,000 from the $16,000 the brokerage company paid the two co-defendants for their recovery. The prosecutor attacked McGee's credibility because he was a disbarred attorney, because his statements were designed to exonerate himself, because he had no supporting evidence, because his co-defendant contradicted McGee by telling police someone unrelated to Rothstein gave the pair the securities, because the thieves could fence the stolen securities for far more than 9 ½ cents on the $1 ($13,000 / $137,000) that McGee claimed they accepted, and because the deceased Rothstein was unable to refute the testimony. The prosecutor emphasized in his closing arguments that it was inconceivable Rothstein was ever involved. "Arnold Rothstein was not a public philanthropist. He never endowed any home for disbarred layers. This statement of McGee's was an afterthought. I couldn't challenge McGee's statement of the recovery of the securities from Rothstein, but it must have brought smiles to the faces of those who knew Rothstein's reputation as a business man to think that Rothstein would have invested $13,000 in those securities in order to do McGee a favor." The jury deliberated just 3 ½ hours before acquitting the pair of having fenced the stolen securities back to the brokerage firm in an extortion scheme. It is ironic that defendant McGee's testimony, which praised Rothstein for recovering the stolen securities without profit to help McGee rehabilitate his legal career, and the bucket-shop bankruptcy testimony that commended Rothstein's conduct, would be reversed by phony organized-crime writers to forever brand Rothstein as a mythical criminal mastermind of these types of crimes. (The prosecutor's quote is from the May 15, 1929 *New York Times*.)

What seemed a certainty to the DA and the NYPD was that the two co-defendants conspired with the messenger, who was acquitted in a separate trial of pocketing the money and falsely claiming he was robbed. The two co-defendants seemed to have mistakenly believed that by fencing the securities back to the company in the guise of good Samaritans, it eliminated any concern about criminal prosecution. However, the plot went awry because the DA realized the co-defendants behavior more resembled that of co-conspirators. Each of the three participants received roughly a year's pay from the company for returning the securities. All three perpetrators ultimately lucked out because the two juries did not understand the legal issues involved in either trial.

ADDENDUM K – Chapter 5 – page 64

THE LIFESTYLES OF PROFESSIONAL LAS VEGAS SPORTS HANDICAPPERS AND POKER PLAYERS

The type of back-and-forth cash bankroll borrowing that went on between Rothstein and Costello goes on between serious gamblers everywhere. My personal knowledge about professional sports bettors and poker players comes from handling their business, hanging around them, and studying their behavior. I opened the first sports book in a Las Vegas Strip casino at the *Castaways Hotel* in 1976. *The Hole In the Wall* became America's most popular sports book, and for years we put up the first betting line in the nation. At 9 a.m. every morning, about 35 men stood with paper in hand, writing as we put up our odds. A few of these men represented Nevada's other legal books, and the rest rushed to payphones to pass on the information to the country's largest illegal bookmaking syndicates so they could quickly open for business, which was at noon on the East Coast, a hour before the National Anthem at the various sports stadiums.

In addition, the *Castaways'* poker room was always part of contestant conversation at every major poker tournament around the globe. My casino had low limits, but it had the fastest action games in the world. We designed the games so players would repeatedly re-raise. Players quickly re-raised each other in rotation at the $4 - $8 maximum-limit games. Even with these low limits, most pots were over $300 and they occasionally exceeded $1,000, as players tossed chips into the pots in rapid sequence. This led higher-limit players to regularly join in because of the fast action and large pots.

I observed the betting patterns of Las Vegas' top professional sports handicappers and poker players, the best in the world. This was their only source of income, and every one of them experienced long-term winning and losing streaks that lasted for months. This means that they had to tightly hold on to their winnings, so they could cover gambling losses during the inevitable, upcoming, long draught while also paying their living expenses.

Incidentally, gambling to make a living is neither fun nor exciting. Professionals specialize in one area, such as sporting events, horseraces, or poker games. The sport or horse handicapper typically spends 12 hours a day seven days a week studying everything in writing they can find about their field. The poker players have a relatively low expected hourly profit, when the losing hours are thrown in, so they must play long hours to make a living.

All these professionals must be highly disciplined. They must wait patiently for the right sporting game match-up, horse competition, or card hand before making the plunge. It is tedious, hard work that requires total concentration. Obviously, these men choose their careers because they like a specific type of gambling, but I never met one who said they enjoyed doing it for a living or who recommended anyone follow in their footsteps.

In contrast to these professionals, the Young Turks of Prohibition played for the sheer thrill and lost overall, although at a relatively slow rate because they were indeed knowledgeable. Rothstein was a unique combination of these two groups, the Young Turks and today's professional gambler. He played for the excitement, often throwing discretion to the wind and wagering against the odds, but he was able to make his living from gambling because he possessed such exceptional poker and horserace betting skills when he needed to come back. He was the most brilliant of all time. The Young Turks and Rothstein "bet with both fists" (hands filled with chips or cash) whenever a favorable situation presented itself, or the mood struck them, so all occasionally went broke. The next day, they were able to pay their gambling debts, cover their living expenses, and have a pocketful of cash to get back into action by borrowing between themselves and with other committed high-stakes gamblers. With this lifestyle, their survival depended on keeping their word. They always paid their gambling and loan debts on time, so the next time they got into a tight spot, they could quickly borrow large sums from recent winners.

I became well acquainted with this cash-exchange ritual during the 13 years I managed the *Castaways Hotel* and the *Silver Slipper* casinos on the Las Vegas Strip that had very popular low-limit poker rooms. The table-game and poker-room executives and I loaned regular poker players $20 to $40 out of our pockets whenever they asked for it. The players usually wanted the money to get back into action, but they sometimes needed it for necessities. I loaned a few of the best up to $200, so they could jump back into our fast-action games and go after the big pots.

In all those years, not one of these players ever failed to pay me back as soon as they started winning again. My executives informed each other about the various players' patterns, and especially notified each other about unusual changes in behavior. Yet no executive ever reported to me that a poker patron had failed to reimburse. We were these players' banking system that they knew they could always borrow from, as long as their balance was zeroed out. The poker fraternity survives by exchanging money. This has nothing to do with the illegal collection of interest known as *loan sharking,* but everything to do with having friends who will readily help each other survive during a bad streak without interest or profit.

ADDENDUM L – Chapter 5 – page 79

ORGANIZED CRIME BOOKS LACK CREDIBILITY, AND
ROTHSTEIN AND TORRIO WERE NOT MENTORS TO LUCIANO ET AL

The writers about early organized-crime who focus on Luciano, Costello, Lansky, and/or Siegel use the basic premise that they were teenage hooligans. This forces these writers to explain how they transformed into the nation's most successful Prohibition violators and illegal casino operators, leading peace advocates, the most respected men in the underworld, and powerful overworld political influences. To pull this off, they created the ploy of two mentors who supposedly corrected these punks' allegedly errant ways. These writers asserted New-York-to-Chicago Mafioso transplant Johnny Torrio (Chapter 6) taught the Young Turks to shun greed because there was enough business for everybody, and to abandon violence and vengeance in favor of peaceful coexistence. Unfortunately, Torrio epitomized the exact opposite of these virtues. He was actually the most violent, vengeful, and treacherous gangster of them all in order to feed his insatiable financial greed and craving for total domination of all crime. The reality is Torrio had no influence on the Young Turks, having left New York a decade before Prohibition began while they were still children. In reality he never met a single one of them at any time. The writers responsible for this nonsense never learned that it was Sicilian Chicago businessman Mike Merlo, who kept the peace in the Windy City primarily by keeping the dangerous Torrio in line. These writers also are unaware how many people Torrio ordered killed for profit including his own uncle "Big Jim" Colosimo who single-handedly had already made him a wealthy man. Talk about insatiable greed and utter lack of loyalty.

Writers about early organized crime typically refer to Torrio in his later New York years as a highly respected elder statesmen and advisor to organized crime, but Jimmy Blue Eyes, who was the renowned east-coast underworld peacemaker for almost six decades, never once encountered these writers' fanciful man of peace. Jimmy told me, "Torrio was out of action long before I came into power (early in Prohibition). No one ever mentioned his name. He must've retired or gone into his own business after returning to New York. The Easterners [New Yorkers] did not like or respect Torrio and Capone because of their whorehouses in Chicago, but it was their business." The disdain the criminals of that era held for pimps and exploiters of women cannot be overemphasized. Whatever their personal attitudes towards Capone, the Young Turks had to deal with him because he was an aggressive powerhouse in the underworld in which they imported booze and later operated casinos.

These writers about early organized crime embellished their charade by inventing a second mentor role in the lives of the Young Turks played by gambler and political fixer Arnold Rothstein (Chapter 5). These writers' first fallacious claim was that Rothstein supplied the initial financing for the large-scale rumrunning operations of Luciano and Costello, but Costello inherited the operation intact when his boss Bill Dwyer went to prison several years into Prohibition. Rothstein's detailed estate records prove he never had substantive investments or businesses other than a few illegal casinos he leased, and he never accumulated more than enough money to use as a bankroll in the next high-stakes no-limit poker game. Whenever he had any excess cash, he loaned it to other gamblers who in turn lent to him during his losing streaks. While these writers fixated on who financed the early rumrunners, all the major Prohibition leaders remained tight-lipped their whole lives about who their sources were except for the big three importers. Costello and Moe Dalitz both revealed their liquor supplier was Joe Kennedy, while Luciano relied on Canada's Samuel Bronfman, who built the worldwide whiskey conglomerate Joseph E. Seagrams & Sons. None dealt with Rothstein in booze and none ever heard of him being involved. Jimmy Blue Eyes emphasized, "Everyone was on their own," making it clear each Prohibition gang developed its own financing, liquor and raw materials sources, and political and law-enforcement protectors. There was no dominate Prohibition money supplier because the Roaring 20s' stock market boom produced many venture capitalists interested in funding this highly-profitable, rapid-turnover business. This is why this book focuses instead on what could be learned about how the leading bootleggers conducted their huge liquor importing and manufacturing businesses.

These writers' second contrived assertion about Rothstein was that he mentored these allegedly uneducated street punks and their partners to apply standard business principles to their illegal activities. While Rothstein was a creature of the night along marquee-glowing Broadway, these writers' depiction of him as the prince of darkness who directed crime in New York City is without substantiation and debunked in Addendum J above. In reality, Rothstein was a total loner. Jimmy Blue Eyes said, "None of my associates ever mentioned Rothstein's name," and Rothstein's only business experience was as the owner and not the operator of a few high-limit illegal casinos and floating crap games. More importantly, the Young Turks were never involved with street gangs or the Mafia. Luciano and his partners were either born in the U.S. or immigrated by age 9, making it all but inevitable that each grew up with basic American business attitudes. Indeed, all were pragmatic by nature, and they united because of their shared values long before they later encountered Rothstein, enjoying the nightlife in the city's many upscale nightclubs and casinos during the Roaring '20s and Prohibition.

The cornerstone of the Young Turks' power in the underworld and the overworld was the strength of their word, which was absolute. In contrast to the Young Turks' exceptional reputations, Torrio was the leading proponent of following up peace pacts with murderous sneak attacks, and Rothstein had far more enemies who wished him ill than friends who trusted him. These writers could have easily learned that their imaginative contentions about Torrio, Rothstein, and the Young Turks were all untrue by studying the numerous documents available to them at the time they wrote.

An interesting aside concerning trustworthiness involved the nation's two biggest poker and crap players. Rothstein ranked number one during the first three decades of the 1900s until his death, and then Nick "The Greek" Dandolas ascended to this throne for the next three decades of the century. One evening late in the Roaring 20s, the two played craps against each other in New York. Both Rothstein and The Greek offered illegal bookmaker and later Reno casino owner Eddy Rollins a piece of their action. He told me, "I didn't want to be involved with either one's action. I was afraid Rothstein might put in balonies [bad dice], and Nick wouldn't pay." Surprisingly, Eddy's statement is not an indictment on either gambler's integrity because he elaborated that he never knew either man to do anything wrong. But with big money at stake and no way of knowing if either had the cash to back up his losses, he did not want to be connected with it. That night both men bet using markers, and Eddy told me, "I watched Nick drop $180,000 to Rothstein. The next day he delivered the cash." As a major horse bookie, Eddy traveled to the nation's highest-stake poker games to book side bets on races of up to $20,000 per horse with the players and any spectators.

Rothstein, unlike Torrio, was relevant to the careers of the Young Turks, but not for the reasons concocted by these writers. Rothstein was important in pioneering wide-open, up-scale illegal casinos which the Young Turks would specialize in after Prohibition, and he was the top political kingmaker in the Big Apple when Luciano and Costello became key players in that field. As the country's biggest gambler, Rothstein shared the Young Turks' passion for wagering, making this their main topic of conversation whenever they met. As these young denizens of the night ventured between the restaurants, nightclubs, casinos, and shows dotting Broadway, they occasionally joined Rothstein's booth in Lindy's delicatessen as he held court with the city's movers and shakers, including the gang leaders.

Six major early organized crime books contain all the errors mentioned above, as well as many more. Later writers about Luciano, Costello, their associates, and/or Rothstein depend on one or more of these six books as their primary reference sources because no new documents surfaced after these books were published. The first book to focus on Rothstein's life was *The Big Bankroll: The Life and Times of Arnold Rothstein* by Leo Katcher (1958), but it is pure fiction (see Chapter 5). While Rothstein received two IOUs from Costello totaling just over $35,000, this book claimed it was just one IOU for $40,000 without giving the date or year the note was signed. The next five crime books give different versions about the number of IOUs and their total value, and all are wrong. Next came the *Green Felt Jungle* by Ed Reid and Ovid Demaris (1963), whose highly fantasized account of Las Vegas' history is exposed in a later volume in this series about Nevada in the 1950s and 1960s.

The third and fifth books were devoted to Costello's life. Neither *Uncle Frank: The Biography of Frank Costello* by Leonard Katz (1973), nor *Frank Costello: Prime Minister of the Underworld* by his attorney George Wolf with Joseph DiMona (1975), offers sources or substantiates its alleged facts. The third book was by Costello's nephew, who was never involved with and knew nothing about organized crime or his uncle's criminal life, let alone his personal lifestyle. However, he took advantage of the February 19, 1973 *New York Times* obituary of his uncle that stated, "He [Costello] cherished the sobriquet Uncle Frank, as if it made him an elder statesman or benefactor." Despite the nephew's euphemism, no one in the underworld referred to him as "Uncle Frank." The nephew embellished about his Uncle Frank in the third book by writing, "Costello and Rothstein frequently were involved in business deals with each other," and "Arnold Rothstein was one of Frank Costello's close associates in those days [the 1920s]." No such business dealings were found by Congressional investigations or by Rothstein's and Costello's estates in the voluminous pages of business papers both left at the times of their death.

The fifth book about the Prime Minister was by Costello's long-time attorney, George Wolf, who expanded this story about the pair's alleged business relationships without validation when he wrote, "The [Rothstein's] executors discovered many notes on various deals between Frank and Rothstein." This is confounding because Wolf wrote about his client's many legal problems and listed the important dates when he described the issues, but he failed to give the amounts, dates, or reasons for any of these notes. Furthermore, Rothstein's estate executors reported to the court that no such notes existed. He wrote Costello's purported biography, which was publicized as containing his inside legal knowledge and viewpoints, but he left out every pertinent detail about the business dealings he claimed he had the records for, unlike the way he documented his client's legal problems.

The fourth and sixth books were both fraudulent autobiographies. *The Last Testament of Lucky Luciano* by Martin A. Gosch and Richard Hammer (1974), and *Meyer Lansky: Mogul of the Mob* by Dennis Eisenberg, Uri Dan, and Eli Landau (1979), were clearly hoaxes. Both books make the typical errors about Costello and Rothstein business dealings and loans, as well as all the others mentioned above, and they create a bunch of new ones. (Many details about these two fraudulent autobiographies are in Addendum M for Chapter 7 about Luciano, in Addendum BB for Chapter 10 about Luciano, and in Addendum DD for Chapter 14 about Lansky.)

ADDENDUM M – Chapter 7 – page 144

THE AUTOBIOGRAPHIES ABOUT LUCIANO AND LANSKY ARE HOAXES

Luciano's background presented in the text was taken from the testimonies of Luciano and the prosecution and defense witnesses in his 1936 prostitution-booker trial, his police records, and the FBI's 548-page file on Luciano. The preparation for and testimony in the trial became the subject of *Lucky Luciano: The Man Who Organized Crime in America* by Hickman Powell. He was a friend and employee of prosecutor Tom Dewey, so Powell tried to make Luciano look as bad as possible to make his boss' action more heroic. However, even Powell had to admit that the extensive six-month investigations by the NYPD and Dewey's prosecutorial staffs found nothing to shake or impeach Luciano's trial testimony about his life. They found no evidence that Luciano ever broke any law besides gambling, rumrunning, and the early selling of one packet of opium rap. Had Luciano indeed committed other types of crimes, it would have been risky for him to deny them in his trial testimony because the prosecutor's large staff would likely have been able to expose him as a perjurer, destroying his credibility with the jury.

Powell's book said Luciano had "frequent" arrests, but they "never amounted to more than a few days' detention." A fundamental rule of crime reporting is to list a subject's specific arrest and conviction records. Thus, this *New York Time's* crime reporter, who possessed the prosecutor's complete files, damaged his sincerity by failing to identify the arrests he claimed existed. The other fraudulent biographers about Luciano report that he was arrested for a number of serious crimes, but every one of their books fails to list the dates, cities, or details, making it doubtful any of their allegations are true. These authors' credibility is further damaged because their lists are very different from each other and also from both the records of the FBI and the Special Prosecutor, despite both having diligently tried to trace down all his records.

Books, movies, and television portray the younger years of both Luciano and Lansky based on two books – *The Last Testament of Lucky Luciano* by Martin A. Gosch and Richard Hammer, and *Meyer Lansky: Mogul of the Mob* by Dennis Eisenberg, Uri Dan, and Eli Landau. The American authors of the Luciano book claimed it was his official autobiography, and the Israeli authors of the Lansky book said it was his authorized autobiography. Historians long ago discredited the Luciano book as a hoax, and the Lansky book plagiarized the Luciano book and included additional ridiculous fabrications. Well-documented facts prove both books are pure fiction. The close associates of Luciano and Lansky always denied either man ever talked to these authors or anyone else about their criminal activities or personal lives.

Both books present events that were popular parts of underworld myth at the time of their publication, but have since been proven to have never happened. Similarly the major events in which Lansky and Luciano were actually involved but were unknown to the public were not included. It is inconceivable that Lansky and Luciano would have failed to include their actions that made them true American patriots, and they certainly would not have taken credit for despicable acts that never occurred. (Many details about these two fraudulent autobiographies are in Addendum L for Chapter 5 about Rothstein, in Addendum BB for Chapter 10 about Luciano, and in Addendum DD for Chapter 14 about Lansky.)

ADDENDUM N – Chapter 8 – page 159

THE FALSE SWORN CLAIMS OF MURDER, INC.'S EXISTENCE BY RELES AND PROSECUTOR TURKUS

The first two Murder, Inc. trial juries heard long dissertations on the history of U.S. organized crime by Brooklyn gang member Abe Reles. Much of this informant's testimony was repeated by Brooklyn Assistant DA Burton Turkus, who prosecuted the cases, as fact in his book *Murder, Inc. - The Story of the Syndicate*. All of Reles' grossly untrue assertions were fabricated to fit the facts of the Murder, Inc. trials to elevate these cases to the level of an organized-crime conspiracy punishable by death. Turkus' and Reles' three primary claims in the Murder, Inc. cases were presented in the text. Both the Assistant DA and the killer informer ridiculously maintained the following fictions:

1- The American Mafia ceased to exist at the end of Prohibition.
2- At that time every U.S. gang was inexplicably absorbed into a national Syndicate led by Johnny Torrio.
3- That is when Torrio also created a centralized-murder organization to handle every gangland killing nationwide. (In reality Torrio retired from Chicago-gang leadership five years into Prohibition and had nothing to do with any major gang afterwards - see Addendum L above.)

The inventive Prosecutor and informer also made the following untrue declarations beginning with their complete revisionism of the genesis of U.S. gang development. Turkus and Reles claimed the country's first criminal gangs developed just prior to World War I to handle violent labor/management conflicts because the informant's gang specialized in labor racketeering. They left out the previous century of professional street gangs in big cities that operated with impunity in return for giving illegal and violent support and protection to politicians' interests. In addition, labor unions were not a major factor prior to World War I.

Since the Murder, Inc. juries were made up of respectable citizens with no knowledge about the underworld, Reles and Turkus made their fantasy chronicle sound familiar and plausible by throwing in the names of infamous gangs and hoodlums who had been disparaged in newspapers. For example, the duo completely altered the purpose and membership of the Unione Siciliana, an ethnic business-networking fraternity made up of Sicilians from all walks of life but primarily the rich and powerful including Mafia leaders. Without presenting a stitch of evidence, Reles falsely called the Unione an "ugly, savage, murderous" criminal gang that opposed the Mafia and had different members.

All of Reles' testimony about the American Mafia was untrue. He asserted the Mafia was an Italian organization, even though he was well aware that it was made up solely of Sicilians. He knew that every Sicilian street tough who lived in his Brownsville district of Brooklyn chose to become associated with the Mafia division headed by Albert Anastasia, while the district's Italian and Jewish punks joined Reles' gang. Reles' also made the absurd claim that Luciano's ascension to the Boss of Bosses was "a definite windup to Mafia as an entity and a power in national crime." Reles never explained why at the moment Luciano became the most powerful hoodlum in American history, he immediately turned everything over to the retired Italian Torrio and stepped aside.

The cohort of Brooklyn Assistant DA Turkus in fabricating this underworld history was Manhattan DA Dewey. At Luciano's trial four years earlier, Dewey had presented exactly the opposite image of the gang leader in his opening and closing arguments to the jury and to the press. Dewey had told his 1936 jury that Luciano personally directed every major crime in New York City, but Reles testified in 1940 that Luciano had already relinquished his power two years earlier in 1934. Obviously either Dewey's or Turkus' jury presentations had to be totally false. Actually both were. Dewey's long and extensive investigation proved that Luciano was never involved with any crime except for his Prohibition and illegal gambling operations. Turkus and Reles falsely claimed to the Murder, Inc. juries that when Luciano allegedly transferred all his power to Torrio, he issued an edict and, "some thirty to forty leaders of Mafia's older group all over the United States were murdered that day and in the next forty-eight hours!" This was a rehash of the *Night of the Sicilian Vespers* folklore that crime authors claim happened following the 1931 murder of Maranzano, but police records prove conclusively that no other major U.S. hoodlum of any ethnicity was murdered within weeks of Maranzano's killing (detailed in Chapter 3).

Turkus and Reles description of their fabricated Murder, Inc. operation contained several aspects that cannot be reconciled and make no sense when compared with each other or with reality. For example, the pair claimed Murder, Inc. was composed of "250 professional shooters" who lived in cities across the country. Since they gave no information about these murderers, it is unclear whether they meant that Torrio somehow found 250 new hired killers roaming the countryside, or he absorbed the enforcers who were already part of every gang. If the gangs' existing killers were used, he gave no rational reason for creating Murder, Inc. to replace a system that already worked effectively. No matter whether the shooters were new or established, neither the prosecutor nor the informant explained why Torrio elevated gang killing to a professional status that required large payments instead of continuing the long-established policy of having members kill for free for the good of the gang when ordered by their leader. Turkus and Reles presented incongruent numbers, and Turkus never explained why Torrio had such an excess of assassins on the payroll. Turkus claimed 250 professionals committed 1,000 murders over a decade, which works out to one killing every two-and-a-half years per shooter.

Two of Turkus' main points contradicted each other. He pointed out time and again how difficult it was to obtain a corroborating witness to each of the three Brooklyn murders because gang leaders were highly secretive. He repeatedly wrote that leaders never talked to more than one man at a time, and they never told anyone their motives for wanting someone killed. America's gang leaders were indeed exceptionally tight-lipped as he wrote, so this raises a huge question - how could Reles have learned the inside details of every gangland murder in the country like he claimed? Remember Turkus' whole case in the Murder, Inc. trials relied on Reles' supposed expertise about extensive inside secret knowledge about American gangland. Turkus wrote that Reles' possessed all-embracing knowledge about underworld murders across the country. "The Kid rattled off names, places, facts, data of one manslaughter after the other, days on end, without once missing [messing] up. He recalled not only the personnel involved, but also decent people who had an unwitting part in some angle of a crime. That way, if you please, he kept his promise to uncover corroboration." Reles' "fellow felons seemed forever to have been apprising him of the fulfillment of plans and contracts." Reles also explained the entire inner workings of the top bosses, what they did and why, even though Turkus earlier wrote that these leaders had contact only with their lieutenants always on a one-on-one basis, and Reles' was a bottom-level street punk.

Since Turkus claimed Reles had far-reaching, detailed inside information about numerous murders, it raises another question. Why did the Prosecutor and the informer never reveal the name of one of these alleged 1,000 murder victims, or the identity of even one of the 250 shooters, to the police, prosecutors, and press? The only men they ever identified were the three victims, seven defendants, and eight state's witnesses in the so-called Murder, Inc. trials, all of whom spent their lives in the Brownsville section of Brooklyn. Yet Turkus wrote, "I prosecuted the board of directors of the death department of this cartel, and sent seven men to the electric chair. (One other received eighty years.) Five of these seven were members of the self-styled Brooklyn combination, the branch office that served as the firing squad for all of the organization. The other two were ranking magnates in the national underworld." Actually all seven defendants belonged to the same small gang that exploited local residents and businesses in their neighborhood. However, Turkus never had a clue about its structure despite information from nine members, who became his state's witnesses during the two years he prosecuted the three murder trials. Turkus' book and opening and closing statements to the Murder, Inc. juries revealed even greater ignorance about the rest of the underworld he discussed. Turkus repeatedly had gang subordinates give orders to their leaders, and he had members of one gang give orders to members of other gangs.

Reles clearly lied repeatedly on the witness stand. He testified in the first two Murder, Inc. trials that he had been with Lepke Buchalter every day during the two years he hid out. He claimed he took Lepke for drives and walked with him in the streets next to Brooklyn police headquarters. Like the rest of Reles' testimony, this is hard to believe. Many NYPD officers in that era were accused of being on the take and/or being violently brutal, but no one said the cops were either stupid or incapable of recognizing a local fugitive from justice walking along the street near their precinct. Reles' contradicted these claims he made in the Murder, Inc. trials prior to receiving the plea-bargain incentive to lie at trial. In earlier testimony to a federal grand jury he swore he had no idea where Lepke was hiding. Both Murder, Inc. trial defense teams used Reles' grand jury testimony to challenge his credibility at trial, so he came up with a whopper of a tale to create a good reason for having lied earlier. Reles claimed that Lepke's goons threatened him just as he was about to enter the grand jury room to testify. However, it is inconceivable that Lepke's associates could have threatened Reles, who was surrounded by a cordon of six police guards around the clock. In this situation the gang leaders would have delivered a cryptic offer or threat to his wife for her to slip to him in the private sanctity of his protected suite bedroom. It is important to note that not one of Turkus' other eight informants were contacted or bothered by Lepke's associates.

The important issue is not how many times Reles lied while testifying, but whether he ever once told the truth. He was a bottom-feeding psychopath who knew nothing about the goings on in his gang except for the orders that were given to him. He conjured up the whole yarn about Murder, Inc. to obtain a get-out-of-jail-free card, and he wielded it to send four of his fellow gang members in two trials to the electric chair.

ADDENDUM O – Chapter 8 – page 161

THE FALSE PORTRAYAL OF LEPKE BUCHALTER
BY TURKUS IN HIS BOOK *MURDER, INC.*

Lepke Buchalter's background, arrest record, and criminal activities are taken from the records introduced at his trials and two of his FBI file documents - FBI Headquarters' Internal Memo August 19, 1935 and FBI New York City Office's Case File January 28, 1938. This documented information is very different from the story presented by Brooklyn Assistant DA Burton Turkus, the man who prosecuted all three Murder, Inc. trials, in his book *Murder, Inc. - The Story of the Syndicate.* His 493 pages are riddled with so many contradictions, inconsistencies, and factual errors that an academician would need a whole book to present them all. Turkus painted Buchalter as a far more powerful criminal than the facts justified, and ensuing writers about organized-crime have repeated his fictitious description. As an example, Turkus wrote in several sections of his book that Lepke controlled the employee unions for several major New York City industries, but this information came solely from two gang informants who testified as Assistant DA Turkus had directed them to do. Turkus failed to produce one piece of documented evidence, a single union member, or one business owner who could corroborate these punks' allegations despite all of the prosecutor's public bravado about possessing detailed information. Turkus created the impression that Lepke and Gurrah directed all labor racketeering in New York City even though the much larger and far more powerful Mafia gangs controlled several of the largest local unions.

Turkus' images of Lepke were sometimes contradictory. His primary claim was that Lepke headed Murder, Inc. and was the most homicidal hood of them all, but Turkus failed to identify who any of these numerous alleged victims might have been. Turkus shamelessly wrote exactly the opposite position in his book's introduction. He said Lepke, along with Luciano and Costello, "were and are the modern type who believe in arbitration," rather than the "breed, who settled everything with a bullet."

Turkus maintained throughout his book that Lepke was a powerful and infamous gang leader. He even asserted that when Lepke was running as a fugitive, the nationwide search got more publicity than the Charles Lindbergh' baby murder. To put this false claim into perspective, practically all Americans have heard of the Lindberg kidnapping, which is usually referred to as the *Crime of the Century*, but virtually no one except organized-crime buffs has heard of Lepke. After contending before trial juries, in press conferences, and in the early part of his book that Lepke was a nationally prominent gangster, Turkus completely contradicted himself in later chapters. He admitted that Lepke was unknown not only to the public but even to the Brooklyn DA's staff until the end of his career. Turkus wrote, "[Lepke was] little publicized until 1939" at the end of the two-year manhunt. Until "the file on the Lepke case was dropped on my desk, I was almost unaware of the Lepke case." "Lepke's name had not previously been mentioned [in the DA's office]. That was in the spring of 1940," a year after he was taken into custody. Turkus' two versions about Lepke - that he had great notoriety nationwide but he was totally unknown in his hometown crime base of Brooklyn - could not have been more contradictory or inconsistent.

ADDENDUM P – Chapter 8 – page 166

COLUMNIST AND BROADCASTER WALTER WINCHELL
REVEALED DIRT ON J. EDGAR HOOVER'S TARGETS

Newspaper columnist Walter Winchell's 3,908-page FBI file is larger than the file for any major gangster's of his era. Winchell's file contains copies of his syndicated newspaper columns as well as FBI agent summaries and evaluations of these articles and his radio broadcasts. These assisted Hoover in advising Winchell how to handle each scandal "properly" on his rumor-mongering broadcasts and writings. His file also contains letters between Winchell and the Director, but these appear to be selected because the pair maintained a steady exchange of correspondence for over 30 years. Winchell's file also contains information about his behavior, both professional and personal.

Walter Winchell's background and high standing with Hoover is described in FBI Headquarters Internal Memo May 24, 1960. It was an evaluation of whether Winchell's request to give singer Bobby Darin a tour of the FBI offices should be approved. It states, "Walter Winchell, born 4-7-97, New York, New York, has been a newspaperman since 1922, and has been a columnist with the *New York Mirror* since 1929. He has been active in radio and television and currently serves as narrator for the weekly television series *The Untouchables,* a Desilu production, in which actor Robert Stack portrays prohibition agent Eliot Ness. It was recently reported in the press that Winchell's staccato narration of *The Untouchables* will soon be released in a record album. Winchell is on the Special Correspondent's List and, of course, is a long-time personal friend of the Director. It is noted that in the interest of expediency, the file review on Winchell was limited to a check of recent abstracts, which reflected no unfavorable information."

ADDENDUM Q – Chapter 8 – page 166

THE FBI'S TWO-YEAR WORLD-WIDE MANHUNT
FAILED TO FIND FUGITIVE LEPKE BUCHALTER

Hoover's quote about Walter Winchell was taken from the FBI Director's Summarization on his stationery of the two-year search and capture of the fugitive Lepke Buchalter. No date is visible on the document. Hoover wrote about the search as if it was a great drama. "A manhunt that encircled the continental United States and extended into Mexico, Costa Rica, Cuba, England, Canada, France, Puerto Rico and Carlsbad, Germany. Summary reports alone succinctly setting forth contacts of Shapiro and Buchalter, number over a thousand pages, to say nothing of the thousands of reports of Special Agents of the Federal Bureau of Investigation working in every section of the United States." Hoover left out that while the FBI searched the world for Buchalter, the gangster never left his rented room in Brooklyn the whole two years. In addition, Lepke's FBI file is not thousands of pages but just 184.

The book *The FBI Story, A Report to the People* by Don Whitehead with a forward by J. Edgar Hoover was a revisionist flack history of the Director's allegedly great contribution to law and order. Hoover gave the author selected FBI files, summaries like the preceding one that was prepared for political propaganda, the Director's forward for the book, and the FBI's official endorsement.

ADDENDUM R – Chapter 8 – page 170

THE FALSE CLAIMS BY PROSECUTORS DEWEY AND TURKUS
THAT MURDER, INC. HARBORED FUGITIVES

Manhattan DA Dewey and Brooklyn Assistant DA Turkus asserted for years to trial juries and the press that Lepke Buchalter and Jake "Gurrah" Shapiro headed the fictitious Murder, Inc. They alleged that it was a huge national crime organization specializing in the protection of criminal fugitives running from their local jurisdictions. But a trial proved that while Murder, Inc.'s leaders Lepke and Gurrah were fugitives on the run they were harbored from the law by their family members rather than other criminals around the country.

Two and one-half months after Lepke voluntarily surrendered to J. Edgar Hoover, a federal jury on November 6, 1939 convicted five people of harboring the two fugitives. The wives of Lepke and Gurrah owned two clothes-manufacturing companies whose employees arranged to give each wife $250 every week while their husbands were in hiding. The prosecution showed that the employees knew that these funds did not represent profits or salary payments to the women, and that this was the exact amount the women turned over to their holed-up husbands for living expenses. The five employees could give no explanation to the jury what these funds were for other than to assist in harboring the two fugitives, so the jury convicted. The five, including Gurrah's brother and his brother-in-law, received one-year prison sentences.

ADDENDUM S – Chapter 8 – page 172

FOUR LINGERING QUESTIONS ABOUT THE GUILT
OF THE THREE MURDER, INC. TRIALS' DEFENDANTS

The three Murder, Inc. homicide trials have left four nagging questions about the guilt of the seven executed defendants. The first is - was any guilty of the single murder for which he was convicted? The only certainty in these three cases is that every prosecution witness testified at trial he was guilty of one or more of these murders, but all had a powerful motive to lie. Each was facing serious charges and strong cases, and the prosecution offered each a free pass in return for testifying that one or more hoods they knew was involved with him in one of these murders. No other evidence tied any of the seven defendants to one of these murders. It is important to remember that every one of these defendants were tight-lipped with associates and the press their entire lives. None ever complained to reporters that they were innocent of the many crimes for which they were charged during their careers, but all maintained to the moment of their executions that they had nothing to do with the so-called Murder, Inc. killing cases for which they were convicted.

The second question is – did Prosecutor Turkus' handpicked blue-ribbon juries convict because they impartially and fairly examined the testimony in each case or because of political loyalty to the Assistant DA? When the juror pool was questioned at the beginning of the Lepke case, it became apparent that the type of *upstanding* citizens who were chosen lacked any commitment to seeing justice done. Almost all tried to get out of actually spending time administering justice by serving, which makes it obvious their primary motivation for being on this elitist-juror list was to gain political points with the Assistant DA. The pool list of 250 members were told to appear as jury candidates, but 26 (10%) did not bother to show up. On the first day of the trial, 129 (58% of those who did show) gave the judge various reasons to avoid jury duty. The remainder offered similar evasive excuses, so it took five weeks with 22 court sessions, some extending late into the evening, before the judge was finally able to pressure 12 of these *respectable* citizens to do their sworn duty and sit on the jury. This second question has a corollary - did any of the unwilling and uncommitted jurors who did serve actually evaluate the evidence, or did they just do their perceived duty to the Assistant DA by convicting no matter how weak the merits of their political ally's case?

The third question is - did Prosecutor Turkus' unsubstantiated speculations about the nature of Murder, Inc. qualify for presentation to the jury, or did the prosecution create a "poisoned atmosphere," as claimed by Lepke's attorney in his appeal? Prosecutors in opening arguments often overstate their case and then fail to back it up during the trial testimony, but prosecutors are not permitted to say anything during closing arguments that is not supported by the evidence presented at trial. State witness Reles ranted about the Murder, Inc. organization, but neither he nor Turkus backed up a single allegation by presenting any supporting testimony or documentary evidence whatsoever or any corroborating evidence from the other state's witnesses from Reles' gang. Both Turkus and Reles talked about all kinds of unspecified murders but did not demonstrate that they had ever occurred, let alone that they were perpetrated by their fictitious Murder, Inc. fabrication. Turkus was guilty of prosecutorial misconduct by presenting as inconvertible fact a mammoth national criminal conspiracy that never existed, and for which not a scintilla of evidence has ever been found by any law enforcement agency, government investigation, or historical researcher. A legitimate judge would have shielded the jury from such whimsical and unsupported hearsay speculation.

The fourth question is - if the defendants were indeed guilty, was the death penalty uniformly imposed and equitable under New York's death penalty law? First-degree murder carried an automatic death penalty, but juries in that era typically convicted defendants charged with a single killing with second-degree murder that carried a maximum sentence of life imprisonment, unless there were special disgusting circumstances. The only extenuating situation in these three cases was the totally false prosecution presentations that a national killing organization of monstrous proportions known as Murder, Inc. existed, and that its chief homicidal maniacs were these defendants. If the three juries gave these seven defendants death sentences at least partially because of this Murder, Inc. mumbo jumbo, which is likely, then the first-degree murder convictions and the automatic death penalty they carried resulted from a perversion of the justice system. The only thing we can be certain of is that every state's witnesses went free even though all admitted being guilty of at least one of these murders, while every defendant was executed despite a reasonable likelihood that some or all seven were innocent of any involvement in the murder for which they were charged.

ADDENDUM T – Chapter 9 – page 180

THE INFORMANTS' TESTIMONIES EXPLAIN
HOW EASILY THE POLICE COULD HAVE KILLED RELES

NYPD detectives guarded Reles and three other informants in a suite at the Half Moon Hotel on the Coney Island boardwalk prior to and during Lepke Buchalter's Brooklyn Murder, Inc. trial. The NYPD report declared that it was the custom of the police to look into the four bedrooms of their charges every 15 minutes, and the five detectives on duty insisted Reles and the other three informants were asleep when they looked at 7:10 a.m. on the morning he flew out the window. The only entrance into the suite was under the eye of one of the guards. This report significantly left out where the other four detectives were stationed that morning, but the report's assertion that they routinely checked the bedrooms implies all were bunched together in the living room. Given the fact that NYPD officers were stationed at every entry into the hotel to stop a gangster invasion from slaughtering the prosecution witnesses, this enormous waste of manpower in the living room amounted to at least gross incompetence and more likely dereliction of duty. Contrary to the NYPD report, the three other gang member informants testified that the detectives sat in each of their four bedrooms while they slept. This would have been logistically sound because the detectives were there both to protect them from the gang members they were testifying against and to prevent the informers from trying to escape. It must be remembered that these informants were being held involuntarily on plea deals for very serious charges.

They had placed the witnesses on the hotel tower's middle floor instead of in the penthouse suite to make escape more difficult. If they were in the twelfth-floor penthouse, it would have been easy for an informant's confederate to rent a room, carry in a short rope in a suitcase, walk up to the roof, drop the rope down to the informant's bedroom window, pull him up, and give him a disguise to walk past the officers at the front door. The sixth-floor suite complicated any escape attempt. Reles would have had to tell his wife during their private conjugal visits to have two pals rent rooms separately and each bring in a suitcase containing a 60-foot rope. On the roof they would have had to link the two ropes together, dropped one end of the combined 120-foot rope to the ground, and let Reles grab the rope outside his bedroom window to shimmy down because it is unlikely he was in any physical condition to pull himself up a six-story rope to the roof. The only way the detectives could have prevented an escape by rope was by having one detective sit in the bedroom of each witness whenever they were in it. The reason a minimum of five detectives was always on duty in the suite around the clock was so one could sit in each of the four informant's bedrooms while the other one watched the front door in the living room. On practically every shift except the morning Reles dove out his window, a sixth detective was on duty to cover the positions of the other five during bathroom breaks.

In analyzing the veracity of the two contradictory sets of statements about whether the detectives sat in each informant's bedroom, the gang member witnesses make immense sense. They had no reason to lie, and they testified to this arrangement in Lepke's Murder, Inc. trial before Reles was thrown to his death and before the detectives' guarding policies were brought into question. The witnesses gave their testimony in open hearings under cross-examination. In contrast, the NYPD report and the written statements of the guards on duty were prepared in a private office by NYPD Captain Frank Bals and his handpicked detectives. They had good reason to lie. They also lacked credibility because they had failed to protect Reles, and then they had concocted and planted the evidence for the wacky bed-sheet-and-telephone-wire-cord escape cover-up that makes no sense of what happened that historic morning. (Bals' pathetic explanation before the Kefauver Committee is in Addendum U next.)

ADDENDUM U – Chapter 9 – page 183

THE TESTIMONIES BY DA O'DWYER AND
NYPD CAPTAIN BALS LACKED CREDIBILITY

DA Bill O'Dwyer and NYPD Captain Bals clearly operated as a team at the time of Reles' plunge, and the pair went to ridiculous lengths a decade later to make his death seem to be an accident. At the March 1951 U.S. Senate Kefauver Committee hearings, Bals testified, "I imagine they all [five police guards] fell asleep at the same time," but this possibility was discredited by all three of the surviving informers who testified the five detectives were in different rooms. Bals postulated, "Reles attempted, from all indications, tied a bed sheet to a piece of wire, piece of telephone wire." "That wire was tied on to a radiator and as he got down the window he only had one sheet. The only place he could go is the window below. The sheet pulled out of the wire, the sheet gave way, and he fell on the roof below." In reality, Reles could not have slipped off the wire and fallen as Bals claimed because this would not have launched him 25 feet away from the wall. It is amazing the Senate investigators let Bals get away with this wacky testimony. Bals testimony then got even weirder. He stated he believed Reles had lowered himself from this sixth-floor room with the intent of re-entering the hotel by a fifth story window and "kid" the sleeping detective guards by reappearing on the sixth floor free of custody. Bals did express the opinion that Reles was too much of a coward to be a suicide.

DA O'Dwyer was the Kefauver Committee's next witness, and Chief Counsel Rudolph Halley told him, "Bals made a spectacle of himself before the Committee, and he gave the flimsiest excuse possible about the death of Reles." This incredulousness seemed to cause O'Dwyer to confuse his testimony between four different positions. He first said, "He tried to escape." Second, he testified that Reles was trying to get to the room below, but refused to ascribe motive or claim to know what was in Reles' mind, even though it is the responsibility of the DA in suspicious death cases to determine this. Third, O'Dwyer testified the next day and this time backed up Bals' belief that Reles was trying to get into the room below but "not trying to escape." Fourth, O'Dwyer contradicted his own conclusion that Reles' had tried to escape. He testified that the four informants had not shown the slightest desire to escape during their incarceration of more than a year. On the contrary they were all "deathly afraid" of underworld attempts on their lives, and were only too glad to be guarded closely by the detectives. Thus, O'Dwyer completely repudiated his and Police Captain Bals' position that Reles was trying to escape. Bals also undermined their escape position when he testified about taking Reles and Tannenbaum to Los Angeles to testify in the murder arraignment of Ben Siegel. The NYPD Captain said that Reles had many opportunities to escape during that trip but made no effort to take advantage of them.

The Committee's Chief Counsel asked O'Dwyer, "Wasn't that worth the greatest endeavor in the world to find out who was culpable in reducing this man Reles to a corpse so that the evidence goes out the window and you can't prosecute the arch criminal, Anastasia? How much of a trial and hearing did you have on these fellows that had charge of Reles?" O'Dwyer replied that he took the medical examiner's statement that it was caused by a fall without any other investigation or questioning of witnesses why he fell.

Chairman Kefauver said, "The important question" is "apparently there were five men in the apartment or the room of Reles, and he was fully dressed at 7 o'clock in the morning, early in the morning, and he got out of the window. It is apparent on the face of it, that these police officers weren't paying attention." O'Dwyer replied that he and the Police Commissioner "looked over the medical examiner's report, and we were both satisfied that it narrowed down to police negligence; and that the best you could have in the case was a police trial, which was held in a trial room, and the men, as I remember it, were punished," but they were not punished.

The May 1, 1951 Kefauver Committee Report stated, "Despite the admitted importance of Reles to what he conceded was the most important murder case his office had, O'Dwyer was content to label his escape through death as the result of negligence; he never fixed the responsibility. He personally appeared to absolve the five policemen guarding Reles from blame at their departmental trial, and he rewarded their superior, Bals, as well as Moran who apparently ordered the removal of the 'wanted cards' which in effect closed up the investigation on Anastasia and his associates, with intimate personal friendship and financial preferment through lucrative city positions." Most intriguing are O'Dwyer's career-long government appointments that rewarded his subordinates who so badly failed in protecting Reles and in prosecuting arch-criminal Anastasia.

ADDENDUM V – Chapter 9 – page 186

DA AND MAYOR O'DWYER'S CLOSE CONNECTION TO FRANK COSTELLO

Bill O'Dwyer's failure to perform his Brooklyn DA prosecutorial responsibilities and his association with high-ranking organized-crime figures was the focus of the Kefauver Committee's March 1951 hearings. O'Dwyer, his clandestine political patron Frank Costello, and his political operative James Moran gave similar testimony, but they attempted to distance themselves from these criticisms. Their testimony did reveal intriguing information about their relationship presented in the text.

The authors about early organized crime jumped on the campaign charge by O'Dwyer's mayoral opponent that O'Dwyer met with Costello in 1942 to obtain his approval to run for mayor in 1945. These writers wanted to illustrate the profound political power of Costello, but they lacked understanding of how politics works. Political kingmakers do not prohibit someone from entering a race, but rather decide which of the potential candidates the political machine will endorse and finance. These writers' suppositions failed to mention that the campaign was still three years away, and that O'Dwyer had recently campaigned for and lost the 1941 mayoralty election. He did not need a secret meeting to get anyone's permission to run a second time. Every one at the O'Dwyer-Costello meeting undoubtedly attended for political networking for future election aid, but the timing of that meeting did not correlate with any known current political developments.

ADDENDUM W – Chapter 9 – page 187

MAYOR O'DWYER WAS AN ERRATIC POLITICAL MANIPULATOR

Once O'Dwyer became Mayor, he became an erratic political manipulator. Remember Franklin Roosevelt always distanced himself from the corruption of Tammany Hall, which in turn opposed his nomination at the 1932 Democratic presidential convention. Later during O'Dwyer's successful

1945 Mayoral campaign, President Roosevelt's wife Eleanor pleaded privately with O'Dwyer to clean out the criminal associates and graft from the Tammany political machine. She and FDR apparently had distanced themselves far enough that they did not realize O'Dwyer was the most mobbed up and corrupt politician of them all.

O'Dwyer used President FDR's wife's suggestion for reform as a Machiavellian cover for replacing Tammany's leadership that had loyally supported his campaign. Long-term Tammany Secretary Bert Strand testified before the Kefauver Committee, "O'Dwyer's actions were always confusing, contradictory, and irrational. He changed the leadership in Tammany Hall almost as often as he changed his mind. The public, however, was apparently misled by all his artful double talk into believing that O'Dwyer sought to *reform* the organization, when actually his only objective was to control it. And he did control it! With the aid of his current cronies at the time, he forced a change in leadership in 1947, and Frank Sampson became an innocent beneficiary of O'Dwyer's strange political maneuverings. In rapid succession, came Hugo Rogers and Carmine DeSapio. In his five years as Mayor, O'Dwyer was for and against anybody and anything dependent upon his queer temperament."

ADDENDUM X – Chapter 9 – page 202

MAYOR O'DWYER INSTIGATED NYPD CORRUPTION, AND THE HARRY GROSS CASE

Mayor O'Dwyer appointed his close friend Third Deputy Commissioner Bill O'Brien to be Police Commissioner after LaGuardia's appointee Wallander retired in February 1949. He left the department after 35 years to join a private company. O'Brien had joined the NYPD the same year as Captain Frank Bals, and when O'Brien would later retire, the pair would work together in Florida real-estate transactions. O'Brien quickly abolished the Police Commissioner's Confidential Squad that investigated allegations of police dishonesty. It had been the department's strongest check on wrongdoing within its ranks.

Shortly after O'Brien became Police Commissioner, Brooklyn DA Miles McDonald began an investigation into charges of graft by members of the NYPD in connection with Brooklyn gambling. This probe culminated in September 1950 with the arrest of Harry Gross, New York City's largest illegal OTB (Off Track Betting) operator. Gross testified at this trial that he operated mostly in Brooklyn but also in Manhattan and Queens. He set up 27 horse-betting rooms in 1942 in the back of candy stores, restaurants, garages, factory lofts, a laundry, and a barbershop. He also ran eight telephone horse-wagering rooms. He ended up operating 35 until September 1950 "when I was pinched." He was given a 12-year penitentiary sentence for bookmaking.

Gross then turned state's witness and amazed the public by identifying the names, dates, and amounts of payoffs to 120 crooked cops in multiple NYPD departmental trials during May 1952. Gross proudly stated that because of his extensive bribery network none of his employees was ever arrested during the eight years he operated. He testified that he paid protection money for his enterprises to all levels of five major police units, including patrolmen on street beats, plainclothes detectives, supervisors, and high officials in the Police Commissioner's office. Gross paid a standard $200 a month to each cop on the take, which was a substantial addition to a patrolman's salary. Gross' revelations caused a wholesale reorganization of the NYPD.

In these NYPD trials, Gross stunned everyone by accusing former Mayor O'Dwyer's five key political appointees and long-time close personal friends of accepting bribes to protect his gambling operations. The five were Bals, O'Brien, James Moran, John Murtagh, and Bill Whalen, former Chief of Detectives. Police Commissioner O'Brien was the first to quit a week after Gross was arrested to avert Acting Mayor Impellitteri's threatened dismissal. Gross testified that O'Brien started taking payoffs in 1943 when he was just an inspector. Bals made out like a bandit during the two months he ran "the Mayor's Squad" in 1946. Gross paid Bals $200 a month for each of his 35 horse and telephone rooms totaling $7,000 monthly, about double his annual salary.

Gross testified that Commissioner of Investigation Murtagh removed the city's bookmakers' telephone numbers from his files. Gross testified that Moran came to him for O'Dwyer's 1949 Mayoral reelection campaign and demanded a "political assessment of $1,000 for each horse room" if he wanted to continue operating. Remember, O'Dwyer and every one associated with him always testified at investigations that they knew nothing about and could never find any illegal gambling activities in New York.

ADDENDUM Y – Chapter 9 – page 202

JAMES MORAN WAS THE POLITICAL FIXER FOR MAYOR O'DWYER

Bill O'Dwyer's close friend, confidant, and fixer of his corrupt schemes was James Moran. The two initially met when Moran was an obscure court attendant. Then O'Dwyer became Brooklyn DA, and he promoted Moran to chief clerk despite his lacking any legal training. Moran made the office's major prosecutorial decisions and directed the NYPD detectives assigned to the DA's office. This allowed him to enforce and cover up O'Dwyer's political manipulations. During O'Dwyer's Army service, Moran handled O'Dwyer's personal financial affairs. When O'Dwyer resigned as DA to run for Mayor of New York in 1945, Moran also quit. Six weeks after O'Dwyer was sworn in as Mayor in 1946, he appointed Moran as First Deputy Fire Commissioner. Then in 1950, outgoing Mayor O'Dwyer rewarded Moran with a lifetime appointment as Commissioner of the Board of Water Supply. This allowed him to overrule decisions made by engineers despite no training in engineering. What a way to run the country's biggest city!

Soon after Moran's lifetime appointment, the city's firemen's union president testified before the Kefauver Committee that when he was Deputy Fire Commissioner he gave a total of $55,000 in union funds as cash "gifts" to Moran to preserve his friendly attitude toward requests of the city's firefighters for improved salaries, pensions, and working hours. The day after his testimony, Mayor Impellitteri ordered Moran to quit his tenure-for-life post as Water Commissioner for violating his *during-good-behavior* clause by taking the cash payments and for his friendship with racketeer Costello.

Six weeks later on May 8, 1951, Moran was convicted of perjury in New York federal court for lying under oath to the Kefauver Committee and was sentenced to five years in prison. The Committee found he lived well within his salary, convincing them he was kicking the graft up to O'Dwyer. They offered him a sentencing deal if he would finally tell the truth, but he remained silent to protect his friend and former boss.

Nine months later on February 5, 1952, a jury quickly found Moran guilty of 23 counts of extortion for being the "guiding genius and protector" of extorting New York City's 1,600 fuel-oil installers. Moran hired the Fire Department inspectors, who required the installers to charge residents a fixed schedule of illegally-high fees, and to kick back graft in return for oil-burner installation permits. This was not bribery for approval of defective or improper installations, but extortion of payments for approving proper installations. Even though Moran never acknowledged sharing his extortion and bribe moneys, the judge characterized Moran's mentor and close friend, former Mayor O'Dwyer, as "a shining example of everything a public official should not be," before sentencing Moran to 15 ½ to 28 years in state prison.

In an effort to either impress the judges handling his various cases, or to respond to mute pangs of conscious about a career devoted to dereliction of duty and criminal acts, Moran began attending night classes at St. John's University on ethics and Christian theology prior to entering Sing Sing on March 13, 1952 to begin the first of his two concurrent sentences. While in prison he was convicted a third time for federal income tax evasion and given an additional 2 years. During the decade of his 50's, Moran spent a total of 10 ½ years in prison for the three offenses. Afterwards in his 60's he became a stenographer in his son's law firm. Six years into his tenure, he was riding on the subway when he suffered a fatal heart attack.

ADDENDUM Z – Chapter 10 – page 203 and 214

LUCIANO'S CONTRIBUTION TO THE ALLIED VICTORY IN WORLD WAR II IS CONFIRMED BY MULTIPLE SOURCES

Governor Dewey appointed State Commissioner of Investigation William Herlands in 1954 to conduct an official but private inquiry into the possible collaboration of organized crime leaders with the Navy during World War II. Herlands and his staff of six interviewed 57 key witnesses. Half were high-ranking Naval officers, and most of the rest administered justice in New York State. A handful of major hoodlums or their attorneys also voluntarily testified. Every key fact included in the Herland Report was corroborated by at least two witnesses in sworn testimony at the hearings. Some of the chief witnesses also testified in other federal, state, and local hearings, and their other statements were always consistent with these but less detailed.

The U.S. Navy cooperated with the state investigation only after the Governor promised to never reveal the findings publicly. Dewey kept his word. He buried his copy of the Herlands Report in his personal files, and he maintained his vow of silence because Naval leaders warned him that if he ever revealed Charlie Luciano's involvement they would publicly disavow any knowledge. But five years after Dewey's death in 1971, his family turned the official state report and his personal files over to a strong Dewey supporter, author Rodney Campbell. He wrote *The Luciano Project: The Secret Wartime Collaboration of the Mafia & the U. S. Navy* in 1977, 23 years after the Report was completed and more than three decades after the incidents actually occurred.

Campbell's book unfortunately suffers from two weaknesses. First, the information other than from the Herlands Report was clearly a rehash from earlier fraudulent crime books. Second, Campbell was extremely biased in favor of Dewey. Like Dewey's publicist Hickman Powell in *Ninety Times Guilty* and Assistant DA Burton Turkus in *Murder, Inc. - The Story of the Syndicate,* Campbell never wrote a single critical word about Dewey. All three were effusive in their accolades deifying Dewey as the flawless, perfect American politician.

What is important here is the accuracy of Campbell's presentation of the 1954 Herlands Commission Report findings, and also the many credible multiple sources that independently substantiate all or at least parts of every fact offered by Campbell. Equally significant is that no inquiry nor any individual ever contradicted anything Campbell said about Luciano's World War II assistance to Naval Intelligence. For example, a *New York Times* reporter was allowed to read the official summary of the original copy of the Commission Report, and his newspaper published it, listing every important underworld contribution to the war effort that Campbell presented. (The reporter read it at Chase Manhattan Bank after a co-executor of Dewey's estate gave permission, and it was published by the *New York Times* on October 9, 1977 shortly after Campbell's book was released.)

In addition, the FBI obtained Naval Intelligence approval to conduct extensive secret interviews with several of the key Naval participants in the Herland inquiry soon after it was completed. These FBI interviews independently confirm every major point in Campbell's book. This was a few years after the events occurred, so the facts were fresh in the officers' memories. The FBI interviews were conducted two decades before the Freedom of Information Act went into effect in 1967, so the officers talked freely believing their statements would always remain buried in the FBI's confidential files. Everything they told the FBI was identical to what Campbell wrote later that they testified to at Herlands' hearings. Further, Campbell's presentation of the Herlands Commission Report's findings correspond with specific facts available from many other sources. These include the Manhattan DA's office, the New York State Department of Corrections, the State Board of Parole, court legal briefs, and press interviews with some of the principals years later.

Campbell's book described these wartime intelligence events in detail. He included the dates and locations of the main events and many quotes from the 57 key participants. If his book had inaccuracies, many of these people would have complained to the press, but not one did. Campbell wrote about the contribution of many Naval Intelligence officers, New York officials from various government agencies, underworld leaders, and their attorneys. A large majority were still alive when his book was published, and since all were retired, they could have spoken out if they disagreed with what he wrote without interference from former supervisors. Significantly, the Navy neither refuted nor concurred with any part of Campbell's narrative despite having long ago officially denied any association with Luciano and his intimates. Dewey's family retained the original report, and they never criticized the author's handling of the documents they had entrusted to him.

The Navy may have publicly denied any involvement with Luciano, but it secretly admitted Luciano's role in confidential communications to the FBI. A 1946 letter from the Office of the Chief of Naval Operations "acknowledges that Luciano was employed as an informant," according to FBI Headquarters Memorandum May 17, 1946. The FBI document further states, "The letter from the Office of Chief of Naval Operations sets out that in 1941, the security of the port of New York was a matter of great concern, not only to the Third Naval District, but to the Secretary of the Navy and the President of the United States, and further that in accordance with the directive issued by the Secretary of the Navy, the activities of the District Intelligence Organization in the Third Naval District were expanded to afford the required coverage in the port of New York." The FBI document continues, "The Navy points out that because of the large Italian population in New York City, every effort was made to obtain any and all information concerning the Mediterranean area, which might be useful in planning operations in that theater. Haffenden was placed in charge of collecting such intelligence and submitted numerous reports on information assembled from all available sources in the New York Area." It is clear that Naval Operations knew the crucial nature of Luciano's mission.

Top Naval brass made other acknowledgements to the FBI about Luciano's War contributions. "The Office of Naval Intelligence [internal] investigation in July, 1945, reflected that Haffenden utilized informants sent to him as a result of arrangements he made with Luciano through Luciano's attorney, Moses Playoff," from FBI Memorandum January 5, 1953. "On May 10, 1946, the Navy advised (the Director of the FBI) that Haffenden's action in behalf of Luciano were known or authorized by Naval authorities," from FBI Internal Memorandum January 29, 1954.

The Navy officially admitted Luciano's World War II efforts publicly in 1959 in the final episode of a new three-part radio series *Profiles in Crime*. Key government officials were permitted to go into detail during interviews. A FBI report about the program stated, "The Navy Department in Washington furnished an official answer in a statement released by Lieutenant Commander Hunt to the effect that in the Spring of 1942, Naval Intelligence was utilizing all available sources of information and Luciano was contacted to exploit his influence on possible criminal sources of information." The radio show was broadcast on March 30, 1959 by MAC New York, from FBI Internal Memorandum to the Director May 13, 1959.

Haffenden headed the War intel effort, and several times over the years he publicly credited to the press Luciano for his contribution. For example, when Luciano's presence in Havana became a political football, Haffenden held a New York press conference on February 27, 1947. He explained, "Luciano was called on through Polakoff and Lanza for information available from Sicilians living in New York City" to gather pre-invasion information about Sicily. This was given large coverage by the *Havana Post* and the *Kansas City Times* using that dateline.

Haffenden also spoke out at a critical time. Following Luciano's application for clemency, Haffenden sent a letter on his behalf to Charles Brietel, Secretary to Governor Thomas E. Dewey of New York, dated May 17, 1945. Haffenden said, "I am confident that the great part of the intelligence developed in the Sicilian campaign was directly responsible to the number of Sicilians that emanated from the Charlie "Lucky" contact. Additional assistance on various subjects came from this same informant which can be explained to you in detail at a later date." The FBI New York Office inserted this letter in a May 14, 1946 report.

Despite this mass of corroborating evidence from so many different official and credible sources, every writer about early organized crime has stated that Luciano made no more than a token contribution to the War effort. While falsely denying that Luciano is a great American war hero, these same authors accused him of all kinds of bad deeds that either did not occur or of which he was not a participant in any way.

ADDENDUM AA – Chapter 10 – page 215

THE FBI INQUIRIES OF LUCIANO'S WAR INTEL EFFORTS FOR POLITICAL DIRT COMPLIMENT HIM

The FBI's inquiry into Luciano began over the conduct of his deportation departure, rather than his War intel contributions, because New York City Mayor Fiorello LaGuardia sent a letter to the FBI Director and his boss, the U.S. Attorney General. LaGuardia included a copy of his February 10, 1946 Sunday radio broadcast in which he alleged that Costello visited Luciano on Ellis Island and then attended a party aboard ship. FBI Headquarters directed its New York City office to investigate the circumstances surrounding these two incidents. It was referred to as "a discreet inquiry to ascertain the facts" because of their political nature. The New York City Office reported its findings to the Director in reports dated February 25, 26, and 27, and May 5, 1946. The FBI determined that Luciano's departure was handled properly, but J. Edgar Hoover expanded the inquiry into trying to find out the reason why Governor Dewey pardoned Luciano after having prosecuted him so vigorously. This inquiry is how the FBI learned about Luciano's important War intel contributions.

The deportation and the War intel issues both concerned a major gangster, but they also involved possible political corruption or at least curious backroom intrigue. Luciano's FBI file is a typical example of Hoover's use of the FBI to monitor Constitutionally-protected political activity rather than to fight major crime. Luciano's 548-page file contains almost nothing about his criminal career. Director Hoover had no interest in the country's most powerful hoodlum until he saw the possibility that investigating Luciano might provide scandalous file records about a leading Governor and Presidential candidate that could be used as blackmail to influence his policies, positions, and appointments.

The FBI did not even start a file on the country's most powerful hoodlum until the end of Luciano's criminal career. The first document was dated August 28, 1935, less than a year before he was framed into prison with a long sentence. This FBI report states, "An individual signing his name as xxxxx by letter dated February 14, 1935, made the statement that Meyer Lansky and Charles Luccio (sic), alias 'Lucky' is the head of the underworld in New York City and also alleged that the individual is connected with other well known racketeers and gangsters. The writer evidently had reference to Luciana." After listing Luciano's arrest record, this sparse report concludes, "The Bureau's files reflect no further information in connection with this individual."

The second document in the FBI's files was dated seven years later on October 16, 1942. It was created because of the INS's outstanding deportation warrant against Luciano that was to be imposed when he was released from prison. The FBI closed this case since he was "being held for his maximum sentence until 1986."

The third document in Luciano's file was dated February 21, 1946, more than a decade after the first. The FBI initiated this inquiry two weeks after Luciano boarded a ship for exile in Italy in reaction to Governor Dewey's surprising pardon and exile. While Hoover ignored Luciano during all the years he was involved in criminal activity in the U.S., the Director launched his first major investigation of this Italian citizen after he was barred from ever returning to the U.S. under threat of having to complete his long prison sentence. Hoover clearly had no interest in Luciano or his criminal activities. The Director was searching for possible dirt that might emanate from all the political furor over his pardon. Dewey had been the Republican candidate for President two years earlier and he would be again two years hence. Hoover's main goal for the FBI was to collect and store scandalous, embarrassing information on every major politician, so he could blackmail them into framing their policies the way he directed.

ADDENDUM BB – Chapter 10 – page 222

THE TWO FRAUDULENT AUTOBIOGRAPHIES
THE LAST TESTAMENT OF LUCKY LUCIANO (1974)
MEYER LANSKY: MOGUL OF THE MOB (1979)

The Hollywood movie and television industry perpetuates myths about Luciano and his associates based on the fictions contained in the fraudulent Luciano and Lansky "autobiographies." In Martin Gosch's airport statement at the time of Luciano's death, it is telling that he mentioned a possible movie project but neither a book nor conducting a series of interviews with the infamous hoodlum. Gosch made these book claims later, despite having no writing experience or credentials for Luciano to have chosen him. Actually the book project did not began until after Gosch's death, when his wife, who inherited the book royalty rights, teamed up with freelance-writer Richard Hammer. Hammer claimed he wrote from handwritten interview notes loaned by Gosch's wife who, upon their return, inexplicably burned them. She claimed that her husband had met with Luciano 30 times over the last four years of his life, while Gosch wrote in his preliminary text that the meetings were only during the last 10 months. She also declared that she had witnessed some of the interviews at their home in Spain, but Italy had revoked Luciano's passport. He would have been arrested if he tried to leave Naples or he tried to enter Spain or any other European country. Mrs. Gosch had no evidence to back up her claim that her husband also flew to Italy on many occasions to interview Luciano. She had no trip expense statements, no tax return business deductions, or a single person in either country who knew about a single meeting between her husband and Luciano.

In response to *New York Times* reporter Nicholas Cage's crushing expose, the publisher tried to protect the more than $1 million generated in pre-sales by quickly declaring the company possessed Gosch's interview tapes, handwritten notes, a signed agreement with Luciano, and verification by law-enforcement authorities. But under mounting press scrutiny, the publisher was forced to admit that not one of the claims in its publicity, its advertising, and on the book's jacket-cover was true. Little, Brown & Co. still managed to make a profit with the fraud by replacing ads claiming Luciano dictated it on "tapes" with disingenuous ads that the book created "a storm of controversy," which the reader should decide for himself. Even though the two top men's nudie magazines proudly proclaimed that they offered their reader/lookers quality literary articles, both succumbed to the fraudulent profit bandwagon. Without indicating to their readers that *The Last Testament of Lucky Luciano* was a complete sham, *Penthouse* serialized it, and *Playboy* made it a Book Club selection. The promotion of this enormous literary hoax revealed an astounding lack of integrity by the nation's publishing industry.

Cage's well-documented exposé revealed that the Gosch-Hammer book quoted Luciano as saying he participated in meetings and events that would have been impossible because he was either imprisoned or dead at the time. The book has Luciano directing the activity of members of rival gangs, and it placed major gangsters in the wrong gangs and positions of authority. While Gosch-Hammer acknowledged that the *Night of Vespers* did not occur, they wrote that Luciano admitted killing lots of people at the time of Maranzano's murder, which is disproved by police records. Gosch-Hammer had Luciano deny the rumors that he helped the World War II Sicilian invasion for which he was a bona fide patriot, and they did not have him complain about how DA Dewey had framed him. Gosch-Hammer also had Luciano say that a person who kills a Mafia leader cannot take their place, when many transfers of power have been by lieutenants killing their leaders, including Luciano killing first Masseria and then Maranzano. The book is filled with so much nonsense that it would take a whole book to respond to all the major factual errors.

Luciano's lawyer Polakoff said that in the 65-page section of the book in which he was directly involved, "not 5 percent of the accounts bear any resemblance to reality." Gosch-Hammer had Luciano identify the wrong attorney as handling his trial defense, and they say his bond "was quickly posted," when it is documented that he never made bail. Crime authors Peter Maas and Hank Messick told reporter Cage that most of the Mafia information in the alleged autobiography had already appeared in previous books. Gosch-Hammer not only put issues in Luciano's mouth that had been presented in earlier books and since disproved, but they even repeated spelling errors from other books illustrating the extent of their plagiarism.

The FBI's internal evaluation in its Memorandum October 2, 1974 concluded that Gosch's *The Last Testament Of Lucky Luciano* was a complete fraud. This included his own admission, and the FBI's evaluation that he had a reputation as a serious liar. The FBI analysis concluded, "With respect to Gosch's personal veracity, Bureau files reveal that he was described in 1962 by the Chief of the United States Narcotics Bureau in Rome as being completely untrustworthy, a liar, and an opportunist who was trying to take advantage of his association with Luciano to produce a movie about the dead mobster. And in 1962, Gosch told the [FBI's] Bureau's Legal Attaché in Madrid that his movie script about Luciano had been largely 'made up out of the whole cloth' and bore little resemblance to anything that had actually occurred. In 1972, Gosch appeared at FBIHQ [FBI Headquarters] and unsuccessfully attempted to secure our help in converting the script (which he said had had Luciano's approval) into book form."

Five years after the publication of *The Last Testament of Lucky Luciano,* three Israelis authored *Meyer Lansky: Mogul of the Mob.* Lansky told friends that he gave just one newspaper interview in his life to paint a rosy, publicity-puff picture for the Israeli government, when he was opposing extradition to the U.S. to face criminal charges. The interviewer, Uri Dan, and his two associates, Dennis Eisenberg and Eli Landau, later published a book, claiming it was Lansky's autobiography based on many hours of interviews. But Lansky denied to associates he was ever interviewed for a book. Lansky's closest friend after the death of Ben Siegel was Jimmy Blue Eyes, who lamented to me, "The Israeli autobiography was all bullshit. Meyer was really upset about his name drug through those lies, but what could he do? The books always lied about us." Two other men said Meyer told them he never contributed to the so-called autobiography, according to author Robert Lacey in *Little Man: Meyer Lansky and the Gangster Life.* (See Addendum DD)

The authors possessed no substantiation of any kind that they ever met with Meyer after the newspaper interview. Their book contains photos of 14 pages of documents, but Lansky's signature appears on only two letters he sent to author Dan. Unbelievably, Lansky's letters make it clear that no book interviews ever took place. While the authors claimed they conducted the interviews between 1971 and 1978, Lansky wrote Dan on November 7, 1976 near the end of this process that he had no interest in contributing to a book. He wrote, "Uri, your suggestion to me to write for posterity is worth a serious thought but I don't want to rush anything. Whether I will ever devote myself to writing a book isn't definite as of now and I doubt if ever while I'm alive. I'm not interested in discussing this writing with anyone else, only Uri Dan will I talk to, and their [sic] it dies. Money doesn't interest me at present. What I'm interested in knowing from you is what the outline would have to be to make my biography saleable. After I am aware as to what you want to know about me, I will then decide whether I am interested in writing in the future." The letter makes it obvious that no deal had been negotiated or interviews conducted prior to 1977, and in fact no outline was later discussed by them.

Lansky sent author Dan his second and final letter a year later on October 28, 1977. In it Lansky expressed his desire to visit Israel, but he made no mention of a book. However, at that time the text would have had to have been close to finished. It was turned in by the fraudulent authors the next year in 1978, so it could be edited before publication in 1979. Yet at the end of 1977 Lansky did not mention or ask anything about the supposedly nearly-completed book's progress. Lansky resided in the U.S. during the alleged interview period, and the authors have no evidence they traveled to meet him where he resided. The authors also have no memos to or from Lansky, and no document signed by Lansky. The authors have no contract, no authorization, and no endorsement signed by him, nor any payment to him, even though Lansky's letter brought up the issue of receiving compensation.

Even though *The Last Testament of Lucky Luciano* had been thoroughly discredited by the press and the publishing industry, the Lansky book copied many of its errors and added a bevy of ridiculous fabrications because the three Israeli's knew nothing about American culture. Their history of American organized crime is bizarre. They make the Jewish Lansky top dog in the Mafia and Luciano his underling. They have Lansky directing all major crime in the U.S., and being the financier of the mob, even though the vast majority of Mafia leaders would not discuss business with him because he was not Sicilian. The authors say Lansky and Luciano ordained that "The smallest man in every outfit should always be given a chance to talk to the boss if he has a grievance," despite the fact that every Mafia leader insulated himself from his members through his lieutenant. The authors claim Lansky invented most types of major financial crime, even though all existed before he was born. They gave Lansky psychic powers to predict major political events, economic conditions, and underworld killings years in advance, so he could plan and direct the correct strategies to deal with them. They accused Lansky of supplying law enforcement with incriminating evidence against many major East Coast gangsters. On the contrary, Lansky was trusted in the underworld because he never talked to nor assisted the authorities. In addition, Lansky actually knew nothing about the other gangsters' illicit businesses because all in that era kept their businesses and crimes secret.

Everything in their book about Las Vegas, the *Flamingo,* and Siegel is incorrect. Most of it is made up and the rest copied from erroneous sources. They claimed the *Flamingo* was the first Strip hotel instead of the third, and they said it was the first casino in Las Vegas, when a number of licensed casinos had operated downtown for the previous fifteen years. Indeed Siegel owned a couple of these before building the *Flamingo.* Their description of Las Vegas at the time they published was even incorrect. They refer to Siegel as *Bugsy,* an offense that would have caused Lansky to permanently walk out on the authors (see Nickname in Chapter 16). Their book has so many factual errors that it would take a set of encyclopedias to adequately refute them all.

The weaknesses in the biographies supposedly about Luciano, Costello, Lansky, and Rothstein are detailed in the Endnotes for Chapter 5 about Rothstein. At the beginning of my first interview with Jimmy Blue Eyes, I explained that I spent my career conducting historical research because I wanted to present what actually happened in the building of the Nevada casino industry. He replied, "I'm fascinated by history. I'm only talkin' to you because I respect your searching for the truth. But the lies have been told about Meyer (Lansky) and Ben (Siegel) and Charlie (Luciano) for so long and so many times, you can't change anything. The lies are now the world's reality. No one's goanna believe you." (Many details about the two fraudulent autobiographies are in Addendum L for Chapter 5 about Rothstein, in Addendum M for Chapter 7 about Luciano, and in Addendum DD for Chapter 14 about Lansky.)

ADDENDUM CC – Chapter 14 – page 294

THE POLICE SURVEILLANCE OF MY INTERVIEWS WITH JIMMY BLUE EYES

Vincent "Jimmy Blue Eyes" Alo's two adult grandsons lived in Las Vegas and worked in the casino business, and they and their families became good friends with my wife and I. Both grandsons supported my historical research, and they too were curious about their retired grandfather's former criminal life. Over a period of years, whenever Jimmy came from Florida to visit his family in Las Vegas, one of his grandsons would ask him if he would talk to me, but he always demurred until April 1, 1995. That day in a telephone call from Florida to his family in Las Vegas, Jimmy said he would talk with me during his upcoming visit with them.

This planned meeting could have potentially produced severe career problems for me because Nevada gaming licensees are prohibited from any association with organized crime figures, and at that time, the FBI listed Jimmy as "a semi-retired capo in the Genovese crime family." Fortunately, my historical research was well known and had always been accepted by the State Gaming Control Board, the Las Vegas Metropolitan Police Department (Metro), leading politicians, top attorneys, casino-industry leaders, and the University of Nevada System for which I had been an instructor of the course "Casino Operations and Management" during the decade of the 1970s. In addition, my historical research project was a serious sociological academic study of organized crime and the Nevada gambling industry, which had been initiated by the School of Criminology at the University of California, Berkeley in 1967 and after it was ordered by the Federal Selective Service System (explained in the Introduction). I was still concerned, so I asked my Las Vegas gaming attorney if interviewing Jimmy could create career difficulties for me. After considering the implications, he laughed and told me, "They can't make a frail 91-year-old man Public Enemy Number 1."

I now had the go-ahead to interview Jimmy Blue Eyes, but his family had told me about an ongoing problem he had with the Las Vegas police. Each time Jimmy visited, he obeyed the law by registering as a convicted felon with Metro within two days of arriving in town. When detectives from Metro's Criminal Intelligence Section (CIS) learned he was in town, they would park outside Jimmy's son's home, and they would knock at the front door to ask what he was doing in town. He would explain he was simply visiting his family. This fragile old man did not want difficulty with anyone, and these intrusions really upset him, so after his wife's death, he rarely visited his family.

I came up with a solution to try and benefit not only Jimmy and his family but also Metro's CIS. It would allow Jimmy to visit his family more often without being bothered by detectives knocking at his door, and it would save Metro's CIS detectives time by no longer having to confirm where he was staying. I had worked with Detective John Nicholson of the Organized Crime Bureau in the CIS for many years on cheating cases whenever he, or I, was warned someone planned a major theft from one of the two Strip casinos I managed, or others I consulted to. I was the first Las Vegas casino manager to have Metro and the Gaming Control Board arrest gambling sharks. Previously, thieves were escorted off Las Vegas casino properties by security guards, sometimes rather roughly.

After Jimmy's grandson approved my proposed solution, I made the following suggestion to Detective Nicholson on April 4, 1995. I offered to report to him the date Jimmy planned to arrive in Las Vegas each time he wanted to visit. This would give CIS knowledge Jimmy was in town before the time he registered as a felon. More importantly to me, by telling Detective Nicholson where I was going to meet Jimmy for each interview, CIS would know where he was staying. Thus, Detectives would no longer have to confirm his location by sitting parked for long hours waiting for him to walk out of the house or to knock at the door and upset him.

Jimmy's upcoming arrival date was for April 8, 1995, but he did not make that flight. I called Detective Nicholson to tell him that the trip was off. Four days later on April 12, 1995, I received a call at midnight from Jimmy's grandson. The family was celebrating Jimmy's arrival with a small reunion by doing up the town. The happy throng wanted me to be at his son's house the next morning at 9:30 a.m., and I spent most of the night preparing my interview questions from all of my resource material. Early the next morning I called Detective Nicholson at his office desk to notify him of Jimmy's arrival, but I was told he was out of town and could not be reached.

None of the other Metro detectives I knew worked in Detective Nicholson's division, so I had no one to report to. I did not know that he had taken my proposal to his Lieutenant, and that his boss was the one who had approved the arrangement. When Jimmy arrived, he first registered with Metro before going to stay with his son. Since no one in the CIS office knew that I had tried to notify Detective Nicholson, the Lieutenant assumed I had reneged on my offer to mediate, so he had two detectives park down the block from Jimmy' son's house to conduct surveillance. I soon arrived for my first two-hour interview. We were interrupted when the two detectives knocked at the front door to confirm that he was staying there. After talking to them in the doorway, Jimmy rejoined his grandson and me at the dining room table. He told us the detectives stumbled and stammered so much trying to explain why they were there that, "I actually felt sorry for them."

My primary goal had been to save Jimmy from receiving the inevitable intrusive knock at his door during this visit, but these plans were nullified when Detective Nicholson left town. I trusted Detective Nicholson because we knew each other well, and he absolutely kept his word. In contrast I had no idea who his supervisory Lieutenant was, nor that he had approved this agreement. When

Jimmy Blue Eyes registered with Metro, the Lieutenant was aware the CIS office had not received a call from me. He made no inquiry to find out if I had acted in good faith by attempting to notify Detective Nicholson about the time and location of my interview. The Lieutenant must have been very angry because he then broke protocol. Metro is a Clark County agency that investigates criminality, and its CIS is highly secretive and protective of its information. Thus Metro has rarely contributed evidence to a Gaming Control Board investigation because it is a state agency that investigates its own regulation violations with civil penalties. The Board is not a law enforcement agency any more than is the Tax Commission, which before creation of the Board handled gaming control and casino licensing.

Yet, the Lieutenant had a detective fill out an organized-crime police report, describing my entering and leaving Jimmy's son's home with papers in my hand. These were my detailed historical research interview notes. This Metro CSI report also listed my background in the casino industry. At that time, I was licensed as a key executive as a member of the board of directors of the *Riviera Hotel-Casino* on the Las Vegas Strip, as well as President at the *Oasis Hotel-Casino* in Mesquite, Nevada, so the Lieutenant sent a copy of the CIS's report of a licensee's visit with Jimmy to the Gaming Control Board. The Lieutenant knew that the Board considered any association with organized crime to be the most serious offense for license denial or revocation. He had to have expected that the Board would almost certainly ban me from the industry and end my career.

He was right about the Board; my meeting with a capo in the nation's largest Mafia gang raised a big red flag. Whenever an allegation or a question is brought up about a licensee, Board agents investigate, and they never close a case until they can file additional paperwork to appropriately explain or justify no further action. When the Board Agent, who was assigned to investigate this CIS report, called me to inquire what it meant, I was stunned to hear such an incriminating document existed. I explained to the Agent that I had acted in good faith and had tried to contact Detective Nicholson just as I said I would. When the truth came out about the legitimacy of my academic research and that I was trying to assist Metro, the CIS Lieutenant did not want to send the Board a statement that he had supplied an erroneous report about my activities. Instead he had Detective Nicholson send me a personal letter explaining my legitimate actions and copied it to the Board to satisfactorily close my case.

Detective Nicholson's April 29, 1995 letter stated:

> On April 4, 1995 you called to inform me of a potential meeting that might be of some interest to me. I would like to take this opportunity to thank you for sharing that information with myself and LVMPD. Since you are in the process of writing a book about the early history of Las Vegas and the Organized Crime Figures of that era, it is often necessary for you to interview possible or known criminal elements that were formally involved in the time frame that you are concerned with. When you became aware that such an interview might take place with Vincent (Jimmy Blue Eyes) Alo, you were quick to notify me and did not object to being put under surveillance at that meeting. Subsequently, such an encounter did take place and your information was useful to us. Again may I say that I sincerely appreciate being made aware of this situation. I hope you will continue in the future as you have in the past to make us aware of any similar situations should they arise. Good luck on your continuing historical work.
> Sincerely,
> Detective, LVMPD, Organized Crime Bureau, Criminal Intelligence Section

Based on the information in this letter, the Board closed my case. Under the circumstances, the Board Agent in charge considered my visit with Jimmy to be so trivial that he saw no need for further discussion. Thus, he never notified me about my case's closure. For some time I remained very worried about the possible impact of the Metro CIS organized-crime report that had been sent to the Board. As the length of the silence grew, my stress level increased, until I finally called the Agent in charge to ask where my case stood. He told me that when the Board received the Detective's letter explaining the details of my meeting with Jimmy Blue Eyes, everyone there had a good laugh about my being an investigative target over my academic interest in organized crime. This allowed me to finally let go with a big sigh of relief. Thank goodness!

ADDENDUM DD – Chapter 14 – page 298

THE STRENGTHS AND WEAKNESSES OF *LITTLE MAN* ABOUT LANSKY

The falseness of the two alleged autobiographies - *The Last Testament of Lucky Luciano* and *Meyer Lansky: Mogul of the Mob* - was documented in Addendum BB above. Robert Lacey, author of the biography *Little Man: Meyer Lansky and the Gangster Life,* reacted very different to these two phony autobiographies. He rejected the *Last Testament of Lucky Luciano* because, as he wrote, "My own research has more than confirmed the doubts cast on their [authors'] veracity by critics." Interestingly Little, Brown and Company published both the discredited Luciano book and Lacey's book with its criticism of their other book. In contrast, Lacey relied heavily on *Meyer Lansky: Mogul of the Mob,* despite its being a rehash of the Luciano book he discredited and despite containing many additional fictions. This is particularly surprising because Lacey quoted two men who said Lansky never contributed to an autobiography. Lansky's Israeli friend Joseph "Yoskeh" Sheiner told Lacey that Lansky had confided in him, "I have given one interview against my wishes and inner judgment," referring to a newspaper interview Lansky gave Israeli journalist Uri Dan to improve his image with the Israeli government where he sought citizenship in that country.

Dan and two associates later wrote *Meyer Lansky: Mogul of the Mob,* claiming it was his autobiography based on many hours of interviews, which Lansky denied ever occurred to not only Sheiner but also writer Paul Sann. Despite publishing these two disclaimers attributed to Lansky, Lacey repeatedly quotes the phony autobiography by Dan and also Sann's notes. Sann was the *New York Post's* executive editor who approached Lansky in the mid '70s to write his autobiography. Sann said Lansky flirted with the idea in a few long-distance phone calls during which he was so "evasive" and vague as to make his answers meaningless. Despite this, Lacey repeatedly quotes Sann's notes. Lacey also used information from earlier fabricated crime books. Thus, the Lacey book is as dubious concerning Lansky's youth and his illegal Prohibition and gambling activities as the Luciano and earlier Lansky books. Lacey did interview some of Lansky's offspring and social friends from late in his life, but they knew nothing about his criminal activities. (Many details about these two fraudulent autobiographies are in Addendum L for Chapter 5 about Rothstein, in Addendum M for Chapter 7 about Luciano, and in Addendum BB for Chapter 10 about Luciano.)

Robert Lacey made one important contribution in his book by being the only author to obtain complete, un-redacted (or non-blacked-out) records of the U.S. Department of Justice, FBI, IRS, and INS, courtesy of the Israeli government. While historians usually accept government documents as fact per se, these complete records allowed Lacey to discredit the reliability and even the veracity of many of these agencies' informant files. He also exposed weaknesses in these investigative intelligent operations and questioned their goals, revealing major government misconduct. These government agency documents are extremely valuable because some parts reveal for the first time secret government surveillance and investigative operations, and the parts that can be validated give us a previously unforeseen look into the personal life of *Public Enemy Number 1.*

ENDNOTES & TIMELINES

HOW THE SOURCE DOCUMENTATION IS PRESENTED

The historical research for this series of books was conducted over almost five decades by rigorously collecting the available facts about the backgrounds, careers, interrelationships, values, and lifestyles of the men who built the Nevada casino industry. Following this, the political and sociological dynamics surrounding these men's careers was exhaustively analyzed. These endnotes provide three types of support information for the material in the text.

1- The information in the text was found in a variety of sources, which are identified in these notes to assist historians interested in further study or to confirm the accuracy of their use in this text. For every quote, the name of the person who said it and the source where it was found are identified either in the text or in these notes. Quotes taken from gambling-industry pioneers who contributed to my research are listed as "my interview." Facts contained in most consecutive sentences in the text are from different sources, so a complete documentation would require a book much longer than this one. The simple but effective solution was to not identify the specific newspaper sources because most information was obtained from the combined reportage of six daily newspapers from 1930 on - the *New York Times,* the *Chicago Daily Tribune,* the *Los Angeles Times,* the *Las Vegas Review Journal,* the *Las Vegas Sun,* and Reno's *Nevada State Journal.* Historians, scholars, interested readers, and critics can easily obtain more detailed information about each issue by going to these newspapers or other local papers for the multitude of dates listed in the notes below. The importance of newspapers in crime investigations is described in the Introduction.

This research included many types of documents and in-depth interviews with 582 Nevada gambling-industry pioneers. My interviewees provided valuable eyewitness accounts that confirmed, corrected, and expanded on the newspaper reports. In addition to my interviews and the newspaper sources, many documents were used, and each is identified either in the text or in these endnotes. They include Congressional hearings, FBI files, legislative and court records, books and magazines, and unpublished documents. In the text these are cited by source type – for example, "in testimony before the U.S. Senate Kefauver Committee."

2- The names of people who appear only briefly in a single incident are listed just in these endnotes in order to be available to historians, without cluttering, complicating, or slowing reading of the text. These people are clearly identified in the text according to their relationship to the event. For example "an eyewitness" or "his girlfriend."

3- Dates in the text are replaced with the length of time in days, weeks, or months between pairs of related events to make the time frame clear. The dates for all major events are presented in the endnotes, and the key dates for related events are listed in chronological order to create clear historical timelines. These groups of related dates will be an invaluable research resource and validation aid to historians who may wish to quickly look up the event and study specific facts in more detail. I wish such timelines had been available to me, but I had to search out each individual incident. Historians can look up every event in the six listed newspapers that were repeatedly used or in other local papers. Usually, the stories appear on the day after the date of an incident in the morning editions but occasionally on the same day as the event in the evening editions.

When the FBI releases document pages under the Freedom of Information Act, it usually redacts (blacks out) the names of everyone except the file subject. Thus, quotes of FBI documents in the text and in the endnotes may contain five small x's in quotes ('xxxxx') to indicate a redacted name was in the quote of an FBI document.

Notes
INTRODUCTION

THE EXTENSIVE NEWSPAPER RECORDS
i- The quote by Vincent "Jimmy Blue Eyes" Alo is from my April 13, 1995 interview. Every quote and paraphrase by Jimmy in this book comes from my interviews with him.

ii- The Harrison Narcotics Tax Act criminalized certain drugs for the first time in 1914 by requiring regulation and taxation of the production, importation, and distribution of opiates. This Act created the Bureau of Narcotics under the IRS in the Treasury Department. In 1930 as the federal effort against Prohibition was losing momentum, Congress renamed it the Federal Bureau of Narcotics (FBN) and upgraded it to an agency under the Treasury Department. In July 1973 President Richard Nixon issued an Executive Order to transform FBN into the Drug Enforcement Administration (DEA) under the Justice Department to establish a single unified command to combat "an all-out global war on the drug menace."

iii- The first fraudulent autobiography was *The Last Testament of Lucky Luciano* (see Chapter 10), and the second *Meyer Lansky: Mogul of the Mob* Chapter 14). Also see Addendums.

iv- The quote by Vincent "Jimmy Blue Eyes" Alo is from my April 13, 1995 interview.

v- The two quotes by Bob Cahill are from my May 20, 1968 interview.

Notes Chapter 1
THE PROHIBITION OPERATIONS OF LUCIANO & COSTELLO

PROHIBITION - IDEALISM WITH UNINTENDED CONSEQUENCES
1- The founder of the colony of Georgia was James Oglethorpe. Some of this information is from *Rumrunners, Moonshiners And Bootleggers* on The History Channel 2002. The three terms – moonshiners, rumrunners, and bootleggers – are used interchangeably for Prohibition violators in this text for varieties sake.

2- The number of alcohol suppliers and consumption both grew dramatically during Prohibition according to the politicians, businessmen, and researchers who studied it at that time. We have only these observers' accounts because the violators did not keep written records of production, wholesale distribution, or retail sales.

3- The rate of alcohol and drug offenses is from a 1930 analysis. Federal prison cost increases were between 1915 and 1932.

PROHIBITION'S MANY NEW SOURCES OF ALCOHOL
4- Frank Wilson's quote is from his *Special Agent: 25 Years With The American Secret Service.*

5- Wine production and grape-growing acreage for 1918, 1920, and 1925 are based on federal government records.

SMUGGLING FOREIGN LIQUORS
6- The legalities of U.S. territorial waters during Prohibition is described in www.EagleSpeak.us/2009/08/sunday-ship-history-rum-war-of.html.

THE LUCIANO & COSTELLO IMPORTING OPERATIONS

7- This info about the operation and corrupting influence of Dwyer's and Costello's gang is documented by testimony in the federal Prohibition cases against Bill Dwyer in July 1926 and Costello in January 1927. The prosecutions' cases were based on the testimony of gang leaders, crew members, and a number of corrupted Coast Guardsmen, all of whom had pled guilty.

8- The comparison between the buying power of the present value of the dollar and its value on these historic dates was calculated by using the official U.S. average Consumer Price Index (CPI) for the given calendar year. This index, calculated since 1913, represents changes in prices of specified goods and services purchased for consumption by urban households with 1913 used as the base of $1. In the text, the value of the U.S. dollar's buying power that is presented in every example is the amount that could be bought in 2009 compared to the amount in the year specified. In this example, $50 million could be bought in 2009 compared to $4 million in 1924 based on a ratio of the dollar at $12.55 to $1. The home page of the official U.S. Consumer Price Index is www.bls.gov/cpi/, and the ratios used here were produced at www.USInflationCalculator.com.

9- Costello and Luciano operated very differently according to documentation and statements by their associates, but few details about Luciano's business ever surfaced.

The quote is by Vincent Alo who everyone knew as "Jimmy Blue Eyes" so this name is always used. Every quote and paraphrase by Jimmy in this book comes from my interviews with him. Jimmy's grandson repeatedly asked him over many years to grant me an interview. His grandson respected my long-term historical research, but he had a personal interest. He told me, "I know my grandfather was a hoodlum because of what is said in the papers, but I don't have any idea if he was a little one or a big one." Jimmy finally agreed to become the only one in his group to break the code of silence. I ruminated for days about how to begin that first interview. I was afraid he would instinctively clam up if I started talking about organized crime, but that was the whole point of the interview. I still had no opening strategy, when we sat down across from each other at his son's dining room table. We stared, as he waited for me to say something. Finally, I blurted out, "I understand you were close to Meyer Lansky and Ben Siegel." Fortunately, at 91 he wanted to reminisce, and the memories poured out. He started with, "Charlie Lucky [Luciano] and I were best friends, and Meyer and Ben were best friends. After that Meyer and I were second best friends and lifelong associates."

THE COSTELLO & DWYER RUMRUNNING TRIALS

10- Dwyer was arrested for Prohibition violations on December 4, 1925, and his trial was held in July 1926. He went to prison in 1927. The IRS won the Dwyer judgment in May 1939, and the quote was by Assistant U. S. Attorney Frank Parker. Dwyer bought the NFL Dodgers in 1930 and disbanded them in 1945. Costello was found not guilty on January 20, 1927, and the U.S. Attorney abandoned attempts to retry him in 1942.

THE BIG THREE IN LIQUOR & GAMBLING

11- The relative sizes of the three biggest Prohibition gangs presented in the text are based on two sources. First is the evaluations by members of two of these three partnerships from their personal knowledge of each other's operations while they were competing and dealing with each other. In my interviews, Luciano's partner Jimmy Blue Eyes and gang leader Moe Dalitz both volunteered this ranking for the three premier rumrunners. Second is an analysis of their relative size and success based on the known size of their importing and manufacturing activities, and the affluence of their retail consumer markets.

Notes Chapter 2
THE HISTORY OF THE AMERICAN MAFIA

AMERICA'S POWERFUL STREET GANGS & THE DEVELOPMENT OF THE MAFIA

12- The police and political corruption scandals and investigations were well publicized in the city's newspapers. In addition, a century of gang unlawfulness and corruption in New York City is described in *The Gangs of New York: An Informal History of the Underworld* by Herbert Asbury. His research was based on New York City newspaper morgue records from the early 1800s to the early 1900s until Prohibition. Martin Scorsese produced a film version of this book as *Gangs of New York* in 2002.

JOE MASSERIA'S MANHATTAN/BROOKLYN MAFIA GANG

13- Ignazio "Lupo the Wolf" Saietta killed Salvatore Morello in their Sicilian hometown in 1899. Saietta's former Sicilian associates killed NYPD Lieutenant Joseph Petrosino there on March 14, 1909. Lupo went to prison for counterfeiting in 1910, and he was pardoned in 1921. Lupo was sent back to prison on July 15, 1936, and he died on January 13, 1947.
Joe Masseria's two arrests were in 1907, and he was imprisoned for theft in June 1913.

THE AMERICAN UNIONE SICILIANA POLITICAL POWER BASE

14- Authors usually do not spell Unione Siciliana with an *a* at the end, but this was the spelling on the September 17, 1985 Illinois incorporation paper shown on the *St. Valentine's Day Massacre* A&E The History Channel 1996. The "padrones" system is described in *The Italians in Chicago 1880-1930: A Study in Ethnic Mobility* by Humbert S. Nelli.

15- The quote by Hickman Powell is from his book *Lucky Luciano: The Man Who Organized Crime in America.* Powell was a New York Times crime reporter and a close friend and appointed government employee in PR positions for DA Thomas E. Dewey. Powell had unfettered access to the Prosecutor's criminal files.

16- The quote is by a witness who was the proprietor of the Henley Brothers' women's wear shop from the August 9, 1922 *New York Times.*

17- The quote by Joe Bonanno is from *A Man of Honor: The Autobiography of Joseph Bonanno,* as are all quotes and paraphrases by Bonanno in this book.

18- The quote by 19-year-old witness Jack Kahane is from the August 12, 1922 *New York Times.*

19- The quote is by 8-year-old shooting victim Agnes Egglineger from the August 12, 1922 *New York Times.* The shot street cleaner was Joseph Schepis.

20- Masseria was issued a concealed-weapon permit on January 23, 1922. Morelli was killed and Masseria was fired at on May 8, 1922. Masseria did the duck on August 8, 1922, and he murdered Valenti on August 11, 1922.

LUCIANO & ASSOCIATES BECOME RANKING MAFIOSI

21- Henry Hill's autobiography *Wiseguy: Life in the Mafia* (1985) was adapted into the movie *Goodfellows* (1990). Paul Vario was a division leader in New York City's [Gaetano "Tommy"] Lucchese crime family. Henry Hill, who was half-Italian and half-Irish, could not become a member of the Mafia gang so he reported to Vario under an associate's status.

LUCIANO'S ECUMENICALISM IN AN INSULAR SICILIAN CULTURE

22- The quote by Mickey Cohen is from *Mickey Cohen: In My Own Words by Mickey Cohen,* as are all quotes and paraphrases by him.

Notes Chapter 3
THE YOUNG TURKS EMBROILED IN CONFLICT

PROHIBITION TESTED THE TOUGHEST
23- Attorney George Wolf's three quotes in this chapter are from his *Frank Costello: Prime Minister of the Underworld.*

24- The quote by attorney Moses Polakoff about his client Charlie Luciano is from a 1980's interview broadcast on *Time Machine: Allied With the Mafia* by the A&E TV channel on January 1, 1994.

VENGEANCE IS NOT MINE
25- The two quotes are by NYPD Patrolman Blanke from the October 18, 1929 *New York Times.* Four NYPD detectives beat up Luciano on October 16, 1929.

26- The Siegel bombing quote is from FBI Memorandum from the Los Angeles office to Director Hoover July 22, 1946 summarizing Siegel's criminal record.

THE YOUNG TURKS CAUGHT UP IN THE SICILIAN-AMERICAN WAR
27- In Chicago, Lombardo was murdered on September 7, 1928, and Aiello on October 23, 1930. In Detroit, Milazzo was killed on May 31, 1930 and La Mare on February 6, 1931.

28- Masseria ordered Bronx Mafia leader Tom Reina killed on February 26, 1930, replacing him with an associate, Bonaventura "Joe" Pinzolo. Maranzano in turn, had Pinzolo's lieutenant Gaetano "Tom" Gagliano murder his boss in his Manhattan office and take over on September 5, 1930. Maranzano also ordered the killings of another gang leader, Mafredi "Al" Mineo, and his associate Steve Ferrigno as they left a building believed to be a Masseria safe house on November 5, 1930. Mineo was replaced by Frank Scalise, but he later stepped down to make way for his lieutenant, Vincent Mangano, when the warring gang leader Scalise supported ultimately lost.

LOOKING FOR AN EXODUS TO A QUAGMIRE
29- Masseria survived another hit attempt on November 5, 1930. Maranzano created an opening to Luciano in early 1931. Masseria was killed on April 15, 1931.

FROM THE FRYING PAN INTO THE FIRE
30- Maranzano was approved for citizenship on May 5, 1930. He held a meeting of America's Mafia leaders in late May 1931 and was elected Unione Siciliana branch president in July 1931. Maranzano was murdered on September 10, 1931.

31- Two authors presented evidence no major murders occurred on the Night of the Sicilian Vespers. These two books are *The Mob: 200 Years of Organized Crime in New York* by Virgil W. Peterson and *East Side, West Side: Organizing Crime in New York, 1930-1950* by Dr. Alan Block. The writers about early organized crime who published the totally untrue books about additional gang leaders murders the night that Maranzano was killed tied it into an ancient event, but even the old story of the *Night of the Sicilian Vespers* may be more legend than fact. Centuries ago, the French conquerors allegedly had their tax collectors stand outside Sicilian churches before evening worship, or *vespers,* to drag tax debtors off to jail.

32- Luciano and Masseria were busted for gambling on March 1, 1930.

Notes Chapter 4
LUCIANO'S ERA OF PEACE – LEADERSHIP & LIFESTYLES

MAFIA VIOLENCE, CLEVELAND & MOONSHINE, & THE CRIME CONFERENCE

33- Kleinman pled guilty to tax evasion in November 1933. The quote is from the FBI Memo for Director Hoover June 1, 1939 concerning the History of the Mayfield Road Gang.

34- The quote by Moe Dalitz is from my July 2, 1969 interview.

35- The St. Valentine's Day Massacre occurred in Chicago on February 14, 1929, and the Atlantic City crime conference ended on May 16, 1929.

THE YOUNG TURKS MAKE FRIENDS

36- The first quote is from *Lucky Luciano: The Man Who Organized Crime in America* by Hickman Powell. He was a close friend and government employee appointed by DA Thomas Dewey. Powell's book covers Luciano's trial and Dewey's prosecution. Powell tried to tarnish Luciano's reputation as much as he could, but even he had to admit Luciano's peace-loving nature and his efforts to eliminate underworld violence and save lives.

The second quote is from a press conference held by author Peter Mass after Costello died to tell about his experiences with the hoodlum. Mass learned a great deal about Costello's character during two months of extensive interviews about his past. He intended to write Costello's autobiography late in his life, but the retired crime leader canceled the project, deciding it was too soon to put into print parts of his life and what he knew about others' lives.

37- Sammy "The Bull" Gravano admitted committing 16 murders in his 1990s' state's witness testimony at the trials of Vincent "The Chin" Gigante and John Gotti, the leaders of New York City's two largest Mafia gangs. Gravano was Gotti's lieutenant as the pair shot their way to the top of the gang that had been headed decades earlier by Albert Anastasia (Chapter 9).

BACK TO A NORMAL LIFE

38- The quote by Polly Adler is from her *A House Is Not A Home.*

39- All four quotes in this paragraph are from my interviews. The first was by Siegel's Las Vegas attorney Lou Wiener on July 22, 1970, and the second by Siegel's bookmaking associate Jack Richards on January 18, 1968. The third was on June 3, 1969 by Mark Swain who directed Siegel's Lake Mead yacht. Every quote by Swain in this book comes from my interviews with him over a 30-year period. The fourth quote was by Jimmy Blue Eyes on April 13, 1995.

THE REPEAL OF PROHIBITION

40- Utah ratified repeal of Prohibition by being the 36th state to vote wet on November 7, 1933. President Roosevelt proclaimed that the 21st Amendment had been ratified on December 5, 1933 repealing the 18th Amendment that became law on January 16, 1920 to begin the 14 years of the Noble Experiment.

41- Molaska Corporation was incorporated in Columbus, Ohio on November 25, 1933, and liquor became legal again on December 5, 1933. Hank Messick wrote about his investigation of Molaska, Inc. in two books - *The Silent Syndicate* (about Moe Dalitz's Little Jewish Navy) and *Lansky.* His descriptions of Molaska's incorporation papers and his interviews with Prohibition Agent Robert Bridges, who was assigned in Cleveland in 1933 when these events occurred, are combined in the text with newspaper reports about this business venture. These multiple sources bear each other out. While newspaper reporter Messick appears to have conscientiously written only what he was told, he failed to verify the authenticity of these statements and failed to document his sources for future researchers.

42- The announcement by Federal Alcohol Control Administration Director Joseph H. Choate, Jr. was on June 16, 1934.

43- The Zanesville raid was on January 19, 1935. Molaska declared bankruptcy on March 2, 1935 and went out of business on November 16, 1935. Before this bankruptcy the new Molaska Company, Inc. was incorporated on October 9, 1935.

44- Lewis S. Rosenstiel was the subject of an 18-month investigation by the New York Joint Legislative Committee on Crime and then public hearings during the first three months of 1971 into his business and personal connections with organized crime to examine "the infiltration of organized crime into business, politics, and officialdom." Rosenstiel's Prohibition ties to Costello and Lansky are in *From The Secret Files of J. Edgar Hoover* edited with commentary by Athan Theoharis, *J. Edgar Hoover: The Man and His Secrets* by Curt Gentry, *Little Man: Meyer Lansky and the Gangster Life* by Robert Lacey, *Official and Confidential: The Secret Life of J. Edgar Hoover* by Anthony Summers, and my interviews with Jimmy Blue Eyes.

Samuel Bronfman, who became wealthy during the Prohibition era, was indicted on December 11, 1934 for non-payment of Canadian excise taxes from liquor-smuggling sale revenues. A judge using tortured reasoning dismissed these charges on June 14, 1936. The Kefauver Committee Final Report August 31, 1951 presented Bronfman's organized-crime connections. Jimmy Blue Eyes told me in interviews that Bronfman was a major supplier to them, and information is also in *Little Man: Meyer Lansky and the Gangster Life* by Robert Lacey.

Joseph Kennedy contacted Costello for help in bringing liquor into the U.S. early in Prohibition, according to author Peter Maas who discussed this in his interviews with Costello on February 26, 1973. Kennedy and Costello were partners during and after Prohibition when they imported Scotch whisky. "I help Joe Kennedy get rich," Costello told Maas. Dalitz told me in an interview on October 11, 1969 that Kennedy was his chief supplier, and Jimmy Blue Eyes told me Kennedy was a major supplier for Costello. Kennedy was identified as Dalitz's supplier in my interview with his business partner and resort executive Mark Swain on April 20, 1971, Dalitz's key Strip resort executive and former Las Vegas Police Chief Ray Sheffer on June 20, 1969, and Gaming Control Board Chairman and former newspaper investigative reporter Ed Olsen on August 14, 1969. Kennedy's Prohibition ties are also in *From The Secret Files of J. Edgar Hoover* edited with commentary by Athan Theoharis, *J. Edgar Hoover: The Man and His Secrets* by Curt Gentry, *A Man of Honor: The Autobiography of Joseph Bonanno* by Joe Bonanno, and *Uncle Frank: The Biography of Frank Costello* by Leonard Katz. It is important to note that Joe Kennedy started investing in the stock market with almost no money in 1919 just before the beginning of Prohibition. The stock market went up six times during the decade of the Roaring 20s, and he was out well before it crested. His financial records do not show any other meaningful income, but at the end of Prohibition, starting with practically nothing, he and his heirs were spectacularly wealthy for generations to come. This analysis was conducted for *The Kennedys: Dynasty and Disaster* by John H. Davis and *The Fitzgeralds and the Kennedy's: An American Saga* by Doris Kearns Goodwin.

45- The quote is from FBI Memorandum from the New York City office to Director Hoover November 7, 1946 concerning the physical surveillance of Siegel attempting to raise additional funds for his *Flamingo* project in early October 1946. The FBI's file on Moe Dalitz contains 2,729 pages of documents. The information about Williams is from *Edward Bennett Williams for the Defense* by Robert Pack.

A WORD THAT OPENED DOORS

46- Attorney George Wolf's two quotes are from his *Frank Costello: Prime Minister of the Underworld.*

47- Ted Binion knew all the pioneers well because he was the son of legendary casino operator Benny Binion, and a partner and the casino manager in the high-wagering-limit *Horseshoe Club* in downtown Las Vegas. His interview is from the October 8, 1975 *Las Vegas Today.*

48- The quote by Lou Wiener was from a social breakfast I had with him on July 26, 1995.

Notes Chapter 5
NEW YORK CITY POLITICS & THE MOB

THE CORRUPT POLITICAL MACHINES

49- A continuing series of major political and police graft scandals involving Tammany Hall politicians are documented in the official records of the Board of Aldermen and various investigations from the early 1800s.

A HIGH-STAKES GAMBLER EXTRAORDINAIRE

50- The two raids of Rosenthal's casinos were in early 1909, and his apartment was raided on April 15, 1912. He locked the cop in on July 11, 1912, and Rosenthal was killed on July 16, 1912. The shooters were executed on April 13, 1914 and NYPD Lieutenant Becker on July 30, 1915.

51- The quote by Fallon is from the October 27, 1963 *New York Times.*

52- The quotes about Tony Costello's floating crap game are by Miami and Las Vegas illegal sports bookmaker Hallie Tutino from my interview on March 13, 1992.

53- The history of the Saratoga Springs resort town in upstate New York and Rothstein's casino operation are presented in *Such Was Saratoga* by Hugh Bradley.

54 - The quote by Rothstein is from the October 27, 1963 *New York Times.*

55- The NYPD announced at Arnold Rothstein's death that he had never been arrested. The local police had his entire record because he was a native New Yorker, who had lived in the city his whole life. Despite the facts, various crime authors claim he had an arrest record. However, their fabricated lists do not contain arrest dates or names of the boroughs in which the unspecified crimes allegedly occurred. The lists of charges by the various authors are different which further undermines their credibility. These authors could not accept that Rothstein was a very successful professional gambler, so they claimed he was a criminal mastermind, despite the fact that the NYPD never linked him to one single crime besides his illegal gambling. Not one person ever accused him of committing any other crime.

56- The two quotes by Rothstein are from the November 7, 1928 *New York Times.*
The Big Bankroll: The Life and Times of Arnold Rothstein was written by *New York Post* reporter Leo Katcher. Crime books written since the original Katcher book use it as the authority on this scandal, but Katcher's logic about this case is astoundingly tortured. He sensationalized his book by denying the popular belief that Rothstein was to blame for the fix. While Katcher was technically correct that Rothstein did not dream up the swindle or finance it, he ignored the facts presented in this book. Rothstein discussed the fix with every participant and was intimately involved in the planning of the fraud; it was necessary for his gambling/bookmaking associates to use his name to get the players to join in the fix; and no record existed of whether or not he placed bets on those games because he wagered with illegal bookmakers privately and in secret. Even though he attempted to discourage the participants, it is difficult to understand how he could have been more embroiled as the principal figure and therefore why Katcher and the ensuing authors failed to recognize that his reputation for being involved in the fix of the World Series was indeed deserved.

ROTHSTEIN'S TIES TO THE YOUNG TURKS

57- Rothstein died on November 6, 1928, and his estate obtained court judgments against Costello of $25,272 and $10,122 on April 5, 1929. The case was dormant until mid 1942, and Costello's affidavit was on July 16, 1942. After the September 1943 arbitrator's ruling in favor of the estate, Costello paid the two amounts on October 1, 1943 and on December 3, 1943, according to FBI Headquarters General Investigative Intelligence File about Costello February 24, 1954.

THE MAN & THE MYTH

58- A judge denied probate for Rothstein's will on April 16, 1929.

THE LEGAL & POLITICAL MACHINATIONS OF THE ROTHSTEIN KILLING

59- The quote by the McManus defense attorney is from the December 19, 1928 *New York Times.*

60- The quote by Will Rogers is from the November 14, 1928 *New York Times.*

61- The two quotes by DA Banton in the Rothstein murder case are from the December 5, 1928 *New York Times.*

62- The reporter's quote about Rothstein's murder case in the December 23, 1928 *New York Times.*

63- The two quotes by Nigger Nate about the poker game in the Rothstein murder case are from the November 30, 1929 *New York Times.*

64- The overall quote about the Rothstein murder decision is by the reporter, and the two quotes by McManus are from the December 23, 1928 *New York Times.* The Park Central Hotel attendant who held in jail as a material witness was Bridget Farry.

65- Rothstein died on November 6, 1928. The DA announced he would not try McManus on December 13, 1928. The NYPD Commissioner was forced to resign on December 14, 1928. The NYPD was reorganized on December 22, 1928. The NYPD shake up was announced on January 8, 1929. The announcement that McManus was going to trial was on September 27, 1929. Nigger Nate was sentenced in January 1932 for his September 1928 crimes. The directed verdict to acquit McManus was on December 5, 1929. The first quote by DA Thomas Crain about the Rothstein murder case is from the December 6, 1929 *New York Times,* and the second quote about his case analysis is from the January 16, 1930 *New York Times.*

66- The quote by DA Crain about planning to get McManus to admit guilt in the Rothstein murder case under immunity is from the January 16, 1930 *New York Times.*

67- The quote by DA Crain after interviewing McManus believed him to be innocent in the Rothstein murder case is from the April 17, 1930 *New York Times.*

WHO SHOT A. R.?

68- The quote by Park Central Hotel electrician Vincent Kelly is from his testimony in the December 3, 1929 *New York Times.* The timekeeper was Thomas McGibney and the watchman was Thomas Calhoun. Rothstein's chauffeur and confident was Eugene Reiman.

69- The quote by NYPD Detective Patrick Flood is from the December 3, 1929 *New York Times.*

70- The quote by DA Crain are part of his conjectures from the January 16, 1930 *New York Times.* The gun was spotted by taxi driver Al Bender, and retrieved by NYPD Patrolman John Rush.

71- Chief Medical Examiner Dr. Charles Norris' quote is in the November 7, 1928 *New York Times.*

72- DA Crain's quote about his McManus interview is from the April 17, 1930 *New York Times.*

73- The quote by Rothstein refusing to comment is from the November 6, 1928 *New York Times.* Rothstein accidentally shot himself on November 4, 1928 and died on November 6, 1928.

LUCIANO & COSTELLO AS POLITICAL KINGMAKERS

74- Frank Cullotta headed the home and business burglary division of the 1970s and 1980s Las Vegas professional street gang that was depicted in the 1995 movie and book *Casino.* He was also the gang's chief murderer. After he joined the protected witness program and testified in trials against his associates, he conducted a 1993 seminar for the detectives in the Criminal

Intelligence Section of the Las Vegas Metropolitan Police Department about how the gang operated and corrupted public officials. These statements and quotes are from that seminar.

75- Costello gave detailed testimony about himself the entire day of October 25, 1943 in a New York City magistrate's disbarment hearing. Costello admitted knowing a couple dozen of the biggest Prohibition gang leaders, including Capone, but denied acquaintance with Capone's associate Johnny Torrio because Torrio had left New York a decade before Prohibition began.

76- Mayor O'Dwyer's Kefauver testimony is in the May 2, 1951 *New York Times.*

77- Mellon's quotes are from *The Good News About the Recession: Maybe it will finally teach Americans how to compete globally* by Daniel Gross in a January 16, 2008 *Newsweek Web Exclusive* article.

78- The 1932 Democratic convention political maneuvering is detailed in *Happy Days Are Here Again: The 1932 Democratic Convention, the Emergence of FDR – and How America Was Changed Forever* by Steve Neal, and in *The Man Who: The Story of the 1932 Democratic National Convention* by Richard Oulahan. Dewey's political report was on November 30, 1937.

Notes Chapter 6
CAPONE'S CHICAGO & THE UNIONE SICILIANA

THE CHICAGO EMPIRE OF JIM COLOSIMO & JOHNNY TORRIO

79- The quote by Torrio is from the February 24, 1929 *Chicago Daily Tribune.*

80- Colosimo was born February 16, 1978, and he married madam Victoria Moresco in 1902. Reform Mayor Harrison, Jr. served from 1911 to 1915. The bribery arrest of Torrio's underling, ex-cop Harry Cullett, was on February 25, 1914. Sergeant Birn and Detective Sloop were killed on July 16, 1914, and Captain Ryan resigned on July 25, 1914. World War I was declared on July 28, 1914. Torrio opened the Burnham Inn in 1916. Thompson became mayor on May 15, 1915. Funkhauser was fired on July 31, 1918, and exonerated on February 10, 1922. Info from Herbert Asbury's *The Gangs of Chicago: An Informal History of the Chicago Underworld,* and Carter H. Harrison's *Stormy Years: The Autobiography of Carter H. Harrison*

81- Thompson was elected Mayor in 1915 and reelected in 1919. Shots were fired at Prosecutor Hoyne's son on May 24, 1920, but Crowe was elected Prosecutor in November 1920. Hoyne was Prosecutor from 1912 to 1920. Lennington Small was elected Governor in 1921 and reelected in 1925. The quote by Jonas is from his speech to the initial meeting of the Cook County Citizens Commission as reported in the November 29, 1927 *Chicago Daily Tribune.*

82- Minnie Oehlerking's father rescued her on October 22, 1921. The Guziks were convicted on February 17, 1922, and the Appellate Court ruled on March 19, 1922. But the Guziks were pardoned on June 20, 1923. With the Guziks Blue Goose opening their pardon was revealed on September 26, 1923, and the quote by AG Brundage is from that date's *Chicago Daily Tribune.* The Guziks' appeal was withdrawn on October 3, 1923. Harry was arrested for pimping at the Blue Goose on January 18 and on September 6, 1924, and the building was torched on February 26, 1926. Mona Marshall was the prisoner who led to the June 1, 1907 fine. Harry's underage charge was on September 25, 1912, and his recruiting clearing house charge was on November 16, 1914. Viola Davis was the captive girl in the March 4, 1922 arrest.

83- The quote by Judge Renz Jennings at the sentencing of Charles Guzik is from the August 23, 1951 *Chicago Daily Tribune.* Charles Guzik pled guilty on August 17, 1951, and Warden Lon Walters Jr. was fired on August 30, 1953.

TORRIO BROUGHT IN AL CAPONE & THE CICERO MOVE

84- Capone's slot fine was on April 14, 1921. His FBI file contains 2,397 pages of documents.

85- The quote by Torrio about his business goals is from the February 9, 1936 *Chicago Daily Tribune.*

86- Colosimo married in 1902. Colosimo imported Torrio in 1909, and Colosimo's Café opened in 1910. Colosimo divorced Moresco on March 29, 1920 to marry Winter, and he was murdered on May 11, 1920. The Porter who saw a man run out after the Colosimo shooting was Joe Gabreala.

87- Capone was slashed in 1923.

88- The quote by Torrio to Vogel is from the September 22, 1926 *Chicago Daily Tribune.* The Cook County Sheriff backing Torrio was Peter Hoffman.

89- The quote by Judge Edmund Jarecki about domestic terrorism against Cicero's April 1, 1924 election is from the April 3, 1924 *Chicago Daily Tribune.*

90- Dever was elected on April 3, 1923, and Torrio entered Cicero in October 1923. Cicero's election riots were on April 1, 1924, and the first Cicero election attack was on Democratic clerk candidate William Pflaum. Capone was charged with voting terrorism in Stickney on July 2, 1926, and the quote was by the reporter of the September 22, 1926 *Chicago Daily Tribune.*

91- Howard was murdered on May 8, 1924, and the motive was finally found a quarter century later in December 1959 in a rusted safe in the office once used by State's Attorney Investigator Captain Dan Gilbert. He had listed summaries of confidential informants' statements for cases during the 17 years he occupied the office. The quote is by Howard's murder eyewitness, 75-year-old retired carpenter David Runelsbeck, from the May 9, 1924 *Chicago Daily Tribune.*

92- The quote by Monsignor Rempe at Merlo's funeral is from the November 14, 1924 *Chicago Daily Tribune.*

93- The quotes by O'Banion and his killer are from the February 16, 1936 *Chicago Daily Tribune.*

94- The quote by "a Catholic Clergyman high up in the councils of the Church" about O'Banion's funeral is from the November 15, 1924 *Chicago Daily Tribune.*

95- The quote by Chicago Police Chief Collins about the death of O'Banion is from the November 11, 1924 *Chicago Daily Tribune.*

96- Merlo was elected Unione president after Anthony D'Andrea was murdered on May 11, 1921. O'Banion was arrested for the Sibley Warehouse theft on January 22, 1924, and police raided the Sieben Brewery on May 19, 1924. Merlo died on November 9, 1924, and O'Banion was killed on November 10, 1924. Tony Genna was killed on July 8, 1925

97 - The quote by Capone about being shot is from the December 21, 1924 *Chicago Daily Tribune.* Bullets missed Capone on December 21, 1924, and his chauffeur Sylvester Barton was grazed on January 12, 1925. The other two occupants in the car were Percy Haiter and Capone's cousin Charles Fischetti who were unscathed.

98- Torrio pled the first brewery charge on December 17, 1923, and the Torrio-O'Banion Sieben Brewery was raided on May 19, 1924. Torrio was sentenced for the Sieben Brewery Torrio-O'Banion brewery on January 17, 1925, and Torrio was wounded on January 24, 1925. Torrio entered jail on February 9, 1925 and was released on October 6, 1925. Torrio was arrested for moonshining in New York on April 22, 1936. Torrio was indicted by the IRS on September 4, 1937, pled guilty on April 10, 1939, and was paroled in 1941. He died on April 16, 1957.

CAPONE AFTER TORRIO

99- St. John left Cicero in mid 1925. The first quote is from a St. John interview on the 1996 A&E television channel show, *American Justice: The Chicago Mob.* The second quote is from a St. John interview on the Court TV channel.

100- The liquor accounting-record raid was on April 6, 1925, and the judge's records hearing was on April 10, 1925.

101- Minister H. C. Hoover raided Capone on May 16, 1925. The minister's investigator David Morgan was beaten on July 7, 1925. The second bombing of the Chicago home of minister Elmer Williams was on January 15, 1926.

102- The Torrio-Capone beer war with Spike O'Donnell raged from 1923 to 1925. The Sheriffs of Cook County during Prohibition were Peter M. Hoffman who was elected in 1922 and took office in 1923, Charles E. Graydon who was appointed in 1927 after Paddy Carr died right after taking office following the 1926 election, and William Meyering who was elected in 1930 and took office in 1931. Frank Loesch was Special Prosecutor of fraud and violence at the polls, and he headed vice and alcohol investigations while working in the Illinois Attorney General's office and the Cook County State's Attorney. The Illinois Police & Sheriff's News published by the Combined Counties Police Association contained another study.

103- The two quotes by Fred Weiss were from the October 13, 1926 *Chicago Daily Tribune*.

104- The Weiss-Capone gang war began in mid 1926. Klondike and Spike O'Donnell were both beer runners, but they were not related and were in different jurisdictions – Klondike was in Cicero while Spike was in southwest Chicago. Klondike members James Doherty and Thomas Duffy were killed with Prosecutor McSwiggin on April 27, 1926. Weiss' raid on the Hawthorne where Capone gangster Paul Valerie was wounded was on September 20, 1926, and Weiss was murdered on October 11, 1926. Policeman Healy killed Drucci on April 4, 1927. The two hoodlums with Drucci were Albert Singel and Henry Finkelstein, while the four other policemen present were Lieutenant Bill Liebeck, Sergeant Mat Cunningham, and patrolmen Al Ruff and Dennis Kehoe.

105- The state's top investigator was Special Prosecutor Frank Loesch. His quote is from the February 17, 1931 *Chicago Daily Tribune*, and Chicago Mayor Thompson's quote is from the October 21, 1956 *Chicago Daily Tribune*. Capone's large bribe to Thompson was for the April 5, 1927 mayoralty election he won. *Tribune* attorney Howard Ellis won the huge judgment against the mayor on July 12, 1928.

LEADERSHIP OF THE UNIONE SICILIANA & THE MASSACRE

106- Merlo died on November 9, 1924. Angelo Genna was murdered on May 25, 1925, Mike Genna on June 13, 1925, and Tony Genna on July 8, 1925. Amatuna was killed on November 10, 1925.

107- Weiss was murdered on October 11, 1926. Capone's drive-by of the Aiello Bakery was on May 28, 1927. Capone shot himself on September 15, 1927. Police discovered the planned ambush of Lombardo on November 9, 1927, and five men were arrested for their plot against Capone on November 20, 1927. Capone was kicked out of LA on December 13, 1927; police surrounded his mother's Chicago home on December 17, 1927; and Capone paid a fine for concealed weapons on December 22, 1927. The Aiello bakery interior was shot up on January 4 ,1928. Capone moved into his new Miami home in June 1928. Dominic Aiello was killed on July 19, 1928 and the three remaining Aiello brothers abdicated their Chicago interests.

108- Brooklyn District Attorney William F. X. Geoghan's request that President FDR return Lupo the Wolf to prison included the minutes from the NYPD departmental trial of Detective Arthur Johnson, according to the July 16, 1936 *New York Times*.

109- McGurn's hat was riddled on March 29, 1926. McGurn and innocent bystander real estate agent Nick Mastro were shot on March 7, 1928 and McGurn was shot at on April 17, 1928. Yale was murdered on July 1, 1928. Lombardo was murdered on September 7, 1928, and his bodyguard who died days later was Joseph Ferraro. Lolordo was killed on January 8, 1929.

110- Production of the Tommy Gun began in 1919, and the Kansas City Massacre occurred on June 17, 1933, four years after Chicago's St. Valentine's Massacre on February 14, 1929. Kansas City's horrific slaughter of lawmen is detailed and solved for the first time in "All *Against* The Law" by Bill Friedman 2013 (see BillFriedmanAuthor.com). Some of this info about the Tommy Gun is from *The Gun That Made the Twenties Roar* by William J. Helmer 1969 Macmillan Publishing Company.

111- The two quotes by Emil Thiry about McGurn's boxing abilities are from the February 21, 1954 *Chicago Daily Tribune*. McGurn's sanity test was on August 17, 1927. The Reputation Law became effective on July 6, 1933; McGurn was arrested on August 26, 1933; and found guilty on September 6, 1933. The Illinois Supreme Court invalidated the law on April 21, 1934.

112- McGurn and Accardo were arrested for concealed weapons on February 1, 1930.

113- The St. Valentine's Day Massacre was on February 14, 1929, and McGurn was arrested on February 27, 1929. Scalisi was arrested on March 6, 1929. McGurn and Scalisi were bailed on May 2, 1929. Scalisi, Anselmi, and Giunta were killed on May 7, 1929, and the Atlantic City crime conference began on May 14, 1929. The quote is from Assistant State's Attorney Harry Ditchburne when McGurn's Massacre charges were dismissed on December 2, 1929. McGurn's display of force for Union President Frank Abbott was on December 14, 1929. Scalisi and Anselmi killed two detectives on June 13, 1925. The convictions of Scalisi and Anselmi for killing officer Harold Olson were on November 11, 1925, and their acquittal for murdering officer Charles Walsh was on March 18, 1926. The retrial and acquittal for murdering officer Olson was on June 23, 1927. The press usually spelled the Unione President's name *Guinta,* but the spelling on his tombstone is *Giunta.* McGurn and his girlfriend were arrested for violating the Mann Act on June 25, 1929 and were convicted on July 21, 1931, but the U.S. Supreme Court reversed their conviction on November 7, 1932.

114- Massacre warrants were issued for Burke on April 2, 1929, and he killed a policeman in Michigan on December 14, 1929. Burke's live-in companion Viola Brenneman told police he was away from their residence the day of the Massacre. Burke was captured on March 26, 1931 and pled guilty to the policeman's murder on April 28, 1931. Assistant State's Attorney Harry Ditchburne was the Prosecutor who met with Burke over a Chicago St. Valentine's Day plea deal. Burke died on July 10, 1940. Bolton was arrested by the FBI on January 8, 1935.

CAPONE'S PHILADELPHIA STAY & BACK IN CHICAGO

115- The quote by Capone about writ efforts is from the March 18, 1930 *Chicago Daily Tribune.*

116- The Massacre was on February 14, 1929. Arresting Philadelphia Detectives James Malone and John Creedon attended the Jack Sharkey and Bill "Young" Stribling fight in Miami Beach on February 27, 1929. The three Unione Siciliana Chicago branch murders were on May 7, 1929, and the Atlantic City convention began on May 14, 1929. In Philadelphia Capone and Frank "Rio" Cline were arrested at 8:30 p.m. and sentenced at 11:30 a.m. the next morning May 17, 1929. The quote by Ralph Capone Jr. about not talking is from the March 16, 1930 *Chicago Daily Tribune.* Ralph Capone Jr. was placed on probation for burglary in March 1948, and he committed suicide on November 9, 1950. The quote by Elizabeth Marie Capone's attorney Henry Kalcheim is from the September 24, 1960 *Chicago Daily Tribune.* Much of the info about the arrest was publicly confirmed by Philadelphia Department of Public Safety Director Lemuel Schofield. Capone was released from the Philadelphia prison on March 17, 1930.

117- Capone proposed his city-wide beer immunity on October 28, 1930, and he banned distribution of competitors' foreign-liquor imports at the beginning of February 1931.

118- Brothel worker Heitler was killed on April 29, 1930. Reporter Lingle was murdered on June 9, 1930, and Police Commissioner Russell stepped down on June 16, 1930. Murderer Brothers was caught on December 21, 1930, and he was convicted on April 3, 1931. The Illinois Supreme Court affirmed Brothers' conviction on February 19, 1932 and he died in 1950.

119- Joe Aiello went into hiding in Buffalo when his brother Dominic Aiello was killed on July 19, 1928, and he returned to Chicago on May 29, 1929 after the peace conference ended on May 17, 1929. Capone was released from prison on March 17, 1930. A war broke out at the beginning of June 1930. Zuta survived on July 1, 1930, and he was killed on August 1, 1930. Joe Aiello was killed on October 23, 1930 after hiding out at the residence of his partner-manager Pasquale "Patsy Presto" Prestogiacomo.

120- Capone was released from the Pennsylvania prison on March 17, 1930, and the Chicago Crime Commission's Public Enemy list was on April 23, 1930. Judge Lyle issued first mass gangster vagrancy warrants on September 16, 1930. The IRS raid of Capone was on September 25, 1930, and Lyle issued his second warrants on October 15, 1930. Lyle announced his mayoralty candidacy on December 25, 1930. The editorial quote is from the April 9, 1931 *Chicago Daily Tribune*. The FBI began the Ten Most Wanted Fugitives list on March 14, 1950.

THE IRS IMPACT ON CAPONE

121- The St. Valentine's Day Massacre was on February 14, 1929, and Herbert Hoover was inaugurated on March 4, 1929. The IRS was officially named the Bureau of Internal Revenue until 1953, but it has always been an agency within the Department of the Treasury.

122- Capone was to appear in court on March 12, 1929, and the Judge postponed this to March 20, 1929. Capone was sentenced for contempt on March 2, 1931. The quote by Capone about this conviction is from the *For Capone: Six Months* article in the March 9, 1931 *TIME Magazine*.

FBI Director Hoover's handwrote notes about the U.S. Attorney were on FBI Chicago Office Memo to Hoover February 27, 1931, and on FBI Headquarters Internal Memo March 1, 1931.

123- Johnson directed the IRS investigation and prosecution against Capone, and he swore under oath to Congress that *The Ship* records were confiscated in the Berwyn Minister's raid. In contrast, lead investigator Wilson wrote they were picked up in the raid after the murder of Assistant State's Attorney William McSwiggin, but no record of such a raid seems to remain.

124- The building of the case is from Johnson's testimony to a Senate Judiciary Subcommittee on March 29 and April 2, 1932, and *"Undercover Man: He Trapped Capone"* by Frank J. Wilson from *Collier's* Magazine. Wilson was named Secret Service Chief on December 31, 1936.

125- Capone was indicted by the IRS on June 5, 1931. His compromise offer was rejected on June 13, 1931, and he pled guilty on June 16, 1931. The Judge warned Capone to withdraw his guilty plea on July 30, 1931 (the quote by Judge Wilkerson about Capone's plea deal is from the July 31, 1931), and he accepted Big Al's withdrawal on September 8, 1931.

126- The four quotes are from *"Undercover Man: He Trapped Capone"* by Frank J. Wilson from *Collier's* Magazine.

127- D'Andrea was caught with a gun on October 10, 1931. The quote by Judge Wilkerson about D'Andrea's gun toting is from the October 29, 1931 *Chicago Daily Tribune*. D'Andrea was President of the Sicilian Union from 1934 to 1941.

128- Capone's trial began on October 5, 1931, and he was convicted on October 17, 1931. Before Judge Wilkerson went on the bench, his political associate was former Illinois Attorney General Edward Brundage. Capone was sentenced on October 24, 1931. Wilkerson was nominated on January 12, 1932, and the quote he requested no resubmission on December 6, 1932 is in a letter to President Hoover. Capone's Supreme Court appeals were dismissed in May 1932 and on May 2, 1933. Prohibition was officially repealed on December 5, 1933.

129- Capone was transferred to the Atlanta Penitentiary on May 4, 1932. Alcatraz was transferred to the Justice Department in January 1933, and Capone was moved there on August 19, 1934.

Capone was stabbed on June 27, 1936. Capone's mistress was diagnosed with syphilis in 1928, and Capone was tested and found sane on February 16, 1938 but declared insane on July 22, 1938. It was decided to treat the intermittent mentally-ill Capone in prison on December 19, 1938. Capone was freed from prison on November 16, 1939, and he died on January 25, 1947. The IRS indicted Torrio on September 4, 1937. Capone's deposition was in early 1938, and Torrio pled guilty to tax evasion on April 10, 1939. Louis La Cava was the employee who had testified against Capone. Capone's son was arrested on August 7, 1965, and he changed his name on May 9, 1966. The first quote by Al Capone's son about his petty larceny is from the August 8, 1965 *Chicago Daily Tribune* and the next two about changing his name are from the May 10, 1966 *Chicago Daily Tribune.*

130- Butch O'Hare graduated from Annapolis in 1937, and his father Eddie O'Hare, Sr. was murdered on November 8, 1939. Butch was honored in April 1942 and was killed in 1943. ORD Airport was renamed for O'Hare in 1949.

ELIOT NESS & THE FBI VERSUS CAPONE

131- McSwiggin was killed on April 27, 1926, and the Arrowhead was raided on May 10, 1926. Capone was charged with Madden's IRS Unit Volstead violations on October 1, 1926, and he was charged with the Ness violations on June 12, 1931.

132- The quote about Ness controlling the organization's monies is from FBI Internal Memorandum November 18, 1939. The FBI's file on Eliot Ness contains 129 pages of documents including eight other reports about his Industrial Safety Committee including Memos from Hoover to the U.S. Attorney General and to the Secretary to President Roosevelt. They are dated December 4, 19 (two), 20, and 26 (two), 1939; January 11, 1940; and October 5, 1942.

133- The quote by law-enforcement officers is from FBI Memorandum December 28, 1942. Hoover's handwritten note is on FBI Memorandum to him July 26, 1944. The FBI's Ness file contains five other reports about his National Police Advisory Committee work. They are dated November 15, 1941; October 5, 1942; and April 5, August 7, and December 7, 1943.

134- Ness' Chicago raids began in 1928, and he raided his first brewery in early 1931. The FBI soon rejected Ness, and Cleveland hired Ness in December 1935. War in Europe began in September 1939, and the Presidential Proclamation was on September 6, 1939. Ness fled the accident on March 4, 1942, and resigned on April 30, 1942. Ness visited New York in 1955, and he died on May 16, 1957.

135- The FBI's first Capone document was dated June 20, 1928 and the second on March 2, 1930.

Notes Chapter 7
LUCIANO & TOM DEWEY

SPECIAL PROSECUTOR TOM DEWEY

136- The gang war flared in 1928 and 1929, and Diamond was killed on December 17, 1931. Coll was murdered on February 8, 1932. LaGuardia took office as New York City's mayor in 1934, and Dewey was sworn in as Special Prosecutor on June 29, 1935. Schultz was killed on October 23, 1935, and the three associates killed with him were Otto Berman, Abe Frank, and Bernard Rosenkrantz. The first quote about Luciano saving Prosecutor Dewey is from *Murder, Inc. - The Story of the Syndicate* by Burton B. Turkus, and the other three quotes are from *Twenty Against the Underworld: An Autobiography of a District Attorney and His Fight Against Organized Crime* by Thomas E. Dewey.

DEWEY TURNS HIS SIGHTS ON LUCIANO

137- The quote by Wolf about Luciano saving Prosecutor Dewey is from the attorney's *Frank Costello: Prime Minister of the Underworld.*

138- Hickman Powell wrote *Lucky Luciano: The Man Who Organized Crime in America,* and as Dewey's official publicity man had a reserved front seat at Luciano's trial.

139- Dewey admitted in a series of late 1937 *Saturday Evening Post* articles over which the Special Prosecutor held approval power that he bizarrely went after Luciano because he saved his life. Schultz was shot on October 23, 1935, and the police raids were on January 31, 1936.

140- The backgrounds of Hot Springs and Madden are presented in Bill Friedman's "All *Against The Law.*"

141- Luciano's quote about the National Guard is from the April 5, 1936 *New York Times.*

142- The quote by Arkansas AG Bailey is from the April 7, 1936 *New York Times.*

143- The quote by Arkansas Gov. Futrell at extradition hearing from April 7, 1936 *New York Times.*

144- The quote by Dewey at the bail hearing was from the April 19, 1936 *New York Times.*

145- Dewey's own investigator questioned Luciano's involvement in prostitution booking in *The D. A.'s Man* by Harold R. Danforth and James D. Horan.

146- The quote by Dewey in his opening statement from the May 12, 1936 *New York Times.*

147- The quote by Luciano at the bail hearing is from the April 19, 1936 *New York Times.*

148- The quote by Dewey at the end of the trial is from the June 8, 1936 *New York Times.*

149- The three quotes, the first two by Dewey and the third by his Deputy Assistant Steinberg, riding roughshod over constitutional rights are from Tom Dewey's *Twenty Against the Underworld: An Autobiography of a District Attorney and his fight against organized crime.* The quote by Tom Dewey is from his book.

150- Luciano vacationed in Hot Springs beginning in early March 1936, and he was arrested on April 1, 1936. Dewey swore the false second charge on April 5, 1936 for an alleged incident occurring on June 24, 1935. The trial began on May 11, 1936.

151- The two quotes by Barbizon-Plaza Assistant Manager Frank Brown are from the May 28, 1936 *New York Times.*

152- NYPD Patrolman Heidt was dismissed on August 31, 1936, and was reinstated six weeks after the December 17, 1937 court decision. The quote by Heidt was from the September 1, 1936 *New York Times* and the court's ruling was from the December 18, 1937 *New York Times.*

LUCIANO'S TESTIMONY ABOUT HIS BACKGROUND

153- The quote by Dewey and by Luciano at trial are from Hickman Powell's *Lucky Luciano: The Man Who Organized Crime in America.*

154- The first three documents in Luciano's FBI file are dated August 28, 1935 which contained the quote, October 16, 1942, and February 21, 1946. They were Internal Memos referencing current interest in him that was expressed by other government agencies or politicians, a list of his arrests, and sparse summaries of his personal background. When the second and third Memos were written, he had been imprisoned 6 and 10 years respectively so his illegal activities had ceased long before.

155- The quote by Luciano is his testimony from the June 3, 1936 *New York Times.*

156- The quote by bookmaker Henry Goldstone is his testimony as a defense witness from the June 3, 1936 *New York Times.*

157- Luciano was convicted for opium selling in 1916 and for crap shooting in Miami on March 1, 1930. His first *New York Times* mention was on October 18, 1929.

THE VERDICT

158- The three quotes in these two paragraphs by Defense Attorney Barra in his closing arguments are from the June 5, 1936 *New York Times.*

159- Luciano was found guilty on June 7, 1936. The quote about Luciano's reaction is by the reporter in the June 8, 1936 *New York Times.*

160- The history of the jury-selection process is from *Kaleidoscope of Justice: Containing Authentic Accounts of Trial Scenes From All Times and Climes* by Dean H. Wigmore.

161- Richard Wright, the highly-respected long-time Las Vegas criminal attorney, explained the legal nuances of Luciano's trial to me in a two-hour interview on April 22, 2004. He presented the basic points of law, the typical court procedures of that World War II era, and how they would be handled today.

162- The quote is by the Judicial Council from the February 5, 1938 *New York Times.*

163- The Judicial Council quote about the un-American system is from the January 17, 1939 *New York Times.*

164- The two quotes by Prosecutor Dewey are from the February 23, 1938 *New York Times,* and the two by Chairman Robinson lying about the merits of the Assembly bill are from the February 20, 1938 *New York Times.*

165- The quote is from a letter to the editor by Jacob Landy in January 30, 1941 *New York Times.*

166- The Judicial Council's recommendation was in its fourth annual report to the Legislature on January 15, 1938. The Senate passed a bill on February 2, 1938, and the Assembly killed a bill on March 8, 1938. The Supreme Court ruled in favor of blue-ribbon juries on June 23, 1947 and March 29, 1948; and the Democratic Legislature eliminated them in 1965.

167- Tom Dewey falsely defended blue-ribbon juries in his *Twenty Against the Underworld: An Autobiography of a District Attorney and his fight against organized crime.*

168- The quote by Dewey is false about the purpose blue-ribbon juries from his *Twenty Against the Underworld: An Autobiography of a District Attorney and his fight against organized crime.*

169- Judge Philip J. McCook sentenced Luciano on June 18, 1936. The quote by Luciano proclaiming his innocence to is from the June 19, 1936 *New York Times.*

170- The quote by Luciano's friends about his framing by Dewey is from *Uncle Frank: The Biography of Frank Costello* by Leonard Katz.

171- The quote by Dewey admitted Luciano would not have associated with pimps from his *Twenty Against the Underworld: An Autobiography of a District Attorney and his fight against organized crime.*

172- The quote by Dewey agreeing with Valachi's statement that Luciano was not a pimp is from his *Twenty Against the Underworld: An Autobiography of a District Attorney and his fight against organized crime.*

173- Polly Adler's eight quotes in these three paragraphs are from her *A House Is Not A Home.*

174- The hiding of state's witnesses from an appeal is from *Lucky Luciano: The Man Who Organized Crime in America* by Hickman Powell.

175- Luciano's new trial motion was filed in March 1937, and retrial hearing held April 20, 1937.

DEWEY'S FOIBLES & PROSECUTION OF POLITICAL OPPONENTS

176- Dewey was elected Manhattan DA in November 1937.

177- Dewey went after Genovese in mid 1937 for Boccia's 1934 murder. Dewey had no clue about Costello as revealed by Powell's *Lucky Luciano: The Man Who Organized Crime in America.*

178- Dewey lost his first race for NY governor in 1938. Dewey convicted Hines in February 1939.

450 Chapter 8 Endnotes

Notes Chapter 8
MURDER, INC. & LEPKE BUCHALTER

A DA INVENTS MURDER, INC.

179- Alpert was killed on November 25, 1933 and the second indictment on February 2, 1940 named Abe Reles, Martin "Bugsy" Goldstein, and Anthony "the Duke" Maffetore. The two quotes by DA O'Dwyer are from the February 3, 1940 *New York Times.*

180- The quote is from *Murder, Inc. - The Story of the Syndicate* by Burton B. Turkus and Sid Feder. All quotes by Turkus are from this book.

181- DA O'Dwyer testified about Reles to the U.S. Senate Kefauver Committee in March 1951, a decade after Reles turned state's witness.

THE STORY OF MURDER, INC.

182- The quote by DA O'Dwyer before Kefauver is from the March 20, 1951 *New York Times.*

183- Costello testified in a New York City magistrate's disbarment hearing October 25, 1943.

THE MURDER, INC. TRIALS & INFORMANT ABE RELES

184- The first two testimony quotes by Reles are from the March 18, 1941 *New York Times,* and the quote by Judge Franklin Taylor is from the September 16, 1940 *New York Times.*

185- Reles became a state's witness on March 22, 1940. Abbundando and Maione were convicted in the first Murder, Inc. trial on May 23, 1940. They were executed on February 19, 1942. Goldstein and Strauss were found guilty in September 1940 and executed on June 12, 1941.

"LEPKE" & "GURRAH" INDUSTRIAL RACKETEERS

186- This FBI description of Lepke Buchalter's and Gurrah Shapiro's kickback and shakedown rackets of legitimate businesses is taken from a Headquarters' Internal Memo Summary date unclear but containing information indicating it was written in late 1947. This document is in the FBI file of Ben Siegel.

187- The reward for Lepke and Gurrah was issued on November 8, 1937. Gurrah surrendered on April 14, 1938.

188- The quote by Moe Dalitz is from my October 11, 1969 interview.

189- Former FBI official Sullivan's two quotes are from the May 15, 1973 *Los Angeles Times.*

190- Abner "Longie" Zwillman was an underworld political ally of Luciano and the Young Turks, and his Newark, New Jersey base was 20 miles from the illegal casino operations of his friend Adonis. Zwillman's FBI interview statements were summarized in an Internal Memorandum for Director Hoover November 30, 1938 from long interviews on November 9 and 10, 1938.

191- J. Edgar Hoover's improper collection of personal information and his misuse of confidential FBI information is detailed in "All *Against* The Law" by Bill Friedman.

192- The quote by Whitehead about Winchell's involvement in the Buchalter arrest is from his book *The FBI Story, A Report to the People* Random House 1956 with a forward by J. Edgar Hoover. Winchell's quote is from his radio broadcast on August 20, 1939 four days before Buchalter surrendered.

193- Hoover's three other cowardly and botched personal arrests are detailed in "All *Against* The Law" by Bill Friedman, as is Hoover's huge FBI publicity machine that included books, movies, radio show series, and comic book series mentioned earlier.

194- Hoover's quote about the FBI's fugitive hunt for Buchalter was taken from his Headquarters' Internal Summarization, but the date is unclear. The document contains information that indicates it was written in late 1947, and it was misfiled in the FBI file of Ben Siegel.

195- Orgen was killed on October 16, 1927. FDR was inaugurated on March 4, 1933, and Cummings was AG from March 4, 1933 until January 2, 1939. The Kansas City Massacre occurred on June 17, 1933. Hoover was born on January 1, 1895, and he was appointed director of the DOJ's Bureau of Investigation, the early name for the FBI, on May 10, 1924 at age 29. A Federal Jury found Buchalter guilty of Antitrust Law violations of New York's rabbit-fur dressing trade on November 8, 1936 and he received a two-year sentence. DA Dewey indicted Lepke for extortion of the garment industry on March 1, 1937, and on March 8, 1937 a U.S. Circuit Court sent the fur case back for retrial due to insufficient evidence to link Lepke with the crime. On the retrial of the fur business for Antitrust Law violations Buchalter failed to appear in court on July 6, 1937. U.S. AG Cummings offered a $2,500 reward for information about Lepke on November 8, 1937. FDR appointed Frank Murphy AG on January 2, 1939 replacing Homer Cummings who resigned at age 68. FDR appointed Francis Biddle AG on September 5, 1941. Music publishing executive Irving Penn was murdered on July 25, 1939 because he resembled union official Philip Orlovsky, and DA Dewy offered a $25,000 reward for Buchalter on August 7, 1939. Fugitive Lepke surrendered to the FBI on August 24, 1939, and his wife Beatrice was convicted for harboring her husband on November 6, 1939. While Lepke was a fugitive he was indicted for narcotics importing and a Federal Jury convicted him on December 20, 1939 resulting in a 14-year sentence.

LEPKE THE POLITICAL PAWN FOR A PRESIDENCY

196- The quote by Bonanno is from *A Man of Honor: The Autobiography of Joseph Bonanno.*

197- Lepke's voluntary surrender "bust" was on August 24, 1939, and he was convicted in federal court on December 20, 1939. The Court of Appeals ruled on New York custody on January 9, 1940. Dewey convicted Lepke in March 1940, as Reles became a state's witness. Rosen was murdered on September 13, 1936. Turkus took over the Lepke case in March 1941, and convicted him of murder on November 30, 1941.

DEWEY'S POLITICAL MACHINATIONS

198- Brooklyn Assistant DA Turkus wrote in his book *Murder, Inc.* that two of his state's witnesses - Moey "Dimples" Wolinsky and Abe Reles - confirmed to him that the FBI's J. Edgar Hoover and U.S. Attorney General Frank Murphy approved Lepke Buchalter's voluntary surrender deal. Both officials guaranteed that Lepke would be tried only for the narcotics violations and that he would remain in federal custody protected from Dewey and state prosecution.

199- Lepke challenged his transfer for trial in New York for the bakery industry-extortion case, but lost his appeal to the U.S. Circuit Court on January 10, 1940. A Manhattan Grand Jury indicted Lepke again for garment-industry extortions on January 16, 1940. DA Dewey prosecuted Lepke for the bakery extortion and obtained a guilty verdict on March 2, 1940. Brooklyn's indictment of Lepke for the murder of Joe Rosen on September 13, 1936 was made public on May 27, 1940. DA O'Dwyer began trying to get custody of Lepke from the feds on September 20, 1940 and succeeded in arraigning him in Brooklyn on May 9, 1941. Lepke's trial began on September 15, 1941, and the blue-ribbon jury was finally selected on October 17, 1941. Lepke and lieutenants Emanuel "Mendy" Weiss and Louis Capone were convicted of first degree murder on November 29, 1941. Special Prosecutor Dewey was elected Manhattan DA in 1937. He was the Republican nominee for New York Governor in four elections, losing in 1938 and winning in 1942, 1946, and 1950. The U.S. Supreme Court decided the final Lepke case appeal on June 1, 1943. Governor Dewey formally demanded President Roosevelt surrender Lepke to the state on September 1, 1943. U.S. AG Biddle's letter dated November 29, 1943 was in the November 30, 1943 *New York Times.* Lepke joined his two associates in the Sing Sing death house block on January 22, 1944; all three were executed on March 4, 1944; and the Republican convention was held in late June 1944.

200- The first quote is by defendant Weiss from the March 5, 1944 *New York Times,* the second by Lepke's attorney Hyman Barshay is from the November 27, 1941 *New York Times,* and the third of Lepke's last statement through his wife is from the March 5, 1944 *New York Times.*

201- Joe Valachi testified before the U.S. Senator McClellan hearings on September 27 and October 1, 1963. Bobby Kennedy was U.S. AG from January 20, 1961 to September 3, 1964. AG RFK demanded J. Edgar Hoover focus on organized crime for the first time, and the AG also created multi-agency strike forces to get the job done. This will be detailed in a future volume about Nevada in the 1960s because of its impact on the Nevada gambling industry in that era.

DEWEY'S POLITICAL AMBITIONS & SARATOGA SPRINGS

202- All four quotes in these five paragraphs are from the March 17, 1951 *New York Times.* The quotes in order are by Detective Walter Ahearn, Senator Tobey and agreed to by State Police Inspector Charles LaForge, Chief Inspector McGarvey, and Senator Tobey.

203- The two quotes in these two paragraphs are by Senator Kefauver from the March 18, 1951 *New York Times,* and by Senator Tobey from the October 12, 1950 *New York Times.*

Notes Chapter 9
BILL O'DWYER, ABE RELES, & ALBERT ANASTASIA

ABE RELES WENT WHERE?

204- The quote is the reporter's detailed summary of the detectives' conjecturings in the November 13, 1941 *New York Times.* Reles died on November 12, 1941. The executive who first noticed Reles' prone body was William Nicholson, chairman of the Coney Island Draft Board.

205- The quote and conclusions are from the Kings County September Grand Jury's December 21, 1951 presentment.

206- Gurino fled into the church on September 11, 1940.

207- The quote by Mrs. Reles is from the November 13, 1941 *New York Times.*

208- Info about Reles' murder is also from the following sources. The NYPD and the Brooklyn DA's investigations, press releases, and press conferences. The criminal investigation into the circumstances surrounding Reles' death by the 1945 Special Kings County Grand Jury. An extensive investigation of the circumstances surrounding Reles' death that was conducted by the September Kings County Grand Jury, which released the testimony and presentment on December 21, 1951. The 1951 U.S. Senate Kefauver Committee hearings testimony, and the May 1, 1951 Kefauver Committee Report. The December 1952 New York State Crime Commission hearings. *Murder, Inc. - The Story of the Syndicate* by Burton B. Turkus.

RESTRICTED & SECURELY-PROTECTED ACCESS

209- The sardonic quote by detectives about Reles is from the November 14, 1941 *New York Times.*

210- The quote by Reles being tough is from the November 14, 1941 *New York Times.*

NULLIFYING A MURDER INVESTIGATION

211- The quote by O'Dwyer in Kefauver testimony is from the March 16, 1951 *New York Times.*

212- There are four quotes in these three paragraphs. The first quote by Kefauver Chief Counsel Rudolph Halley is from the March 20, 1951 *New York Times.* The next two quotes by Mayor LaGuardia are from the November 14, 1941 *New York Times.* The fourth quote by DA O'Dwyer in his Kefauver Committee testimony is from the March 20, 1951 *New York Times.*

THE CONSEQUENCES FOR MURDER

213- Mayor LaGuardia's letter demanding NYPD information was dated November 6, 1941, and Reles was murdered on November 12, 1941. Captain Bals' resignation effective date was

December 3, 1941, and his resignation quote is from the December 4, 1941 *New York Times.* DA O'Dwyer then joined the Army on June 1, 1942.

214- DA O'Dwyer ordered the investigation on June 3, 1946. Deputy Police Commissioner Bals retired in January 1947. Bals P.O. box and illegal-gamblers' bribery scheme were made public later by the Kefauver Committee in 1951. The quote by NYPD Commissioner Wallander about the grafting spree in the previous paragraph is from the June 25, 1946 *New York Times.*

215- The quote by Bals to the Kefauver Committee is from the March 16, 1951 *New York Times.*

O'DWYER'S RELATIONSHIP WITH COSTELLO & TAMMANY

216- The Costello-O'Dwyer association became public in December 1942.

217- The two quotes by O'Dwyer to Kefauver are from the March 20, 1951 *New York Times.*

WHO WAS BEHIND RELES' MURDER?

218- Lepke's trial began on September 15, 1941, and the blue-ribbon jury was selected on October 17, 1941. Reles died on November 12, 1941. Lepke and his lieutenants Emanuel "Mendy" Weiss and Louis Capone were convicted of first degree murder on November 29, 1941.

ANASTASIA WAS DOMINANT IN BROOKLYN

219- O'Dwyer served as Brooklyn DA in the early 1940s, and he was New York City's Mayor from 1946 to 1950. His administrations suffered from a pervasive pattern of blatant prosecutorial and police corruption. O'Dwyer's failures to prosecute major criminals, especially Albert Anastasia, for serious crimes were investigated and exposed by the 1945 and 1951 Special Brooklyn Grand Juries, the 1951 U.S. Senate Kefauver Committee inquiry, the December 1952 New York State Crime Commission hearings, as well as several criminal trials and internal NYPD departmental trials.

The FBI's file on Anastasia is 180-pages with FBI Internal Memorandum Background Summaries on September 26, 1952, October 15, 1952, and February 25, 1954. It should be noted that the first document in his file is dated September 26, 1952, when he was 50-years old, late in his criminal career and three decades after Prohibition began. Much of the FBI's information about Anastasia is copies of newspaper articles or taken from the book *Murder, Inc. - The Story of the Syndicate* by Burton B. Turkus and Sid Feder.

220- The quote by Tony Anastasia is from the December 14, 1952 *New York Times.*

221- Albert Anastasia's first arrest was in 1920, the retrial in 1922, and the assault arrest in 1923.

222- The December 20, 1952 *New York Times* description of Anastasia was made at his December 19, 1952 New York State Crime Commission appearance.

223- The quote by Brooklyn DA Beldock was from the October 31, 1945 *New York Times.*

224- The five quotes in these two paragraphs by union attorney Mannino in Kefauver testimony are from the December 19, 1952 *New York Times.* Mannino was union counsel from 1938 to 1940 and Brooklyn Democratic chairman from 1938 to 1939.

225- The five quotes in these two paragraphs by union worker insurgent committee attorney Protter in Kefauver testimony are from the December 19, 1952 *New York Times.*

DA O'DWYER SHIELDED ANASTASIA

226- The information in this section is from the same sources as the previous section # 219 above.

227- Panto organized a longshoremen's revolt and soon disappeared on July 14, 1939, and the grand jury inquiry was in 1945. The two quotes by DA Beldock in a Brooklyn grand jury investigation in these two paragraphs are from the October 31, 1945 *New York Times.*

228- Attorney Protter's Kefauver quote is from the December 19, 1952 *New York Times.*

229- The two quotes of attorney Mannino's testimony to the Kefauver Committee about O'Dwyer's statements to him in these two paragraphs are from the December 19, 1952 *New York Times.*

230- O'Dwyer was elected DA in November 1939. He began his longshoremen's investigation on April 30, 1940, and filed away Heffernan's July 15, 1940 report. The quote from Heffernan's report presented to the Kefauver Committee is from the December 19, 1952 *New York Times.*

231- The quotes by New York Crime Commission Chairman Joseph Proskauer and by Heffernan are from the December 19, 1952 *New York Times.*

232- Camarda was killed on October 2, 1941 by Salvatore Sabbatino, VP of Sabbatino & Co. The quote by Sabbatino is from the October 3, 1941 *New York Times.*

233- Diamond was killed on May 25, 1939, and Panto disappeared on July 14, 1939. DA O'Dwyer announced the location of Panto's body at the beginning of 1941, and it was uncovered on January 29, 1941. Camarda was killed on October 2, 1941.

234- The two quotes by DA O'Dwyer in these two paragraphs were reported by the September Kings Country Grand Jury and are from the December 22, 1951 *New York Times.*

235- Four investigations concluded DA O'Dwyer failed to prosecute Anastasia in two strong murder cases - the 1945 and 1951 Brooklyn Special Grand Juries, the 1951 U.S. Senate Kefauver inquiry, and the December 1952 New York State Crime Commission hearings.

236- In these two paragraphs the 1945 Brooklyn Special Grand Jury report quote is from the December 14, 1952 *New York Times,* and the 1951 Brooklyn Special Grand Jury report quote is from the December 22, 1951 *New York Times.*

237- O'Dwyer left the Army and returned as Brooklyn DA in February 1945.

238- The Brooklyn Special Grand Jury October 29, 1945 presentment quote about O'Dwyer is from the February 7, 1946 *New York Times.* The quote by DA Beldock about not prosecuting Anastasia is from the October 31, 1945 *New York Times.*

239- DA Beldock impaneled the Additional Kings County Grand Jury on September 19, 1945, and its presentments were issued on October 29, 1945, December 20, 1945, and January 31, 1945. O'Dwyer was elected New York City Mayor on November 6, 1945, and Democrat Miles McDonald defeated DA Beldock. Kings County Judge Franklin Taylor expunged the two Grand Jury presentations on February 6, 1946.

240- The two quotes in these two paragraphs are from the May 1, 1951 Kefauver Report.

THE PANTO MURDER BOMBSHELL

241- Assistant DA Heffernan testified in the December 1952 New York State Crime Commission hearings that Murder, Inc. informant Tannenbaum revealed the details of Panto's murder to him on February 7, 1941. The following four investigations concluded that DA O'Dwyer was criminally malfeasant for failing to prosecute Anastasia for Panto's murder: the 1945 and 1951 Brooklyn Special Grand Juries, the 1951 U.S. Senate Kefauver Committee inquiry, and the December 1952 New York State Crime Commission hearings.

242- The quote by AG Towe to the press was from the December 20, 1952 *New York Times.*

243- The quote by O'Dwyer with a false defense is from the December 19, 1952 *New York Times.*

244- O'Dwyer resigned as Mayor in September 1950 and as Ambassador to Mexico late in 1952.

Notes Chapter 10
LUCIANO IN PRISON

LUCIANO & THE WAR

245- The boat sinking average rate was for the period from December 1941 through March 1942. The *S.S. Normandie* burned on February 9, 1942.

246- The quote by Polakoff is from an interview on *Time Machine: Allied With the Mafia* broadcast by the A&E TV channel on January 1, 1994.

247- Lanza created the two unions in 1920, and he was first investigated in 1931. He was first charge in 1933, and Lanza was acquitted on October 18, 1933. He was found guilty of separate conspiracy charges on November 14, 1935 and on March 7, 1938. Lanza was indicted for extortion on January 17, 1941, he and four gunmen pled guilty on January 12, 1943, and Lanza was given a 7 ½- to 15-year sentence on January 29, 1943.

248- The quote by Dewey about Assistant DA Hogan and the women is from his book *Twenty Against the Underworld: An Autobiography of a District Attorney and his fight against organized crime* Double Day & Co. Inc. 1974.

249- The quote is from Rear Admiral Carl Espe's July 26, 1954 letter to the Herlands' investigation.

250- Pearl Harbor was attacked on December 7, 1941, and the espionage project began on March 26, 1942. Luciano first said "No" and then agreed in late May 1942.

251- The quote by Polakoff about inmate assistance is from the January 28, 1954 *New York Times.*

252- The quote by Commander Haffenden is from a letter to his Third Naval District supervisors on July 25, 1945 and was contained in Luciano's FBI file report dated May 14, 1946.

253- The two quotes by the Navy Intelligence agents are from *The Luciano Project: The Secret Wartime Collaboration of the Mafia & the U. S. Navy* by Rodney Campbell.

254- Lanza pled guilty on January 12, 1943, and Dewey paroled him in 1950. Lanza's brother-in-law, P. Vincent Viggiano, was appointed by Justice Samuel Di Falco in January 1949, based on to FBI Headquarters General Investigative Intelligence File February 24, 1954 about Frank Costello. Lanza was arrested for parole violation in February 1957 and released in July 1960.

255- The quote by Haffenden's boss is from *Mussolini: Italy's Nightmare* a 1995 A&E Biography.

256- The quote by Marsloe is from an interview on *Time Machine: Allied With the Mafia* broadcast by the A&E TV channel on January 1, 1994.

257- Genovese's U.S. Military job in Italy is from FBI Memo November 17, 1944. Genovese spoke three languages, and actor George Raft, who grew up with Luciano's associates, introduced Genovese to the Army while he was on a USO Camp Show Tour in Italy after the invasion.

258- The Allies' Casablanca conference was held on January 14 to 24, 1943, and the Axis North African armies surrendered on May 12, 1943. The Sicily assault began on July 10, 1943, and the German's evacuated Sicily on August 17, 1943. Mussolini was overthrown on July 25, 1943, and he was rescued by the Germans on September 1, 1943. Italy surrendered on September 3, 1943 and declared war against Germany on October 13, 1943. Mussolini was hanged on April 28, 1945, and Hitler committed suicide on April 30, 1945. German forces in Italy surrendered May 2, 1945.

LUCIANO'S LEGAL MANEUVERS

259- Luciano appealed to his trial Judge Philip J. McCook to suspend two sentences on February 8, 1943. Polakoff's three quotes to the Judge are from the February 9, 1943 *New York Times.*

260- The quote by Commander Haffenden is from a letter to his Third Naval District supervisors on July 25, 1945 and was contained in Luciano's FBI file report dated May 14, 1946.

261- The quote by New York Judge Philip J. McCook denying Luciano's sentence suspensions is from the February 11, 1943 *New York Times.*

262- Luciano petitioned Dewey on May 8, 1945, and Dewey pardoned Luciano in January 1946.

263- The quote by Polly Adler is from her book *A House Is Not A Home.* The FBI quote and another like it are in FBI Headquarters Memorandums of April 18, 1946 and May 9, 1946.

264- The INS issued Luciano's deportation order in November 1936. Luciano sailed on February 10, 1946.

A WINTER IN THE CARIBBEAN

265- The quote by an agent is from the FBI Habana Internal Synopsis March 22, 1947.

266- Luciano arrived in Cuba at the end of October 1946. The lifestyle of Luciano in Havana was described by the *Havana Post* on February 23 and 25, 1947. The FBI investigated Luciano's 1946-47 winter visit to Havana and prepared reports dated February 10, 12, 14, 19, and 25, 1947, a detailed internal synopsis by agents in the Habana office dated March 22, 1947, and another from the Italian office dated February 18, 1959. This section of Luciano's FBI file also contains numerous Havana newspaper articles in both English and Spanish and a few are from the U.S. All the information in this section of the text was taken from a newspaper article unless it is noted as quoted or paraphrased from one or more of these seven FBI reports.

267- The *Tiempo En Cuba* article was published on February 16, 1947. The two quotes by Ruark, a daily syndicated Scripps-Howard columnist, was from his column published on February 21, 1947 but carried a dateline for the day prior.

268- The quote by Luciano is from the February 23, 1947 Cuban *Havana Post.*

269- The quote is from FBI Habana Internal Synopsis March 22, 1947.

270- Arthur M. Schlesinger, Jr. wrote about Anslinger, the Federal Bureau of Narcotics, and the Kefauver Committee in *Robert Kennedy and His Times.*

LUCIANO IN EXILE

271- Luciano, his friend Lansky, and their attorney Polakoff made statements to the press during the years Luciano lived in Italy that he loved New York City and desired to be there.

272- All quotes in this section are taken from the FBI's translation of an Italian magazine series entitled *The Secret Life of Lucky Luciano* in the three issues of *L'Europe* dated January 11, January 18, and January 25, 1959, except for the four quotes in the last two paragraphs in this section whose sources are presented in the next two footnotes. All of the info in this section is taken from this series of articles, the FBI Internal Memo to the Director February 18, 1959 and January 22, 1959 regarding the Luciano surveillance, and the six primary U.S. newspapers.

273- The FBN's Siragusa arrived in 1951. Florita became police head in early 1954. The Naples court ruled in favor of Luciano in March 1958. The quote about the Appellate Court interview of Luciano concerning the 1957 Apalachin meeting is from the July 25, 1958 *New York Times.* The quote about the Appellate Court's Luciano ruling and the quote about the FBI's investigative conclusions are from FBI Internal Memo to the Director January 22, 1959.

274- Luciano married in 1949, and Igea died in late September 1958. The quote by Luciano about marriage is from the January 27, 1962 *New York Times.*

THE LAST TESTAMENT OF LUCKY LUCIANO

275- Luciano died on January 26, 1962. His funeral was described in FBI Internal Memorandum to the Director February 19, 1962.

276- Adonis did not attend Luciano's funeral from the *Rome Daily American* January 30 1962.

277- The quote by the U.S. Consulate spokesman is from the January 29, 1962 *New York Times.* The quote by Luciano's brother Bartolo is from the February 8, 1962 *New York Times.*

278- Cage's *New York Times'* expose was published on December 17, 1974.

Notes Chapter 11
THE ACTION CROSSED THE HUDSON RIVER

JOE ADONIS IN BROOKLYN

279- Adonis was arrested five times from 1926 to 1931.

280- The quote is from a *Collier's* Magazine two-part series about Costello, *"America's No. 1 Mystery Man"* by Herbert Asbury April 12 and 19, 1947.

281- DA Dewey harassment arrest of Adonis for the truck hijacking was on September 16, 1937, and Dewey's report to the Governor was dated November 30, 1937. The quote by Manhattan DA Dewey is from the May 27, 1951 *New York Times.*

282- The quote by Adonis' attorney Leo Healy is from the October 25, 1940 *New York Times.*

283- Amen's two phony kidnapping trials were in October 1940 and February 1941, and the Prosecutor withdrew the phony extortion and kidnapping charges against Adonis on February 24, 1941. LaGuardia was elected New York City Mayor in 1933, 1937, and 1941, while DA Dewey was elected New York Governor in 1942, 1946, and 1950.

284- The quote by alleged victim Isidore Juffe is from the October 26, 1940 *New York Times.*

BEN MARDEN'S *RIVIERA*, & WILLIE MORETTI IN NEW JERSEY

285- Ben Marden's *Riviera* opened in 1932 and burned on Thanksgiving Day 1936.

286- The quote by Guarino "Willie" Moretti is from the December 14, 1950 *New York Times.*

287- Willie Moretti married and settled in East Paterson in 1927. The two quotes by Willie Moretti about power and politics are from the December 14, 1950 *New York Times.*

288- The quote by Willie Moretti about character is from the December 14, 1950 *New York Times.*

289- New Jersey's AG raided casinos in June 1944, and the Cliffside casino closed on June 16, 1944. The defense attorney's letters about the politically-based raids sent on August 23, 1944.

FRANK ERICKSON: FROM NEW YORK TO NEW JERSEY

290- Costello's quote to the McFarland Committee is from the April 28, 1950 *Chicago Tribune.*

291- Lehman held the hearing on September 12, 1936. The quote of the LaGuardia harangue is from the April 8, 1939 *New York Times.*

292- The two quotes by Mayor LaGuardia are from the April 15, 1939 *New York Times.*

293- Erickson was arrested for bookmaking five times between 1919 and 1928. He obtained a pistol permit in 1934 and 1939, and he appeared before Herlands on April 14, 1939. Erickson surrendered for the perjury charge on May 6, 1939.

294- The quote by Mayor LaGuardia against Erickson is from the June 8, 1939 *New York Times.*

295- The quote by Queens County Judge Thomas Downs in Long Island City to Assistant DA J. Irwin Shapiro is from the June 8, 1939 *New York Times.*

296- Dewey's two quotes about LaGuardia are in his autobiography *Twenty Against the Underworld.*

297- Erickson moved his bookmaking headquarters to Broadway in 1927. He moved his wire room to New Jersey in 1934, and his cash transactions in March 1939.

298- Erickson was robbed in April 1941. The obituary quote in the March 3, 1968 *New York Times.*

299- Erickson stopped the lottery in 1936, according to the 1939 Herlands Report ordered by the Mayor. Erickson invested in Tropical Park in Miami in 1935 and sold it in 1941.

THE MORETTIS WORKED FOR ERICKSON & ADONIS

300- The three testimony quotes by Adonis at the trial of former Bergen County Prosecutor Walter Winne are from the April 2, 1954 *New York Times.*

301- The quote is from FBI General Investigative Intelligence File February 24, 1954 summarizing Costello's background.

ERICKSON HELPED THE GOVERNMENT - OOPS!

302- Erickson's statement to the Kefauver Committee in the previous paragraph was read by his attorney Harold Corbin, and that quote and Erickson's quote in this paragraph are both from the March 13, 1951 *New York Times.* The quote by U.S. Attorney J. Edward Lumbard is from the February 12, 1954 *New York Times.*

303- Erickson testified before the McFarland Committee on April 28, 1950, was indicted for bookmaking on June 1, 1950, and pled guilty on June 18, 1950. He was indicted for contempt of the U. S. Senate on July 25, 1951, and the charges were dropped on February 11, 1954. He was sentenced for income-tax violations on December 15, 1953. The Moreland Act Commission hearings were held in March 1954. Erickson died on March 3, 1968.

EVERYTHING UNRAVELED FOR ADONIS

304- Ambrose married the Senator's niece in 1933, began his fraud in 1948, and pled guilty to fraud on January 8, 1951.

305- La Mare was killed on February 6, 1931. The two quotes by Bennett to Kefauver are from the February 9, 1951 *New York Times.*

306- Ford died in 1947, and the Kefauver hearings about his company were held in Detroit in February 1951. Adonis sold his interest in Automotive Conveying Company in July 1951, and purchaser Chiri was arrested in Apalachin in 1957.

307- The quote by DA Hogan about Adonis is from the November 28, 1950 *New York Times.*

308- The *New York World-Telegram* quote is from *Murder Inc.* by Burton B. Turkus.

309- Federal Judge John F. X. McGohey's quote is from the February 17, 1953 *New York Times.*

310- The four quotes by the U.S. Court of Appeals are from the June 25, 1953 *New York Times.*

311- The quote by U.S. AG Brownell, Jr. is from the January 31, 1954 *Los Angeles Times.*

312- The quote by Adonis to the INS is from the April 28, 1953 *New York Times.*

313 The quote by the Italian Foreign Office is from the August 6, 1953 *New York Times.*

314- Bergen County Judge Lester Drenk's quote is from the February 3, 1954 *New York Times.*

315- Adonis was facetiously charged in Manhattan of gambling in New Jersey on November 9, 1950. Adonis was indicted for operating Bergen County casinos on January 24, 1951 and pled no defense on May 21, 1951. Adonis was indicted for Kefauver Committee contempt on July 25, 1951; the 15 counts were dismissed on February 16, 1953; and the Appeals Court final acquittal was on June 24, 1953. Adonis was indicted by Bergen Country for birthplace perjury on February 17, 1953, and for similar Kefauver perjury on April 24, 1953. He was released from Trenton State Prison for the gambling conviction on July 16, 1953. A deportation warrant was issued on February 20, 1953, and a deportation order was issued on August 5, 1953 that was upheld on appeal on December 17, 1953. AG Herbert Brownell, Jr.'s deportation quote about Adonis is from the January 31, 1954 *Los Angeles Times.* Adonis was convicted of Bergen County perjury on January 18, 1954, and Kefauver perjury on April 9, 1954. Adonis proposed voluntarily exile on November 14, 1955 and departed on January 3, 1956.

REFORM CAUGHT UP WITH WILLIE & SOLLY MORETTI

316- Adonis, Erickson, and Willie and Solly Moretti closed their gambling businesses in early 1950. Willie Moretti visited California in 1943, testified before the Kefauver Committee on December 13, 1950, testified before the Bergen County Grand Jury in May 1951, and was murdered on October 4, 1951. As an aside, Willie Moretti bailed Bonanno out of a detention center in 1924, shortly after the future Mafia leader arrived in this country, according to Bonanno's autobiography *A Man of Honor: The Autobiography of Joseph Bonanno.*

317- This New York City gangland power struggle will be detailed in the *Tropicana* section of a future volume about Nevada in the 1950s.

318- The quote by Moe Dalitz is from my July 2, 1969 interview.

ADONIS IN EXILE

319- Adonis was arrested in Italy in May 1971 and exiled in June 1971. Adonis died at age 69 on November 26, 1971. The first quote by Adonis is from the November 27, 1971 *New York Times,* and his second quote is from the June 21, 1971 *New York Times.*

320- The mourner's quote at Adonis' funeral is from the December 7, 1971 *New York Times.*

Notes Chapter 12
THE ACTION MOVED INTO CAJUN COUNTRY

COSTELLO FROM YOUTH THROUGH PROHIBITION

321- No official record of Costello's birth exists. He gave various dates for his birth on government documents and in interviews that covered a five-year span from 1891 to 1896. The various birth dates he used and their sources are in FBI Headquarters Memorandum September 5, 1952. The date used here Costello listed on his petition for naturalization of January 26, 1891. Costello was the subject of the two-part series *America's No. 1 Mystery Man* by Herbert Asbury in the April 12 and 19, 1947 issues of *Collier's Magazine.* These two investigative articles extensively detailed the information available about Costello at that time and became the basis for three biographical books about him, but none credits Asbury's articles or any other sources. None has a bibliography, endnotes, or other documentation. Only *Uncle Frank: The Biography of Frank Costello* by Leonard Katz has an index. It and *Frank Costello: Prime Minister of the Underworld* by his attorney George Wolf were published soon after Costello's death. *This Is Costello On The Spot* by Robert H. Prall and Norton Mockridge was originally published four years after the two articles.

322- Costello's first two arrests were in 1908 and 1912 under the name Costello. He was arrested for carrying a concealed revolver in Manhattan on March 13, 1915 under the name Frank Saverio, his mother's maiden name. He pled guilty on March 26, 1915 and was sentenced to the penitentiary on April 5, 1915, according to FBI New York Office Memorandum to the Director June 3 and 4, 1935 and November 24, 1944. The quote by Judge Edward Swann is from the September 2, 1943 *New York Times* and from *Frank Costello: Prime Minister of the Underworld* by his attorney George Wolf. Costello's no-weapon policy quote is from my interview with Jimmy Blue Eyes and also from his attorney Wolf's biography of Costello.

323- Siegel's concealed weapon permit is taken from FBI Headquarters Summary Report December 16, 1946 in Siegel's file.

324- The CIA-Mafia murder attempts against Castro will be detailed in a future volume about Nevada in the 1960s.

325- Attorney George Wolf's quote is from his *Frank Costello: Prime Minister of the Underworld.*

326- The quote by the U.S. Bankruptcy Referee is from *"America's No. 1 Mystery Man: Conclusion Of Two Parts* by Herbert Asbury in the April 19, 1947 *Collier's Magazine.*

327- Costello started his slot operation in 1928 and his slot-route figures are from *The Mob 200 Years of Organized Crime in New York* by Virgil W. Peterson.

328- A Federal Court imposed the injunction against seizing slots in 1931, and the U.S. Circuit Court of Appeals revoked the injunction in 1933 according to FBI SAC NYC Office Memo to the Director November 2, 1944 concerning Costello's general information. The slot raids and Mayor LaGuardia's press picture-op was on February, 24, 1934.

COSTELLO & PHIL KASTEL IN LOUISIANA

329- The quote by a Long critic is from *The Story of Huey P. Long* by Carleton Beals.

330- Louisiana Governor O. K. Allen's letter was dated July 20, 1934. The quote by New Orleans' Mayor Walmsley about the Senator Long is from the August 5, 1934 *New York Times.*

331- The quote about wicked is by the reporter in the September 2, 1934 *New York Times.*

332- The Kingfish met with Costello in August 1935.

333- The FBI New York Office Memo to the Director October 23, 1935 quote about Costello's deal with Long, and the info about the slots and the police is from FBI SAC New Orleans August 19, 1937 letter to the Director. The FBI's file on Huey P. Long contains 1,818 pages.

334- The quote by Costello about Long to Kefauver is from the March 14, 1951 *New York Times.*

335- Senator Huey Long was mortally shot on September 8, 1935. This analysis of the shooting is a summary of the statements by witnesses and State Police bodyguards.

336- The first professional forensics' investigation of the involvement of Dr. Weiss was done 56 years later in 1991. The lead investigator's scientific lecture was given on February 21, 1992.

337- This info is from *Katrina Reveals Poverty Reality* by Kelley Beaucar Vlahos September 9, 2005 FOXNews.com, and *Not Much Has Changed: President Bush made some bold promises to help the Gulf Coast's poor after Katrina. Too bad he hasn't kept them* by Michael Eric Dyson's Web-Exclusive Commentary Special to Newsweek August 25, 2006 MSNBC.com.

338- The partners in Costello's slot-machine company were indicted for tax evasion on October 9, 1939, and the Judge ordered their acquittal on May 15, 1940.

339- The quote by Kohn is from *Uncle Frank: The Biography of Frank Costello* by Leonard Katz.

340- The four quotes about Mayor Morrison concerning Costello's New Orleans slots are from FBI Headquarters Memorandum September 22, 1949.

341- The quote by Kastel about the Beverly Club is from the March 18, 1956 *New York Times.*

342- The quote by Kefauver about Marcello is from the January 28, 1951 *New York Times.*

343- Costello began New Orleans slots and other route operations in 1935 and sold the routes in 1948. Costello opened the Jefferson Parish casino in late 1945. Sheriff Clancy appeared before Kefauver a second time on February 7, 1951 to report all casinos were closed.

COSTELLO AS LEADER

344- Costello's Copa meetings are from FBI General Investigative Intelligence File February 24, 1954 based on surveillance in October 1946, and from NY SAC to Hoover Summary November 7, 1946 about Siegel's activities in New York City from October 5 to 10, 1946.

345- The quote by Costello about his doctor is from the February 27, 1973 *New York Times.*

346- The three quotes by Mickey Cohen are from *Mickey Cohen: In My Own Words* or from an interview he gave in 1957 to Mike Wallace on ABC television.

347- Costello was on the cover of the November 28, 1949 *Time Magazine.* The quote Mass repeated by the doorman is from the February 27, 1973 *New York Times.*

348- The FBI summarized the newspaper articles about Costello's psychiatric sessions. "According to various accounts in NYC newspapers, exact dates not known, Dr. Richard Hoffmann has been ascertained to be Costello's personal psychiatrist. According to these newspapers, Dr. Hoffmann said Costello had come to him in the early part of 1947 because he did not sleep well and his mind was troubled. According to further newspaper accounts, in the early part of 1949, Richard Hoffmann, Jr., the son of Costello's psychiatrist, was appointed secretary of the Department of Marine Navigation of the City of New York" when O'Dwyer was Mayor. This quote is from FBI General Investigative Intelligence File February 24, 1954.

349- The quote by Mass about Costello is from the February 27, 1973 *New York Times.*

350- The quote by Bonanno is from *A Man of Honor: The Autobiography of Joseph Bonanno.*

351- The quote about Costello is from *America's No. 1 Mystery Man: Frank Costello* by Herbert Asbury in the April 12 and 19, 1947 *Collier's* Magazine.

352- Costello's 1957 shooting will be detailed in the *Tropicana* section in a future volume about Nevada's casino industry in the 1950s.

353- Frank was married to Loretta "Bobbie" Geigerman on September 23, 1914 from FBI Internal Memorandum to the Director June 4, 1935. The quote by Costello's attorney George Wolf is from *Frank Costello: Prime Minister of the Underworld.*

354- The quote by Mass about Costello and Lansky is from the February 27, 1973 *New York Times.*

355- The quote by the NYPD detective-lieutenant is from a 1928 interview and included in *Uncle Frank: The Biography of Frank Costello* by Leonard Katz.

THE FBI HAUNTS COSTELLO

356- The pair of robbers were Nicholas Montone and Charles Cali. The interview quote about how the robbers targeted their victims is from FBI Washington Office Special Agent in Charge March 1, 1937 letter to the FBI Director.

357- The two quotes by Costello are from his long voluntary formal interview in New York City FBI Office Memorandum to the Director June 12, 1935.

Costello's 2,456-page FBI file is divided into 14 parts. The first two parts are about Costello's possible involvement in the Bell jewelry robbery. The first part is 345 pages of FBI internal documents about the case's evidentiary and prosecutorial facts beginning April 11, 1935 and ending February 15, 1954. The second part is 411 pages of newspaper clippings pertaining to the case beginning on February 6, 1935 and ending on November 10, 1945. The FBI arranged its file documents and articles by date received. This is a proper method of filing, but it distributed information about specific aspects of this case in distant locations in these files because it was learned at different times during the investigation. This made assembling all this data into a coherent whole a monumental task.

358- The two quotes by Costello are from a FBI Jacksonville Florida Office report to the New York City Office and to the Director dated June 12, 1935.

359- The following books are among several that use FBI's records to focus to some degree on Hoover's publicity machinery -

G-Men: Hoover's FBI in American Popular Culture by Richard Gid Powers.

J. Edgar Hoover: The Man and His Secrets by Curt Gentry.

From The Secret Files of J. Edgar Hoover edited with commentary by Athan Theoharis.

Official and Confidential: The Secret Life of J. Edgar Hoover by Anthony Summers.

J. Edgar Hoover: The Man In His Time by Ralph de Toledano.

The FBI Story, A Report to the People by Don Whitehead with a forward by J. Edgar Hoover.

All Against The Law by Bill Fricdman

360- The quote by J. Edgar Hoover about stolen jewelry is from the May 31, 1935 *New York Times.*

361- The jewel robbery at the Miami-Biltmore Hotel occurred on January 26, 1935. Cali was arrested for stealing bicycles on February 2, 1935, and two days later, Montone flew the jewelry to New York where he was arrested for the Miami robbery on February 8, 1935. Scaffa received the payoff from Lloyd's on March 6, 1935 and turned over the gems that evening. Montone sent a telegram to Scaffa on March 11, 1935 and he flew to Miami to confer on March 13, 1935. Scaffa cut a deal with Miami's law enforcers on March 15, 1935 and flew back to New York. Montone's case was nolle-prossed on March 17, 1935. Chief Bryant was given the key and reported finding the gems in his car on March 18, 1935. Bryant voluntarily came clean with the FBI on April 20, 1935, the day Scaffa lied to a Federal Grand Jury. The FBI's Hoover praised Scaffa's helpful role on April 23, 1935. The gunmen were convicted of armed robbery on April 24, 1935 and sentenced to 25 years on May 13, 1935. Scaffa was arrested for perjury on May 29, 1935 and convicted on July 26, 1935. Scaffa, Costello, and the three casino operators were arrested for conspiracy under the Federal Stolen Property Act on May 31, 1935. Nelson was arrested and accused of being part of this conspiracy on August 31, 1935. Scaffa was sentenced for perjury on September 16. 1935. The case was Nolle prosequised against all defendants including Costello on June 3, 1937.

362- The FBI's first investigation of Costello was after the 1935 jewel robbery on July 10, 1946.

363- Hoover's denial of the Mafia is well documented by repeated assertions to Congress, and it was part of the conflict detailed in *Bobby and J. Edgar: The Historic Face-Off Between the Kennedys and J. Edgar Hoover That Transformed America* by Burton Hersh.

364- The two quotes about an FBI Internal Summary of Costello are from FBI SAC NYC Office Memorandum to the Director November 2, 1944.

365- The NYPD put phone taps on Costello and Stern on February 14, 1935. The FBI tapped Costello's home from April 19 to 30, 1935, based on FBI Headquarters Memo May 17, 1947.

COSTELLO'S BUSINESSES

366- Roosevelt Raceway hired Pinkerton's detectives in 1943. The Commission threatened revocation in 1946, and Roosevelt employed Costello until 1950. The Moreland Act Commission hearings were in the fall of 1953.

367- How Costello put together the Whitely deal was revealed in hearings by the New York State Liquor Authority and the Kefauver Committee, as well as NYPD investigations.

368- The quote by Presiding Justice Bayes about Sanger is from the July 14, 1939 *New York Times.*

369- Sanger was acquitted of perjury on July 13, 1939, and Haim's liquor license expired on February 29, 1948. Costello clearly had an interest in it. Two years after the revocation, the Kefauver Committee revealed that Costello had told a Treasury Agent in 1939 that he had an interest in the Whitely Distillery liquor distributorship in the U.S. In addition a 1935 FBI wiretap recorded Costello frequently calling from his office to Alliance Distributors, but the FBI kept its files secret from local criminal investigations and prosecutions.

370- Costello created the 79 Wall Street Corp in 1944 and sold in 1950. Costello's Wall Street purchase is from FBI Internal Summary July 10, 1946. The quote about Costello's investments is from a November 24, 1944 follow up to FBI SAC NYC Office Memorandum to the Director November 2, 1944. Costello also bought his Long Island estate in 1944.

371- The two quotes about Costello are from *America's No. 1 Mystery Man: Frank Costello* by Herbert Asbury in the April 12 and 19, 1947 *Collier's* Magazine.

372- Three men attempted to rob Costello's apartment on March 24, 1951.

COSTELLO'S POLITICAL SCANDALS & LEGAL ENTANGLEMENTS

373- The two quotes by Costello to a New York U.S. Attorney are from *"America's No. 1 Mystery Man: Conclusion Of Two Parts"* by Herbert Asbury in the April 19, 1947 *Collier's Magazine.*

374- The quote is by the reporter about Costelloisms from the October 28, 1950 *New York Times.*

375- The Democratic Party nominated Thomas A. Aurelio for Supreme Court Justice on August 23, 1943. The following morning, Aurelio telephoned Costello, and DA Hogan's staff transcribed their conversation from the wiretap. Hogan issued his statement on August 28, 1943 revealing the political connection between the hood and the nominee. The next day, the August 29, 1943 *New York Times* blared the headline story "Gangster Backed Aurelio for Bench."
    The second two quotes by Costello and Magistrate Aurelio are also from the August 29, 1943 *New York Times,* as is the quote by DA Hogan in the next paragraph.

376- The first quote by Judge Benedict Dineen about Aurelio is from the September 19, 1943 *New York Times.* The Court of Appeals Judge ruled in Aurelio's favor on October 30, 1943. The second quote by the unanimous decision of the Appellate Division (state Supreme Court) is from the November 2, 1943 *New York Times.*

377- The quote by Mayor LaGuardia about Aurelio is from the November 8, 1943 *New York Times.*

378- The quote by Assistant Manager Frederick Chapey is from the June 23, 1944 *New York Times.*

379- The quote by Mayor LaGuardia is from *"America's No. 1 Mystery Man: Conclusion Of Two Parts* by Herbert Asbury in the April 19, 1947 *Collier's Magazine.*

380- Costello left envelopes containing cash in the taxi on June 14, 1944, and the trial to establish the money's owner was held in January 1947. Costello's quote is from *"America's No. 1 Mystery Man: Conclusion Of Two Parts* by Asbury in the April 19, 1947 *Collier's Magazine.*

Notes Chapter 13
JOE E. LEWIS & COSTELLO'S COPACABANA

JOE E. LEWIS, MACHINEGUN McGURN, & THE COPA

381- The quote by Lewis' former wife Martha Stewart is from *The Joker Is Wild: The Story of Joe E. Lewis* by Art Cohn.

382- The quote by McGurn is from *Capone: The Life and World of Al Capone* by John Kobler

383- Lewis was attacked on November 8, 1927, and he opened at the Rendezvous again on January 28, 1928. In *The Joker Is Wild: The Story of Joe E. Lewis,* author Art Cohn said in his Entrance Chapter, "Joe disapproves of many passages. We are friends, but when truth and friendship were at odds, I chose truth in the name of friendship." Joe E.'s first-hand accounts of his life would have been preferred especially since the book differs from many facts in the available documents presented in this text.

McGURN AFTER CAPONE

384- The first quote by an unidentified shooter is from the February 15, 1936 *Chicago Daily Tribune.* The second quote by bowling alley proprietor William Aloisi is from the February 16, 1936 *Chicago Daily Tribune.*

385- Oak Park Police Lt. Harry Wilson's quote is in the February 16, 1936 *Chicago Tribune.*

386- McGurn was murdered on February 15, 1936. McGurn's brother Anthony Gebardi was killed on March 3, 1936.

387- McGurn's hat was riddled on March 29, 1926. McGurn and innocent bystander real estate agent Nick Mastro were shot on March 7, 1928. McGurn was shot at while running on April 17, 1928. McGurn and Tony Accardo were arrested together for concealed weapons in the car on February 1, 1930. McGurn's double quote is from the February 15, 1936 *Chicago Tribune.*

JOE E. LEWIS PERSEVERED

388- Joe E. Lewis's quote about covering up his slashing is June 5, 1971 *New York Times'* obituary.

389- The quote by Joe E. Lewis about his throat slashing for going to work at the Rendezvous nightclub is from the June 23, 1961 *Chicago Daily Tribune.*

390- The quote by Sammy Davis, Jr. is from his *Why Me? The Sammy Davis, Jr. Story.* The quote by Bobby Darin about his career is from the biographical movie *Beyond the Sea* 2004.

391- These three entertainment reviews succinctly describe the differences in Joe E.'s performance level before and after his Copa engagement. Before the Copa engagement, Ed Sullivan acknowledged Joe E. had again risen to the top of the bill in Chicago but offered no praise in his April 11, 1940 *Looking at Hollywood* column. After Joe E.'s Copa transformation, he received this before and after rave review by Will Davidson in his December 26, 1943 column, and Joe E.'s current standing was acclaimed by Claudia Cassidy in her December 31, 1944 *On the Aisle* column. All three articles were printed in the *Chicago Daily Tribune.*

392- The quotes by Runyon and Joe E. are from *The Joker Is Wild:* by Art Cohn.

393- The quote by Mayor O'Dwyer for Robinson is from the November 29, 1949 *New York Times.*

394- Abraham Lincoln's quote on Robinson's tombstone is from TheEverGreensCemetery.com.

395- Robinson died on November 25, 1949. Some of the info about his life is from the New York City Department of Parks & Recreation's NYCGovParks.org, the November 11, 2007 Virginia *Richmond Times Dispatch,* the Encyclopedia Britannica's concise.Britannica.com, *Contemporary Black Biography* at Cengage Learning's library reference arm The Gale Group at Gale.Cengage.com, Actor All Media Guide 2010, and *Green Oasis in Brooklyn: The Evergreens Cemetery* by John Rousmaniere. Photos of Robinson's funeral procession and tombstone are in DigitalJournalist.org, Flickr.com and FindAGrave.com.

396- The quote by Friars Club Director of Communications Barry Dougherty was in a February 27, 2008 E-mail to me. He added, Joe E. Lewis "helped keep the Friars alive during their bad times in the '40s and '50s" when he was billed as "King of the Nightclubs." Dougherty reaffirmed Joe E.'s name remained on two facilities in a telephone call on October 23, 2014.

397- The quote by *Sands Hotel* GM Loveland about Martin is from my interview on March 6, 1969.

398- The quote by *Sands* General Manager Archie Loveland about Dean Martin is from my March 6, 1969 interview. The quote by Martin is from the November 8, 1987 *Chicago Daily Times.*

399- Dean Martin's pal Frank Sinatra publicized himself as the top draw of Las Vegas high-rollers, but the *Caesars Palace* and *Riviera* Strip resorts' crowd counts and casino win figures prove Dino, just as Joe E. Lewis before him, was tops in this class by himself.

COSTELLO'S COPACABANA

400- Phil Silvers starred in the *Phil Silvers Show* TV series 1955-1959 playing the part of Master Sergeant Ernest G. Bilko for 142 episodes.

401- Morey Amsterdam starred in the *Morey Amsterdam Show* TV series 1948-1950 for 13 episodes, and he was one of the four main cast members in the *Dick Van Dyke* series 1961-1966 for 158 episodes.

402- Costello opened the Copa on November 1, 1940. The final performance of comedy duo Martin and Lewis before breaking up was at the Copa on July 25, 1956. Some of the info about the Copa in this section is also from the pictorial book *The Copacabana* by Kristin Baggelaar; *Food Is Tops, Too At the Copacabana* by Robert W. Dana is a 1953 review of the nightclub's food in www.BigBandsAndBigNames.com/Baggelaar.html; and www.thecopacabana.com.

403- Belafonte's quote is from his autobiography *My Song: A Memoir of Art, Race and Defiance.*

404- The statement about the Mafia wives and girlfriends is from an interview of New York City gangster Henry Hill on *"Empire of Crime: A Century of the New York Mob"* A&E 1996, and also in Hill's biography *Wiseguy: Life in a Mafia Family* by Nicholas Pileggi 1986 and the movie *Goodfellas* 1990. The quote by Lewis is from his autobiography *Jerry Lewis in Person.*

405- Both quotes by NYPD Detective George Collins are from September 8, 1944 *New York Times.*

406- The quote by Costello's attorney George Wolf and the quote by NYPD Police Commissioner Lewis Valentine are both from the September 21, 1944 *New York Times.*

407- LaGuardia ordered the NYPD to investigate the Copa in November 1943. The Commissioner's statement was in September 1943 The NYPD Copa ownership hearings were held in September 1944, and the Copa reached a compromise with the city on September 30, 1944. The first quote is from *"America's No. 1 Mystery Man: Conclusion Of Two Parts* by Herbert Asbury in the April 19, 1947 *Collier's Magazine.* The second quote from Monte Proser's agreement with Costello is from the October 1, 1944 *New York Times.*

408- Costello closed the Copa to the public for the Salvation Army dinner on January 24, 1949. The quote of the Copa's statement is from the March 10, 1949 *New York Times.*

Notes Chapter 14
THE ACTION SETTLED UNDER THE PALMS

"JIMMY BLUE EYES'" EARLY CAREER

409- The quote by Nick Pileggi was from our telephone conversation on October 16, 1995. Every quote and paraphrase by Vincent "Jimmy Blue Eyes" Alo in this chapter and this book comes from my interviews with him.

410- The FBI internal memo quote about Jimmy Blue Eyes was given to me by Criminal Intelligence Section Detective John Nicholson of the Clark County, Nevada Metropolitan Police Department Organized Crime Bureau in a discussion on December 3, 1993.

JIMMY BLUE EYES JOINED "POTATOES" KAUFMAN

411- The quote by Virginia Kaufman about her mother Josephine Kaufman's death is from the December 3, 1911 *Chicago Daily Tribune.*

412- Duffy killed his girlfriend on February 20, 1924, and he was killed later that night. Marian Kaufman relinquished the stolen ring to police on February 27, 1924. Potatoes Kaufman beat the officer on May 16, 1924.

413- The two quotes by Kaufman are from the March 11, 1930 *Chicago Daily Tribune.*

414- Circuit Court Judge Harry Fisher's two quotes are from the April 12, 1931 *Chicago Tribune.*

415- Police busted the *Sheridan Wave* in June 1928. The Police Commissioner began investigating illegal casinos in April 1929, and he closed the *Sheridan Wave* in June 1929.

416- Potatoes was divorced in 1925. Potatoes opened a casino inside the *Hollywood Country Club* in late 1935.

417- Potatoes opened the *Colonial Inn* in 1937. The two quotes by Harry Katzen are from my March 22 and 29, 1996 interviews.

MEYER LANSKY'S EARLY CAREER

418- The "Charlie the Bug" nickname for Lansky was in the August 29, 1940 *Los Angeles Times.*

419- Lansky's family moved to the Lower East Side in 1914. Meyer's first two arrests were in October and November 1918. He was charged with Prohibition violations in January 1929 and November 1931. The group roust was in 1933. Lansky's felonious-assault arrest was on March 6, 1928, and the INS hearing was in 1957.

LANSKY JOINED JIMMY BLUE EYES

420- The info of Costello's home is from Miami FBI Office Memo to Director October 16, 1953.

421- Gulfstream Park opened on February 1, 1939, and it reopened on December 1, 1944. The *Colonial Inn* reopened in December 1945. *Greenacres* opened on November 1, 1946.

422- The quote in the paragraph above and the four quotes in this paragraph by Freddie Ayoub are from my interview on February 6, 2004. He worked with Dino Cellini in several locales, including Steubenville, Ohio, where they both served their dealing apprenticeships. Freddie went on to be a key casino executive at casinos in countries around the world.

MIAMI'S S&G BOOKMAKERS & ILLEGAL CASINOS

423- *S&G* was created in 1939.

424- The quote by Sy Freedman is from my interview with him on March 22, 1996.

425- The quotes by Miami Councilman Melvin Richard and Police Chief Short were in testimony before the Kefauver hearings and are from the March 1, 1951 *New York Times.*

426- This quote is from the Kefauver August 18, 1950 Interim Report. Erickson was ousted from the Miami resorts in 1947.

427- The S&G takeover and Florida gambling corruption were exposed by a Pulitzer-Prize winning *Miami Herald* investigation in 1948, and by in-depth testimony before Kefauver in 1950.

428- Governor Warren's special personal Gambling Investigator W. O. "Bing" Crosby told Sheriff Sullivan which bookies to arrest in January 1949. Continental Press shut down its service to S&G on February 28, 1949, and disconnected the whole state from March 5 to 14, 1949. "The raids ceased as soon as Russell, an associate of Johnston in the Capone mob, was taken in as a member of the S. & G. Syndicate," according to the Kefauver February 28, 1951 Preliminary Report. Russell paid $20,000 to S&G in March 1949, and S&G bought the boat in February 1950. S&G dissolved in late 1950. The five original S&G partners were Sam Cohen, Charles Friedman, Jules Levitt, Ed Rosenbaum, and Harold Salvey.

429- The quote by Dade County Sheriff Jimmy Sullivan is from the September 15, 2002 *Miami Herald,* and it is a summary of a Pulitzer-Prize winning 1948 expose of Miami corruption.

430- The injunction against the *Colonial Inn* was issued on February 12, 1948.

LANSKY'S HIGH-END SARATOGA CASINO & OTHER BUSINESSES

431- The early Saratoga Spring's casino was described in *Such Was Saratoga* by Hugh Bradley.

432- Luciano invested in a Saratoga Springs casino in the late 1920s, and Lansky and Costello opened casinos there in the late 1930s to the early 1940s.

433- The quote by Paul Bryant is from my discussion with him on July 18, 1994.

434- This testimony was by Milton Hammergren, former Wurlitzer Corporation Vice President and Sales Manager, before the U.S. Senate Rackets Committee in 1963.

435- Wurlitzer cut its deal with Accardo in 1940. Lansky formed Emby for Wurlitzers in 1942 and sold it in 1948.

KEFAUVER TOOK ON FLORIDA LAW ENFORCEMENT

436- Committee Chairman Kefauver's quote is from the September 20, 1950 *New York Times.*

437- The two quotes are from the August 18, 1950 Kefauver Interim Report about Florida.

438- The quote by Broward County Sheriff Clark is from the July 23, 1950 *New York Times.*

439- The quote is from the February 28, 1951 Kefauver Committee Preliminary Report,

440- The two quotes are from the April 12, 1951 Florida House of Representatives resolution.

441- Miami City Manager Danner was fired on June 2, 1948. The Miami casino legalization drive began in late 1949. Governor Warren's letter was issued on February 22, 1950. The Kefauver Interim Report was dated August 18, 1950. The Kefauver quote was on September 19, 1950. J. Edgar Hoover's refusal to investigate organized crime and supply information to the U.S. Senate is documented from official FBI records in "All *Against* The Law" by Bill Friedman. Sheriff Clark testified before Kefauver on July 15, 1950. Sheriff Clark was suspended on July 21, 1950. Governor Warren's third letter to Florida sheriffs and police chiefs was on August 7, 1950. The S&G felony gambling indictments were served in September 1950. Sheriff Sullivan was indicted on October 16, 1950, and five of his deputies were indicted on November 6, 1950. The Florida Supreme Court ruled on April 9, 1951. The Kefauver Preliminary Report was dated February 28, 1951. The Kefauver Committee Final Report was dated May 1, 1951. The Florida House voice vote dismissing the Governor's charges was on May 28, 1951.

442- The quote from Florida Governor Warren's letter is from the June 17, 1951 *New York Times.*

EVERYTHING CAME UNDONE FOR LANSKY & HIS PALS

443- The quote is from Kefauver Committee Interim Report #3 May 1, 1951.

444- Saratoga Sheriff Hathorn's quote to Kefauver is from the August 18, 1951 *New York Times.*

445- The first three quotes by Supreme Court Judge Leo Hagerty are from the January 1, 1954 *New York Times,* and the fourth quote is from the 12-31-53 *New York Times.*

446- The quote by Commissioner Leonard is from the August 30, 1951 *New York Times.*

447- The century-long history of Saratoga Springs gambling is described in the previous section of this chapter, and all the political intrigue and protection of these casinos by Governor Tom Dewey is presented at the end of Chapter 8. The *New York Times* article about the Lanskys' vacation was on June 29, 1949. The Kefauver Committee hearings were in 1950 and 1951. Lansky and Jimmy pled guilty to a Broward gambling charge in September 1950. The Kefauver New York City hearings were held in February and March 1951, and Dewey countered on March 29, 1951. Seven men were indicted for *Arrowhead Casino* interests on September 8, 1952. Lansky pled guilty to gambling on February 18, 1953, and he was released from jail on July 21, 1953. Sheriff Hathorn resigned on August 17, 1951. Republican Leary was indicted on July 25 and September 9, 1952, and he was found innocent on December 9, 1953. Dr. Leonard resigned on August 22, 1951, won the November election, and resigned again on January 1, 1952. He was indicted on April 30, 1952, and this was dismissed in 1955.

Notes Chapter 15
CHICAGO FROM PROHIBITION TO UNION TAKEOVERS

CAPONE TURNED TO UNION RACKETEERING

448- The quote by businessman Becker is from the March 20, 1943 *Chicago Daily Tribune.*

449- The quote by Fitchie is from the January 21, 1939 *Chicago Daily Tribune,* and the quote by Sumner is from the October 20 1934 *Chicago Daily Tribune.*

450- Fitchie was kidnapped on December 21, 1931, and the IRS Federal Court hearing was held on October 19, 1934. Humphreys lost his IRS appeal on January 28, 1942, and he settled his tax bill on September 3, 1952.

451- Capone's North-Side gangland nemesis Roger Touhy's quote is from his *The Stolen Year's.*

452- Capone's Sanitary Cleaning Shops was incorporated on April 25, 1928. Capone's efforts to control city departments were blocked during the last two weeks of April 1930. Humphreys targeted laundry unions in 1931, Rosenberg was murdered on January 11, 1932, and the Jury acquitted on May 5, 1934. The union contract was signed on November 6, 1937.

453- The quote by Roger Touhy is from his *The Stolen Year's.*

454- Capone entered prison on October 17, 1931. Touhy tried to kill Humphreys on April 28, 1933 and September 8, 1933. In between these two attempts, Humphreys was indicted by the IRS on June 27, 1933, and he was arrested for tax evasion on October 26, 1934. Touhy was charged and convicted for Factor's alleged July 1933 kidnapping, and Federal Judge John Barnes ruled for Touhy on August 9, 1954. This case is detailed in the *Stardust Hotel* section of future volume about Nevada in the 1950s and 1960s. Guzik's gambling finances were published on October 24, 1941. Humphreys was indicted by the IRS on June 2, 1933, and he pled guilty to tax evasion on October 26, 1934. Humphreys failed to appear before the Grand Jury on June 25, 1965, was charged with lying on August 19, 1965, and died on November 23, 1965.

THE RISE OF FRANK NITTI

455- Courtney was State's Attorney from 1931 to 1942. Policeman Albert Magoon was shot to death in a speakeasy on December 12, 1932. Chicago's *A Century of Progress Exposition* opened May 27, 1933.

456- Nitti's exclamation to God is from the December 20, 1932 *Chicago Daily Tribune.*

457- The quote by CPD Detective Lang and the one by his partner Detective Miller are from the April 6, 1933 *Chicago Daily Tribune.*

458- The quote by CPD Detective Chris Callahan is from the April 7, 1933 *Chicago Daily Tribune.*

459- The quote by Nitti is from the April 7, 1933 *Chicago Daily Tribune.* Francesco Nitto was born on January 27, 1886 and officially became Frank Nitti and a U.S. citizen on February 25, 1925, at age 39. Nitti was indicted for IRS evasion on March 22, 1930, and he was captured on October 31, 1930. He pled guilty on December 20, 1930; Capone was imprisoned for IRS evasion on October 17, 1931; and Nitti was released from prison on March 24, 1932. Nitti was arrested in the car chase on May 30, 1932. He was shot by Detective Lang on December 19, 1932, and Newberry's body was found on January 7, 1933. Detective Callahan testified on April 5, 1933, and Detective Lang was convicted and then freed on September 27, 1933.

CHICAGO'S MAYORS CERMAK & KELLY

460- Cermak's first quote is from *The Five Weeks Of Giuseppe Zangara: The Man Who Tried To Kill FDR* By Blaise Picchi. Cermak's second is from the March 6, 1933 *Chicago Tribune.*

461- Early exploratory surgery was from *"The Five Weeks of Giuseppe Zangara: The Man Who Tried to Kill FDR"* by Blaise Picchi which was helpful on a few issues.

462- Zangara's first quote is from *The Five Weeks Of Giuseppe Zangara: The Man Who Tried To Kill FDR* By Blaise Picchi. His next two quotes are from *Chicago Tribune* on February 16, 1933, and March 21, 1933. Zangara's fourth is from the February 16, 1933 *New York Times.*

463- The quote by Secret Service Chief Reilly is from the June 2, 1957 *Chicago Daily Tribune.*

464- The quote by Zangara is from the February 17, 1933 *Chicago Daily Tribune.*

465- The first quote by Zangara is from the March 21, 1933 *Chicago Daily Tribune,* and his last two quotes are from *The Five Weeks Of Giuseppe Zangara: The Man Who Tried To Kill FDR* By Blaise Picchi.

466- The two quotes are from *Chicago Daily Tribune* Editorials on February 17 and March 7, 1933.

467- Cermak was inaugurated Mayor on April 9, 1931. Nitti was wounded on December 19, 1932, and Cermak was shot in Miami on February 15, 1933. FDR took the oath of office on March 4, 1933. Cermak died on March 6, 1933; Zangara was executed on March 20, 1933; and Kelly took office as Chicago Mayor on April 17, 1933.

NITTI'S POLITICAL POWER & UNION TAKEOVERS

468- The quote by Bioff is from *After Capone: The Life And World of Chicago Mob Boss Frank "the Enforcer" Nitti* by Mars Eghigian Jr.

469- Prignano of the 20th Ward was killed on December 29, 1935, and Bolton of the 2nd Ward was killed on July 9, 1936. Hinky Dink was held captive from 1933 when he was 75 until his death on October 9, 1946.

470- The quote by Humphreys is from the March 24, 1943 *Chicago Daily Tribune,* and the quote by McLane is from the June 3, 1940 *Chicago Daily Tribune.*

471- The quote by McLane to the bailiff is from the December 3, 1940 *Chicago Daily Tribune.*

472- Humphreys threatened McLane in his office on August 4, 1939, McLane testified to the County Grand Jury on June 4, 1940, and Nitti was acquitted on December 2, 1940. McLane lost reelection on January 6, 1941.

473- The quote by gangster Rio and the one by Bioff are from the October 7, 1943 *New York Times.*

474- The quote by the Chicago gangsters is from the October 7, 1943 *New York Times.*

475- Browne and Bioff met in 1932. and their IATSE negotiation with Balaban was in early 1934. The IATSE election was in June 1934, and Maloy was murdered on February 4, 1935.

476- The quote of Bioff's testimony is from the October 20, 1943 *New York Times.*

JOHNNY ROSSELLI WAS THE MAN ABOUT TOWN

477- Rosselli moved to Los Angeles in 1924, and the Dempsey - Tunney fight was in 1927. Rosselli's five arrests for robbery in LA were from January 28, 1925 to June 3, 1932. He was arrested with Cornero on May 1, 1926, and with Dragna on July 29, 1930. The Monfalcone burned in August 1930. Rosselli's reputation is from multiple sources - the Kefauver Committee, an undated *Los Angeles Examiner* morgue file from late in Prohibition contained in FBI LA Office to Headquarters September 26, 1960 surveillance record, and my interviews with underworld figures and casino executives who dealt with him in Los Angeles or Las Vegas. Rosselli's quote is from FBI Internal Memorandum Summary Background September 16, 1947. The other quotes in this section are by Mark Swain from my interviews. He was Moe Dalitz primary enforcer, and Swain teamed up with Rosselli in committing a couple murders that are described in my upcoming book about the Nevada gambling industry in the 1950s. The FBI's file on Johnny Rosselli contains 1,228 pages of documents.

IATSE'S HOLLYWOOD-MOVIE-INDUSTRY EXTORTION

478- The quote in Wilkerson's telegram to Bioff is from the November 25, 1943 *New York Times.*

479- *The Jazz Singer* opened in 1927, and the abortive IATSE Hollywood strike was in 1933. The Chicago theater strikes were on November 30 and December 1, 1935. The IATSE officially won its Hollywood jurisdictional battle in the April 1936 contract negotiations and began the Hollywood movie extortion. Schenck's "loan" to Bioff followed the 1937 union contract. Rosselli supplied goons in the 1933 and 1937 Hollywood strikes.

480- Bioff was sentenced for pandering on February 23, 1922, and the Appellate Court affirmed his conviction in February 1923. State's Attorney Courtney started the extradition process on November 23, 1939, and Bioff began his sentence on April 15, 1940. Bioff was released on September 20, 1940, and the AFL adopted its hands-off union-official' misconduct policy on November 19, 1940.

481- The Senate Committee held Chicago hearings in October 1933.

482- The quote by Harry Warner about Bioff is from the March 22, 1943 *New York Times.*

483- The IRS audited Schenck in 1939, and Bioff and Browne were convicted on November 6, 1941. Circella pled guilty on April 7, 1942. Carey was murdered on February 2, 1943. The racketeers were indicted for the Hollywood extortion on March 19, 1943, and Nitti committed suicide that afternoon.

THE IATSE RACKETEERING TRIAL & PARDONS

484- The two quotes by federal officials are from the February 10, 1960 *Chicago Daily Tribune.*

485- The quote in Warden Sanford's letter is from the June 21, 1948 *Chicago Daily Tribune.*

486- The quote by the Tavern owners is from the May 13, 1948 *Chicago Daily Tribune.*

487- The Editorial quote is from the April 11, 1950 *Chicago Daily Tribune.*

488- The two quotes by Assistant U.S. AG Boris Kostelanetz are from the March 3, 1948 *Chicago Daily Tribune,* and the two quotes by Federal Judge John Bright are from the May 13, 1948 and the March 6, 1948 *Chicago Daily Tribunes.*

489- Boris Kostelanetz was the extortion Prosecutor. Louis Campagna, Philip D'Andrea, Paul Ricca, Charles Gioe, and John Rosselli were convicted and sentenced on January 6, 1944 and they went to prison on April 7, 1944. FDR died on April 12, 1945. Warden Joseph Sanford's letter was dated July 21, 1945, and the convicts were transferred about August 15, 1945. Ragen was shot on June 24, 1946. The slots were operated prior to the November 5, 1946 election while Michael Mulcahey was Cook County Sheriff. Bernstein paid the Chicago IRS collector on November 1, 1946, and the gift taxes were paid on May 28, 1952. The mail-fraud charge was dismissed on May 6, 1947. They filed for parole on July 3, 1947, and the

Prosecutor's and Judge's objection letters were dated July 9, 1947. Dillon met with the Parole Board on August 6, 1947, and the gangsters were paroled on August 13, 1947. Wilson resigned on August 31, 1947. The U.S. House hearings ran from September 25, 1947 To June 21, 1948. The Committee's letters to Truman for information were dated October 2 and 4, 1947. Clark was appointed Attorney General in 1945 and to the Supreme Court in 1949. The bugged Chicago conversation was overheard by the FBI in 1964 from J. Edgar Hoover: The Man and His Secrets by Curt Gentry.

BIOFF & RICCA AFTER PRISON

490- Bioff and Browne were freed on December 22, 1944, and the gangsters were paroled on August 13, 1947. The *Riviera Hotel-Casino* opened on April 20, 1955, and Bioff was murdered on November 4, 1955.

491- The quote by the INS District Director is from the October 12, 1962 *Chicago Daily Tribune.*

492- Ricca entered the U.S. on August 10, 1920, and became a citizen on September 27, 1928. The Teamsters purchased Ricca's home in 1956, and Hoffa became International President in 1957. The INS filed its first brief on March 6, 1957, and Ricca's citizenship was canceled on June 8, 1957. The IRS convicted Ricca on May 29, 1958, and he was ordered deported on January 26, 1959. Ricca was again ordered deported on October 21, 1961, and the Supreme Court refused to hear his appeal in October 1962. The INS accepted Ricca's 47 unwelcome letters on October 11, 1962. He was arrested for perjury on April 28, 1966, and a jury freed him on November 25, 1967. The quote by CPD Lieutenant Michael O'Donnell is in the November 14, 1971 *Chicago Daily Tribune.* Ricca died on October 11, 1972, and the priest's quote is in the October 15, 1972 *Chicago Daily Tribune.*

Notes Chapter 16
GO WEST YOUNG MAN

SIEGEL FOLLOWED THE STARS TO HOLLYWOOD

493- Mayor LaGuardia ordered the Costello slot raids and held his picture-op on February, 24, 1934, and Siegel moved out of New York on March 2, 1934, according to a FBI Background Summary about Siegel for the Director on July 22, 1946.

MICKEY COHEN REPRESENTED CLEVELAND

494- The seven quotes by Mickey Cohen in this section are from *Mickey Cohen: In My Own Words.* All the other quotes of Cohen in the rest of this chapter are also from his autobiography.

JACK DRAGNA REPRESENTED CLEVELAND

495- The quote by Jack Richards is from my interview on April 22, 1968, and the quote by Mark Swain is from my interview on February 16, 1972. All quotes by Swain in this chapter are from this interview or the ones on April 14, 1969 and October 4, 1974. All quotes by Richards are from this interview or the one on February 19, 1968.

496- The description of Dragna's appearance is from the Los Angeles FBI SAC R. B. Hood letter to Director Hoover on December 12, 1946.

BEN SIEGEL'S EARLY LIFE & ARREST RECORD

497- Siegel's Background Summary was sent by the FBI Los Angeles Office to the Director on July 22, 1946. Siegel's FBI file of 2,421 pages of documents was begun in early 1934.

498- Siegel's gambling and vagrancy arrest was on February 28, 1930, and the quote is a statement by the June 22, 1947 *New York Times.*

499- All quotes of author Dean Jennings in this chapter are taken from his book *We Only Kill Each Other: The Life and Bad Times of Bugsy Siegel.* Jennings biography has the only kernels of truth ever published about Siegel because Jennings conducted the only first-hand interviews about Siegel prior to my extensive research. He talked to several people who knew him socially while he lived in Hollywood. This information is interesting, but limited because the interviewees had no knowledge about his businesses, criminal interests, or associates in Southern California. They knew nothing about his earlier New York activities or later life in Las Vegas. Jennings failed to identify any sources for his information except for the interviewees who spoke about his Hollywood social life. Jennings states author Ovid Demaris gave him his personal file for the *Green Felt Jungle,* but this is a highly contrived, fictionalized account, and the fraud perpetrated by its two authors in the *Green Felt Jungle* is exposed in a future book in this historical. Only Jennings' book and the FBI's Summary Report contain any reliable information about Siegel's arrest records. However both fail to identify their sources, and both contain demonstrable errors, so doubt remains about the data they did not document.

500- Siegel's first arrest was with his partner Lansky for a minor Prohibition violation in January 1929, and it was dismissed according to Author Robert Lacey in *Little Man.* Siegel was convicted of gambling on February 28, 1930. The roust occurred in 1933 according to the FBI, but it was in 1931 according to Jennings, who wrote his book 20 years after the FBI Summary was prepared. Jennings claimed Siegel was busted for a concealed weapon in April 1928 at age 22. Siegel's legal concealed-weapon permit is from FBI Headquarters Summary Report December 16, 1946, and the details about it are presented in Chapter 12. Jennings' preposterous and undocumented rape charge allegedly occurred in 1926.

501- Siegel was 33 when this early 1939 incident occurred. Although he was older and more mature than when the rape charge was allegedly filed, it is typical of what every woman said about him. Gladys' experience with Siegel is related in her daughter Susan Berman's autobiography *Easy Street: The True Story of a Mob Family.*

SIEGEL'S INFAMOUS TEMPER & HIS MONIKER "BUGSY"

502- The quote by Lou Hershenberg is from my interview on March 2, 1992.

503- The two quotes by Jack Walsh are from my interview on August 28, 1968.

504- The first *New York Times'* article about Siegel was on October 30, 1935. The remaining 12 articles were written between 1939 and 1943, years after Prohibition ended. The 566 *Los Angeles Times'* articles were from 1939 through 1985.

505- The two quotes by the Prosecutors - Assistant U.S. Attorneys John Doyle and William Young - are from the September 4, 1939 *New York Times.*

506- The *Bug and Meyer Mob* was mentioned in only two of the nine articles the *New York Times* published about Siegel during his lifetime. They were on September 4 and 29, 1939.

THE LIFE-LONG PARTNERSHIP OF SIEGEL & LANSKY

507- Lansky lived in Brooklyn from 1911 until he moved to the Lower East Side in 1914.

508- The quote by Robert Lacey is from his *Little Man: Meyer Lansky and the Gangster Life.*

509- Dave Stearns quotes in this and the previous paragraph are my interview on August 7, 1969.

510- The quote by Lou Wiener is from my interview on December 2, 1971.

THE MURDER, INC. CASE OF "BIG GREENIE"

511- LAPD Detective Lt. Lloyd Hurst's quote is from the January 31, 1942 *Los Angeles Times.*

512- The quote by LAPD Investigator Lloyd Yarrow was what Siegel had said to him and is in the January 31, 1942 *Los Angeles Times.*

513- DA Fitts' quote of Manhattan DA Dewey's letter is in the August 17, 1940 *Los Angeles Times.*

514- Siegel's first quote is from the August 23, 1940 *Los Angeles Times,* and his second quote is from the June 27, 1941 *Los Angeles Times.*

515- The quote by U.S. Commissioner David B. Head is from the May 30 1941 *Los Angeles Times.*

516- The quote by Abe Reles is from the November 13, 1941 *Los Angeles Times.*

517- The quote of Tannenbaum's trial testimony is from the January 29, 1942 *Los Angeles Times.*

518- The quote by Ben Siegel is from the February 6, 1942 *Los Angeles Times.*

519- The quote of Tannenbaum's testimony is from the October 2, 1941 *Los Angeles Times.*

520- The quote by the Sheriff Biscailuz about Deputy Sheriff James Pascoe is from the December 11, 1940 *Los Angeles Times.*

521- The quote from Ben Siegel is from the May 26, 1944 *Los Angeles Times.*

522- The two quotes by George Raft are from the July 18, 1944 *Los Angeles Times.*

523- Siegel's hotel roust occurred in 1933. Big Greenie was deported in 1935, and He was indicted for extortion in 1937. Greenie was murdered on November 22, 1939 after threatening to squeal. Lepke surrendered to Hoover and the FBI on August 24, 1939. Siegel was jailed for contempt from September 28 to October 3, 1939 for refusing to testify about not harboring Lepke. Reles testified to the Lepke-harboring Federal Grand Jury in September 1939, and he turned state's witness in Brooklyn in February 1940. Turkus flew to LA in July 1940 with his New York depositions, and the LAPD arrested Siegel on August 16, 1940. Reles and Tannenbaum testified before the Los Angeles Grand Jury on August 20, 1940. Lansky visited Siegel in jail in late August 1940. The articles by the *Los Angeles Times* and the *New York Times* about Reles were both on December 8, 1940. The two DA's asked the judge to dismiss Siegel's murder charge on December 11, 1940. DA O'Dwyer and Bals vacationed in LA in February 1941. Siegel was arrested for harboring Lepke on April 16, 1941, and Siegel testified against his removal to Brooklyn on May 27, 1941. Big Greenie's murder case was reopened in September 1941. The Grand Jury reindicted Siegel following Tannenbaum's second appearance on September 22, 1941. Siegel voluntarily surrendered to the second murder indictment on October 10, 1941. Reles flew out his Atlantic City hotel window on November 12, 1941. The Judge dismissed Siegel's second murder charge on February 6, 1942. Siegel was arrested for bookmaking on May 25, 1944, and he pled guilty and was fined on September 11, 1944. Siegel's remaining Los Angeles and Las Vegas conflicts and their outcomes are detailed in the next volume in this historical series.

SIEGEL'S LOS ANGELES BUSINESS INTERESTS

524- The histories of Annenberg and the wire services are in the next volume of this series.

525- LAPD Captain Lynn White's quote to Kefauver is in the April 22, 1950 *New York Times.*

526- The only info available about this 1935 News Service deal came from testimony by John Rosselli and a LAPD Captain before the Kefauver. Normile operated Agua Caliente Race Track in 1938 and 1939. Annenberg's *Nationwide News* ceased operation in 1939.

527- The quote by Chief Deputy DA Williams is from the August 17, 1940 *Los Angeles Times.*

528- Three men had knowledge about Siegel's investment in the S.S. Rex – his bookmaking associate Jack Richards; Jimmy Lloyd who had a minor interest in the Rex and who would later become a Reno casino owner; and Harry Bloomfield who Siegel brought from New York to become the ship's bookkeeper to protect his interest.

529- Siegel's interest in casinos is from FBI Los Angeles Office Background Summary to the Director July 22, 1946, and Rosselli's interest is from an undated *Los Angeles Examiner* morgue file from late in Prohibition contained in FBI Los Angeles Office Surveillance Record to the Director September 26, 1960.

530- English passenger Richard Gulley's quote is from the January 19, 1939 *Los Angeles Times.*

531- English passenger Richard Gulley's quote is from the January 19, 1939 *Los Angeles Times*.

532- The Metha Nelson sailed from Long Beach on September 19, 1938. Captain Hoffman wired the mutiny charges against the two crewmen - Charles Segal and Abraham Kapellner – on November 2, 1938, and they were arrested upon arrival in San Pedro, California on November 28, 1938. The Metha arrived back in San Pedro on January 10, 1939; the Grand Jury no-billed the crewmen on January 18, 1939; and Customs searched Siegel's home the next day.

HOLLYWOOD'S HOODLUM SOCIALITES

533- The quote by Lou Wiener is from my interview on July 22, 1970. The quote by Jackie Fields is from my interview on August 7, 1969.

534- The quote about Siegel is from an August 23, 1940 *Los Angeles Times* article.

535- The quote by Dean Martin is from the book *George Raft* by Lewis Yablonsky.

536- The quote is from the California Governor's Commission on Organized Crime Report in the May 11, 1953 *Los Angeles Times*.

537- The three quotes are by society columnist Paul Coates, the first in the November 28, 1962 *Los Angeles Times*, and the last two in the December 7, 1962 *Los Angeles Times*.

538- Siegel and the Countess sailed to Naples on April 8, 1939 and returned on June 6, 1939. Germany set off World War II in Europe on September 1, 1939.

539- Siegel met with Luciano in prison on November 24, 1944.

540- The quote from Tom Douglas about di Frasso is from the January 5, 1954 *Los Angeles Times*.

541- The quote by Major Riddle is from my interview on February 10, 1970.

542- The obscene-conversation quote is from FBI Memo from the Los Angeles office to Director Hoover July 20, 1946. Hill's description is from a 60-page FBI Summary from 8-46 to 10-46 unclearly dated, and from FBI Salt Lake City Newman to Hoover Memo January 9, 1947.

543- The quote by Major Riddle is from my interview on February 10, 1970.

544- The Kefauver Committee quote by Senator Tobey and the one by Virginia Hill are from my interview with Cliff Jones on April 14, 1969.

545- Chick Hill's interview is in *We Only Kill Each Other: The Life and Bad Times of Bugsy Siegel*. Siegel's close Las Vegas associates told me Epstein subsidized Hill, and this was also openly rumored in Chicago underworld circles, according to Virgil Peterson's Kefauver testimony.

NEVADA'S INVITATION TO A HOOD

546- Nevada legalized casinos in March 1931, and Prohibition ended on December 5, 1933. Nevada legalized off-track horserace books in 1941.

BIBLIOGRAPHY REFERENCES

BOOKS

Adler, Polly. *A House Is Not A Home* Rinehart Books 1953

Asbury, Herbert. *The Gangs of Chicago: An Informal History of the Chicago Underworld* New York: Thunder's Mouth Press, An Imprint of Avalon Publishing Group 1940

Asbury, Herbert. *The Gangs of New York: An Informal History of the Underworld* Alfred A Knopf, Inc. 1927 (The 1998 reprint reports Martin Scorsese did a film version of this book)

Baggelaar, Kristin *The Copacabana* Arcadia Publishing 2006

Balboni, Dr. Alan. *Beyond the Mafia: Italian Americans and the Development of Las Vegas* University of Nevada Press Reno, Nevada 1996

Balsamo, William and George Carpozi, Jr. *Under the Clock: The True Story of the Mafia's First 100 years* New Horizon Press 1988

Beebe, Lucius. *Snoot if You Must* NY: D. Appleton-Century Co., Inc. 1943

Belafonte, Harry. *My Song: A Memoir of Art, Race and Defiance* Vintage Reprint edition 2012

Bergreen, Laurence. *Capone: the Man and the Era* NY: Simon & Schuster 1994

Berman, Susan. Easy Street: *The True Story of a Mob Family* The Dial Press 1981

Block, Dr. Alan. *East Side, West Side: Organizing Crime in New York, 1930-1950* New Brunswick, New Jersey: Transaction Books 1985

Bonanno, Joseph with Sergio Lalli. *A Man of Honor: The Autobiography of Joseph Bonanno* Simon and Schuster 1983

Bradley, Hugh. *Such Was Saratoga* Doubleday, Doran and Company, Inc. 1940

Burrough, Bryan, *Public Enemies: America's Greatest Crime Wave and the Birth of the FBI, 1933-34* New York: Penguin Books 2004

Campbell, Rodney. *The Luciano Project: The Secret Wartime Collaboration of the Mafia & the U. S. Navy* McGraw-Hill Book Company New York 1977

Carpozi, George Jr. *Bugsy: The Bloodthirsty, Life of Benjamin "Bugsy" Siegel* New York: SPI Books, a division of Shapolsky Publishers, Inc. 1973

Castleman, Deke *Las Vegas Compass* American Guides, Inc. 1991

Cohen, Mickey as told to John Peer Nugent. *Mickey Cohen: In My Own Words* Englewood Cliffs, New Jersey: Prentice-Hall 1975

Cohn, Art. *The Joker Is Wild: The Story of Joe E. Lewis* New York: Random House 1955

Cook, Fred J. *A Two-Dollar Bet Means Murder* The Dial Press 1961

Cooney, John. *The Annenbergs: The Salvaging of a Tainted Dynasty* New York: Simon and Schuster 1982

Cooper, Courtney Ryley with an introduction by J. Edgar Hoover. *Ten Thousand Public Enemies* Lovat Dickson and Thompson 1935

Corti, Count. *The Wizard of Hamburg and Monte Carlo* Thornton Butterworth Ltd. 1934

Creigh, Alfred *History of Washington County from Its First Settlement to the Present Time* 1871 B. Singerly 1871

Danforth, Harold R. and James D. Horan. *The D. A.'s Man* Crown Publishers Inc. USA 1957

Davis, John H. *Mafia Dynasty: The Rise and Fall of the Gambino Crime Family* New York: HarperCollins Publishers 1993

Davis, Sammy Jr. and Jane and Burt Boyar. *Why Me? The Sammy Davis, Jr. Story* Farrar, Strauss and Giroux 1989

Demaris, Ovid. *The Last Mafioso: The Treacherous World of Jimmy Fratianno* Times Books 1981

de Toledano, Ralph. *J. Edgar Hoover: The Man In His Time* Arlington House, New Rochelle, New York 1973

Dewey, Thomas E. from his prepared papers as edited by Rodney Campbell. *Twenty Against the Underworld: An Autobiography of a District Attorney and his fight against organized crime* Double Day & Co. Inc. 1974

Eghigian, Mars Jr. *After Capone: The Life And World of Chicago Mob Boss Frank "the Enforcer" Nitti* Nashville, Tennessee: Cumberland House Publishing 2006

Eiscnberg, Dennis, Uri Dan, and Eli Landau. *Meyer Lansky: Mogul of the Mob* New York and London: Paddington Press Ltd. 1979

Fonzi, Gaeton. *Annenberg: A Biography Of Power* Weybright & Talley 1970

Friedman, Bill. *All Against The Law: The Criminal Activities of the Depression Era Bank Robbers, Mafia, FBI, Politicians, & Cops* Old School Histories 2013 (see BillFriedmanAuthor.com)

Gentry, Curt. *J. Edgar Hoover: The Man and His Secrets* New York: W. W. Norton & Company 1991

Gosch, Martin A. and Richard Hammer. *The Last Testament of Lucky Luciano* Boston: Little, Brown and Company 1974

Goulart, Ron. *Line Up: Tough Guys (Owney Madden, Al Capone, Arnold Rothstein, Legs Diamond, Roger Touhy, Machine Gun Kelly, John Dillinger, Alvin Karpis, Dutch Schultz, Louis Buchalter-Lepke, Bugsy Siegel, Frank Costello, Joe Adonis, and Lucky Luciano)* Sherbourne Press, inc. 1966

Harrison, Carter H. *Stormy Years: The Autobiography of Carter H. Harrison* The Bobbs-Merrill Company Publishers 1935

Helmer, William J. & Arthur J. Bilek. *The St. Valentine's Day Massacre: The Untold Story of the Gangland Bloodbath That Brought Down Al Capone* Nashville, Tennessee: Cumberland House 2004

Hersh, Burton. *Bobby and J. Edgar: The Historic Face-Off Between the Kennedys and J. Edgar Hoover That Transformed America* New York: Carroll & Grat Publishers 2007

History of Tammany Hall "documented by official records of the Board of Aldermen and various investigations"

Hoover, J. Edgar. *Persons in Hiding* Boston: Little, Brown, & Co. 1938.

Hoover, J. Edgar with Ken Jones. *The FBI In Action* New American Library 1957.

Humble, Ronald D. *Frank Nitti: The True Story of Chicago's Notorious "Enforcer"* Fort Lee, New Jersey: Barricade Books 2007

Jennings, Dean. *We Only Kill Each Other: The Life and Bad Times of Bugsy Siegel* Englewood Cliffs, New Jersey: Prentice-Hall, Inc. 1967

Katcher, Leo. *The Big Bankroll: The Life and Times of Arnold Rothstein* Da Capo Press, A Member of the Perseus Books Group 1958 and printed 1994

Kobler, John. *Capone: The Life and World of Al Capone* Fawcett Crest Book 1971

Lacey, Robert. *Little Man: Meyer Lansky and the Gangster Life* Little, Brown and Company 1991

Lait, Jack and Lee Mortimer. *Chicago Confidential* New York: Crown Publishers and American Book - Knickerbocker Press 1950

Lewis, Brad. *Celebrity Gangster: The Incredible Life and Times of Mickey Cohen* New York: Enigma Books 2007

Lyle, Judge John H. *The Dry and Lawless Years* Englewood Cliffs, New Jersey Prentice-Hall 1960

Messick, Hank. *Lansky* G. P. Putnam's Sons 1971

Messick, Hank with Joseph L. Nellis. *The Private Lives of Public Enemies* Peter H. Wyden 1973

Messick, Hank. *The Silent Syndicate* The Macmillan Company 1967

Nash, George H. *The Life of Herbert Hoover* New York: W. W. Norton & Company 1996.

Neal, Steve. *Happy Days Are Here Again: The 1932 Democratic Convention, the Emergence of FDR – and How America Was Changed Forever* New York: HarperCollins Publishers, Inc. 2004

Nelli, Humbert S. *The Italians in Chicago 1880-1930: A Study in Ethnic Mobility* New York, New York: Oxford University Press 1970

Newton, Michael. *Mr. Mob: The Life and Crimes of Moe Dalitz* Jefferson, North Carolina and London: McFarland & Company, Inc., Publishers 2007

Ogden, Christopher. *Legacy - A Biography Of Moses & Walter Annenberg* Little, Brown & Company 1999

Oulahan, Richard. *The Man Who: The Story of the 1932 Democratic National Convention* New York: The Dial Press 1971

Parr, Amanda J. *The True and Complete Story of Machine Gun Jack McGurn* Leicester, UK: Matador an imprint of Troubador Publishing Ltd. 2005

Peterson, Virgil W. *Gambling: Should It Be Legalized?* Springfield, Illinois: Charles C. Thompson Publisher 1951

Peterson, Virgil W. *The Mob 200 Years of Organized Crime in New York* Green Hill Publishers, Inc. 1983

Picchi, Blaise. *The Five Weeks of Giuseppe Zangara: The Man Who Tried to Kill FDR* Chicago: Academy Chicago Publishers 1998

Pileggi, Nicholas. *Casino: Love and Honor in Las Vegas* New York: Simon and Schuster 1995

Pileggi, Nicholas. *Wiseguy: Life in the Mafia* Simon and Schuster 1985

Potter, Claire Bond. *War on Crime: Bandits, G-Men, and the Politics of Mass Culture* New Brunswick, New Jersey: Rutgers University Press 1958

Powell, Hickman. *Lucky Luciano: The Man Who Organized Crime in America* Barricade Books 2000 (originally *Ninety Times Guilty* in 1939 with afterword by Ed Becker)

Powers, Richard Gid. *G-Men: Hoover's FBI in American Popular Culture* Southern Illinois University Press 1983

Prall, Robert H. and Norton Mockridge. *This Is Costello On The Spot* Greenwich, Connecticut: Gold Medal Books by Fawcett Publications, Inc. 1951 and updated after the Costello shooting in 1957

Rabushka, Alvin. *Taxation in Colonial America* Princeton University Press 2008

Rappleye, Charles and Ed Becker. *All American Mafioso: The Johnny Rosselli Story* Doubleday 1991

Reid, Ed and Ovid Demaris *The Green Felt Jungle* Pocket Books, Inc. 1963

Reid, Ed. *The Mistress and the Mafia: The Virginia Hill Story* Signet Books 1972

Riddle, Major A. as told to Joe Hyams *The Weekend Gambler's Handbook* Random House 1963

Roemer, William F. Jr. *Accardo: The Genuine Godfather* New York: Donald I. Fine, Inc. 1995

Roemer, William E. Jr. *Roemer: Man Against the Mob* New York: Donald I. Rine, Inc. 1989

Schlesinger, Arthur M. Jr. *Robert Kennedy and His Times* New York: Ballantine Books, a division of Random House 1978

Schoenberg, Robert J. *Mr. Capone: The Real - and Complete - Story of Al Capone* New York: Quill - William Morrow 1992

Sciacca, Tony. *Luciano: The Man Who Modernized the American Mafia* New York City: Pinnacle Books 1975

Sifakis, Carl. *The Mafia Encyclopedia: From Accardo to Zwillman* New York: Facts On File Publications, Inc. 1987

Summers, Anthony. *Official and Confidential: The Secret Life of J. Edgar Hoover* New York: G. P. Putnam's Sons 1993

Theoharis, Athan editor and commentary. *From The Secret Files of J. Edgar Hoover* Chicago: Ivan R. Dee 1991

Tosches, Nick. *Dino (Martin): Living High in the Dirty Business of Dreams* New York: Doubleday 1992

Touhy, Roger. *The Stolen Year's* Pennington Press 1959

Tuohy, John W. *Capone's Mob Murdered Roger Touhy: The Strange Case Of Touhy, Jake The Barber And The Kidnapping That Never Happened* Fort Lee, New Jersey: Barricade Books 2001

Turkus, Burton B. and Sid Feder. *Murder, Inc. - The Story of the Syndicate* Farrar, Strauss and Young, New York 1951

Twain, Mark. *Roughing It* Signet Classics 1886

Whitehead, Don with J. Edgar Hoover forward. *The FBI Story, A Report to the People* Random House 1956

Wigmore, Dean H. *Kaleidoscope of Justice: Containing Authentic Accounts of Trial Scenes From All Times and Climes* Washington Law Book Co. 1941

Wilkerson, W.R. III. *The Man Who Invented Las Vegas* Ciro's Books (self-published in name father's nightclub) 2000

Wilson, Chief Frank J. & Beth Day. *Special Agent: 25 Years With The American Secret Service* London: Frederick Muller Limited 1966

Wolf, George with Joseph DiMona. *Frank Costello: Prime Minister of the Underworld* Great Britain: Hodder & Stoughton Limited 1975

Yablonsky, Lewis. *George Raft* McGraw-Hill Book Company 1974

Zion, Sidney. *Loyalty and Betrayal: The Story of the American Mob*, a companion to and with interviews from the Fox TV Special executive producers Bill Couturie and Nicholas Pileggi. San Francisco: CollinsPublishers, a division of HarperCollins Publishers 1994

Zuckerman, Michael J. *Vengeance Is Mine: Jimmy "The Weasel" Fratianno tells how he brought the kiss of death to the Mafia* Macmillan Publishing 1987

MAGAZINE ARTICLES

America's No. 1 Mystery Man: The First Of Two Parts - An Account Of The Career Of Frank Costello And Of His Strange Empire Herbert Asbury *Collier's* Magazine April 12, 1947

America's No. 1 Mystery Man: Conclusion - Further Revelations Of The Power Of Frank Costello Herbert Asbury *Collier's* Magazine April 19, 1947

Los Angeles – 'America's Wickedest City:' Cleans Up Its Gambling, Graft and Girl Rackets in *Look* Magazine September 26 1939

Mickey Cohen: The Private Life Of A Hood Dean Jennings *Saturday Evening Post* Magazine September 20, 1958 (The 1st of a series of 4 articles)

Mickey Cohen: The Private Life Of A Hood Dean Jennings *Saturday Evening Post* Magazine September 27, 1958 (The 2nd of a series of 4 articles)

Mickey Cohen: The Private Life Of A Hood Dean Jennings *Saturday Evening Post* Magazine October 4, 1958 (The 3rd of a series of 4 articles)

Mickey Cohen: The Private Life Of A Hood Dean Jennings *Saturday Evening Post* Magazine October 11, 1958 (The 4th of a series of 4 articles)

Undercover Man: He Trapped Capone Frank J. Wilson as told to Howard Whitman *Collier's* Magazine April 26, 1947 (The first of a series – How Scarface was enmeshed in the toils of the law)

Unholy City: Los Angeles Cracks Down On Its Crooks and Sinners George Creel *Collier's* Magazine September 2, 1939

A&E & HISTORY CHANNEL PROGRAMS BIBLIOGRAPHY

Joe Bonanno: The Last Godfather A&E Biography 1996

Rumrunners, Moonshiners And bootleggers The History Channel 2002 A&E Television Networks

Mussolini: Italy's Nightmare A&E Biography 1995

Walter Winchell: The Voice of America A&E Biography 1995

St. Valentine's Day Massacre The History Channel 1997 A&E Television Networks

Empire of Crime: A Century of the New York Mob A&E 1996

Time Machine: Allied With the Mafia broadcast by the A&E TV channel on January 1, 1994

"Bugsy:" The Real Flamingo Story, Gambling On The Mob A&E Biography 1995

Vegas and the Mob A&E American Justice 1996

Eliot Ness: Untouchable The History Channel 1997 A&E Television Networks

History's Mysteries: The True Story of the Untouchables The History Channel 1999 A&E Television Networks

REFERENCE FBI FILES BIBLIOGRAPHY

Aiuppa, Joseph– 294 pages
Anastasia, Albert – 180 pages
Buchalter, Louis "Lepke" – 184 pages
Capone, Al – 2,397 pages
Cohen, Mickey – 1,755 pages
Costello, Frank – 3,045 pages
Dalitz, Moe – 2,729 pages
Darin, Bobby – 73 pages
Factor, John "Jake the Barber" – 154 pages
Genovese, Vito – 186 pages
Giancana, Sam -186
Lewis, Joe E. – 18 pages
Long, Huey P. – 1,818 pages
Luciano, Charlie "Lucky" – 548 pages
Nelson, "Baby Face" – 225 pages
Ness, Elliot (actually Eliot) – 129 pages
Raft, George – 127 pages
Rosselli, Johnny – 1,228 pages
St. Valentine's Massacre – 107 pages
Siegel, Benjamin – 2,421 pages
Sinatra, Frank– 2,403 pages
Spilotro, Tony "The Ant" – 240 pages
Winchell, Walter – 3,908 pages
Zwillman, Abner "Longie"– 747 pages

Made in the USA
San Bernardino, CA
30 August 2016